AFRICAN HISTORICAL DICTIONARIES
Edited by Jon Woronoff

Historical Dictionary
of
ETHIOPIA

by

Chris Prouty
and
Eugene Rosenfeld

African Historical Dictionaries, No. 32

THE SCARECROW PRESS, INC.

METUCHEN, N.J., & LONDON

1981

Library of Congress Cataloging in Publication Data

Rosenfeld, Chris Prouty.
    Historical dictionary of Ethiopia.

    (African historical dictionaries ; no. 32)
    Bibliography: p.
    Includes index.
    1. Ethiopia--History--Dictionaries. I. Rosenfeld,
Eugene, 1915-   . II. Title. III. Series.
DT381.R57   963'.003'21   81-8729
ISBN 0-8108-1448-X   AACR2

CONTENTS

EDITOR'S FOREWORD

Few countries in Africa have a more glorious history than Ethiopia; few have had as tragic a past. These two aspects of a nation that has struggled to survive over centuries have never been more poignant than today. Ethiopia has only just passed through the convulsions of the death of an old regime, one tracing its roots back to Biblical times, into the confusion of the birth of a new regime. Seemingly torn apart by antagonisms among its constituent peoples and threatened with dismemberment by its traditional foes, it is still struggling to remain intact.

It is not unusual in such circumstances that less should be known about Ethiopia now than a decade or two ago when things were more settled. This dictionary will help trace some of the people and institutions whose fate was not easy to follow. It also informs us about new leaders and groups that have risen, sometimes quite suddenly, to take their place. However, despite the amazingly comprehensive view of Ethiopia as it was until recently, is today, and may perhaps be tomorrow, great attention is paid to more remote history. Added to this are useful entries on the ethnic groups that inhabit the land, their customs and practices, and an overall view of the economic and cultural situation.

This volume was written by Chris Prouty and Eugene Rosenfeld, whose interest in Ethiopia has continued since 1965, when Mr. Rosenfeld was first posted as director of the United States Information Service in Addis Ababa and Chris Prouty, his wife, took courses in Ethiopian history at the university. Rosenfeld has specialized in politics of the modern period and Prouty has concentrated on the Menilek period and the history of Ethiopian women. She is presently working on a biography of Empress Taytu Betul. Their varied interests combine to make this African dictionary particularly broad and rich.

Jon Woronoff
Series Editor

PREFACE

We have received the personal help and advice of Gustav
Aren, Bereket Habte Sellase, Clifton Brown, Donald Crummey, Haggai
Erlich, Peter Garretson, Marilyn Heldman, Bonnie Holcomb, Willi
Loepfe, Richard Pankhurst, Donald Paradis, Kay Shelemay, Zewde
Gebre Sellase, Zewde Bairu, and most particularly, Richard Caulk.
None of them is responsible for any mistakes or omissions in this work.
The Ethiopian embassy in Washington D. C. provided up-dated infor-
mation whenever it could.   We are especially indebted to the Area
Handbook for Ethiopia (see Bibliography) for statistics up to 1970.

Regarding Transliteration

Commonly, those writing about Ethiopia beg off troubling to
transliterate from Ethiopic script on the grounds that Ethiopianists
have yet to agree on a single system of transliteration.   However,
the late Stephen Wright laid down accurate rules in 1964 in the
second issue of the Journal of Ethiopian Studies.   The Journal as
well as other publications of the Institute of Ethiopian Studies at
Addis Ababa University did adhere to them.   Shorn of the numerous
diacritics required in Wright's system, which are a trial for typists
and typographers, his rules were still applied to the orthography of
the Ethiopian portion of the Encyclopaedia Africana (1977).   Without
diacritics, however, Wright's rules produce few spellings that
Ethiopianists use.   A modified system has been adopted here with
the assistance of Richard A. Caulk (Rutgers/Camden).   For spellings, our dictionary is indebted to the excellent indexes provided
by Sven Rubenson (1976), Tadesse Tamrat (1972), Donald Crummey
(1972), and Edward Ullendorff (1976), and the biographical dictionaries of Heruy Welde Sellase (1922-23) and Mahteme Sellase Welde

Mesqel (1968, 1969), whose works are in our Bibliography. Valuable guidance is provided in "The Ethiopian Writing System, " a chapter in Bender, et al., Language in Ethiopia (1976). A number of women's names, seen only in the accounts of European travelers whose caprices of transcription cannot always be sorted out, may be faulty.

Without diacritics, it has not been possible to represent the spelling of a word with precision. For the non-specialist, the simplest equivalents are the most serviceable. Glottalized "s" and "ch" are represented as "ts" and "tch" and glottalized "k" as "q. " For glottalized "p, " as in "Ityopya" and other borrowings from Greek, nothing has been added (the "p" itself being used only in rare loan words). Similarly, for the two kinds of "z" which the Ethiopic syllabary represents by separate characters, no indication is given here. Ethiopic has a character for "y. " This leaves only five Roman letters to do duty in representing the seven vowel markers by which the thirty-odd basic characters of Ethiopic are modified in writing. A deplorable, if inevitable overworking of one Roman letter results when the diacritics are scrapped: in our case "e. " For the seven vowel orders of Ethiopic, "e" has been used to indicate the first, fifth and sixth orders. The second order is represented by "u, " the third by "i, " the fourth by "a, " and the seventh by "o. " All the first order "h" vowels are written as "ha" as they are pronounced. Doubling of consonants, which sometimes affects meaning in Ethiopic but is not indicated in writing, has occasionally been used. Our symplified system cannot be even approximately phonetic in the way that Ethiopic script itself is.

For Arabic, the Roman forms of J. S. Trimingham in Islam in Ethiopia (see General Works) have been followed where possible. For Ethiopia's unwritten languages, no solution has yet been found to correct the deformation that has occurred when they are transcribed by authors writing in Amharic and Ge'ez. Colloquial variants of Muslim names and local variants of Ge'ez and Amharic names have not been included as a rule. Ethiopians writing in Roman script followed no particular system, any more than the foreign explorers and journalists. Such idiosyncrasies have been glossed over.

A few place names have become so well established that no effort to alter them for the sake of congruence has been made; though as often as possible that spelling which fits this dictionary's system has been placed in parenthesis after it. The well-known spelling of personal names, as in "Haile Sellassie" has been discarded in the interest of accuracy, hence, "Hayle Sellase. "

We apologize only for the deficiencies of the simplified system, and for inaccuracies of spelling. (See ONOMASTICS in the Dictionary for more information on the naming system.) We have eschewed the usual glossary and defined Amharic terms in the text.

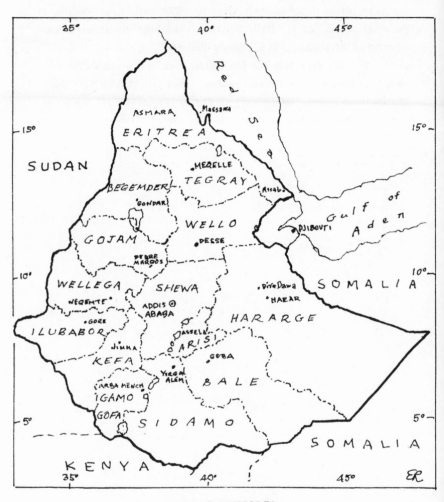

Map of ETHIOPIA

Showing the 14 Administrative
Divisions (Provinces)
and their capitals

INTRODUCTION

The end of monarchy in 1974 was the end of a political system, but not the end of traditional ways of life that have taken centuries in their formation. Since the economy is about 85 percent agricultural, it is in this area that the socialist government intends to develop a fairer share of the wealth, though the energy of its leaders is distracted by two conflicts: one old--the dispute in the Ogaden with Somalis, and one very old--the Eritrean secessionist movement. Progress in any field is hampered by tensions within the country produced by past conquests that expanded the size of the country and imposed Amhara cultural, religious and political dominance.

The Land and the People.

With a land area of more than 470,000 square miles, Ethiopia is bounded by the Sudan on the west, Egypt on the north, the Red Sea, Djibouti and Somalia on the east, and Kenya on the south. The spine of the country is a 700-mile long plateau, averaging 7,500 feet elevation, which is mountainous but with large fertile areas. This plateau is cleft by the Great Rift Valley and falls away to the north, west and south to lowlands.

Climatically, the high mountain areas vary from below freezing to 60° F.; most of the plateau at the five to eight thousand feet elevation is a temperate zone from 60° to 85° F., whereas the lowlands are hot, either arid as in the Ogaden region and the Danakil desert on the east or more lush and tropical in the south and west. Most of the year is dry, but there is a fairly heavy rainfall between mid-June and mid-September.

Population is estimated at from 25 to 27 million. Although the largest ethnic group is generally recognized as the Oromo (often called Galla) who comprise roughly 40 percent of the total, the dominant people have long been the Amhara-Tegray (often called the Abyssinians) complex, comprising perhaps 30-35 percent. The balance consists of a dozen or more groups, none larger than 500,000, the most prominent among them being the Gurage, Afars, and Somalis.

Languages

An estimated 95 languages (and dialects) are used, but the

official language is Amharic.   Tegrigna is mostly limited to Tegray province.   More widely spoken is Oromo, though it must be written in the Amharic script, an event of the mid-19th century under the sponsorship of missionaries.   Arabic is spoken by pockets of Muslims and on the border areas of the Arabic-speaking countries. There is a great deal of language interchange and bi-lingual capability.

        Marxist-Leninist terminology has necessitated the issuance of a Progressive Dictionary (Addis Ababa, 1976) which uses words borrowed from English (common in the Amharic press before the revolution), or assigns a new meaning to an "old word, " or creates a new word by derivation from an Amharic or Ge'ez root.   The same need by the Eritrean Popular Liberation Front has produced the Tegrigna Vocabulary (1975).

Religions

        A key factor throughout history has been the Ethiopian Orthodox Church, which espouses a Monophysite creed.   State and Church have been inextricably mated.   Though there are only a few Jews (Felashas), Old Testament Judaism is apparent in Ethiopian religious customs.   Islam is the faith of possibly half the country's inhabitants but is practiced in a far less rigid way than in the Middle East. There are many groups holding animist beliefs who have much affected both Christianity and Islam.

Education

        Secular, government-sponsored public schools became an earnest endeavor only in 1942.   Enrollment at all levels, primary to university, would be one million if 1970 prediction rates were steady.   Still that represents less than 3 percent of the population in elementary and secondary schools.   At Addis Ababa University the student body is at present less than 3, 000.   There are about 3, 000 Ethiopians (and Eritreans, as they prefer to be called if pro-separatist) studying at U. S. universities with about the same number attending universities in Britain, France, Italy, Cuba, and Eastern Europe, including the Soviet Union.   The literacy rate was optimistically estimated at 10 percent in 1970; the present government has announced it has raised this rate to 25 percent since 1974.

Health Conditions

        Life expectancy is low, and infant and child mortality high, though intense activity in the development of treatment facilities has been carried on by foreign missionary societies, government, and international organizations.   The World Health Organization has announced the eradication of smallpox.   About 80 percent of the population still relies on traditional medical practitioners.   Cholera has virtually been eliminated, but malarial, parasitic and gastro-intestinal illnesses are common, and there is a high number of incidences of syphilis, tuberculosis, typhoid and eye ailments.

Economy

Agriculture accounts for the subsistence of most of the people. Large cattle herds provide meat and their skins are used for various domestic products as well as hides for export. Rancid butter is an important by-product, used not only in cooking but as a hair cosmetic and a prime component of medical prescriptions. There is no large-scale dairy industry except in Eritrea. Honey is the basic component of the national drink, tej (honey beer), and also is used medically. Coffee is the chief cash crop and accounts for at least 48 percent of foreign exchange earnings; other exports are lentils and other pulses, and oilseeds. A small industrial sector includes sugar processing, cement, paper, bricks, shoes, glassware and textiles for domestic consumption. All are nationalized, as are all financial and insurance institutions.

Regions

The 14 administrative divisions (announced in 1968) were formerly called "provinces" (retained in this text for historical recognition). The present government has made two minor changes; the old names are in parentheses.

Region	Capital
Arisi (Arusi)	Assela
Bale	Goba
Begemder	Gondar
Eritrea	Asmara
Gamo-Gofa (Gemu-Gofa)	Arba Mench
Gojam	Debre Marqos
Hararge	Harar
Ilubabor	Gore
Kefa	Jimma
Shewa	Addis Ababa
Sidamo	Yirga Alem
Tegray	Meqelle
Wellega	Neqemte
Wello	Desse

These regions are further divided into 103 awraja (sub-regions), 505 woreda (districts) and 949 miktel woreda (sub-districts), all responsible to the Ministry of Interior. In addition there were about 210 municipalities responsible to a Department in Addis Ababa. These numbers changed from time to time. The Derg (present government) has retained the same structure but changed almost all of the appointees and appointed military men to awraja, posts through-

out Eritrea and Wello and added Peasant Associations in an effort
to increase participation in political power at the local level, and
Urban Dwellers Associations (kebelle) in municipalities for the same
purpose.

Communications

Telephone, telegraph and telex services connect about 80 percent of the municipalities.   A railroad connects Addis Ababa with
Djibouti, a distance of 486 rail miles, and 191 rail miles connect
Massawa with Asmara and Agordat.   In western Eritrea there is a
short spur line between Teseney and the Sudanese rail system.
Deep-water ports at Massawa and Assab are import and export
points as well as through the port of Djibouti by agreement with that
government.   The road network totals about 15, 000 miles with about
4, 800 all-weather roads in the central plateau and going to the ports.
Mule, donkey and camel tracks are relied on by the predominantly
rural population.   Domestic airlines connect 42 towns and cities and
flights from Asmara and Addis Ababa provide cross-Africa service
and go to the Middle East and Europe.

The government communicates to the people primarily by
radio which reaches more than 20 percent of the total population.
Television is of minor importance, received only in Addis Ababa
and environs and Asmara.   There are newspapers and magazines
with a circulation related to the literacy rate.

Calendar and Time

The Ethiopian calendar runs seven years behind the Gregorian
at the beginning of its year and is eight years behind at the end.
The first day of the Ethiopian year, 1 Mesqerem 1962, corresponds
to 11 September 1969 and the last day corresponds to 10 September
1970.   There are 12 months of thirty days each and one month of
five days (six in a leap year).   The day begins at sunrise, not midnight.   The day that an event has occurred is more often expressed
in terms of the holy day, than a calendar date; for example, "His
horse ran away on Mikael. "   Each day of the month is dedicated to
some holy figure.   Years are denoted in sequences of four--Matthew,
Mark, Luke and John in turn.   Non-Christians have other ways of
defining the passage of time depending on whether they are Muslim
or worship other gods.

Historical Overview

The Ethiopian state had its origins in the Aksumite kingdom
formed about the first century A. D.   In the fourth century, the
court adopted Christianity, had a written language, and was in contact with the Byzantine empire, Egypt, and India.   With the rise of
Islam in seventh century, the Aksum kingdom became isolated with

the severing of old sea routes, though sporadic contacts with the
Coptic Patriarchate in Egypt were managed.   The Aksumites ex-
panded south and in the early 12th century a new imperial center
and a new line of kings called the Zagwe were established in Lasta.
Their overthrow in 1270 is represented as the restoration of the
Solomonic line.

From 1270 to 1520 there was further territorial expansion,
consolidation of the church, a flowering of religious literature and
a resumption of diplomatic contacts through the Muslim barrier that
occupied the coast and the land route to Egypt.   This process was
disrupted by an Islamic invasion from the coastal Muslims that
ravaged and destroyed much of the Christian culture in a 15-year
sweep through the Ethiopian highlands.   Their defeat, with the help
of a Portuguese military force, led directly to an attempt by Catholic missionaries to bring the Ethiopian Church and State back to the
"true faith. "   Once the emperor was converted to Catholicism, the
reaction in the country was violent: Monophysitism was re-estab-
lished, the missionaries were expelled and the country reverted to
isolationism.

A new ethnic factor was emerging in the same period.   A
people called the Oromo (or Galla) had begun a slow, steady migration from an area in the southwest, probably more in search of
land than with the notion of conquest, but they were in constant conflict with the Christian structure until by adaptation they infiltrated
it.

The establishment of a fixed imperial capital at Gondar, with
appropriate castles and beautiful churches, created a suitable setting
for monarchs but it ended the mobile capability of the imperial army
to keep in touch with the outlying regions of the country.   This led
to the Zemene Mesafint and almost a century of anarchy and civil
war.

The "modern" period (1855-1980) represented by the reigns
of Tewodros II, Yohannes IV, Menilek II, Zewditu, Hayle Sellase
I, and the revolution has been a period of extraordinary eventful-
ness.   Despite internal wars and external enemies along with
famine, disease and poverty--all the ills that can afflict mankind--
Ethiopia survives.

THE DICTIONARY

ABEBE AREGAY, <u>Ras</u> (1903?-1960). The son of <u>Afanegus</u> Aregay and Askale Gobena (daughter of Menilek's most famous general), he was one of two police chiefs in Addis Ababa at the time of the Italian entry in 1935. He became a renowned resistance leader operating in northeast Shewa until 1941 when he and his troops came out of hiding to escort the returning Hayle Sellase into the capital. Confirmed as a <u>ras</u>, he was for a short time mayor of Addis Ababa. His ministerial posts included War (1942-3 and 1947-9); Interior (1949-55); and Defense (1955-60); he held governorships of Sidamo (1941-2) and Tegray (1943-47) and was chairman of the Council of Ministers when he was shot during the abortive coup of December 1960. His wife was Qonjit Abnet, and his son, Daniel.

ABEBE BIQILA (1932-1973). Ethiopia's first world-renowned sports hero (marathon, Rome Olympics, 1960) came out of the Imperial Bodyguard. He was promoted to Captain after his first win, but his military and athletic career ended tragically when he was paralyzed in an automobile accident in March 1969. He died October 1973.

ABERA KASA (1905-1936). One of the three sons of Kasa Haylu (q. v.) who lost their lives fighting Italy. With his brother Asfa Wessen, a small number of soldiers, and <u>Abune</u> Petros (q. v.), he attacked Addis Ababa in July 1936. It <u>was a</u> disaster; Abera surrendered a short time later and was executed 21 December 1936.

ABEY ABEBA, Lieutenant-General. Scion of noble Shewan landowners, he held several ministries and became President of the Senate in 1964 although his main career was in the Army. He was married briefly to Hayle Sellase's youngest daughter, Tsehay. Gen. Abey was one of the military leaders executed on 23 November 1974 by the Provisional Military Administrative Council (q. v.).

ABREHA (King, c. 325-350). The first Christian ruler at Aksum who is said to have reigned with a twin brother, Atsbeha. Abreha is assumed to be the same as Ezana (who had a brother Sayzana) whose conversion to Christianity is known from inscriptions in Greek and Ge'ez. The brothers are saints in the synaxarium, memorialized on 4 teqemt (14/15 October).

ABREHA.   The Ethiopian viceroy of the colony in Yemen in the
  sixth century.   He is credited with building a great church at
  San'a (present capital of South Yemen) and for leading an expedition against Mecca in 570.   Muslim tradition recalls that
  this attempt to challenge the religious and mercantile supremacy
  of the Prophet's home town was "miraculously" defeated.

ABU ANJA.   Mahdist general whose forces defeated Tekle Haymanot's
  army in January 1888, then ravaged Gondar.   Despite this,
  Yohannes IV appealed to him and the Khalifa to help him repel
  the Italians later in the year.   The appeal was rejected as
  Yohannes was informed there could be neither peace nor alliance until Ethiopia's rulers became Muslims.   Abu Anja died
  of an illness 29 January 1889, at Metemma.

ABU BAKR, Sultan of Zeyla (c. 1815-1885).   An Afar who became
  governor of Zeyla in Issa territory and succeeded in monopoliz-
  ing the caravan trade from the coast into Shewa.   He was an
  ally of the Egyptians and was also a French protégé; he died at
  sea returning from a visit to France and was succeeded by one
  of his 11 sons.

ABUN.   Title of the head of the Ethiopian Church, equivalent to
  "metropolitan" or "bishop. "   From the 4th century to 1958 the
  abun was chosen by the Coptic Patriarchate in Alexandria.   The
  man knew no Amharic or Ge'ez (the language of liturgy) and
  was expected to spend the rest of his life in Ethiopia and never
  marry.   Since the Ethiopians paid a great deal of money to
  Egypt for the appointment they preferred the candidate to be
  young.   Zera Yaqob (q. v.) in the 15th century broke with tradition and had two men sent and Yohannes IV in 1881 imported
  four men, Petros, Luqas, Matewos and Marqos, to aid in
  the expansion of Christianity.   Matewos, assigned to Menilek of
  Shewa, became primate when Menilek became emperor in 1889
  and on his death in 1927 was succeeded by Qerelos.   The
  Ethiopianization of the office in 1950 occurred with the naming
  of Abune (the "e" is added before a proper name) Baselyos
  (q. v.).
      The first abun was Frumentius (q. v.) (c. 331 A. D.).   One
  abun notable for knowing the language and customs of Ethiopia
  on arrival was Sawiros (c. 1080) for he was the nephew of
  the preceding bishop and had lived with his uncle in Ethiopia.
  Much time could elapse before the death in office of one abun
  and the appointment of another, due not only to slow communication but political disagreements between Egypt and Ethiopia.
  Abune Selama arrived in 1841, thirteen years after the death of
  Qerelos (c. 1828); and Atinatewos in 1869, three years after
  the death of Selama in Emperor Tewodros' prison at Meqdela.
  The abuns played a largely ceremonial role, much honored and
  led a comfortable life on lands granted by the crown, except
  for those occasions when they were in conflict with the monarch
  (as in Selama's case); day-to-day management was in the hands
  of the Echege (q. v.) the highest office for an Ethiopian.

ABYSSINIA. The name by which the country was widely known until after World War II. It comes from a corruption of an Arabic word "habesh" which means "mixed breed. " The Habeshat
people, who lived on both sides of the Red Sea, are believed to
have begun their migratory settlement on the African coast about
the 7th century B. C. Marco Polo mistakenly used the
"Abash" to denote a "very large province that constitutes Middle
India. " Ethiopians frequently call each other "habesha" but they
might resent such use of the word when used by non-Ethiopians.
Some of the peoples in the far south of the country have been
known to refer to Christian highlanders from the north as
"habeshi. "

    "Abyssinians" is still used to denote those people of the
highlands, distinct from Oromo (Galla) or other ethnic groups
as those who are Monophysite "Christian-Amhara-Tegrayan, "
with common linguistic and cultural roots--the carriers of those
traditions that give Ethiopia its uniqueness among nations.

ACADEMY OF ETHIOPIAN LANGUAGES. Reorganized after the
Revolution, it was previously known as the Academy of the Amharic Language (1972). Its director is listed as Comrade Dr.
Amsalu Aklilu and is under the Ministry of Culture and Sports.
It now has three divisions: a Dictionary Committee; a Committee of Alphabets and a Committee for foreign terminology.
Twelve languages spoken in Ethiopia are to be included in a
written system. The Academy's declared priority task is to
prepare definitions of the 700 most important words and phrases
used in the study of Marxism-Leninism and short dictionaries
of such terminology have been produced in Amharic and Tegrigna.

ADAL, Sultanate of (Adel, Adaiel, Adela, Adem, etc.). Adal
evolved into an independent kingdom when the militant members
of the Welasma dynasty of Ifat, headed by Sa'd ad-din, migrated to an area northeast of Harar, rather than submit to the
rule of Amde Tseyon (1314-1344). The Welasma militants took
the title of sultans of Adal about 1415. Sultan Ahmad Badlay
invaded Dewaro in 1445 and was defeated and killed by the
soldiers of Zera Yaqob (1434-1468). Muhammad, Ahmad's
son, promised tribute to Be'eda Maryam (1468-1478), was called
"king" and 10 years of peace followed. Power then passed into the hands of a more aggressive family whose armies deci-
sively defeated the Christian emperor in 1474, and Adal was
not attacked for many years. This peace was nullified by the
emir of Harar, Mahfuz, whose aggressions brought the army of
Lebna-Dengel (1508-1540) to Fetegar (near Harar) in 1516. The
Welasma clan watched as the Adal changed sultans five times in
two years, then a Welasma became sultan and transferred military headquarters to Harar in 1520/21. An Adalite soldier (not
a Welasma), Ahmad ibn Ibrahim supplanted the sultans, adopted
the religious title Imam, launched a jihad (holy war), and won
his first decisive victory over imperial territory in 1529. His
armies occupied Ethiopia until 1543 when they were thrown back

to Harar and finally dispersed into the desert regions of Awsa.
The area controlled by Adal rulers is within the Ethiopian state
today, with the exception of Zeyla and its environs (now called
Republic of Djibouti). Descendants of the Welasma dynasty
live in the region of the Borqena river and have served the
Shewan kings Sahle Sellase and Menilek with the title of abegaz
(governor of a frontier province).

ADAL TESSEMA see TEKLE HAYMANOT, KING

ADDIS ABABA (Abeba). Capital of Ethiopia, situated in the center
of the country, toward the southern end of the 700-mile-long
plateau, at an altitude of approximately 7,800 feet. It has a
temperate climate, ranging from 58° to 65° F. year-round,
with the rainy season running from June to September. Addis
Ababa, which means "New Flower" in Amharic, was so named
by Empress Taytu (q.v.) wife of Menelik II who decided in
1887 that the new capital should be established there. In Shewa
province, it is the center of Amhara life and culture and is
the political, financial and communications center of the country.
With a more temperate climate than the previous capital at
Entotto, Addis Ababa was also far better situated strategically
and particularly served Menelik's plans for expansion southward.

ADDIS ALEM. In 1900, Menelik toyed with the notion of moving
his capital 20 miles to the west of Addis Ababa, set up only a
dozen years before. By 1902 a motorable road had been built
and the new town of Addis Alem ("New World" in Amharic)
began to take shape: it had a water system, a Russian-staffed
clinic, the legations of Italy and Russia and the church of
Maryam. Menelik changed his mind in 1903 and the houses
were knocked down and transported to build the town of Gennet
which became one of his retreats. The church, copied from
Maryam at Aksum, survived as a royal endowment.

ADDIS AMET (New Year). Amharic name for the religious festival
of the New Year. Occurring on September 11 of the Gregorian
calendar, it is thus around the same time as Rosh Hashanah,
the Jewish New Year, and is similar in purpose. It also marks
the end of the rainy season and thus the return to work and
harvest.

ADEN. Name for the former British protectorate in South Arabia,
of the port city (occupied 1839) for the territory, and the Gulf
of Aden. This body of water, into which flows the Red Sea
from the north, runs in an east-west direction from Djibouti
for about 600 miles to Cape Guardafui, at the tip of the Horn
of Africa, and the Arabian Sea. The area, now part of the
Democratic Republic of the Yemen, was one of the main jump-
ing-off points for the migrations to Abyssinia from South
Arabia in the centuries before Christ, and a significant commercial and communications link between the Middle East and the
African mainland in the 19th century.

ADULIS.   An ancient port located south of Massawa where an inscription (c. A. D. 277-90) was found recording the first campaign of an Aksumite king into South Arabia, a campaign in
the Semen and one against the Beja.   A first century travel
account described the town as a "fair-sized village."   Cosmas
Indicopleustes found it a flourishing port in A. D. 525, trading
with Arabia, Persia and India.

ADWA (Adowa, Adua).   One-time capital of Tegray, believed to
have existed in the 6th century, as it was mentioned by an en-
voy of Justinian to the king of Aksum (20 miles to the west).
It became an important commercial center and customs collec-
tion depot.   It was the provincial seat of Webe Hayle Maryam,
Neguse Welde Mikael, and Kasa Mercha.   The latter defeated
Tekle Giyorgis just outside the gates in July 1871 and became
Yohannes IV.   The Hewett agreement of 1884 (see ADWA,
TREATY OF) was signed there and it was on the heights of
Abba Gerima surrounding it, that Ethiopia defeated Italy in
March 1896.   Asmara has superseded it as capital of Tegray.

ADWA, BATTLE OF.   Site of the crucial defeat of the Italians by
the forces of Menilek II on 1 March 1896, though "Adwa" is
the name given to the whole conflict beginning 7 December 1895
when the advance guard fought and won against the Italians at
Amba Alage, followed by the siege of Meqelle 7-20 January
1895.   The Ethiopian army consisted of about 100,000 men; the
Italians had four brigades totaling 17,700 men, including 7,000
native troops.   Casualties were heavy on both sides, the
Italians losing 50 percent, and the Ethiopians an estimated 10
to 15 percent.   Immediate consequences of the Ethiopian victory
were proof of its independence from Italian claims in the Treaty
of Wetchale (q. v.), and the respect of European nations who soon
established legations in Addis Ababa to deal directly with a
sovereign power.   Celebration of "Adwa" day is a national holiday in Ethiopia, and is marked by military parades.

ADWA, TREATY OF (3 June 1884).   Yohannes IV signed this treaty
with Rear Admiral Sir William Hewett on 3 June 1884 respecting relations between Egypt and Ethiopia, with Great Britain as
guarantor.   There were seven articles, of which the first three
were significant: I. Free transit through Massawa to and from
Abyssinia for all goods; II. Bogos to be restored to Abyssinia
on 1 September 1884--when the garrisons of Kasala, Amedeb and
Senhet (occupied by the Egyptians) had left the country, all
buildings and their contents would become the property of Yohannes IV; III. The Ethiopian emperor will facilitate the with-
drawal of the Egyptian troops from the aforementioned garrison
towns to Massawa.   Yohannes met his obligations under the
treaty, but Italy, after occupying Massawa in 1885, violated the
free-transit provision, despite a promise to Great Britain not
to do so.

AFAR.   An ethnic group of Hamitic origin in eastern Ethiopia, also

known as Danakil (Arabic) or Adal.   Upwards of 10,000 live in
a dry, barren region called the Danakil Depression, where they
work the salt flats of Lake Karum, providing pure, white,
ready-to-use salt for a large area of northeastern Africa.
These tablets of salt (amole) were once the currency of Ethiopia.   The Afar roam the area north of the Djibouti-Addis Ababa
railway.   An estimated 50,000 share the former colony of
French Somaliland, now known as the Republic of Djibouti.
They resemble Somalis but speak a different language and do
not think of themselves as Somali.
     In the past the Afar were under Tegray rule and in the
south under Shewan hegemony.   In recent years the lower Awash
valley Afars were led by Sultan Ali Mira Hanfere (Anfari) until
his self-exile in June 1975; they have been reluctant to adopt to
the rural land reform program of the Derg (q.v.).   After the
sultan left, his people rampaged the Tendaho cotton and sugar
plantation.   Tendaho was a sore point with the Afar as the
central government had expropriated some 52,000 hectares, thus
depriving the Afar of a large section of grazing land.
     The Amhara took six campaigns to subdue the Afar who to-
day remember and resent their conquest by Ras Darge (q.v.).
The Boran and Guji Afar define their history as good "before
the Amhara" and bad afterward.   During the Italian occupation
the Afar rated the Italians as less oppressive, and the occupiers
permitted open season on the Amhara (see ADAL, SULTANATE
OF).

AFARS AND ISE (Issa), Territory of see DJIBOUTI, REPUBLIC
OF

AFERSATA.   Ethiopian "judicial" custom used when a crime was
     committed in a village or small area.   All local inhabitants
     were rounded up and held in an enclosure, sometimes for as
     long as two weeks, until the guilty person was revealed.   Often
     as many as four or five thousand people would be brought in,
     confined and addressed by the elders who would forbid almost
     all activities until the culprit was found.   Those who failed to
     register at the afersata would be fined, thus providing a good
     source of revenue.   In 1933 the emperor modified this prac-
     tice, limiting the days and hours it could take place as well as
     the distance from which people had to come.   The Italians
     maintained this system when they occupied Ethiopia (1936-1941).

AFEWERQ GEBRE IYESUS (1868-1947).   In 1894, after an argument
     with Empress T'aytu over the murals and panels he was paint-
     ing at Entotto Raguel church, he went with Alfred Ilg (q.v.) to
     Switzerland, swearing never to return until she was dead.   He
     and his fellow students in Switzerland, Gugsa Darge and Kelew
     Amanuel, were persuaded to defect to Italy during the war of
     1895-96.   Afewerq married first a relative of Ilg's, then an
     Italian, Eugenia Rossi, in 1904.   He was attached to the Orien-
     tal Institute in Naples and wrote two Amharic grammars, the
     first Amharic novel, a guidebook with many of his political

ideas for Ethiopia, and a biography of Menelik II. His writings
in Amharic were highly regarded for their purity of language
and won for him the reputation as "father" of modern Amharic
literature. He returned to Ethiopia when Zewditu (q. v.) became
empress, headed a trade mission to the United States in 1918,
served as director of customs at Dire Dawa, and as president
of a special court in Addis Ababa to adjudicate disputes between
Ethiopians and foreigners. From 1931 to 1935 he was Ethiopian minister to Italy and was pro-Mussolini. A collaborator
from 1936-1941 he was chief of the Ethiopian court system.
After the liberation, he was exiled to Jimma where he died in
1947.

AFRICA HALL. Constructed in the late 1950s and offered as Ethiopia's contribution to the United Nations organization on the understanding that it would serve as quasi-headquarters for the
United Nations in Africa. It now houses the U. N. Economic
Commission for Africa. An impressive structure, it is also
used for a variety of international conferences dealing with African affairs, including those of the Organization for African
Unity (q. v.). This move by Hayle Sellase succeeded in attracting greater world attention to Ethiopia and enhanced his position
as one of Africa's elder statesmen.

AGAME. A sub-province of Tegray in northeastern Ethiopia comprising an area from the high plateau down to the Red Sea, and
populated largely by the Afar (q. v.). The large Teltal salt
plain is its most important geographical feature. From this
plain came the amole (salt money) which was legal tender in
most parts of the country until late in the 19th century. Enderta, in Agame, was a starting point, from earliest times, for
Tegrayan caravans transporting large blocks of salt.

AGEW (Agaw). Important ethnic group which formed the original
population of the north and central Ethiopian plateau. Their
language, also called Agew, was a strong influence on the development of Amharic and found its way into other dialects in
Ethiopia because it was picked up and used by immigrant Semitic
groups of the pre-Christian millennium. The Agew are considered the progenitors of the Ethiopian "type" ethnically and
linguistically. In the 10th century the Agew revolted and attacked the expansion of Christianity in order to re-establish
Hebraic-pagan religious dominance and observance. The
Felasha (q. v.) are believed to be descended from the Agew.
Another descent group lives south of Lake Tana in Agewmeder;
their language, Awiya, was probably the purest extant form of
the original tongue, but is believed to have died out.

AGORDAT. An administrative division of western Eritrea where the
predominant language is Tegrigna. The town of Agordat is a
terminus of the country's northern railroad which runs from
Massawa to Asmara, Keren and Agordat. It was the scene of
a battle between the Mahdists and Italians in December 1893.

AHMAD IBN-IBRAHIM see ISLAMIC CONQUEST

AIR FORCE. Regent Teferi Mekonnen hired two French pilots in
    1929, and bought four bi-planes from France that had mounts
    for machine guns and were capable of small-bomb drops. By
    the time the Italians invaded in 1935, this air force nucleus
    had become 13 planes and four pilots. In 1947, the emperor
    turned to Sweden for training officers and appointed General
    Sodergren to build an effective air force with 18 Saab trainers
    and two squadrons of Saab-17 light bombers. In 1958, U.S.
    jets were introduced under a military agreement with the USA,
    though General von Lindhal (who replaced Sodergren) was in
    command throughout 1960. His second-in-command, Brig.-Gen.
    Asefa Ayene succeeded him in 1962, recognized for his part in
    ordering reluctant Ethiopian pilots to strafe and bomb Addis
    Ababa in 1960 to help put down the coup d'état against the em-
    peror.
        The Air Force has flown combat missions in the Congo
    (1960-62 and 1967); a squadron of fighters and transport planes
    went to Tanzania in 1964 to support Pres. Nyerere; and most
    recently under the Derg has attacked in the Ogaden and in
    Eritrea. It has done rescue work during floods and famine,
    assisted the East African Locust Service, and trained students
    from Nigeria, Somalia, Kenya, Uganda and Tanzania (pre-1974).
    Its present strength is hard to determine. In mid-1970 there
    were seven fighter and transport squadrons, a helicopter unit,
    a training command, central maintenance workshop, command
    headquarters and academy at Debre Zeyt, a flying school at
    Dire Dawa where it has also trained pilots for the national air-
    line.

AIRLINE, ETHIOPIAN (EAL). Created by Imperial Charter in 1945,
    it was organized under a Government contract with Trans-World
    Airlines (TWA) requiring the General-Manager, Secretary-
    Treasurer and Head of Technical Services to be TWA personnel
    and permitting TWA to have 25 percent ownership. This stock
    option was relinquished before 1950. Victor Harrell took over
    as General-Manager in 1952, heading a staff that was totally
    American, but following a training program financed by USAID
    the airline became fully Ethiopianized and the TWA contract
    was eventually terminated by the late 1970s. The concern for
    efficiency and service made the EAL one of Africa's best and
    in 1962 it became first on the continent to use jets (Boeing
    720-Bs) and the first to China. It also has service to Rome,
    Paris, London, Frankfurt, Athens, Karachi, New Delhi and to
    East and West Africa. Highly useful for both tourism and com-
    merce it also markedly improved internal communications and
    administration.

AKKELE GUZAY. Specifically referred to in pre-Christian litera-
    ture as one of three highland provinces of Ethiopia. Close to
    Muslim areas and tribes of the Massawa region it was still
    loyal to Monophysite Christianity. Its main language is Tegrigna.

Originally Cushitic, its colonization by South Arabian traders
and settlers led to an important infusion of Semitic culture and
language into the two powerful areas of Akkele Guzay and Aksum.   Its influence, along with Aksum's, grew until the 7th
century when the center of power began to shift southward
toward the Shewan region.   Akkele Guzay in more recent centuries was the subject of Catholic proselytization via the Portuguese, the French and, most recently, the Italians.

AKLILU HABTE WELD (1912-1974).   Prime Minister from 1961 to
1974, he was a younger brother of Mekonnen Habte Weld, also
a confidant and favorite of Hayle Sellase's.   Aklilu was educated in France where he remained during the Italian occupation.
He returned with a French wife after the liberation and promptly took up a series of high-level government appointments, ulti-
mately becoming the Minister of Foreign Affairs in 1943.   He
was a key negotiator in the Anglo-Ethiopian Agreement of 1944,
which rectified the rather one-sided agreement of 1942, and in
1945 signed the United Nations Charter in San Francisco.   He
was active in getting U. N. approval, first for Eritrea's federation with Ethiopia in 1952, then for unification in 1962.   Aklilu
was a skilled and loyal bureaucrat, favoring and supervising
more modern administrative procedures in government; his
power to appoint Cabinet ministers, however, was subject to the
Emperor's veto.   He was virtually "thrown to the wolves" by
the emperor in the half-way measures taken to stem the widespread dissent of early 1974.   Though no longer Prime Minister,
he was among those arrested, then executed on November 24,
1974.

AKSUM (Axum).   The name of the ancient kingdom in northern
Ethiopia which exists today mainly as a holy city with archaeological sites, which offer evidence of its establishment in the
first century.   Ezana (q. v.), its 4th century king who decreed
Christianity as the state religion, built huge stone stelae whose
inscriptions give the history of his reign; one of these stelae
was taken to Rome by the Italians as booty from their 1935 invasion.   An Aksum king once occupied Yemen across the Red
Sea, and Meroe to the northwest.   Aksum declined by the 7th
century when the Persians ended Christian rule in South Arabia,
and cut off trade.
    The ark of the covenant, believed to have been brought
from Jerusalem in the 10th century B. C. is said to rest in the
sanctuary of St. Maryam Tseyon, and is the basis of Aksum's
status as Ethiopia's holiest place.

ALEMAYEHU TEWODROS.   Son of Emperor Tewodros II (q. v.) by
Terunesh Webe.   Before he died, Tewodros expressed the wish
that Alemayehu be educated in England.   The boy became a
ward of Queen Victoria after being taken to England by Captain
Speedy who had been with the Anglo-Indian expedition of 1868.
The young prince went to Rugby but died of a pulmonary ailment
in November 1879 and was buried at St. George's Chapel at Windsor.

ALEQA. A title meaning "chief" that described the administrator
of large churches and monasteries, with consequent wealth and
power. He could be a layman or a member of the clergy, and
many were men of great learning. Aleqa Gebre Hanna was head
of a church in Gondar when he devised a new style of liturgical
dancing (peculiar to the Ethiopian Orthodox Church). Though it
was rejected by the conservatives of Gondar, his son carried
the style to Debra Tabor, from which it spread. He was famous for his wit and mastery of the double entendre (see
POETRY) and became a popular figure at the court of Menilek
II (1889-1913). Some eighteen aleqas were famous enough for
either wit, biblical scholarship or diplomacy to be mentioned in
the biographical list of Heruy Welde Sellase (q. v.). A variant,
"Shaleqa, " is a military title meaning "chief of a thousand men. "

ALEXANDRIA, Coptic Patriarchate of. The link with Alexandria was
established in the 4th century when the Patriarch there appointed
Ethiopia's first bishop. Despite interruptions the See of St.
Mark kept its privilege to name a Copt as abun of Ethiopia for
fifteen centuries. The Ethiopian church became independent in
1948--effective in 1950 with the appointment of an Ethiopian to
head the church.

ALEYU AMBA (Haylu amba; Hailiamba). Town which contained the
central market of Shewa and in which live a large community of
Hararis, many of them merchants. The leading member of this
group was usually named by the Emir of Harar as his consul
and was recognized as such by the King of Shewa. The town
was a center of the amole trade (see AGAME). Some slaves
were traded in this market but the great slave market of Shewa
was at Abdul Rasul, a few miles from Aleyu Amba.

ALI ALULA, Ras (1818-1866?). Elected to rule by a Yejju Oromo-
Christian council in 1831 when he was a minor. His father was
Alula Gugsa and his mother Menen Leben Amede (q. v.). His
widowed mother dominated the regency council appointed to guide
him, living near his seat at Debre Tabor, until he came of age.
He was married to Hirut Webe, daughter of the lord of Tegray
who tried and failed to unseat his son-in-law in 1842. A converted Christian, he was too tolerant of Muslims for the other
Christian princes, and spent most of his term of office putting
down rebellions. His putative daughter, Tewabech, married
Kasa of Qwara (see TEWODROS II) which did not prevent that
chief from defeating Ali in June 1953 and forcing him to flee.
His flight was aided by Hayle Melekot of Shewa and he is presumed to have lived safely among his Yejju relatives until his
death about 1866.

ALI MIRA HANFERE (Anfari), Sultan. A religious and political
leader of the Afars, 13th in a line of sultans in a domain with
300 years of history. Shortly after the Provisional Military
Administrative Council took power in 1974, it requested Ali
Mira to come to Addis Ababa for discussions on how to per-

suade the Afar to adapt to rural land reforms programs being
set up by the Derg. Suspecting this as a trick to imprison or
execute him, Ali Mira fled to European exile and his tribe rebelled against the Derg, invading the Tendaho Plantation in
1975. Prior to his exile, Ali Mira had been a minority stock-
holder of the Tendaho Development Corporation and had control
of about 80 percent of the lowland plains.

ALL-ETHIOPIA FARMERS ASSOCIATION (AEFA). National peasant
organization set up by Derg proclamation in September 1977 as
part of its overall Marxist scheme to "politicize the masses
and radicalize the intelligentsia. " It is the centralized control
over all peasant groups which are the rural counterpart of the
urban kebelle (q. v.).
     The objective of the AEFA is to "agitate, educate and en-
lighten members so they may be able to safeguard the gains of
the struggle so far, and step up production in the days ahead. "
     The AEFA is the top of the bureaucratic structure aimed at
organizing and effectuating the Derg's land reform program:
distributing small holdings of land to all farmers, keeping them
informed of national policy, assisting them in solving economic
and social problems, and thereby improving agricultural production.
     Under this system, peasant associations (q. v.) elected rep-
resentatives to regional groupings and these, in turn, sent appointed delegates to the AEFA. In theory, this would provide
a chain of command and information that would reach into every
one of the country's 556 districts (woreda). The central government earlier had tried to use university students as their con-
duit to the farmers (see ZEMECHA) but this campaign failed
when the farmers preferred their independence to any dictation
from the center for them to collectivize, especially by largely
uninformed students, many of whom were pursuing other political
aims or were disgruntled at being sent away from the cities.

ALL-ETHIOPIA SOCIALIST MOVEMENT. Also widely known as
Mei'son, this avowedly Marxist group was, like the Ethiopian
Peoples' Revolutionary Party (q. v.) an outgrowth of the turmoil
surrounding the overthrow of Hayle Sellase in 1974. Never fully
accepted or authorized by the ruling Provisional Military Administrative Council, or Derg, Mei'son had a heavy overlay of Oromo nationalism and was committed to general support of the Derg.
Among those who formed the group was Hayle Fida, educated in
France and other European countries where for 14 years he had
been in exile. He returned immediately after the revolution and
helped shape this group which quickly allied itself to the Derg,
its policies and methods.
     Hayle Fida's primary effort was to establish a central po-
litical party that would eventually supersede the ruling military
council, but the Derg was clearly opposed to any such development. Instead, the Derg appointed Hayle Fida to POMOA (q. v.)
but tolerated the Mei'son publication, "Voice of the Masses. "
Opposition to Mei'son's ambitions came not only from the Derg,

which feared loss of political control to such a party, but also from many radical intellectuals who believed a Mei'son-controlled party would be a government arm and not representative of "people."

Mei'son preferred a "provisional revolutionary government" and accepted an alliance with the military dictatorship as the most efficient way to achieve the feudalism-to-socialism transition. They theorized that socialism would come about not as a result of any mass popular movement but by a "revolution from above," which would weed out dissenters as well as "capitalists, feudalists and bureaucratic bourgeoisie."

A statement in April 1976 by Mengestu Hayle Maryam (q.v.) on behalf of the Derg seemed to endorse Hayle Fida's points, as the latter had become his political adviser. But it also appeared to accept some of the policy aims of the Mei'son's bitter rivals, the EPRP even though the latter were strongly anti-Derg. Establishment of POMOA and the Yekatit 66 (q.v.) School had the purpose of politicization and radicalization around the country by instructors (cadres). Many young Marxist-Leninists were named as cadres and in fairly short order the two units were dominated by Mei'son delegates. The Derg, highly concerned, supplanted most of the Mei'son people with loyal military men who belonged to <u>Abyot Seded</u> (see COOPERATIVE OF MARXIST-LENINIST ORGANIZATIONS).

One of the reasons that Mei'son lost favor was the hyper-militancy of Germa Kebede, chairman of one of the <u>kebelle</u> (q.v.) in Addis Ababa. The epitome of Mei'son's terrorist mentality, Germa was personally responsible for killing 24 "counter-revolutionaries" and "anarchists" early in 1977; a few weeks later he executed nine people, including a pregnant woman, after torturing and blinding them. This outrage provoked a large demonstration and, in March, the Derg executed Germa and several collaborators in a public square. The Derg was particularly annoyed at Mei'son for opposing the execution on the grounds that Germa was a "good revolutionary."

With its representatives in virtual control of both the urban and peasant associations--"grass roots" politicking that the Derg was either unwilling or unable to do--Mei'son continued to challenge the Derg in a power struggle. Having set up Seded as a counterpoise, the Derg outlawed Mei'son in December 1976. Seded members were ordered to uproot the Mei'son, and by February 1977 thousands on both sides had been killed. Hayle Fida was arrested but most Mei'son leaders went underground. Dr. Negede Gobeze, a Mei'son leader who had remained in Europe, was smuggled back into Ethiopia by the Cubans; he sought to rally the Mei'son remnants. When his existence in Addis Ababa was discovered, the Derg sought to arrest him but he took refuge in the Cuban Embassy. Eventually he managed to leave the country, reportedly spirited out in a Cuban Embassy group headed by Ambassador Jose Noved.

Reports from Addis Ababa indicate that both the Soviets and Cubans have urged Derg leaders to relent toward Mei'son in the interest of "unity." But Derg chairman Mengestu Hayle Maryam has continually opposed the development of any mass movement, such as Mei'son, that might be a potential replacement for the governing PMAC.

ALULA ENGEDA QUBI, Ras (c. 1847-1897).   As the son of a peasant without hereditary rights to land, Alula's promotions were based on ability and service.   He became the most trusted army commander of Yohannes IV and was a formidable adversary of the Mahdists, the Italians and Catholic missionary efforts.   He served with distinction in the two wars with Egypt in 1875 and 1876, and defeated the Mahdists at Kufit in September 1885.   That same year the Italians occupied Massawa and began to move inland.   After an ultimatum to withdraw, Alula attacked a 500-man column at Se'ati and wiped them out on 26 June 1887--the Italians call it the "Dogali massacre."   When Britain and Italy protested, Yohannes backed Alula, but privately rebuked him for acting without orders.   After the death of Yohannes, Alula gave his loyalty to Mengesha Yohannes (q. v.), exhorting him not to relinquish Tegrayan independence to the new emperor, Menilek II (q. v.).   In June 1894 Alula reluctantly accompanied Mengesha to Addis Ababa to submit to the emperor.   Alula remained with Menilek amicably, though he was impatient with Menilek's delay in challenging Italian incursions into Tegray.   He fought at Adwa in March 1896, and was rewarded with the governorship of half of Tegray by Menilek.   He died 15 February 1897 from wounds received in a minor skirmish with Hagos of Shire.   He had three daughters from Bitwata whom he divorced in 1878 at the request of Yohannes IV, to marry Amlasu Araya Demtsu, Yohannes's cousin, by whom he had a son.

AMAN MIKAEL AMDON, General.   Brought out of semi-retirement (former Commander of the Third Division), he was named Chief of Staff of the Armed Forces by Hayle Sellase in July 1974, in response to demands of the Armed Forces Co-ordinating Committee.   Born in the Sudan of Eritrean parents, he was a long-time resident in Shewa.   Aman was a popular figure; he had been a senator for 10 years and was considered a moderating influence on the committee attempting to take over the country.   He fell out with the more radical members of the Provisional Military Administrative Council, which took over from the Coordinating Committee, as he advocated a peaceful solution to the Eritrean "problem," as well as trials for arrested government officials.   He was killed resisting arrest at his home the night of 23/24 November, 1974.

AMBA.   Flat-topped mountains with almost vertical sides that have been formed by millennial erosion, and almost impervious to invasion or capture.   Virtually every provincial leader selected an amba to use as his strong-hold where he could keep his treasures and imprison his rivals.   Typical was Meqdela (q. v.) which was long a center of operations for Emperor Tewodros II. A number of ancient monasteries are situated on ambas.   Amba

Wehni, described by Jeronimo Lobo in the 1630s, inspired Dr. Samuel Johnson's Rasselas. Amba Geshen in Gojam, reputed to be the place where the True Cross was kept, was a safe haven used by Emperor Zera Yaqob and by King Tekle Haymanot.

AMDE TSEYON (Emperor 1314-1344). Son of Yekuno Amlaq (q. v.), he is credited with the consolidation of the Solomonic dynasty, after the rule of the Zagwe (q. v.), and as a forceful commander who halted Islam's incursions and widened the frontiers of his empire, subjugated Damot, Gojam and Begemder. A literary renaissance occurred during his reign, its greatest work being the Kibre Negest (q. v.). He is a saint in the synaxarium and his life was chronicled by an eye-witness.

AMEDE LEBEN, Dejajmach. Chief of the Oromo of Were Himeno, succeeding his father, Imam Leben in 1815; staunchly Muslim, he was accused of plotting with Egypt's Muhammad Ali to conquer all of Ethiopia in 1838. When his nephew, Ras Ali Alula (q. v.), still a minor in 1831, was selected as ruler of north-central Ethiopia, he served on the regency council but was superseded in influence by his stepsister Menen, the boy ruler's mother. He was succeeded on his death in 1839 by his son, Imam Leben.

AMEDEB. Garrison post of Egyptian troops on Ethiopian territory at the time of the Ethio-Egyptian clash of 1875. The Adwa Treaty (1884) that emerged from that conflict specified that Yohannes IV would facilitate the safe evacuation of Egyptian troops from Amedeb, as well as those at Kasala and Senhet, in return for the stores and munitions to be left behind. Egyptian units were finally relieved by Ethiopian forces attacking the Mahdist besiegers in 1885.

AMHARA (People and Province). Politically and historically, the Amhara are the dominant culture group of Ethiopia from which virtually all its rulers have come. Their language is Amharic, the religion is Monophysite Christianity; subsistence over the centuries has been through cultivation of cereal grains. With the Tegrayans, with whom they share all these characteristics except language, the Amhara constitute the main power groups that other peoples of the world have called "the Abyssinians." Important influences on the development of the Amhara were the Aksumites and, some centuries later, the Agew (q. v.). While there is no Amhara province today, earlier maps located an area called Amhara between Gojam and Wello. Always a numerical minority of the population, the Amhara, for most of the past few centuries, have dominated Begemder, Gojam, Wello and Shewa (see Tegray).

AMHARIC. The national language spoken by approximately eight million people as a mother tongue (also called Amharigna), and as a second language by about five million others: totaling

about half the population. In government primary schools it
was replaced as the language of instruction by English after the
sixth grade. Written Amharic has 282 symbols and is written
from left to right in contrast to other Semitic languages. The
complex grammar is mastered by relatively few scholars. Vir-
tuosity in spoken Amharic is much admired: wit, oratory, insult, poetry bring prestige to their practitioners. Verb forms
contain both the sex of the person addresséd and his rank relative to the speaker. Except for legal cases and martial boasting, loud speech indicates loss of self-control and disrespect.
There is a movement towards calling the alphabet "Ethiopian"
rather than "Amharic" because it is also used to write Tegrigna
and other languages. Nothing was written in Amharic before
the 18th century. All manuscripts were written in Ge'ez (see
GE'EZ; LITERATURE; POETRY).

ANKOBER. A former capital of Shewa province built by King Sahle
  Sellase (1813-1844). Its church, Medhani Alem, was the site
  of Menilek II's (q.v.) marriage to Taytu Betul in 1883 and it
  was the checkpoint for all caravans and foreign expeditions en-
  tering Shewa, and served as a state prison for political detainees under Menilek II.

AQABE SE'AT. Once the title given to the chief ecclesiastic of the
  imperial court, translatable as "appointment." It also became
  the name of the system whereby Hayle Sellase would see his
  ministers at specified times during the week.

ARABIC. One of the Semitic dialects that succeeded the Aramaic
  of Christ's time, found its way to Ethiopia and was used by
  northern Muslim groups and along the Red Sea coast. As a result, some Arabic words were incorporated into other local dialects but Arabic never supplanted any of these despite some
  similarities in grammar and sound. Arabic has been less
  prevalent in recent years in Ethiopia partly because of the
  spread of Amharic, Tegrigna, Galligna and other tongues, partly
  because fear of the surrounding inimical Muslim countries such
  as the Sudan, Egypt and Somalia has led Ethiopian rulers to attempt to curtail the language.

ARAYA DEMTSU, Balgada (c. 1810-1889). Tegray noble who rebelled against Webe (the "outsider" from Semen) in 1840; he
  was imprisoned by Webe for 15 years, then given command of
  Tegray by Tewodros II. Shortly thereafter, he was imprisoned
  at Meqdela where he remained until released by the Anglo-Indian
  Expedition of 1868. He held high commands under his nephew,
  Emperor Yohannes IV; both of them died fighting the Mahdists
  in March 1889. His title balgada meant he was the comptroller
  of the salt trade.

ARCHITECTURE. One of the earliest examples of permanent construction (apart from the stele at Aksum and the rock-hewn
  churches of Lalibela and Tegray) was directed by the Jesuit

Pero Paez who believed in demonstrating the European technology of 1614.   Apart from their ability to construct round,
conical-roofed huts and churches similarly styled, the Ethiopians knew little or nothing of other building materials.   Paez
found a quarry, directed the making of stone-cutting tools and
saw to the building of Maryam Gemb, a castle at Gorgora.   An
Indian craftsman brought in by the Portuguese found limestone
for use as mortar.

The fact that there was no fixed capital, nor significant urban settlements, made no demand for government buildings or
monumental structures.   Not until Fasiledes (q. v.) established
a permanent capital at Gondar in the 17th century, did the arts
and skills of architecture and construction have an outlet.   The
Gurage (q. v.) in the 19th century acquired a reputation as builders, but in the field of design Europeans were relied on primarily (see CHURCHES).

ARMAH, King.   Possibly an aprocryphal figure, but believed to be
the king of Aksum in the 7th century A. D. who befriended those
disciples of Prophet Muhammad who had fled persecution in
Arabia.   Some scholars believe that without Armah's support
and assistance, Islam might not have survived.   The only positive response to Muhammad's proclamation urging the world's
rulers to "worship the One God, " came from Armah, a Christian monarch.   As a result, it is believed, Muhammad issued
a prohibition against any offensive moves against Ethiopia, an
edict respected until the 16th century.

During Armah's reign, Ethiopian occupation of South Arabia
ended, but he continued to control the Red Sea area and favored
good relations there because of mutual trade.   He continued his
predecessor's policy of allowing Muslim refugees to come to
Ethiopia; when Muhammad asked him to permit these exiles to
return, Armah agreed and the émigrés were sent to Medina
where the Prophet had fled to escape his antagonists in Mecca.

ARMED FORCES.   Ethiopia's army, efficient, disciplined and well-
equipped with modern weapons evolved over centuries of warfare, fighting off attacks, civil war, and wars of conquest.   Local leaders maintained their own armies.   This was especially
true during the contentious Zemene Mesafint (q. v.).   Constant
skirmishing led to a mercenary soldiery who would shift their
allegiance to the leader who offered the best chance at booty.
In 1853 it was estimated that more than 200, 000 men, plus
their camp-followers, made up a fragmented fighting force.
Women carried loads, cooked, tended the wounded and shared
all the hazards of war.

When Emperor Tewodros II came to power in 1855 he made
a start at reorganizing his followers into a drilled, disciplined
force that was paid regularly and punished severely for looting.
Yohannes IV continued these efforts, hiring British Sergeant
John Kirkham to be a military adviser, though the Ethiopian
soldiers did not take willingly to drilling; nonetheless the armies
of Yohannes successfully defeated two European-trained armies

from Egypt and their reputation as fighters was sufficient to keep Menilek's Shewan army disinclined to meet them in combat.

Menilek II was the most successful at acquiring weapons and controlling marauding by the establishment of granaries for his soldiers to draw provisions from. His military campaigns were timed to allow his men to return to their land from June to September for the planting season and then again for harvest. His provincial governors were required to provide men, food and material for his standing army and he carefully controlled the number of guns they were allowed to distribute among their own forces. Menilek's army was around 80,000 men when he faced the Italians in 1895; the number swelled to 150,000 as loyal chiefs brought their armies in support.

The army had no clear division of forces into infantry, artillery and cavalry. Most men walked hundreds of miles to battle; those who had mounts constituted the cavalry. Menilek had a small number of men trained by a French instructor to use artillery.

As Regent, Ras Teferi, sent men for training to the British in Kenya, to the Italians in Tripoli and to St. Cyr in France. As emperor, he brought in a Belgian Military Mission, and staffed a Military Academy at Holeta in 1934 with Swedes. The war with Italy came too soon to enable this effort to have any effect on army efficiency. It was reopened in 1941 under British direction. An Air Force Academy was established at Debre Zeyt (Bishoftu) in the 1950s with Swedish advisers, and in 1953 the first United States Military Assistance group was sent in. Subsequent years saw military teams from India, Japan, and Israel, while the Norwegians advised on the formation of a navy, based at Massawa. Members of various services were sent also to the United States, Yugoslavia and Britain for training. A radical departure for Ethiopian armies was the despatch in May 1951 of a battalion to Korea as a contribution to the United Nations Forces. In another U.N. action in the Congo in 1960, some 3,300 Ethiopian Army and Airforce men took part.

Members of the Imperial Bodyguard fomented the 1960 uprising that failed and in 1974, army men, both officers and enlisted, succeeded in deposing the emperor (see DERG).

The Ethiopian Armed Forces are rated as one of the best trained in Africa, although it has required the assistance of Cuban troops and Soviet "advisers" to contain Somali attacks in the Ogaden as well as guerrilla activity in Eritrea. In 1977-78 a new eight-division army was created, and about 100,000 men were drawn from the semi-organized peasant militia. See also AIR FORCE.

ARMENIANS. It was to her Armenian purchasing agent, Matewos, that Empress Elleni (q.v.) confided her letters to the King of Portugal in 1509/10 initiating a long history of trust between trader and monarch. The worldwide dispersal of Armenians included many who became residents of Ethiopia where their

talents in artisanship and trade flourished. Early in the 19th
century, Armenians were observed in metal work and tanning
at Adwa, and the descendants of an Armenian-Ethiopian gold
worker, Werqe Karapet held positions at Tewodros's court, and
were translators and envoys for Yohannes IV. One, Mercha
Werqe was for a time the imperial treasurer. Werqe Karapet
himself completed diplomatic missions for three provincial
rulers, Sebagades of Tegray in 1812, Webe of Tegray in 1832
(to the Na'ib of Arkiko) and Sahle Sellase of Shewa in 1843.

Menilek II used Bogos Macarian (i.e. Polos Magarean) as
his envoy to Egypt in 1875 and Sarkis Terzian and Dikran
Ebeyan as purchasing agents and go-betweens in many state
matters. Terzian accompanied Haj abd-Allah Sadiq to the U.S.
in 1905 to deliver gifts from Menilek to Theodore Roosevelt.

Armenian emigration spurted after the Turkish pogroms in
1895-96, but even more arrived in Ethiopia in the 20th century.
Many found employment on the Franco-Ethiopian railway, and
others settled as small entrepreneurs and artisans in various
parts of the country. By 1935 there were an estimated 2,800
Armenians, exceeded only by Indians, Arabs and Greeks in the
foreign population. They built their own school in 1918, a
sports club in 1930, and a church in 1935 (see INVESTMENT,
FOREIGN).

The Armenian Church shares the Monophysite creed with
the Ethiopian church but in the bitter conflict over the Ethiopian
church and convent in Jerusalem (q.v.) sided with the Copts who
had taken it over in 1820. The Armenians, however, did provide subsistence rations for the Ethiopians who were starving,
for many years until Yohannes IV undertook to improve the finances of the Jerusalem community.

The Armenian Patriarch, with the approval of the British,
dispatched his Archbishop, Issac de Kharpet (or Sanak) and a
priest, Dimothéos (or Timotêos) Saprichean to intercede with
Tewodros II in 1867 to release the European captives. They
were too late to have any effect and spent most of their two
years in the country in the custody of W̲a̲g̲s̲h̲u̲m̲ Gobeze. Their
account, published in Armenian, French and later in German,
is an invaluable source for the period 1868-1870.

ARSI (Arisi, Arussi). Both the description of an area and a grouping of Oromo people living beyond the Awash river southeast
of Shewa. Though they describe themselves as descended from
the 17 sons of "Arsi," they are much mixed with the Sidama
population. Islam spread among them only in the last half of
the 19th century, but their religious practices remain a blend
of animist and magical practices. Highly efficient warriors,
they were brought under the imperial umbrella only after several military campaigns led by R̲a̲s̲ Darge (q.v.) in the 1870s
and '80s. The shrine of Shaikh Hussain is guarded by the Arsi.

ARTICLE XVII (Treaty of Wetchale). The Italian version of this article committed Menilek II to conduct his foreign relations
through Rome, while the Amharic translation said the emperor

could use Italy if he wanted to. The mistranslation did not
surface until Menilek received letters from Queen Victoria and
Kaiser Wilhelm in 1890 referring substantive matters to the
good offices of Italy. Protracted negotiations resulted only in
counter accusations of bad faith and trickery. Menilek informed
European powers of the mistake in translation immediately, and
denounced the entire treaty in Feb. 1893.

ARTS see PAINTING; MUSIC; HANDICRAFTS; POETRY; DANCE

ARUSI see ARSI

ASFA WESSEN, Meredazmach (1916-). Eldest son of Hayle
Sellase I and regarded as heir-apparent although the Ethiopian
throne was not inherited necessarily through primogeniture.
He first married Welette Israel, daughter of Ras Seyum of
Tegray (q.v.); then Medferiyashi-Werq Abera Damtew. During
the 1960 Imperial Guard revolt (see COUP, 1960), he was put
forward by the rebels as monarch, but it was generally believed that his broadcast statement of support for them was
forced with a gun at his back. On the emperor's return, he
was in apparent disgrace, and on future trips abroad he accompanied his father. Despite carrying out a number of
government functions, Asfa Wessen was never allowed to gain
experience in leadership or government. He had a reputation
as a progressive because of a number of discerning decisions
while a judge of the imperial court. Paradoxically, his poor
health in 1974 lengthened his life. He was in London for
treatment at the time of the deposition of his father and is of
this date safely in exile. His daughter from his first marriage, Ejjegayehu, died of medical neglect in 1977 while in detention; her children escaped to the United States.

ASMARA (Asmera). Capital and main city of Eritrea, located at
the northern end of the central Ethiopian plateau and has, like
Addis Ababa at the southern end, an altitude of about 7,500
feet and a temperate climate. Developed under Italian tutelage,
it took on the physical structure and amenities of an Italian
town. It is a communications, commercial and administrative
center second only to Addis Ababa, connected by railway to
Massawa, Keren and Agordat and its airport is one of the most
modern in Africa.

ASRAT. A form of land taxation which was begun by Menilek II in
1878. Farmers preferred providing the government with one
tenth of their crop to quartering soldiers in their houses.
These unwelcome boarders often remained as virtually permanent
residents. Local officials or elders would determine the size of
the crop and the amount to be paid. This system, which went
by different names and regulations according to the province or
language group, remained in force through the Italian occupation
but was eventually superseded by more specific tax levies under
Hayle Sellase.

ASRATE KASA, Ras (1918-1974).   Descended from the Shewan royal
    house (see KASA DARGE) he was appointed to govern, in turn,
    Begemder (1942-44 and 1952-56); Wellega (1944-46); Arussi
    (1946-52); Shewa (1956-57). He became vice-president of the
    Senate in 1957 and its president from 1961 to 1964 and was the
    emperor's representative in Eritrea from 1964. He moved
    quickly to coordinate military action against the 1960 rebellion
    and was unrelenting in his demand for severe penalties. After
    the emperor's overthrow he was clearly marked for execution
    by the Derg in November 1974.

ASSAB (Aseb).   A port on the Red Sea just north of the territory
    of the Afars and Ise (Djibouti). It was an ancient port of entry
    for seafarers and colonizers from South Arabia. In 1869 it
    was sold to an Italian shipping company by the local sultan.
    It was soon taken over by the Italian government (though not
    voted an Italian colony until 26 June 1882) and through agree-
    ment with the Sultan of Awsa a trade route was pioneered to
    Shewa. It never was able to compete with the Obok (Djibouti)-
    Harar-Shewa route, nor with Massawa's facilities, and fell into
    disuse. In 1967, the Soviet Union's aid to Ethiopia was the
    establishment of crude-oil bunkers and port development of
    Assab; a U.S. company built a refinery there.

ATSME GIYORGIS GEBRE MESEH (1821-1914).   An historian of the
    Oromo people ("Ye-Galla Tariq"). First educated in monastic
    schools, he then learned Arabic from Muslim traders, then
    Latin from Catholic missionaries who converted him. He served
    Menilek II as a courier and provided intelligence to that
    monarch before the conquest of Harar in 1886. He was a
    critic of Menilek's contacts with the Khedive of Egypt and an
    early warner on the implications of Article 17 (q. v.) of the
    Treaty of Wetchale.

AUSSA see AWSA

AUSTRALOPITHECUS AFARENSIS.   Scientific name for species of
    hominid whose fossil bones were found by anthropologists at
    sites near Hadar in the Afar region of Ethiopia. Similar re-
    mains were found in Tanzania by scientific expeditions between
    1973 and 1977. The name, which means Afar ape-man, was
    applied to creatures estimated to have lived in these East Afri-
    can areas between 2. 9 and 3. 8 million years ago. A report
    published in January 1979 identifies these as fossils of a new
    species of man believed to be from 600, 000 to 800, 000 years
    older than any heretofore discovered.
        Although its countenance was ape-like, the Afar species
    was analyzed anatomically as "an upright, bipedal creature we
    can definitely place in the zoological family of man. " Some 57
    different skeletons were identified: 22 from the Tanzanian site,
    and 35 from the Afar region, with the Tanzanian fossils in the
    older time period. Since the sites are 1, 000 miles apart, it
    was assumed that the creatures were nomadic, possibly mi-

grating to Afar from their earlier habitat to the south. The announcement was made by the Museum of Natural History of Cleveland, Ohio.

AUSTRIA. In 1853, Konstantin Reitz, the Austrian consul in Khartoum, and his secretary, Theodor von Heuglin, tried and failed to negotiate a treaty with Webe of Tegray. Von Heuglin returned to explore the coastal areas near Massawa in 1857, and in 1861 accompanied Werner Munzinger (q. v.) on a trip into the highlands. Austrian explorers H. Schubert, T. Kinzelbach and H. Steudner were also on this exploration. Two Austrians held high rank in the Egyptian invading forces of 1876 (see EGYPT).

The Austro-Hungarian empire (1867-1918) sent military observers with the British expedition of 1868 and its foreign office took the advice of Bismarck in 1872 to ignore Yohannes IV's letter (13 August 1872) and envoy (John Kirkham) who complained of Egyptian attacks. Philipp Paulitschke and K. von Hardegger explored the Zeyla-Harar route in 1885 just as Egyptian forces were evacuating Harar.

Attempting to replace the ubiquitous Maria Teresa taler, Menilek II purchased a minting machine from Austria in 1904 and employed Willy Hentze to operate it. Only a few coins were produced and Hentze left in 1905 just as an official mission arrived headed by L. von Hoehnel and including Frederic Bieber and Baron A. von Mylius. After von Hoehnel signed a trade treaty with Menilek II, 21 March 1905, he left Austro-Hungarian affairs in the care of the Italian legation and with Bieber traveled to Kefa. Bieber returned to Kefa in 1909 and again in 1913; his published research on Kefa is a major resource for historians.

In April 1913, a resident Austrian, Karl Schwimmer became the honorary consul, but two years later these duties were assigned to the German legation. Dr. Erich Weinsinger renewed the role of honorary consul in 1925 for two years, after which Austria was again represented by Germany. In 1936 Austria recognized the annexation of Ethiopia by Italy. After the end of the Allied occupation of Austria in 1955, diplomatic relations were resumed through Austria's mission in Cairo. Not until 1963 was an embassy opened in Addis Ababa headed by Dr. Hermann Cohn; relations have been maintained after the 1974 revolution.

Austria's most visible impact on Ethiopia was the Maria Teresa taler which began circulating around 1805 (see CURRENCY). Alfred Abel, an expatriate Austrian, was a long-time commercial and banking adviser to Hayle Sellase.

AWSA (Aussa), Sultanate. Fertile oasis in eastern Ethiopia, about 150 miles from the port of Assab; peopled about 1577 by a Muslim clan who were united in their hatred of the neighboring Ise and highland Oromo who raided them constantly. This well-watered area came under the control of nomadic Afar and its sultanate disappeared about 1672. Most important of its

latter-day rulers was Sultan Hanfari Muhammad (1862-1902).
By agreement with Italy and then Menilek II, he allowed arms
caravans to traverse his territory safely.

AYLET (Ailet).   Village in Eritrea on the coastal plain near Massawa between Se'ati and Ginda. In the 1860s it was a point of
contention between Egypt and Ethiopia, both laying claim to
ownership.   Aylet was attacked by Alula (q. v.) in October 1883
trying to dislodge the Egyptians and assert Ethiopia's claims.
Aylet is the site of some hot springs that are a mecca for
people seeking cures for syphilis, rheumatism, fevers and
dysentery.

AYSHAL, Battle at (29 June 1853). Site, in Gojam, of one of the
bloodiest battles of the entire Zemene Mesafint.   By 1852,
Kasa Haylu had decided to disobey orders from his nominal
master, Ras Ali Alula (q. v.), who was still in control of most
of the princes and areas of northern Ethiopia.   Ali sent his
troops to capture the rebellious Kasa but the latter, having regrouped his forces during the rainy season and having won support from the lowlands, of which he was native, finally clashed
with Beru Goshu, Ali's chief lieutenant, at Gur Amba.   Beru
was killed and his army dispersed; Kasa went on to other victories and openly declared his intention to smash Ali and re-
unite Ethiopia under his rule.   Ali then led his forces--spear-
headed by his hitherto undefeated Oromo cavalry--to the inevitable clash, this time at Ayshal, on 29 June 1953.   Kasa and
his Amhara warriors routed the cavalry and forced Ali to flee;
the victory at Ayshal marked the beginning of the reign of
Tewodros II.

AZMARI see MUSIC

- B -

BALCHA SAFO, Dejazmach (c. 1862-1936).   Found castrated, while
still a boy, on a raid into a Gurage area, he became a ward
of Menilek II after being educated by Ras Mekonnen.   In 1882
he was appointed keeper of the stores at Entotto and then
treasurer of the imperial court.   He commanded the artillery
during the Welamo campaign of 1894 and during the war of
1895-96; then became governor of Sidamo.   In 1908 he was appointed governor of Harar; unpopular with the merchants there
for onerous customs levies, he was removed in 1910.   He opposed Lej Iyasu and was active in his deposition in 1916.   In
1928, hostile to the Teferi Mekonnen regency, he repaired to a monastery for seven years, reappearing in 1935 to fight the Italians.
To commemorate his death, a hospital in Addis Ababa was named
for him.

BALE.   A district that covers almost 10 percent of the country;
it borders the Ogaden desert from which it is separated by the

Webi Shebeli river. Its northern border with Arussi consists
of fertile, cool highlands and it slopes down to the hot and arid
lowlands on the border with Somalia. Its sparse population of
Oromo, Somali, and others was incorporated into the empire
between 1885 and 1891 by Ras Darge and Dejazmach Welde
Gabriel and the Amhara political and social system was imposed.
A simmering resentment against expropriation of lands and a be-
wildering tax system administered by governors whom they saw
as corrupt and unfair, led to a rebellion in 1963, partly financed and abetted by the new state of Somalia. It took the
central government seven years to establish its control (see
REBELLIONS).

BANKS. The stimulus for the chartering of the first "Bank of
Abyssinia, " was Menilek II's wish to relieve himself of dependency on French financing of the railroad. The charter was
granted on 10 March 1905. It was an affiliate of the National
Bank of Egypt and had a branch in Harar. By far the largest
share of the stock was owned by British subjects and only a
small percentage by Ethiopians. Menilek was disillusioned with
the bank barely three months after it opened and did not entrust
even the royal treasury to it, though his trust increased by
1907 through the good work of its first manager, D. McGillivray.
A rival bank was considered by Empress Taytu in 1909; it
lasted about eight months, collapsing when the coup d'état
against her succeeded in March 1910.
    In 1931 the bank became state owned as the "Bank of
Ethiopia, " and in 1943 a charter was granted in the name of
"State Bank of Ethiopia. " There is also the "National Bank of
Ethiopia, " created in December 1963 and the Commercial Bank
of Ethiopia, which was established as a share company. The
Development Bank, 1951, grew out of the Agricultural Bank of
1945. The Investment Bank of Ethiopia was established, August
1963, and the first private one, Bank of Addis Ababa, was
founded 1964. All banking is now nationalized.

BARYA and KUNAMA PEOPLE. These names describe two negroid
tribes that live in the Barentu area of Eritrea on the Sudan
border, from whence the Barya may have moved around the 13th
century. The Kunama are called "Bazen" by the Abyssinians,
and "Baza" by the Sudanese and are more numerous (about
15,000) than the Barya (about 9,500). An 1861 estimate of
100,000 Kunama appears high, though there is no doubt they
were decimated in raids by the Egyptians and the Abyssinians
to take them as slaves. Both are sedentary agriculturalists
living in settled villages, and both had a matrilineal descent
system before the Barya were forcibly islamized (about 1856),
thereby removing the equality of women that had existed. The
Kunama retained the matrilineal system. Until the Swedish
missionaries realized they should concentrate on the women in
the 1920's, the number of converts between 1866-70 was 4 or 5.
The first books printed in the Kunama tongue came in 1903 as
a result of the Swedish mission. Today, about a third of the

Kunama are Christian, either Roman Catholic or Protestant;
the Barya remain Muslim. Although the practice is officially
discouraged, the word "Barya" along with "Shankalla" has been
used to jibe at people with negroid characteristics.

BARYAU GEBRE TSADEQ, Ras (?-1878). A deputy governor of
Tegray under Tewodros II, he was defeated by Kasa Mercha
(Yohannes IV) at Debre Sina in September 1867. He was reinstated as governor of Tegray in 1871 and played a commanding
role in the two battles with Egypt in 1875 and 1876. Yohannes
IV appointed him to Hamasen in 1878 where a few months later
he was killed by the rebel, Welde Mikael Selomon.

BASELYOS, Abune (formerly Echege Gebre Giyorgis) (1881-12 Oct.
1970). The first Ethiopian-born bishop of the church in 16
centuries; he was consecrated 14 January 1951 and raised to
Patriarch in 1960. Continuing the tradition of the religious-
political structure of the nation, he was appointed to the Senate
in 1957. He was succeeded by Abune Tewoflos who was "replaced" by a candidate of the Derg in 1976, Abune Tekle Haymanot.

BE'EDA MARYAM (Emperor 1468-1478). He became emperor at
the age of 22 and was confronted with great difficulties in maintaining a widespread domain after the aggressive expansionism
of his father (Zera Yaqob). He avoided conflict with neighboring sultanates, particularly Adal (see IFAT), making an armistice with its sultan. This permitted him to send an expedition to quell the Felasha (q.v.) of Semen. The armistice col-
lapsed with the death of the Adal sultan and his successor began the attacks forcing Be'eda Maryam to reduce his empire
during the last four years of his reign. There are fine descriptions of the royal court and the positions of the queens
(Jan Sayfa, Romna, and "Bealte-Shehna") and the queen-mother
(Elleni) in his chronicle. He convened a council in 1477 to hear
proposals on severing the spiritual dependence on Alexandria,
but was influenced by the abbot of Debre Libanos to veto it.

BEFANA. Consort of Menilek from 1865 to 1882. From previous
husbands she had a number of children, one of whom married
Menilek's first cousin, Meshesha Seyfu and another married
Muhammad Ali (see MIKAEL, Ras). The ambitious Befana
sought promotion of her sons, and to that end drove a wedge
between Menilek and Meshesha Seyfu, the heir apparent, ordering her daughter to divorce him. She was an accomplice in a
rebellion against Menilek in 1877; briefly rusticated she returned
to court and Menilek's favor until he married Taytu (q.v.).
She died about 1887 in seclusion at Debre Libanos monastery.

BEGEMDER (Begamder, Bagamdir). A major province, bordered
by Semen and Wello to the east, Gojam to the south, and the
Sudan on the west. Early in the 14th century, it was defined
only by the river Beshilo and the upper course of the Tekkeze

on the east and the southeastern shore of Lake Tana.   Its main
city, Gondar (q. v.) was for almost 200 years the imperial
capital.   Its second city is Debre Tabor (q. v.).

BEJA.   One of the major ethnic groups (Cushitic) residing between
the Nile and the Red Sea; differentiated by anthropologists today as "Hamito-Semitic. "   In the 5th century, Herodotus referred to the Beja as "Blemmyes. "   They retain physical
characteristics, customs, and a language described a thousand
years ago.   There are four main federations, of which only
one, the Beni Amer (q. v.), lives on the Ethiopian side of the
Sudan border.

BEKAFFA (Emperor 1721-1730).   Much folklore is attached to his
name which means "the inexorable" in the Oromo tongue, and
his reign, centering on his incognito travels around the country
to see that justice was done.   His employment of an Oromo
regiment to destroy the ambitions of rebellious nobles opened
the door to stronger influence of the Oromo at court.   His wife,
Welette Giyorgis (see MENTEWAB, Etege), who outlived him by
40 years, had a greater impact on Ethiopian history.

BELEN   see   BOGOS

BELEW TEKLE HAYMANOT   see   TEKLE HAYMANOT, KING

BELGIUM and Ethiopia.   The consul in Alexandria, Edouard Blondeel van Cuelenbroeck, explored the possibility of a Belgian
colony in northern Ethiopia during a year's travel 1841-42.   In
Brussels his recommendations were well received but came to
naught.   Belgian military observers accompanied the British
expedition of 1868 and an agent of Leopold II investigated the
Italian administration of Eritrea in 1892 and 1893.   Belgian
imports of iron, enamelware, hardware and ammunition constituted a small factor in the trade figures of 1900.   An Antwerp
based company was formed in 1901 to explore for gold in
Ethiopia (majority stock-holders were Italian); it was liquidated
in 1910.   A certain Dr. Goffin, about whom little is known,
tended to the ailments of the royal house in 1901 and was hired
to join the French scientific expedition headed by Duchesne-
Fournet in 1902.   In 1906 official relations were negotiated by
H. Henin who was accompanied by an engineer, Fritz Boulvin,
but Belgian affairs were handled by the French legation until
the appointment of Maxime Gerard in 1923.   Two Belgian com-
panies established coffee plantations in Arusi in 1912, but these
were abandoned as losses by 1935.   Advisers on police and
military training were hired in 1929, but were recalled by their
government as Italian forces neared Addis Ababa in 1936.   Belgian troops participated in retaking Ethiopia in 1941; a contingent
cooperated in an attack at Gambela to stifle the attempted return
to power by a son of ousted monarch Lej Iyasu.   Belgium maintains an embassy in Addis Ababa, and has provided modest economic assistance after its own recovery from World War II.

BENI AMER.   Tribal group of the Beja (q.v.) who straddle the
northern Ethiopia-Sudan border with about 60,000 living in
Eritrea and half that number in the Sudan.   They began forming
in the 16th century and over the next 100 years were incorporated into the Funj Confederation of Sennar.   Their paramount
chief, the diglal, received from the Funj a three-horned cap
as symbol of authority which is still worn today.   Some speak
To-Bedawe and others Tegrigna.   In the first half of the 19th
century Muhammad Uthman al-Mirghani and his sons preached
among them and Islam took hold.   There are Mirghani centers
at Kasala and Keren; other Beni Amer revere the tomb at
Agordat of Sayyid Mustafa.   There is a seasonal migration to
pick cotton in the Sudan.   Despite the diverse origins of the
tribe (Beja, Arab, Tegre) there is a general uniformity of law
among them based on organized rulers and serfs.

BENI SHANGUL (Bani Shangul).   Used to describe the area next to
the Sudan (Blue Nile to the north) and the people who live in
it, of Berta tribe.   Though a mélange, they regard themselves
descended from a single family whom they trace back to 1720.
Islam (Tijaniya order) was established among them by 1855.
They were conquered 1897-98 by imperial forces under the command of Ras Mekonnen (q.v.) but their leader, Shaikh Khojali,
preserved their autonomy by regular tribute of alluvial gold.
Menilek II granted the gold-mining concession there in 1899 to
an English company but stipulated they were not to interfere
with local gold working.   They and other Nilotic peoples have
been labeled pejoratively as "shankalla" although this was officially discouraged by Emperor Hayle Sellase.   Many Beni
Shangul were brought to the capital as slaves; slave trading
was a business in the Shaikh Khojali family conducted with
Sudan-based traders as well as with Ethiopians.   The area is
now a district of Welega.

BEREKET HABTE SELLASE, Dr. (Bereket-ab-Selassie) (1932-).
Eritrean-born law graduate of the University of London who became the Attorney General in 1962 and helped to organize the
law school (q.v.).   Known for his "radical views and attitudes,"
he resigned from the government and was "exiled" to Harar in
1967; the governor of Hararge province made him mayor of the
city 1968-70.   In 1970 he returned to Addis Ababa and was later
appointed Vice-minister of Interior but asked to be relieved in
1972 to join the World Bank in Washington D.C.   In June 1974
he returned to Addis Ababa to take charge of the inquiry into
the conduct of the arrested "ancien regime."   After the shooting
of Gen. Aman Mikael Amdon (q.v.) with whom he had sought
a peaceful resolution to the Eritrean "problem," he escaped.
After two years of working with Eritrean displaced persons he
joined his family in the U.S.   He is now a professor at Howard
University, Washington D.C.

BERU GOSHU see GOSHU ZEWDE

BERU WELDE GIYORGIS, Aleqa. Senior administrator of ecclesiastical affairs in the early part of the reign of Yohannes IV.
In 1869 he carried the 20,000 talers to Egypt to secure a new
bishop whom he escorted back to Ethiopia. In 1872 he transferred his loyalty to Yohannes's reluctant vassal, Menilek, and
became his envoy to the Khedive of Egypt. Returning in November 1875 with a contingent of Egyptian troops led by Werner
Munzinger (q.v.), Beru and Munzinger were both killed in
Awsa when attacked by Danakil tribesmen.

BETE ISRAEL ("house" of Israel) see FELASHAS

BEYENE YEMER, Lej. A Tegrayan sponsored by Empress T'aytu
for appointment, in October 1901, as the first head of Posts
and Telegraph, and later named by Menilek II as Minister of
Posts and Communications. In mid-1911, Beyene Yemer and
others were imprisoned for having supported Ras Abate in his
attempted coup some months earlier. Subsequently Beyene was
released and named Foreign Minister by Lej Iyasu (q.v.) who
not long afterward, in a typically capricious move, replaced
him with one of his favorites, a court minstrel.

BEZEBESH (Betsabeh) (Queen of Shewa). A Menz lady of good
family, who after being widowed became the wife of Sahle
Sellase, ruler of Shewa. She had four daughters from her first
husband who were married and divorced to suit the political aims
of her second husband, whose active counselor she was. By
Sahle Sellase she had two sons: Hayle Melekot (father of
Menilek II) and Seyfu. Some allege she was too quickly
resigned to the conquest of Shewa by Tewodros II in 1855.
Usually she was distant with the foreign white men who entered
Shewa, but made an exception for the Frenchman, Rochet
d'Héricourt and the Italian priest, Father Massaia. She died
about 1870-71, at Sela Dengay.

BLACK LIONS (Tequr Ambesa). One of the resistance groups
formed after the Italians occupied Addis Ababa in May 1936,
formed by a number of young, educated Ethiopians including
several graduates of Holeta military school, and headed by Dr.
Alem Werq. They convinced Ras Emru (q.v.) to be their
leader. Although they disapproved of the emperor's departure
to exile, they reaffirmed their support for him. Among these
"Lions" were Yelma Deresa (q.v.) and Tedesa Mercha who
survived to write their history in 1950. A number of hit-and-
run engagements against the Italians succeeded, but the force
was surrounded in December 1936, though many escaped to
join other groups. Ras Emru and Yelma Deresa were among
those taken to Italy to be displayed as important captives (see
PATRIOTS).

BOGOS or BELEN. Both a region and an ethnic group, it is the
most northerly district of Tegray, divided from that province
by the Mereb River. Its border with Egypt was so poorly de-

fended by Tegray rulers that its people, the Belen (Bogos), were prey to slave and cattle raiders from the Egyptian-Sudan. Keren, its capital (also called Senhet), was occupied by the Egyptian agent, Munzinger (q. v.) in July 1872. The return of all of Bogos was guaranteed by the Adwa Treaty (q. v.) in 1884 but the Italians, despite a promise to fulfill the terms of that treaty, annexed Bogos; this occupation was legalized in 1889 by the Treaty of Wichale signed with Menilek II. Italy retained control of Bogos until after World War II.

The people comprise two main tribes: the Bet Teqwe and the Gebre Terqe of about 15,000 each, representing, it is believed, two different waves of migration into Bogos from Lasta and Tegray by Agew peoples in the 13th or 14th century. They displaced or absorbed the Tegre (q. v.). They became Christians (though it was noted in the 1840's that they had neither churches nor priests), but took on the protective coloration of Muslims in the mid 19th century in an attempt to save themselves from the depredations of Egypt and the Beni Amer. The Gebre Terqe were slower to become Islamized because of the assiduous efforts of Roman Catholic and Swedish Evangelical missionaries; about one-fourth of the population is Catholic today. The Belen are agriculturalists, have a social system which keeps women debased, hereditary chieftainship, and serfs who, though they own their land and have freedom of movement, may never cross into the status of simager (ruling class).

BORANA PEOPLE. Believed by some ethnologists to be the seminal branch of the Oromo (q. v.) because of their rigid observance of the gada (q. v.) social system. They speak a dialect of the Oromo tongue and live in an arid prong of Ethiopia along the border of Kenya, into which area many Borana have migrated; the Kenya Borana cross back periodically to participate in rituals. On the Somalia side, when the cattle-herding Borana moved westerly in time of drought and the camel and goat-herding Somali moved into their abandoned lands, frequent conflicts resulted. Under Menilek II, in 1899, the Borana were brought under imperial administration. Other Oromo respect the Borana and pilgrims from much of Ethiopia (mainly Welega and Shewa) travel to the ceremony of leader selection (the qallu) held at the shrine of Oda every eight years.

The Borana have expert astronomers who calculate their calendar on a lunar system. A Borana time reckoner can tell day, month, year and gada period from memory, keeping track of years ceremonially, not arithmetically. Their noted historian, Arero Rammata, was able to recount, in 1969, an oral history covering four thousand years. The only irregularity in Borana history was the Italo-Ethiopian war of 1936 when they extended their gada period by three years to avoid a confrontation with Italian troops; it was compensated for in the scheduling of the next gada period.

BORDERS. Present-day Ethiopia was delineated by agreements after the war with Italy that ended in March 1896. A statement regarding his country's boundaries was made by Menilek in a circular letter to the European powers 21 April 1891 but it included territory southeast and southwest of Addis Ababa that he had not yet conquered.   The statement recognized the agreement he had made with Italy 2 May 1889 and 1 October 1889 over a border with the Italian colony of Eritrea.   Menilek's sovereignty over Lake Assal was accepted by Italy in September 1890; Italian extension into the Danakil plains was approved May 1908.   Eritrea was reincorporated into Ethiopia in 1962, ten years after it had been transferred from British Trusteeship to federated status with Ethiopia as a result of a U. N. General Assembly decision.

The border with British Somaliland was agreed 14 May and 4 June 1897; the border with independent Somalia (1960) is in dispute in reference to the Haud and Ogaden (q. v.).

Demarcation with Anglo-Sudan was settled 15 May 1902 and ratified with minor modifications by independent Sudan 29 July 1972.

With British East Africa, border fixing began 29 January 1903 and again in December 1907.   It was amended 29 September 1947, then in 1950/51 a joint commission was formed to demarcate the border.   Kenya received its independence from Britain in 1963; the commission continued its work and declared a result in 1968 which was finally accepted by both Kenya and Ethiopia 9 June 1970.

The French Somaliland border was agreed to on 20 March 1897; on 5 September 1945 an additional protocol on tracing the frontier was signed.   16 January and 2 November 1954 France and Ethiopia delimited the boundary between Ethiopia and the French Territory of Afars and Ise (Issas), now the Republic of Djibouti.

BORUMEDA, Council (May-June 1878).   Two months after Yohannes IV won the submission of Menilek of Shewa, he presided over the meeting between his ecclesiastical advisers, determined to eliminate doctrinal disputes, most particularly the Sost Lidet (three-birth) heresy at the Debre Libanos monastery in Shewa. A letter was read from the Alexandrian patriarch, supporting the Orthodox position of Yohannes: those who did not recant the Sost Lidet and failed to take the precaution of fleeing had their tongues cut out.   Menilek and Adal Tessema of Gojam were present as were the two rival claimants to leadership of the Wello clans.   Yohannes selected Muhammad Ali who agreed to be baptized a Christian and was made a Ras (see MIKAEL OF WELLO).   A Christianizing campaign was announced: non-Christians could not hold government office though Muslims already in such posts were given three months to convert or resign; all other Muslims were given three years in which to convert, while pagans had two years.

BRUCE, Sir JAMES (1730-1794).   Scottish traveler and consul-general at Algiers for Great Britain.   He learned Arabic and some Ethiopic preparing for his venture into Ethiopia where he

dreamed of finding the Nile source. In 1769 he arrived at
Massawa and traveled much of northern Ethiopia for two years,
meeting almost every figure of importance and enjoying a
favored position with the royal women at Gondar (see MENTE-
WAB, Empress). He took back to England many Ethiopian
manuscripts (25 are in the Bodleian Library) and wrote
"Travels to Discover the Source of the Nile" (1790) re-kindling
an interest in Ethiopia that had lapsed for a hundred years.
Bruce's claim of discovering the Nile source was incorrect as
others (Pero Paez and Giovanni Gabriel) had been there before
him.

- C -

CANDACE (Kandake). The ancient title for the queen of Nubia;
often misused as the name of the queen herself (see MEROE).

CAPITALS. The Christian emperors abandoned Aksum about
A. D. 750 and ruled from another capital farther south until the
Zagwe (q. v.) usurped the throne and built Lalibela which
served as the imperial capital, as well as a site of pilgrimage,
until this dynasty in its turn was overthrown in 1270. Thereafter, for over three hundred years until the founding of Gondar
(q. v.) in 1636, each emperor moved his seat of government
whenever he felt it necessary for the exercise of strategic
military control, or when natural resources to support a populated camp had been exhausted. Strategic and other considerations made certain camps repeated favorites from reign to
reign. Zera Yaqob (1434-1468) did stay at Debre Berhan for
12 years and built a palace there; Gelawdewos (1540-1559)
built a capital at Wej, though no building traces remain; and
Sartsa Dengel (1563-1597) kept his residence in Wegera for
many years. Fasiledes's (1632-1667) choice of Gondar as a
fixed capital was based on luxuriant resources of wood and
water, its good defensive position and the convenience of the
nearby trade routes to the Sudan. It was the center of empire
for 200 years. Tewodros II (1855-1868) moved the capital to
the residence of the Yejju warlords he had supplanted, Debre
Tabor (q. v.). The royal treasury and the books which he
plundered from Gondar, were stored on Amba Meqdela, but he
regularly returned to Debre Tabor to camp between campaigns.
Yohannes IV (1871-1889) made similar use of this strategic
place although he built a stone palace at Meqelle in Tegray,
his natal province, as the formal capital. On Menilek's assumption of the throne in 1889, his new town, Addis Ababa (q. v.),
automatically became the imperial capital (see HARAR, IFAT
and ISLAM for Muslim capitals).

CAPTIVES, EUROPEAN (1863-1868). The provocation for the
British invasion of Ethiopia (see GREAT BRITAIN) in 1867-8
was the imprisonment by Tewodros II of Her Majesty's Consul,

Duncan Cameron, on 2 January 1864 and the subsequent detention of a second embassy, sent to secure Cameron's release,
that arrived January 1866.

The ostensible cause for putting Cameron in irons was his
protest when Tewodros had beaten and chained the Rev. Henry
Stern and his colleague, Mr. Rosenthal, for presumed insults.
The two German-born missionaries were sponsored by a
British Society.

Tewodros had welcomed Protestant missionaries if they
had manual skills and would confine their conversion efforts
to the Felasha and the Oromo. They built roads, carts and
taught youths entrusted to them at Gafat where Tewodros had
granted them land. The missionaries thrived, married and
multiplied. They remained safely, though under surveillance,
at Gafat after Stern, Rosenthal and Cameron had been incar-
cerated at the state prison at Meqdela.

Tewodros released the missionaries and officials in the
care of the head of the second embassy, Hormuzd Rassam, in
April 1866, but rearrested the lot on the pretext that they had
not paid a farewell call on him. After that, the artisan-
missionaries who could make armaments were at Gafat or Debre
Tabor, and the others were kept under restraint at Meqdela.
Some 61 men, women and children were at Meqdela when the
British army defeated Tewodros's army on 11 April 1868. Except for Cameron and Stern, who suffered great deprivation, the
freed Europeans were found to be in excellent health.

CELU see LABOR UNIONS

CHALCEDON, Council of. Site of the fourth council of the Catholic
    Church, held on 8 October 451. The council declared as
    heresy the Christological definition that Christ's natures, the
    human and divine, were perfectly united, which became known
    as Monophysitism. The Patriarchs of Syria and Alexandria
    attending the conference left the Catholic Church at this time
    over this issue. The ancient site of Chalcedon is now the vil-
    lage of Kadikoy on the outskirts of Istanbul, Turkey.

CHAMBER OF DEPUTIES. Set up in the late 1940s as a Parlia-
    ment whose members were virtually appointed by the Emperor;
    it evolved, as a result of the 1955 Constitution, into an elec-
    tive body, with quadrennial terms of office. With no political
    parties to represent, these contests were on a personal level
    and incumbency was no insurance of re-election. Members
    ranged from notables and landowners to popular teachers and
    educated "radicals. " It represented the countryside of the
    provinces rather than the sycophants of the capital. The Cham-
    ber could veto or amend government-sponsored legislation and
    could summon ministers for questioning. But it could easily
    be by-passed by Imperial decree and the monarch could veto
    undesirable legislation or dissolve the Chamber. The absence
    of political parties was, on balance, helpful by not thus allow-
    ing the growth of ethnic constituencies, but the consequent lack

of political organization prevented effective communication between deputies and the electorate.

CHILOT see JUDICIAL SYSTEM

CHINA and Ethiopia.   Contacts with northeast Africa probably began
around the 3rd century B. C. by traders working out of Alexandria.   In the 6th century A. D. , Ethiopian merchants secretly
imported silkworms from China, thus bypassing the Persians
who held a monopoly over silks coming from India.   Most of
China's trade with East Africa--luxury goods such as porce-
lains, carpets, and gold-brocaded garments--funnelled through
Zanzibar to what is now known as Kenya, Somalia, Tanzania,
and Ethiopia.   In return the Chinese bought gold, ivory and
slaves.   Chinese coins were also often used as currency.   Emperor Ping, circa 5 A. D. , received a live rhinoceros, the
origin of China's interest in the animals' horns which when
powdered are allegedly aphrodisiacal.   China-East Africa trade
hit a peak during the Sung Dynasty (960-1280).
        Early 19th-century records show China buying salt and
sharks' fins and selling silk.   Napier brought Chinese coolies
with him on his 1868 expedition to build a supply railway from
the port of Zula a number of miles into the interior.
        Diplomatic relations were established with Communist China
in 1965, an outgrowth of China's involvement in East and Central Africa with its construction of the Tan-Zam railroad between Tanzania and Zambia.   Trade between China and Ethiopia
was minimal at this time but looked as if it might expand in
the mid-1970s when the Chinese sought to work more closely
with the revolutionary Derg after the 1974 overthrow of the emperor.   Sharply increased Soviet influence with this ruling military junta served, however, to vitiate such Chinese moves.
The Peoples' Republic of China continues to have an embassy in
Addis Ababa.

CHIQA-SHUM.   Literally "mud-chief" the title is an ancient one for
a person appointed to the office from among the rist-holders
to act as intermediary between the gult-holder and other
peasants--the position rotates to all elder rist-holders before
anyone has a second term.   It is the nearest thing to a mayor
in a rural area, and he also represented his parishioners' complaints to the meslenie (q. v.) on the next level of authority.
He supervised assessment and collection of taxes at harvest
time, and received no compensation except tax relief and sometimes fields set aside for his special use.   In certain areas
(e. g. Damot) the chiqa-shum must be descended from the first
holder, a genealogical process known to the inhabitants though
unwritten.   His term of office was a year, during which time
his duties could range from overseeing land transfers, dis-
seminating orders from higher authority, and hearing divorce
cases.   The office was a stabilizing factor during the civil
wars and violent changes of authority in the 18th and 19th centuries, as he could not be displaced by any outside authority.

During their occupation, the Italians tried to eliminate the office but found they could not do without it. Some of the privileges of the office were removed after 1942; though as early as 1907, Menelik II decreed that the lands of a deceased childless person could go to his or her parents, not to the chiqa-shum. The office was transposed by the land reform act of 1975 and the formation of peasant associations (see LAND TENURE).

CHURCH, ETHIOPIAN ORTHODOX. Along with its sister churches in Monophysitism--the Coptic Church of Egypt, the Syrian Jacobite, the Armenian and the Church of Malabar of South India--the Ethiopian Church is one of the oldest Christian congregations in the world. About A. D. 331 Christianity became the religion of the court at Aksum, and the Monophysite interpretation defined by the dissidents at Chalcedon in A. D. 451, its creed. The Monophysites opposed the Chalcedon formula of two natures in the person of Christ, holding that in Christ, the two natures were perfectly combined at birth into one uniquely divine human form. The Ethiopians call this belief "tawahedo" (union).

The impetus that spread Christianity came with the arrival of the nine saints (q. v.) at the end of the 5th century; they moved out of Aksum to spread the word. Evangelization followed closely upon the expansion of the Ethiopian region in the 14th century and during the reign of Zera Yaqob (1434-68) the rituals and organization of the church became more or less what it is today.

It is the only church extant that preserves liturgical dancing; it condones both male and female infant circumcision, and infant baptism which is renewed annually by immersion on Timqat (see HOLIDAYS). Communion is irregular; men and women are segregated to receive it and must be sexually pure for 24 hours prior to the sacrament; menstruating women, or those who have not completed the 40 day post-natal purification period are banned from church services. The fasting calendar (q. v.) is the most rigorous among the world's religions, and along with the observances of Saints' days (many indigenous saints have been added to the usual saints of the Christian church) determine the rhythm of daily life. Veneration for the Virgin Mary alone takes 33 days each year.

Developing in isolation from other churches, and in proximity to peoples with animistic beliefs, the Ethiopian Church has been syncretic, tolerating demon spirits, as well as providing amulets to protect people from the "evil eye, " and inventing magic formulas to cope with the exigencies of life. The Church retains many Judaic elements, including distinctions between clean and unclean food, method of slaughtering animals, and observance of the Sabbath on Saturday as well as Sunday.

Separating itself from the Coptic Patriarchate of Alexandria has taken 16 centuries. In 1929, Alexandria agreed to consecrate five Ethiopians as suffragans to the abun, and in 1950 when the last Coptic abun died, the first Ethiopian bishop was appointed.

A theological college was added to the centuries-old training schools in music, liturgy, dance, theology, and history in
1943. Amharic has replaced Ge'ez in some centers, making
the services more intelligible to the people. The Church
joined the World Council of Churches in 1955 and sent observers
to the Second Vatican Council (1962-65) indicating its sympathies
with ecumenism. Until the revolution of 1974 the Church controlled an estimated one-third of the land and its income; however, it had already lost much of its political power when its
monopoly of education was reduced in the 1930's and by the
1955 constitution that made the emperor "head of the Ethiopian
Orthodox Church. "
     Even with the loss of its economic resources, the Church
is likely to survive as a force in the lives of the people,
though modifications of food taboos, fasting and reduction of
holidays are likely to keep pace with the pressures for economic
development (see EDUCATION; RELIGION; MONASTICISM;
JERUSALEM; CLERGY; GE'EZ; CHURCHES; "NINE SAINTS").

CHURCHES. In 1962 the estimated number of churches in Ethiopia
     was about 16, 000 serving a Christian population of perhaps 10
     million. Building a church was considered the spiritual duty of
     well-to-do men and women (some 41 churches were credited to
     Ras Gobena (q. v.) and his wife, Ayeletch). Construction began
     with the blessing of a replica of the Ark of the Tabot: the Ark
     remains in the innermost circle (meqdas) of the church to which
     only priests and kings had access. All churches, round or
     square, have a threefold division modeled on the Hebrew temple.
     The outer ring (qene mahlet) is where hymns are sung. The
     next circle is where communion is given (qeddest). Though the
     circular church, usually perched on a hill, is the most common
     form, rectangular and octagonal buildings exist in Addis Ababa
     and Asmara. The most famous square church is Maryam
     Tseyon at Aksum, built in the 6th century, destroyed and re-
     built only in 1655; another is Maryam Tseyon of Addis Alem
     built in 1902 and Trinity Cathedral in Addis Ababa (1941).
     Tabots are dedicated most frequently to Maryam, Giyorgis and
     Mikael.
     The foundation dates of churches reflect periods of political
     history: the most recently incorporated areas such as Sidamo,
     Ilubabor, Arsi, Kefa, Welega, and Hararge have churches
     founded after 1907, though Harar city has Christian institutions
     built soon after Menilek's conquest of 1887. Most of the
     churches of central Gojam were founded before 1706. In Tegray
     only 14 of its churches were built in the more than three centu-
     ries between 1532 and 1869; during the reign of Yohannes IV
     (1871-1889) 19 new churches were built.
     There has been almost no new church construction since the
     revenues of the church establishment and the patronage of
     wealthy land owners have been eclipsed by the 1974 revolution.

CIRCUMCISION. Both male and female infants are circumcised by
     Christians, Muslims, Felashas, and some animists. The age

for the operation ranges from 5 days after birth for Amhara
girls (7th day for males) to 7 years of age among the Beni
Amer (who do not circumcise girls).   The Harari boy can be
circumcised anytime between birth and 15, and the girl is
generally operated on before she is 12.   The Gurage of Soddo
do their children just after birth, but the Western Gurage wait
till their children are 8 to 10 years of age.   The rationale for
excision of a girl's clitoris (clitoridectomy) is that it will help
to preserve her virginity until marriage, and discourage her
from faithlessness after, as the operation is believed to lessen
sexual enjoyment.   The Mensa ensure virginity by infibulation,
or sewing up the vaginal opening.   Needless to say, vaginal
infection and difficulties in urination and menstruation are the
consequences for many women.   Although the Fetha Negest
(q. v.) cites St. Paul as saying circumcision means nothing,
the Orthodox Church (both Coptic and Ethiopian) interprets it
as necessary.   The Fetha Negest does not even speak of circumcision for women, but it has the force of ancient practice
behind it.   Efforts to abolish female mutilation have been defied by the strength of the custom.

CIVIL SERVICE.   The first attempt to set up some kind of central
    administrative structure was made by Yohannes IV.   Menilek II
    expanded this but it was still relatively small, inexperienced
    and inefficient.   The hiatus between Menilek's incapacity in
    1909 and the 1916 Regency headed by Ras Teferi saw a dwind-
    ling of even this small bureaucracy.   Teferi, with his reformist
    approach, tried to encourage and expand the existing service but
    not until he was crowned Emperor in 1930 was he able to give
    it both form and substance.   His emphasis on centralization re-
    quired administrative machinery and a civil service to man it,
    so he brought into the fledgling ministries whatever educated,
    well-born and loyal persons were available.   He also sent scores
    of qualified youth to study abroad, assuring them of responsible
    government positions on their return.   The Constitution of 1931
    makes no specific mention of a civil service but refers to the
    "machinery of State, " "posts and offices in the service of the
    State, " and gives the Emperor the power to "lay down the or-
    ganization and the regulations of all administrative departments"
    as well as to "appoint and dismiss ... civil officials and to de-
    cide as to their respective charges and salaries. "
        The Italian occupation of 1936-41 improved the governmental
    infrastructure to some extent but resulted in the execution of
    many civil servants who refused to collaborate.   On his resto-
    ration, Hayle Sellase moved promptly to remedy this gap, even
    though he had to use some of the former collaborators.   As the
    overseas students returned, they were placed in ministries
    dealing with economic development, education, health, finance,
    engineering and military technology, largely to be able to deal
    with the increasing numbers of foreign advisers and assistance
    programs that proliferated in Ethiopia after the end of World
    War II.

The Revised Constitution of 1955, with its more liberal approach and greater stress on centralized modernization, required a marked increase in the civil service. This new Constitution mentions the "duty" of every Ethiopian to "perform public services ... when called upon to do so, " and specified that "the appointment, promotion, transfer, suspension, retirement, dismissal and discipline of all ... Government officials and employees shall be governed by regulations made by the Council of Ministers and approved and proclaimed by the Emperor. "

The extreme unrest of early 1974 led to promises of reform. One of the first was to give salary and pension increases to lower-paid government workers, a group comprising over 40 percent of the civil service. But this and other palliatives failed to prevent the Revolution or the Emperor's overthrow in September. In early 1975, the ruling Derg promulgated its nationalization program, based largely on ideas of lower-level civil servants who had been selected and promoted to high advisory and administrative posts. Three new ministries were established: National Resources, Industry, Public Works and Housing. Some 30, 000 additional civil service jobs resulted, making the total personnel in the public sector around 100, 000. Many of these were shifted to a reorganized Ministry of Land Reform and Administration (a pre-revolution department) to carry out the radical proposals for land reform, a key program of the Revolution.

CLERGY.   Estimated in recent years to number up to 100, 000 throughout the country, Ethiopian Orthodox Church functionaries have been in a decline since the 1974 Revolution but the priesthood is still believed to attract young men as a career.   In ascending order or rank, debtera are the lowest, functioning as scribe, deacon, chorister, or farmer of church land; he prepares sacramental bread, fetches holy water and assists at Mass, which requires two priests and three debtera. A debtera must be married by communion and live with his wife for 40 days before he can become a priest (qes) and may not divorce, or remarry if his wife dies. Priests are ordained and must have mastered the 14 varieties of chants for regular masses and some special ones; he conducts marriages, communions, baptisms, hears confessions, and when his duties are done lives like his neighbors: farming, marketing, weaving, and joining his fellows in drinking and idle conversation. He wears a white turban and carries a cross. Abba, or "father" can be the title of a priest, but qes is more common.

A memher (master) is the head of a monastery which attracts unwed debtera, widowed priests, and anyone who is ready to renounce the world. A monk becomes a legal nonentity which frees him from paying taxes or debts--a strong motivation.   Women--who have no other role in the church other than to be generous to it and observe the many fasts and rituals--may also renounce the world and take up residency at a monastery.

At the imperial court there was an aqabe se'at as its chief churchman, as well as a qes atse, chaplain to the monarch. There is an office of leqa debtera, to supervise the debtera and leqa memheran, or "chief of the learned men." The echege (q. v.) was the church office second only to the abun, head of the church, equivalent to metropolitan or patriarch. A special office of honor is to be a nebura-ed, which is chief of the sacred district of Aksum, site of the Ark of the Covenant, alleged to have been spirited away from Solomon's court in Jerusalem by Menelik I. Aleqa, a layman, manages one or several monasteries or churches (see MONASTICISM; CHURCHES).

CLOTHING. The style, quality and fabric worn have long been an indication of status and ethnic group; ranging from the brief leather skirt decorated with cowrie shells to the embroidered velvet or silk capes and shirts worn by the well-to-do Amhara-Tegray families. The most "Ethiopian" sight is the cotton dress, always white, worn by the women, and the shamma (or shawl) she wraps herself in. Border designs, skirt length, sleeve style, neckline and quality of the soft, porous hand-loomed cotton varies, and women now frequently wrap their heads in carefully pleated and styled turbans. A caftan style was more common in Tegray and Gojam than Shewa; noble women were allowed gold embroidery on them and their capes. Both the shamma and the kuta (double-layered shamma) are worn by men, even over a European-styled jacket.

Loose trousers of length varying from above the knee to ankle and a loose shirt were worn by men. One fashion, the jodhpur, adopted by Tewodros II when he saw the style worn by the British Consul Plowden, is now common. Tewodros decreed that only the group he designated could wear velvet or silk shirts and the unfavored were to wear cotton. Menilek II popularized the wide-brimmed felt hat atop a head bound with a muslin kerchief (Menilek was bald). The banna, a length of black wool produced in Menz district is also common. Wealthy men wear a barnos, a tailored cape made of this wool.

Marriage is marked by the giving of clothing to both bride and groom. Mourning is marked by wearing dirty clothes. On Timqat in January, the annual renewal of baptism for Christians is celebrated by washing clothes and giving new outfits to children. The shamma lowered to the waist has long been an indication of respect; raising the shamma to cover the nose asserts superiority and covering the mouth, equality.

COFFEE. For centuries, a valuable agricultural product and a mainstay of Ethiopia's early 17th-century trade with India. Even today it is the top foreign exchange earner and the major source of tax revenue (48 percent of total export earnings from 1972-77). As early as the 15th century, ships calling at Red Sea ports took large quantities of Harari coffee. The unsubstantiated belief is that coffee got its name from Ethiopia's Kefa province; another story is that it was found around Harar in the 15th century and taken to Arabia. Rather than use it simply as

a beverage, many Ethiopians enjoy it as a food, grinding up
the beans and mixing the powder with butter and honey to form
billiard-size balls for a quick meal. It was native to the moist
lowlands where it grew wild. When it was brought north by
Oromo cultivators it flourished at an altitude of 5-6,000 feet.
The Church originally opposed coffee drinking because Muslims
and pagans inbibed it, but this attitude changed by the mid 19th
century and today Ethiopians use an average of eight pounds
per person annually. In 1893 Menilek II established a coffee
monopoly with Tessema Nadew and Welde Giyorgis; coffee production and exports increased steadily. The government coffee
board was established in 1957 to encourage cooperative societies,
assist in marketing and improve quality. Most of the Ethiopian
coffee crop goes to the United States. One of the 67 members
of the International Coffee Agreement (1962), Ethiopia is the 15th
largest coffee exporter.

COLLEGIO ETIOPICO (Rome). In 1529 the Vatican bought a hos-
pice behind St. Peter's for the pilgrims who had come to Rome,
usually via Jerusalem; it became known as Santo Stefano dei
Mori and became the inspiration of Ethiopian studies in Europe.
It was renamed in 1919 "Pontificio Collegio Etiopico" and is the
only theological college within Vatican City and the one to which
the bishop for Ethiopia's Catholics is attached.

COMMUNICATIONS see FILMS; NEWSPAPERS; RADIO; RAILROADS;
AIRLINE; POSTAL SERVICE

CONSTITUTIONS (1931 and 1955). Drafted by Tekle Hawaryat (q.v.)
Ethiopia's first constitution was modeled on the Imperial Japanese Constitution of 1889, though more simplified and more em-
phatic about imperial power. It was primarily an instrument
for securing national unity under the centralized rule of the emperor, who was declared the dynastic heir in an uninterrupted
line from Menilek I, son of Solomon, King of Israel. It confirmed the emperor's executive power over both central and provincial government, and control of legislature and judiciary. It
recognized (subject to limitation by law and emergency powers)
freedom from illegal arrest, imprisonment and expropriation and
from searches of home and correspondence; but not freedom of
speech, association and religion which were in the Japanese
model. At least it established a Senate, though it was appointed
by the emperor, and a lower house which was named by the
nobility and local chiefs.
     In 1955, after some six years preparation, the revised con-
stitution was announced which respected a changing political climate. Like the first one, the revision was submitted to the
prominent power elite of the country for approval. It did provide for freedom of speech, religion and assembly, and an
elected Parliament. A Committee on Constitutional Revision
was set up after the attempted coup d'état of 1960. Only one
of its recommendations was adopted when the Prime Minister
was permitted in 1966 to select other ministers.

COOPERATIVE OF MARXIST-LENINIST ORGANIZATIONS
(E'ma'le'deh).   At least six organizations professing Marxist-
Leninist doctrines sprang out of the intense political activity
following the 1974 revolution.   Five of them, temporarily,
joined in this cooperative, familiarly referred to as E'ma'le'deh
(EMLD).   Its members were Abyot Seded (Flame of the Revolution) founded by Mengestu Hayle Maryam in August 1976 before
he became the strongman of the Derg (q. v.) in February 1977.
It was set up primarily to counter the ultra-radical efforts of
Mei'son (q. v.) which withdrew from EMLD in August 1977;
Ma'le'red which was reputedly of a Maoist cast; Wes League
(Proletarian); E'cha'at (Ethiopian Oppressed People's Organization) which was originally a part of Mei'son.   After the Derg
outlawed Mei'son in December 1977, many of its members
joined the other four groups.   Also of Marxist orientation but
not a member of EMLD was the anti-Derg Ethiopian Peoples'
Revolutionary Party (q. v.), which was also opposed to Mei'son.

COOPERATIVES.   Among the highly individualistic Amhara, cooperative associations have been rare until the 20th century when
under the impact of the Gurage people who did organize themselves into cooperative assistance societies, they too developed
edir (q. v.) and equb groups.   The Harari have the afocha.   The
Dorze (q. v.) were among the first ethnic groups to organize
themselves a business cooperative to make and market their
weaving products in the capital.   In Proclamation 71 of 1975,
peasant associations were encouraged to establish cooperative
societies of two types: service, and agricultural producers.   A
government source gives 2000 service cooperatives organized by
1977.

COPTIC CHURCH.   Copts were Egyptians who converted to Christianity in the second and third centuries and developed their own
language, Coptic, a combination of Greek and Arabic, to translate the Bible.   Their patriarch was one of early Christendom's
most powerful figures.   The Monophysite doctrine was developed
by the Copt Eustichius, who led his followers out of the Council
of Chalcedon in 451, forever to be divided from the See of St.
Peter in Rome.   The patriarchate is in Alexandria, though the
Patriarch usually lives in Cairo.   He chose Ethiopia's first
bishop in the 4th century and each bishop thereafter (until 1950)
was a Copt.

COUNCIL OF MINISTERS.   Menelik II, stating frankly he would appoint a cabinet after the European model in October 1907, made
the names and positions public in January 1908:   Justice, War,
Interior, Commerce, Foreign Affairs, Finance, Agriculture and
Public Works, plus the ancient offices of court scribe (Tsehafi
T'ezaz) and palace administrator.   A Health Minister and one
for Post and Telegraph were named shortly after.   It was a
start towards division of functions, though no real change occurred in dividing authority.   In 1930 Education and Fine Arts
was added, Mines in 1938, and by 1966 there were Communica-

tions, Information and Tourism, Land Reform and Administration, National Community Development and Planning and Development. There have been changes in ministerial titles since the revolution of 1974 and of course Ministers of Pen and Palace have been abolished.

COUP D'ÉTAT, 27-28 September 1916.   Though Menilek II was
   dead, and Lej Iyasu was acting emperor, he was never crowned.
   He had proved so ineffective, capable of libertine behavior, and
   had so alienated the church and Amhara nobility by his apparent
   sympathy with Islam, that a group of clergy and noblemen appealed to Abune Matewos to excommunicate him, relieve them of
   their oaths of loyalty, and approve the nomination of Menilek's
   daughter, Zewditu, to be empress in his place, with Ras Teferi
   as regent.   Iyasu was in Harar at the time, and after a telegram arrived ordering his arrest, protested his Christianity,
   and rode out of town on horseback, eluding capture for four
   years (see IYASU and MIKAEL OF WELLO).

COUP D'ÉTAT (attempted), 13-17 December 1960.   Seen by many as
   the ideological precursor of the 1974 revolution, this unsuccessful attempt to depose the emperor and bring economic and
   political reforms was led by Germame Neway (a graduate of the
   University of Wisconsin, U.S.) and his elder brother, Major
   Mengestu Neway, commander of the Imperial Guard, a force of
   nine battalions.   They began careful planning and recruitment
   to their Council of the Revolution in mid-1960, drawing on army
   officers already disaffected over pay scales.   Knowing that rumors of an army rebellion had reached the palace, they were
   provoked into premature action, and used the absence of the emperor on state visits (West Africa, then Brazil).   The Crown
   Prince Asfa Wessen was taken into custody the night of 13 December; in the morning contingents of the Imperial Guard took
   over the State Bank, Ministry of Finance, radio and two telecommunications stations; dignitaries and ministers were arrested.   Not a shot had been fired.
       Left at large, however, was a coterie of senior army and
   airforce officers, Patriarch Baselyos, Asrate Kasa and others
   who quickly mobilized for a counter-coup.
       Copies of the revolutionary proclamation were distributed,
   and the Foreign Affairs Ministry notified the foreign press of
   a change of government.   The Crown Prince was asked (forced,
   he said later) to record the proclamation on tape.   It was
   broadcast on the afternoon of 15 December and it was announced
   he would lead a representative people's government and that Ras
   Emru had been appointed Prime Minister.   Mengestu Neway met
   with the students at the University, secured their support, and
   with the Crown Prince and Emru tried to negotiate a peaceful
   take-over with the counter-revolutionary group.
       In the late afternoon of 14 December, an Amharic leaflet
   signed by the Patriarch appealed for loyalty to the emperor and
   excommunicated the rebels, a powerful tool and unsettling to the
   general public; two loyalist generals (Mered Mengesha and

Kebede Gebre) denounced in leaflets the "few treacherous officers" and reaffirmed their own loyalty to Hayle Sellase.
Asefa Ayene, senior Ethiopian commander of the Air Force at
Nazeret, was contacted as well as the territorial units at
Gondar, Harar and Dire Dawa and an airlift began bringing soldiers to Debre Zeyt, close to the capital.   The Crown Prince
made another broadcast on 15 December criticizing the actions
of Mered Mengesha and Kebede Gebre and raising the salaries
of the army.
      The counter-coup military forces began firing on the after-
noon of 15 December.   Hundreds of civilians were killed in the
streets of Addis Ababa, and planes strafed and bombed the city.
As army forces neared the palace where the rebels had their
detainees, Germame Neway and others sprayed the room with
machine guns.   Some 18 were killed or seriously wounded.
      The night of 17 December the emperor returned.   Some
rebels had fled up the slopes of Entotto; many were killed by
local people, some committed suicide.   Germame and Mengestu
Neway evaded capture for a week, then as soldiers approached,
Germame shot his brother and killed himself.   Mengestu however, survived to be tried and executed 30 March, 1961.   An
estimated 3,100 people were arrested of which 400 were freed,
2,000 released on bail and 700 imprisoned (figures given by
government).

COUP D'ÉTAT (attempted), 3 February 1977.   By the autumn of
1976, groups of students, teachers, labor unions and some
moderate landowners had begun underground agitation against
the Derg, urging greater democratization.   Most active among
these was the Ethiopian Peoples Revolutionary Party (EPRP).
The military campaign in Eritrea had suffered serious reverses
and Gen. Getachew Nadew, the commander there but an oppo-
nent of the Derg's Eritrea policy, had been executed.   Guerrilla
attacks in the Tegray countryside mounted by the monarchist
Ethiopian Democratic Union, plus EPRP-fomented urban strikes,
sabotage and assassination of Derg members, created confusion
and tension within the Derg.   Major Mengestu Hayle Maryam,
the Derg's vice-chairman who was blamed for this unrest because of his ruthless tactics, was shifted to the figurehead
chairmanship of the Council of Ministers.   Gen. Teferi Bante,
a moderate who had replaced the executed (November 1974)
Gen. Aman Mikael Amdon as Derg chairman, was given authori-
tative control.   But the more dynamic Mengestu secretly regrouped his followers; his "Flame Brigade" broke into an emergency Derg meeting, from which Mengestu had absented himself,
and murdered Teferi Bente and five of his cohorts.   Mengestu
then seized control, announcing that these "executions" had
foiled an "attempted counter-revolutionary coup d'état " and
accusing his victims of having conspired with the EPRP and the
EDU.   The bloody "Red Terror" then ensued, resulting in the
deaths of thousands throughout the country.

COUPS D'ÉTAT (attempted against Hayle Sellase I).   Strictly de-

fined, there were only three "sudden strokes": the first in
1928 against his regency for Empress Zewditu (q. v.); the
second a plot to assassinate him in 1951; and third the coup
of 13-17 December 1960 (q. v.). The other actions ranged
from armed rebellion to individual dissent: In 1932 Gojam's
Haylu Tekle Haymanot conspired in the escape attempt of deposed "emperor" Lej Iyasu (q. v.); that same year Ras Gugsa
Wele of Begemder marched his army towards Shewa--his
forces were scattered by the first use of Ethiopia of small
bombs and leaflets (denying Gugsa propaganda that the emperor
was Catholic) from an airplane. Gugsa himself was killed in
a skirmish with Ras Mulugeta Yegezu. In 1942 Tekle Welde
Hawaryat (q. v.) was arrested on suspicion of treason and held
without trial for two and a half years; on release he was
honored with various offices, then arrested again for presumed
complicity in 1961 with others who wanted the development of a
more constitutional monarchy. In 1944, resistance hero Belew
Zelleqe was hanged with other officers, including the son of Haylu Takle Haymanot, for plotting to seize power in Addis Ababa.
In 1951 a plot to assassinate the emperor, led by Negash Bezebeh, was uncovered and the conspirators were rusticated (see
REBELLIONS).

CROWN COUNCIL. Rulers of ancient times usually had a close
circle of people they trusted and consulted, but a Crown Council
as such, was named as an advisory body to the emperor only in
the Revised Constitution of 1955. It was in existence since 1941
and was composed of the elite: Ras Kasa Haylu, Seyum Mengesha, Haylu Belew who were the heads of the royal lines of
Shewa, Tegray and Gojam; Adefresew and Mekonnen Endalkatchew
of the Shewan nobility, Ras Abebe Aregay and the Patriarch
Baselyos, the Crown Prince and the Duke of Harar and some
others. After the death of Ras Kasa in 1956, the Duke of Harar
in 1957, and others shot during the 1960 attempted coup d'état,
the council appeared to fade away. In 1966 new members were
named and it revived as a consultative body for the emperor.

CUBA and Ethiopia. Cuba became involved in Ethiopian affairs as
an outgrowth of its close ties to the Soviet Union and their joint
policy of assisting revolutionary regimes in Africa in the mid-
1970s. One of these recipients of Soviet attention was Somalia
which the Soviet Union provided with military aid as an apparent
counterpoise to continuing U. S. arms aid to Ethiopia. With the
overthrow of Hayle Sellase in 1974 by a Marxist-oriented military junta, the Soviets moved into the vacuum created by the
Derg's (q. v.) antipathy to America's "imperialist" policies.
U. S. military assistance to Ethiopia inevitably ended in April
1977. The USSR's decision to shift its attention from Somalia
to Ethiopia's "young revolutionaries for whom the Soviets would
do much" (remark attributed to Soviet Foreign Minister Gromy-
ko in November 1977) led to the renunciation by Somalia of its
Friendship Treaty with the USSR and expulsion on 13 November
1977 of some 3, 500 Soviet advisers. At the same time, So-

malia broke diplomatic relations with Cuba.   In mid-July 1977
"insurgents" belonging to the "West Somali Liberation Front"
began a successful series of attacks in the Ogaden, long disputed between them and Ethiopia.   An estimated 2,000 Cubans
and 1,000 Soviets landed in Ethiopia and Raul Castro, Cuban
defense minister, visited Ethiopia, reportedly to coordinate with
the Russians and Ethiopians on military operations in the Ogaden.   The first week in February 1978, the Ethiopians moved
against the Somali "irregulars," who by this time had occupied
much of the Ogaden and had almost captured Harar.   Cuban
pilots were reported as flying Soviet "Migs" in this campaign.
As the Ethiopian drive gained momentum, the U.S. warned
Ethiopia (11 February 1978) that if they crossed the Somali
border, the U.S. would provide Somalia with defensive weapons.
They did not cross the border.   In a matter of weeks, Somali
guerrillas, aided by regular Somali troops, were pushed out of
the Ogaden with the assistance of an estimated 12,000 Cubans.
   Press reports claimed in mid-May, when Ethiopia turned
its attention to halting the secessionist movement in Eritrea,
that from 15,000 to 17,000 Cubans were part of the Ethiopian
forces.   This would be Cuba's second largest contingent in Africa, second only to the reported 19,000 soldiers (plus 4,000 civilians) stationed in Angola.   A report on Cubans in Ethiopia of
30 May 1978 said the Cubans were reluctant to commit any
troops to the offensive in Eritrea.   Subsequent press items have
indicated, however, that some Cuban forces have been involved
in the area.

CURRENCY.   Ethiopia is only partly a money economy; in remote
   areas farmers and herdsmen still use a barter system.   Bars
   of salt substituted for currency at the same time the Maria
   Teresa taler was in use in the 19th century.   When the Italians
   occupied Eritrea in 1891 they circulated a coin resembling the
   taler but using the image of King Umberto.   In 1893, Menilek
   decreed a Menilek taler with six coins of lower denomination,
   three of silver and three of copper; they were minted in Paris.
   The people continued to prefer the Maria Teresa taler, and
   melted the Menilek issue for jewelry.
      The Ethiopian dollar, pegged to the U.S. dollar (1 Ethiopian
   dollar equaled U.S. $0.40), was made legal tender in 1945.
   Notes were issued in 1, 5, 10, 20, 50, 100 and 500 denominations and coins in values of 1, 5, 10, 25, and 50 cents.   In
   1977, the Provisional Military Administrative Council decreed
   the official currency unit to be the birr, which comes in coins
   of four denominations--1, 10, 25 and 100 cents.   One U.S.
   dollar is equivalent roughly to 2.07 birr.

- D -

DA GAMA, CHRISTAVÃO see PORTUGAL and Ethiopia

DAGNA.   Slightly lower in rank than the village head (see CHIQA-

SHUM) and a man "knowing the law" who served as local judge.
The dagna would often hold court in a market, seated in a small
booth together with the melqagna (district governor's deputy), and
the neggadras, chief officer of the market and a customs official.
Cases arising in market disputes would come before them and
were dealt with rapidly by the dagna after conferring with his
two colleagues. The dagna at a municipal office could also
solemnize the registry-office type of marriage.

DAHLAK ARCHIPELAGO. To protect their Red Sea commerce,
Muslims occupied these islands off Massawa (q.v.) in the 7th
century; inscriptions on tombstones (taken to museums in
Treviso, Modena, and Cairo) give the names of the reigning
families in the 12th and 13th centuries, who engaged in considerable commerce. Great cisterns for the storage of water
have been found as these islands share with Massawa one of the
hottest climates in the world. Its present day inhabitants are
mainly Tegre-speaking, and their only resource is fishing for
pearls and mother-of-pearl, and sparse herds of goats and
camels.

DAMOT. Once a powerful animist kingdom, and the speculative
base of the aggressive queen (see GUDIT) of the Bani-al Hami-
yah in the 10th century, when it was located south of the Abbay
(Blue Nile). In the 13th century it was ruled by King Motelami
who attacked the southern Shewan region, but was converted to
Christianity by St. Tekle Haymanot (q.v.), and absorbed into
the empire during the reign of Amde Tseyon (1314-1344). It
was still largely animist in the early 16th century according to
the Portuguese Father Alvarez. During the Oromo expansion
of the 16th and 17th the inhabitants migrated across the Abbay
to its present location in northwest Gojam. Its army was an
independent force in the 19th century whose leader opted to
bring when called by Ras Ali Alula (q.v.) though their nominal
governor was Dejazmach Goshu. Much reduced in size, it is
now the sub-district Dega-Damot; still very isolated, with no
road or telephone (in 1966) connecting it to the provincial capital of Debre Marqos.

DARGE SAHLE SELLASE Ras (c. 1825-1900) and Family. A pater-
nal uncle of Menilek II, Darge was a general and trusted adviser
to his nephew. He was among the prisoners of Tewodros II, released from Meqdela by the British expedition of 1868. When he
returned to Shewa he was made governor of Marabete and later
resided at Salale. He acted in the short-term cooperation negotiated with Wagshum Gobeze for Menilek in 1869, was the peace-
maker between Menilek and his cousin Meshesha Seyfu in 1877,
and between Menilek and Yohannes IV in 1888. He was popular
for his bravery, generosity and religiosity except in Arussi
which he conquered after repeated bloody campaigns. He had
four sons and three daughters by three wives. His son Gugsa
was sent to Switzerland for education in 1894 but disgusted his
father by defecting to Italy. His other sons died in the service

of Menilek: Shewa Regged in 1882, Tessema in 1906 and Asfa
in 1907. At the time of the 1869 agreement with Wagshum
Gobeze, his daughter also Tessema, was married to the Wagshum's half brother, Haylu Welde Kiros (see KASA HAYLU).
She divorced him in 1881 to marry Welde Tsadiq, her father's
clerk, who was named kentiba (mayor) of Addis Ababa in 1900.
His daughter Tsehay-Werq was famous for her independence of
court etiquette, was a good shot and horsewoman, learned to
do unaristocratic things like knitting and sewing and never married. When Empress Zewditu came to power in 1916 she was
forbidden to come to Addis Ababa.

Though an old man, Darge's death in 1900 was hastened by
the drastic indigenous treatment for syphilis.

DAWIT I (Emperor 1382-1411). When he came to power, one legend
explains, the Egyptians decided to discontinue the gifts and
tribute they had long paid Ethiopia for the use of the Blue Nile
(Abbay). Dawit promptly threatened to divert the river and the
Egyptians, just as promptly, resumed their tribute. Dawit also
is believed to have invaded Egypt and punished the Mamluk sultan for persecuting Christians. The peace agreement was celebrated by Dawit who sent 21 camel loads of Ethiopian curiosities
to the sultan. In return, the Egyptians sent Dawit some religious
relics including fragments of the "true cross." Observance of
this event, Mesqel, is the most important on the religious calendar and transcends fact.

A Felasha (q. v.) rebellion against Christian conversion in
Semen was put down by Dawit between 1394 and 1400 and Gojam's
transition into a Christian province began in Dawit's time. Re-
pelling attacks by the Muslims of Adal, Dawit drove the Adal
leader to Zeyla where he was killed in 1403.

In opposition to the Coptic patriarch's strictures against observing the Saturday Sabbath (a Hebrew practice) a pro-Saturday
movement (see Ewostatewos) grew so powerful that on arrival of
the new Coptic abun in 1398, Dawit called their leaders together
and gave the prelate a free hand in disciplinary action, and the
dissidents were confined four years. After Dawit's conquest of
Zeyla, he responded to pressures from the pro-Sabbath faction,
released the detainees and in 1404 decreed freedom to worship
on the Sabbath, thus undermining the prestige of the abun. This
is now seen as an example of religious nationalism which would
be carried even further by Dawit's son Zera Yaqob.

Dawit sent one of several Florentine craftsmen at his court
as leader of an embassy to Europe in 1402 to elicit support for
a campaign against Islam. Three of his queens were Dingil-
Sawana, Tseyon Mogasa and Egzi Kebra. Four of his sons succeeded to his throne in turn: Tewodros I (1411-1413); Yeshaq
(1413-1430); Hezba-Nagn (1430-1433), and Zera Yaqob (q. v.).
His sister Zera Ganela, was renowned as a nun under the name
"Barbara."

DAYR ES-SULTAN (Der-es-Sultan) see JERUSALEM

DEBEB ARAYA, Fitwrari (?-1891). Though a cousin of Yohannes
  IV (q. v.) he rebelled and raided caravans coming from Massawa throughout 1883-84; part of the negotiations with Hewett
  (see ADWA, TREATY OF) were concerned with handing Debeb
  over as he had been captured at Suakim and was in British
  custody. Debeb escaped and continued his marauding and collaboration with Italian troops until 1888 when he came into
  Asmara and asked pardon; Yohannes IV asked his advice on
  dealing with the Italians; in February 1889 he defected back to
  Italy. Debeb was killed fighting in September 1891, his claims
  to be the ruler of Tegray stilled forever.

DEBRE BIZEN. A religious community founded by the priest
  Filipos (c. 1323-1406) in Hamasen about 1390-91 for followers
  of Ewostatewos (q. v.) dedicated to observance of the two Sab-
  baths--Saturday and Sunday. By the time of Zera Yaqob
  (1434-68) it consisted of 8 monasteries and 3 convents (with
  more than 1100 nuns resident). The head of the female community had unusual independence; she could confer the monastic
  habit herself and confessions were made through her, then re-
  layed through a lay brother to the head of the community.

DEBRE DAMO. Founded in the sixth century, it is Ethiopia's
  oldest monastery, located on a rocky hill near Adigrat in
  Tegray, and is accessible only to men, who pull themselves up
  by a rope hanging down, using foot holes cut into the rock.
  The site was chosen by Ze-Mikael Aregawi (one of the nine
  saints; see CHURCH, ETHIOPIAN ORTHODOX). The church
  there was probably not built until the 15th century. Its construction of alternating layers of stone and wood in rectangular
  form with the ceiling painted with floral designs, animals and
  crosses is considered one of the most beautiful in the country.
  Despite the ban on women, the Empress Seble Wengel (q. v.),
  her daughters and their attendants were in refuge there in
  1541. Noted religious figures who once resided there were
  Iyesus Moa (d. 1292) (see MONASTICISM) and St. Tekle Haymanot (q. v.).

DEBRE LIBANOS. One of two important monasteries called Debre
  Libanos is in Tegray and the other is in Shewa. The site of
  Shemezana (in Tegray) was chosen by Abba Yem'ata (one of the
  nine saints; see CHURCH) in the 6th century. Its abbot was
  known to be a power during the reign of Lalibela (1225-1268).
  The Shewan site was chosen by St. Tekle Haymanot about 1284,
  and a church was built there 57 years after his death in 1313.
  Originally named Debre Asbo, it was renamed by Emperor Zera
  Yaqob (1434-1468) who utilized many Debre Libanos alumni for
  his vigorous Christianizing campaign and granted the community
  extensive lands and liberal revenues. Its manuscripts and
  buildings were burned in 1531 at the onset of the Islamic conquest (q. v.) and the surviving monks took the tabot of St. Tekle
  Haymanot to Azezo near Condar. The tabot was brought back
  at Menilek's order in 1889.

During the controversies over celebration of the Sabbath in the 15th century, Debre Libanos clerics were firmly committed to the Alexandrian position against it, but went along with the compromise arranged by Zera Yaqob, agreeing that both Saturday and Sunday would be celebrated. In the disputes over the nature of Christ, Debre Libanos in the late 18th century formulated the doctrine Tsegga-Ledj (3 births), an heretical view in the eyes of the Orthodox church. Not until Yohannes IV in 1878 decreed its abolishment, did Debre Libanos relinquish this dogma.

The prior of Debre Libanos was, at the same time, the leader of the monastery and the highest ranking Ethiopian of the church (until 1950 when an Ethiopian was allowed to take the higher office of bishop).

The rocky caves of Debre Libanos became the burial site for the elite faithful in many cases and the water coursing from the rocks a mecca for pilgrims believing in its healing powers as well as giving them a 7 year remission for their sins. It possesses a renowned library and was declared a legitimate place of asylum for fugitive thieves and murderers about 1881. Menilek II had a church started which took 12 years to build (1881-1893) and had to be rebuilt in 1906. On the urging of Empress T'aytu Betul a cloister for nuns was built in 1909, restoring an institution that had been wiped out 4 centuries earlier.

DEBRE TABOR. Leaving the crumbling palaces of Gondar to the powerless holder of the imperial title, Ras Gugsa Mersu (q. v.) established Debre Tabor about 1800 attracted by its good defensive position in a mountainous area and its many springs. He and his sons are buried there. His grandson, Ras Ali Alula (q. v.) built four churches during his reign before he was forced to flee by Kasa of Qwara (Tewodros II) in 1853. The town had been razed in battles fought in 1835 and 1842 but survived to become Tewodros's capital after he ravaged Gondar in 1866. Yohannes IV built his residence at Samera, an hour's mule ride away, and built the church of Heruy Giyorgis in the city; the relics of his reign are there. After Addis Ababa became the capital, Debre Tabor declined, though it was an important market on the caravan track connecting Gondar with Lalibela and Addis Ababa. Ras Gugsa Wele, ex-husband of Empress Zewditu (q. v.) rebuilt and renovated its churches when he was governor of Begemder 1918-1930. In April 1936, the occupying Italians built a road from Gondar, via Debre Tabor to Desse; the first mosque was built, wells were dug and eucalyptus planting extended.

DEBTERA. Though only the first step on the clerical ladder, the debtera ("scholar") have had a relationship to the educational system and power structure that transcends their religious office. They could read and write therefore they were indispensable to emperors, kings, nobles and on down the table of rank. Their skills as scribes were embellished by their knowledge of

ecclesiastical matters and law which they were called upon to
interpret; they are the dancers and choristers of church services. Liq ("one who excels in knowledge") is a title given to
some. Their learning awed the people who ascribed occult
powers to them as well; debtera are still asked to write amulets
for the paying customer to wear around his neck to protect him
from evil. Even with the growth of secular education they still
function as purveyors of traditional education, conducting
schools in the churchyard or their homes.

DEL WENBERA, Bati. The daughter of Imam of Zeyla in the 16th
century and wife of Ahmad ibn-Ibrahim (see ISLAMIC CONQUEST)
whose invasion of Ethiopia was successful for some 13 years.
Del Wenbera accompanied Ahmad on his expeditions and bore
him two sons during the fighting in Tegray in 1531 and 1533.
She interceded to save the life of Minas, brother of Emperor
Gelawdewos (q.v.) and exchanged him for her son who had been
captured by the Christians. After her husband was killed in
1543, Del Wenbera made her way to Harar where she married
her husband's nephew on condition that he avenge her husband's
death. Nur's army fought Gelawdewos in 1559, and though
Ahmad's death was avenged by the killing of the emperor, the
days of the Muslim city state were numbered.

DENQENESH HAYLU, Weyzero see DINQINESH HAYLU, Weyzero

DERESGE, BATTLE OF (9 February 1855) see TEWODROS II

DERG. Ahmaric word for committee or council which became the
popular and journalistic designation for the Provisional Military
Administrative Council which rules Ethiopia. Originally it was
a secret dissident army faction that emerged early in 1974 as
the voice of servicemen opposed to the top generals close to
Hayle Sellase, and demanding better pay and conditions. As the
Coordinating Committee of the Armed Forces, this early Derg
surfaced forcefully in April 1974 and arrested most of the cabinet although still claiming loyalty to the emperor. Little further
action was taken until 26 June when it organized another purge, ar-
resting many leading figures of the bureaucracy, army and nobility.
    At this point it added police and other security elements as
members, listed a series of social and political demands and
established its slogan of "Ethiopia Tikeem" ("Ethiopia First").
This so-called "creeping coup" took several months to burst
into a clear revolutionary action with the overthrow of the emperor in September and the Derg's seizure of power under the
title of Provisional Military Administrative Council with Gen.
Aman Mikael Amdom (q.v.), earlier installed as Army Chief of
Staff by Derg demand, as Chairman. Actual membership of the
Derg was believed to be around 120, many of them enlisted
men. Their program was vague, not particularly radical, but
clearly dictatorial with the aim of toppling the existing order
and restructuring the feudal, monarchical society.
    Underground radical groups were sharply critical of the
Derg as an undemocratic military junta without visible social

or political direction. When the Derg's attempts to work out a rapprochement with Eritrean secessionists failed, and internal problems increased, unrest mounted sharply. On 23-24 November, the Derg moved swiftly to execute Gen. Aman and 59 leaders of the former government, army and monarchy, among hundreds who had been imprisoned.

Soon after, the Derg seemed to follow a more Marxist orientation. It promulgated a peasant-reform "land to the tiller, " program, took repressive action against dissidents (including students who were demanding a civilian regime), established peasant associations and urban units (see KEBELLE), disclosed increased dependency on the U. S. S. R. and Cuba, and under its "anti-imperialist" slogans made a sharp break with various "western" countries, particularly the United States.

Among the very few Derg leaders who had been publicly identified was Major Mengestu Hayle Maryam, 39, 1st Vice-Chairman. Atnafu Abate, although slightly older and more senior to Mengestu, was 2nd Vice-Chairman. After Gen. Aman's execution, Gen. Teferi Bante, former commandant of Holeta Military Academy, was named chairman. These three became well-publicized as the top leadership of the government. Mengestu soon emerged as the real strong man, but his thrust for personal power was opposed by many in the Derg. One group was sharply critical of his Eritrean policy and demanded a Derg session to discuss it; Mengestu had them assassinated as "counter-revolutionaries. " As Mengestu's problems multiplied, so did dissatisfaction within the Derg. In an attempt to stamp this out, Mengestu called for a Derg meeting but his rivals managed to put through a reorganization at the end of 1976 which relegated Mengestu to a less influential role. He bided his time, however, and in February 1977 set a trap for Gen. Teferi and four of his associates who were Mengestu's main opposition. All five were assassinated along with four of Mengestu's supporters who were supposed to meet with them, shot down as "counter-revolutionaries" by the Derg's security forces (see FLAME BRIGADE). Mengestu thus emerged as undisputed leader.

DERVISHES see MAHDISTS

DESTA DEMTEW, Ras (1892-1937). A loyal supporter of Hayle Sellase when he was regent (for Zewditu) he was rewarded with the hand of Tenagne Werq Hayle Sellase and the provinces of Sidamo and Borana in 1924. One of the Shewan nobility through his father Fitwrari Demtew (Menilek II's envoy to Russia in 1895), still he favored modernization which he observed on visits to Europe and the United States; he pushed through road building, education projects, favored scientific medicine and a pure water supply. He was commander-in-chief of military forces in southern Ethiopia in 1935 and harassed the Italians in a series of guerrilla actions until he was captured and executed in 1937.

DEVELOPMENT THROUGH COOPERATION CAMPAIGN.   Colloquially
known as zemecha (q. v.) this short-lived project was apparently
an outgrowth of the University service idea (q. v.).   The Derg
proclaimed its "land to the tiller" reforms in 1975 and--seeking
to use the high school and university students to carry the message to the countryside, and at the same time get the radical
students who opposed them out of Addis Ababa (as had Hayle
Sellase through University Service)--formed the zemecha.   The
students, essentially against the Derg because of its militarian-
ism and harshness, tried to make their zemecha into an anti-
Derg force and toward a collective system of agriculture.   The
Derg objected to collectivization, fearing it would alienate the
independent-minded farmers, most of whom were tilling their
own land for the first time.   By June 1976, the zemecha ended,
the students were dispersed and the peasant associations, which
on the whole had rejected the students' ideology and methods,
were in an even stronger position.

DINQINESH HAYLU, Weyzero (d. 1838).   The revered matriarch of
Gojam's royal house; her descendants ruled Gojam, Damot and
Agew-meder for most of the 19th and 20th centuries.   Because
she was the daughter of Ras Haylu (grandson of Empress Mentewab), her son, Goshu, asserted royal lineage for his father
was only a converted Oromo, Zewde Salim of Damot.   Zewde
Salim, battling with Ras Gugsa Mersu, placed his wife in safety
at Mahdere Maryam, and his son with Oromo relations in 1807.
She never saw him again.   Gugsa Mersu broke his promise to
restore Dinqinesh if Zewde would pay him a ransom in gold;
instead, he hunted him down and imprisoned him until his death
in 1818.   Faithful Dinqinesh would not marry again; she and her
sister, Trungo, passed through Tegray in 1814, took ship for
Jerusalem where she lived piously and penuriously as a nun until her death.

DIPLOMACY, FOREIGN.   As of July 1979, there were 67 countries,
the Organization for African Unity, the Palestine Liberation Front
and eight international organizations represented in Addis Ababa.
For countries which have had a significant history of contacts
with Ethiopia see AUSTRIA, BELGIUM, EGYPT (UAR), FRANCE,
GERMANY, GREAT BRITAIN, ITALY, PORTUGAL, RUSSIA
(USSR), SPAIN, SUDAN, SWEDEN, TURKEY, UNITED STATES,
and YEMEN.

DIPLOMATIC MISSIONS, SPECIAL.   In a sense, the visit of the
Queen of Sa'ba (see MAQEDA) to Jerusalem to study Solomon's
methods of government in the 10th century B. C. may be considered the first special mission; 14 centuries elapse before the
verified spasmodic missions to Egypt to acquire abuns (q. v.).
These ostensibly religious delegations were diplomatic as well,
given the nature of the Ethiopian polity and the Muslim-Christian
interaction.   The use of foreigners as envoys was often essential
for their language facility: Dawit I (1380-1412) sent his Florentine craftsman, Antonio Bartoli, to Europe in 1402 and Zera

Yaqob (1434-1468) dispatched Pietro Rombulo to India and then
to Affonso of Aragon (who ruled Naples and Sicily as well). It
was a second attempt to forge a Christian alliance with Affonso
against Islam, the first was made by Emperor Yeshaq in 1428.
Dowager Empress Elleni (q. v.) sent her Armenian trader-
supplier, Matewos, to Portugal in 1509/10 offering cooperation
to oust the "infidels" from the Holy Land and asking for military
aid against the encroachment of Islam on her borders. Her
grandson Lebna Dengel (1508-1540) sent Abba Tsaga-zeab to
Portugal where he remained from 1527-1539 pursuing the matter.
The Armenian, Goggia Murad, served three emperors on missions to India from 1658-1707.

A real interest in the exchange of diplomatic missions began
with Tewodros (1855-1868). His rival, Neguse, abetted by the
Catholic missionaries sent Abba Emnete and Lej Taqaye to
France in 1859 seeking aid against Tewodros. Tewodros wrote
letters to European governments and asked foreigners to carry
them; his dispatch of Johann Flad to London in 1866 hardly
qualifies as a diplomatic mission, for Tewodros kept Flad's
wife and children as hostages against his return with the foreign
craftsmen he wanted from England. The emperor's diplomatic
tentatives were doomed when he detained two British diplomats
(see CAPTIVES, EUROPEAN).

Yohannes IV appointed Henry King, a London merchant, as
his honorary consul there in 1870, and immediately after sent
Aleqa Beru and Mercha Werqe to complain about Egyptian incursions. These envoys were stopped at Alexandria on the pretext
of possible costs to the British government; they wanted these
contacts to be made through the Aden residency. In 1872 Yohannes sent his military aide, John Kirkham to England, Austria
and France to plead for aid against Egypt. Apart from diplo-
matic-religious missions to Egypt to acquire abuns in 1871 and
1881, he sent Memher Gebre Egziabeher on a fruitless mission
to make a peace settlement in Cairo after the Ethiopians had
defeated Egypt in two wars, 1875 and 1876. Mercha Werqe succeeded in reaching England in 1884, heading a widely publicized
3-week special mission from Yohannes, who had just signed the
Adwa treaty (q. v.); and in July 1888 two priests represented
Ethiopia at the Kiev celebration of the 900th anniversary of the
Russian Orthodox Church.

Menilek, when King of Shewa, sent Abba Mikael to Italy in
1872 to inquire into trade possibilities, setting in motion a
record number of special missions for any imperial reign to
date. Between 1889 and 1911, there were 11 delegations: to
Italy, Russia, Anglo-Sudan, Anglo-Egypt, Turkey, France, Germany, Austria. One to the U. S. in 1905 turned out to be a bo-
gus envoy after he was received by President Roosevelt. A
trade mission went to the U. S. in 1919 after going to Paris to
congratulate the Allies on their victory. A delegation attended
Ethiopia's acceptance as a member of the League of Nations in
1923. Ras Teferi (Hayle Sellase I) visited Egypt, France and
Italy in 1924 and Dr. (Martin) Werqneh Eshete (q. v.) went to
the U. S. in 1927 to seek help on a dam project and to India to

recruit teachers; Heruy Welde Selasse undertook missions to
Japan in 1931 and to Greece in 1933; conferees attended the
Economic Conference of 1933 in London and Desta Demtew went
to Washington D. C. the same year.   Ethiopia established legations and embassies gradually after 1931 (Italy, first).

DIVORCE.   Civil marriage (kal kidan) can be dissolved at the request of either party; negotiations about property settlement
are usually the main issue.   Rapid divorce and rapid remarriage
have long characterized Ethiopian society and no opprobrium is
attached; in fact, the Amhara male is defined as an adult (mulu
saw) only after several years of married life, resulting in
children, one or more divorces and remarriages.   The Church
though disapproving of more than one marriage, has been unable
to enforce its preference.   Five, even ten, divorces have not
been uncommon among leading Ethiopian historical figures both
male and female.
        Divorce is prohibited after qerban (communion marriage),
unless special dispensation is obtained from the Church.

DJIBOUTI, REPUBLIC OF.   Centered around its capital of Djibouti
city, an excellent port on the Gulf of Aden, the new republic attained its independence in June 1977 after 115 years of French
tutelage.   Islam is the main religion, shared by its two main
ethnic groups--the Somalis and the Afars (q. v.).   In the 19th-
century "scramble for Africa, " the British, French, and
Italians sliced up much of the Horn of Africa, the French taking
over the area containing Djibouti, between British and Italian
Somaliland on the South and the area to the northwest eventually
known as Eritrea.   During this period the French and Ethiopians
worked out arrangements for building a railroad from Djibouti
to Addis Ababa, thus giving the Ethiopians an important outlet
to the sea and the French access to both revenue and trade advantages.   The post-World War II drive for independence in Africa pushed the French to hold referendums in 1958 and 1967
on interim alternatives to colonial rule.   This resulted in a
name change in 1967 to the French Territory of the Afars and
Ise (Issas) but growing demands for independence were finally
realized 10 years later.   The young republic, with a population
of about 250, 000, has an area of less than 15, 000 square miles.

DOGALI, BATTLE OF see TEDALE

DORZE PEOPLE.   A group of about 20, 000 who fall into the ethnic
classification Ometo and live in a closely settled 15 square-mile
area of the Gemu-Gofa highlands.   They speak their own dialect
of the Sidama tongue.   They are known for their lyrical singing,
their uniquely designed basket-shaped houses of woven bamboo,
and their tradition of community responsibility and cooperation
to settle inter-group conflicts.   Dorze who have settled in urban
centers maintain a strong emotional attachment to their highland
home and many return for Mesqel Day every September.   After
the 1898 conquest of the highlands of Gemu-Gofa by Hapte

Giyorgis (q.v.), many slaves, including Dorze, were brought
to Addis Ababa and settled on the property of Hapte Giyorgis
at the foot of Entotto mountain.   Already skilled at weaving,
a low-status occupation despised by the Amhara, some were
sent to Ankober to learn how to weave the shamma (see
CLOTHING) and within a few years the locally made product out-
stripped foreign imports in quality and sales.   "Dorze" became
synonymous with "weaver" despite the fact that all weavers were
not Dorze.

DRAMA.   Plays other than improvised skits on festive occasions are
a new phenomenon.   Many books in Amharic are called "plays"
but lack dramatic development and structure; stage directions
are mixed in with dialogue and might be called versified narrative.   Playwrights Tsegaye Gebre Medhen, Mengestu Lemma,
Taezazu Hayle have mastered the classical form and in both English and Amharic have expressed historical and social themes.
Only the subtlest symbolism could get through rigid censorship;
one notable production in 1970 "Face of the Earth" managed to
snipe at attitudes toward marriage, death, witchcraft, prostitution, courts, press, and radio.   Even translations of "Hamlet"
and "Othello" were censored for placing "kingship" into dis-
repute.
   A national theatre was inaugurated in 1955; by 1960 it had
a staff of 85 musicians, dancers and actors; a folkloric orchestra played traditional instruments and there were two
"western" style ensembles.   The Creative Arts Center of the
university, directed by Tesfaye Gessesse (also an author) persisted in efforts to develop Ethiopian drama.   Plays by foreign
groups (English, American, French, German) have been produced
in the capital drawing an audience from the multi-lingual public.

- E -

ECHEGE.   Abuns (bishops from Egypt) had the prestige of highest
office in the church, but the second in line, an Ethiopian
Echege held the real power and influence.   They were appointed
from Debre Libanos monastery in Shewa, a priority established
by St. Tekle Haymanot (c. 1215-1313) and ran the temporal affairs of the church: maintenance of buildings, land and property,
discipline and settlement of disputes among clergy.   The appointment was made by the emperor and could be revoked by him;
demotion involved great loss of property, and of the privilege
of wearing white silk garments and the red umbrella.   Menilek
II made a bitter enemy of Echege Tewoflos when he made Gebre
Sellase, a priest at his Shewan court, Echege six days after his
own coronation as emperor.   Tewoflos who became nebura-ed
(q.v.) of Aksum abetted the reluctance of Ras Mengesha Yohannes (q.v.) to acknowledge Menilek as suzerain.   Regent Teferi
Mekonnen (Hayle Sellase I) replaced the 1917 Echege for opposition to his "modernization."   The office was merged with that
of abun in 1950-51 when the highest office became "Ethiopianized."

ECONOMIC COMMISSION FOR AFRICA.   A United Nations regional
   body which began work in 1958.   It was established in Addis
   Ababa as the result of intensive lobbying by the Ethiopian
   Government and Hayle Sellase personally.   The emperor provided a brand-new building called Africa Hall.   These moves
   marked for the emperor a definite turning away from Europe
   and the Middle East toward Africa and its problems as a prime
   target for his policies.   Establishment of the UNECA in Addis
   Ababa led naturally--but not without more pressure from Hayle
   Sellase--to the setting up of the headquarters of the Organization for African Unity, also in the Ethiopian capital, in 1963.
   (see UNITED NATIONS, INTERNATIONAL MEMBERSHIPS)

ECONOMIC DEVELOPMENT.   Relative to its potential and measured
   by "western" standards (per-capita income, mortality rates,
   literacy) Ethiopia is an under-developed country, though except
   for periods of drought, natural disaster (see FAMINES) and war
   it has provided enough food for its people.   Ninety percent of
   the population engage in subsistence agriculture and maintain
   large herds of livestock.
      Using "modernization" and "industrialization" as synonymous
   terms for "progress," imperial authority from Tewodros II to
   Hayle Sellase I (exception: Yohannes IV) has viewed the import-
   ing of foreign technology as essential for economic development
   which has had little impact on the farmer or herdsman, the
   basic unit of Ethiopian wealth.   Industrialization, aided by
   foreign governments and foreign private investment, has developed electric power, sugar cultivation and refining, salt
   processing, beer, cotton yarn, textiles, cement, metal tools,
   tires, rubber and canvas footwear, bottle and glass manufacture
   and petroleum products.   Ethiopia in the 1960s was one of the
   most "aided" countries in Africa.
      A highway building program, supplementing what was built
   by the Italians during their occupation, was embarked on; still
   in 1968 only 20 percent of the country lay within 20 miles of
   an all-weather road.
      Planned economic development in the nature of five-year
   plans was instituted in 1957.   The first plan concentrated on industrial development.   The second plan aimed at but did not
   achieve a substantial re-distribution of land, the bulk of which
   remained in the hands of big land owners, the church and the
   crown.   An onerous tenure system (75 percent of the crop as
   rent, frequent payment of land tax) was declared illegal in 1944;
   the Agricultural and Industrial Development Bank was opened in
   1945 for farm loans and the tithe was abolished in 1967, but
   the peasant farmer remained the poorest segment of the population, in terms of assets.   The third five-year plan favored
   large-scale commercial farming by exempting tractors, pesti-
   cides and fertilizers from import duties; small loans would not
   be granted by the Agricultural and Industrial Development Bank
   without collateral amounting to 125 to 200 percent of the total
   loan, thus working against those already disadvantaged in
   property or real wealth.   Mechanized agriculture which could be

afforded only by those already well-off, or on government farms, diminished the need for tenant labor, accelerating their displacement and poverty. Government policies concentrated on increasing crops for export. Incentives to increase their own food production by adopting agricultural innovations, conserving trees or water or investing in improved soil fertility were non-existent for the subsistence farmer.

The Derg (q. v.) nationalized crown land in 1975, abolished all private rural land ownership and made all land used for agricultural purposes the collective property of the Ethiopian people. In one stroke it aimed to change "feudalism" into "socialism," by encouraging the development of peasant associations (kebelle). Reports to date indicate increased food production has resulted, though much remains to be done to secure the farmer against price fluctuations, climatic conditions beyond his control and provide assistance in education, irrigation, afforestation and health (see INVESTMENT, FOREIGN).

EDIR (eder, eddir). Communal associations like the edir, a kind of funeral society, are of fairly recent origin. Members contribute a small amount monthly, or whenever the need arises, to the common fund to defray costs of burial, and are obliged to attend funerals of other members. Edir have become more common in towns, taking the place of the family and relatives in this function (see EQUB; MAHEBER).

EDUCATION. Traditional education was the exclusive province of the church in the case of Christians, and for Muslims by teachers of the Koran, except for the relatively small numbers educated by foreign missionaries. In church schools boys (never girls) learned the Psalms of David and other religious texts in Ge'ez (q. v.) by rote. Those who elected the priesthood continued through a demanding curriculum that could take more than 20 years to complete. A lay order of the church, the debteras (q. v.), learned to write as well as read, hence constituted the only literate population.

An edict of Menilek II in 1907 established secular education for both boys and girls; however, he was forced to put its implementation into church hands and enrollees were primarily the children of the privileged. Secular education advanced in 1925 with the Teferi Mekonnen School in Addis Ababa which had an enrollment of 300 by 1931. A special education tax of 6 percent on imports and exports was assigned to the school. In 1927 a school for freed slaves was supervised by Dr. (Martin) Werqneh Eshete (q. v.). A school for girls, the first since one opened in Eritrea in 1877 by Swedish missionaries, was financed by Empress Menen in 1931. The Italian occupation not only stifled school growth but set it back because so many people just educated were killed. About 200 Ethiopians were educated abroad during the occupation.

By 1944 some 25, 000 pupils attended government six-year schools growing to 338, 000 by 1968; many foreign teachers were brought in from Canada, the United Kingdom, Sweden, India and

the United States.   Amharic was the medium of instruction
through the sixth grade, then classes were taught in English.
In private schools run by Protestant and Catholic groups, and
various foreign communities there were an additional 113,000
students (in 1968).

In 1951, University College opened (now called University
of Addis Ababa, q.v.).   In Asmara, a Roman Catholic University was established in the 1960s.   By the early 1970s, enrollment in both was about 3,300 with another 1,800 in colleges
overseas.   Adult education, pioneered by the Swedish Evangelical mission in the 1870s continues to receive attention from
foreign missions, private organizations and the government.
The present government has restructured education to fit its
ideological objectives.

EGYPT (United Arab Republic) and Ethiopia.   Establishment of a
consulate in Addis Ababa in 1928 climaxed centuries of mutual
hostility between these two nations.   Repeated incursions by
Egypt under its pashas (rulers empowered by the Ottoman empire) into Ethiopia, had a mixture of motives both religious and
economic (slavery and control of the Nile were but two of
them).   These invasions increased in the 19th century with the
occupation of Kasala in 1834, and Metemma in 1838 from where
they incessantly raided the imperial capital, Gondar.   In 1846,
the ailing Ottoman empire ceded to Egypt the port of Massawa
from which attacks westward on the highlands around Keren
were made.   In 1875 Harar was occupied by the Egyptians, then
two invasions by Egyptian armies in 1875-76 were repulsed by
Yohannes IV, effectively ending the Egyptian threat to Ethiopia.
Weakened further by financial bankruptcy, Egypt fell under
British occupation in 1882; this led to the loss of Egyptian control over the Sudan and to the occupation of the Red Sea Coast,
an area formerly under Egyptian control, by European colonial
powers.

Ethiopian slaves were preferred in Egyptian households and
that trade persisted even into the 20th century.   Despite hostilities, Ethiopian spices and coffee were briskly traded for manu-
factured goods available in Cairo.   Alexandria was the seat of
the Coptic Patriarchate which named the head of the Ethiopian
church until 1950 and Jerusalem, as the mecca for Ethiopian
Christians, maintained a steady flow of contacts and pilgrims.
(See MUHAMMAD; ISLAM; COPTIC CHURCH; MAHDISTS; ADWA
TREATY OF 1884.)

The Egypt of the pharaohs regularly traded with the land
of Punt, which encompassed the area that became the Ethiopian
empire.   The papyrus boats which sail today on Lakes Tana,
Hayq and Zway, the eye cosmetics and jewelry of women in the
highlands can be said to represent Egyptian influence from antiquity.

ELECTIONS.   In 1956, the Ethiopian parliament, itself an appointed
body founded in 1931, put forward an Electoral Law Proclamation.   Ethiopians (both men and women) voted in September 1957

for the first time for national representatives. A reported 30
percent of the eligible electorate voted. With widespread il-
literacy, most people comprehended neither issues nor the process and deputies to the chamber continued to be largely appointed. The third election held in 1965 drew votes from more
than half the registered voters. Elections were held every four
years until they were suspended in 1974 (see ERITREA; CHAM-
BER OF DEPUTIES). A registered voter had to be 21 and
"regularly domiciled" in the district he voted in. Candidates
had to own land to the value of E$1000 (U.S. $400 in 1961) or
movable property worth E$2000 (U.S. $800); for a largely land-
less peasantry this effectively maintained the status quo.

ELECTRIC POWER. Electric power was first generated into the
palace of Menilek II in 1905 and the erection in 1911-12 of a
hydroelectric plant on the Aqaqi river brought power into Addis
Ababa. Still by 1959 less than 1 percent of the population
lived in houses lit by electricity. The Qoqa (Koka) dam was
completed in 1960/61 and doubled the amount of available electricity. Eritrea, under the Italians, developed electric energy
earlier and faster.
　　Power generating facilities are a government corporation.
Most of the existing plants in 1967 were thermal but hydroelectric plants at Addis Ababa, Jimma, Debre Berhan, Dire
Dawa, and Asmara exceeded thermal production. After Qoqa
dam (Awash I), Awash II was built and operable in December
1966. Awash III was completed in the 1970s.

ELLENI, Weyzero (of Hamasen). A widow, she was appointed
governor of part of her district by Webe (q.v.) in 1839 after
she personally appealed to that lord; Webe sent troops back to
Hamasen (q.v.) with her, as there was opposition to her sex,
as well as a long-time rivalry with another Christian clan, the
Tsazega. Elleni wished to rule till her sons, Welde Mikael
and Mered Selomon, came of age. In 1842, forces that she led
suffered a defeat, but she was permitted to retain her liberty
and the accoutrements of power. Webe then imposed over the
rivals his own district supervisor, whose methods of tax collection were repressive to both clans. Under the guise of common problems, Elleni invited a rapprochement with the Tsazega,
but in a cruel trick trapped them, and her sons killed their
leader. Welde Mikael and his brother went to Tegray to explain
their actions to Webe who pardoned and detained them. In a
counter act of cruelty, Elleni and her two young grandsons were
murdered by the Tsazega chief in 1851.

ELLENI (Helena, Illeni), (Empress 1434-1468). Favored with the
title Eteqe (literally meaning in Ge'ez, "sister of the country")
over the two other wives of Zera Yaqob (q.v.), she was still a
power during the reign of her stepson, Be'eda Maryam (1468-
1478) and maneuvered the choice of his son, Lebna Dengel, as
emperor in 1508. A Muslim princess from Hadeya, she converted to Christianity, commissioned two religious texts and

rebuilt many churches. Her knowledge of scripture and elegant
Amharic was noted in the chronicle of Be'eda Maryam. With
the encouragement of Pero da Covilham (see PORTUGAL and
ETHIOPIA) she offered the support of Ethiopia against the spread
of Islam in a letter to the King of Portugal in 1509/10. The
letters did not arrive in Lisbon until 1514 and the favorable response came back with her emissaries (Matewos and Tsaga-zeab)
only in 1520, by which time she had retired to her estates in
Gojam where she died about 1522. Elleni's initiative with Portugal led finally to their help in 1541, enabling the defeat of the
Muslim occupiers (see ISLAMIC CONQUEST).

E'MA'LE'DEH see COOPERATIVE OF MARXIST-LENINIST ORGA-
NIZATIONS

EMPERORS. The oft-stated claim that 225 emperors and one empress (Zewditu)--from Menilek I (10th century B.C.) to Hayle
Sellase (1930)--were descended from Solomon and Maqeda
("queen of Sheba") is unprovable. A reasonably reliable estimate is over a hundred between A.D. 330 and 1930. Royal
chronicles are available from the reign of Lalibela (d. 1225)
while information about rulers prior to him are found in the
history of the patriarchs of the Coptic church in Egypt with
whom Ethiopian monarchs corresponded, in manuscripts of the
Ethiopian Church on the lives of distinguished priests, and in
accounts by infrequent travellers on the Ethiopian coast. The
inscriptions on the stelae at Aksum (see EZANA) certainly establish a "King of Kings" in about A.D. 330.
     The so-called "unbroken" line of descent is a fiction (see
ZAGWE; ZEMENE MESAFINT; SHEWAN DYNASTY). Succession
was based not on primogeniture, but often on the judgment of
the incumbent emperor and his advisers as to the best qualified
of his children and/or near relations. Physical perfection was
desired as well as having a royal ancestor. The fact that emperors were frequently polygamous and produced numerous pro-
geny eased the problem of finding a royal connection. Illegiti-
mate birth was no bar to eligibility. At one point during the
Zemene Mesafint (1769-1855) there were an estimated 15 imperial candidates to draw from. The imperial title was neguse
negest ("King of Kings"); he could be addressed as Atse, and
the general public used "Janhoy" to cry out for his attention.

EMRU HAYLE SELLASE, Leul-Ras (c. 1894-1980). Known as the
"red ras" for his liberal views on land reform and his frequent
attempts to present the views of discontented radicals to the emperor (whose second cousin he was; they were raised together
in Harar), he was named by the leaders of the coup d'état of
1960 (q.v.) as Prime Minister and tried unsuccessfully to prevent the bloodshed that occurred between them and government
loyalists on 17 December 1960.
     During the Italian invasion he was in command of troops
that fought and lost the battle of Shere; he escaped to join the
resistance group called the "Black Lions." Surrounded in De-

cember 1936, he gave himself up to the Italians so that most of
his band could escape. He spent seven years in Italian prisons
until liberated by the Allies in 1943.

He was made governor of Begemder on his return, having
already been governor of Harar (1916), Wello, and Gojam
(1933); then became ambassador to the United States (1947-1954)
and India (1954-1959). He was a keen supporter of a non-
political civil service and of responsibility to central authority
rather than to provincial and parochial loyalties. He allowed
his home to be used as a clubhouse for overseas-returned students where reform of autocratic government was the principal
subject discussed. He and his wife, Tsege, had five daughters
and one son (Mikael Emru, who had a diplomatic career like
his father: Washington, 1959-1961, and Moscow, 1961-1965);
his daughter Yemesrach was the wife of Lorenzo T'ezaz (q. v.)
and daughter Yodit (q. v.) the highest ranking woman in the
Foreign Office. Despite his long association with Hayle Sellase and his position as one of the leading members of the old
nobility, he was spared by the Derg. He died in August 1980
and was given a state funeral by the Derg.

ENDALKACHEW MEKONNEN, Lej (1926-1974). As the son of a
   former Prime Minister, Mekonnen Endalkachew (q. v.), and
   member of the prominent Addisge family clan, he had singular
   advantages and opportunities. Educated at Oxford, he returned
   to Ethiopia at the age of 25 to enter government service. He
   was Vice-Minister of Education (1958) then Ambassador to
   Britain; Minister of Commerce; and in 1966 was sent as Ambassador to the United Nations, reportedly because his ideas were
   too progressive. After the Provisional Military Administrative
   Council (Derg) took power, he was asked to serve as transitional
   Prime Minister. His cooperation with the Derg was both futile
   and fatal; he was among the 60 government and military leaders
   executed on 23-24 November 1974.

ENNARYA, Kingdom of (Inarya, Inar'it). References to this area
   during the reign of Yekuno Amlaq (1270-85) establish it as an
   ancient kingdom. It was invaded by the Oromo of neighboring
   Limu at the start of the 18th century and a hundred years later
   was organized into a monarchy and had adopted Islam. Though
   smaller than the original kingdom, Limu-Ennarya, as it was
   now known, was well known throughout the country. Bofo, its
   king, better known by his "horse name" Abba Gomol, ran a
   prosperous realm, centered at Saka, the marketplace. Hundreds
   of caravans from October to May transited the market taking
   ivory, skins, incense, musk, gold, spices and thousands of
   slaves north through Gojam and east through Harar to the coast.
   Abba Gomol (d. 1837) abdicated in favor of his son, Abba
   Bogibo-Ibsa in 1825. He ruled until his death in 1861. Any
   threats to trade routes were met by war, though Abba Bogibo
   made many marital alliances with Jimma (in 1841 his daughter
   married the Jimma king's son) and with Gera and Guma. His
   son-in-law broke the peace after his succession in 1855, and

Limu-Ennarya united with Gera and Guma in 1859 and killed
him in battle.   Abba Bogibo's son did not have the talents of
his father, and after 1861 wars were frequent and trading in
Ennarya was affected.   Wars of the Gibe valley kingdoms did
not come to an end until Menilek II annexed the lot in the
1880s, completing the expansion to the southwest begun by his
grandfather, Sahle Sellase in the 1840s.   Ennarya is presently
within the Limu awraja (district) of Kefa province (see OROMO).

ENSETE.   The cultivation, consumption, and use of the by-products
of this versatile plant (ensete edulis) defines a group of Gurage
and Sidama people living in Sidamo province (eastern part) into
a particular cultural cluster.   Known as "inset" in Sidamo,
"hutta" in Kefa, "uarki" in Oromo, "kojo" in Amharic and
"guna-guna" in Tegrigna, its use as food is disdained elsewhere.
The preparation of flour is a lengthy and laborious process;
once pulp is freed from the pseudo-stem it is fermented three
months; eventually it is roasted on large baking pans as a large
thin bread or boiled with oil to a porridge.   Fibers of the ensete are used for ropes and leaves are used for thatching;
women fasten their skirts with a girdle of ensete fibers.   Plantations of ensete are fertilized with cattle manure; they use a
pointed bamboo stick, a wooden mattock to weed and work the
soil and a knife as their only implements.   Ensete is reproduced by offshoots from six-year-old plants.   Though no scientific study has been made of the nutritive values of ensete, the
ensete eaters possess an excellent physical appearance.   The
plant was brought to Europe in 1853 and has spread over the
world as a popular ornamental plant with an average height of
five or six meters.   It is also called the false banana.

ENTOTTO.   Settlement on the heights above Addis Ababa believed
to have been an encampment of Emperor Lebna Dengel (1508-
40); it became Menilek's fourth capital as King of Shewa,
(after Letche, Were Ilu and Debre Berhan) in 1881.   A Swiss
architect-engineer Alfred Ilg and two Swiss carpenters were
responsible for much of the building.   After Menilek's marriage
to Taytu Betul in 1883, she supervised the construction of Entotto Maryam church and he actively participated in the building
of Entotto Raguel church--both declared official places of asylum
soon after their completion.   Entotto had a cold and windy climate, its wood supply was exhausted and Taytu preferred the
temperate climate below and the hot springs of Finfinne (Felwu-
ha), so the move to the new capital began 1886-7.   Menilek returned to Entotto to be crowned as emperor in November 1889.
Taytu repaired to a house she had built beside the church after
Menilek's death in 1913 and lived there till her own demise in
1918.

Hayle Sellase stopped to pray at Entotto Maryam church before making his triumphal return to Addis Ababa with British
colonel Orde Wingate in May 1941.   After the 1960 coup attempt, peasants around Entotto helped round up the insurgents
who had fled there.

EQUB. A type of savings and social organization of fairly recent
   origin. Members make regular payments of a fixed sum for
   the privilege of receiving a large lump sum at some point in
   their lives from a lottery drawing. The day of the pay-out is
   also a social occasion. A member can win only once and must
   remain in the society until everyone has drawn once. It is
   most common among low- and middle-income groups like clerks,
   servants, peasants, policemen, etc. (see EDIR; MAHEBER).

ERITREA. Named by the Italians in January 1890 after the Roman
   Erythraeum Mare (now Red Sea), it contains an area of some
   60,000 square miles, and was acquired by treaty with Menilek II
   in 1889. When the Italians exceeded the agreed-upon borders,
   Menilek declared war (see ADWA, BATTLE OF). Its capital is
   Asmara at 7,500 feet above sea level; its port is Massawa (q.v.)
   to which it is connected by a railway and an all-weather road
   down the escarpment to the sea. The Eritrean population of
   about 3,400,000 is largely Tegrigna-speaking, about half-
   Christian and half-Muslim, with a scattering of Catholics.
      Italian governors (Ferdinando Martini--1898-1906--followed
   by Salvago-Raggi, De Martino, Cerrina-Ferroni, Gasparini,
   Zoli, Astuto dei Lucchesi, and Daodiace) developed public-
   administered medical services, agricultural improvements, and
   Italian-flavored public amenities. With the Fascists in power
   in Italy, previously relaxed racial attitudes changed for the
   worse. Eritrea was the strategic base from which Italy
   launched its conquest and occupation of Ethiopia (1935-41).
      Eritrea was administered by Britain (Stephen Longrigg, J.
   M. Benoy) from 1941 until it was transferred to Ethiopia on a
   federated status in 1952 by a United National General Assembly
   resolution. With a more advanced political structure than the
   rest of the empire, Eritrea had a desire for separatism that
   was bound to grow, so the federated status was undermined by
   the imperial government which would not tolerate Eritrean control over police, local administration, and taxation or with
   its own elected assembly.
      With U.N. acquiescence, Eritrea became part of Ethiopia
   in November 1962 by vote of the Eritrean assembly, which by
   then had been purged of all anti-annexation elements. Since
   then various insurgent organizations have fought for secession
   through underground political action and guerrilla warfare (see
   ERITREAN LIBERATION GROUPS).
      The central government takeover by the Derg (q.v.) in
   1974 did not alter Ethiopian government policy that Eritrea was
   Ethiopian. At first the Derg seemed to favor some form of
   federation, and the Marxist opposition group in Addis Ababa
   (see ETHIOPIAN PEOPLES' REVOLUTIONARY PARTY) es-
   poused the Eritrean cause. But the need to prevent any loss
   of territory or prestige drove the Derg to seek a military solution and complete domination of Eritrea. By late 1978
   Eritrean resistance, which appeared to have won a number of
   battles, and controlled virtually every urban center except for
   Asmara and Massawa, was being steadily pushed out of the cities

by heavy attacks organized by the Ethiopians and their Russian
and Cuban advisers.   (There was no clear evidence that Cuban
troops had participated in the fighting.)   Still, by mid-1979,
partisan groups claimed to have repulsed a number of Ethiopian
attacks and by early 1980 were reported to have opened a
counter-offensive.
     It was clear by late April 1980, however, that all urban
centers were in Ethiopian hands although guerrilla spokesmen
said "the countryside still belongs to the revolution. "   The only
northern town still believed under rebel control by that date
was Naqfa, but frequent clashes took place in the mountainous
rural areas.   Foreign observers reported the general feeling
that a large-scale Ethiopian offensive was scheduled for Sum-
mer 1980 as a final drive to crush the Eritrean rebellion.
     On the diplomatic front, Sudan President Nimeiri, with
the backing of Egypt's Anwar Sadat and Somalia's Siad Barre,
was seeking to mediate the conflict, primarily with the aim of
shutting off any further flow of Eritrean refugees into the Sudan
where 500, 000 had already settled (see SUDAN).

ERITREAN LIBERATION GROUPS.   By April 1980, at least three
     main Eritrean liberation groups were in action against Ethiopia.
     The Eritrean Liberation Front (ELF) had its origins in the
     early 1950s but was not formally named until 1961.   It was
     largely Muslim and received support first from the Sudan and
     Ba'athist Syria.   Later China (via South Yemen), Iraq, Somalia,
     Saudi Arabia and the Palestinian al-Fatah contributed.   Local
     highway bands collected "taxes" to help the movement (see
     SHIFTA).
          The Eritrean Peoples' Liberation Front (EPLF), a smaller,
     more radical and ideologically concerned group, publishers of
     a monthly, Vanguard, in Tegrigna was formed by a splinter
     group of the ELF and attracted support from Libya, Iraq and
     Syria.   Its strength grew after 1974, following three years of
     conflict with the ELF.   There were further splits with parts of
     the EPLF returning to consolidate with the ELF.   This group-
     ing, now called "Eritrean Liberation Front-Peoples' Liberation
     Forces" was more pro-Western and is headed by Osman Saleh
     Sabbe.   A middle-group of the EPLF preferred to maintain a
     non-aligned status; its chief is Mohammed Nur ad-Din Amin,
     while a Soviet-leaning group led by Ahmad Nasser, is called
     the Eritrean Liberation Front-Revolutionary Council.   The latter
     group (ELF-RC) is under fire from the other two for allegedly
     carrying on secret negotiations with the Derg with Soviet spon-
     sorship.   The ELF-PLF and the EPLF argue that the only ef-
     fective and lasting negotiations would have to involve the United
     States, the Soviet Union and all three rebel groups.

ESKENDER (Alexander) DESTA (-1974).   Son of Tenagne Werq
     Hayle Sellase and Ras Desta Demtew.   Educated in Britain, he
     then became commander of the nascent Ethiopian navy, 1955.
     Many considered him to be the most progressive possibility in
     the royal family to succeed Hayle Sellase until he was executed
     by the Derg in 1974.

ETHIOPIAN DEMOCRATIC UNION.   Organized by a number of
leading figures in the Hayle Sellase government, army, nobility
and business groups.   Formed in London by those who had
managed to escape after the Emperor's overthrow, the EDU
included in its leadership Mengesha Seyum (q. v.), and Nega
Tegegne, ex-governor of Begemder.   Denying that it wished
to reinstitute the monarchy, the EDU favored a democratic,
primarily free-enterprise system.   With reported Sudanese
government support, the EDU mounted guerrilla attacks in the
north from its bases in the Sudan, and was allowed to transmit
Ethiopian-language broadcasts against the Derg and its policies.
Although it had some success toward the end of 1976, the EDU,
now based in Khartoum, was unable to foment the widespread
popular uprisings in the north that it had hoped for.

ETHIOPIAN ORTHODOX CHURCH   see   CHURCH, ETHIOPIAN
ORTHODOX

ETHIOPIAN PEOPLES' REVOLUTIONARY PARTY.   One of the radical political groupings which emerged in the aftermath of the
1974 Revolution.   Earlier it was known as the "Democracia" group
and was primarily a leftist student movement.   It became known
as the EPRP with its primary purpose to oppose the Derg.
To bolster its position, the EPRP obtained support from
teachers, technical and white-collar workers, and other anti-
regime forces: it also made overtures to the Eritrean Peoples'
Liberation Front with which it signed a joint communique expressing solidarity in April 1976.
Espousing "scientific socialism" and using Marxist terminology, the EPRP was nevertheless clearly in favor of democratic
forms and opposed the Derg's authoritarian "fascism. "   The latter criticism arose from the Derg's many executions, arrests
of leftists and unionists, and refusal to permit anything but
state-controlled labor groups.   Another distinction between EPRP
and the All-Ethiopia Socialist Movement (Mei'son-q. v.), a
Marxist-Leninist faction that originally supported the Derg and
its hard-line policies, was an ethnic one: EPRP was largely
Amharan and Tegrayan; the other had a strong Oromo (Galla)
and Gurage base.
EPRP favored the transition of feudalism to socialism via
a "provisional peoples' government" that included all democratic
groups--something of a neo-Maoist approach.   This meant that
any military dictatorship was unacceptable, although the EPRP
conceded that some of the Derg's economic reforms had merit.
Their program, published in August 1975, indicated that their
main thrust lay less in the direction of what reforms were
needed than how the government's power should be employed.
EPRP wanted a civilian temporary regime whose national assembly would draft a constitution and appoint a provisional
government which included various "progressive" elements--
workers, peasants, students, soldiers, even merchants who
were "right-minded. "   On the touchy problem of Eritrea, the
EPRP favored self-determination, even up to secession--a position originally taken by Mei'son but later reversed.

Although some of the EPRP's adherents were quite conservative, even capitalist, they supported it largely because of its anti-Derg posture and because of their general belief that a new Ethiopian socialism could be compatible with Western-style democracy. Indeed, most of the leaders of both the EPRP and the Mei'son were Western-educated.

For a while, the EPRP enjoyed some freedom of operation. It suffered a setback when the Confederation of Ethiopian Labor Unions, an independent labor organization which the EPRP backed, was shut down by the Derg. In mid-1976, the left wing of the EPRP split off to form the Ethiopian Communist Party. Subsequent to this, the verbal conflict between the EPRP and the Mei'son shifted to violence; the EPRP was accused by the Derg of attempting to assassinate Maj. Mengestu Hayle Maryam (q. v.) then vice-chairman of the Derg. In the days following this attempt, hundreds were reported killed, most of them student activists on both sides. One result was that a number of the more conservative elements in the country, in and around such important towns as Dire Dawa and Jimma, gave increasing political and financial support to the EPRP.

Violence among the various factions and the Derg escalated during the December 1976-February 1977 period, with a "Red Terror" countering the EPRP's alleged "White Terror"; an estimated 5,000 were assassinated or executed around the country (see Kebelle). While the Mei'son suffered sharp political setbacks, the EPRP was virtually crushed. By early 1979 it was believed to exist only in small groups around Gondar. Moves to establish some kind of civilian-led political party continued to be frustrated by the Derg, although with the return to relative internal quiet, the Derg was reported readying a party based on the army-controlled Abyot Seded faction (see COOPERATIVE OF MARXIST-LENINIST ORGANIZATIONS).

ETHIOPIC. Defined as the particular script or lettering used for various languages in the country. Amharic, for example, is considered to be the prime example of Ethiopic writing. "Ethiopic" sometimes is used to refer to the classical language Ge'ez (q. v.).

EWOSTATEWOS (c. 1273-1352). The founder of a monastic community, Seraye, whose insistence on observing the Sabbath on Saturday as well as Sunday brought him into conflict with the established church. He left Ethiopia about 1337, via the Holy Land and Cyprus and settled in Armenia where he died 14 years later. He taught against the Alexandrian position on the Sabbath (which rejected it as a Jewish custom) and his followers were persecuted and isolated until the reign of Dawit (q. v.) who decreed their protection in 1404. Dawit's son Zera Yaqob personally presided over the Council of Debre Metmaq (in Shewa) in 1450 when the Ewostatewans were vindicated and the Saturday Sabbath observance was formally restored to the Ethiopian Church.

EZANA and SAYZANA (also known as Abreha and Atsbeha).   Tutored
by the Hellenized Syrian Christians, Frumentius (Fre'mnatos)
and Aedesius, Ezana and his brother (some say they were twins)
and their mother, Sawya (or Sophia) became Christian in the 4th
century.   Ezana ascended the throne between A. D. 320 and 325.
Inscriptions on the obelisks at Aksum detail a kingdom on both
sides of the Red Sea and extending into Semen and Welqit, and
parts of present day Sudan and Somalia.   He introduced the
title "king of kings, " and like his predecessors minted coins
with Greek inscriptions for his external trade.   The Ge'ez
language became distinct from Sabean during his reign and he
introduced new words such as "Egziabeher" (God).   Ezana is
presumed to have died fighting on his western borders and his
body was brought back to Aksum and buried in a rock-hewn
church still in existence.   His brother, Sayzana, conquered the
Beja tribes (q. v.) as he ruled the next 14 years after his death,
and is buried at the same site.   Both have been canonized as
"Abreha and Atsbeha" celebrated 14 October each year.

- F -

FAMINES.   For such a fertile country, Ethiopia has suffered an
unusual number of devastating famines.   Famines have been recorded in the royal chronicles in 1540, 1543, 1567, and in the
late 1770s.   The famine of 1888-1892 began with the spread of
rinderpest from Indian cattle unloaded at Massawa by the
Italians to feed their troops.   The disease spread through all
the cattle of Ethiopia; without his beasts the peasant had neither
meat to eat nor means to till the soil.   One-third of the population died.   Drought and famine were reported in 1913-14,
1921, 1953, 1958-59, 1961, and 1964 in certain areas.   In the
wake of the famine of 1970 some 200, 000 people are said to
have perished.   There was so much negligence and corruption
attendant on the distribution of emergency grain shipments from
the U. S. and Europe, and a cover-up by the imperial government, it was a factor in the downfall of Hayle Sellase.   Aside
from drought as a cause of these disasters, analysts agree that
the appropriation of the fruits of a farmer's labor by the nobility and the clergy through the centuries of exploitation have
created the bare subsistence state of the farmer, which is
quickly promoted to starvation when the rains are delayed or
non-existent.

FASHODA, "CRISIS AT" (1898) (now known as Kodok).   France in-
volved Ethiopia in its challenge to Britain's control of the upper
Nile valley believing that the interests of Ethiopia coincided
sufficiently with France's need for the cooperation of Menilek II.
The French dispatched Captain Marchand from West Africa in
February 1896 and obtained Menilek's agreement by a conven-
tion (20 March 1897) kept secret by both parties, to establish
Menilek's authority on the right bank of the Nile so as to help
Captain Marchand when he arrived on the left bank at Fashoda.

Menilek did not want to offend the British or the Mahdists at this time and managed to delay the expedition headed by Tessema Nadew (q. v.) who was accompanied by two Frenchmen and three adventurous Russians.   When they reached the Nile 22 June 1898, the Russians helped their exhausted French friends by swimming out to plant the French flag.   The expedition withdrew, and by the time Marchand got there, 16 days later, Fashoda was deserted.   Marchand's presence at Fashoda irritated Britain to the brink of war with France and he was forced to evacuate on 3 November 1898.   While Menilek's calculated duplicity frustrated France, there was no coordination between the Frenchmen sent from Paris to Ethiopia to effect the rendezvous with Marchand.

FASILEDES, (Emperor 1632-1667).   On his assumption of authority, three months before his father's (Susneyos) death, his first task was the re-establishment of the Ethiopian Church and the ruthless eradication of all Catholic adherents; the Jesuits were banished, and ports were closed to Europeans, whom Fasiledes considered more threatening than Islam.   There was an expansion of Islam at this time as more Oromo adopted this religion, expressing both a preference for its simplicities, and resentment of Christian Amhara dominance.

Fasiledes built a large palace and swimming bath at Gondar, giving that city its unique appearance in today's Ethiopia.   Some historians opine that his adoption of a fixed capital contributed to the weakening of the monarchy, as it restricted his capacity for lightning campaigns against rebel movements and encouraged factionalism within the court itself.   Fasiledes spent much of his reign adjudicating the heated and violent doctrinal disputes within the church.   His son Yohannes I inherited these problems on his succession in October 1667.

FASTING.   The rigorous fasting requirements of the Ethiopian religion, the most severe in the Christian world, are also an important economic and social factor in the national life.   Most Christians devote part or all of 165 days a year to fasting; for the deeply devout the figure is higher--220 days.   The impact on productivity is obvious and can be counted among the reasons for famines (q. v.).   Fasting means no food or drink is allowed before early afternoon, and after that no meat, fowl, milk or eggs; only grains or pulses may be eaten.   This is required every Wednesday and Friday, except those days during the eight weeks after Easter.   There is a month-long fast before Pentecost, two months before Christmas, generally observed only by clergy and elders.   Universally observed is the fasting during the eight weeks before Easter, three days before Lent, two days before Christmas and 16 days before the Assumption of Mary in August.

Slave traders in the 15th century seized Ethiopian families largely during Lent when they were too weak to resist.   In civil wars, it was considered "uncivil" to initiate wars during a long fast.

FAZUGHLI. Located in the mountainous, far western area of the
    country, Fazughli is near the Sudanese border and was part of
    the old province of Beni Shangul. It was a legendary source
    of gold and was reputed to be an important motive, around the
    1820s, for Egyptian plans of conquest of both the Sudan and
    Ethiopia. Muhammad Ali, the Egyptian ruler, sent his son
    Ismail to take Fazughli but Ismail was diverted by the need to
    fight recalcitrant inhabitants of the Nile Valley.
        Fazughli was something of a mystical jinx to Muhammad
    Ali. Ismail was killed in 1822 in pursuit of the gold mines,
    and in 1825, an Italian mineralogist hired to assess the area
    died in Khartoum before he could set out. Muhammed Ali per-
    sisted, however, and acting on the reports and rumors of some
    of his officers carrying out his expansionist campaign in the
    area, sent in 1837 a number of mining engineers headed by an
    Austrian named Rossiger. When stories came back that gold
    had been found in the mountains between Fazughli and Atbara,
    Muhammad Ali was fully occupied with the battles on the
    Ethiopian border and the crisis in Syria and Arabia, but he
    was determined to inspect his new-found riches and appropriate
    the territory for his own. On his arrival in Fazughli, however,
    he discovered that the reports of treasure were greatly exag-
    gerated; besides, the area was far from subdued.

FELASHA (Falasha). Some 25,000 (once numbering about 150,000)
    concentrated in areas north of Lake Tana, the Bete Israel
    (House of Israel) as they call themselves, practice a unique
    form of Judaism. Some believe they are descendants of people
    who, in the 10th century, sought to replace Christianity with
    remembered Judaic traditions; others believe they were an
    Ethiopian tribe that resisted conversion to Christianity. They
    pray in Ge'ez, the liturgical language of the Ethiopian Church
    and practice male and female circumcision. There are
    Felasha monks (not a part of Judaism) and their literature
    comes mainly from Ethiopic sources. Before becoming caste-
    differentiated (they make pots and do metal work) they were a
    political unit. Yeshaq (1413-1430) deprived them of their land
    after his conquest of their capital at Wegera and proclaimed,
    "He who is baptized in the Christian religion, may inherit land
    ... otherwise let him be a felasi (exile). " A group of Felasha
    blacksmiths were required to travel with the royal army to
    make swords and daggers, others settled in monastic-type com-
    munities. A resurgence of power under their leader Gedewon
    (q. v.) in the Semen mountains was put down by Susneyos (1605-
    1632) in 1624. They broadened their skills into building and
    masonry and constructed the first stone castle at Guzere, built
    churches at Gorgora and Azezo and many houses in Gondar and
    were rewarded with lands and titles like azmach (commander).
        Their decline into a despised (by the Amhara) caste was
    complete in the early 1800s. Tewodros II permitted missiona-
    ries from the "London Society for Promoting Christianity
    Amongst the Jews" to work among them in 1860, though in a
    dispute that came before him in 1862, he ruled that they did

not have to convert. The best known of the Felashas who did
convert at that time was Mikael Aragewi who was taken to
Europe and returned to establish a school for his people in
1874. Professor Tamrat Amanuel, a Christian convert who
reverted back to his origins, opened a school in Addis Ababa
for Felashas in 1924. Studies of the language, culture, and
history of the Felashas have engaged many scholars since the
first one, J. Halévy in 1867.

The claim of the royal dynasty of Ethiopia of its descent
from King Solomon has led, not without reason, to its being
termed a "Jewish dynasty." The contacts between the "black
Jews" of Ethiopia and the state of Israel worsened after Hayle
Sellase broke diplomatic relations with Israel in 1973. The already fragile economic status of the Felashas has worsened
under the revolution and pressure groups to "save Ethiopian
Jews" have been formed in the United States and in Israel
where a few hundred had emigrated by 1980.

FETHA NEGEST. Literally, "Laws of the Kings"; it was produced
by Ibn al-Assal in the 13th century as a compilation from Old
and New Testament sources, canons of the councils of Nicea
and Antioch and Roman and Byzantine laws, for the use of
Coptic Christians living in Muslim Egypt. It was introduced
into Ethiopia in the middle of the 15th century, though the first
record of its use was in the chronicle of Sartsa Dengel (1563-
1597); it might well have taken many years to transcribe and
translate from Arabic to Ge'ez (q. v.).

There are 22 chapters on spiritual law, and 29 on temporal
conduct with rules for marriage, property and its inheritance,
and definitions of crimes and punishments. Developing vocal
interpretations of the Ge'ez manuscript, kept in a monastery,
into a functional reference book in Amharic probably took centuries. It was translated into Italian in 1899 and into English
for the first time in 1968 (by Abba Paulos Tzadua, ed. by
Peter L. Strauss).

The Fetha Negest forms the basis of customary law in contemporary Ethiopia as well as underpinning the penal code of
1930 with the justification, "We [Hayle Sellase] have noted on
the eighth page of the ... Fetha Negest the principle ... 'act
according to ... conditions of times and seasons'. "

FIKKARE IYESUS. An apocalyptic work which predicted that Christ
would bring a man named Tewodros to power after a long period
of corruption, perversity and lawlessness. The prophecy was
widespread and it mingled with some legendary elements of the
life of Tewodros I, who ruled Ethiopia briefly at the beginning
of the fifteenth century. Tewodros I is celebrated in the
Ethiopian synaxarium and belief that his namesake would restore
peace and prosperity was especially strong during the tribula-
tions of the Zemene Mesafint (q. v.). Kasa Haylu chose Tewodros
II as his throne name in 1855, confident he was the predicted
savior of Ethiopia.

FILMS. Though there is no film industry, two feature films have
been made in Ethiopia by foreign trained film makers and one
by a French linguist who filmed, with Ethiopian talent, the
story of Arthur Rimbaud when he lived in Harar.   Elala Ibsa's
Hirut, Who Is Her Father (1966) was shown in every major city
where there was a cinema, but did not make back production
costs.   Most successful has been Hayle Gerima's Harvest:
3000 Years which has English subtitles for its Amharic sound
track; this film has commanded international attention.   There
are some 22 movie theatres in Ethiopia, eight of them in Addis
Ababa, showing foreign films after censorship.

FLAG. The national colors were established as green (top), yellow
and red in horizontal bands when Abune Matewos blessed the
flag on 1 March 1897.   The flag, as a national symbol, was a
fairly new concept at that time, though pennants and banners
had been used in the past to distinguish a military unit; Yohannes IV used a flag, seen in 1879, of crimson, white then
blue at the bottom and later one of two red bands separated by
a yellow one on which the imperial lion was embroidered.

FLAME BRIGADE. A group of army and police officers and men,
hand-picked by Mengestu Hayle Maryam in 1976 to form his
personal strong-arm and execution squad.   It was used to reinforce Mengestu's control over all branches of the armed
services and in February 1977 assassinated a number of high-
ranking Derg officers allegedly to prevent a reported overthrow
of Mengestu (see COUP D'ÉTAT [attempted], February 1977).

FOLKLORE. An abundant stock of proverbs embellishes conversation and reveals much of Ethiopian attitudes towards authority,
religion, women, men, parents, children, illness--every aspect
of culture.   Anecdotes about great feats of shrewdness, one of
the most admired virtues, are the "twice-told" tales of the
hearth.   Improvised funeral songs praising the deceased are
remembered and repeated.   Boasting songs after battle, known
as fuqara, achieve renown for originality.   Court satirists
were expected to make comment on current events in verse, of
sufficient ambiguity so as not to insult those in authority, but
make a point.   Some of this unwritten lore has been retrieved,
written down, and analyzed by historians who find in them clues
to actual occurrences (see POETRY; LITERATURE).

FOREIGN POLICY (1855-1980). Tewodros II (1855-1868) feared
Turko-Egyptian expansion from the Sudan and along the coasts
in collusion with Ethiopian Muslims.   He tried for an alliance
with an unresponsive Great Britain and British technical aid.
From 1871-1889 Yohannes IV had to contend with more de-
liberate aggression by Egypt, then by a new enemy, the Italians,
who encroached from Massawa (1885) at the very time that he
provoked the Mahdists into a border war.   Belatedly, and unsuccessfully, he tried to pit his two enemies against each other.
Menilek II, while still Yohannes's vassal succeeded in inducing

both Italy and France to sell him weapons and to recognize his expansion in return for promises of trade and privileges. Once emperor (1889) he attempted to balance Italy with France, then France with Russia and Britain. After the Battle of Adwa (q. v.) the European Powers and the United States sent resident and other missions to Addis Ababa. Menilek used their interests to delimit Ethiopia's much enlarged frontiers and gain material aid. In January 1908, however, he committed Ethiopia to an unequal treaty which placed foreigners under consular jurisdiction and limited the government's right to impose customs duties. He obtained admission to the International Postal Union, Ethiopia's first international membership.

From the coup of 1916 until the third (counting Dogali as the first) Italo-Ethiopian war, a concerted effort was made to place Ethiopia on an equal footing with other nations. Membership in the League of Nations from 1923 worked at first to ward off Anglo-Italian deals on spheres of influence, but failed to protect Ethiopia once Italy attacked. During his exile, the emperor worked to preserve his claims to the throne and territorial integrity. Allied with the British, at last, from 1940, he succeeded in offsetting their colonial ambitions by making use of the Americans and renewing aid from Sweden and other, smaller industrialized states of Europe to whom he had appealed in the 1920s. He committed Ethiopia to participation in the United Nations actions in Korea and in the Congo and mediated in inter-African disputes; that between Ethiopia and Somalia (q. v.) has not been resolved by either negotiation or war. After the 1974 revolution, Ethiopia adopted a pro-Soviet orientation.

FORESTRY. Deforestation of Ethiopia was proceeding at a destructive pace when Menilek II was persuaded (1904), after he had stripped Menangesha forest of wood to build Entotto and Addis Ababa, that he must adopt a tree planting policy. The Australian eucalyptus was introduced, a fast-growing tree that can be cropped every ten years, while new shoots sprout from the roots of the felled tree. Menilek backed up his policy by decreeing severe punishment for those who cut down trees without permission and exempted from taxation lands sown with these trees. Addis Ababa owes much of its character to the graceful and fragrant eucalyptus, as elsewhere in the country. The disadvantage of the eucalyptus is its absorption and transpiration of moisture. The cassia siamca was recommended by a forestry adviser in 1964 as a substitute. A forestry program in each province was placed under the Ministry of Agriculture, but there are no recent reports on progress in encouraging a substitute to the eucalyptus or the present status of conservation.

FRANCE and Ethiopia. Exploration by Frenchmen after the brief stay of physician Charles Poncet at the royal court in 1699 began in 1835 with the arrival of E. Combes and M. Tamisier, followed by J. Dufey and L. Aubert-Roche in 1837, Théophile Lefebvre (sent by Ministry of Commerce and Agriculture) in 1839, Army captains Ferret and Galinier in 1840, and Rochet

d'Héricourt in 1839, 1842 and 1848.   The latter took to France
the Amharic text of a treaty with Sahle Sellase of Shewa, dated
7 June 1843.   The validity of this "treaty" cited by France in
subsequent dealings with Ethiopia, is questioned by modern experts.   Some of the voluminous notes of the d'Abbadie brothers,
Antoine and Arnauld, who traveled Ethiopia between 1838 and
1848 have been published; others are in the Bibliothèque
Nationale in Paris and in the Vatican Library.   There was a
French consul at Massawa from 1841 to 1885 when Italy took
it over.

   Justin de Jacobis, head of a French Catholic mission in
Tegray, pressed the French government in the 1850s to become
more closely involved with Ethiopia.   Napoleon III welcomed
the envoys of Neguse, a rival of Emperor Tewodros II, in
Paris in 1859 but no serious commitment followed.   The Gaston
LeMay mission to Yohannes in 1885 offered a treaty and
scholarships in France to Yohannes IV, but nothing came of it.
Father Taurin de Cahagne of the Harar mission 1881-1899 was
a vigorous proponent of French official efforts to thwart Italian
and British tentatives.   The Italians expelled the French-
staffed Catholic mission in Eritrea at the end of 1894 for their
pro-Ethiopian, anti-Italian actions.

   With the purchase of Obok in 1862 for use as a re-fueling
stop for ships heading for Indo-China, it was a short step for
France to acquire nearby Djibouti and advance inland developing
French Somalia (now Republic of Djibouti).   From Djibouti,
traders and adventurers flowed into Harar and Shewa (P. Arnoux,
L. Chefneux, A. Savouré, L. A. Brémond, A. Rimbaud (the
poet), P. Labatut, P. Soleillet) and Menilek II used them as
messengers, negotiators and arms and goods suppliers.   The
most important of these was Léon Chefneux (1853-1927) who was
active on railway development and arranged for minting of
Ethiopia's first currency and first postage stamps.   Casimir
Mondon-Vidhailet, correspondent for Le Temps, produced
columns favorable to Ethiopia from 1894-1898 and, as well as
acting as a semi-official representative, acquired a number of
valuable manuscripts for the Bibliothèque Nationale.

   A legation was established in 1897.   The minister, Leonce
Lagarde, negotiated the frontier line between the French coastal
zone and Ethiopia and arranged French transit across Ethiopia
to the Nile in 1898 (see FASHODA).   A special envoy, Anton
Klobokowski, persuaded Menilek II to sign an agreement 10
January 1908 granting more favorable terms to France on the
railway rates.   He had the help of a French national, Dr.
Joseph Vitalien who was Menilek's doctor; medical politics were
deliberately pursued by the French.   One French doctor (born
in Russian Georgia) not connected with the legation, Dr. Paul
Mérab, published his invaluable researches and memories of
personalities and politics of Ethiopia from his stay in 1908-
1914 and 1922-1929.   The French legation was never loathe to
meddle in internal affairs, expediting guns and ammunition when
it suited their purposes on several occasions: in 1910 to insure the downfall of Empress Taytu, in 1916 to assist the over-

throw of Lej Iyasu, and 1930, when they did not forbid two
privately employed French pilots from hurling a few bombs
and leaflets over the camp of Ras Gugsa Wele (q. v.).   About
15 Ethiopians who had been trained at St. Cyr were called into
action by Hayle Sellase just before the Battle of May Tchew
(March 1936).

On 7 January 1935 Pierre Laval made a secret agreement
with Mussolini renouncing French interests in Ethiopia; he
ceded part of French Somalia to Italy and released shares in
Djibouti-Addis Ababa railroad for Italian purchase in exchange
for Italian support should Germany attack France.   Although
Léon Blum, French Socialist Premier who succeeded Laval,
refused to recognize Victor Emmanuel as emperor of Ethiopia,
Marshal Pétain as leader of Vichy France accepted the Italian
occupation.   Only in 1945 were Ethiopian-French diplomatic relations restored and Ethiopia agreed to French direction of the
railroad, as it had in the past.   This was due partly because
France had sent troops, in agreement with Hayle Sellase, to
Dire Dawa to protect the railroad workshops during the Italian
occupation and because the French, fearing Italian takeover of
Djibouti, had clandestinely provided arms, money and technical
help to Ethiopian resistance forces.   Free French officers and
men also had participated, under British command, in the 1941
drive that culminated in the Liberation.

Apart from the economic significance of the railroad,
there had been French influence in subtler ways: French
schools (opened in Addis Ababa and Harar in 1907) were attended by children of the elite who then went to France for
higher training (at least 50 in the 1930s); there were more
Ethiopian students in France than anywhere else.   The Napole-
onic Code was basic to the drafting of the Civil and Commercial
Code and had some influence on the predominantly British-type
Civil and Criminal Code.

Newspapers (q. v.) in French began publishing in 1904.
Scholarship by French scholars in Ethiopian studies has been
extensive: Jules Perruchon, René Basset, Maurice de Coppet,
Marcel Cohen, Joseph Halévy, Jacques Faitlovich, and Joseph
Tubiana, for example.   French archaeologists supervised the
founding of archaeological studies in Addis Ababa in 1952.

FRUMENTIUS (Fre'mnatos).   Though the missionary activities of
Frumentius and his brother Aedesius are deemed the introduction
of Christianity in Ethiopia about A. D. 331, it is likely that only
the court at Aksum was converted and that Christianity spread
only after the arrival of the nine Syrian missionaries in A. D.
480.   The brothers, shipwrecked, were taken to Aksum and
given protection and employment.   Their patron king died and
his widow asked them to tutor her sons (see EZANA) and she
and they embraced the faith.   Frumentius went to Alexandria to
request the Patriarch to send a bishop to the nascent Christian
kingdom.   The Patriarch chose him and he returned, as "Abba
Selama" and is revered as a saint.

- G -

GADA.   A generation-grading form of social organization among the
   Oromo (q. v.) that produced automatically a warrior class; the
   significant factor in the 16th and 17th centuries migration-
   conquest of today's southern Ethiopia.   Gada is 1) a concept
   standing for a whole way of life; 2) the institutional framework;
   3) that period of eight years during which one gada class stays
   in power.   The latter limitation provided a turnover considered
   the most democratic among Ethiopian peoples.   The newborn
   male child enters the grading system exactly forty years behind
   the father, regardless of the father's age, so father and son
   are always five grades apart.   Women acquired status and
   privilege by virtue of their relationships with the men passing
   through the gada system.   Each grade's responsibilities guaranteed that a man could not raise children nor hold office until
   he had shown an ability to produce food or herd cattle, and
   had been to war.   Traditionally and still true of the Borana
   (q. v.) area a man may marry only in his 32nd year and only in
   his 40th may he raise a child and be elected by his peers to
   leadership as the Abba Gada.
        By the 19th century, major adaptations had been made in the
   spread-out Oromo groupings, though from available research it
   is not clear how much the system survives.

GAKI SHEROCHO, (king of Kefa 1890-1897) (Kenito, Gali Sheroko,
   Kafa-Tatchini).   With his father he resisted invasions from
   Gojam in 1880 and 1881; in 1882 Menilek sent Ras Gobena
   (q. v.) with an army and Gallito (his father) agreed to pay
   tribute (slaves, musk, coffee) to Shewa; which he did only when
   threatened.   In 1897, Gaki Sheroko was captured and kept in
   custody at Ankober until his death in 1919.   His memory is
   cherished in the songs of the Kefa (q. v.) highlands.

GALLA.   A word in use for four centuries to describe the Oromo
   people (q. v.); it probably means "immigrants. "   As it is dis-
   liked by many Oromo as a term used by their overlords, it is
   being eliminated.   Thus their language, Galligna, is now called
   Oromigna.

GAMES.   Gebata (in Oromo called sedaka) is a parlor-type game in
   which the aim is to accumulate as many pebbles as possible by
   moving them around a board with six holes on each side.   This
   game is played all over Africa and Asia.   Chess (senteraj)--
   with rules more similar to the 6th-century Persian game than
   to the 15th-century European one--was played primarily by court
   figures and has gone out of style; played primarily by court
   figures (noble versus noble or noble versus servant) and occasionally by women (Empress Taytu (q. v.) was known for her
   skill at the game).   Priests were forbidden to play both gebata
   and chess.   The Ethiopian game had a one color board with
   squares effected by strips sewn on it.   Often the game was
   played with much spirit, accompanied by shouting, with servants

moving the heavy ivory pieces at the direction of their masters and knocking captured pieces off the board with force.

Also popular are verbal games, such as riddles, and a type of cross-examination, called tetayaq, which indulges the national fondness for litigation (see SPORTS).

GAMO-GOFA see GEMU-GOFA

GASHA. An unstandardized unit of land measurement introduced in Shewa in 1879-1880 by Menilek II; each gasha then to be classified as fertile, semifertile, or poor, for the purpose of taxation. The lands of peoples defeated by the armies of Menilek were measured with a rope (a qelad) about 133 cubits long. A cubit was roughly the length from the tip of the elbow to the tip of the middle finger of a very tall man. The size of a gasha varied with the type of land; for example in Thertcher where the land was less fertile a gasha measured about 43 hectares while in Burqa, fertile area, a gasha was about half that. Once measured, the land was apportioned between the conquerors and selected local leaders; the former owner of the land became a share-cropper in effect (see GEBERE). Gasha also referred to the shield carried by the conquering soldier who was rewarded with land; hence application of this word.

GEBBI (Ghibbi). The residence of an emperor, provincial noble, or chief, gebbi applied to that ensemble of buildings that serviced him. It is now more specifically the old palace of Menilek II in Addis Ababa. The cabinet met at the gebbi; many state entertainments were held there and the weekly petitioners for justice formed their lines there up to 1974, though Hayle Sellase resided at the Jubilee Palace (built with Italian reparations after 1942). Menilek's gebbi was built in stages after the decision to move the capital from Entotto to Addis Ababa in 1887. After a fire in 1892, construction started over and work was completed on the elfign (private apartments), the gebbi, the aderash (banquet hall), and other houses (for cooks, weavers, jewelers, saddlers, etc.) by January 1894.

GEBER. A tax which the landholder paid in kind; honey, butter, cereals, oxen, cloth, labor, etc. to the provincial governors. Geber was called by various names depending on the produce in question; traditionally, it dates from the reign of Emperor Yekuno Amlaq in the 12th century. The governor determined the geber according to the total quantity of land a person held. For example, one ox and about 19 kilos of honey was tax for 20 gashas (q.v.) of land. It is now paid in cash.

Also the name of a feast given twice yearly by the lay administrator of a parish for all priests and debteras. It describes the banquet given by the monarch for his subjects, to celebrate a military victory, a coronation, the visit of a distinguished guest, etc. Thousands of people flocked to the palace and were served in descending order of rank, in relays; women were excluded. Wives of visiting dignitaries were served in the private apartments of the empress.

GEBERE (gebbar, gabbar). A person who has rist land (inheritable) and pays geber (land tax) to a government representative. The word is derived from the Ge'ez verb, "gebre" ("he worked"). Today it is a tax paid in cash, while formerly it was paid in kind--such as honey, grain, firewood, and labor. Some of the duties of gebere included the provision of cooked food, honey beer, grain and hay for the mules, firewood for a traveling official of the government and giving his time and mules to carry the supplies of the governor across his region. The latter and the "gifts" of money when a baby boy was born to an official were abolished by Teferi Mekonnen in the 1920s. A "numbered" gebere was a rist owner in an Oromo region, paying geber according to the number of livestock or other things he possessed; he was also required to devote labor, like building a house for an official. After 1933, gebere could pay 30 talers a year in lieu of physical labor.

Gebere were created primarily out of the conquered peoples of the southwest. Soldier-settlers (neftenya) were allotted between two and ten gebere each; a higher-ranking soldier could be given 15 to 20 farmers each. The soldier-settler, in turn, was obliged to dispense justice in disputes between gebere, provide food from their larders during famine or just before harvest time when their geberes' supplies were usually exhausted. Though part of Menilek II's colonization policy of the 1880s meant predictable hardship for those colonized, the system also produced peace and increased productivity in areas that had had constant civil war.

The term "gebere," in the sense of describing a serf, is now out of date. It was applied to that land to which private ownership had been established by payment of the land tax until 1975, when systems of land ownership and taxation were changed by the Derg under the program called "land to the tiller."

GEBRE EGZIABEHER MORODA, Dejazmach (c. 1870-1924). The eldest of the seven sons of Moroda Bekere, moti (king) of Leqa in eastern Wellega. His father sought peace with the forces of Tekle Haymanot of Gojam (q.v.) which invaded his kingdom in 1881 and agreed to tribute, baptism and the grant of local autonomy with the title of dejazmach. Menilek challenged Tekle Haymanot's suzerainty over Leqa by sending in Ras Gobena's army (1882). Moroda retained his title and privileges under Menilek and about 1885 sent this eldest son (whose Muslim name was Kumsa) to Menilek's court where he learned Ahmaric and Ge'ez. Menilek stood as his godfather when he was baptized Gebre Egziabeher. He succeeded his father in 1889 and Menilek appointed him governor of extended lands in eastern Welega, from which he gathered his tribute in gold and ivory. He abolished forced labor, supported education and welcomed members of the Swedish Evangelical Mission who established Mekane Yesus Church (q.v.) in Sibu, one of his districts.

GEBRE HEYWET BAYKEDAGN (1886-1919). Born near Adwa and

educated at the Swedish mission in Eritrea, then in Germany
and Austria, he returned to Ethiopia as interpreter with a German mission to Menilek in 1905 and stayed to become a scribe
at Menilek's court.   As a translator for the German doctor
who was treating Menilek in 1909, he ran afoul of Empress
Taytu; in November the same year he exiled himself to the
Sudan where he worked for Sudanese intelligence.   After his
return in 1911 he worked at the palace then in 1914 was appointed head of customs at Dire Dawa but was soon removed
for siding with Ras Teferi (Hayle Sellase).   After the coup of
1916 (q. v.) he recovered his offices, but succumbed to the influenza epidemic of 1919.   His polemical writing, published in
1912 and posthumously in 1924 advocated economic self-sufficiency and radical changes in education, administration, and management of the state's finances.

GEBRE SELLASE WELDE AREGAY (c. 1844-1912), Tsehafi T'ezaz.
As the author of Menilek II's chronicle (published in French in
1930 and 1932 and in Amharic in 1966) he was well-educated by
the church system.   He began his career as a scribe for
Befana, Menilek's consort, became secretary to Menilek about
1876, and was particularly influential in the decisions regarding
church administration.   The title, Minister of Pen, was given
to him in 1907 and subsequently he became nebura-ed of St.
Maryam Tseyon of Addis Alem, the first, outside of nebura-ed
of Aksum, to bear that title.

GEBRU DESTA, Kentiba (mayor) (c. 1853-1950) (formerly "Gobbaw"
or "Gobao").   Educated from 1868-1879 in Jerusalem, Switzerland and Germany, he became a Protestant convert and learned
German, French, English and Arabic.   On his return from
Europe he taught in the Felasha (q. v.) school at Jinda; set up
a school in Gudru in 1881 at the request of Tekle Haymanot of
Gojam; and in Bale taught at the missionary school from 1883-
1886.   He returned to Jerusalem, taught in Syria then in
Tanganyika, and in Aden.   He married Martha Bender who died
six months later from cholera in Harar where Gebru was employed by Ras Mekonnen.   From his remarriage he had six
children (see SENEDU GEBRU).   After a mission to Jerusalem
in March 1891 regarding Ethiopian property, Mekonnen appointed
him comptroller and chief of police for Harar.   In 1895 at the
request of Menilek II he served as aide to Ras Darge in Addis
Ababa during the first war with Italy, and after the war was
appointed chief official of Gondar for two years.   His services
as envoy, interpreter, protocol adviser and tutor (to Lej
Iyasu) were varied and interspersed with periods of being out
of favor.   His missions out of the country for Menilek were:
1) to ask the Mahdists to return Ethiopians captured at Metemma
in 1889; 2) attend coronations of Edward VII (1902) and George V
(1911).   Empress Zewditu sent him with the delegation to congratulate the Allies on victory to Paris in 1919 and Hayle Sellase
sent him to the U. S. in 1930.   He was appointed to the Senate
in 1931 and reappointed after the 1941 restoration having spent

2 years in prison in Italy for alleged complicity in the attempt
on Viceroy Graziani's life in 1937.

GEDEWON (Gideon) (ruler of the Felashas 1586-1624). He took over
leadership after the attack of Sartsa-Dengel (1563-97) on the
Felasha stronghold in the Semen mountains when many died or
committed suicide to avoid capture. When Susneyos (1607-32)
was on the throne, Gedewon supported pretenders, and was the
object of royal reprisals. After a two-month siege in 1615/16
he gave up the man he supported to Susneyos and withdrew;
eight years later he was killed for supporting yet another pretender (see FELASHAS).

GE'EZ (Gi'iz, Gheez). Also called Ethiopic, the language evolved
out of Sabean, which had been brought to the highlands by immigrants from South Arabia in the first century A.D. It
ceased being a spoken language in about the 10th century but
continues to be a literary and ecclesiastical tongue to the
present day. It has 182 phonetic symbols (26 characters with
7 variations each), and is learned by rote by young lads from
debteras (q.v.) in the churchyard; they can read it but don't
understand it and cannot translate it into Amharic (q.v.), the
living language. Those who learn to write it as well as read
it are those who became debteras. The Bible was translated
from Greek into Ge'ez in the 6th century and remained in that
inaccessible form until the 19th (see MISSIONS, PROTESTANT).
A vast number of Ge'ez manuscripts (some in European libraries) contain Ethiopia's early history; Europeans became aware
of it in 1513 when a book of prayers was printed in Rome.
The royal chronicles that exist from the 13th century are all in
Ge'ez; the first in Amharic were not written until the time of
Tewodros II (1855-1868).

GELAWDEWOS (Emperor 1540-1559) (Claudius). Eighteen years old
on accession, he took advice for a time from his mother Seble
Wengel (q.v.) while he studied the arts of war. In 1540 the
Muslim occupation--with its attendant plundering of churches and
monasteries, forced conversions and general slaughter--was at
its peak. In 1543 his army, supplemented by the army of Tegray and 200 Portuguese musketeers who had survived an earlier
encounter with the Muslim commander, was victorious.
    Gelawdewos wrote or dictated the "Confession of Faith"
which reaffirmed the Monophysite doctrine and defended the
special nature of the Ethiopian Church against the Jesuit priests
who had come with the Portuguese. His interests ranged from
irrigation projects to poetry composition. He lost his life in
1559 fighting the last remnants of a Muslim army, mistakenly
seeking battle when his soldiers were weakened by the Lenten
fast.

GEMU-GOFA (altered in 1980 to Gamo-Gofa). The area presently
called by this name is a consolidation (since 1942) of a variety
of societies (about 60) ethnically divided between Konso and

Ometo peoples.   It includes the Dorze and Welamo who are
dealt with in this text.   Its capital is Arba-Minch (or Mench)
("40 springs"); it lies between Kefa and Sidamo and stretches
from Lake Abaya to the Kenya border.
    The highlands were conquered in 1898 by Hapte Giyorgis
(q.v.).

GERMAME and MENGESTU NEWAY see COUP D'ÉTAT (attempted),
13-17 Dec. 1960

GERMANY and Ethiopia.   J. Potken of Cologne heard a mass said
by Ethiopian priests in Rome and printed their words in 1513;
it was the first publication in Ge'ez (q.v.).   Another visitor to
Rome, Job Ludolf, met the learned Abba Gregory from Amhara
province and with his help, under the patronage of Duke Ernst
of Gotha, published a book in 1661 which initiated Ethiopian
studies in Europe.   A physician, lawyer and linguist, Peter
Heyling, made his way to the court of Fasiledes in 1634.   He
spent 18 years in Gondar, married a relation of the emperor,
taught Greek and Hebrew to the clergy, translated the Gospel
of St. John into Amharic, but was murdered by the Pasha of
Suakin as he returned to Europe in 1652.   Explorers and
naturalists such as E. Rüppell (1831-1833), Georg Schweinfurth
(in Ethiopia intermittently 1865-1882) and Wilhelm Schimper
(1837-1874); and Protestant missionaries like C. Kugler, J. L.
Krapf, C. W. Isenberg, Johann Flad, J. Mayer, T. Waldmeier
and H. A. Stern provide accounts in German of events and personalities of the 19th century.
    Official contacts took place after Germany's reunification in
1871; Gerhard Rohlfs who had represented the King of Prussia
during the British expedition of 1868, returned in 1881 to deliver a noncommittal letter to Yohannes IV from Kaiser Wilhelm
I, who had been advised by Bismarck to stay out of the quarrel
between Egypt, Ethiopia and Britain.   From 1890-1895, the
Kaiser always sent polite answers to Menilek's appeals for support for his stand on the Treaty of Wetchale while giving
de facto recognition to the Italian claims.   Germany embargoed
arms to Ethiopia just before the Italo-Ethiopian war of 1895-96.
Nor did Germany join the first rush to establish legations in
Addis Ababa after Menilek defeated Italy.   Only in February
1905 did a special mission headed by Friedrich Rosen negotiate
a commercial treaty, and in May 1906 a legation was established.
An Ethiopian mission went to Germany in 1907, shopped for munitions in Hamburg and sought German support for resolution of
Ethiopia's problems in Jerusalem (q.v.).   Relations with Germany were checked in 1909 over Menilek's irritation with a
German doctor (Steinkuhler) who had accused palace personnel
in league with Empress Taytu of trying to poison Menilek.   This
caused the departure of Steinkuhler, Alfred Zintgraff, a foreign
policy adviser, and the German tutor of the heir-apparent Lej
Iyasu.   This crisis did not affect the high regard Menilek had
for the Halls, a German-Ethiopian family who were descendants
of Moritz Hall who had worked for Emperor Tewodros (see

CAPTIVES, EUROPEAN). The alleged pro-German sympathies
of Lej Iyasu who had been cared for as a child by Catherine
Hall, contributed to his downfall in 1916. During the second
World War, Germany supported its Italian ally in Ethiopia. In
the post-war era, the West German government provided substantial amounts of economic and technical assistance in road
building, welding and radio electronics, and maintained a
hospital at Bahr Dar, and a leper station; the German school
is an important educational facility in the capital and many
Ethiopians have gone to Germany for higher education. Both
East and West Germany maintain relations with the present
government.

Scholars August Dillman, Franz Praetorius, E. Mittwoch,
Elke Haberland, E. Hammerschmidt and explorers C. von
Erlanger and Oscar Neumann (in 1900), F. J. Bieber (in
1873 and 1904) are among those contributing to resources in
German on Ethiopia. The Frobenius Institute in Frankfurt
supports Ethiopian studies.

GIDADA SOLON, Qes (priest). Blinded at the age of four from smallpox, he became a beggar after the death of his father a few
years later. He was found at the age of 20 by Presbyterian
missionaries who converted and educated him. He learned
English and Braille and when the gospels arrived in Braille,
he translated them into Oromo and read them aloud to his
people. The Amhara shum (q.v.) at Burqa Bedessa forbade
him to teach; nonetheless he achieved a great reputation as a
preacher.

GIMIRA people. Residing in an area south of Kefa, they were so
often raided for slaves, and so wantonly slaughtered, an estimated 100,000 people (1935 figure) have been reduced to about
10,000. A 1973 field study (W. Lange) corrects the mistakes
written about them by 19th century European travellers, traces
their varieties of divine kingship and belief systems, and di-
vides them into two ethnic groupings: Tolu (with 7 sub-groups)
and Dizu (with 10 sub-groups of which 2 have been extinguished).
The "Tolu" represent the descendants of the indigenous population and the "Dizu" the descendants of an immigrant elite with
cultural-historical links to the Jenjero, an iron-working culture.
First, they were preyed on by the Oromo kingdoms (mainly
Kefa) and later by Amhara governors from Welde Giyorgis in
1897 to Taye Tekle Maryam in 1930. After two years of active
resistance against their predators from 1932-1934, the anti-
slavery law of 1923 was implemented and they were saved from
extinction, though not cultural atrophy.

GOBENA DACHE, Ras (c. 1819-1889). The most important Oromo
leader (from Abichu) to pledge loyalty to Menilek in 1865 when
the young prince escaped Meqdela to claim the throne of Shewa.
Gobena's territorial acquisitions for Menilek earned him the
title of ras in 1878. In 1881-82 he "persuaded" the Oromo
kingdoms of Jimma, Limu, Goma, Guma, Gera, Jenjero, and

Leqa to pay tribute to Menilek after challenging an effort by
Tekle Haymanot of Gojam to the same end.   In 1886 he repelled
(whether by force or diplomacy is not certain) a Mahdist (q. v.)
advance in western Welega (the province he governed) and led
an attack on the Mahdists in October 1888.   His army and
wealth were as great as Menilek's, sources say.   His wife,
Ayeletch Abarasa was the mother of most of his sons--Abdi
(d. 1870), Mered (d. 1887), Dellenso, Garedew and Wedajo
and daughters Menna (d. 1887) and Askale.   His son, Wedajo,
was married to Menilek's daughter, Shewa Regga before her
marriage to Ras Mikael of Wello.   Ayeletch managed his vast
estate at Falle (Shewa) during Gobena's frequent absences.   At
Menilek's side on the Wello-Begemder border when the King
of Shewa declared himself emperor in March 1889, Gobena died
in July before seeing Menilek's coronation.

GOBEZE, Wagshum (c. 1836-1872).   The bearer of the hereditary
title in Lasta after his father had been hanged by Tewodros II
in May 1858; he remained in hiding for seven years.   In 1864-
65 he emerged at the head of an army supported by his mater-
nal uncle, Meshesha Tedla, and his mother's second husband,
Welde Qirkos.   He invaded Tegray in 1866 defeating Tewodros's
deputy there; married Denqenesh Mercha, sister of Kasa
(Yohannes IV).   He did not interfere when the British expedition
under Col. Napier marched to Meqdela, nor did he help them.
Soon after Napier had defeated Tewodros, Gobeze proclaimed
himself Emperor Tekle Giyorgis, but was not anointed as there
was no abun (q. v.) in Ethiopia.   His beleaguered reign ended
10 July 1871 when he was defeated by his brother-in-law, Kasa
Mercha, near Adwa; imprisoned on Amba Selama, he died in
captivity in 1872.   See additional entry, TEKLE GIYORGIS II.

GOJAM.   The eastern half of Gojam is one of the oldest entities of
the Christian empire; its eastern and southern borders are
sharply defined by the gorges carved by the river Abbay (Blue
Nile) which rises at Lake Tana and is propelled by the magnificent Tissisat Falls.   The river gorges were natural bar-
riers; the Christianization and Semitization of the Agew (q. v.)
settlers began in the 12th century but made no great impact until the reign of Amde Tseyon (1314-1344).   By the mid-18th
century, all but the unfertile areas on the Sudan border of
western Gojam was settled by Amharic speaking Christians.
The ruling family had intermarried with the Gondarine dynasty.
Today's western Gojam was not incorporated until 1897-1899,
under the command of Tekle Haymanot (q. v.).
      During the Zemene Mesafint (q. v.) under Haylu Yosedeq
(d. 1794), Mered Haylu (d. 1821) and Goshu Zewde (d. 1852)
Gojam's princes warred with the overlords of Begemder, made
forays beyond the Abbay in the south and fought each other;
from 1855 to 1868 they resisted the efforts of Tewodros II to
collect tribute from them.   From 1870 to 1901 Gojam was
ruled by Adal Tessema, a grandson of Goshu Zewde.   He was
granted the title of negus (king) by Yohannes IV in 1881; he

benefited from the lucrative trade in slaves, ivory and musk
which transited Gojam en route to the Sudan or to Massawa.
After the death of Tekle Haymanot in 1901 efforts were made
to end the autonomy of Gojam; the title of negus was not given
to any of his descendants. His sons competed for succession
and in 1907 Menilek named Haylu Tekle Haymanot as ras. In
1932 he was deposed for disloyalty to Hayle Sellase and a Shewan governor was appointed (see EMRU, Ras). During the
war with Italy, Haylu Tekle Haymanot was a collaborator, but
could not "deliver" Gojam; it was a center of resistance, and
a sense of solidarity was retained. In 1942 a dynastic appointee
was named, Ras Haylu Belew; he served until 1957 except for
1945-1951 when the Shewan Kebede Tessema was appointed.
1960-1968 another Shewan, Tsehayenque Sellase was governor; a
rebellion in Gojam forced his removal and Dereje Mekonnen replaced him (see REBELLIONS, PEASANT).

The farmers of Gojam have resisted with success, sometimes with violence, every attempt by the central government
between 1942 and 1968 to alter their tax system and measure
their land; this has often been inaccurately ascribed more to a
resentment against Shewan overlords than to their real griev-
ances about lack of roads, schools, medical services, a share
in government and bare subsistence. Strong regional sentiments
still obstruct interference from Addis Ababa's military government.

GOLD. Gold has been a royal monopoly since the beginning of im-
    perial history. It has been expected as tribute from subject
    kingdoms, and possession of it in the form of jewelry has been
    permitted only to royal family members up to the end of the
    19th century. Laboriously panned, mainly in Welega, from
    river beds, and mined in Nejo (Beni Shangul) and near Asmara
    (Tegray), production increased in the early years of the 20th
    century with the introduction of more modern methods through
    concessions given to foreigners by Menilek II and in Eritrea by
    Italian companies. Very few figures are available, but it ap-
    pears clear that the country does not have rich resources on
    the nature of Ghana, Zaire, or South Africa.

GOMA (now part of Gemu-Gofa province). One of the Oromo king-
    doms, transposed from its earlier Sidama character by inter-
    marriage and adaptation of custom with the Oromo migrants of
    the 17th century. It became Muslim (Tijanya order) in the
    early 19th; the reigning family, Awallini, claimed descent from
    a Somali shaikh called Nur Husain who emigrated from Mogadiscio
    about 1780; others claim their ancestor was a Muslim from Go-
    jam. In 1878 their abba-boku (carrier of the scepter) was known
    to be closely advised by his powerful mother; that same year a
    pestilence carried off two-thirds of the population. It was con-
    quered by Beshah Aboye for Menilek in 1886, though as early as
    1883 they were sending tribute to the Shewan king. They speak
    the Metcha dialect of Oromo and are settled cultivators of
    maize, cotton and coffee.

GONDAR. The administrative center of Begemder province and the country's fifth largest city; it was for nearly 200 years the imperial capital. At seven thousand feet above sea level it is situated about 40 miles due north of Lake Tana. Fasiledes (1632-1667) is said to have pitched his tent near a sycamore tree (still standing) and ordered the construction of a castle, seven churches, a number of bridges and a large bath with a three-story pavilion beside it. The remnants of these buildings and those constructed by his successors, show a European influence, and make Gondar the city most redolent of an imperial past. Iyasu I (1682-1706) did much to establish the city as a center of religious culture; its schools of religious dance, painting, poetry and textual studies are considered among the most elite in the country, and survived the decline of Gondar's political power. Between 1769 and 1855 "emperors" lived in Gondar, but political strength lay in the largest military camp elsewhere. Tewodros II punished the clerical resisters of his policies by pillaging Gondar in 1866; Wagshum Gobeze ("Emperor" Tekle Giyorgis) began restoration of its churches in 1868, and Yohannes IV continued that work. The Mahdists almost destroyed it in 1887 burning 44 churches to the ground. The castles are still in the process of being rehabilitated; much was done by the Italians who also built roads and modern buildings. The battle of Gondar in late 1941 was one of the critical struggles that enabled the Ethiopians with British assistance to complete the liberation. The World Health Organization, in cooperation with U.S. aid, established the country's first public health college in Gondar in 1953 and now students in government schools far outnumber those taking religious studies. Nonetheless, at least until 1974, clergy dominated the town's administration. The city was divided into districts marked by the location of churches and the town council consisted of the heads of these churches.

GOSHU ZEWDE, Dejazmach of Gojam c. 1825-1852. As hereditary chief of Gojam he was part of the wars, negotiations, betrayals and reconciliations that characterized the Zemene Mesafint (q. v.) until his death during the battle with Kasa Haylu (Tewodros II) in 1852. By his wife, Sahalu, he had two sons, and by other women, 3 daughters and another son. The latter, Beru, he was forced to legitimize and promote at the insistence of Empress Menen (q. v.) who preferred Beru as her daughter's husband, to Tessema, who was his son by Sahalu. Beru survived release from his imprisonment by Tewodros only a few months and was killed at the end of 1868 in a power struggle with a cousin in Gojam. Tessema had died about 1856, but his son Adal became King Tekle Haymanot of Gojam.

GOVERNMENT. Ethiopia was an absolute monarchy with councils called into session at the wish of the monarch, but few actions were undertaken without the advice and consent of the clerical hierarchy. As long as provincial heads provided soldiers when called upon and tribute, they were permitted autonomy. Rules of conduct and responsibilities of emperors were set down in

the Kebre Neqest (q. v.) and the Fetha Neqest (q. v.) which were
observed as it suited the exercise of unchallenged authority.
Menilek II's division of responsibility in the form of cabinet
posts (Interior, War, Foreign Affairs, etc.) reflected an already
de facto division under other names and ranks.   The Constitution
promulgated under Hayle Sellase in 1931 established a two-
chamber parliament and provided a form for centralization and
recognized certain civil rights, which could be suspended at the
emperor's will.   Even with the more liberal constitution of 1955
and reorganization in 1966, what government undertook and how
it went about it was still a matter of personal relationships between the emperor and his senior officials.   The table of organization below the emperor was Crown Council, Private Cabinet,
Parliament, Prime Minister, Council of Ministers, then Ministries and Agencies.   There was also the Aqabe Se'at, or a weekly appointment between individual ministers and the emperor; and
the Minister of Pen (Tsehafe T'ezaz) who saw to the publication
of the Negarit Gazeta in which all laws were published.
    The revolution of 1974 suspended the constitution and func-
tions as of this date as a military dictatorship.

GRAGN ("the left-handed"; Ahmad ibn-Ibrahim al-Ghazi; "Ahmad
    Guray" in Somalia) see ISLAMIC CONQUEST; DEL WENBERA

GREAT BRITAIN and Ethiopia.   The publication in 1790 of the
    Abyssinian adventures of James Bruce (q. v.) during 1769-1771
    elicited British interest in Ethiopia.   Then Viscount Valentia
    (1804 and 1805 at Massawa) sent Henry Salt to the highlands
    (1805 and 1810).   He was followed by Nathaniel Pearce, who
    lived twelve years in Tegray, where William Coffin also re-
    sided from 1810 until his death.   In 1830, Samuel Gobat of the
    Church Missionary Society was the first foreigner allowed to
    advance beyond Tegray to Gondar since Bruce.
        In 1841-1843, Cornwallis Harris led an Anglo-Indian mission
    to Shewa and signed a poorly understood and consequently moot
    treaty of commerce with King Sahle Sellase.   At court, Harris
    encountered the surgeon Charles Johnston, who lived in Shewa
    during 1842.   In 1843 Charles Beke was exploring in Gojam.
    An adventurer, John Bell, served Ras Ali Alula and then Em-
    peror Tewodros from 1841 until his death in 1860; Mansfield
    Parkyns resided in Tegray from 1843-1846, and Walter Plowden,
    Bell's traveling companion in 1844, was named the first British
    consul at Massawa in 1847.   By the time of Plowden's death at
    the hands of a rival of Emperor Tewodros in 1860, British-
    sponsored Protestant missionary-artisans, many of German-
    Swiss extraction, were living at Gafat under the patronage of
    the emperor.
        In 1862, Tewodros trusted the second British consul, Dun-
    can Cameron who was going on home leave, with a letter for
    Queen Victoria.   Soon after his return in June 1863 without an
    answer, he was chained after protesting Tewodros's trial of
    two of the missionaries for allegedly insulting him.   This in-
    cident led to the punitive British expedition of 1868 (see CAP-

TIVES, EUROPEAN) which took as loot many of the valuable manuscripts now in the British Museum, where their preservation and accessibility has served scholarship.

An English soldier with the expedition, John Kirkham, became the military adviser to Yohannes IV in 1869, but no more diplomats were appointed to Ethiopia until 1897, though Werner Munzinger (q.v.) represented both France and Great Britain at Massawa from 1868-1871. The emperor sent Kirkham as his envoy to Britain and Europe in 1872, to protest Egyptian aggression on his borders, and appointed Henry King as his honorary consul in London. Egypt nevertheless attacked Ethiopia and though they were repulsed in 1875 and 1876, the peace process took ten years. General ("China") Gordon was employed by the Khedive to negotiate in 1877 and 1879 but only in 1884, Britain, having taken over Egypt and needing Ethiopian cooperation against the Mahdists (q.v.) sent Vice-Admiral Sir William Hewett to offer a treaty to Yohannes IV. An agreement was reached (see ADWA, TREATY OF) but it was violated as far as the Ethiopians were concerned within the year. Britain abdicated its responsibility for enforcing the treaty to Italy, when that nation occupied Massawa in 1885. A mission headed by James Harrison-Smith in 1886 failed to reconcile Ethiopian resentment of Italy and in 1887, Gerald Portal's conciliation mission also failed. Only the Mahdist threat in Yohannes's rear prevented Ethiopia from attacking Italy.

From 1890 to 1895, Emperor Menilek II continually protested Italy's interpretation of the Treaty of Wetchale (q.v.) by which Rome claimed Ethiopia as its protectorate. Only after Italy's defeat in 1896 were Ethio-British relations opened by the James Rennell mission and the subsequent appointment of James Harrington as minister to Addis Ababa. Relations were strained in 1906 when Britain, France and Italy made an agreement over their respective spheres of influence should the Ethiopian empire crumble in the event of Menilek's demise; the monarch was reassured only by strong guarantees of Ethiopia's independence. Borders with the Sudan, Egypt and British Somalia were established by treaties between 1897 and 1906, and Britain established consuls in Gambela, Dire Dawa, Gondar and Gore.

Relations were interrupted from 1935-1941. Britain recognized the Italian occupation, but gave refuge to Hayle Sellase and finally organized a Commonwealth army that freed Ethiopia in 1941. Britain administered Eritrea from 1941-1952 and provided advisers to the emperor in the fields of finance, education and economic and military development, though the number diminished steadily both because of economic troubles in Britain and as a result of the emperor's diversification policy on foreign aid.

Among the many British scholars in history and linguistics of Ethiopia are C. F. Beckingham, G. W. B. Huntingford, E. Wallis Budge, Steven Wright, Edward Ullendorff, Richard Pankhurst, Spencer Trimingham, Neville Chittick, Christopher Clapham, and Richard Greenfield.

GREECE and Ethiopia. The word "Ethiopia" is rooted in Homer's
9th century B.C. and Herodotus' 5th century B.C. use of the
word "aethiopes" to denote people with skins darker than
Greeks--its literal meaning is "burnt skin." Coins, inscriptions, and tablets testify to 1st century A.D. contacts with
Greeks, and in the 4th century, two Hellenized Syrian brothers
introduced Christianity to the Aksum (q.v.) court (see FRUMEN-
TIUS). Despite divergent positions taken at Chalcedon (q.v.)
some hundred years later, there are some similarities between
Greek and Ethiopian Orthodoxy. Before the irruption of Islam
which sealed Ethiopia off from Greek or any other influence,
Greek language, its numerical system, and some law affected
the mountain kingdom.
        In the diaspora after Byzantium fell to the Turks in 1463,
a number of Greeks made their way to Ethiopia; several held
positions of honor at the courts of Iyasu I (1602-1706), Bekaffa
(1721-1730) and Iyasu II (1730-1755). Empress Mentewab and
her son Iyasu II studied Greek and letters were written in that
language to the Greek Patriarch of Alexandria (though the Coptic
Patriarchate named Ethiopia's bishops) inviting priests, carpenters, and goldsmiths, and asking for holy books. A Greek
clerical mission arrived in 1755, but Iyasu died soon after and
conditions were too unsettled for any ecumenical discussions.
        Even after Greece became a nation again in 1829-1830,
defeating their Ottoman overlords, the country remained poor
and barren and the diaspora continued. Greeks came in as
craftsmen and traders, farmers and builders; many married
Ethiopian women, and though they tended to form separate communities they integrated well into Ethiopian life, and since
Greece was a weak nation, did not look to the Ethiopians like
the advance guard of an invasion. Despite their manifest contributions, Greeks were derogated by other Europeans as inferior and not worthy of being counted as "Europeans"; thus
they were ignored socially along with Armenians, Indians, Arabs
and Ethiopians. Hence, the accepted wisdom that Sir Richard
Burton was the first European to visit Harar overlooked the fact
that a Greek businessman had been there some ten years before
him.
        The first official envoy was Demosthenes Mitzakis, sent in
1879, largely as a result of the persuasive articles in Athenian
newspapers by Ioannis Kotzikas, a merchant of Kasala, who was
sympathetic to Ethiopia and its aspirations. Kotzikas had defended Tewodros II, and made an unsuccessful effort to deter
the British expedition of 1868, on the grounds that retrieval of
the European hostages could be managed without bloodshed.
Kotzikas was of course interested in economic ties between
Greece and Ethiopia.
        Mitzakis was present when Yohannes IV conferred with
General Gordon in 1877 about an Ethio-Egyptian peace treaty,
provoking Gordon to ascribe a sly influence on the Ethiopian
emperor when Yohannes refused Gordon's unacceptable terms.
In 1884, Mitzakis returned, and was given a medal by Great
Britain for his assistance to the Hewett Mission that did succeed

in getting a treaty of peace (see ADWA, TREATY OF).   As a
result of Mitzakis' rapport with Yohannes, a Greek physician,
Nicolas Parisis, was sent to attend the emperor from February
1885 to June 1886.   Parisis was a thorn in the side of the
Italians who were busy trying to justify their occupation of Massawa.
      After a Greek consulate was opened in 1918, a commercial
treaty was signed in 1922.   The consulate appears to have been
established in response to the pleas of successive British consuls in Addis Ababa from 1900 to 1911 that dealing with the
crimes and disputes of Greeks under their protection was taking
up all their time.   Nevertheless the British employed Photius
Zaphiro, Ioannis Gerolimato and M. Michaelidis as consular
agents and border inspectors.   The names of Greeks who served
the Ethiopian crown would make up a long list.   A few were
Athanase Sourvis (secretary to Menilek II); Andreas Kavadias
(founded first newspaper in 1902); Iakovos Zervos (physician to
Hayle Sellase); Giyorgis Fotis (soldier, tailor, trader to Yohannes IV, Menilek II); Pierre Pêtridès (counsellor in Ethiopian
embassies in Cairo and Turkey and adviser to the Foreign Affairs ministry 1955-1974).   A journal Abba Salama published in
Athens was founded in 1970 and is devoted to research into the
Greek-Ethiopian connection; it is edited by the former Metropolitan of the Greek church in Aksum, Methodios Fouyas.

GUDIT, queen (?) (Gwedit, Yodit, Judith).   Sources agree that
      there was a 10th century woman who seized power and mobilized
      persecution of the church of Ethiopia, destroying monuments and
      artifacts at Aksum, but her origins and motives are not clear.
      Variously described as a king's daughter reduced to prostitution
      or a pagan converted to Judaism who becomes an avenging ruler
      for some thirty years, her existence is certain in a letter
      written from the king of Abyssinia to Patriarch Philothéos, whose
      term of office was 979-1003 A.D., complaining about her.   In
      Amharic she is called "Esato," and in Teltal "Ga'ewa."

GUGSA MERSU, Ras (ruler of north central Ethiopia, c. 1803-1825).
      The consolidator of Yejju Oromo power during the Zemene Mesa-
      fint (q.v.); the power initiated by his great uncle, Ras Ali I who
      died in 1788, urging his family to respect the Christian religion,
      to which they converted from Muhammadanism in a superficial
      way.   Gugsa married a daughter of Emperor Tekle Giyorgis
      (on and off the throne six times between 1799-1800) and had 4
      daughters and 4 sons but not all from the same mother.   The
      relative peace during his rule was partly due to the marital al-
      liances he arranged between his daughters and the Christian
      lords (Hirut to Hayle Maryam of Semen in 1812; Welette Tekle
      to Maru of Dembya; Aster to Welde Rafael; Trungo to Wagshum
      Kenfu).   Gugsa made a new capital at Debre Tabor.   His sons
      succeeded him in turn: Yeman 1825-1828; Marye 1828-1831;
      Dori, three months.   His grandson Ali Alula (q.v.) was the
      last of the line to hold power.

GUGSA WELE, Ras (1877-1930). The son of Wele Betul and Ras
   Mikael's sister, he had a good religious education at his
   father's seat of government, Marto, in Yejju; he had a
   reputation as a poet, amateur musician (on the begenna, a
   harp-like instrument), bibliophile and for generosity to the
   church. He commanded troops at the battle of Adwa 1895-96.
   A favorite of his aunt, Empress Taytu, he spent some time at
   court and she negotiated his marriage (in 1900) to Zewditu, the
   daughter of Menilek II; he was named a ras and made governor
   of Begemder in 1901, a post he lost when Taytu's power was
   clipped in 1910.
       He and Zewditu were separated as a pre-condition for her
   being named empress in 1916. She succeeded in having him reinstated as governor of Begemder. In 1929 he was ordered to
   quell a rebellion in Yejju and was accused of a variety of dere-
   lictions: failure to deal with the rebels, secretly corresponding
   with the Italians in Eritrea, failure to trap Lej Iyasu, marching
   on Addis Ababa with hostile intent. Whatever the truth, he was
   killed in a battle with government forces on 31 March 1930; two
   days later his ex-wife, Empress Zewditu, died.

GULT (gwilt) see LAND TENURE

GUNDET, BATTLE OF (14-16 November 1875). Some 2,500 Egyptian
   troops landed at Massawa and Senhet between August and October
   1875; they proceeded inland to the border of Tegray and Yohannes
   IV declared war on 23 October. Shaleqa Alula engaged some
   troops on the 14th, and the full force (an estimated 60,000 men)
   surrounded the Egyptians the night of the 15th and defeated them
   in a one-hour battle. Yohannes captured the Remington rifles
   used by Egypt, 18 artillery pieces, ammunition, supplies and
   20,000 talers.

GURA, BATTLE OF (7-9 March 1876). Keeping the defeat at Gundet
   (q.v.) secret, the Khedive of Egypt formed a new expeditionary
   force on 26 November 1975; an estimated 11-12,000 troops de-
   barked at Massawa 11 January 1976. Two-thirds of the force
   advanced to Gura and one-third to Kayakhor by the first week in
   February. Yohannes IV moved out with a force (estimates vary
   from 45,000-200,000 with the lower figure more likely) from
   Adwa on 3 February; three weeks later they were 4 hours from
   Gura. Sheleqa Alula commanded the advance guard that attacked
   near Kayakhor on 7 March and pursued the retreating Egyptians
   to Gura a few miles away. 8 and 9 March the Ethiopians attacked Gura fort and despite heavy losses from the artillery
   fire from the fort, managed to capture thousands of rifles and
   some 15 cannon. The Egyptians sued for peace.

GURAGE PEOPLE (Gerawege, Gerage). There are 14 (some say
   16) groups in the Gurage cluster, further defined by the language
   or dialect spoken by each. The "western" group formed a political federation in the mid-19th century consisting of seven
   clans; they inhabit an area around Lake Zway (in Shewa) and are

ensete (q. v.) cultivators like their neighbors in Sidamo. Some claim descent from a Tegrayan noble who came to conquer them in the 14th century. "Eastern" Gurage (Soddo) trace their origins to the Harar area, from which they fled during the 16th-century invasion of Ahmad ibn-Ibrahim. An attempt at unifying the western Gurage under one leader was allegedly made by a Christian commander of Sartsa Dengel (1563-1597) who came to relieve them of Oromo raids. This commander's descendants were overthrown by King Sahle Sellasse between 1832-1840. Menilek II incorporated both western and eastern Gurage into the empire by 1889 after many campaigns. An estimated 50,000 speak Guragigna, a language that has defied agreement among linguists as to its classification.

Women are excluded from land ownership. Gurage men weave and market cloth, and only certain sub-castes tan hides or smelt iron; pottery is a woman's craft. The Soddo Gurage follow Amhara Christian custom circumcising in infancy both boys and girls. The western group circumcises at the ages of 8 and 10 both boys and girls (clitoridectomy).

Christian, Muslim (Shaikh Budella cult), and traditional Gurage belief (in the god Waq) systems co-exist, though one or the other dominates in a given area. Both in the country and in the cities, the Gurage are adept at forming cooperative self-help societies (see EDIR; EQUB).

- H -

HADEYA, KINGDOM OF (Hadya). A Sidama people superficially Muslim before their subjection by Amde Tseyon (1314-1344) who took their king, Amano, to his court and many of them as slaves; the cooperative males formed a contingent in his army which suppressed a Felasha (q. v.) revolt in Wegera in 1332. Hadeya was mentioned by an Arab writer about 1250 as the place where slaves who had been rendered eunuchs were brought for medical treatment before being shipped to the middle east through the port of Zeyla. An Hadeya princess became the wife of Zera Yaqob (1434-68) (see ELLENI). The Hadiya reverted to animism as the Oromo spread among them in the 16th century. The northern portion, led by Umar Beksa in 1878 had slave trading relations with Jimma and Limu and there was a resurgence of Islam. The Shewan army under Hapte Giyorgis (q. v.) in 1883 met stiff resistance but control was effected. They are part of Shewa province now; speak an eastern Cushitic dialect; are Muslim; and cultivate ensete.

HAMASEN. Northern district which, together with Seraye and Akkele Guzay, makes up the central area of Eritrea. Tegrigna is the language of the two most prominent tribes, the Mensa and the Marya. It was part of the Aksumite empire until the 8th century.

In the 1820s two clans living an hour apart at Hazega and Tsazega vied for power, a rivalry that continued through the

reigns of Tewodros and Yohannes IV until 1889-90 when Italy,
in defiance of the limits set by the Treaty of Wetchale (q. v.)
occupied the area.   A strong Catholic mission existed there in
1869 and an agricultural colony had been set up at Shotil.   A
sizeable proportion of the populace is Muslim, although Christianity is the official religion.   Much of the Eritrean opposition
to control from Addis Ababa is based in the Hamasen area
(see ELLENI OF HAMASEN; WELDE MIKAEL SELOMON).

HANDICRAFTS.   For centuries the Ethiopian peasant has relied entirely on his own skills, inventiveness and ingenuity to produce
tools and equipment.   This self-sufficiency in the absence of
any industry, or cash with which to purchase imported goods encouraged a functional and often artistic group of handicrafts.
Despite their total dependence on those craftsmen and women
who made cloth, pots, agricultural implements and weapons, the
Amhara looked down on the Oromo, Gurage or Felasha who produced them.   Both Tewodros II and Menilek II cautioned the
people to give up this snobbish attitude, to little avail.   Some
ladies of importance were proud of their ability to spin thread,
but the process of weaving was relegated to Oromo or Gurage
men.
    Fine cotton and a silky thread used in embroidery were
crafted in Gondar in the 1800s and Shewa's weavers were admired, but none can match the hand-woven shamma (see
CLOTHING) made by a Dorze weaver.   Imported Indian and
American cotton affected Harar's output in the 1880s, but in the
hinterlands did not affect production.   Tailoring was men's work.
Crude needles were made; imported needles were counted as
part of the extraordinary booty collected by Tewodros II when he
defeated Webe of Semen (q. v.) in 1855.
    Carpets made of wool and goats' hair, colored with natural
dyes were famous in Semen and Gondar.   Today a more refined
and handsome carpet in beige, black and brown designs brings
high prices and is produced by young lads attached to a church
and young women at the government handicrafts center.
    Leatherworkers made saddles, shields, scabbards, cartridge
belts, bags, pouches, musical instruments; brass and copper
workers create incense holders, bells, chains and decorate the
harnesses and shields, sword hilts, mule collars and jewelry.
Gold work was limited as it could only be worn by the aristocracy, but silver, largely obtained from melting down money
such as the Maria Teresa taler and the coinage introduced by
Menilek II (to the dismay of the government), was fashioned into
jewelry.   Horn and ivory (now quite rare) was carved into drinking cups, tooth and ear picks, combs, tattooing points and chess-
men.
    Earthenware is the province of women who make food recep-
tacles as well as the gulelat, a clay object mounted on the top
of a hut.   The Oromo are known for water and butter jars
ranging in size from 2 to 60 litres, called gumbos, artistic in
shape and often ornamented with simple designs.   Perishable
pottery figures are sold by the Felasha.

Woodworking is mostly functional, though certain carved stools and chairs are prized and figures of animals and people produced. Basketry is also functional and artistic, employing vari-colored reeds. The round tray-like table (messob) on which Ethiopian food is served (made watertight with the juice of the qulal tree--candalabra euphorba) is often a work of art. The church has been an important patron for hand-crafted items such as crosses held in the hand, placed on top of a stave, and small ones as neck pendants, all in a great variety of design. Painting is often a craft rather than an art, as the same religious or historical theme is painted over and over.

HAPTE GIYORGIS, Fitwrari (d. 12 Dec. 1926). Of obscure origin, he won his rank serving with Ras Gobena (q.v.) in the conquest of the Hadeya in 1883 and retained the title as War Minister in 1908 though he had been made dejazmach after his heroism at Adwa in 1896 and named ras-werq in 1909. He conquered Konso and Borana in 1897 and the Gemu-Gofa highlands in 1898. As chairman of the council of ministers authorized by Menilek in 1908, he steered his way skillfully through the crises of Empress Taytu's (q.v.) downfall, and Lej Iyasu's eccentricities until December 1913 when he left Addis Ababa with his wife, Altaye-Werq, for his vast estates many miles from the capital. He returned a year and a half later, supported the choice of Zewditu for the throne and master-minded the entrapment of Ras Mikael in 1916. Popular and respected he was a power to be reckoned with; Regent Teferi's "modernization" plans were opposed by him but he stayed in his ministerial post until his death.

HARAR (Harer). The capital of Hararge province in eastern Ethiopia; at an elevation of 5,000 feet, the area is fertile and well-watered and is productive in sorghum grain, vegetables, and coffee. The walled inner city (built 1551-69) has five quarters, each named for one of its five gates and these are further divided into about 65 neighborhoods, each named after a Muslim saint or hero in the city's history. It is a center of Sunni Islam. About 1520 it was near the site of the Adal Sultanate (q.v.) which rivaled the Ethiopian empire for control over the eastern rift, but fell into decay after the death of Ahmad ibn-Ibrahim (see ISLAMIC CONQUEST) in 1543. Eighteen emirs ruled it from 1647 to 1887. When Richard Burton gained access for ten days in 1854, disguised as an Arab trader, it was a flourishing entrepot of no political importance beyond the environs of the walls, outside of which Oromo were settled and Somali nomads roamed. Occupied by Egypt 1875-1885, it revived as a trading center for slaves, coffee, ivory and hides, attracting European traders (one was the poet, Arthur Rimbaud) and a Catholic mission. The British, after occupying Egypt in 1882, obliged the Egyptians to evacuate Harar. Taking advantage of the vacuum, Menilek II occupied Harar after a brief battle with its last emir, Abd Allah, and appointed his cousin, Mekonnen, as its governor in January 1887. The Franco-Ethiopian railroad bypassed it in 1902, but it is connected by a motor road to Dire Dawa, where the train stops for passengers and goods.

It became an important military, administrative and educational center with about 16, 000 students enrolled in secondary schools and teacher training.   The 3rd division of the army is stationed outside the walls assigned to guard the border with Somalia, and Holeta Military Academy is there (see HARARI PEOPLE).   Harar is also the chief center for growing khat, (q. v.) a mild stimulant.

HARARI PEOPLE.   The Oromo and Amhara residents of greater Harar call the inner city residents Adare.   There are about 18, 000 in the old city who have a distinct language and culture; an overlapping social framework is divided into ahli (kinship network), marinyet (friendship group) and afocha (neighbor).   The latter concerns itself with the expenses of weddings and funerals in a cooperative way--roughly equivalent to the edir of the Amhara.   A school, Au Abadir, named for their legendary 10th-century ancestor, was established in 1972, to counter the central government's effort to spread the Amharic language and restrict Islamic religious instruction.   The imperial government tried to utilize the afocha to solve local problems.   The Derg, since 1975, has imposed the kebelle (q. v.), as afocha groups declined a political role, resenting in particular land reform which restricted individual holdings to 10 hectares.

HAYLE GIYORGIS (Neggadras 1900-1917; died 1924).   His ability to increase Menilek II's treasury between 1900 and 1908, as the neggadras (q. v.) of Addis Ababa, earned him the honorific of balemwal (favorite) from the emperor, and the description by the secretary at the British legation as the "richest man in ready money in Abyssinia. "   He served in the post of neggadras for 17 years, expanding its function to cover everything from awarding monopoly-concessions in which he participated as revenue sharer, to comptroller of the Franco-Ethiopian railroad, and reorganization of the police.

He was a competent administrator, and had a reputation for fairness, although a consummate opportunist: when Empress Taytu fell from her position of power in 1910, he divorced her niece and married Tessema Nadew's (who had become Regent) niece.   When Tessema Nadew died, Hayle Giyorgis repudiated her and married Sehen Mikael, the half-sister of Lej Iyasu who had just become emperor.   His equivocal position in 1916, before the overthrow of Lej Iyasu, whose adviser he had become, led to his forced removal from office by Regent Teferi Mekonnen in July 1917.

HAYLE MELEKOT (king of Shewa 1847-1855) see SHEWAN DYNASTY

HAYLE SELLASE I (Emperor 1930-1974).   Born 23 July 1892 in Harar to Yeshi-emabet Ali (d. 1893/4) and Ras Mekonnen (q. v.) he was named Teferi Mekonnen.   He learned to write and read

both Ge'ez and Amharic from clerical tutors and became fluent
in French through foreign tutors; after his father's death in
1906 he joined the sons of other nobles at Menilek's court and
in 1907 attended the new Menilek II school in Addis Ababa,
while his elder half-brother, Yelma, became governor of Harar.
Yelma died in October 1907 and despite pressure on Menilek
from Mekonnen family partisans, Teferi was not appointed in
his place (see BALCHA). Not yet 16, in April 1908, he was
made governor of part of Sidamo and in 1910 returned to Harar
as governor. Married and with one daughter (Romane Werq)
he was divorced and married Menen Asfaw (q. v.) and from this
union were born six children: Tenagne Werq (q. v.), Asfa
Wessen (q. v.), Zenebe Werq (d. 1933), Tsehay (d. 1942),
Mekonnen (d. 1957) and Sahle (d. 1962).

After Menilek's grandson and heir, Lej Iyasu, left the capital in 1916, his deposition was announced and Menilek's daughter,
Zewditu, was crowned empress, with Ras Teferi as regent and
heir to the throne (see SHEWAN DYNASTY). Teferi's policies
dominated her reign and were directed at 1) international recognition, 2) expanded education, 3) abolition of slavery, 4) elim-
ination of opposition. To those ends Ethiopia joined the League
of Nations in 1923 and the regent toured Jerusalem, Cairo and
Europe in 1924; some schools were opened (many by foreign
missionaries who were encouraged by the regent with grants of
land); anti-slavery measures began to be enforced; Iyasu's
father, Ras Mikael (q. v.), was defeated in an attempt to march
on the capital (1916) and Iyasu was captured and imprisoned
(1921); an attempt to get rid of Teferi was frustrated in 1928
and Empress Zewditu was forced to grant him the title of negus
(king).

Ras Gugsa Wele (q. v.) who ignored orders to report to
Addis Ababa was defeated and killed in a battle with government
troops. On Zewditu's death, Ras Teferi was crowned Emperor
Hayle Sellase I on 2 November 1930.

A start at centralization of administration, financial regula-
tion, army training and education was interrupted by the Italian
invasion. Earlier, in 1931, a constitution had been approved by
the rulers of each region in 1931 that provided a minimal start
towards wider participation in government; foreign advisers were
employed to establish a military academy, advise on legal and
foreign affairs and develop state education. The world economic
depression affected prices for Ethiopia's coffee and hide exports
and revenue to finance these programs was insufficient due to a
chaotic tax system. As the Italian army approached Addis Ababa in May 1936, Hayle Sellase, his family, along with religious
and political advisers, fled the country. He made his speech
appealing in vain for sanctions on Italy in Geneva on 30 June
1936, then took up residence for five years in Bath, England
(see ITALY and Ethiopia).

Ethiopia was liberated in May 1941 with the help of British
Commonwealth troops. The restored emperor, in the immediate post-war period dealt with myriad problems: maintaining
independence from his benefactors (the British administered

Eritrea until 1952, the Ogaden and "reserved areas" until 1955, the railway until 1946), at the same time he received financial aid from them; insurrections (Gojam, Tegray, Harar, etc.); re-definition of provinces; appointment of governors and ministers of proven loyalty to himself--all fraught with rivalries left over from the occupation as well as intense regional feeling. Economically and socially he had a mild head-start based on the new roads, bridges, hospitals, schools and municipal buildings built by the Italians with Ethiopian forced labor; but economic planning was not undertaken until 1955, and policies were based on a desire to "modernize."

Banks, communications, large and small industry, handicraft training and marketing, electric power, an oil refinery, domestic and international airlines, medical services, a trained army, tiny navy, air force, police force, a legal code, agricultural projects, secondary schools, a university, teacher training college, a law school, college of agriculture, technical schools, public health college, business school--all became realities with the assistance of United Nations agencies, Sweden, West Germany, Israel, Norway, U.S.S.R., Czechoslovakia, Yugoslavia, Japan and the United States.

Though the emperor took the lead in inter-African involvement (see ORGANIZATION OF AFRICAN UNITY) and United Nations (q.v.) actions, little progress was made resolving relations with the Eritrean independence movement or the conflict with Somalia over the Ogaden.

The subsistence way of life of most of the inhabitants of the country scarcely changed; efforts at land reform failed repeatedly. After the challenge to his authority in the abortive coup of 1960 (q.v.) minor improvements were offered, and the emperor promised to delegate more power to parliament which discussed but did little about the need to redistribute the big landholdings that supported the power of the elite and the church. In 1973, a combination of drought resulting in famine in Wello province, and the evident corruption and inefficiency in the distribution of aid led to a crescendo of criticism and unrest. The army in Eritrea mutinied in February and forced the mass resignation of the cabinet. The emperor appointed the progressive Endalkachew Mekonnen (q.v.) as prime minister, and a committee was formed to draft a new constitution. This was not enough for militant students who periodically disrupted Addis Ababa. Thus began the "creeping revolution" (April-September), organized by junior army officers; they eventually dethroned the emperor on 13 September 1974. In November they executed 60 imprisoned leaders associated with the old regime but kept Hayle Sellase under house arrest at the gebbi (q.v.). His death at 84 on August 27, 1975 was announced. He was buried without a funeral service at a place never announced (see COUPS D'ETAT).

HAYLE SELLASE I PRIZE TRUST. A private charity trust of the Emperor's instituted in 1947 and linked to the Hayle Sellase I Foundation. At one point it had a budget of some $2.5 million a year, part of the monarch's income from the St. George's Brewery. It supported hospitals, orphanages, an umbrella factory which employed 230 blind and crippled workers, and provided scholarships for blind students at Hayle Sellase I University and overseas. It has given awards, each worth about $1,700, to Ethiopians for literary and artistic achievement, social work and civic betterment, and to foreigners for humanitarian, agricultural, industrial and intellectual contributions to Ethiopia. It was abolished in 1974 in the aftermath of the Revolution and its assets taken over.

HAYLU TEKLE HAYMANOT, Ras (c. 1868-1951). Youngest son of King Tekle Haymanot of Gojam (q.v.) and Wz. Wessen, he was originally named Seyum. At the age of 14 he was made a governor of Dega and Damot, and in 1896 was appointed governor of Metcha upon his marriage to Askale Maryam Mengesha Atikim, one of his eight marriages. When his father died in 1901 Seyum, who by this time had taken the name Haylu, was made governor of Gojam, but upon being convicted of false accusations against other chiefs he was sentenced to death, a punishment commuted by Emperor Menilek to five years in prison. Reinstated in 1910 he married Asalefetch Wende, whom he divorced when her aunt, Empress Taytu, was deposed shortly after. Haylu supported Lej Iyasu and gave him his daughter, Seble, as wife.
    Haylu's business operations were extensive and he continued them between 1932-1935 when he was again imprisoned for intrigues against the emperor, part of his continuing desire to become "king of kings." He collaborated with the Italians, but Gojam remained a center of resistance. After the restoration in 1941 he was confined to Addis Ababa where he died in 1951.

HEALTH see MEDICINE, MODERN; PUBLIC HEALTH MINISTRY

HERUY WELDE SELLASE, Blattengeta (1878-20 Sept., 1939). He was the author and publisher of some 28 of his own works which include stories, histories, and social philosophy, in Amharic; a linguist, diplomat (missions to Paris, Geneva, Japan, U.S.) and foreign minister in 1930. His title means "master of the pages" and was a civil honorific. He came from Merhabete district to Menilek II's court at Entotto and served at Entotto Raguel church and as a secretary to the monarch. For Hayle Sellase he was a trusted adviser and edited the civil and ecclesiastical codes. He went into exile with the emperor and died in England.

HEWETT TREATY see ADWA, TREATY OF; BRITAIN and Ethiopia

HEYLING, Peter (c. 1607-1652) see GERMANY and Ethiopia

HOLIDAYS (religious and secular). Except for "Adwa Day" (March 2), which commemorates the Ethiopian victory over Italy in

1896; "Martyrs Day" (February 19), which honors those who
were executed by order of General Graziani in revenge for the
attempt on his life in 1937; and "Liberation Day" (5 May: from
the Italians), most holidays have a religious significance. The
celebrations of Hayle Sellase's birthday and coronation are now
cancelled.

New Year's day, 10/11 September, also celebrates St. John
the Baptist; 27/28 September is Mesqel (q. v.) for discovery of
the "true cross" when after religious ceremonies a huge bonfire
is set and drinking, eating, dancing and singing begin--this day
crosses religious lines and most people except Muslims, celebrate it; St. Mikael's day, 20 January, presents elaborate chant-
ing and dancing by the clergy, followed by feasting and dancing.
Christmas, 6/7 January, is marked by hockey games, genna
(see SPORTS) and religious services. The most solemn day is
Epiphany, Timqat, as the baptism of Jesus is observed by renewal of baptism, either by priests sprinkling holy water or immersion in a nearby river. New clothes are given and all old
ones washed. During an eight-week Lent in April/June no
gaiety is permitted until the feast at the end; in August on the
13th day of a 16-day fast for the Assumption of Mary, the buhe
occurs, and whole wheat bread is cooked and eaten to the sound
of country people cracking their whips, sometimes in a contest
in which two teams lash each other until one gives up--a game
going out of style. There are six fixed religious holidays per
month, three additional ones yearly, and eight movable ones according to the calendar announced in churches on New Year's
day in September.

Animist societies have their own special days for the god
they worship and Muslims observe their traditional calendar.
Mesqel, occurring as it does at the end of the rains, is now
celebrated as a day of excitement with a bonfire, if not prayers
and chants, throughout most of the country (see PILGRIMAGES).

HORN OF AFRICA. A geo-political term that describes that vast
    spearhead of land jutting into the Indian Ocean south of the Ara-
    bian peninsula. It comprises four states: the Somali Republic
    along the coast of the Indian Ocean; the French Territory of
    Afars and Issas at the southern end of the Red Sea; Ethiopia in
    the center; and the Sudan which stretches deep into the Sahara
    and north to Egypt. The highlands of Ethiopia, quite unlike any
    other African area, and the two Niles, the Blue and the White,
    are its most distinctive features; the rest is bush, desert or
    wasteland. The Horn, a region almost the size of Europe, is
    diversely populated by people of different religions, races,
    languages, traditions and attitudes, united only by geography
    and the consequences of history. Most of its population leads a
    marginal existence. They all belong to the Organization of Af-
    rican Unity (q. v.); all are striving to realize an effective agri-
    cultural policy. Relations between them remain subject to an-
    cient animosities and modern political rivalries.

HORSE NAMES see ONOMASTICS

HUMAN RIGHTS, STATUS OF. The United Nations, despite its
widely-approved but unenforceable Declaration of Human Rights,
specifically enjoins U. N. action against a country's domestic affairs. As a result, private organizations, such as Amnesty International (AI) conduct investigations and collect information;
over the years, AI has won a reputation for credibility. Its report for 1961 summed up Hayle Sellase's government's violations: detention or unfair trial of political opponents, especially
in Eritrea; harsh conditions of imprisonment; use of torture;
use of death penalty for both political and criminal offenses;
killing of civilians in war zones, particularly Eritrea. Since
1974, when a new government took charge, AI has noted: Derg
decrees November 1974 and July 1976 permitted death penalty
or prison terms for a range of political "crimes" that includes
"anti-revolutionary activities." Kebelle (urban-dwellers or
peasant associations) have been imposing sentences on defen-
dants, none of whom are allowed local counsel; the death
penalty was then carried out without possibility of appeal. The
first excesses were the shooting of some 59 political detainees
(linked to the previous government) by firing squad, without
trial, 23-24 November 1974. Derg forces killed large numbers
of students and protest marchers on 1 May 1975 and 1976. In
April 1977 Kebelle posses killed some 500 young people gathered
at a rally. Random shootings and massacres, even of young
children occurred in May 1977 and in November, mass arrests,
tortures and summary executions--estimated at 5000 between December 1977 and February 1978. An estimated 30, 000 political
detainees are held in detention camps, regardless of sex or
age. Prison conditions, never very good, fell to deplorable
levels under the Derg. Appeals from AI to the Derg to respect
Human Rights Declarations, which the regime claims to adhere
to, have been rejected as "counter-revolutionary propaganda;"
however, in September 1981 they released 549 political prisoners.

HUSSAIN, Shaikh. A Muslim mystic and teacher of the Sufi order,
revered as a saint in Arsi where he is said to have introduced
Islam in the 13th century. The village where he is believed to
be buried attracts some 30, 000 visitors in February every year
who come from Harar and the provinces in the southeast; they
carry a Y-shaped staff as an identifying symbol.

- I -

IFAT, SULTANATE OF (Yifat, Wafat, or Awfat in Arabic histories).
The Welasma house had made Ifat into the most powerful of the
Muslim kingdoms ringing the south and east of the Ethiopian
massif, by 1285; its leaders controlled the trade route from the
coast to the Christian-controlled highlands. By 1332, Ifat interference with the caravans of the emperor, expansionist forays
and the killing of a Christian ambassador returning from Cairo
brought the armies of Amde Tseyon (1314-1344) into Ifat. The
citadel of its kings, as described by Arab writers in the middle
of the 13th century, was richly furnished and prosperous; after

1332 it was ruled by appointees from the Welasma dynasty who
promised to obey the Christian king.   Militant members of the
family, unwilling to be subjugated to the imperial power, migrated to an area east of Harar where they created the sultanate
of Adal about 1415.   Ifat was re-invaded from that direction by
the armies of Islam in 1531.   Christian control was re-
established by Susneyos (1607-32) but Islam remained the dominant religion.   The name, Ifat, now refers to a small district
in eastern Shewa inhabited by the Argobba.   See also ADAL,
SULTANATE OF.

ILG, ALFRED (1854-1916).   Ilg came to Ethiopia in January 1879
from Zurich, a graduate of the Polytechnic there.   For 27
years he performed a variety of technical, purchasing and diplomatic commissions for Menilek, surviving the jealousies of
the court and the competitive self-interests of various Europeans
by putting the interests of Ethiopia first.   He built houses and
churches, a bridge over the Awash (1886), repaired, designed,
invented, translated, and went to war (1889, 1893).   But it was
his piping of running water into the palace in Addis Ababa that
gained him a mention in the royal chronicle of Menilek.   Menilek granted him the railway concession in 1894 and a gold mining
one in 1898.   He was appointed counselor of state for foreign
affairs in 1897, a role he had played for many years, arguing
Ethiopia's case against Italy from 1890-1896.   He married in
Zurich in 1895; his wife, Fanny, joined him in Ethiopia in 1897
bringing with her one of Ilg's commissions from Menilek, the
new Ethiopian flag.   Ilg had a son and two daughters from an
Ethiopian liaison and Menilek allowed him to purchase land for
their mother's security.   The Ilgs departed in 1906 and he sent
his resignation to Menilek in 1907, kept in Zurich by family demands and his knowledge that the physical and mental powers of
his patron were on the wane.

IMRU HAYLE SELLASE see EMRU

INDIA and Ethiopia.   Indian silk, cotton, pepper and kohl have been
sold to the Ethiopians since antiquity; in return went ivory,
aromatic herbs, and slaves.   "Portuguese" India (1500-1600)
sent about 70 Indians of various skills with the military aid mission of 1541.   They and their descendants built the first churches
of stone, as one of their number discovered usable limestone for
mortar, near Gondar about 1626.   One of them designed the
palace of Fasiledes (1632-1667) in Gondar, as many Indians remained after the expulsion of Jesuits in 1633.   From the
thousands of slaves taken to India from the 13th to the 15th
centuries arose a clan of rulers of Bengal between 1486 and 1493.
They were called "Hapshis," a corruption of "Habeshat" (q.v.).
In southwest India, Ethiopian slaves serving as soldiers established such a reputation it was said "a good soldier must be
an Abyssinian."   The district of Janjira in the Bombay area is
often called "Habsan," another form of "Habeshat."   Fasiledes
sent a diplomatic mission to the Moghul emperor, Aurangzeb

(1659-1707); the mission returned with a copy of the Koran and 2,000 rupees to build a mosque in Gondar.

British India provided the officers and escort for Britain's official mission (1841-43) to King Sahle Sellase, and Indian footsoldiers were the mainstay of the British expedition of 1868 as well as the British army of liberation in 1941. The fall of Keren that year was ascribed to the valor of Indian soldiers.

Indian traders (there was a firm in Harar in 1888) increased their numbers in Ethiopia after 1897 when Great Britain established a legation in Addis Ababa for the protection of Indian nationals; the legation sponsored a number of Indian workmen to build Menilek's palace. In 1923, Dr. (Martin) Werqneh Eshete (q.v.) visited India to recruit Indian teachers, and by 1927 Hindus had built their first crematorium and established a school. The Indian population had reached some 4,500 by 1935, about equally divided between Hindus and Muslims, almost all of them in commerce. They lived in Harar, Dire Dawa, Tchertcher, Awash, and Addis Ababa. The occupying Italians exiled Indian merchants; when the latter tried to return after the Liberation they encountered much reluctance on the part of the Ethiopian government. Britain requested exceptions for those who owned businesses prior to 1935.

Independent India (1947) established diplomatic relations in 1950. When the military academy in Harar was opened in 1958, it was under the management of officers of the Indian army. The Ethiopian Ministry of Education employed several hundred Indian teachers for secondary schools in 1959 and for a number of years afterward, at the same time sending Ethiopian students to Indian schools and universities; other scholarships were provided by the Indian government, U.S. AID, and others. The Indian community in Ethiopia built the Gandhi Memorial Hospital for children in 1955; its director was an Indian doctor, Dr. Rama Rao. An Indian textile company (Birla) invested in the Indo-Ethiopian Textile Mill at Aqaqi with the aim of making Ethiopia self-sufficient in cotton. The factory opened in April 1960.

INDUSTRY see ECONOMIC DEVELOPMENT

INSTITUTE OF ARCHAEOLOGY. Established by agreement with the French government in 1952, it published the results of excavations and study in Annales d'Éthiopie, presently suspended.

INSTITUTE OF ETHIOPIAN STUDIES. Founded in Addis Ababa in 1962, under the direction of Richard Pankhurst, it rapidly developed a magnificent library for the use of scholars and a museum (under the direction of Stanislaw Chojnacki) on the premises of the old Ras Mekonnen palace adjacent to the University. From 1963 to 1975 it published the Journal of Ethiopian Studies twice a year, sponsored numerous conferences, and issued a number of other monographs. Its present director is Dr. Taddesse Tamrat.

INTERNATIONAL MEMBERSHIPS. Though Ethiopia printed its first stamps in 1893/4 it was not admitted to the Postal Union until

November 1908; joined the League of Nations in 1923 and International Labor Organization the same year though until 1963 only government representatives attended the annual meetings. The ILO has a regional office in Addis Ababa. The Confederation of Ethiopian Labor Unions joined the ICFTU in March 1964.

Ethiopia joined the International Red Cross in July 1935, the International Coffee Agreement in 1962. As a founding member of the United Nations (1945) Ethiopia is a member of all the U.N. specialized agencies.

INVESTMENT, FOREIGN. Menilek II (1889-1913) initiated and encouraged foreign investment of both money and skills in Ethiopian economic development by granting special concessions to individuals and nations. Greek, Armenian and Italian traders helped to earn foreign exchange by the sale of Ethiopian farm products and profited also from the import of machinery, textiles and various consumer goods. A number of these, such as the Zecou family from Greece, and Armenians like the Darakdjians, came to Ethiopia early in the 20th century, eventually becoming Ethiopian citizens. Italian businesses, a number of which had been established earlier in the colony of Eritrea, flourished during the 1936-41 occupation.

Under Hayle Sellase the pace was stepped up and, supported by President Truman's "Point Four" policy, plans were drawn for larger-scale industrial development mostly under government ownership but also aimed at attracting foreign capital. From the 1940s, until the revolutionary Derg took over the reins of government and nationalized virtually all means of production, scores of businesses and industries sprang up around most of the urban centers.

Some examples were the Wonji Sugar Estate, with Dutch involvement; Darmar Tannery (Darakdjian); United Oil mills, producing vegetable oil and soap from oilseeds grown around the Harar area (Zecou); Diabaco Cotton Mills (British); the Indo-Ethiopian Textile Mill at Aqaqi (Birla Brothers from India); Tobacco Monopoly (British-directed but state-owned); Ethiopian Fibre Co. (Egyptian and British); Ethiopian Abattoir Co. (Besse & Co., French) and various shoe factories, usually American owned.

Power projects such as the Qoqa Dam were government-owned but largely foreign-financed, with plans drawn by Norwegian engineers and construction done by Italians as part payment for reparations arising out of the 1936-41 occupation. Airline development had much U.S. Government financing and technical direction (see ETHIOPIAN AIRLINES), and Tendaho Plantation, an agricultural development project administered by the British firm of Mitchell Cotts & Co., was a successful experimental complex. It contained 52,000 hectares of land taken from Afar grazing areas and is devoted to production of sugar and cotton. The plantation was set up after an agreement with the Sultan of the Afars (q.v.) whose large share-holding in the corporation lapsed when it was nationalized by the Derg. Nationalization of almost all of the above projects has taken place since 1974.

ISLAM.   Because the Christian king gave refuge at Aksum to the
Prophet Muhammad's disciples who had fled persecution in
Mecca about A. D. 622, Muhammad was said to have excepted
the Abyssinian state from any jihad (holy war).   Still, a
gradual penetration into East Africa proceeded from the time
Muslims occupied the Dahlak islands off Massawa about A. D.
650 to protect their Red Sea commerce.   With Islam firmly established in Yemen, Egypt and the upper Nile, Ethiopia was effectively isolated from Christendom.   Trading and political relations continued through this Muslim barrier, and the imperative
acquisition of their bishop from Alexandria compelled the rulers
of Ethiopia to have periodic communication with the rulers of
Egypt.
      Muslim principalities were established along the coast from
Massawa to Zeyla and inland to the highlands of Shewa where
the Mahzumite sultanate existed in A. D. 989 until its conquest
by the sultanate bordering it, Ifat (q. v.), in 1285.   Greater Ifat
also included smaller entities like Mora and Adal (q. v.) until
Ifat was conquered by Amde Seyon in 1332, followed by Fetegar,
Wej, Dewaro, Bale (q. v.) and Hadeya (q. v.).   In 1443, a letter
from Emperor Zera Yaqob to the Mamluk sultan in Cairo cited
the freedom he granted Muslims in Ethiopia as he protested the
persecution of Christians in Egypt, repetition of a similar protest made in 1290.   Trade security superseded strictly religious
issues and relations would be peaceful when trade wasn't inter-
fered with.   New factors affected Islamic relations with Ethiopia
as the Ottomans conquered Syria, Egypt, North Africa and the
Arabian coast between 1512-1519 and met opposition from the
naval power of Christian Portugal; in 1507 the Ottomans failed
to uproot a Portuguese settlement on the island of Socotra which
blocked the entrance to the Red Sea and by 1538 the Portuguese
commanded the Indian Ocean.   However, the Turks managed to
supply arms to a Muslim warrior (see Islamic conquest) who
re-conquered all the Muslim principalities as well as the Christian provinces between 1528 and his death in 1543.   Muslim
power fell back but still mustered sufficient strength to kill Emperor Gelawdewos in battle in 1559.
      Ethiopians transferred their fear of Islam to a horror of
Catholicism provoked by the proselytizing priests attached to the
Portuguese military mission that had helped them defeat the
jihad; Fasiledes (1632-1667) initiated pacts with the Ottoman
pashas of Massawa and Suakim to keep the Catholics out; the
price was the peaceful propagation of Islam.   Theological controversies had weakened the Ethiopian church and the simple
doctrines of Islam found fertile ground in the highlands of Ethiopia where Muslim traders did business.   Yohannes I (1667-1682),
alarmed at the progress of Islam, called a council at Gondar,
where it was decreed that Muslims must not commingle with
Christians.   The Muslims (called Jabartis) joined ranks with
other penalized communities (Felashas, Armenians and Parsees)
who were debarred from owning land or engaging in agriculture.
About 1755, the control of the Solomonic dynasty passed into the
hands of an Oromo clan of Yejju who had adopted Islam; some of

its leaders switched to Christianity to ease their acceptance at court and marry into the impoverished royal family. They controlled northern Ethiopia for the next 100 years (see ZEMENE MESAFINT). Emperor Tewodros IV ended their hegemony in 1855; one of his aims was to convert or expel all Muslims.

Egypt, under Muhammed Ali, had expanded into the Nile valley in 1820-1830 and aimed to conquer Ethiopia. Egypt's motives were more geopolitical than religious; a network of forts and two invasions in 1875 and 1876 failed. The emergence of a militant Shi'ite sect, the Mahdists (q. v.) on the border of Sudan in 1881, constituted a new threat, replete with demands that the Christian emperor become Muslim; they mounted many raids and battles, in one of which Yohannes IV was killed in 1889. Mahdist power waned after their defeat at Omdurman in 1898 but was not eliminated until the following year. Within Ethiopia, Mahdist efforts at subversion had met with little success despite hostility towards Yohannes IV's edict that all Muslims convert, a campaign launched in 1878 which made little progress. Menilek II restored religious freedom when he became emperor in 1889, though he imposed Christian overlords over most of his conquests of non-Christian lands to the south and southwest; as long as taxes and tribute came in, there was little interference with religion.

The age-old fear of Islam returned after Menilek II's death in 1913; his grandson, Iyasu (whose father had been one of the Wello leaders forced to convert in 1878) succeeded and showed great sympathy for Islam; it was the needed pretext to depose him.

Equal rights to civil and military rank for any native of Ethiopia were written into the 1931 constitution, but social prejudice kept Muslims inferior in the power structure; they have their own courts and schools and in predominantly Muslim regions hold important posts. During the occupation the Italians supported the building and repair of mosques, seeking to undermine church influence which was so bound up with nationalist sentiment.

Today, an estimated one-third of the population is Muslim, but each community possesses different characteristics reflecting ethnicity, historical factors and their proximity to animists and Christians. The present government has reduced the number of Christian holidays celebrated and recognized certain Muslim holidays in an effort at accommodation. However, the coincidence of strong Muslim support for Eritrean independence and the hostilities with Somalia over the Haud and the Ogaden, keeps Muslim-Christian relations from being cordial.

ISLAMIC CONQUEST, 1527-1578. Under the command of Ahmad ibn-Ibrahim al-Ghazi, a Muslim force defeated the Christian battalion that had some to collect the tribute refused by the king of Adal in 1527. Two years later Ahmad's army won a decisive victory over the Christians at Shembera Kure; they occupied Dewaro and Shewa in 1531; Amhara and Lasta in 1533 and invaded Tegray in 1535. Emperor Lebna Dengel became a

fugitive as the invaders controlled two-thirds of the empire and
the royal women found safety in the Debra Damo monastery.
On Lebna Dengel's death in 1540 his son, Gelawdewos (q. v.),
inherited a small demoralized army, plagued by desertions.
Given heart by news that Portuguese ships were at Massawa in
February 1541, an appeal for military aid was answered by 400
volunteers under the command of Christavão da Gama.   Joined
to the army of Tegray and accompanied by the Queen mother,
Seble Wengel (q. v.), they administered the first check to
Ahmad's army of occupation early in 1542.   Ahmad retreated,
then acquired from the Turkish Pasha of Zebid 900 Arab, Turkish and Albanian mercenaries who helped win the next encounter.
There were heavy casualties, including half of the Portuguese
contingent, and da Gama was captured and beheaded.   Ahmad
confidently dismissed his mercenaries.   Seble Wengel and her
female colleagues who had acted as a medical corps for the defeated army, escaped capture.   In October 1542, Emperor
Gelawdewos, who had been in Tegulet, (Shewa) during the first
two battles, linked his army with the northern group in Semen.
They took the offensive and won a decisive victory near Lake
Tana on 21 February 1543.   Ahmad was killed, his army dispersed and his wife, Bati Del Wenbera, reached Harar with
some survivors.   She married her husband's nephew, Nur,
with the proviso that he renew the conquest of Ethiopia.   Campaigns were mounted in 1545, 1550, 1554 and in 1559 Nur's
army killed Emperor Gelawdewos who had unwisely put his troops
into battle at the end of a fasting period and had ordered them to
attack before they were in a position to surround the Muslims.
        In the north, the Ottoman Turks had taken control of Mas-
sawa and soldiers had moved into Agame where they profaned
churches; a Muslim queen, who headed the independent tribes
of Mazaga (lower Welqit), was raiding with success.   She was
defeated by the Tegrayans in 1557 and the Turks were forced to
fall back and confine themselves to Suakin, Massawa and Arkiko.
Harar's military capability was not extinguished until 1577 by
Emperor Sartsa Dengel (q. v.) who then turned to a new threat
in Tegray from an alliance between the Turks and a rebellious
Tegray lord.   In 1578 Sartsa Dengel defeated them, but a peace
agreement with the Turks was not obtained until 1589 (see
PORTUGAL and Ethiopia).

ITALO-ETHIOPIAN WAR CAMPAIGN (1935-36).   The small border
    clash in December 1934 known as the Wel Wel incident (q. v.)
    was the pretext used by Mussolini to move into Ethiopia in force
    on a "legal" basis, although this did not occur until October
    1935 because of the need to bring in supplies, munitions and
    men from staging areas in Eritrea.
        On October 5, Adwa and Adigrat capitulated without a shot
    fired after the Italians moved across the Mereb River, generally
    accepted as the border between Eritrea and Ethiopia.   Meqelle,
    capital of Tegray, fell a month later, again with little opposition.
    Mussolini, Italy's Fascist Premier, was elated at these victories
    but pressed his commander, Marshal de Bono, to drive south-

ward.   De Bono, claiming he needed time to supply his forces for impending attacks in mountainous Temben province, temporized so long that Mussolini replaced him with Marshal Badoglio in late November.

The Ethiopians retreated, enticing the Italians to extend their lines precariously but Badoglio was as eager for victories as Il Duce.   Then the Ethiopians, despite the lack of heavy weapons, struck back in late December in a "Christmas offensive" and the Italians were routed by Ras Emru's (q. v.) column at Dembequena Pass.   At the same time, forces under Ras Kasa and Ras Seyum linked up in Temben and Ras Mulugeta pushed back toward Meqelle.

Badoglio sent urgent pleas for reinforcements and Mussolini promptly despatched three more divisions but Badoglio had been forced to retreat to Aksum and Amba Tsellere.   In a panic at these reverses, and at Mussolini's direction, Badoglio began to bomb military and civilian areas indiscriminately and to drop canisters of "special liquids"--poison gas of various kinds--in violation of Italy's signature on the 1926 Geneva Convention.

This illegal but effective warfare enabled Badoglio to regroup and with his new troops began a January offensive in Temben. The Ethiopians counter-attacked, besieged and almost wiped out the garrison at Waryau.   Lack of communications prevented the Ethiopians from bringing all their forces to bear.   Badoglio's columns escaped this final coup-de-grâce and, once again, using heavy bombing and poison gas, bought a respite.

The situation for the Italians, however, was bad enough for Mussolini to initiate secret peace feelers via a Palestinian, Shukry Yasr Bey, for a possible compromise peace.   In the meantime, Gen. Rodolfo Graziani, in Italian Somaliland in an essentially anchored position, was happy to get orders to make a diversionary attack toward Negelle in the southeast.   By mid-February, also employing aerial bombardment and poison gas, Graziani had taken Negelle.

During this time in the north, Badoglio began to move toward the steep, rocky stronghold of Amba Aradom with over 70, 000 men, the largest force ever used in a colonial war and, after three days of relentless bombing and artillery barrages, severely damaged the Ethiopian force under Ras Mulugeta using his bombers to decimate the Ethiopians.   The clash, known as the battle of Enderta, was over on 19 February.

Badoglio next moved to eliminate the forces of Kasa and Seyum and pushed northwestward for the second battle of Temben. With 200, 000 men under his command, as against 60, 000 Ethiopians, Badoglio expected quick victory and did not expect the frenzied waves of attacking Ethiopians that almost routed the Third Army and Eritrean Corps of the Italians.   But air power again proved decisive and Seyum's fleeing army was virtually destroyed; the second battle of Temben was over on 29 February. Badoglio then struck at Emru's forces in Shere with the same result.   The northern area was now conquered and Badoglio pushed toward Addis Ababa for final victory.   He met little opposition to his march on Gondar and other towns in that area.

The only obstacles that remained were the units under the personal command of Emperor Hayle Sellase camped at May Tchew (q.v.), some 400 miles north of Addis Ababa. His plan was to hit Badoglio with a surprise attack, but this never was carried out because of delays for prayer, discussion and changing decisions. Without the element of surprise, the Ethiopians were no match for the Italians whose defenses were able to turn back wave on wave of furious Ethiopian attacks. Aided by the Azebu (Raya)/Oromo tribesmen, the Italians pushed the emperor's forces toward Lake Ashenge where they carried out another aerial massacre.

By the time Hayle Sellase and the remnants of his force reached Addis Ababa, near the end of April, the capital was in turmoil. At the urging of his advisers the monarch departed for Djibouti by rail on 5 May before Badoglio entered the city in triumph at the head of mechanized columns. With Graziani moving westward through the Ogaden against little opposition, the war of armies and battles was over. The guerrilla war of resistance (see PATRIOTS; BLACK LIONS) began shortly afterward; hostilities along these lines continued until British Commonwealth forces, under Brigadier Sandford and Col. Orde Wingate, liberated Ethiopia on 5 May, 1941 when the Emperor finally returned from exile, symbolically leading these troops into Addis Ababa.

ITALY and Ethiopia. Early contacts by Italians were made in the 15th century when artisans from the city-states of Florence and Venice went to Ethiopia and worked for its emperors. Ethiopian priests went to Rome and Florence even before their formal attendance at the Council of Florence in 1441; a steady trickle of pilgrims led to the founding of the Collegio Etiopico (q.v.) in 1539, at the Vatican.

Italians were members of both the Lazarist missionary initiative in 1838 and the Capuchins in 1846. One of the Lazarists, Giuseppi Sapeto, saw the need for a Red Sea fueling station after the Suez Canal opened in 1869 and purchased the port of Assab for the Rubattino Shipping Company; it was abandoned when Egypt occupied it. Egypt's power waned by 1882 and the Italian government occupied Assab and Massawa in 1885, signifying their political interest in Ethiopia.

Since Italy had become a nation again (March 17, 1861) it entered the colonial power game late, but more than 70 Italian expeditions, backed by commercial and geographic societies went to Africa in the last half of the 19th century--the one with the most far-reaching implications for Ethiopia--was headed by the Marchese Orazio Antinori, arriving in Shewa in October 1876. The Italian Geographical Expedition was willing to become an extension of government interest, unlike the Italian Capuchin, Father Massaia, (in Shewa from 1868-1879) who resented the House of Savoy's curtailment of papal power. A Milan trade mission (headed by Dr. P. Matteuci) visited Yohannes IV in 1879, but Yohannes was only interested in what the Italians could do to free his port of entry, Massawa, from Egyptian-

British interference with his arms imports. The Italian foreign office then concentrated on Menilek through envoy Count Pietro Antonelli, who fed Menilek's appetite for arms and rivalry with his suzerain, Yohannes IV. Antonelli pioneered the trade route from Assab to Shewa and on 21 May 1883 concluded a Trade and Friendship treaty with Menilek; another agreement was signed 20 October 1887, though in the north, in January of that year, Ras Alula had attacked an Italian column moving into Ethiopian territory (see TEDALE). Yohannes IV was on the brink of war with Italy in 1888 over their refusal to evacuate Ethiopian lands but, threatened with aggressive action from Menilek and a Mahdist army massing on his Anglo-Sudan border, he offered reconciliation and withdrew to fight the battle in which he would lose his life.

Antonelli signed the Treaty of Wetchale (q.v.) with the new emperor, Menilek II on 2 May 1889; Article III drew the border between Italian-occupied Eritrea and Ethiopia. An Ethiopian delegation (see MEKONNEN, Ras) went to Rome to witness the ratification and to purchase armaments with the four million lira credit granted by the Italian parliament. Violations of the border prescribed by Article III, and Italy's attempt to prove it had been given a protectorate over Ethiopia by Article XVII (q.v.) led to a rupture of diplomatic relations and finally war (see ADWA, BATTLE OF). Though Italy was defeated in 1896, she retained her colony of Eritrea, and established a legation in Addis Ababa in 1897, and commercial agencies in various locations. In August 1928 the regent, Teferi Mekonnen (Hayle Sellase) signed a 20-year Friendship treaty with Italy which provided for a free-trade zone at Assab and joint construction of a road from Assab to Desse.

Between 1927-1934 Italy built a number of hospitals and clinics throughout the country, serving both their health needs at the same time providing for the collection of intelligence. Using the pretext of the "incident at Wel Wel" (q.v.) in December 1934, Mussolini's black-shirts invaded and conquered Ethiopia between October 1935 and May 1936 and occupied it until May 1941. They joined it administratively to Somalia and Eritrea as the "Italian East African Empire."

Diplomatic relations were resumed in 1948; a considerable amount of Italian influence is still apparent in the urban centers of Ethiopia, particularly in Eritrea, where Asmara is almost a mirror image of an Italian city; thousands of Italian farmers, mechanics, businessmen flourished in the country until recently. The country with the largest number of resident Ethiopians is Italy. Scholarship in Ethiopian studies, notably by Ignazio Guidi, Enrico Cerulli, Carlo Zaghi, C. Conti Rossini, Lanfranco Ricci, as well as the memoirs of hundreds of Italians who lived, fought, doctored, explored, and constructed in Ethiopia, make the Italian language a sine qua non for students of Ethiopian history. The Rassegna di Studi Etiopici is the oldest journal in the field, founded in 1941.

IYASU I (Emperor 1682-1706). The son of Yohannes I (1667-1682) and Seble Wengel (described as a dark-skinned lady from Sennar), he succeeded to the throne at the age of 22 and inherited the religious controversies that plagued his father's reign. He sponsored councils to resolve the doctrinal differences in 1684 and 1686, but unity was not attained. He led at least nine campaigns against different Oromo clans between 1685 and 1705. An Armenian, Goggia Murad, held a high office at his court and was employed as a diplomatic envoy to India. He and one of his sons suffering from a skin ailment were seen by the French physician, Charles Poncet, who visited his court 1699-1700. Poncet reported that the monarch had eight sons and three daughters, not all from his legal wife, Melakotawit (Welette Tseyon). Poncet noted her regal bearing and curiosity about French women, and also remarked that Iyasu consulted his sister, Elleni, several times a week. The monarch was eager to learn the use and preparation of medicines. Grief-stricken over the death of a favorite concubine in 1705, he withdrew to a monastic island in Lake Tana. In his absence, abetted by Melakotawit, his son Tekle Haymanot claimed the throne and had his father assassinated. He in turn was murdered and Melakotawit was publicly hanged in October 1708.

Iyasu I was called "the great" for his reorganization of taxes and customs fees, trade development, friendly relations with Egypt, impartial administration of justice and the establishment of higher religious studies at Gondar.

IYASU MIKAEL, Lej (uncrowned emperor 1913-1916). Son of Menilek II's daughter Shewa Regga and Ras Mikael of Wello; designated heir to the throne (unofficially in June 1908) on 18 May 1909 at the age of 13, shortly after his marriage to the great-niece of Empress Taytu, Aster Mengesha Yohannes. Tessema Nadew (q.v.) was named as regent 29 October 1909 and Iyasu undertook some imperial duties. After the coup d'état against Empress Taytu of March 1910, Iyasu divorced her niece and married Seble Wengel Haylu. His coronation was blocked for several reasons, mainly because Menilek II, though incompetent to rule, remained alive until 1913. There was also opposition to him based on his father's Oromo origins, and his own immature behavior. He conferred the title of negus on his father in 1914, granting him Begemder and Gojam, thus agitating hereditary families of those provinces as well as the Shewan elite. But it was his absenteeism, casual attitude toward Christian practice, and evidence of sympathy with Islam that precipitated his downfall. He was deposed while on one of his frequent sojourns away from Addis Ababa (see COUP D'ÉTAT, 27-28 September 1916), but escaped capture for five years. He was eventually trapped by Ras Gugsa Araya and spent the next 14 years as a prisoner. The fact of his existence inspired support for his return to the throne from time to time, by those who opposed Hayle Sellase, who had married Iyasu's niece, Menen. Iyasu died in 1935. One of his sons, Yohannes Iyasu, was proposed as leader of the resistance movement against the Italians in 1939, but this was vetoed by a representative of the exiled Hayle Sellase.

IYESUS MOA, Abba (d. 1292).   Founder of a monastic community
at Debre Estifanos (St. Stephen's) on Lake Hayq in 1248 and the
spiritual backer of Yequno Amlaq, his pupil, who restored the
Solomonic dynasty in 1270.   Tradition states that Yekuno Amlaq
then granted to the abbots of Debre Hayq the title of Aqabe-Se'at,
the most influential ecclesiastical adviser to the court until the
last appointee (Negede Iyesus) was executed by a Muslim general
(see ISLAMIC CONQUEST) in 1535.   A manuscript of the "Four
Gospels" inscribed by Iyesus-Moa is a treasured possession at
the monastery today.

- J -

JABARTI (Jabara, Jiberti, Djeberti, etc.).   Generic term for Muslims scattered throughout the Christian highlands who practice
Islam but also observe some customs of the Christians among
whom they live.   The word appeared about the 12th century as
the homeland of Ifat (q. v.) near Zeyla before it expanded inland, and was then used to describe all the Islamic principalities of southern Ethiopia.   Since antiquity Jabarti also described Muslim enclaves among the Amhara and Tegray to whom
they would offer military services.
      Many are merchants and artisans, trades often scorned by
the Amhara-Tegray people.

JERUSALEM.   The old city has represented to Ethiopian Christians
for centuries the only point in the outside world they aspired
to visit; not only because Christ was buried there but because
it is enmeshed with the mystique of "Solomon and Sheba."   It
was in Jerusalem in the late 13th century that Europeans first
heard of the "land of Prester John" (q. v.); and it was from
Jerusalem that Ethiopian monks went to Florence, Rome and
Cyprus in the early years of the 15th century.
      For the Eastern Orthodoxies, the enclave of convents,
churches, altars and grottos arranged around the Church of the
Holy Sepulchre (by 1149 it looked more or less as it does today)
has been the site of the most unholy contention, particularly
between the Copts, Armenians, Greek Orthodox and Ethiopian
Orthodox for centuries, centered around claims to the curiously
Arabic-named convent, Dayr-es-Sultan (haven of the sultan);
but it may once have been called Dayr-es-Sultan al-Habash, or
"haven of the sultan of Abyssinia."   The first documented use
of that name appeared in 1687.   The convent is located on the
roof of the chapel (or crypt) of St. Helena.
      Copts and Ethiopians lived together in the convent in the
late 18th century--both communities in an impoverished state.
The Copts were persecuted in Egypt and the Ethiopian empire
was in disarray.   With the restoration of Coptic prestige in
Egypt under the rule of Muhammad Ali (1805-1849), the Copts
asserted dominance over their fellow Monophysites, the Ethiopians, by keeping the key to the convent and its chapel, but
permitted them to live in the cells; however, for a period be-

tween 1863 and 1905 the Copts prevented them from using the
chapel except for an occasional holy day. In 1905, Menilek II
sent a delegation to Jerusalem and at the same time deposited
a large sum of money for the relief and sustenance of the
resident priests, nuns and pilgrims and they were given a du-
plicate key to the chapel. Within the precincts of the Basilica
they hold rights to nine altars and chapels; outside the Basilica,
to Dayr-es-Sultan and outside the old city, the grotto of David
on Mt. Zion, and altars in the Church of Mary at Gethsemane,
the house of St. Elizabeth (on the Jordan road) and in the
Church of the Nativity in Bethlehem. As of 1964 there were
18 Ethiopian monks living in the convent of Dayr-es-Sultan and
one Copt, who is there for the purpose of safeguarding Coptic
rights, so the absolute entitlement only to Ethiopia is still un-
resolved.

JEWS see FELASHA

JIBUTI see DJIBOUTI

JIMMA, SULTANATE OF (also called Jimma Abba Jefar). Abba
    Jefar ("lord of the dapple-grey horse") was the war title of
    Tullu, king of Jimma with his capital at Hirmata (now it is
    Jimma and the capital of Kefa province). The monarchial sys-
    tem that evolved in this primarily Oromo populated area had a
    relatively recent history. Abba Jefar I (1830-1855) was pre-
    ceded by Abba Faro, Magal and Rago, but a Muslim merchant
    converted Abba Jefar and though most of those close to the
    ruler converted, large numbers held to the traditional Oromo
    beliefs. Abba Jefar was succeeded by his second son, Abba
    Rebu, who maneuvered his older brother Abba Gomol out of
    the way. Abba Rebu's role was punctuated with the confisca-
    tion of property held by wealthy merchants, and he was over-
    thrown by them in 1859. His elderly uncle, the Abba Boku,
    succeeded but concerned himself in his two-year reign with the
    building of mosques and Muslim ritual. Abba Gomol returned
    to rule 1861-1878 and was so successful in increasing trade it
    was irresistible to expansionist Menilek, king of Shewa. Abba
    Jefar II (Muhammad ibn-Daud) was only 17 on accession; four
    years later he opted for cooperation with Menilek (in 1882) and
    in return was granted a measure of independence. He assisted
    in the conquest of Kulo (1889), Welamo (1894) and Kefa (1897),
    and was allowed to govern Jenjero and Gera sultanates. His
    annual tribute to Menilek was the largest any area of the em-
    pire paid; Jimma was the principal slave trading center. It
    was divided on the Sidama (q. v.) system into 70 districts (koro),
    each governed by an Abba Koro and the whole surrounded by a
    thorn fence (gudema) pierced by gates (kela). Abba Jefar en-
    couraged teachers of the Koran to settle in his kingdom, and
    also welcomed the Evangelical missionaries (they were Ethio-
    pian converts) at his capital, Jeren, in 1884 over strong pro-
    tests from prominent Muslims, and employed one of them as
    secretary for his Amharic correspondence. Before his death

in 1932, Abba Jefar turned over authority to his grandson, Abba
Jober; the kingdom ceased to exist in 1933, and was administered
from Addis Ababa.

JUDAISM (Influence of).   King Solomon symbolizes the Judaic link
    with Ethiopia because of his legendary encounter with Maqeda
    (q. v.) from which Menilek I was born.   When Solomon died
    (922 B. C.) the kingdom was split into two sections, the northern
    becoming Israel, the southern, Judea, whose people became
    known as Judeans or Jews, the current generic term for all
    Hebrews.   While it is difficult to pin down the dates of the
    sporadic migrations from South Arabia into Abyssinia, it is be-
    lieved that they took place during the early part of the first
    millennium before Christ (see FELASHA).
        Maqeda, the Kebra Negest reports, elected to worship the
    God of Israel, but many animist religions were present in the
    pre-Christian (4th century A. D.) Ethiopian kingdom.   The Ark
    of the Covenant at Aksum (q. v.) legend says, is the same one
    stolen from Jerusalem by Menilek I, who refused his father's
    offer of his kingdom, preferring to return to his mother's land.
    No church is built in Ethiopia without a procession and the
    placement of a replica of the Ark (the tabot) first; further most
    churches are divided into three areas, similar to synagogues.
        Only Jews and Ethiopians perform circumcision on the
    eighth day after birth; dietary laws in Ethiopia are Old Testa-
    ment inspired, and Ethiopia alone among Christian nations has
    rejected the doctrine of Pauline Christianity that biblical law
    lost its binding force at the coming of Christ; and the liturgy
    of church service is largely from the Hebrew Bible.   Many
    Ethiopic words are derived from early Hebrew, and a number
    of magical rites to ward off evil spirits are similar to ancient
    Hebraic ones.   The six-pointed "Star of David" was part of the
    imperial insignia and can be seen on the gates and fences of
    Menilek II's palace grounds in Addis Ababa.   The September
    New Year is similar to the Jewish Rosh Hashanah, and Mesqel,
    the commemoration of the finding of the True Cross, timed as
    a harvest festival is like the Jewish Sukkoth.   Ethiopian Easter,
    Fasika, has overtones of the Jewish Pesach, both in name and
    nature of the observance.   Mourning customs bear a striking
    resemblance to the Jewish week of shiva.
        Controversy over observing the Sabbath (and circumcision)
    arose as early as the 11th century in Ethiopia, for in 1238 the
    Copts rejected the Sabbath as a Jewish custom, and instructed
    the Ethiopians to follow suit.   After three centuries of disputa-
    tiousness (see EWOSTATEWOS) it was upheld formally in 1450.

JUDICIAL SYSTEM.   Based on the medieval Fetha Negest (q. v.),
    the traditional central legal system was influenced by western
    concepts first during the reign of Menilek II, then with Hayle
    Sellase I's "modernization. "   Finally the cancellation of previ-
    ous systems by the Provisional Military Administrative Council
    (see DERG) after the 1974 Revolution marked a radical shift,
    particularly in property law.

TRADITIONAL SYSTEM. Despite the power of absolute monarchs, judgements were locally oriented and pragmatic. Following the Fetha Negest's dictum that a judge has to be impartial and not compassionate, for "in judgement there is no compassion," litigants would take their turn under a system that encompassed a wide range of courts and appeals machinery, sometimes through 15 different venues. On the lowest level were roadside courts where passing travelers might be called upon to decide a case. Similar courts were set up in large markets but established officials were the judges (see DAGNA). Enforcement of the decision rested on public pressure. The next appeal was to the village headman (see CHIQA SHUM), or to a special functionary. Each litigant had guarantors who would provide bail or pay required penalties. The first court for the more important or criminal cases was that of the district governor's deputy, the melqenya; appeals went next to the governor, then to the central court at the emperor's capital before judges appointed to represent each of the provinces who would hear appeals from the respective districts. Penultimate step was the Afa Negus (mouth of the king), then from him to the emperor who, two days a week, presided over the court called the chilot. It served as a court of last resort: the chilot heard the final appeal of those who believed they had been unjustly judged in lower venues but were ready to accept the emperor's decision; it rarely heard civil cases brought by those who preferred to go directly to an imperial judgement rather than through lower courts. The emperor usually spent an hour or more as head of the chilot, customarily standing. He heard cases from women on Tuesdays, all in camera.

EUROPEAN INFLUENCE. Menilek II announced judicial reform in March 1908; this divided the country into six districts with two judges in each, with appeal to the Afa Negus who, that same year, also assumed the duties of Minister of Justice. This revamping, devised largely by the Europeans around Menilek, buttressed the emperor's policy of greater centralization. The Supreme Court was the emperor alone who could decree the death penalty, heretofore a power held also by provincial governors. Three scribes were assigned to each court, an attempt to keep civil records for the first time. Punishments were rigorous; habitual thieves would have a hand or foot amputated; rebels suffered heavy and cruel punishment but mercy was not unknown. Relatives of a murder victim could carry out the death sentence themselves on a convicted killer, or alternatively could levy "blood-money."

SPECIAL COURTS. Ecclesiastical tribunals tried cases involving priests, church property, heresy and divorce (when there had been a communion marriage). In the 1890s, foreigners came before a special court where an Ethiopian judge and the consul of the accused's country sat in judgement. Muslims had access to a separate legal system, endorsed by Hayle Sellase in 1942 as a way "to achieve national unity." Islamic courts had long existed in such southwestern Muslim kingdoms as Jimma (q.v.), but only in religious matters did the shari'a, the Islamic canon law, apply and even then sentences had to be approved by the provincial governor.

Hayle Sellase's "modernization" of the legal system, completed in 1965, had four levels from District Courts to the Supreme Imperial Court which included the chilot.   Actually, in most parts of the country, local systems prevailed but the new system was generally accepted as necessary for the country's future development.   Records show that most of the cases scheduled for the post-1965 District Courts never came to trial as the litigants preferred to use their local institutions (see QALLITCHA).

POST-REVOLUTIONARY SYSTEM.   Under the Provisional Military Administrative Council (PMAC), after the 1974 Revolution, attempts were made to set up legal venues more closely related to local needs but these have largely been superseded by political events.   Various urban and rural tribunals (see KEBELLE; PEASANT ASSOCIATIONS) have the power to settle disputes; as political, rather than legal, bodies they appear to have replaced the established courts.   Also, by virtue of the Special Penal Code Proclamation of Nov. 16, 1974, military tribunals officially replaced the former criminal courts.   Proclamation No. 47, on "the Government Ownership of Urban Lands and Extra Houses," was issued by the PMAC in July 1975.   This was the basis for the kebelle tribunal structure and powers which thus bypassed the existing courts on questions concerning urban land and housing.   Proclamation 104, issued in January 1977, extended the kebelle tribunals' writ to cover certain criminal and civil matters.   This has been interpreted as a mandate to carry out "revolutionary justice" which has resulted in prompt execution, by kebelle guards, of "counter-revolutionaries," after summary hearings.   Such a terminal veto of any appeal, counter to the traditional system, was carried to its extreme in 1977 when the "Red Terror" instituted by the Derg claimed thousands of casualties, including imprisonment, torture and executions without even the questionable legal process of the kebelle tribunals.

- K -

KALEB (Caleb) (King of Aksum c. 514-c. 543).   Known also as "Elle-Atsbeha", his existence is verified by Cosmas Indicopleustes, merchant and writer of the 6th century A.D. and Procopious, a Byzantine historian who served Justinianus (527-565).   Kaleb responded to Justinian's (518-527) request to wage war on Dhu Nuwas of Himyar (present-day Yemen) who had converted to Judaism and was persecuting Christians in retaliation for Justinian's persecution of Jews.   Kaleb's expedition (A.D. 525) annihilated the Himyarite army.   Gold, silver, and bronze coins have been found from his reign.   He abdicated in favor of one of his four sons and took up the monastic life; his saint's day in the Ethiopian calendar is 20 genbot (28 May).

KASA DARGE, Ras (1881-1956).   As the son of Darge Sahle Sellase
   (q. v.) his claim to the throne was equal to Hayle Sellase's, but
   he was consistently loyal to his cousin.   Known as a devout
   churchman, he was an active participant in designing the Constitutions of 1931 and 1955.   Three of his sons were killed by
   the Italians, only Asrate Kasa (q. v.) escaping that fate.

KASA HAYLU (of Qwara) see TEWODROS II

KASA HAYLU, Leul-Ras (1881-1956).   The son of Haylu Welde Kiros
   (half-brother of Emperor Tekle Giyorgis (q. v.)) and Tessema
   Darge, daughter of Darge Sahle Sellase.   He cooperated in deposing Lej Iyasu in 1916; and though more of a scholar than a
   soldier, he was appointed to command the northern armies in
   1935 and after defeat lived in exile in Jerusalem until 1941.
   On his return he was named crown councillor.

KASA MERCHA see YOHANNES IV

KEBELLE.   Basic administrative mechanism for control of Ethiopia's
   cities established by the Derg (q. v.) in 1974.   It is a neighborhood revolutionary council also known as the urban-dwellers' association.   Its rural counterpart is the peasant association.
       Evidently modeled after the workers' soviets in the USSR
   and the peoples' communes in China, the kebelle is the funda-
   mental urban unit, each one generally representing and controlling
   a small city area comprising 500 or more families (roughly 3, 500
   to 4, 000 persons) mainly in Addis Ababa and some other cities;
   there is at least one in every town of more than 2, 000 population.
   The kebelle has a 15-man policy committee which selects a chairman who then appoints various subcommittees on youth, education,
   women's affairs and "public safety. "   It has a representative at
   the next higher level (keftanya) which has jurisdiction over six to
   twelve kebelle.   Each of the keftanya sends a delegate to a central council which then elects the Mayor and Deputy Mayor who
   are, in effect, the political, administrative and ideological functionaries who run the city system.   In 1978, the mayor of Addis
   Ababa was Soviet-educated Dr. Alemu; his deputy was Yohannes
   Heruy, a lawyer who had attended universities in Britain, West
   Germany and East Germany.
       The kebelle has a number of specific administrative tasks:
   it collects rents on houses confiscated from private renters;
   acts as a form of tribunal (see HUMAN RIGHTS VIOLATIONS);
   is in charge of police protection; provides personnel for schools,
   health stations and other social services; runs fixed-price shops
   selling sugar, salt, oil, grain, etc. in competition to private
   merchants in the various market-places, and oversees other
   similar municipal functions.   One of the kebelle's main tasks is
   to politicize the masses and it is responsible for conscripting
   men into the "peoples' militia. "
       Kebelles supervise schools and form kindergartens; they
   "re-educate" designated "reactionaries" who were either high officials in the former government or were moneyed "exploiters"

who owned businesses or rented houses.

The kebelle's enforcement power lies with its armed guards, who have killed thousands of dissident, demonstrating youths and students. Dues for membership in the kebelle are minimal but frequent "charity fairs" are held around the city or town and much money has been so raised.

KEBRE NEGEST (Kibra Negast). The foremost creation of Ethiopic literature, its title means "Glory of the Kings." Its author, Yeshaq the nebura-ed of Aksum, compiled it early in the 14th century from the Old and New Testaments, from apocryphal literature, Book of Enoch, Book of the Pearl, and borrowings from Coptic, Syriac, Arabic, Greek, rabbinical literature and the Koran. Its purpose was to support the claims of the Solomonic dynasty "restored" in 1270, its author making his own embellishments to the "Queen of Sheba" story, already in the Old Testament and the Koran in basic form.

KEFA (Kaffa, kingdom then province; see also GAKI SHEROCHO). The first account of this kingdom was by Francisco Alvarez (in Ethiopia 1520-1526) who gained his information second hand. It was claimed at the end of the 16th century that Sartsa Dengel (q.v.) had converted them to Christianity and indeed some medieval churches have been found testifying to some early contacts. The Keficho fall into the Omotic ethnic grouping and have their own language; they may have originally migrated from the Damot highlands and absorbed the residents of the area as their slaves; they in turn were absorbed by the Oromo migration of the 16th centuries and a monarchy with divine kingship developed. The kings (tati) did not lead their own conquests into surrounding areas, which were done until 1870, staying behind a veil invisible to the people. Their kingship mystique was so powerful, that when Menilek conquered the area in 1897, he had the Kefa king's crown taken out of the country--it was returned from Switzerland in the 1950's, to the museum in Addis Ababa. Much of Kefa's rich-coffee producing lands, after the conquest, were held by Ras Welde Giyorgis (q.v.), Ras Getachew and his sister, and Dejazmach Taye. The slave trade continued into the 1930's, though Ras Getachew (governor 1926 and again in 1933) no longer took part personally, on order of the central government.

KEMBATTA (Kambata). Located between (former) Gurage-land and Welamo, it was conquered by Menilek II between 1890 and 1893; the people, nominally Christian, practice many old Cushitic rites and are of mixed Sidamo and Amhara-Tegray ancestry. About 75,000 people believe their royal house was descended from an Amhara Solomonic king; the dynasty is named after Oyeta, a daughter of a religious leader and it is from that status group their ruler is selected. The Kembatta were mentioned in a hymn of Yeshaq (1412-1427) and sparse accounts place them as an independent kingdom from that time.

KENFU HAYLU, Dejazmach (d. 1839). The elder half-brother of
Kasa Haylu who became Tewodros II; they had different mothers.
Kenfu's was the powerful Welette Tekle, judged to be the
"first lady of Gondar" in 1830. Kenfu served Ras Ali Alula
(q. v.) as governor of Qwara district 1832-1839, while his half-
brother attended religious school in Qwara, and then served in
his army. Kenfu is renowned for his defeat of the Egyptian
army on his border in 1837.

KEREN (also called Senhet) see BOGOS

KHAT (Catha edulis or celastrus edulis). This plant when chewed
is a mild narcotic, producing a pleasant insomnia in small
doses and slight intoxication in larger amounts. Muslim men
(only women said to possess occult powers are permitted to
chew it) have used it for centuries; an early account reported
it kept scholars from falling asleep over their books. Amde
Tseyon's chronicler (early 13th century) writes that the Muslim
enemy intended to plant khat in the lands of the Christians when
he beat them.
     Ethiopia is the main commercial producer (on the Harar
plateau), exporting the leaves to South Arabian customers. It
plays a great part in Muslim social life; great chewings take
place at festivals of birth, circumcision, marriage and tomb
vigils. In Arabic it is qat, and gofa to the Oromo. It has
some nutritive values; workers may chew it in the early morning then work until evening without stopping. Its only identi-
fiable chemical pharmacological component is non-methylated
ephedrine, a derivative of which is used for the relief of asthma
and some allergies.

KOLUBI (Qulebi) see PILGRIMAGES

KONSO (people and area). An estimated 55, 000 people, defined as
part of the Lacustrine grouping because they live in the area of
the Great Rift Valley lakes. The Konso are centered in Gemu
Gofa, and are divided into 9 tribes, and speak a Cushitic-based
language with close similarities to Oromo. "Konso" is derived
from the name of a wooded hill in a market area. Menilek II
imposed an Amhara governor there in 1897 and they were incorporated as taxpayers. The Amhara insisted that the previously
naked men wear trousers. They are a generation-graded society, settled on farms and adept at using the stones of their
rocky environment to build terraces against flooding, wall their
towns, and make tools. They are devoted to male dominance
(they worship a male sky God) and phallic symbols are atop
their priests' head gear and huts. Women may not own property and are seen as weakeners of men in sexual intercourse,
hence the custom of men's dormitories so they may stay apart
from women. Women may witness ceremonies only from a distance. A Norwegian Lutheran Mission School and clinic and a
government school are established. They have hostile relations
with the Borana and resent the Amhara who look down on them.

KUNAMA see BARYA

KWER'ATA RE'ESU. The name of an icon whose name means "the
    striking of his head," the Ge'ez version of the "Crown of
    Thorns" and an allusion to the biblical verse (Mark 15:19) "they
    smote him on the head." An icon of this name appears in the
    time of Dawit I (1380-1412); a different one (of foreign origin)
    was carried on campaigns by Yohannes I (1668-1682) and it be-
    came customary to swear loyalty by it. It was captured by the
    Sudanese enemy in a battle and purchased back by Iyasu II
    (1730-1755). The painting disappeared from Meqdela fortress
    in April 1868 and though Yohannes IV requested the British
    government to search for it among the Ethiopian manuscripts
    taken to the British Museum, it was not found. It turned up in
    the private possession of Richard Holmes, the archaeologist of
    the British Museum, who had been with the British forces at
    Meqdela in 1868. His widow sold it at Christie's in 1917; it
    was resold in 1950 to a purchaser who outbid the Ethiopian em-
    bassy. It disappeared until 1980 when it was located in a
    private collection in Portugal.

- L -

LABOR UNIONS. The 1955 constitution guaranteed the right to
    form worker's associations in conformance with law. Unions,
    as such, were not legal until 1962. The first collective bar-
    gaining agreement was signed in March 1964 at the Bahr Dar
    Textile Factory; then came agreements covering workers of the
    Wonji and Shewa Sugar Estates; six contracts by 1966 encom-
    passed 10,000 employees. In April 1963 the Confederation of
    Ethiopian Labor Unions (CELU) was recognized. Between
    March 1970 and 1974 membership grew from 50,000 in 119
    unions to 250,000 in 164 unions (less than 20 percent of em-
    ployed industrial workers). They called their first general
    strike 7-11 March, 1975 and won all of their demands. In
    September 1974 as the military Derg overthrew the emperor,
    the CELU was the first to reject the military junta, preferring
    a "people's government." in 1975 a strike of workers at air-
    lines, telecommunications, banks, insurance companies, and a
    few industrial plants called a strike to protest the Derg's attempt
    to control the CELU; soon after the CELU was outlawed. By
    mid-1977 the only workers not in a union under government con-
    trol were the employees of bank and insurance companies.

LALIBELA (Emperor c. 1185-1225?). One of the Zegwe (q.v.) em-
    perors, named as a saint and the legendary builder of the 11
    rock-hewn churches at his capital, then named Roha, but now
    called Lalibela after him, in Lasta province. His wife, equally
    pious, was Mesqel Kebra. The church building probably began
    in the reign of one of his predecessors, and it is likely that
    Egyptian workmen were involved; the Zegwe emperors maintained
    good relations with the sultans of Egypt. It is unlikely that

Lalibela made the pilgrimage to Jerusalem as his hagiographer says, but other details are plausible: that he wandered in self-exile during the reign of his brother (Harbe) and that his half-sister tried to poison him. Struggles over succession were characteristic.

The eleven rock churches are a remarkable architectural achievement and became accessible to tourists by air travel in the 1960's; pilgrimages on foot and horseback have long attracted the intrepid laity and priests (see ROCK-HEWN CHURCHES).

LAND TENURE. The land, in Ethiopian tradition, belongs to God: He passes it on to the emperor, His anointed on earth; the monarch, in turn, grants it to deserving individuals as gult or rist.

The term "gult" (land granted as fief) was in use as early as the time of Amde Seyon (1314-1344); gult was held temporarily at the pleasure of the monarch and its holder became the judicial and administrative authority of these lands, entitled to collect taxes in kind, or labor. Rist, though it could be confiscated for treasonous or criminal actions, was more or less equivalent to private property and could be inherited, sold and subdivided. In addition to gult, specific lands held by the crown were the source of supplies to the court. The property holdings of individuals were expressed in terms of which gults and which rists they held. So great were the variations--according to provinces and their relatively autonomous lords--that the history of land tenure defies summary.

Begemder, under Iyasu II (1730-1755), was reportedly the first province to institute some measurement system. In 1800, Ras Gugsa, to break the power of the Begemder nobles, confiscated all gult and rist land and reallocated it, reviewing these grants every 12 months.

To reduce the power of the church, which was believed to control up to one-third of all the land, Tewodros II (1855-1868) confiscated much of its gult land, thus incurring the wrathful opposition of the religious establishment, a factor that led to his downfall. Wagshum Gobeze restored these gults as soon as he claimed the throne in 1869. Yohannes IV (1871-1889) was generous with gults for the church, especially in Aksum where he even purchased land and gave it to them so it would not be subject to confiscation. In Hamasen and Tegray, Yohannes and his commander-in-chief, Ras Alula, established that title to the land would go to squatters after 40 years' occupancy. The Fetha Negest states that land should belong to those who cultivate it. Muslims, previously barred from owning land, found it expedient to convert to Christianity, under Yohannes' edicts of 1878, for then they could own land.

In 1879-80, Menilek II instituted land measurement in Shewa, a system that was extended to territories that he conquered. Royal surveyors measured land into gashas (q.v.) that varied according to the fertility of the land, poorer soil being divided into larger plots.

Progress in security of rist rights was advanced under Menilek II, and land in Addis Ababa was measured, and ownership established by written title.   Much land confiscated from Oromo tenants was restored to them as rist.

The Constitution of 1931 stated that "except in cases of public utility, determined by law" no one could deprive an Ethiopian subject of his property.   This was welcomed in the north where 90% of the Tegrayan and Amhara farmers owned land either individually or communally.   In the south, where the large majority of peasants were tenants, this constitutional provision seemed another way of insuring that the privileged landowners and the church need never share their large holdings.

A decree of July 1934 stated that all land in the empire was to be measured; it was not done until after the Italian occupation. Measurement of land was the necessary prelude to a tax on the amount of land held, though distinctions were maintained in many areas according to the fertility of the land.   Land reform, generally understood to mean breaking up the large holdings held by the elite and the church, made little progress although Hayle Sellase I, in the face of mounting unrest, offered some ineffective palliatives.   After his overthrow in 1974 and the ascendancy to power of the Derg (q. v.), radical changes occurred. All property of the nobility was confiscated and in proclamations issued between March 1975 and September 1977 following the Derg's policy of "land to the tiller," a framework was developed to distribute 10 hectares to each farm family and new political and social organizations were set up (see PEASANT ASSOCIATIONS).

Response to this move was mixed, among farmers and between urban and rural populations.   Small farmers were stimulated to increase production: they were freed from onerous taxes and got better returns for their produce; city consumers complained over the higher prices that resulted from the scarcity caused by a breakdown in the distributive system and by greater on-farm consumption.   Farmers in the south welcomed the reforms and new organizations.   Those in the north feared that their large, communally owned farms would be subject to government takeover.

All in all, the Ethiopian land-reform experiment could be considered as among the most successful in Africa, at least from the peasants' viewpoint.   Since he was prevented by Derg decrees from hiring farm laborers, the farmer had to work his own land himself, but he no longer had to pay rent which in many cases amounted to over half of his crop.   Many of the peasants, however, often withheld crops to create higher prices. The Derg, lacking an enforcement system in rural areas, found it increasingly difficult to police this traditional farmer's tactic.

LAW, CODIFICATION OF.   Steps toward a written legal code (apart from the Fetha Negest) were taken in 1923 (a law covering contracts and sales set interest rates at 9 percent) and in 1930/32 (Abyssinian Criminal Code and Decrees relating to Loans, Arms and Slavery). Culpability was defined in descending order: a man who knows the law and breaks it, the forgetful man, the countryman, the monk, the poor ignorant man, the stranger, the ignorant woman, the imbecile or invalid, the non-Amharic speaking and the child under 12. A codification commission was formed in 1954; it worked with drafts written by Swiss and French lawyers and included Ethiopians and foreigners familiar with Ethiopian custom. They worked in secrecy; interested groups had no chance to read, comment or complain about the codes which were far too complex for a country so long dependent on customary law. The Penal and Civil codes were published in 1957 and 1960 respectively. These were followed by Commercial, Maritime, and Criminal and Civil Procedure Codes by 1965 (see JUDICIAL SYSTEM).

LAW, CUSTOMARY. Apart from the 17th-century law book Fetha Negest (q. v.) the law was customary and what the emperor decreed. It was purveyed by messenger, called out in the market place, or announced in church. Each area had its own set of standards and its own way of dealing with transgressors. To all the obvious vagaries of human behavior (stealing was often treated as a more serious crime than murder) was added the crime of insulting or abusing authority, and the crime of heresy.

LAW SCHOOL. A faculty of Law was established in 1963 (under the direction of an American, James Paul) as there were only 19 university-trained lawyers in the country, most of them graduates of McGill University, Canada. Adjective law was Anglo-Saxon while substantive law was based on continental concepts, especially French, Swiss, Italian and German. By 1967 there were 1, 000 students enrolled in Addis Ababa, and resident courses in Asmara and Jimma. Two LL. B programs, one daytime and one in the evening, graduated their first students in 1966 and 1967. A diploma course and a certificate course were conducted in English, with some in French.

LEAGUE OF NATIONS (1920-1946). Initially rejected because of the existence of slavery within its borders, Regent Ras Teferi Mekonnen guaranteed an attack on the problems and Ethiopia was admitted on 28 September 1923. Publicity given to an Ethiopian challenge, 12 June 1926, to League members caused Great Britain and Italy to back away from a deal in which Italy would support British interests in the Lake Tana area, and Britain would support Italy's wish to build a railway from Eritrea to Italian Somaliland. In December 1934, Ethiopia asked League arbitration over the Italo-Ethiopian skirmish at Wel Wel (q. v.). It was turned down. On 3 January 1935 Ethiopia sent a telegram to the League informing it that Italian troops were massed on the Ethiopian frontier; the League referred it to direct negotiation between the two countries. After this defeat, Hayle Sellase made his famous appearance in Geneva 30 June 1936. On 14 May 1938 the League voted in favor of recognizing Italy's right to remain in Ethiopia.

LEBNA DENGEL, Emperor (1508-1540). As he was only 12 years
old on accession, he was advised by a regency that included
his mother, Na'od Mogesa, and the Dowager-empress Elleni
(q. v.). In 1517 he won a battle against the Adal (q. v.). From
1520-1526 he was host to a Portuguese mission, who had come
in response to Elleni's offer of an alliance against the Muslim
powers of the Red Sea, unaware that he would soon be on the
run threatened by the renewed strength of the Adal (see ISLAMIC
CONQUEST). By 1539 he had fled to the isolated monastery of
Debre Damo, where he died in September 1540. His wife,
Seble Wengel, gave him four sons and two (?) daughters. One
son was killed by the Muslim enemy, and one, Minas, was captured. His daughter, Amate Giyorgis, was influential in the
reigns of Gelawdewos, Minas and Sartsa Dengel, 1540-1597.

LEGESSE, ASFA, Lt. Member of the Provisional Military Administrative Council (Derg) and chairman of its committee on political and military affairs, essentially an ideological and propaganda unit. Legesse is considered the leader of the pro-
Soviet faction of the PMAC and is in an important position to
influence country-wide political organization and indoctrination.
His move to become vice-chairman of the Derg, after the execution of vice-chairman Lt-Col. Atnafu Abate in November 1977,
was rejected by the PMAC chief, Lt-Col. Mengestu Hayle
Maryam.

LIBRARIES. The National Library of Ethiopia was established by
an order of 1930, but did not take form until 1944. The
largest and best-equipped library is at Addis Ababa University
(formerly Hayle Sellase I University); it opened in 1961. The
U. S. Information Service operated libraries of several thousand
volumes in both Addis Ababa and Asmara. These were almost
all in English, although there were a few volumes in Amharic.
USIS also ran small reading rooms in Meqelle, Gondar, Jimma,
Neqemte, Harar and Dire Dawa, linked to the local secondary
school. Other libraries were run by the British Council, the
West German Goethe Institute and the Alliance Française. All
were closed by the Derg beginning in 1977. Centers run
by the U. S. S. R. and the German Democratic Republic are still
in operation, and the British Council re-opened in 1980.

LION OF JUDAH. The lion, mentioned in the Old Testament, has
been a symbol of power and protection, referring both to God
and to temporal control, and was commonly used to refer to
all of Israel and several of its enclaves, particularly Judah,
which was regarded as the royal tribe (Genesis 49:10). Not
until the early 16th century, when the Portuguese were active
in Abyssinia, were the two concepts blended: the lion as the
symbol of ruling power, plus Solomonic descent as the sine
qua non for ascent to the throne. From then, Ethiopia's "king
of kings" (also a Biblical term) became known as "The (Conquering) Lion of Judah, " with the six-pointed star of David as
part of the insignia. Both David and Solomon were of the tribe
of Judah.

LITERATURE, RELIGIOUS. Great collections of manuscripts exist
throughout the monasteries and churches of Ethiopia and in the
important libraries of Europe. The lives of saints, commentaries, hymns, prayers and chronicles of emperors were all
hand-written in Ge'ez until the Amharic chronicle of Tewodros
II (1855-1868). A school of calligraphy and a school for book-
binding trained people for these tasks. Often they made copies
and sold them. Writing materials, parchment, ink (black and
red) and pens were prepared. The oldest known manuscript
dates back to the 13th century, but there may have been older
ones that either deteriorated from climatic conditions or were
destroyed in the 10th century by the anti-Christian raids of
Gudit (q. v.) or in the 16th-century destruction of churches during the Islamic conquest (q. v.).
    A printed Bible in Amharic was brought into the country by
agents of the Church Missionary Society in 1856; and the first
printing of teaching and religious books was done inside the
country at (Omtulo) Emkullo in 1885 on a press installed by the
Swedish Evangelical Mission (see MISSIONS, PROTESTANT;
KEBRE NEGEST).

LITERATURE, SECULAR, AMHARIC. Books in Amharic dominate
the literature, though writers of Tegrigna and Oromo origin
are beginning to include phrases and sentences in their own
languages in their books. The first novel to be printed in Amharic was Tobbya by Afewerq Gebre Iyesus, in 1908; it was
followed by a drama written by Tekle Hawaryat in 1911/12.
The fiction and non-fiction of Heruy Welde Sellase began in
1923 with the establishment of the Berhanena Selam Press, and
his own press, Goha Sabah. The entire output of stories and
plays has not exceeded 250 creations by about 128 writers,
which however, is the highest number of books in the vernacular
in all of the sub-Sahara. Stories have tended to be didactic and
moralistic whether the themes were love and marriage, education,
history or political (see DRAMA; POETRY; PRINTING; FOLK-
LORE).

LORENZO T'EZAZ, Blattengeta (1900-1947). An Eritrean, educated
in France, who drafted Hayle Sellase's appeal to the League of
Nations in 1936 against Italy's aggression. He remained as
Ethiopia's representative, protesting against the lifting of sanctions against Italy. During the occupation he facilitated contacts
between the emperor, who was in hiding in England, and resistance leaders, making a secret trip into occupied Ethiopia to
gain information on collaborators, guerrilla strength and Italian
morale prior to the liberation. He was Minister of Foreign Affairs 1941-2; Minister of Posts 1942-3; President of the Senate
in 1943 and Ambassador to Moscow 1943-47. He was married
to Yemesrach Emru, daughter of Emru Hayle Sellase (q. v.).

LUDOLF, JOB see GERMANY

- M -

MAHDISTS.   Members of an Islamic order (sometimes derogatively
    called Dervishes) who were marauding nomads resident in the
    Sudan and followers of al-Mahdi, the title assumed by a mes-
    sianic figure, whose real name was Muhammad Ahmed ibn
    Sayyid Abd Allah.   In 1887 they were particularly aggressive
    in western Ethiopia, forcing Emperor Yohannes IV to divert at-
    tention from Italy's colonial incursions in the north.   They often
    used hit-and-run guerrilla tactics, at one point dashing in from
    the Sudan to savage Gondar, then withdrawing.   In 1889, at
    Metemma, they suffered heavy losses at the hands of Yohannes'
    army but in the final moments of the battle Yohannes was
    fatally wounded and the Ethiopians, disorganized, stopped their
    attack and retreated.   This marked a high point for the Mah-
    dists who continued their depredations inside the Sudan until
    they were crushed at the battle of Omdurman on 2 September
    1898 by British forces under Gen. Herbert Kitchener.

MAHEBER.   The most prevalent type of rural association inspired,
    legend says, by the Last Supper.   Membership is either male
    or female, depending on the sex of the saint on whose day they
    prepare a convivial feast; the opposite sex may come as guests.
    In urban settings the maheber has become less of a religious
    occasion than for having a good time.   It is frequently a vehicle
    for cooperative assistance to members who have come to the
    city from the same rural area.

MAHTEME SELLASE WELDE MESQEL, Blattengeta (1902-   ).   The
    son of a secretary to Empress Taytu (q. v.), he was educated in
    France where he studied agriculture.   From 1941 to 1946 he
    was secretary to Crown Prince Asfa Wessen, then became in
    turn Vice-Minister and then Minister of Agriculture 1949-1958;
    Finance 1958-60; Education 1960-61; Public Works 1961-66,
    member of the Crown Council.   Something of a scholar and
    author, he compiled the Zekra Nagar ("Things Remembered")
    published in 1942/1949-50, which despite some inaccuracies and
    a hagiographical flavor, provided valuable biographical notes and
    copies of letters and documents on the Menilek II and early
    Hayle Sellase periods.

MAQEDA, Queen of Saba (Sheba).   Her story is the national epic of
    Ethiopia and is told in the Kebre Negest (q. v.).   She went to
    Jerusalem in the 10th century B. C. to learn the wisdom of
    Solomon and returned to Ethiopia to have his child, Menilek I.
    When the lad was 22, she abdicated in his favor; thus the foun-
    dation of the Solomonic dynasty.   It has been called a "silly
    fantasy" since the revolution.   In Arabic legends, she is called
    "Bilkis. "

MARRIAGE.   Each of the many ethnic groups has different marital
    customs; and there are variations in Christian marriage as well.
    In general: damoz is a contract between a man and a woman

for a specific length of time with agreed upon remuneration for the woman but no claim upon her partner's estate. Children of such unions are regarded as legitimate with rights of inheritance equal to children born in full wedlock; kal kidan (or serat) is a binding civil contract entered into by the parents. Often the girl goes to live with her prospective in-laws until she reaches the age of puberty; a kind of long engagement called madego. The virginity of the bride is subject to confirmation when the marriage is consummated. This kind of civil marriage is the most common, and is sometimes called semanya ("80") because the traditional fine for breaking one's word was 80 Maria Teresa talers, so this is called the "eighty-bond. " Feasting accompanies the ceremony and a list of assets brought to the marriage by each partner is witnessed and consulted for fair division of property in case of divorce. A genealogical check has been made well in advance of the contract to ensure there is no consanguinity between the spouses for seven generations removed.

Between ruling families, marriage has almost always been political, used to cement an alliance or in case of divorce, to break one off. Even poor rural families respect that the interests of the fathers are decisive in selecting a mate. Priests are often present at these weddings, but their presence is not indispensable.

Qurban or marriage by communion is extremely rare, since divorce is forbidden unless special dispensation is obtained from the church court. Couples who have lived together for many years under kal kidan will sometimes undertake this religious blessing towards the end of their lives. The Civil Code passed in 1960 abolished damoz in law, though in practice, this "marriage for hire" or "marriage by the month" still exists. Muslims of course follow Islamic law in marriage and divorce, but the Christians and Muslim customs have interacted to the extent that Ethiopian Muslims practice polygamy less frequently than in the Middle East; and the frequent marriage and divorce pattern of Christians reflects the influence of polygamy.

MARTIN-WERQNEH, Dr. see WERQNEH ESHETE MARTIN

MARTYRS DAY (19 February). A commemoration of the three-day massacre of unarmed men, women and children and burning of their houses that followed the attempt on the life of the Italian viceroy, Rudolfo Graziani, on this day in 1937. The number who died was well in excess of two thousand.

MARYA PEOPLE. Some 25, 000 Marya claim to be descendants of a Sahlo warrior who settled among Tegre-speaking people in the second half of the 14th century; they were mentioned earlier in the hagiography of the monk, Ewostatewos, who was on his way through their area in 1337 on his way to Jerusalem. They are divided into the "red" Marya and the "black"; the black are considered the "first born" and intermarry freely. They live in strictly defined plateaus; the "black" in the more fertile area

which may account for them being twice as numerous as the
"red." Once Christian, between 1820 and 1835, the "black"
Marya joined the Islamic faith of their serfs (Tegre). Each
tribe is independent with its own hereditary chief, but the
"black" head is paramount.

MASSAWA. The name applied first to the outermost island of two,
it is now connected to the mainland (now also called Massawa)
by a rail causeway. Its architecture is redolent of its
Turkish-Arab history, for it was not under Ethiopian administration until after World War II, despite its significance as
the gateway to and from Ethiopia for trade and communication.
Before its occupation by the Ottoman empire in 1557, the
neighboring Dahlak archipelago (q. v.) had been occupied by
Muslims who took control of the area in the 7th century from
the declining kingdom of Aksum. The Turks delegated control
to a chieftain of the Belew who was titled Na'ib (deputy) in
1589. He and his successors were notorious for some 250
years for their onerous taxes on goods going in and out of the
port and harassed Ethiopian pilgrims going to Jerusalem and
Muslims going to Mecca equally. The na'ibs kept their power
during successive Egyptian and Turkish periods of ownership.
In 1865 the lease of Suakin and Massawa, which had lapsed
after the death of Egypt's leader, Muhammad Ali, was renewed
in favor of Khedive Ismail (1863-1879); he appointed the Swiss,
Werner Munzinger (q. v.) as governor of Massawa in 1871.
Forced to curtail their empire, a bankrupt Egypt withdrew from
Massawa in 1885, and the Italians occupied the port and from
there began their encroachment into the highlands leading to
their defeat at the Battle of Adwa in 1896. In the peace treaty
with Menilek II, they retained Eritrea and Massawa. In 1952
with the federation of Eritrea and Ethiopia, Massawa again became Ethiopian. The small Ethiopian navy is based there; a
railway connects it with Asmara, Keren and Agordat. Its
necessity to Ethiopia is a vital pawn in the continuing battle
over Eritrean secession.

MAY TCHEW, BATTLE OF (31 March 1936). The final battle
of the Italian invasion was fought near Lake Ashenge, in the
hills surrounding the market town of May Tchew on 31 March
1936. Some 30,000 troops under the personal command of
Hayle Sellase attacked the position of the Italian army at
5:45 a.m. The Ethiopians had been in position on 21 March
but war councils had delayed them long enough to give the
Italians time to strengthen their initially weak defenses and gain
intelligence from defectors. For the first 3 hours the Ethiopians
won some successes, but the equation was altered at 8 a.m.
when 70 aircraft began bombing, though the Ethiopians managed
to shoot down 36 planes with ground fire. At 6:00 p.m. the
Italian army still held, and the emperor ordered a retreat.
The soldiers were without food as their supply train had been
wiped out by bombers. For the next week, the retreating army
was bombed with 73 tons of high explosives and mustard gas,

and harassed by the alienated Azebu Oromo whose loyalty had been purchased by Italy. Ethiopian casualties have been estimated as high as 8,000; the enemy lost about 1,300 men, divided between 900 Eritreans and 400 Italians (see ITALIAN CAMPAIGN).

MEDICAL TRAINING. In 1965 a medical school was added to the university in Addis Ababa, financed largely by Great Britain. A public health college was established in 1953 in Gondar, jointly sponsored by the government, World Health Organization and the U.S. Aid program. Nurses are trained in schools attached to five major hospitals and special courses in midwifery were available to women who agreed to serve in provincial health centers. The paramedics (dressers) were trained at many hospitals and those with advanced training were licensed to operate medical stations and work in schools.

MEDICINE, MODERN. The high rates of malaria, tuberculosis, typhus, intestinal parasites, syphilis, trachoma, leprosy and cholera gave health programs a high priority in the modernization plans of Hayle Sellase I. But even before his reign, Menilek II had been receptive to foreign medical assistance and had decreed compulsory vaccination (as far as supplies went) as had Yohannes IV.

Foreigners, whether medically trained or not, were perceived as the possessors of cures from the medical kits they carried with them. Missionaries, craftsmen, explorers, diplomats--all were obliged to set up consulting hours to gain control of the stream of patients that would appear as soon as their tents were put up. The Italians were the first to combine medicine and diplomacy when they sent Dr. Vincenzo Ragazzi to head their geographical station in 1884; a succession of Italian doctors (Leopoldo Traversi, Lincoln de Castro among others) gave services, though the court tended to monopolize them. The Italian legation in Addis Ababa opened a free clinic in 1901.

A great impact was made by the Russian Red Cross that arrived in 1896 to treat the wounded survivors of the Italo-Ethiopian war. The four doctors and thirteen medical corpsmen with the first mission were replaced in 1897 with a second group who erected a 20-bed hospital which gave free treatments until it was closed in 1906. Menilek II financed a hospital on the site in 1909. In Harar the Capuchin missionaries had opened a leprosarium in 1901 and Ras Mekonnen financed a small hospital there in 1903. Railway company doctors provided good medical service in Dire Dawa in 1902.

With a land grant from the emperor and some financial support, many hospitals were founded by Catholic and Protestant missionaries, notably the Seventh Day Adventists and the Presbyterian Church of North America, and the Sudan Interior Mission. By 1927-9 there were nine hospitals in the provinces and three in Addis Ababa. In 1930 a Public Health bureau was established under the Interior Ministry and rules for the oper-

ation of medical facilities and pharmacies were issued. By
1969 there were 84 hospitals (over 9,000 beds), 531 outpatient
clinics and 64 health centers.   About 20 percent of the population was receiving modern health care.   There were 365 doctors (50 were Ethiopian), 15 dentists, 72 pharmacists, 600
nurses, 91 health officers, 126 sanitarians, and about 3,000
dressers (see PUBLIC HEALTH MINISTRY; MELAKU BAYENE;
WERQNEH ESHETE).   Current figures are not available.

MEDICINE, TRADITIONAL.   The contents of 14th- and 15th-century
prescription booklets show an early Greco-Arabic influence; a
slight sense that prevention is better than cure and that diet and
hygiene are important.   Though regular bathing was uncommon,
washing hands and rinsing the mouth were routine.   People go
to tanquay (sorcerers), special debteras (scribes), and hakims
(Arabic for a medical person) both to prevent and to be cured
of illnesses and a variety of troubles--from catching a thief to
attracting love.   The debtera charged the most, for he could
write Ge'ez words on an amulet (the magic enhanced by the fact
that no one could read it) and give a written prescription after
consulting impressively in his notebook.   Bleeding, fumigation,
inhalation, poultices, massage and cauterization were employed,
as well as pills and suppositories.   Medicines were based primarily on plants and soil taken in honey and melted butter--
palliatives in themselves.   One plant constantly in use was
kosso; it produced violent purgation expelling the worms acquired from eating raw meat.   Men of Menz (a north Shewa
district) and those from Gojam gained reputations as the most
skilled physicians (wuqesa) and Gurage and Oromo were favored
for bone setting and surgery.   Variolation against smallpox was
not unknown.   The sun was considered dangerous and led to the
widespread use of umbrellas made of woven cane.

MEI'SON (or Me'ei'sone)   see   ALL-ETHIOPIA SOCIALIST MOVE-
MENT

MEKANE YESUS, EVANGELICAL CHURCH OF.   A Protestant con-
gregation constituted on 16 October 1921 in Addis Ababa which
in 1959 became the name applied to all sister Lutheran congregations in the country.   There are some 500,000 members, of
which about 3,000 are members of five congregations in Addis
Ababa.   It evolved from the combined efforts of Swedish missionaries, reformist-minded Ethiopian Orthodoxists and the
British and Foreign Bible Society, whose colporteurs of Amharic
and Oromo translations of the Bible distributed their texts.   The
Swedish group played the primary role, relying on indigenous
evangelists, notably Neguse Tashu, Gebre Ewostatewos, Onesimos Nesib (q.v.) and Badima Yalew.   The present general secretary, Rev. Gudina Tumsa, and his wife, Tsehay Tolessa,
were arrested 28 July 1979.   She was released but the Reverend
Gudina's whereabouts are unknown (see SWEDEN and ETHIOPIA;
and MISSIONS, PROTESTANT).

MEKONNEN ENDALKACHEW, Ras Bidwoded (1890-1963). Scion of
the powerful Addisge families of Shewa which rose to promi-
nence during the reign of Menilek II, at whose court he served
as a page. He served Zewditu (1916-1930) and when the regent
was crowned Emperor Hayle Sellase I, Mekonnen became a
district governor, then controller of the Djibouti-Addis Ababa
railway, Minister of Commerce (1926-31), ambassador to London
and the League of Nations (1931-33), mayor of Addis Ababa
(1933-34) and governor of Ilubabor. During the Italian occupation
he worked with the Ethiopian refugees in Palestine. In 1941 he
was named Minister of the Interior and from 1943 to 1957 served
as Prime Minister. His last office was President of the Senate
(1957-61), from which he resigned for health reasons. Mekonnen
made important contributions to Amharic literature; his 20 books
dealt mostly with high-minded themes, whether non-fiction, a
novel or a play. He had 16 children (see ENDALKACHEW
MEKONNEN) by his first wife, Zewditu Mengesha; none from his
second marriage to Yesheshwerq Yelma, a niece of Hayle
Sellase.

MEKONNEN WELDE MIKAEL, Ras (1852-1906). The son of Tenagne
Werq, a daughter of King Sahle Sellase of Shewa, and Welde
Mikael (a general from eastern Tegray who died 1879/80), he
began service to his cousin, Menilek II, at the Shewan court
about 1866, fighting in various campaigns and governing small
districts. His wife, Yeshi Emabet Ali, died in 1894, two years
after the birth of Teferi (Hayle Sellase I). He had an elder son,
Yelma, whom he legitimized after he saved his life at the
Battle of Adwa in 1896.
     When Menilek II conquered Harar in January 1887, he ap-
pointed Mekonnen governor and granted him troops to fulfill his
duties; he expanded his territory eastwards and cooperated with
the French to open the port of Djibouti. He embarked for Italy
in August 1889 with a delegation to witness ratification of the
Treaty of Wetchale (q. v.); while there he negotiated a loan to
purchase arms, with the customs duties of Harar as security.
He made every effort, on Menilek's instruction, to prevent war
with Italy but accepted the inevitable and commanded the advance
guard that left Addis Ababa in October 1895; after Ethiopia's
victory in March 1896 he favored tolerant peace terms.
     In dealing with the British, June 1897, it was Mekonnen
who secured cession of a large area to Ethiopia respecting the
placement of the border line with British Somaliland. In December the same year he took an expedition to secure the
gold-mining district of Beni Shangul on the Sudan border. At
the end of 1898 he served briefly as governor of Tegray after
capturing Mengesha Yohannes (q. v.), with the assistance of Ras
Mikael (q. v.). Returning to Harar in June 1900 he cooperated
with the British on military campaigns against the Somali movement led by Muhammad Abd Allah Hassan until the truce of
1905. He spent three months of 1902 heading a mission to
Paris and London (coronation of Edward VII). He died at
Qulebi, 22 March 1906, on his way to Addis Ababa.

MELAKU BEYENE, Dr. (1900-1940). Armed with a letter from his
relation, Teferi Mekonnen, Melaku Beyene and two colleagues
presented themselves to President Harding at the White House
in 1922. He referred them to Muskingum College, Ohio and
Melaku subsequently graduated as a physician from Howard University in 1935. He recruited several black Americans,
aviators Hubert Julian and J. C. Robinson, an educator, Cyril
Price, and Doctor John West to go to Ethiopia along with Ernest
Work, a white teacher, as education adviser. He married an
American, Dorothy Hadley, in 1931 and returned to Ethiopia
with her and their son in 1935 to work at the American Mission
hospital in the capital and later with the Ethiopian Red Cross in
the Ogaden. They left for England in May 1936 with the emperor and he served as his physician, interpreter and secretary
until he was dispatched to America to garner support among
blacks for Ethiopia--a futile effort, as blacks were the most
economically deprived in a country suffering the depression. He
edited a publication "Voice of Ethiopia" in New York, addressed
his black audiences as "fellow Ethiopians" and sacrificed his mental and physical health to the cause, dying on 4 May 1940.

MENELIK see MENILEK II

MENEN ASFAW (Empress 1930-1962). Born about 1891 to the
Janterar (an old title allotted only to the guardian of the mountain fortress of Ambasel) Asfaw and Sehen Mikael, she was thus
the granddaughter of Ras Mikael and the niece of Lej Iyasu
(q. v.). She married Hayle Sellase in 1911 after leaving her
husband, Lul Seged, by whom she had one child; she had six
children by Hayle Sellase; four of her children pre-deceased
her. After being crowned empress in 1930, she endowed a
school for girls and backed the formation of a woman's association and the Ethiopian Red Cross Society as the Italians were
preparing to invade Ethiopia. She shared her husband's exile
in England and on her return in 1941 she kept her holy promise
never to wear her crown again if God permitted her to return
to Ethiopia. She died after a long illness 22 February 1962
depriving Hayle Sellase of one of his most trusted advisers.

MENEN LEBEN AMEDE (Empress 1840-1853). Her title was given
to her by her son Ras Ali Alula (q. v.) after she married
Yohannes III in 1840; he was one of the royal claimants with no
power. Menen was a force to be reckoned with from the day
in 1831 when she was named a regent for her teenage son, who
succeeded the Yejju Oromo overlords who lived at Debre Tabor
(see GUGSA MERSU). She commanded her own army, ordered
the lives of the residents of Gondar, received foreigners, and
showed devotion to her adopted religion, Christianity. She
negotiated the marriage of Ali Alula to the daughter of Webe,
ruler of Tegray; the marriage of her daughter to Beru Goshu
of Gojam and the marriage of Ali Alula's putative daughter
(Tewabech) to Kasa of Owara. She was betrayed by her husband, Yohannes III, who fled Gondar in 1842 to join the forces
of Webe, but took him back after Webe was defeated by her son.

In 1847 she took her army to attack Kasa of Qwara, was wounded and captured; her son ransomed her at the price of granting her lands to Kasa. After 1853 when Kasa (on his way to becoming Tewodros II) defeated Ali Alula, she disappeared, but is said to have escaped with her son to their relations in Yejju where she died soon after.

MENGESHA SEYUM, Ras (1926-   ). As the great-grandson of Yohannes IV, he has imperial credentials to match those held by Hayle Sellase, to whom he remained loyal. Mengesha's mother came from Wello, and was one of several wives of his father, Seyum Mengesha, Ras of Tegray. After he and his sister, Beyenech, were convicted (in camera, before their father and the emperor) of implication in the 1942-43 Tegray rebellion (q.v.), he was kept under house arrest, then sent abroad for study. On his return he was married to Ayda Desta Demtew, the emperor's granddaughter (Cambridge-educated) by whom he had six children.

After terms as governor of Arussi (Arsi) (1952-55), Sidamo (1955-58) and Minister of Public Works (1958-61), he became governor of Tegray succeeding his father who was killed in the palace shooting in Addis Ababa (see COUP D'ÉTAT). Faced with certain imprisonment if not execution after the 1974 revolution, despite his popular reputation as a "man of the people" in Tegray, he went into exile and with others formed the Ethiopian Democratic Union (q.v.), of which he is president. Ayda Desta did not escape and remains in detention in Addis Ababa.

MENGESHA YOHANNES, Ras (c. 1865-1906). Acknowledged as the son of Yohannes IV and Welette Tekle Sellase (the wife of Yohannes's brother Gugsa) he was named Ras and given a command after the death of his half-brother in 1888, Crown Prince Araya Yohannes. Before his death fighting the Sudan-based Mahdists (q.v.) in March 1889, Yohannes IV named Mengesha his successor, but Menilek of Shewa's quick claim to the throne, based on considerable military and political power, negated the claim of Mengesha. Menilek had to march an army to Tegray in March 1890 to secure his formal, though temporary, submission. Menilek was angered over Mengesha's treatment of the agent he had left behind (Meshesha Werqe) to keep an eye on Tegray and the Italians, but particularly by Mengesha's independence in signing the Mereb Convention of December 1891 with Italy. The Italians, who persisted in calling Mengesha "an effeminate dandy," found him an unsatisfactory ally; but it was not until June 1894 that Mengesha came to Addis Ababa to beg pardon and re-submit, assuming that Menilek would grant him the title negus (king). Menilek did not. Mengesha, apparently without orders from Menilek, attacked the Italians at Addi Ugri in January 1895, and was forced to retreat. His troops fought bravely in the Italo-Ethiopian war (Dec. 1895-March 1896). To insure his future cooperation Mengesha was required to divorce his cur-

rent wife and marry Kefey Wele, the niece of Empress Taytu.
In September 1969, Menilek sent Ras Mekonnen with troops to
Tegray to capture Mengesha, who had declined an imperial
summons.   In February 1899, Mengesha gave himself up; he
was placed in detention at Ankober, where he died in 1906.

MENGESTU HAYLE MARYAM, Lt. Col. (1935-   ).   The dominant
figure in the regime that was formed in the wake of the 1974
revolution.   Supposedly of humble origins, he was raised in the
house of Kebede Tessema (a former governor of Gojam and
commander of the Territorial Army) through whose patronage
he was able to enter Holeta Military Academy.   Ambitious and
energetic in the army, Mengestu rose through the ranks to become a major by the time of the revolution, of which, initially,
he was not one of the prime conspirators.
   He was named First-vice-chairman of the Provisional
Military Administrative Council (q. v.) and was implicated in
the November 1974 assassination of the Council's chairman,
Aman Mikael Amdon, and the execution of 60 members of the
old regime (excluding his patron, Kebede Tessema).   Not known
for his intellectual grasp of socialist theory, Mengestu welcomed
the services of the All-Ethiopian Socialist Movement (Mei'son)
but when this group pressed for establishment of a "people's
party" and for civilian rule, he ordered them to disband.   Late
in 1976, the Derg (q. v.) voted to shift him to the chairmanship
of the Council of Ministers and gave General Teferi Bante control of the Derg.   Almost immediately, Mengestu and his supporters engineered a plot that wiped out Teferi Bente and four
close advisors (see COUP D'ÉTAT, attempted, 3 Feb. 1977)
and moved to stamp out any opposition.   Thousands of people,
mostly young protestors opposed to military rule, were shot.
   Mengestu's ascension to top leadership was greeted with
congratulations for crushing the "counter-revolution" by a number of communist envoys led by the Soviet ambassador; within
weeks, Fidel Castro paid a visit and Mengestu completed the
shift to Soviet and Cuban "advisers."   His leadership, according
to a 1980 report, has taken on an "imperial" cast as he uses
the former emperor's throne at important meetings and his pic-
ture is hung in every public place.

MENILEK II (Menelik) (Emperor 1889-1913).   Born in August 1844 to
Hayle Menekot, elder son of the prince of Shewa, and Ejjegayehu,
a woman employed in the palace of Ankober; his father became
king in 1847 and died in 1855 on the eve of battle with Tewodros II (1855-1868) who ended the nearly 100 years of Shewan
autonomy.   With his mother and a group of nobles, Menilek
was taken to the north with the emperor.   Although Tewodros
treated the young hostage as a son and gave Menilek his
daughter, Alatash, in marriage, Menilek escaped in mid 1865
and took over his patrimony while Tewodros became embroiled
with the British.
   Menilek had good advisers: his uncles, Darge (q. v.) and
Welde Giyorgis (q. v.) and his childhood tutor, Nadew (q. v.).

He was fortunate in securing the loyalty of a superb Oromo commander, Gobena (q. v.) who greatly extended the borders of Shewa in the early 1880's.   These and other conquests, notably the occupation of Harar in 1887, filled Menilek's store-houses with ivory, gold, musk, etc. and silver talers from taxes on the slave trade.   These resources paid for the import of firearms on an unparalleled scale.   Many freebooters from the north were drawn into Shewan service by the prospect of booty and the land grants they might receive for their war services.

Menilek welcomed foreigners and their ideas, but conservative councillors and public opinion, as well as inadequate means, hampered his more audacious projects.   He was insatiably curious about new inventions and had considerable mechanical aptitude; by decree and example he challenged the soldier's and office holder's contempt for manual labor, but was ignored.

In March 1878 he was compelled to submit to Emperor Yohannes IV who recrowned him king (negus) of "Shewa and the Galla lands. "   The Shewan clergy were obliged to adhere to the orthodoxy of the imperial court and the Shewan army had to be deployed at the emperor's behest to Wello in 1882-3 and 1887-8. After Menilek's war with the other chief vassal, Negus Tekle Haymanot at Embabo in June 1882, Yohannes reprimanded Menilek but the Shewan king kept most of the territory he had gone to war over.

Menilek's daughter Zewditu (q. v.) was affianced to Yohannes's heir in October 1882 and the Shewan was left almost free in foreign as well as secular domestic policies.   Menilek gave only token response to Yohannes's appeals for aid against the Mahdists and the Italians 1887-1889.

The Shewan king proclaimed himself emperor after the death of Yohannes in March 1889.   No one was strong enough to challenge him although Mengesha Yohannes (q. v.) proved a reluctant and troublesome vassal.   Italy's willingness to guarantee a supply of arms earlier in the 1880s, and the need to end conflicts with them in the north led Menilek to negotiate Ethiopia's first comprehensive treaty, which he signed 2 May 1889 (see WETCHALE) with Pietro Antonelli, who had been at his court off and on since 1879.   In defiance of the treaty, the Italians persisted in their advance into the northern highlands provoking the second stage of the Italo-Ethiopian war 1894-96.   Defeated finally at Adwa (q. v.) Italy halted its annexations and abandoned the pretense that the Treaty of Wetchale had granted them a protectorate.   The establishment of foreign legations in Addis Ababa that followed, and the start of construction on the railway from the coast to Addis Ababa, permanently altered Ethiopia's relationship to the outside world.

Secular education, printing, postal and telegraph services made modest beginnings under Menilek.   His last years of active rule were concerned with obtaining recognition of the empire's frontiers from the three colonial powers (Britain, France, Italy) which encircled Ethiopia and controlled his access to the sea.   In 1906, Menilek had a cerebral hemorrhage and though he recovered, his strength declined.   His wife, Taytu (q. v.) who

had always been consulted on matters of state, took on by de-
grees the powers of a regent. A "stroke" on 27 October 1909
left him paralyzed and incapable. With no surviving male issue,
he had named his grandson, Lej Iyasu, his heir in March 1909
and tried to provide dynastic alliances in the north for the young
prince, a council of ministers after the European fashion, and a
loyal regent, Tessema Nadew (q. v.); none of which succeeded in
containing the avarice and ambition of various factions at court.
Menilek's death 12 December 1913 was never officially announced.

MENTEWAB (Empress c. 1722-1730; regent-empress 1730-1769).
   The empress whose power and personality came to life in the
   notes of James Bruce (q. v.) just two years before her death.
   She was granted the title Etege (empress) by her husband,
   Bekaffa (1721-1730) and held her status after his death, first as
   co-ruler and re-crowned empress during the reign of her son
   Iyasu II (1730-1755) and his son Iyoas (1755-1769) with the support of her relations from Qwara district. She came to terms
   with the Tegray lord, Mikael Sehul (q. v.) who gained control of
   Gondarine strategy in 1755, by marrying her daughters, one to
   Mikael's son, and one to Mikael himself. After an abortive
   coup against Mikael in 1770, she fled to the estates in Gojam of
   her other daughter, Welette Israel, but returned at the pleading
   of Tekle Haymanot II and Mikael Sehul who guaranteed her safety.
   Her presence lent respectability to their rule. The father of
   her three daughters was Grazmach Iyesus Tarlach.

MEQDELA, AMBA. One of the many flat-topped mountains used by
   the rulers of Ethiopia as fortresses, retreats, and as prisons;
   this one became the last redoubt of Tewodros II in 1868. He
   kept his library, treasury and captives, both European and domestic there. After the Anglo-Indian army defeated the army
   of Tewodros on the plain below it, they stormed the fortress and
   found the body of the emperor who had committed suicide. The
   commander of the Anglo-Indian army on his return to England
   was titled "Lord Napier of Magdala." The amba was then occupied by Mestawet (q. v.), queen of the Were Himeno, and eventually came under the control of the king of Shewa, Menilek II.

MEROE, KINGDOM OF. Once part of ancient Ethiopia, it lies within
   the Sudan border today. It was mentioned in the 4th century
   B.C. as being ruled by a Queen Candace (a generic name);
   another queen of the same name was reigning when the centurions
   of Nero passed through Meroe searching for the sources of the
   Nile in the 1st century A.D. In the 3rd century it was conquered by an Aksum (capital of ancient Ethiopia) king and in the
   sixth century it was christianized.

MESQEL ("cross") FESTIVAL 27/28 September. The feast of Mesqel was sanctioned at the end of the 14th century (see DAWIT I)
   but was mentioned as being celebrated early in the century during the reign of Amde Tseyon (1314-1344). Occurring as it does
   at the end of the rains and the beginning of the New Year (10/11

September) it would appear to be rooted in ancient animist as
well as Hebraic celebrations.   This festival of the finding of
the True Cross begins with morning religious ceremonies in
the open air and is climaxed by the lighting of a great bonfire
on which sticks and yellow flowers (called Mesqel daisies) are
thrown.

MESTAWET (queen of the Were Himeno clan of Wello, 1857-?).
The widow of Imam Leben Amede (d. 1857) who claimed
Meqdela in the name of her son, Abba Watew, as the British
vacated the mountain fortress after razing it to the ground, in
April 1868.   Her martial accomplishments are remembered as
"she fought in battles like a man." She harassed Tewodros II
and his successor, Wagshum Gobeze of Lasta, and kept up an
intense rivalry with another Wello queen, Werqitu.   Her son
lost the struggle for power in Wello in June 1878 when Yohannes IV promoted over him the stepson of Queen Werqitu,
Muhammad Ali (see MIKAEL, Ras).   Mestawet remained a devout Muslim though her son was required to become a Christian
in Yohannes's order of June 1878.   After her son's death in
1880, she still had sufficient power to commit troops to assist
Menilek in his campaign against Tekle Haymanot at Embabo in
1882 and in 1885 was said to be behind the rebellion of Muhammad Qanqe and Abba Jebel (son of Abba Watew) against the
exactions of Araya Yohannes (son of the emperor), the nominal
ruler of Wello.

METEMMA.   A market town at the southwestern corner of Begemder province abutting the Sudan; on the Sudanese side is Qallabat
which was a key point in the slave trade.   A caravan route to
Gondar enabled the Mahdists from this point to vandalize the ancient city in 1888; it was at Metemma that Yohannes IV lost his
life in March 1889 fighting the Mahdists.

MIKAEL, Ras (c. 1850-1918).   Born about 1850, he was raised in
the home of his step-mother, Werqitu, queen of one of the
Oromo houses of Wello.   In 1876, Menilek of Shewa ousted Abba
Watew (scion of a rival Oromo clan) and appointed Muhammad
Ali over the province.   Muhammad sided with Yohannes IV in
that monarch's confrontation with Menilek in 1878, renounced Islam and became a Christian; Yohannes stood as his godfather and
gave him the name, Mikael, and the title of Ras, but did not
make him governor over all Wello until 1886.   His army, one of
the largest and fiercest in the kingdom, fought at Metemma
(1894), the Italian campaign (1895-96) and Tegray (1898).
    He threw his allegiance to Menilek when he became emperor
in 1889, though Menilek appointed his own uncle, Ras Darge
(q.v.) to oversee Mikael until full trust was established; Mikael
proved his loyalty and was given a putative daughter of Menilek's, Shewa Regga, as his wife.   Among his known wives to
that date was Alatash Wende (cousin of Yohannes IV), Manale-
besh (daughter of Menilek's consort Befana).   After Shewa Regga's death in 1897 he married Zennebesh by indissoluble com-

munion rite. Among his known children Derita, Ali, Asi (?),
Tewabech, Sehen (mother of Hayle Sellase's wife, Menen),
Yetemegnu, Zenebe Werq and Iyasu. The last named was the
designated heir to Menilek II.

Lej Iyasu, emperor though never crowned, named his father
a negus (king) in 1914. Dissatisfaction with Iyasu's discharge
of his imperial duties plus the fear that he had reverted to his
father's first religion led to the coup d'état that overthrew him
in 1916. Mikael tried to secure his son's position by marching
on Addis Ababa but was defeated en route, at Segele, on 22
October 1916. He died, in custody, 8 September 1918 after
several years on an island in Lake Zway.

MIKAEL AREGAWI (c. 1848-1931). A Felasha converted to Pro-
testantism at the Jinda mission; he accompanied his mentor,
Johann Flad, to England in 1866 when Tewodros II sent Flad
to acquire European workmen. Mikael Aregawi was educated
in Switzerland and in Germany and on his return to Ethiopia,
opened a school for Felashas (q.v.) which functioned from 1878
until his death in 1931. He made several trips to Europe in
that time, helping Flad to revise the Amharic Bible in 1885
and did the corrections on Heruy Welde Sellase's New Testament which was printed in Addis Ababa with parallel Amharic
and Ge'ez texts.

MIKAEL SEHUL, Ras (c. 1686-1780). From the Turks who held
the port of Massawa, Mikael Sehul had purchased guns which
backed up his position as the ruler of Tegray. About 1749,
after several contests with the Gondarine emperor, Iyasu
(1730-1755), he assented to helping the emperor put down some
rebellions. By the time Iyasu died, Mikael Sehul was far more
powerful than the royal house. In the background stood the
Dowager-empress Mentewab (q.v.) whose reputation was such
that an alliance with her was essential. His son, Welde Hawaryat (d. 1760) was married to Mentewab's daughter, Alatash,
in 1755 and Mikael Sehul married her elder sister, Aster, and
though an old man, produced a son by her. Mikael Sehul is
considered the initiator of the Zemene Mesafint (q.v.) because
he ordered the murder of two emperors (Iyoas in 1769 and
Yohannes II five months later) and placed on the throne Tekle
Haymanot II, (son of Yohannes II) who did Mikael Sehul's bid-
ding.

A rebellion against him in Tegray threatened in 1770 when
he was in Gondar; he took Tekle Haymanot II with him to put
it down. In his absence, a pretender seized the throne with
the connivance of Mentewab. Mikael Sehul and "his" emperor
marched on Gondar and the pretender fled, as did the Dowager-
empress, though Mikael would never have risked harming his
wife's prestigious mother. A coalition against Mikael Sehul
succeeded finally, but he was allowed to die of old age in Temben, his natal province, near Aksum.

MISSIONS, CATHOLIC. From 1555 to 1633 Portuguese Jesuits like

Pero Paez (died 1622) and Affonso Mendez (arrived 1626) proselytized the court and irritated existing doctrinal controversies within the Ethiopian Orthodox Church. Uncharacteristically for the Jesuits, Mendez would not compromise with indigenous practices. He attacked such customs as circumcision, encouraged the eating of pork, and wanted to abolish the Ethiopian religious calendar and import the Latin liturgy, conceding only the use of Ge'ez. The Jesuits provoked the downfall of their eminent convert, Emperor Susneyos (q.v.). His son, Fasiledes banished all Catholics in 1634, and though various missions attempted to return, they were not successful until 1752, when three Franciscans arrived. After nine months at court in 1752 they were dismissed after bringing pressure on the emperor (Iyasu II, 1730-1755) to make a pro-Catholic declaration. An Ethiopian convert, Father Tobias Gebre Egziabeher, was sent by the Propaganda Fide in Rome, but he was forced to confine his activities to the area of Adwa from 1790-1797.

After the expulsion of the Protestants in 1838, a new Catholic effort was initiated by the Lazarist Giuseppe Sapeto, but it was Father Justin de Jacobis of the same order, who arrived the following year, who truly planted the faith. De Jacobis, though not an agent of France, was a proponent of French influence and his advice was sought on the letters and contacts between Tegray leaders who were opposed to Tewodros II, and France from 1840 until his death at Massawa in 1860. Lazarist missions, staffed by indigenous priests, survived in the Bogos area and numbered several thousand adherents. They came into bitter conflict with Yohannes IV in the 1870s for their suspected Egyptian sympathies.

The Capuchins, led by Father Gugliemo Massaia remained in the southwest area from 1849 to 1863. Massaia appeared at Menilek's court after a four year stay in Europe, in March 1868, but the king would not accede to his request to return to his old missions in Kefa. Massaia and his colleague, Father (later, a Bishop) Taurin de Cahagne, were often consulted by Menilek until they were ordered out of the country by Yohannes IV in 1879. The Capuchins insisted on the Latin rite, while the Lazarists were willing to work with the Ge'ez rite, a duality that persists to this day.

Menilek permitted Father Taurin to re-open the Harar mission in 1882. A leprosarium and orphanage were established; in 1905 they published a weekly newspaper in Amharic and French, Le Semeur d'Éthiopie, the first newspaper in the country, and in 1908 a press was established at Dire Dawa. French Lazarists were required to leave Tegray in 1894 by the Italians.

The Consolata mission was permitted to work in Kefa in 1917 (first since Father Jarousseau had been expelled in 1903); they ran a forest concession, had a carpentry workshop which built the first pre-fab houses (brought to Addis Ababa in 1924) and were on excellent terms with local officials and their wives.

Subject, as were all other groups, to the Foreign Mission Law of 24 August 1944, Catholics were restricted to working

only with non-Christian Ethiopians and required to use Amharic
as the medium of instruction in their schools.   A 1970 report
estimated Roman Catholics at 130,000, divided between those
who use the Latin rite and those who follow the Ethiopic (Ge'ez).

MISSIONS, PROTESTANT.   A German Lutheran, Peter Heyling
(q. v.) in 1634, was the first Protestant pioneer in Ethiopia where
he lived under the protection of Emperor Fasiledes until 1652.
Some 150 years later, Henry Salt, after trips to Ethiopia in
1805 and 1809 interested the British and Foreign Bible Society
in producing an Amharic bible, because most Ethiopians, no
matter how Christian, could not read their own bible as it was
in Ge'ez (q. v.).   In 1830 the Church Missionary Society (CMS) in
the persons of Samuel Gobat and Christian Kugler began distribution of the Gospels and the New Testament, and in 1840 the
entire bible was finished and distributed.   The CMS was active
1830-1838 and briefly in 1843 in Tegray and were in Shewa
1839-1842.   Individual Protestants, vocal opponents of the Orthodox Church's veneration of Mary, fasting and other religious
rituals, provoked the expulsions of 1838 and 1843.

The Pilgrim Brethren (trained at St. Chrischona, in Switzerland, but assigned to work under the CMS) entered Ethiopia
in 1855 and as artisan-craftsmen were welcomed by Tewodros II.
The London Society for Promoting Christianity Amongst the Jews
sent the Rev. Henry Stern in 1860 to work among the Felasha.
Missionary work was curtailed in 1863 when Stern was arrested
(see CAPTIVES, EUROPEAN) though Tewodros left at liberty
other missionaries who were able to build houses, roads and
armaments for him.   All but two were confined to Meqdela fortress in 1867 until their release in 1868 by the Napier expedition.

Remote from the scenes of Tewodros' shifts in attitudes,
were the members of the Swedish Evangelical Mission (SEM)
founded in Kunama in 1866.   They had an impact on Ethiopia
in the fields of medicine, literacy and education for women.
Their printing press, the first in the country, at Emkullo
(Omtulo) in 1885, turned out teaching materials as well as bibles
in Tegre, Tegrigna, Oromo and Amharic.   Their literate and
multi-lingual converts provided resource material and translation
services to scholars as well as founding the indigenous Protestant
church, Mekane Yesus (q. v.).   Native evangelists, Gebre Ewostatewos and Neguse Tashu, established self-supporting missions in
Welega and Jimma and acted as secretaries and teachers to the
rulers of those areas beginning in 1904.

The American Seventh Day Adventists (SDA) were in Begemder in 1907 and active in Shewa, Gojam, Welamo, and Wello by
1921, and the United Presbyterians were working in Welega in
1919.   The Sudan Interior Mission, also American, developed an
extensive medical and educational program from 1927 in the
western districts and the same year the German Hermannsburg
Mission began its work in Welega.   By 1935 there were 10
Protestant groups in Ethiopia running 34 schools and 10 hospitals among them.   The Italians expelled all of them in 1935, ex-

cept the German group, Seventh Day Adventists and Presbyterians.   The last named were expelled in early 1937, but six
SDA missionaries and one Swedish nurse remained throughout
the occupation.

Missions resumed operations in 1944 under the decree pro-
hibiting them from converting the Ethiopian Orthodox and re-
quiring all education to be in Amharic.   Protestant parishioners
in 1970 were estimated at 227,000, twice that of Catholics (see
ONESIMOS NESIB; J. H. FLAD; SWEDEN; MISSIONS, CATHO-
LIC).

MONASTICISM and MONASTERIES.   A celibate branch of the clergy
and the monastery as a center of Christian learning were introduced into the Aksum kingdom about A.D. 490 with the arrival
of nine monks from various parts of the Roman Empire.   They
lived at court for twelve years, then spread out to found monasteries (see DEBRE DAMO).   For seven centuries there is little
information, then a notable expansion is documented in the 13th
century with the activities of Iyesus Moa (q.v.), Tekle Haymanot (q.v.), and Ewostatewos (q.v.).   By their own pious example
they attracted disciples and championed higher moral standards,
one going so far as to lecture an emperor on his matrimonial
habits.   The monasteries provided a pool of missionaries to go
with the imperial army to christianize a newly conquered area.
From the time of Zera Yaqob (1434-1468), the monastic order
was represented at court in the person of a monk from Debre
Libanos chosen to be the Echege, highest church office for an
Ethiopian.   He also had authority over all monks and monasteries.

The only qualification for a monk, or a nun was a willingness to renounce worldly pleasure and devote their lives to
prayer, fasting and humble chores.   The monk did not even
have to reside in a monastery, could wander about or even stay
in his own home.   He went through a ceremony in which his
body was declared dead and he was given a cloth skullcap, the
symbol of his status.   He was freed of all debts, a motivation
for some of these renunciations.   The Fetha Negest ruled that
anyone who took up the life of a monk must have the permission
of his wife, and that if he did so to avoid his obligations to his
family he would be excommunicated.

Women were not encouraged to become nuns until they were
50 and widowed.   Nonetheless there were many in the history
of the church who left their husbands and children to join a religious community or to form one (see WELETTE PETROS).
Converts usually grew up beside an important monastery, and
there were many established by the 13th century.   In Amhara
and Shewa, the custom was for monks and nuns to live together.
A source of 1878 says that women were not admitted to Debre
Libanos and lived in their villages, though it has been asserted
that there was a convent there before 1531.   In any case, in
1908 Empress Taytu (q.v.) ordered a house built for the women,
and a "reverend-mother" was named to administer the convent.

MONOPHYSITISM see RELIGIONS.

MUHAMMAD, Prophet (A.D. 570-632).   An Ethiopian Christian com-
    munity living in Mecca was said to have provided a nursemaid
    for the young Muhammad, predisposing him to a special interest
    in Ethiopia.   At the time of persecution of his followers (about
    622) a group of refugees, including his daughter, were sent for
    safety to the king of Aksum.   When it was safe to return, the
    Aksum king sent a generous dowry with one of them who was to
    become a wife of the Prophet.   In fact, Muhammad married
    two of the returnees, and took into his harem the Christian girl
    Mary, who had come with them.   Muhammad's entourage in-
    cluded soldiers of Ethiopian origin; his conversation employed
    Ge'ez words (some 200 words in the Koran are Ge'ez loan
    words derived from other languages such as Greek and Syriac).
    Grateful for the Ethiopian asylum, the Prophet excepted Ethio-
    pia from any holy war (see ISLAM).

MUHAMMAD ABD ALLAH HASSAN, Sayyid (religious teacher, lead-
    er) (1864-1920).   A Somali of the Salihiya order, a celebrated
    poet in a society that conducted its political thinking in poetry,
    and leader of a 20-year jihad against European and Ethiopian
    intrusion into Somali-inhabited areas, and against the Qadiriya
    Sufi order which was less puritanical than his own; the latter
    used the phrase "mad mullah" to describe him, a name his
    enemies used thereafter.   His first adherents came from a
    settlement in the Ogaden that the Ethiopians had attacked; be-
    tween 1900 and 1910 four Ethio-British expeditions tried and
    failed to capture him, though there was a four year truce
    1905-1909 arranged by the Italians.   He died in 1920, still at
    liberty.

MUNZINGER, WERNER (1832-1875).   A Swiss scholar and business-
    man who was deeply involved in Ethiopian affairs.   He settled
    in Keren in 1855, married a lady of the area, and studied the
    language, social, economic and legal life of the Bogos people.
    Appointed vice-consul at Massawa for the British in 1863, he
    served France as well, becoming an ardent protector of the
    Catholic missions in Bogos, and worked to separate this pro-
    vince from Ethiopia.   In 1868 he took an active part in prepa-
    rations for the British expedition against Tewodros.   He joined
    the Egyptian administration as governor of Massawa in 1871,
    then was made commander of the Egyptian troops stationed in
    eastern Sudan.   Instructed by the Khedive to seek the coopera-
    tion of Menilek of Shewa against Emperor Yohannes, he and
    his party of Sudanese soldiers, his wife, and Menilek's envoy
    to the Khedive, Aleqa Beru, were killed by the Afar on 13
    November, 1875.

MUSIC AND INSTRUMENTS.   Most of Ethiopia's musical tradition
    and development has come from church observance and ritual.
    Sacred music and dance (zema) is learned by priests and
    debtera (q.v.) in special church schools, by rote and by study-

ing notation which indicates tempo or one of three categories
of melody (selt).   These courses can take as long as 20 years
to achieve proficiency in all the aspects of church music.   The
hymnary (diqwa), learned early in this training, is ascribed to
Abba Yared (q. v.), reputed to have lived during the 6th century
A. D.   The Yared School of Music in Addis Ababa trains young
Ethiopians in both western and traditional music.

Secular music (zeffan) was performed as an occupation by
azmari, bards and folk-singers, who pass their skills and songs
on to their children.   Azmari celebrate the exploits of patrons
in songs that praise and criticize with clever double-entendre, a
much-admired talent.   Sociologists and historians study these
handed-down ballads for their description of famines, floods,
triumphs and defeats.   The lalibeloch, named after the famous
12th century king, would sing in the hour before dawn with
their faces covered, as they were usually lepers who had to
remain unseen: they performed outside the house of the wealthy
and expected alms.

Songs are composed spontaneously in all parts of the country
among most ethnic groups: singing while working is noted particularly among the Konso (q. v.) and the Dorze (q. v.).   Fuqara
and shilela are the boasting songs of a warrior returned from
battle.   Musho and legso are sung by women to honor the deceased.   Many of these songs are preserved in the historical
literature.

Instruments, many of ancient invention and locally made, include the kerar, a lyre of six to ten strings; the begenna, another ten-stringed lyre or harp; the one-string masenko, played
with a horse-hair bow or plucked; kebaro, two-headed tympani;
the sistrum, a hand-rattle of metal disks shaken for rhythmic
effect; mekwamiya, a prayer-stick; and various small drums,
horns and flutes.   The voice is a basic component as is rhythmic hand-clapping.

European musical instruments first appeared in 1897, as
gifts brought by the Russian, N. Leontiev.   Pianos, harpsi-
chords and a large variety of other western-made brass,
strings, woodwinds and percussion instruments have been
brought in by foreigners, and official bands play on state occasions.   The latest national anthem, "Ethiopia Tikdem,"
(Ethiopia First) was established by the Provisional Military Administrative Council after the 1974 Revolution.

In the cities there is greater interest in more modern musical forms.   There are many Ethiopian love songs played by
local musicians and are featured on radio and television.   A
number of instrumental groups play these and western melodies
at the hotels or clubs.   Traditional music is played by various
"folk" ensembles such as Orchestra Ethiopia, the Patriotic
Association and others with recordings of these traditional
styles and songs played almost constantly at local restaurants
and coffee houses.

- N -

NAPIER, Sir ROBERT (1810-1890).   Commander of the Anglo-Indian
    expedition, January-May 1868 in Ethiopia (see GREAT BRITAIN
    and Ethiopia).

NATIONALIZATION.   Imperial monopolies of gold and ivory were
    enforced during the rule of Menilek II (1889-1913); he granted
    on strict terms a number of short term contracts of the mo-
    nopoly-concession type that provided maximum revenue to the
    treasury under his control, if they succeeded.   The Ethiopian
    share of the railway was entirely government held; the French
    shares, once government owned, have been sold to a private
    company.   In the 1930s the government held the monopoly for
    tobacco, matches and manufacture of alcohol.   The land tenure
    system (q.v.) retained state ownership (gult) of vast tracts of
    farmland.
        One of the first steps taken after the revolution of 1974 was
    the nationalization of all businesses owned by the royal family
    or the gentry, followed by banks and insurance companies.   In
    February 1975, 101 foreign- and locally-owned companies were
    taken over.   The take-over of Ethiopian-owned businesses,
    caused considerable dislocation as the drop in production and
    quality caused almost immediate shortages of goods, with con-
    sequent price rises in processed materials such as shoes, tex-
    tiles and certain foodstuffs.

NAVY.   A naval college was established at Massawa in 1955, with
    a training center for support personnel at Dongolo Gend.   The
    training officers were Norwegian.   Since 1958, a number of
    patrol boats, motor torpedos (Yugoslav make) have acted as a
    coast guard unit off the Eritrean coast.   A seaplane tender,
    and landing craft were re-cycled from the United States as part
    of the Military Assistance Program in the early 1960s.   The
    first commodore was Eskender Desta, Hayle Sellase's grandson.
    He was shot in 1974.

NEBURA-ED.   This ancient title which means "laying on of hands"
    was given only to the head of Debre Tseyon, the church dedi-
    cated to Mary, at Aksum where the Ark of the Covenant al-
    legedly brought from Jerusalem is kept.   It was an honor of
    great magnitude.   Despite the creation of a duplicate nebura-ed
    by Menilek II in 1905 at the church of Debre Tseyon of Addis
    Alem, where he had built a church in a rectangular form simi-
    lar to Aksum's, the investiture was not actually made until
    1911 by Lej Iyasu.

NEGGADRAS ("head of the merchants").   Originating as the name of
    the man who led a caravan consisting of more than ten donkeys
    or mules, it evolved as the title of the man in charge of a
    customs post (kella) as well as the man who supervised the
    market site, renting the stalls and adjudicating all disputes.
    The apotheosis of neggadras was represented in the career of

Hayle Giyorgis who took the office in Addis Ababa in 1900; he collected customs dues, fees for judgments, revenue from his own trading activities, taxes on the local market and received a portion of the taxes collected by the provincial neggadras (there were six).   As much of the trade was conducted by foreigners, it was natural that Menilek, when he made up a cabinet in 1908, designated him as Minister of Commerce and Foreign Affairs.   The office of neggadras was gradually abolished as it was replaced by government tax collectors, and multiple customs from province to province replaced by the single levy.

NEGUSE NEGEST ("king of kings" or "king among kings").   Ge'ez term, which in its earliest usage in pre-Christian times meant "chief of chiefs."   The right to create "kings" (neguse) over whom to rule has been used sparingly.   The "kings" of Shewa simply arrogated the title to themselves until Tewodros II put a stop to it in 1855.   However, as soon as Menilek escaped from Meqdela in 1865, he resumed the practice, at times even using neguse negest, until Yohannes IV put a stop to that in 1878.   He forced Menilek to revert to the title of negus and made it clear it was received by his gracious permission; to rival Menilek in importance, Yohannes IV created Adal Tessema of Gojam, a negus in 1882.   Menilek regranted this title after he became emperor, and appointed no others.   Lej Iyasu made his father a negus in 1914 though he himself had never been actually crowned.   The last man to be made a negus was Welde Giyorgis Aboye in 1917, receiving the title from the first negiste negest (queen of kings) Zewditu (see EMPERORS).

NEWSPAPERS and periodicals.   The first Amharic "newspaper" was a handwritten sheet produced by Blatta Gebre Egziabeher around 1900; a polygraphed newsletter was issued by the Franciscan mission in Harar from 1900 to 1905, then a printing press was acquired and the publication became Le Semeur d'Ethiopie (1905-1911); it was in French with special items in Amharic. In 1902-03 Aimro (intelligence) was circulated by A. Kavadias with the cooperation of Menilek II.   At first it was handwritten and had a circulation of about 24, but rose to 200 when a copying machine was obtained.   Aimro was revived 1911-1916. Le Courier d'Ethiopie was published twice weekly from 1913 to the early 1920s.   Yetwor Ware (war news) was issued from the Italian legation 1916-1918.   In 1925 Regent Teferi founded Berhanena-Selam (light and peace) an Amharic weekly that folded when the Italians invaded in 1935.   A Daily News Bulletin started in 1941 was circulated primarily to foreign embassies.   It was still being printed by the Ministry of Information in French and English up to 1974.   Addis Zemen (new era) an Amharic daily began circulating (first as a weekly) in 1941-42 and had the highest circulation (10,000 in 1970); followed by an English language daily, Ethiopian Herald (started 1945) with 8,000.   It is the main source for the foreign community on government activities.   The editor in the 1960s was Tegenye

Yeteshewerq, a Boston University graduate.   He was executed
by the Derg in November 1974, for suggesting moderation.

Addis Soir a French evening paper began in 1965; Giornale
dell' Eritrea and Il Quotidiano Eritreo are published in Asmara;
Sandek Alamtchin (Our Flag), Hebret, and Andnet were published in Arabic as well as Amharic or Tegrinya.

In sum, there were six dailies and 11 weeklies reported in
1970.   All, of course, were subject to censorship, as they are
under the revolutionary government.   Combined circulation was
about 100,000, in 1970; present figures are not known.

Bulletins and magazines, and scholarly journals proliferated
at an astonishing rate between 1950 and 1970; some appearing
at irregular intervals.   Commerce, highways, development research, geography, medicine, law, education, history, archaeology were some of the special interests served.   No update on
these publications is available, but many have ceased publication.

NINE SAINTS (6th century).   It is verified that nine missionaries
came from various parts of the Roman empire (i.e. Constantinople, Syria, Antioch, Rome) at the end of the 5th century.
Their names were Ze-Mikael (or Aregawi), Pentelewon, Yeshaq
(Issac, or Gerima), Aftse, Guba, Alef, Yem'ata, Liqanos and
Sehma and each has a saints day on the Ethiopian religious
calendar.   They remained at Aksum about twelve years, then
spread out to found monasteries and centers of education, spreading a religion that until then had been more or less confined to
the court at Aksum.   They are believed to have contributed to
the translation of the Bible into Ge'ez, a language that was just
evolving.

- O -

OGADEN.   Barren region in the southeastern part of the country
inhabited by nomadic tribesmen largely of Somali language and
culture.   The area has long been a matter of dispute between
Ethiopia and its neighbor (see SOMALIA and Ethiopia).   This
culminated in an undeclared war in 1978, which assumed international significance (see ORGANIZATION FOR AFRICAN UNITY;
CUBA; RUSSIA).   Hayle Sellase earmarked sizeable budgets for
development projects in the Ogaden both for resettlement and to
establish firmer territorial claims.

ONESIMOS NESIB (c. 1856-1931).   An Oromo rescued from slavery
by the Swedish Evangelical Mission in Tegray who became their
first student and first convert in 1871.   From 1876-1881 he was
in Sweden and on his return married Meheret Haylu, daughter
of an aleqa who had been a secretary to Emperor Tewodros.
She was a student at the girls school at Emkulo (Omtulo) opened
in 1878.   He began his life work: translation of the Bible into
Oromo, revising the work of Debtera Zeneb whose translation of
the scriptures into Oromo had been published between 1870-1877.

With the help of Aster Ganno he finished the New Testament
in 1893, Old Testament in 1897 and went to Switzerland to supervise the printing.

Aster Ganno also helped Onesimos produce the Oromo
reader and spelling book printed at the Swedish Mission Press
in 1894. He had completed a hymn book in 1886; translated
Bunyan's "Man's Heart" and Luther's catechism thereby creating
a body of Oromo reading material in the Amharic script. His
wife died in 1888 and he married Lidia Dimbo. With her and
their children he returned to his roots in the Oromo speaking
area of Welega in 1904 as a lay evangelist and teacher. He and
his colleagues were ordered not to teach in 1906 after complaints
to Abuna Matewos by the Orthodox clergy; he continued to read
the Bible aloud under the protection of Gebre Egziabeher Moroda
(q.v.) and sell the Oromo Bible until his death in 1931 (see
MEKANE YESUS CHURCH).

ONOMASTICS (naming system). There are very few names among
the Christians of Ethiopia that do not have a meaning: e.g.
Tedla--"happiness"; Kasa--"compensation". The latter is often
given when the mother has lost a child prior to this one's birth.
Many names are biblical: Maryam, Iyasus, Solomon. Names
are interchangeable for boys and girls: Zelleqe ("he excelled")
and Zelleqa ("she excelled"). A child's name is not given out
for several weeks after birth for fear of giving assistance to
some evil spirit. A special name is given at baptism. A child
can have a name known only within the family, a "world" name,
a baptismal name, and a new name when ennobled or crowned.
The crown name is fraught with significance and consultation
with religious advisers is essential before selection. In addition, there is the "horse name" for the warrior--he and his
horse share a name during battle. Menilek II was baptized
Sahle Maryam ("mercy of Mary"); he did not change his name
when he became emperor. His "horse name" was Abba Dag-
new ("master of rendering justice") while Yohannes IV changed
his name from Kasa Mircha to be crowned emperor, and bore
the "horse name" of Abba Bezbez ("master of devastation").

There are, however, no family names, for example: the
son (or daughter) of Kebede Tessema becomes Hagos Kebede
and his son can be Alemu Hagos. Women keep their names
when they marry though change in the present time from Weyze-
rit (Miss) to Weyzero (Mrs.) the way they are addressed.
"Welette" means "daughter of" and is a common baptismal
name, often retained for "world use" and must be followed by
another name. The same rule applies for "welde" or "son of."

Numerous names consist of two words, e.g. Hayle Sellase
("power of the Trinity,") and the two parts are inseparable.
Other names, with or without use of their titles (Kantiba,
Dejazmach, etc.) can be properly addressed dropping their
second name. The first part of many compound names can
form a shorter proper name by altering the final vowel to ex-
press possession; hence, Haylu ("His power"), or as in the case
of the historian Atsme Giyorgis who was often called Atsme
(properly "é"), meaning "my".

ORGANIZATION OF AFRICAN UNITY.   Thirty heads of African
states were brought together in Addis Ababa by Hayle Sellase I
in 1963, forming this first cooperative effort on the continent.
The organization has its headquarters in the Ethiopian capital.
The Emperor acted as mediator in the Morocco-Algerian conflict, and Ethiopia responded with troops to help establish order
in Tanzania after its 1964 military revolt.

Ethiopia was much interested, as was Zambia, Somalia and
Burundi, in cooperative efforts with the East African Community
(Kenya, Tanzania and Uganda) in 1967.   The break-up of that
community a few years later aborted this promising regional
economic effort.

OROMO PEOPLE.   The Oromo, or Galla, an estimated seven million, are the largest ethnic group in the country.   They consist
of about a dozen clusters living in 10 of the 12 provinces.
Nearly all speak a mutually intelligible dialect of an east Cushitic tongue (Galligna or Oromigna) but they differ in religion
(animist, Ethiopian Orthodox, Protestant, Muslim), style of
life, and community organization, but most retain some features
of their unique and complex generation-grading system, gada
(q. v.).   Their dispersal, frequent inter-clan animosity, their
adoption of the ways of the people among whom they settled,
their lack of interest in political domination (in contrast to the
highly motivated Christian Amhara-Tegray), are among the
reasons they remained a "minority" to be ruled.

Their migration from their homeland in southern Ethiopia
began in the early 16th century and by the end of the century
there were Oromo settlements as far north as Begemder,
Dembya and Gojam.   By the late 17th century, one group in
Yejju had become Muslim, established dynastic succession,
made a show of Christian conversion and took control of the
Solomonic house in Gondar.   For nearly a hundred years (see
YEJJU DYNASTY) it was the peak of Oromo power, but was effective only over two provinces.

In the southwest small Oromo kingdoms (Ennarya, Jimma,
Gera, Guma) formed in the early 19th century; they raided each
other for slaves; other groups like the Borana (q. v.) and Guji
maintained an egalitarian animist society based on the gada system, in which no man could hold power longer than eight years.

The historical literature is rich and explorers were generally admiring of the industry and bravery of the "Gallas" they
met.   Modern ethnographic and anthropological studies (i. e.
E. Haberland, Asmerom Legesse, Bonnie Holcomb, Herbert
Lewis, E. E. Knutsson, P. T. Baxter, D. Levine, and John
Hinnant) are growing.   The marked upsurge of Oromo nationalism ranging from separate-nation sentiment to the extension
of Oromo influence in the Addis Ababa administration is a vigorous movement; certainly among Oromo students abroad it is
strong, but very difficult to measure within the country.

- P -

PAINTING.   Production of paintings is a small industry as artists
reproduce the same themes over and over in primary colors
outlined in black, on parchment and canvas.   There are scenes
of rural life, the "Battle of Adwa" (q. v.), heroes on horseback,
emperors, saints suffering impassively, and that staple of street
sale to tourists the "comic strip" treatment of the Queen of
Sheba's visit to King Solomon.   Naturalistic murals on the walls
and ceilings of churches intersperse holy figures with political
leaders.
    Rock paintings of great antiquity have been found in several
parts of the country, particularly in Akkele Guzay in Eritrea,
Karora (on the Eritrean-Sudan border) and near Harar.
    Little pictorial art done before the fourteenth century sur-
vives, but skillfully illuminated manuscripts (the Kibran gospels, for example) and icons found in churches and monasteries
were painted in that century.   The style can be attributed to
Byzantine, Syrian and Coptic models but with variations by the
Ethiopian artist in mode and adaptation of the Biblical subject.
Neither perspective, light and shade, nor background detail is
characteristic.   In the recovery period after the destruction of
churches by the Islamic invaders of the sixteenth century, the
output was enormous and changed; a little with a discernible
influence from the Renaissance and Baroque prints brought to
Ethiopia.   More animals and plants appear as the setting was
Ethiopianized and efforts were made to give life to the figure--
eyes had direction, the torso might bend and the arms would indicate movement.
    Individual artists are not easily identified from the past.
One artist of renown was Agenew Engeda (1903-1948), whose
work on murals, manuscripts and church decorations was admired.   He studied in Paris 1932-35 and on his return founded
the first secular art school; a few artists like Skunder Bogassian, Gebre Krestos Desta, Afewerq Tekle and Berhan Mehary,
have been recognized internationally.

PANKHURST, Sylvia (1882-1960); Richard K. P. (1927-   ).   She
    founded, with her husband Silvio Corio, New Times and Ethiopia
    News in May 1935 as a forum in England for Ethiopia's cause
    after Italy occupied Ethiopia.   In 1956 when she took up resi-
    dence in Ethiopia (Silvio Corio died in 1954) New Times became
    Ethiopia Observer.   Her son, Richard Pankhurst, took over
    editorship upon her death, and in 1963 became a co-editor of
    the Journal of Ethiopian Studies.   That same year he founded
    and became the director, until 1975, of the Institute of Ethio-
    pian Studies, Addis Ababa.   He is presently associated with
    the Royal Asiatic Society in London and continues to be one of
    the most prolific writers in Ethiopian studies today.   He is
    married to Rita Eldon, onetime librarian of the National Library
    of Ethiopia and of Addis Ababa University Library.

PATRIOTS ("arbegna" in Amharic; see also BLACK LIONS).   The

designation given to those who took part in the resistance against
the Italians during 1936-1941. Their leaders (e. g. Abebe
Aregay, Mesfin Sellase) were often provincial or local chiefs
from important landowning families who had the resources to
provide fighting equipment as well as sustenance.   Many were
killed in action (e. g. Hayle Maryam Mamo in June 1938), or
executed (e. g. Desta Demtew) but others fought on until the
liberation, harassing Italian troops whenever they ventured out
of fortified towns.   The Church contributed many men to resistance units.   Abune Petros (q. v.) refused to collaborate and
was executed in July 1936, as was Abune Mikael shortly after.
Over 100 monks at Debre Libanos were shot near the monastery
when the Italians discovered a large cache of arms there.
     Scores of women were numbered among Patriots, including
Lekyelech Beyen and Kebeddech, daughter of Tegray Ras
Seyum Mengesha, and wife of Abera Kasa who was shot along
with his two brothers under the pretext of granting them safe
conduct, after their capture.   Virtually every province had a
woman Patriot leader; one heroine, Shewa Regga Gedle, was
sent to prison in Italy in 1937 on suspicion of having taken part
in the assassination attempt on Graziani.   She was allowed to
return in 1939 and promptly joined a sabotage team; captured
and flogged, she escaped and joined the guerrillas again.   Ro-
mana Werq Hayle Sellase (a daughter of the emperor) was captured and her husband (Beyene Mered) shot.   She died in detention in Italy just as the Allies ended Italian participation in the
war (see SENEDU GEBRU).
     Many Patriot leaders who survived the protracted warfare
were disappointed in their rewards after the liberation, were
critical of the emperor for leaving the country and became potential opponents to his regime.   Typical of these were Belay
Zelleqe, Mamo Haylu (son of the collaborating Ras Haylu of
Gojam), Haylu Kebret, Geressu Duke, Tekle Welde Hawaryat
and Negash Bezebeh.
     Belay Zelleqe had been active in Gojam, was given a dis-
trict there, and the title of Dejazmach, but continued his criticism of the emperor and was required to live in Addis Ababa.
He was eventually convicted of plotting to overthrow the emperor and was hanged, along with Mamo Haylu, his fellow-
conspirator.   Haylu Kebret, given a district in Wello, was
hanged for intrigue in 1962.   Geressu Duke, an Oromo, was
vocally critical and sent to govern Gore, far from Addis Ababa;
recalled and angry with the emperor, he nonetheless reported
the (1951) conspiracy of fellow patriot, Negash Bezebeh (and
others).   Negash, who had the honorific of Bidwoded (beloved)
was detained in Jimma the rest of his life, dying sometime
after 1964.
     Tekle Welde Hawaryat, perhaps the most important re-
sistance leader, had always spoken his mind to his longtime
friend, Hayle Sellase, spent 25 years in and out of detention
interspersed with high office (mayor of Addis Ababa: 1942;
Vice-Afa Negus: 1945-16; Vice-Minister of Interior: 1955-57;
Afa Negus: 1957-61) and died by his own hand in 1970, rather
than be arrested again.

The two veterans' organizations, Ethiopian Patriots' Association, whose members are of the clergy, and Ethiopian National Patriotic Association became benign fraternal orders whose prestige could not be ignored. The latter had a clubhouse at which cultural events were produced and published an Amharic newspaper "Voice of Ethiopia" which became the weekly "Addis Reporter" (see MARTYR'S DAY).

PEASANT ASSOCIATIONS. Basic to the land distribution policies of the Derg was the formation of associations to support the new structure as set forth in Proclamation 31, in 1975. Later that year, Proclamation 71 legalized these associations and by 1977, figures released that year claimed, they had a membership of 6. 7 million in 24, 700 units. In addition, 200, 000 peasants formed into "armed defense squads, " and about 2, 000 service cooperatives had been set up. Involvement in rural roadbuilding, running the schools, housing plans and other social developments grew out of this new infrastructure (see ALL-ETHIOPIA FARMERS ASSOCIATION).

This latter decree provided the associations with a large measure of autonomy which enabled them, in a way unforeseen by the Derg, to become both independent of central authority and strongly authoritarian to their members. The proclamation enabled the group to apply for government loans, weakened the trend toward individual farming entrepreneurship and gave obvious encouragement toward communes and collectivization.

Moves to integrate peasant groups into the total political framework included creation of "revolutionary administrative and development committees" which sought to link the peasant associations to the Derg-appointed regional offices and establishment of the AEFA. Farm taxes were almost non-existent--out of annual income of around $300, the farmer paid $1. 50 to the peasant association.

PEASANT RED MARCH (May 1976). The Derg attempted a "populist" solution to the Eritrean problem by offering "self-determination" to Eritrea if it joined a "united revolutionary front. " This offer was rejected by Eritrean secessionists. The Derg then mobilized some 30, 000 northern Ethiopian farmers who were told to take over Eritrea, promising them the conquered areas as their own. Eritrean forces quickly routed this untrained "peasant red march" and many died. Another similar effort in April 1977 also failed.

PETROS, Abune (1882-1936). As a priest named Abba Hayle Maryam, educated at Debre Libanos, he became confessor of Teferi Mekonnen (see HAYLE SELLASE I) and was one of the first four Ethiopians ordained as abun after centuries of (Egyptian born) Copts had held the highest office in the church. His participation in the attack on Italian-held Addis Ababa in July 1936 led to his execution in a public square, an act of outrage that did much to stiffen Ethiopian resistance. His martyrdom is the subject of two Amharic plays, and his statue was unveiled in Addis Ababa in 1946.

PILGRIMAGES. Many Oromo travel every eight years from all
over Ethiopia to the Abba Muda shrine in Borana; another site
is on the slopes of Mt. Bokkaha. The Afar pray for health,
prosperity and success in war at a shrine on Mt. Ayelu. Amharas and Tegrayans make pilgrimages to a variety of church
shrines on the relevant saints' days; praying at Debre Libanos
or Lalibela's churches brings the supplicant closer to God.
Hedar Tseyon brings vast crowds to Aksum's St. Mary of
Tseyon church (Hedar is c. 11 Nov.-11 December) and St.
Gabriel's day in the month of Tahsas (c. 11 Dec.-9 Jan.) provides thousands with a carnival-like celebration at Qulebi
(Kolubi) in Hararge province. The ultimate pilgrimage for a
Christian is to go to Jerusalem and for the Muslim there is
Mecca; each religion respects the other's achievement of these
trips. Large numbers of both Christians and Muslims attend
the annual sacrifice at Lake Besheftu, a fertility rite of pagan
origin. Muslim Gurage honor Shehotch, and pay frequent visits
to this contemporary saint's shrine. The Konta people make
pilgrimages to wherever their gallitcha (q.v.) are buried;
Sidamo elders visit two places, Mt. Bensa and the river Logida.
The Arsi (Arussi) have a special reverence for the burial place
of Shaikh Hussain (q.v.).

POETRY. The most cultivated and developed art form in Ethiopia
is poetry. There are two types: qene and getem. Qene, the
most popular, has about a dozen types, ranging from eleven
verses to two, of which semene-werq, or wax and gold, is most
favored. Qene is composed in Ge'ez and depends on religious
symbolism, but in the semene-werq form it also appears in Amharic and can have secular themes. The apparent meaning is
called "wax" (semene) and the hidden, intended meaning is the
"gold" (werq). Its most admired practitioners achieve a maxi-
mum of thought with a minimum of words in couplets. The
earliest specimens of qene are found in the reign of Eskender
(1478-94) though its invention is ascribed to "Tawanay" a Gojami of the 1300s. Others claim that Yared, the hymn composer
of the 6th century A.D. originated qene. Instruction in qene
for ecclesiastics requires from two to five years and the monasteries of Wadela, Weshara, and Gonj in Gojam are renowned
over all others.
     The punning, double-entendre, and ambiguity of semene-
werq flavor all aspects of Amhara life and the listener must
attend to latent meanings and hidden motives--it is a way of
communicating wit and insult, it is a defense of privacy and
also an outlet for dissatisfactions with parental, religious or
political authority. As long as it is clever, it is tolerated.
     Getem, composed in Amharic, is recited or sung to music.
The publication of a volume of poetry by Selomon Deresa in
1963 marked the first appearance of free verse in Amharic.

POMOA (Political Office for Mass Organization Affairs). Outgrowth
of Peoples' Organizing Political Office which was set up in
April 1976 as a result of a speech by Mengestu Hayle Maryam

outlining the Derg's (q. v.) ideology and aims, particularly the
"politicization of the masses. " Members of MEI'SON (q. v.),
particularly Hayle Fida, who had been close political coun-
selors to Mengestu's faction in the Derg, became important
functionaries in POMOA. They had originally urged establishment of a civilian political party and POMOA was supposed to
organize such a party and act as liaison between it and the Derg.
At this writing this has not yet occurred.

PORTUGAL and Ethiopia. "Discovering" the fabled "land of Prester
John" (q. v.) interested Portugal on her emergence as a maritime power under Henry, "the navigator" (1394-1460). After
Bartolomeo Dias, near the end of the 15th century, opened the
sea route around the Cape of Good Hope up the east coast of
Africa, Pero da Covilham's expedition became the first to
reach the interior of Ethiopia. He lived at the court of Eskender (1478-1494) in the last year of that monarch's life. It was
Pero who suggested to the Dowager-empress Elleni (q. v.) that
Ethiopia seek an alliance with Portugal to prevent encirclement
by Muslims. To that end she dispatched an Armenian merchant
in her service, with letters from her and Lebna Dengel (1508-
1540) for whom she was regent, to Portugal in 1509. Medieval
travel schedules being what they were, the envoy did not return
with an investigatory commission headed by Roderigo da Lima
until 1520. By then Elleni had retired to Gojam and Lebna
Dengel had repulsed an attack from the Muslim Adal principali-
ty, and denied any need for an alliance. The Portuguese left
in 1526, just as Ahmad ibn-Ibrahim began his jihad that would
overwhelm Ethiopia (see ISLAMIC CONQUEST). By 1535 Lebna
Dengel was a hunted fugitive and sent a Portuguese named Bermudez who had remained in the country, to request help. 400
Portuguese, under the command of Cristovao da Gama, arrived
in 1541, and fought with Emperor Gelawdewos (1540-1559) to
defeat the Muslims.

Good will generated by Portuguese help was dissipated in
the next 50 years by the aggressive efforts of the Jesuits (see
MISSIONS, CATHOLIC) who accompanied the musketeers.
Between 1634, when the Jesuits were expelled and 1948, when
Portugal established diplomatic relations (disrupted in June
1963) there was no substantive contact between the two nations.

The unusual architecture of Gondar has been ascribed to
Portuguese influence though it was built after the missionaries
were banished; there are the remains of a bridge over the
Abbay called the "Portuguese" bridge. The lasting contribution
of the Portuguese is the remarkable documentation of the 16th
and 17th centuries by the eye-witnesses Father Alvarez, Manoel
da Almeida, Manoel Barradas and Jeronimo Lobo.

The scholar Esteves Pereira translated from Ge'ez into
Portuguese the chronicles of Emperors Minas, Amde Tseyon,
Susneyos and Gelawdewos; their subsequent translation into
French or English made them accessible to a wider range of
Ethiopianists.

POSTAL SERVICE.   Originally a service for parcels and letters
carried by couriers who often rode on camel relays, especially
between Harar and Djibouti.   They were paid by the emperor
in land grants.   In 1896, Menilek II issued stamps for the first
time, printed earlier in France from designs by Ethiopian artists.   The victory at Adwa provided the occasion for the release
of the new stamps in seven denominations.   Mondon-Vidhailet
(see France), who brought the stamps, was asked to set up an
office of Posts and Telegraphs and this eventually became, in
1909, the Ministry of Posts, Telephones and Telegraphs.   The
year before, French technical experts came to Ethiopia to organize a postal administration and Ethiopia was finally admitted
to the International Postal Union after waiting 12 years for its
application to be acted upon.   The Ethiopian postal service is
reasonably efficient, and has been enhanced by the use of Ethiopian Airlines domestic service.   For much of its existence it
has been a profit-maker for the government.

PRESTER JOHN.   The name assigned by Europeans in the 14th
century to a legendary king of a yet-to-be discovered Christian
kingdom.   The legend spread at the time of the failure of the
Crusades and inspired the Portuguese to search for the land of
incredible riches.   The existence of Abyssinia was well known
in Cairo, Alexandria and Jerusalem.   Henry IV of England,
who visited the Holy Land in 1392-3, heard of Ethio-Egyptian
hostilities during reign of Dawit (1380-1412) and sent a letter
complimenting the monarch on his desire to liberate the Holy
Sepulchre from the Muslims in 1400, addressing him as
"Prester John."

PRINTING.   In October 1863, the Lazarist, Father Biancheri
brought in a press with Amharic type cast from matrices made
in France; he printed an Amharic catechism at Massawa but
when he died a few months later, the Turkish authorities there
destroyed the press.   Religious presses were the only ones
(Lazarists at Keren in 1879, Swedish Evangelical Mission at
Emkullo [Omtulo] in 1885) until the Italian Military Press was
established at Massawa in 1885, and a commercial press in
1890.
     Menilek II purchased a press which was delivered to Addis
Ababa in 1892/3 but had no one to make it work.   The French
Franciscans in Harar brought in a press with both Amharic
and French type in 1905; in 1908 new equipment was bought and
the printing business moved to Dire Dawa where some pam-
phlets for the government were printed as well as the newspaper Le Semeur d'Ethiopie.   Some printing equipment arrived
in Addis Ababa in 1906 and government decrees were produced.
After 1923, when Teferi Mekonnen (Hayle Sellase) established a
press, printing establishments were a fixed feature of urban
life.   Everything printed was and is still subject to censorship.

- Q -

QALLABAT (Gallabat). This town and its market area, Metemma, now are divided with Qallabat on the Sudan side of the border. From the 1820s to 1863 the region was under Ethiopian sovereignty, though from the time of the Egyptian conquest of the Sudan (1820-1840), attempts were made (1838, 1853) to launch attacks on Ethiopia by Egyptian soldiers in the direction of Gondar. Shaikh Jumma paid tribute to both Egypt and Ethiopia in the 1860s, but made it clear he preferred his obligations to Tewodros II. In 1872, the Egyptians arrested Shaikh Jumma and took him to Cairo and by the following year Egyptian garrisons were stationed on a de facto borderline stretching in a semi-circle from Qallabat to Massawa. The stage was set for the Egyptian invasion force of 1874. In 1879 Yohannes IV demanded retrocession of all Egyptian-held posts; not until 1884 through the Treaty of Adwa (q.v.) was this done, but Yohannes IV failed to leave an Ethiopian garrison at Qallabat, and it fell to the Mahdists (q.v.). In 1889 Qallabat/Metemma was the scene of the bloody battle between Ethiopian and Mahdist forces in which Yohannes IV lost his life.

QALLITCHA (Gallitcha). A sort of magician-priest in Oromo society who as those societies became Islamized, could also be called a "fuqara." They have evolved into respected adjudicators in disputes, many people (both Christian and Muslim) preferring the moral enforcement of the society in which the qallitcha functions to the law courts set up by the government.

- R -

RADIO. In 1931 the Ethiopian government signed a contract with an Italian company (Ansaldo) to build a radio station at Aqaqi, but contracted with a Swede (Frank Hammer) to run it in 1932. The Italians refused to hand it over, but Hammer and a French engineer (hired for the same job) persuaded the government to buy a transmitter from France while they trained Ethiopian telegraphers. A provisional station was inaugurated October 1933 and the Italians handed over the Aqaqi installation on 31 January 1935, but retrieved it on their conquest of Addis Ababa in May 1936, though the facility had been wrecked by the retreating Ethiopians. The stations installed by the Italians during their occupation were destroyed by them as they retreated in 1941. In 1953 shortwave broadcasting was resumed, and by 1970 Radio Ethiopia operated from Addis Ababa, Asmara, and Harar and broadcast over five shortwave and mediumwave transmitters in Amharic, English, Somali, Arabic, French and Afar. In 1959, the government authorized the World Federation of Lutheran Churches to build and operate in Addis Ababa a shortwave station; it went on the air in 1963 as Radio Voice of the Gospel and reached 12 other countries in Africa and Asia.

They transmitted news and features in English, French, Amharic, Hausa, Hindi and Swahili, and sometimes added programs in Malagasy, Arabic, Mandarin, Sinhalese, Telugu, Tamil, Farsi, and Fulani. It was taken over by the Derg in 1974.

The U.S. communications station at Kagnew operated a medium wave transmission in Asmera 1954-1970 with programming provided by the U.S. Armed Forces Radio. This was primarily for the approximately 1200 American servicemen and civilians who were assigned to Kagnew but it was listened to by thousands of Ethiopians and others in the Asmara area.

RAILROADS. One line, 191 miles long, was started in 1888 to run from Massawa west up the escarpment to Asmera which was reached in 1908 and was connected with Keren and Agordat by 1920. The second, more important, runs from Djibouti to Addis Ababa, a distance of about 500 miles. Its construction was begun in October 1897, completed up to Dire Dawa by December 1902. The original concession agreement was signed over to Alfred Ilg (q. v.) by Menilek II in 1894, but the project was fraught with financial problems, international rivalries, Ethiopian foot-dragging and raids by desert nomads. The section into Addis Ababa was not finished until 1917. A typical trip (1932) took 30 hours at 15 mph and left Djibouti once a week. It is still French-managed though called "Compagnie du Chemin de Fer Franco-Ethiopien." The line was a frequent target of Somali guerrilla attacks which put the railway out of action for extended periods in 1977 and 1978.

RASTAFARIANS. A Jamaica-based religious sect that took this name after seeing a newsreel in 1928 which showed Ras Teferi Mekonnen being given the crown of a negus by Empress Zewditu. As Hayle Sellase I, he made an official visit to Jamaica in 1966 where he received a wildly adulatory reception by the "Rastas" on his arrival at the airport in Kingston. Cultists made one attempt at settling in Ethiopia but were not made welcome.

REBELLIONS, PEASANT (1942-1970). The Weyene (connotes "solidarity" in Tegrigna) rebellion against the government engaged some 10,000 government troops with British advisers and military assistance (planes and artillery) from June to October 1943. It was prefaced by unsuccessful government action against the Raya (Azebu) Oromo from April to July 1942, whom the government was determined to crush, not only for their refusal to pay taxes but for their notorious cooperation with the Italians in 1935-36. The Raya and Azebo joined the people of Enderta and south Temben under the leadership of Hayle Maryam Redda (of Enderta) who vowed to liberate Tegray from the Shewan-Amhara hegemony and declared war on "Catholics, Protestants, and officials who smoked and wore long pants" (a euphemism for the government appointees). Though Hayle Maryam had a personal grudge (he had been a chief in Enderta 1938-1941 under the Italians and confirmation in this post was

refused after the restoration), the causes of the rebellion went
much deeper than his proclamation would indicate for some
20,000 peasants, well-armed, fought to be relieved of oppressive officialdom.   After their defeat, extremely punitive penalties were imposed.   Hayle Maryam did not surrender until
1946 and was imprisoned for 20 years; he was appointed head
of the militia in Tegray by the Derg in 1975.

From late 1963 to 1970 there was rebellion in Bale (q.v.)
of an entirely different sort and though supported and abetted
by the Somali government, it was not a Somali plot.   The primarily Muslim Oromo and ethnic Somali inhabitants had accu-
mulated resentments from the bloody campaigns of conquest by
Menilek II's armies 1885-1897, and the imposition of Christian
Amhara rule which, with a few exceptions, brought governors
and soldiers with no tolerance for their traditional ways, took
their land and asked for taxes.   The rebellion took the form of
ambushes and lightning attacks that steadily bled the territorial
army (no casualty figures available).   Deserted by their Somali
allies in 1969 and cornered, after intensive aerial bombard-
ments and threats to the peasants who had been their support,
the rebel leaders surrendered one by one; the last, Waqo Gutu,
negotiated his surrender under promise of a pardon, which was
honored.   The years of suffering by the peasants resulted in a
slight improvement in educational and medical services and improved communication with central government.

The period 1968-69 saw an armed rebellion in Gojam,
sparked by the Agricultural Income Tax Proclamation of 1967,
and fueled by cruelty and corruption of local administrators.
Gojami farmers had forced the government to suspend tax
measures they did not like in 1950-51 by more or less peaceful protest and petitions; the 1967 law was not preceded by any
explanation and they ignored the government's request to elect
local people to measure their land for tax purposes.   By February 1968, 65 percent of the population of eastern Gojam (four
of the seven provinces) was in revolt with attacks on district
governors, tax assessors, the auxiliary police force, nech
lebasha (who acted like vigilantes and were hated), and on any
person or group that cooperated with the government program.
There was no clarion call against the emperor (as in Bale and
Tegray), for there was a naive belief that he did not know what
was being done in his name.   Investigative committees were
sent from the capital; the level of violence ebbed somewhat.   In
September 1968 the government offered general amnesty and re-
instatement of those officials the rebels wanted, but they were
ordered to submit all their taxes in arrears by December 1968.
Resistance persisted, and though government troops had been
employed sparingly, in October and November the Airforce
bombed villages, and three more battalions along with 700 police
were sent to Gojam.   All resistance ended by May 1969 and the
peasants were exempted from tax arrears for the 19 years,
1950-1968 (see COUPS D'ETAT).

RELIGIONS.   Monophysite Christianity is practiced by perhaps 50

percent of the population.   Ethiopia is the only country in the
world of Semitic language to have Christianity as the state religion.   Adherents to Islam are thought to rival Christians in
number, but not in unity and some 4-5 million persons are
animists; though the name of their god differs, he is associated
with the sky.   A primitive form of Judaism exists among the
Felasha (q. v.).   Roman Catholics are a small minority as are
various Protestant adherents (see MEKANE YESUS; MISSIONS,
PROTESTANT; MISSIONS, CATHOLIC).

Monophysitism is the belief that in Christ there was but
one divine nature, opposing the formula of the rest of Christianity that there were two natures and one person in Christ.   The
Ethiopians call the belief that Christ was from two natures that
effected a perfect union--tawahedo in Ge'ez.   Other Monophysite
churches are the Coptic church of Egypt, the Syrian Christians
and one in South India.

Religious beliefs of the Ethiopian Christians include other
supernatural beings besides God and the devil, saints and
angels; the zar and the advar must be placated; there is the
feared buda who takes a human form, usually in the manually-
skilled people such as blacksmiths, tanners, potters and
weavers.

RESISTANCE GROUPS see PATRIOTS; BLACK LIONS

REVOLUTION OF 1974.   Not a coup d'état but a "creeping revolution" led to the overthrow of Hayle Sellase I in September 1974.
Months of festering unrest--student protest marches, discontent
by teachers over education policies, demands by isolated army
units for better pay and more privileges, rumblings about famine in Wello province caused by administrative incompetence
and corruption and a sudden rise in gasoline prices reached an
intolerable level in January-February 1974 in Addis Ababa.
Literally unable to govern, the cabinet resigned on 27 February.
Moving to establish some semblance of control, the emperor
named a progressive monarchist, Endalkachew Mekonnen (q. v.)
as premier on 1 March.   Constitutional revision and greater
civil rights were promised; demands of the Confederation of
Labor Unions were agreed to and investigation of corruption
and mismanagement in all sectors was announced.   Not until
2 July did the self-styled Armed Forces Co-ordinating Committee start broadcasting that they were the agents of revolution.
It was still unclear who headed the group of 120 men, though
General Aman Mikael Amdon (q. v.) was its spokesman.   The
Armed Forces committee took an increasingly hard line against
Eritrean secessionists, and favored punishment of all those involved with imperial power either by birth, privilege or appointment, but as the committee refused to accept responsibility for running the government, the powerless Endalkachew
Mekonnen resigned on 22 July.   He was arrested on 1 August
and Mikael Emru, another well-born progressive was named
premier.   Nationalization, eradication of Hayle Sellase's name,
expropriation of royal assets, detention of "enemies of pro-

gress" (including wives and children), banning of strikes and demonstrations, abolishment of parliament, suspension of the Constitution and stringent censorship followed. On 18 November it was announced that Major Mengestu Hayle Maryam (q. v.) was the head of the Executive Committee of the Provisional Military Administrative Council, called the Derg (q. v.). The night of 23-24 November, 59 officials associated with the regime were executed without trial and then Aman Mikael Amdon and several aides died fighting arrest at his home. 13 December, Ethiopia was declared a socialist state and 21 March 1975 the formal revocation of the monarchy was announced (see POMOA; ALL-ETHIOPIA SOCIALIST MOVEMENT; YEKATIT 66 IDEOLOGICAL SCHOOL).

ROCK-HEWN CHURCHES (monolithic). The eleven monolithic churches at Lalibela in Lasta province are among the least known wonders of the world. Little can be substantiated about how and by whom they were built, but tradition states they were constructed during the 13th century reign of Emperor Lalibela (q. v.) who wanted to create a New Jerusalem since the Saracens had taken over the holy city.

Hundreds of rock and cave churches are in use in the northern part of the country and some differ from the Lalibela churches in the refinement of their interior design. Lalibela is distinct for the emphasis on exterior architecture. Most of these churches are well off the beaten path; Lalibela became a star attraction of the Ethiopian Tourist Organization, accessible by air followed by a mule trek or a bumpy ride in a Landrover.

The 126 rock churches in Tegray were given a scholarly description for the first time in 1966 by an Ethiopian priest, Abba Tewelde Medhen Yosef, before an International Conference of Ethiopianists in Addis Ababa. After his death the following year, many foreigners investigated his findings, among whom were two intrepid English ladies, Ivy Pearce and Ruth Plant, who have described many other churches. Only a few are located in the southwest.

RUSSIA and Ethiopia. Fourteenth-century contacts between priests of the Russian and Ethiopian Orthodox churches in Jerusalem were among Russia's earliest sources of information about Ethiopia. General Avram Petrovich Hannibal declared himself of noble Ethiopian birth to Peter I (Czar, 1689-1725). His descendant, the writer Alexander Pushkin, is cited by the Soviets today as a sentimental link between the two countries, though Hannibal's origins are unsubstantiated. Elizabeth (Czarina, 1741-1762) initiated a special guard of "Ethiopians" (slaves purchased for their height and good looks in Constantinople and Cairo) who staffed the Mariinski palace up to 1917.

A Ukrainian mining engineer, E. P. Kovalevsky, led a Russian expedition down the Blue Nile and into eastern Gojam in 1847-48, but made no contact with any government leader. Yohannes IV sought support from Russia (and other nations) in the 1870s for his efforts to oust the soldiers of Egypt from his

borders and was disgusted at the lack of response or even ack-
nowledgment of the gold cross he had sent as a gift for the
Czar; he refused to permit Nicholas Ashinov to visit his
court in 1885, but through Ras Alula at Adwa, gave permission for Ashinov to create a Cossack settlement on some
vaguely defined area in the gulf of Aden, and assigned two
Ethiopians to return to Russia for education.   Yohannes IV sent
gifts to Alexander III (Czar, 1881-1894) and enjoined him to
purchase arms for him.   Well-intentioned public support in
Russia of Ashinov's aims to strengthen ties between Ethiopian
and Russian Orthodoxy raised funds for his expedition.   When
Ashinov landed at Tajura in April 1888 he found a message from
Yohannes IV agreeing to permit monks from Jerusalem to attend
the 900th anniversary of the Russian Orthodox Church to be
held in Kiev.   Ashinov escorted the priests to Russia.   The
Ethiopians were ignored in Kiev, though one of them made a
speech there on 15 July 1888.   After much pressure the Czar
agreed to receive Ashinov and the priests.   By now Ashinov had
acquired French support as well as generous backing from the
Holy Synod (Russia's) and Russian businessmen and was able to
charter a boat from the Russian Volunteer Fleet.   He and
Archimandrite Paissi and about 150 men, women and children
left Odessa on 10 December 1888 and landed at Tajura 18 January 1889, proceeding inland to a deserted fort at Sagallo.   After
repeated requests from French authorities to vacate this spot,
claimed by them, they were shelled by a French gunboat on 17
February, resulting in twenty wounded and five dead (two
children, three women).   This soured the Franco-Russian alliance for six months until mutual self-interest prevailed.   One
member of the Ashinov party, V. Mashcov, made his way from
Obok to the court of Menilek II in mid-1889.   He stayed two
months and planted in the mind of that sovereign some notion
of the might and power of Russia.   Mashcov's favorable articles on Menilek and his people, "the black Christians," re-
fueled the interest of the Russian public and the Holy Synod.
Russia refused to recognize the claims of Italy over Ethiopia
in 1890 and blocked the Italian attempt--at the Brussels anti-
slavery conference that year--to speak as representatives of
Ethiopia.   These policies were based on inter-European rivalries, not on dedication to Ethiopian independence.
     Despite a valid scholarly study in 1887 which pointed out
irreconcilable differences between Russian and Ethiopian orthodoxy, the illusion persisted in Russia that a union of the two
churches was possible.   Two monks accompanied Mashcov on
his second trip, which was official, but by the time Mashcov
reached Shewa in October 1891, he had quarreled with the
monks and they had returned to Russia; so Mashcov made the
overtures regarding the church, but returned to Russia only
with a request from Menilek for an artillery officer to train
troops.   Nothing substantive was done to assist Menilek before
the war with Italy, but evidence of Russian and French sympathy steeled Menilek's determination to stand up to Italy.
The exchange of missions, Nicholas Leontiev to Ethiopia

(March/April 1895) and <u>Fitwrari</u> Demtew to Russia (July/August 1895) led to a Russian Red Cross mission to treat the Ethiopian wounded after the war.   A subsequent medical mission 1898-1906 was crucial to the development of "modern" medicine in Ethiopia.

Diplomatic relations were established with the arrival of P. M. Vlassov in January 1898 and his premises became the most impressive legation in the capital, with a guard of 40 cossacks.   Exploration and services by A. X. Bulatovich, M. P. Dragomanov and N. Kurmakov were a feature of Ethio-Russian relations in this period.   The legation and medical services were reduced after 1906, and the legation closed down after the Russian revolution in 1919; some hundred or so "white" Russians emigrated to Ethiopia in the years that followed.   The Soviet Union established diplomatic relations in 1944 and in 1959 extended four hundred million ruble (US$100 million) credit to the government of Hayle Sellase.   Education of Ethiopians in Moscow increased substantially in the 1960s, one of the graduates being the present leader of the Derg (q.v.).

Technical assistance from Eastern Europe has included the oil refinery at Assab (Soviet Union), hand-tool factory (Poland), fishing industry (Czechoslovakia).   Scholarship in the Soviet Union has been led by Boris Turaev and I. Krachkovsky.   An important guide in English to source material published in the Soviet Union was issued in 1980 (see Darch, Colin in the Bibliography).

- S -

SAHO (people and language).   Of an eastern Cushitic language family, the Saho live in Tegray and Eritrea along the coastal area. They are primarily Muslim, though one Saho group, the Erob in eastern Agame, about 10,000 strong, are Christian.   The largest tribe in the Asawerta (18,000), some of whom could have been nominally Christian under Zera Yaqob (1434-1468) but are now Muslim of the Mirghaniya order (Muhammad Uthman al-Mirghani, 1793-1852) as are the Beni Amer and Habab.   The next largest group are the Meni-Fere (11,000) who have two legends about their ancestry: one that they derive from "Mena" of royal Abyssinian stock, and the other (after they became Muslim) tracing a connection to the Prophet Muhammad.   They are pastoralists and nomadic, now quite peaceful though in the 1860s they appeared in travelers' tales as wild and feared robbers.   They elect their leaders democratically.

SARTSA DENGEL, Emperor (1563-1597).   Of necessity a warrior king, fighting the last attempts at Muslim conquest from the city-state of Harar, and by the Ottoman Turks moving from Massawa into the highlands (see ISLAMIC CONQUEST).   The influence of his mother, Selas Hayle, and his aunt, Amate Giyorgis, up to 1579 and the powerful role played by his wife, Mary-

am Sena, marked his reign. Maryam Sena gave him three
daughters, and from a mistress, Haregawa (a converted
Felasha), he had several sons one of whom, Yaqob, succeeded
to the throne. The Oromo penetration had superseded Islam
as the principal threat to the integrity of the Christian kingdom;
Boran tribes had occupied Shewa and Damot by 1587. Sartsa
Dengel died of illness on his last expedition, to fight the Oromo
in Damot.

SEBAGADES WELDU, Ras (1818-1831) see TEGRAY

SEBLE WENGEL, Empress (1552-1568). The wife, and only one
insofar as records show, of Emperor Lebna Dengel, whom she
married sometime after 1508 since he was only about ten years
old when he acceded that year. Only after the old Empress
Elleni (q.v.) died in 1552 could Seble Wengel carry the title
Etege. She had four sons and several daughters; one son was
killed during the Islamic conquest (q.v.) and another, Minas,
was captured but ransomed by Seble Wengel in 1543 after her
eldest son, Gelawdewos (1540-1559) won victory over the armies
of Islam. She and her daughters and youngest son, Yaqob, had
taken refuge in the monastery of Debra Damo (q.v.) before her
husband's death, and came down from that refuge (accessible
only by lowering and raising a basket) when the Portuguese arrived in June 1541. She and her women companions endured
the hardships of the military campaign as nurses and provision-
ers; her presence had much to do with the return of many de-
serters. Discredited for her injudicious influence during the
reign of Minas (1559-1563) she was still powerful enough to ensure the succession of Minas' son, Sartsa Dengel (q.v.) in 1563
sharing the regency with the boy's mother, Selas Hayle, for a
short time.

SEMENE-WERQ see POETRY

SENEDU GEBRU, Weyzero ("lady"). The first woman elected to
parliament (1957) at the same time she was director from 1946
of the Menen School for Girls, and active in the Ethiopian
Women's Welfare Association. She was married to Major Asefa
Lemma (Vice-Minister of Interior in 1960) after marriages to
Amede Ali and Lorenzo T'ezaz (q.v.) were dissolved.
    As the daughter of foreign-educated Kantiba Gebru Desta
(q.v.) she and her sister Yewub-dar were sent to his Protestant-
mission friends in Switzerland to be educated in 1928. They returned as the war with Italy started. She joined Ras Emru's
(q.v.) resistance group in Gore and was among those captured
and sent to Italy in December 1936. After the war she wrote a
play about the massacre of Yekatit 12 (see MARTYRS DAY), and
other books.

SENHET see BOGOS

SEYUM MENGESHA, Ras (1887-1960) see TEGRAY

SEYUM TEKLE HAYMANOT see HAYLU, Ras

SHANQELLA (Shanqila, Shangalla). An Amharic term used in a
    derogatory way to describe the Hamitic-Nilotic peoples with
    dark skins, thicker lips and kinkier hair than the Amhara-
    Tegray. More specifically means the Berta people of the Beni
    Shangul region. They were much desired as slaves by raiders
    on both sides of the Sudan-Ethiopian border. In 1770, a con-
    tingent of them served as the imperial guard in Gondar, special-
    ly dressed and on horseback. At the coronation of Menilek II
    in 1889 they marched past, dressed in velvet tunics and carry-
    ing swords. In 1899-1900 the Marquis de la Guiborgère, work-
    ing for Ras Mekonnen, was permitted to give marching and
    military training to 200, part of a large number captured on a
    military campaign in Beni Shangul.

SHEBA, QUEEN OF see MAQEDA

SHEWA (Shoa, Showa)--province and dynasty. Geographically it is
    the center of Ethiopia with its capital at Addis Ababa, but only
    since 1889 has it been the political center. Prior to the late
    10th century when the eastern plateau bordering Ifat (q.v.) was
    the site of a Muslim sultanate, little is known, but by the early
    12th century, the original Sidamo inhabitants had become tribu-
    tary to the Christian kings (see ZEGWE) whose base was in
    Lasta. Certainly during the reign of Amde Tseyon (1314-1344)
    the plateau was the center of the Christian empire. It was con-
    quered by a Muslim force in 1531 (see ISLAMIC CONQUEST)
    and occupied for 14 years until Emperor Gelawdewos ousted the
    occupiers. Over the next century Oromo migrants surrounded
    and even dominated parts of Shewa and in the 17th-18th centuries
    it was the most southerly area of empire as the imperial court
    and the head of the monastery of Debre Libanos (q.v.) had moved
    for safety to the north where they remained, establishing Gondar
    as the imperial center.
        Menz, a district in northeastern Shewa on a 10,000 foot
    high plateau, had escaped the Muslim incursion, surrounded as
    it was by protective mountains; about 1700 its chief, Negasse,
    began the reconstitution of the province, and begat a dy-
    nasty that continued and constantly expanded under Sebestyanos
    (1705-1720) and Abeye (1720-1745). Emperor Iyasu (1730-1755)
    granted the title meredazmach (roughly "terrorizing commander")
    to Abeye when he brought tribute to Gondar. Abeye's son, Amha
    Iyasu, had a long rule (1745-1775) and also paid tribute to Gon-
    dar. As Gondar came more under the sway of the Yejju Oromo
    (see ZEMENE MESAFINT) Shewa became more independent.
        During the period 1775-1808 Asfa Wessen started using the
    title ras (prince); he founded Sela Dengay and Ankober and
    doubled the size of Shewa by conquest, dividing it into four dis-
    tricts. For the last 15 years of his rule he was blind, and there
    were some uprisings, including an unsuccessful revolt by his son,
    Wessen Seged, who nonetheless succeeded to the throne.
        Despite his short reign (1808-1813) Wessen Seged was known

for his religious toleration and sensible administration, appointing Muslim governors where Muslims predominated, and rewarding loyal Oromo subjects. His policies excited the hostility of the clergy and the Amhara Christians who arranged his assassination in June 1813. His son by Zenebe Werq Gole (q. v.) of Menz succeeded.

Sahle Sellase (1818-1847) took upon himself the title of negus (king) and carried on the conquests to the southwest. He had a great many "wives" and children but Hayle Melekot, one of the sons of his legal wife Bezebesh, succeeded him. Hayle's son, Menilek II (q. v.), the tenth in the Shewan dynasty line, was destined to return the center of empire to Shewa.

SHIFTA. In ancient times the word had a political connotation applying to someone who rebelled against his feudal lord, and could apply to persons of high status. Kasa Haylu, who became Emperor Tewodros II in 1855, was called a "shifta," as was Susneyos before he succeeded to the throne in 1632. Shiftas were in some cases idealized as "Robin Hoods," handsome, brave, expert singers of challenging war chants, somewhat like the fabled, swashbuckling "highwayman." More recently it applies to any person doing robbery, usually in a rural area, sometimes with a political purpose but mostly for personal profit.

SHIHAB AD-DIN. A Yemenite chronicler who wrote an eye-witness account, "Futuh-al-Habasha," about 1559 on the conquest of Ethiopia by Ahmad ibn-Ibrahim (see ISLAMIC CONQUEST). Though glorifying the jihad, he provided unusual descriptions of the people and the rich decoration of churches and the manuscripts found in them in the early sixteenth century (destroyed by the conquerors). The text was translated into French by R. Basset in 1898.

SHUM. This word for "chief" has several permutations (see CHIQA-SHUM). In the plural "shumament" it can mean "authorities." It can be attached to the title of a court functionary as "gotara-shum" meaning the person in charge of honey and grain stores. Wagshum was the title held only by the hereditary chiefs of Wag, who were believed to be descendants of the Zagwe dynasty (q. v.) though it was not exclusive to one man. Wagshum Gebru commanded an army for Yohannes in 1875 as well as Wagshum Beru, who was governing Wag. Menilek II allowed Wagshum Beru to outrank the rases (princes) at his court in 1894, giving him a gold basin instead of silver, for the customary hand washing, as well as drummers to precede his entrance. In 1909, Menilek appointed a non-Wag descendent as Wagshum; soon after the title faded into insignificance.

The governors of Temben and Agame tended to have "shum" preceding their names, e. g. Shum-Agame Weldu, but that fell out of use by Menilek's time (1889-1913).

Shum-shir became the term for the technique "promote-demote" by which Hayle Sellase rotated offices so that no one person could gather a small empire around himself.

SIDAMA PEOPLE see SIDAMO

SIDAMO (area and people). Of the eight distinct groups of Sidama people, four reside in areas that are part of Shewa province, and three in the area denoted as Sidamo-Borana province. They speak a Cushitic tongue and have an ensete-planting culture as opposed to the Amhara cereal-growing agriculture. Before the Oromo (Galla) migrations of the 16th century they inhabited almost the whole of the southern part of Ethiopia. The Oromo used the term "sidama" meaning "foreigner" and one of the 8 groups retain that name. An interchange of Sidama and Oromo institutions took place, principalities formed, some adopted Islam, others retained animist beliefs, and one group, the Kembata, became Christian. By 1891, all of the Sidama people were incorporated into the empire.

SLAVERY. Domestic slavery and slaves as exports are as old as the state; and though both activities were legally abolished in 1923, they were not effectively erased until the 1940s. Domestic slavery was recognized in the law book of the 13th century, Fetha Negest, with strict rules of behavior for both master and slave. The late 19th-century estimate that slaves constituted as much as a quarter of the population may have been accurate but it was difficult for foreigners to distinguish free men who were tenant farmers and had to pay land rent to an absentee landlord, from slaves. The export trade, engaged in primarily by Muslims with connections in the Middle East where Ethiopian slaves fetched the highest prices, has been estimated for the years 1800-1850 at 1,250,000.

   Whenever pressed by some horrified European, Emperors Tewodros, Yohannes and Menilek would issue an edict forbidding the selling of slaves; edicts that did not apply at all to domestic slaves. Occasionally arrests would be made although slave traders were adroit at changing their routes.

   In 1923 Empress Zewditu (under pressure from her regent, Teferi Mekonnen) established the death penalty for anyone who bought and sold slaves. In 1924 laws were enacted making provision for the freeing of domestic slaves and their offspring. In 1926 Ethiopia signed the International Slavery Convention. Pressed by the British government to do more than these pro-forma actions, Hayle Sellase attached a British adviser (Franz de Halpert) to the Ministry of Interior in 1930. Before the Italian invasion of 1935, considerable progress had been made through the establishment of Anti-slavery bureaus in known slave market areas.

   In the areas they controlled during the occupation, the Italians abolished slavery and claimed that 125,000 were freed and placed in "Villages of Liberty," and that they employed many ex-slaves as salaried workers on road and building projects. The post-war period saw additional legal penalties passed and

enforced, and though authorities are reasonably certain a boot-
leg trade still exists, it is very small, as slavery is also forbidden in those countries which were former customers.

SOMALIA and Ethiopia.   Ancient animosities (see ISLAMIC CON-
    QUEST), the uprising of Muhammad Abd Allah Hassan (q. v.)
    from 1899 to 1920 against British, Italian and Ethiopian colo-
    nialism, its convenience as a staging area for Italian troops
    attacking Ethiopia, along with a continuing dispute over the
    Ogaden (q. v.), have plagued relations between Ethiopia and its
    Muslim neighbor in the horn of Africa.   Ethnic Somalis live on
    both sides of border lines drawn in 1897, 1908, 1948, and
    1954 between Ethiopia and British and Italian Somalilands, of
    which the present republic was formed in 1960.   Somalia re-
    gards itself as the protector of all ethnic Somalis on both sides
    of this line.   Within months of the formation of the new Somalia,
    clashes had broken out between the Ethiopian army and Somali
    nomads over the usual issues of smuggling, stock theft and tax
    collection; this escalated into an all-out war between govern-
    ment forces until February 1964 when a cease-fire was ar-
    ranged through the OAU; continued attempts at a settlement on
    the diplomatic level were disregarded by leaders in the Ogaden.
    In 1978 after a series of successful incursions by Somali
    "volunteers" including disruption of the Djibouti-Addis Ababa
    rail service, Ethiopia called for help from Soviet "advisers"
    and Cuban troops and succeeded in re-establishing an uneasy
    military control over the disputed region.   In late August 1980,
    Somalia claimed that Ethiopia had invaded its northwestern
    frontier but had been driven back; Ethiopia strongly denied it
    had launched any attack.   Earlier in the month, the United
    States and Somalia negotiated an agreement providing the U. S.
    with facilities at Berbera port for U. S. naval vessels.   In re-
    turn, the U. S. was said to be providing about $85, 000, 000 in
    military credits and economic aid, an apparent response to the
    Soviet Union's invasion of Afghanistan in December 1979.   In
    September, Ethiopia sent formal protests about this agreement
    to Pres. Carter and certain Congressional Committees.   So-
    malia and Ethiopia do not maintain diplomatic relations.

SPAIN and Ethiopia.   Ethiopian emissaries went to Spain and to
    Avignon (residence of Pope Clement V) in 1299-1314 and to the
    court of Affonso of Aragon in 1427 and 1434.   The next re-
    corded contact was four centuries later when Abargués de
    Sostén came to the court of Yohannes IV in 1881, with a
    vaguely defined mission of seeking a coaling station for Spanish
    ships along a coast not under the control of Ethiopia at the
    time.   Spain has a legation in Addis Ababa.

SPORTS.   Genna is a type of field hockey where an indefinite num-
    ber of players use curved clubs to stroke a leather-covered
    ball past the defender's goal line.   Gougs is played by large
    groups of horsemen riding furiously towards each other trying
    to unseat their foes by launching long staves at each other.

Wrestling, riding, and sword play were popular sports in the sixteenth century. With the advent of a secular educational system in the 20th century, team sports like soccer and basketball have replaced the ancient competitions, and army installations have provided a variety of sports. It was from the army that Ethiopia's first great international sports heroes came; Abebe Biqila (q. v.) broke both world and Olympic records when, running barefooted, he won the marathon at the Rome Olympic Games in 1960, and in Tokyo in 1964; his teammate, Mamo Welde, won the marathon in 1968.

As the first Olympic gold-medal winner from an African nation, Abebe Biqila was credited with stimulating greater sports consciousness throughout Africa. The unknown Eritrean, Ethiopian Air Force captain Miruts Yifter startled the Moscow Olympics in 1980 by winning both the 5,000- and 10,000-meter races, the only track and field competitor to win two gold medals.

STUDENT MOVEMENTS (Addis Ababa, 1960-1977). The anti-monarchial persistence of the university students, beginning with vocal support for the attempted coup of 1960, helped set the stage for the successful military coup of 1974. They were much influenced by the informality of Peace Corps teachers from the U. S. who supported the notion that freedom of expression was a basic right, and by the presence of students from other African countries (200 scholarships had been granted by the emperor) with whom they found Ethiopia compared unfavorably in development.

They demonstrated, boycotted and went on strike under two umbrellas: The National Union of Ethiopian University Students (NUEUS) and the University Students Union of Addis Ababa (USUAA); by 1968 they had drawn in high school and secondary school students and many teachers. The government responded to their demands occasionally with concessions but more often with guns and tear-gas, beatings, detention and suspension of all assembly and publication rights. The students in turn often used rocks, fire bombs and physical force. They wanted redistribution of land to the oppressed, abolishment of the monarchy, fair exams, expulsion of all foreign teachers (they saw the Peace Corps as part of the U. S. assistance which kept Hayle Sellase in power). They publicized the plight of beggars, who were frequently rounded up and placed in camps for cosmetic purposes, and did much to expose the government's main secret: starvation in Wello province 1972-73. In a brief hiatus in 1970, the students took part enthusiastically in a ten-day sanitation and anti-cholera campaign earning praise from the mayor of Addis Ababa.

The student population after the revolution of 1974, joined other organizations demanding a civilian rather than a military government. They were gunned down by the thousands during the Red Terror (1977-78) (see ETHIOPIAN PEOPLES' REVOLUTIONARY PARTY).

SUDAN and Ethiopia.   Ethiopia's longest frontier (1,600 miles) is
on the west with the Sudan; the Blue Nile (Abbay) rises in
Ethiopia, flows through the Sudan and joins the White Nile at
the capital, Khartoum.   As Sudan was not an independent nation
until 1953, relations between the two countries were conducted
with Sudan's conquerors: first the Egyptians who occupied it
between 1820 and 1840 and founded Khartoum; then with Anglo-
Egypt which was forced to confront the Mahdist (q.v.) uprising
against its rule from 1881-1898.   Ethiopia assisted Anglo-Egypt
(under the terms of the Treaty of Adwa signed with Vice-Admiral
Hewett) in removing its troops from Sudan-based forts under attack by the Mahdists in 1884-1885.   The Gojam king, Tekle
Haymanot (q.v.) suffered a defeat by Mahdist armies in January
1888 when thousands of Ethiopians were taken to Khartoum as
slaves.

Qallabat was a border town trading in slaves and goods; its
chief official paid taxes both to Ethiopia and Egypt in the 1860s
before the Mahdists occupied it.   The largest economic center
in the borderlands between 1904 and 1955 was Gambella, a
steamer port on the Baro-Sobat river.   Kasala, capital of Taka
district, was another key border town.   Borders and grazing
rights were negotiated there between the new Anglo-Egyptian
condominium government and Italian-held Eritrea (q.v.) between
1898 and 1904; further agreements between the condominium and
Ethiopia delimited the rest of the frontier with a 1902 agreement
specifying that Ethiopia would not interfere with the flow of the
Nile.   Ethiopia, however, has always taken the view that this
treaty provision is not valid as it is "an unequal" provision in
an imposed treaty.

With the rise of Eritrean liberation movements in the
1950s, relations soured as the Sudan provided a base of operations and for those (many of them Christians) fleeing the civil
war in southern Sudan.   Sudan renegotiated in 1972 all borders
with Ethiopia, with a few modifications.   In the 1973 Addis
Ababa Agreement, Hayle Sellase was instrumental in mediating
a solution to the civil war between northern and southern Sudan.
It was generally understood that Ethiopia would no longer give
haven to the southern Sudanese if Sudan equally shut out the
Eritreans.

Although diplomatic relations continue, the anti-communist
President Nimeiri of the Sudan took a much harsher line toward
the Marxist Derg after the 1974 revolution in Ethiopia that overthrew Hayle Sellase.   Once again Eritreans are believed to receive sanctuary in the Sudan and some of the anti-Derg guerrilla
movements (see ETHIOPIAN DEMOCRATIC UNION) have used
Sudanese border areas as operational bases.

Reports in April 1980 claimed that close to 500,000 Ethiopian refugees had inundated the eastern Sudan.   The U.N. High
Commission for Refugees stated that Sudan had settled about
42,000 of these, but that this amount was "just a drop in the
ocean," according to a U.N. representative.

SUEZ CANAL.   Its opening in November 1869 enhanced economic

and political importance for Ethiopia and the entire Red Sea
area.   Almost immediately, European shipping began to ply
the canal and fueling stations were required along the coast.
Ports such as Assab and Obok were set up under the control
of various European countries which preferred to bypass
Egyptian-controlled Massawa.   The Khedive of Egypt commissioned Giuseppe Verdi to write the opera Aïda to celebrate the
opening of both the canal and the Cairo Opera House, but it
was not performed until 1871.   The libretto tells of the love of
Radames, an Egyptian captain, for Aida, an Ethiopian princess:
four years after the opera premiered, to great acclaim, Egypt
and Ethiopia were at war.

SUSNEYOS, Emperor (1607-1632).   Remembrance of this emperor's
   disestablishment of the Ethiopian Orthodox Church between
   1614 and 1632 has obscured some of his virtues.   He was a
   grown man with many wives and children when he won a four-
   year struggle for the throne over the supporters of Ze-dengel
   (1603-4) and Yaqob (1597-1603) and had spent most of his life
   as a shifta (q.v.) fighting the Oromo in his father's province
   of Gojam.
      His conduct at court had a democratic flavor: he refused
   to conceal himself behind the curtain that monarchs customarily
   used to keep them from the vulgar gaze, nor did he require
   the baring of the chest and prostration on the ground that accompanied appeals to the emperor.   He discontinued privileges
   for sons of nobility at court and filled their positions with boys
   from Oromo and Agew areas whom he asked the Jesuits to
   educate.   For this behavior his critics said he was debasing imperial dignity and mystery.
      He prohibited the sale of slaves to Muslims in 1619 which
   ended the peace between the crown and the Sultan of Awsa who
   thrived on this trade.   With the help of the Portuguese priests
   and other craftsmen he built several stone churches near Lake
   Tana, a two-storied palace and a bridge over the Abbay (the
   ruins of it can still be seen).   In the end, he admitted he had
   miscalculated the strength of religious orthodoxy in his people,
   took steps to end the religious fratricide caused by the proclamation that Catholicism would become the state religion and asked
   his son Fasiledes to take over the throne.   Three months later
   he died.

SWEDEN and Ethiopia.   The basis for the extensive relations between
   these two countries was laid by Swedish missionaries beginning
   in 1866; they performed much useful work in the fields of education, medicine and printing.   This record disposed Hayle Sellase I
   to ask for political, technical and military experts "with a
   Christian outlook" when he visited Sweden as Prince Regent in
   1924.   Johannes Kolmodin, son of the director of the early
   Evangelical Mission in Eritrea, became his political adviser in
   1931 and on Kolmodin's death in 1933, Eric Virgin replaced him.
   Army officers were brought in to serve as instructors at Holeta
   military school 1934-36.

Sweden's diplomatic relations (mostly involved with the missionaries) were handled by the German Legation from 1911-1919; Britain represented them from 1924 to 1929 when a physician already working in Ethiopia, Knut Hanner, was appointed as consul.

All missionaries (except one nurse) and all the military advisers had to leave the country after Italy occupied Addis Ababa in May 1936. The mission hospitals had been placed at the disposal of the Ethiopian Red Cross during the fighting; a Red Cross team had arrived from Sweden as had an aviator, Carl von Rosen, who flew some 55 mercy missions before the Italian conquest.

In the post-war period, the only texts available to reopen schools were those that had been printed at the Swedish press at Emkullo (Omtulo) many years before. Sweden's foreign economic assistance program provided some 137 experts in various fields by 1947, not counting the returned missionaries (about 103). Beginning in 1952, the number of government-sponsored personnel in Ethiopia began to diminish as those from America increased, though many of the Swedish educational, medical, agricultural and building technologists remained.

Swedish scholarship in Ethiopian studies has relied on the observations of the earlier missionaries who also provided the German staffed Littmann expedition with much of its folk material; publications by K. G. Roden and Johannes Kolmodin are notable. Today Sven Rubenson, for many years a professor of history at the University in Addis Ababa, is a leader in the field of Ethiopian political history.

- T -

TAXATION. From antiquity, taxation took the form of tribute gathered from the farmers and herdsmen by the provincial or district governor, who took a percentage for himself and passed the rest on to the imperial coffers. A local official, the neggadras, collected taxes from market transactions and caravanseries. Menilek II imposed the asrat (q. v.) which, for a tax on one-tenth of his crop, relieved the peasant of the obligation of quartering soldiers.

Taxes, which fell principally on the peasantry, were paid occasionally in money, usually Maria Teresa talers (dollars), but mostly in kind or labor. Rapacious landlords could, by onerous tax demands, force farmers to migrate. Default of taxes could mean confiscation of the peasant's cattle which were then killed and the hides sold. The basic tax in Tegray was traditionally a tithe; this spread to the rest of the country by the end of the 19th century.

Different crops paid different levels of taxes; coffee, for example, as a valuable cash crop, was taxed at a special rate. Livestock in Tegray rated cash payments, perhaps one taler for two oxen, per year. By the 1930s, this levy had doubled.

Trade was assiduously taxed: on goods brought to market,

on articles sold, and by various import and export duties,
generally 10 percent ad valorem. Goods carried between Harar
and Addis Ababa required another 5 percent ad valorem payment. Sometimes, in lieu of cash, taxpayers used bars of
salt.

The first moves to change from the primitive system to a
more cash-oriented taxation were made by Hayle Sellase who
appointed an American adviser, E. A. Colson, to devise a
workable tax mechanism. Broad principles were established in
the 1931 Constitution; these called for taxes in money, labor
and produce, but legislation spelling out the details took a number of years to adopt. The Italians, during their occupation,
sought to curry popular favor by decreeing in October 1935 that
there would no longer be any required "tribute." Continued
Ethiopian resistance against the occupiers, however, eventually
caused the Italians to reimpose various taxes.

Modern Ethiopia has been able to set up a reasonably effective revenue system. Radical changes in land tenure (q.v.)
have meant better returns for the farmer with only minuscule
taxes but this is believed to be changing because of the need to
pay for increased government services. (See also ASRAT;
GABBAR; GEBER.)

TAYTU BETUL (Empress 1889-1913). Born around 1850 to Betul
Hayle Maryam of the Semen nobility and Ye-wub Dar (origins
unknown). She had a younger sister, Desta and two brothers
Alula and Wele. Her brothers were prisoners of Tewodros II
at Meqdela where they met Menilek II, a fellow prisoner.
Sometime after Menilek's escape in 1865 they joined him in
Shewa, while Taytu began a marital career that included a general of Tewodros II, a general of Yohannes IV and a high-ranking
officer of Menilek's, who was the brother of Menilek's then
consort, Befana (q.v.). Taytu's marriage to Menilek, 29 April
1883 was by communion, therefore indissoluble (see MARRIAGE).
Taytu became a strong influence on her husband and a power in
her own right with vast lands to administer, an army of her
own, and a separate palace staff to command.

Unusually well educated for a woman of her time, she was
adept at Ge'ez poetry (q.v.), literate in Amharic, a skilled
chess player and proud of her weaving and cooking skills.
Childless, she was a surrogate mother to the children of nobles
brought up at the palace, and a marital politician in the interest
of alliances that would be useful to her husband and herself.
She held her own in theological debates as a defender of orthodoxy, and took the initiative in securing more security for the
priests and pilgrims in Jerusalem (q.v.). Wary of Menilek's
open-door foreign policy, nonetheless she did not block his
treaty-making with the Italians 1883-1890; but when war with
Italy became inevitable, she put her own life in danger at the
battles of Meqelle and Adwa 1895-96.

She named, and had much to do with the founding of, Addis
Ababa; financed its first hotel; was active in efforts to form an
agricultural loan bank; and saw that Menilek included both girls

and boys in his statement establishing a school in 1907. Her
downfall followed the increase of her personal power to make
government appointments and land grants as Menilek's chronic
illness debilitated him between 1906-1910. In March 1910 she
was obliged to confine herself to nursing Menilek. After his
death in December 1913 she retreated to a semi-monastic life
at Entotto Maryam, a church she had built and endowed, where
she died 11 February 1918.

TCHERTCHER. A district directly east of Addis Ababa through
which the railway from Djibouti travels to the capital. It was at
Tchelenqo in Tchertcher that the battle for Harar was fought in
1887. At that time this normally productive region was suffering terribly from the famine that had enveloped Ethiopia; its recovery was followed by resumption of regular tribute (in kind)
to the emperor. In 1934 it was detached from Hararge province
and was the locus for a pilot-project on various administrative
reforms. Under Dr. Werqneh Eshete revenues were collected
in cash, and salaries paid to officials; there was an active anti-
slavery policy and village schools, medical assistance and earth
roads were started. A new town, Asebe Teferi, was built.
The inhabitants are settled Oromo-Muslim farmers.

TEDALE, BATTLE OF (25 January 1887). Known to the Italians
as the "Dogali massacre, " the encounter was an unexpected victory by the forces of Ras Alula (q. v.); Alula had ordered the
Italians to evacuate their garrisons at Wiha, Se'ati and Zula.
When Alula learned that a 550-man relief column was approaching
to re-supply the garrisons, he poured his 7, 500 troops down on
them, virtually annihilating it. Actually, Emperor Yohannes was
shocked, fearing that instead of deterring further Italian expansion into Ethiopia, Alula had provoked an all-out war (see
ITALY and Ethiopia), and rebuked him privately though Ethiopian
pride was boosted by the victory.

TEGRAY. Since the province of Tegray contains Aksum, site of the
earliest kingdom, the monasteries established by the "nine
saints, " and its people speak Tegrigna, a language much closer
to Ge'ez than Amharic, it is properly considered the birthplace
of Ethiopia. As the area through which all trade and communications passed to the port of Massawa, it was the gateway of
empire and its political orientation was crucial to the state.
      After the Aksumite empire expanded south in the 9th century,
emperors lived in Lasta, Amhara and Shewa. Separatist tenden-
cies of Tegray were apparent in the 13th century and Amde
Tseyon (1314-1344) was obliged to re-conquer Tegray and post a
military colony there. Still Aksum remained the cultural center
of the church and Emperor Zera Yaqob (q. v.) in 1434, undertook
the long journey from Shewa to Aksum to be invested with his
crown. The expansion of Christianity in Shewa and Gojam was
the work of priests trained in Tegray's monasteries.
      Rulers of Tegray were known as the Bahr-negash ("king of
the sea") though they had little actual authority over the "sea"

after the Ottoman empire occupied Massawa in 1557 (see
YESHAQ, Bahr-Negash).   The title changed to Ras by the
time of Mikael Sehul (c. 1740-1780) who was on good enough
terms with the Ottoman governors to acquire muskets which
enabled him to extend his power inland to Gondar; his descendants, Welde Sellase (1780-1816) and Sebagades (1822-1831)
ruled until Webe Hayle Maryam (q. v.), an outsider from Semen,
gained control from 1831-1855.   All of them considered themselves the true defenders of the faith and the Solomonic dynasty
during the Zemene Mesafint (q. v.) until Kasa Haylu (Tewodros
II) defeated Webe in 1855.

Tewodros II was unable to gain the loyalty of all Tegray;
he did succeed in putting down the pretensions of Neguse Welde
Mikael in 1861 who, as a protector of the Catholic missionaries,
aimed to get French help to establish Tegray as a Catholic state.
Tewodros appointed Kasa and Gugsa Mercha of Temben to govern
certain districts in 1864 but in 1867, after much internal warfare, Kasa Mercha declared himself ruler of all Tegray.   He
controlled enough to secure the march of the Anglo-Indian army
to defeat Tewodros in 1868.   Near the capital of Tegray, Adwa,
was the battle in July 1971 that brought Kasa Mercha to the
throne as Yohannes IV (q. v.) and relative stability to Tegray
under Baryau Gebre Tsadeq (1873-1878) except for the attacks
from Egypt in 1875 and 1876.   The Tegrayan general, Ras
Alula (q. v.), and the governor ended the Egyptian threat, but
did not occupy Massawa from which the next danger would
come--Italian colonialism--and end in the splitting of the province into Tegray and Eritrea (q. v.).

The Tegray portion after 1890 was ruled by Mengesha Yohannes (q. v.) who reluctantly accepted the suzerainty of Menilek
II in 1894 in time to have the assistance of the imperial armies
in beating back increased Italian encroachment (see ADWA,
BATTLE OF, 1895-96).

Between the removal of Mengesha Yohannes in 1899 and
1935 when Tegray was occupied by Italy many attempts were
made to administer the recalcitrant Tegrayans by either dividing
the governorship or imposing a Shewan over them.   Seyum
Mengesha was governor at the time of the 1935 invasion, having
shared or alternated authority in Tegray since 1910 intermittently with Gebre Sellase Baryau (d. 1930).

After the end of the occupation the Shewan-Oromo general,
Abebe Aregay, served a term from 1943-1947, at the beginning
of which a separatist rebellion broke out and was put down
with the assistance of the British who were administering
Eritrea.   Seyum Mengesha was then forgiven his sorry record
of collaboration with the Italians after his defeat and capture in
1936, and served as governor from 1947 until he was shot in
Addis Ababa during the attempted coup of 1960 (q. v.).   His son,
Mengesha Seyum (q. v.) governed 1961 to 1974; currently it has
a military governor whose major concern is the prevention of
Eritrean secession.

TEGRE (Language and People).   Used to describe the people who speak this language and the language itself, which is a descendant of Tegrigna, therefore a Semitic tongue, but altered so drastically that speakers of one language cannot understand the other. Tegre was unwritten until Dawit Amanuel at the Swedish Mission translated the New Testament in 1890 and began a dictionary. The language appears to be dying out because of the imposition of Tegrigna in Eritrea where almost all Tegre speakers live, and because Arabic has become widely used in trading.

Tegre means "serf" which was what they were: the Muslim vassals of the Bet Asgede (house of Asgede). In the 19th century, their rulers adopted the language of their subjects as well as their religion, but kept them as serfs. The Bet Asgede is made up of three autonomous groups, Habab, Ad Tekles and Ad Temaryam (all Christian names revealing their former religion). They are primarily nomadic herdsmen, except for the Ad Tekles who have settled in the Keren district. Other Tegre speakers live between Mensa and Belen (Bogos), the Dahlak islands and among the Beni Amer (q. v.).

TEKLE GIYORGIS II, "Emperor" (1868-1871). Born Gobeze Gebre Medhen, he was Wagshum (see shum) in Lasta and rebelled against Tewodros II in 1864, but remained neutral when the Anglo-Indian expedition came in 1868 (see Great Britain) to release the European captives held by Tewodros. He occupied Gondar, proclaimed himself emperor but was not anointed because there was no abun (q. v.); in 1871 he moved his armies into Tegray to gain the submission of Kasa Mercha, whose sister Dinqinesh was his wife. He was defeated and died as Kasa's prisoner in 1872, after Kasa had become Yohannes IV (q. v.). See additional entry, GOBEZE, Wagshum.

TEKLE HAWARYAT, Bejirond (Treasurer and Chief of Stores). A close associate of Hayle Sellase's in the 1920s, he became Minister of Finance in 1930 at which time he proposed a constitution and was assigned to draft it. He had been educated in Czarist Russia (1896-1902) where he studied military science and agriculture; on his return he was employed by Ras Mekonnen in Harar and Jigjiga. He participated in the coup that deposed Lej Iyasu in September 1916 and became Minister of Finance when Hayle Sellase was crowned in 1930.

In 1934, as governor of Tchertcher awraja (district) he was permitted latitude in devising a fairer form of taxation. He left for work in Djibouti with Ethiopian refugees during the occupation and did not return until 1955. Despite his own falling-out with Hayle Sellase, his son Germachew became Minister of Information in 1961.

TEKLE HAYMANOT, Negus of Gojam (c. 1847-1901). As Adal Tessema, he was named to rule Gojam by Tekle Giyorgis (q. v.) in 1870, thus restoring the hereditary family of Gojam and he was given the emperor's sister, Laqetch as his wife. Tekle Giyorgis was defeated by Kasa of Tegray (see YOHANNES IV)

but refused to submit to him until late 1874.   Yohannes granted
him the title, negus on 21 January 1881 and included Kefa
(q. v.) in his bailiwick. This created conflict with Menilek of
Shewa who also claimed Kefa and they went to war in June
1882; Menilek triumphed and captured Tekle Haymanot, two of
his sons, and many Gojami and brought them back to Shewa.
Yohannes IV was furious at his two vassal kings and ordered
Menilek to report to Borumeda with his captives; the emperor
deducted Agewmeder from Tekle Haymanot, and Wello from
Menilek's control and sent both kings home.

In January 1887, Tekle Haymanot fought an army of Mahdists at Metemma; they withdrew, regrouped and returned to
defeat Tekle Haymanot at Sarweha in January 1888, taking
thousands of Gojami into slavery, including two daughters
(Mentewab and Yewub-dar) of the king.   Bitter at the failure
of Yohannes to reinforce him, Tekle Haymanot promised
Menilek he would help depose Yohannes, but even as Menilek
was en route north, the Gojam king decided to make peace with
the emperor.

Tekle Haymanot was one of the first to pledge loyalty to
Menilek when he claimed the throne in March 1889.   He came
to Addis Ababa in June 1890 to pay tribute, and thence to
Kefa, part of which Menilek restored to him.   He did not join
the campaign against the Italians until late December 1895; his
army fought at Meqelle in January and the battle of Adwa in
March.   He died in January 1901.   His sons Belew (d. 1907),
Bezebeh (d. 1905) and Seyum (see Ras HAYLU) quarreled with
him and with each other both before and after his death;
Menilek, both to settle the quarrels and to break the independence of Gojam, divided the province, though Seyum won the
full title of Ras Haylu of Gojam and Damot in 1907.

TEKLE HAYMANOT, Saint (c. 1215-c. 1313). He was descended
from a family of Christian immigrants who had settled on the
western edge of the Shewan plateau.   He became a student of
Iyesus Moa (q. v.) at Lake Hayq, went to Tegray to learn at
Iyesus Moa's alma mater, Debre Damo, for twelve years then
returned to Shewa, settling with his disciples at Debre Asbo
which became known as the monastery of Debre Libanos (q. v.)
a century after his death.   He is said to have played a pacific
role in the deposition of the Zagwe (q. v.) dynasty in favor of
Yekuno Amlaq (q. v.) in 1270.   Icons always depict him standing
on one leg, a feat he performed for several years, demonstrating his miraculous stamina.

TEKLE WELDE HAWARYAT, Afa Negus (1900-1970) see
PATRIOTS

TESSEMA NADEW, Ras (?-1911). His father was Nadew Abba Bahr;
his mother Qonjit Debneh. His father being the tutor-guardian
of Menilek II, Tessema was eased into a favored position at
court before his father's death in 1886.   That year Tessema was
appointed governor of Guma and Ilubabor; by 1892-94 he and

Welde Giyorgis (q. v.) had succeeded in shifting the coffee caravans from the cross-Sudan route to transiting Shewa to the
coast, with the result of a virtual monopoly on the coffee trade
and income for their own treasuries as well as Menilek's.
Tessema Nadew was one of the generals assigned to neutralize
the Afar of Awsa, so they would not be able to assist the
Italians in the war of 1895-96 and immediately after went on
the 9-month campaign to subdue Kefa; and in 1898, under
Menilek's orders, provided half-hearted cooperation to the
French in their effort to reach Fashoda (q. v.).   After being
named Ras in April, 1900, he spent most of his time as adviser to Menilek in Addis Ababa; was named to the board of
governors of the first bank in 1905; named regent and Ras
Bidwoded (beloved or favored) for Lej Iyasu in October 1909.
The heir-apparent moved into his house, but the ailing and
tired Tessema was unable to control him or balk the decisive
moves by Empress Taytu (q. v.) to run the government; he gave
his approval to the plot that stopped her in March 1910.

He had several ex-wives, but married Beletchew Abba Jober
(daughter of the last king of Guma) by communion in 1907 after
many years of a civil marriage; at the same time he confessed
that 30-year-old Welde Rafael was his son and gave him the
name, Kebede.   Before his death 10 April 1911, he brought
his sister's (Abunesh) son, Mekonnen Endalkachew to court;
Mekonnen would continue the family's traditional service to the
crown as Hayle Sellase's prime minister.

TEWODROS II (Emperor 1855-1868).   Born "Kasa Haylu" he was
the son of Attetegeb and Haylu Welde Giyorgis (ruler of Qwara
district).   He was educated in church schools in the scriptures
and some history, law and traditions, then served in the army
of his half-brother Kenfu, until the latter's death in 1839.   He
gained sufficient favor in the service of Empress Menen (q. v.)
to acquire her grand-daughter, Tewabech Ali (d. 1858) as wife
after divorcing a previous spouse; stewardship of a district of
Qwara was part of her dowry in 1845.   He rebelled in 1846
and captured both Empress Menen and her husband (Yohannes
III) when they came with an army to attack him in 1847.   Ras
Ali Alula (q. v.) ransomed his mother, and granted Kasa all
lands west and north of Lake Tana.   In 1852 he made his bid
for supreme power by defeating Goshu Zewde of Gojam; the
next year he routed Ras Ali Alula and Empress Menen, and in
February 1855 defeated Dejazmach Webe of Semen and Tegray.
He chose the throne name of Tewodros II for his coronation on
11 February, demonstrating fulfillment of a prophecy in Fikkare
Iyesus (q. v.) that a man of that name would end corruption, im-
mortality, lawlessness, war, and famine.   His early years
proved a dedication to these ideals, and he quickly brought
the empire into the kind of unified administration that Ethiopia
had not known for a century, subjugating Wello and Shewa before the end of his first year.

Gradually he lost the support of the church hierarchy as he
tried to curb their land holdings.   His imprisonment of Abune

Selama in 1864 and punitive burning of 41 churches in Gondar
in 1866 gained him the implacable hatred of the clergy. Excom-
munication by then meant nothing to him; he had lost control of
most of the empire.

Foreign relations which had begun promisingly with England
and France deteriorated in 1864 when the British consul Duncan
Cameron failed to bring an answer to a letter Tewodros had
written Queen Victoria proposing an alliance. He imprisoned
at Meqdela, or detained at Gafat the missionaries and craftsmen
(see CAPTIVES, EUROPEAN) whose talents he had so admired
and brought on himself the wrath of Great Britain. After the
defeat of the army that remained loyal to him, he shot himself
in the mouth with a revolver Queen Victoria had sent him as a
gift in happier days, on 13 April 1868. His son, Alemayehu
(q. v.), by his third (?) wife Terunesh Webe (d. 1868) was taken
to England and died there in 1879. Among his other children
were Meshesha (who governed Qwara for both Yohannes IV and
Menilek II); and Alatash (wife of Menilek II when he was at
Meqdela, then of Ras Baryau Pawlos of Tegray; she died
c. 1890/91).

TITLES (and Modes of Address). Civil and military titles overlapped
under the imperial regime and almost no person of importance
was without one title or another. The basic military title
azmach (commander) was embroidered as Grazmach (commander
of the left), Kenyazmach (commander of the right), and Dejazmach (commander of the gate). Fitwrari was the commander
of the vanguard. Titles were retained unless the person was
specifically dishonored. Meredazmach (terrorizing commander)
became a title peculiar to the rulers of Shewa. Ras (prince)
was the top rank before negus (king). Ras Bidwoded meant
"beloved, or favored prince. " The English "prince, " "princess"
and "duke" came into common usage after Hayle Sellase returned
from his English exile during the Italian occupation.

Blatta was an executive at court; Kentiba used for the office
of mayor; azaj was the person responsible for overall supervision of the palace, and was also used by the state jailers.

Weyzero and Emabet were high ranking female titles, with
Etege for empress or queen. Weyzero became the mode of address for any married woman in the late 19th century, and Ato
an equivalent for Mister. Ato probably derived from Abeto, a
17th-century princely title.

At the present time, such "western" military titles as
"lieutenant, " "colonel, " and "general, " have superseded Amharic
titles.

TOLA IBN-JAFAR, Shaikh. A Muslim leader of Gerfa in southeast
Wello who instigated a rebellion in 1884, having resisted for six
years Yohannes IV's edict to convert to Christianity. He eluded
capture and fled into the Sudan where he fought with the Mahdists
then returned to Wello, where in 1890 he gathered enough followers to challenge Shewan rule and again escaped. He was an
ally of the Italians in 1895-96, but defected back after they lost

the war.   He was an active proponent of Islam in Wello up to
1916.

TOURISM.   A useful source of foreign exchange until the time of
the 1974 coup d'état.   As a result of the efforts of the Ethiopian Tourist Organization (ETO), headed by Hapte Sellase
Tafesse, its US-educated director, some $15 million (US) was
being earned annually from approximately 110,000 tourists.
ETO had been set up in 1961 as a separate unit but in 1970,
because of its evident success, was incorporated into the
Ministry of Commerce, Industry and Tourism.   ETO estimates
around that time indicated that about 50% of tourists came from
Europe, 25% from North America, and the rest from Asia,
the Middle East and other African countries.   Tourism plans,
which were linked to Ethiopian Airlines' development and promotion, called for significant increases in hotel accommoda-
tions, inland trips on the so-called Historic Route (Aksum,
Lalibela, Gondar, etc.) and hunting safaris.   ETO's well-pro-
moted advertising slogan induced visitors to enjoy "13 months
of sunshine" (see Ethiopian calendar).   The $8 million (US)
International Hilton in Addis Ababa, completed in 1969, was
a focus of tourist attraction until the 1974 overthrow of Hayle
Sellase signaled the temporary demise of tourism.   Hapte
Sellase was one of the government officials imprisoned by the
Derg but it is believed that he is still alive although in deten-
tion.   Recent reports indicate that the government, as of
April 1980, was permitting foreign travel agents to organize
trips and safaris as well as through Ethiopian Airlines.

TREATIES.   Meaningless treaties of friendship and commerce were
arranged between King Sahle Sellase of Shewa with Great
Britain (16 November 1841) and France (7 June 1843) and between Ras Ali Alula (of Begemder and Gojam) and Great
Britain (2 November 1849) and between France and Neguse of
Tegray on 2 October 1859.
Serious treaties by Menilek of Shewa (with Italy 21 May
1883 and 2 May 1889) and by Emperor Yohannes 3 June 1884
(with Great Britain) initiated Ethiopia into the world of international diplomacy.   Menilek, after the peace treaty with Italy
(26 October 1896) signed border (q.v.) agreements with France,
Italy and Great Britain, and typical commercial treaties with
the United States (1903), Germany (1905), Austria-Hungary
(1905), Italy (1906), Belgium (1906), France (1908).   Particularly significant were those with Italy, by which commercial
agents were posted in various markets of the empire, and
with the French which gave her legation judicial privileges
over her nationals working in the country and also reduced
the customs of her goods from 10 to 8 percent.   (See also
DIPLOMATIC RELATIONS; ADWA; WETCHALE.)

TREATY, TRIPARTITE (13 December 1906, London).   Italy,
France, and Great Britain established their spheres of interests and claims in the event of Ethiopia's disintegration after

the death of Menilek II.   They were concerned because Menilek
had been very ill in May 1906 and Ras Mekonnen whom the
European powers considered a suitable successor to Menilek,
had died in March.   Before the signing in London, it was submitted to Menilek in Addis Ababa (July 1906); on December 4
Menilek gave his views in writing stressing that whatever arrangements they made must not infringe on the sovereign rights
of Ethiopia and on 13 December the ambassadors of the respective three countries signed.   One of the stipulations was
prior consultation on all important matters in Ethiopia.   This
was systematically ignored by the heads of legation in Addis
Ababa who competed rather than cooperated.

TURKEY and Ethiopia.   Turkey was the center of the Ottoman empire, which mounted a 16th century attempt to make northern
Ethiopia one of its provinces.   It was defeated but the Ottomans
controlled the coast and the island of Massawa (q. v.).   They
called the territory they held "Habesh" (q. v.) and it eventually
became known as Suakin and Jiddah.   The Ottoman pasha of
Zebid (Yemen) provided arms and men to Ahmad ibn-Ibrahim
(see ISLAMIC CONQUEST) in 1542 to assist his campaign in
Ethiopia; in 1589 the Ottoman pasha of Massawa was replaced
by a local appointee, called the Na'ib.   As the power of the
Ottoman empire declined (losing Greece and Egypt in the 1820s)
so did any threat to Ethiopia, though the Ethiopians persisted
in calling any enemy on their borders "Turks. "   Constantinople
made an ineffectual protest when Italy occupied Massawa in
1885, as they still had a nominal governor there.
    It was over the Ethiopian convent of Dayr-es-Sultan in Jeru-
salem (q. v.) that Ethiopia had continuous negotiations with
Constantinople, as Ottoman control of that city lasted until
1918.   The Ethiopian mission to Russia in 1895 was received
cordially by the sultan on their return trip; special missions
over Jerusalem problems went in 1901, 1904 and 1907; the
Sultan Abdul Hamid sent a mission to congratulate Menilek on
his victory over Italy in 1897 and another envoy in 1904 on
problems never fully explained.   Turkey has maintained diplomatic relations with Ethiopia since 1933.

- U -

UNITED NATIONS.   An outspoken proponent of the concept of collective security, especially after being spurned by the League
of Nations, Ethiopia was active in the formation of the United
Nations Organization and signed as a charter member in San
Francisco in 1945, representing Africa along with Liberia and
South Africa.
    Eritrea became one of the U. N. 's early problems, in its
Trusteeship Council.   Eventually, the U. N. General Assembly
voted to link Ethiopia and Eritrea in a federation (1952); then,
ten years later, the U. N. approved Ethiopia's incorporation of
the former Italian colony.

Ethiopia maintains representation at U. N. Headquarters and
at most of the Specialized Agencies; its ambassador to Washington also acts as its representative in New York.   Under the
Derg, Ethiopia maintains that it is non-aligned, but in most
votes at the U. N. has joined the Soviet bloc.
     Ethiopia assigned 5, 000 troops to the United Nations Com-
mand in Korea from 1950 to 1966, and sent 1, 500 troops to the
Congo in 1960.   Ethiopia is active in the African bloc at the
U. N. and sponsored the Southwest Africa case before the World
Court (1967).   The recipient of U. N. technical aid, Ethiopia has
in turn provided scholarship education for many East Africans.
(See also ECONOMIC COMMISSION FOR AFRICA; WORLD BANK;
ORGANIZATION FOR AFRICAN UNITY.)

UNITED STATES and Ethiopia.   A black American entrepreneur,
     W. H. Ellis, called on Menilek II in 1903 to discuss business
     opportunities.   Encouraged, he departed just before an official
     mission headed by Robert Skinner arrived to offer Ethiopia a
     routine commercial treaty.   Ellis returned with the ratified U. S.
     treaty in 1904, but was unable to obtain concession contracts,
     even for the popular "amerikani, " unbleached muslin, which
     dominated Ethiopia's imports until 1918 when Japanese cloth
     superseded it.   Enamelware, Singer sewing machines, steel
     bars, hurricane lamps and knives filled the trade gap after
     1918.   Exports to the U. S. then and now are hides, coffee and
     beeswax.
          Contacts before the Skinner mission and the establishment
     of a legation in Addis Ababa in 1906 (unstaffed from 1913-1928)
     were rare.   New York Herald correspondent Henry M. Stanley
     informed his readers of the British defeat of Tewodros II in
     1868; some ex-Civil War officers (from both sides) employed by
     the Khedive of Egypt were captured by Yohannes IV in 1875-76;
     the latter detained the Egyptian-employed surveyor L. H.
     Mitchell for two months in 1877 and Mason Bey acted as Khedi-
     val agent at Massawa in 1884-1885.   There were explorers
     Dr. Donaldson Smith (1894), Oscar Crosby (1900) and W. N.
     MacMillan (1903).   An American philanthropist backed the
     Deutsche-Littmann expedition to Aksum 1905-1910; collectors
     from the Field Museum of Chicago explored in 1925-26 and
     1927-28.   There was American participation in the Phelps-Stokes
     educational survey in 1924 and in the Papal visit of 1929.   An-
     thropologist Carleton Coon and his wife made a study trip in
     1933.
          Heruy Welde Sellase visited the U. S. in 1919, after heading
     the Ethiopian delegation to Paris to congratulate the Allies on
     their victory; six students came in 1922, one of whom, Melaku
     Beyene (q. v.), graduated from Howard University as a doctor in
     1935.   In 1927, Dr. Werqneh Eshete (Martin) (q. v.) and in
     1933, Ras Desta Demtew visited the U. S. to obtain aid for a
     dam project at Lake Tana.   A contract with the J. G. White
     company was pending when the 1935 attack by Italy ended all
     negotiations.
          In 1930 a special mission attended the Hayle Sellase corona-

tion; thereafter the emperor employed several advisers from America: Ernest Work on education, A. Everett Colson on finance and J. H. Spencer on constitution drafting. Their work ended with the Italian invasion, but Spencer returned from 1943 to 1960 and assisted in the 1951 constitutional revision (see CONSTITUTIONS), and advised on foreign affairs.

Ethiopia named an honorary consul in New York in 1933, John Shaw, but a legation in Washington was not opened until 1943. President Roosevelt condemned Italian aggression in Ethiopia, but isolationist America was unable to produce anything more substantive than armament embargoes (5 Oct. 1935 and 29 Feb. 1936) which applied both to the aggressor and her victim. In 1935 some 100 American missionaries refused the U.S. consul's advice to leave Ethiopia, since they sought to do some good in the coming conflict (see MISSIONS, PROTESTANT). The U.S. did not recognize Italian annexation.

After World War II, advisers on legal affairs were employed (Albert Garretson, then Donald Paradis) and others in communications, medical services and road building. U.S. Technical Aid began in 1944, and by 1969 there were more than 6000 Americans living in Ethiopia, many of them military personnel stationed in Addis Ababa and at Kagnew Communications station in Asmara. The base was curtailed in the early 1970s and phased out in 1977 at the end of the 25-year lease which coincided with deteriorating Ethiopian-U.S. relations.

Major aid projects were the College of Agriculture at Alemaya, the Public Health College in Gondar, the College of Business Administration, the J. F. Kennedy Library, a power station on the Abbay, supply of equipment and trainers for Ethiopian Airlines (q.v.), staffing of the law school (in cooperation with the Ford Foundation) and teachers for the university. The Peace Corps began service in 1962 with 270 teachers and medical people and reached more than 900 by the late 1960s; the last volunteer left in 1976. The U.S. Mapping Mission made the first scientific estimate of population, and until 1976 the Navy Medical Research Stations studied tropical diseases. Today, a few missionaries remain, and a small embassy staff maintains relations with the present government. Ethiopia asked the United States to recall Ambassador Frederic Chapin in 1980 because the government was angered by the prospect of a U.S.-Somalia military and economic agreement.

Ethiopian studies developed only in the late 1950s and is now of sufficient proportion to justify conferences (Michigan State University in 1972 and the University of Chicago in 1977), and a newsletter has been expanded into a journal, Northeast African Studies (Michigan State University). Since 1974, American scholarship has been enriched by such scholars as Abraham Demoz, Asmerom Legesse, and Bereket Habte Sellase who have joined with Wolf Leslau, Lionel Bender, Donald Levine, Richard Caulk, Robert Hess, Allan Hoben, Harold Marcus, and Donald Crummey (Canadian) and many others to keep the study of Ethiopia a vigorous field.

UNIVERSITY OF ADDIS ABABA.   Began its existence in 1950 as
    University College, generally patterned after the British system.
    Granted a civil charter in 1954, it gradually included a variety
    of specialized colleges until it became, by imperial charter in
    1961, Hayle Sellase I University.   It is now called the Universi-
    ty of Addis Ababa, a change made after the 1974 coup d'état.
        In Addis Ababa are the faculties of arts, education, science,
    engineering (founded by the Ministry of Education and Fine Arts),
    business administration, building technology (with Swedish
    Government support), and agricultural and mechanical arts (a
    joint Ethiopian-U.S. effort originally).   Outside the capital are
    the Public Health College in Gondar, and the College of Agricul-
    ture in Alemeya, both of which were largely USAID funded.
        The teaching faculty was predominantly foreign, with a large
    number of Americans and British, but also including Yugoslavs,
    Canadians, Poles, French, Czechs and Rumanians.   By 1970,
    largely through the work of U.S.-educated Ethiopian administra-
    tors under the direction, during most of the 1960s, of the
    American academic vice-president Edward D. Myers, the Uni-
    versity had expanded to include five faculties of arts, law,
    medicine, education, and science, plus five colleges of technolo-
    gy, public health, agriculture, business administration and theo-
    logy.   Financial assistance came from various nations as well
    as USAID.
        All secondary school graduates could attend the University
    to obtain a degree after four years of study, but they could pur-
    sue work toward a degree only after successfully completing a
    general, first-year program.   They paid no tuition and received
    a small, usually insufficient stipend to pay living expenses.   This
    resulted in sub-standard living and study conditions for most of
    the students and led to much unrest, dissent and ultimately po-
    litical protest which built up in the late 1960s and hit a crescen-
    do in the early 1970s.   This contribution to the tense atmos-
    phere in the capital became part of the "creeping revolution"
    that caused the downfall of Hayle Sellase.   When the Derg took
    over the government, it closed the University, reopening it many
    months later under its new name.   (See also UNIVERSITY SER-
    VICE.)
        The only institution of higher learning in Eritrea is at the
    University of Asmara, founded by an Italian Roman Catholic or-
    der.   It is under the jurisdiction of the Ministry of Education and
    offers courses in law and commerce, arts, and science.

UNIVERSITY SERVICE.   A program of practical work, made manda-
    tory in 1964, which compelled students to work one year in the
    provinces between their third and fourth year.   The government
    purpose was to get the students to relate to the problems of the
    peasants but it turned out to be also a source of cheap labor for
    the Ministry of Education who assigned most of them as teachers.
    Many students opposed their forced migration away from the
    pleasures and conveniences of the capital; some seized it as an
    opportunity to spread firsthand information about the militant
    student movement which was opposed to the emperor (see
    STUDENT MOVEMENT).

- W -

WAL WAL INCIDENT see WELWEL

WARS on Ethiopia. 1527-1543: the Muslim jihad conquered most
of Ethiopia (see ISLAMIC CONQUEST). 1867-1868: the British
army of India defeated Tewodros II at Meqdela in April 1868;
as the mission was accomplished (release of the European captives) the army left immediately. Sept.-Nov. 1875: Egyptian
army invades Ethiopia; defeated at Gundet (Tegray) 16 November.
Jan.-March 1876: Egyptian army again invades; defeated at
Gura (Tegray) March 7-9. Sept. 1885: Mahdist (q.v.) attack
at Kufit repulsed. January 1887: Mahdists routed at Metemma.
January 1888: Mahdists defeat forces of Tekle Haymanot of Gojam,
ravage Gondar, withdraw. March 1889: Mahdists were defeated
at Metemma.
    Italy inflicted a defeat at Se'ati 25 Jan. 1887; the next day
their re-inforcement column was wiped out at Dogali (see Tedale).
Italy won a battle at Addi Ugri (Coatit) in January 1895 but lost
at Amba Alage in December, Meqelle in January 1896 and Adwa
(q.v.) in March 1896. From 3 October 1935 to 31 March 1936,
Italy conquered Ethiopia.
    The undeclared war between Ethiopia and Somalia over dis-
puted territory in the Ogaden began in 1960; in 1978 the disputed area was in the hands of Ethiopia but peace is still not
achieved.

WEBE HAYLE MARYAM (c. 1800-1866/7). Born in Semen to Hayle
Maryam Gebre, its lord, and Mentay, a liaison of his father's,
Webe was selected by the elders after his father's death in
1826, over his "legitimate" brother Merso, to be their chief.
He extended his rule to include Tegray (q.v.) in 1832. In 1842,
in alliance with Beru Goshu of Gojam he took his armies to up-
set the rule of Ras Ali Alula (q.v.), who was also his son-in-
law, but was defeated. In alliance with Ali Alula in 1853 he
fought against Kasa Haylu at the Battle of Ayshal and was defeated. Ali Alula fled, but Webe made peace with the victor
and agreed to send Abune Selama who had been in his custody,
to Gondar and was allowed to return to Tegray. Kasa Haylu,
aware of Webe's ambition to become emperor, ended this possibility by defeating Webe at the battle of Deresge (in Semen,
where Webe had gone in January) on 9 February 1855. Kasa
Haylu had himself anointed as Emperor Tewodros II, in the
church at Deresge, which Webe had prepared for his own coronation. Webe and his sons Kasa and Gwangul were imprisoned
at Meqdela. He was released from his chains in February 1860,
when Tewodros II married his daughter Terunesh. It was a
brief respite. He died at Meqdela in 1867 still a prisoner.
He had a number of wives (Ye-werq Wuha, Ye-werq Maru and
Dinqenesh Sebagades were three) and children. It was his
niece, Taytu (daughter of his half-brother Betul) who would
achieve renown as the empress of Ethiopia in 1889.

WELAMO, KINGDOM OF.   In 1894, Menilek II led an expedition to
annex this area between the Belati and the Omo rivers; except
for Kefa west of the Omo, Welamo was surrounded by peoples
already tributary to the emperor. Kawo Tona Gagga, the Welamo
king, had refused the tribute his predecessors had sent and was
inciting his neighbors to rebel against their governors.   The
high mortality on both sides during this campaign was testimony
to the ability and will of the Welamo to defend themselves; in
the past the Welamo had dug ditches and covered them with
branches to discourage attacks and Tona employed this ruse
again.   It delayed Menilek's victory, but only temporarily.
Legend establishes Christianity in Welamo in the lifetime of
St. Tekle Haymanot (13th century), but evidence is incomplete.
The Welamo-speaking people have oral traditions of a dynasty,
whose fifth ruler, Kawo Kote made the kingdom known in the
late 18th century.

WELASMA DYNASTY see IFAT

WELDE GIYORGIS ABOYE, Ras (1851-1918).   The son of Ayehelu-
shem, daughter of King Sahle Sellase of Shewa, and Meredazmach (governor) Aboye, a commoner who had been appointed by
Tewodros II to rule Shewa in 1858.   Welde Giyorgis and his
brothers, Lemma (d. 1908) and Beshah (d. fighting the Italians
1 March 1896) were long in the service of Menilek II, whose
first cousins they were.   He was married to a relation of
Befana (q. v.), Menilek's consort, and later to Yeshi Emabet,
the cousin of Taytu Betul (q. v.) who became the wife of Menilek
in 1883.
    After the conquests into the southwest, serving under Ras
Gobena (q. v.) he was appointed Dejazmach in 1886 and Ras in
1893.   He fought in the Welamo campaign of 1894; Awsa in
1895-96 and ruled Kefa from 1897-1910.   He was the informed
negotiator with the British in 1902 and 1907 on the borderlines
drawn between his lands and the Sudan and Kenya respectively.
    He and Tessema Nadew (q. v.) shifted the coffee trade route
from going through the Sudan to going through Shewa to benefit
the imperial treasury and their own; joined the Bank of Abyssinia as a governor in 1908.   He spent a year or so in Addis
Ababa as Menilek was seriously ill, but left abruptly for Kefa
in June 1909, the intrigue over royal succession apparently the
cause.   After the downfall of his wife's cousin, the empress, he
was appointed by the Tessema Nadew-Lej Iyasu regency to
govern Amhara, Begemder and Semen; in 1916 he cooperated with
the coup to get rid of the irresponsible Iyasu and was made a
negus (king) in 1917 but died a few months later.

WELDE GIYORGIS WELDE YOHANNES, Tsehafi T'ezaz (Minister of
Pen).   Born about 1902 in Bulga to a leather worker and church-
educated, he became the secretary to Hayle Sellase before the
Italian invasion, shared his exile, and returned to become the
most powerful man in the government from 1941-1955.   Very
few saw the emperor without his office as intermediary.   His

control of appointments to the ministries and to governorships
was absolute; he himself combined the function of Interior
Minister (1943-49) and Justice (1949-55) with the role of principal private adviser.   Inevitably, over fourteen years, he began
to assert himself as a leader in his own right, and his usefulness to the emperor was at an end.   He was "rusticated" as
governor of Arsi (1955-60) then Gemu-Gofa (1960-61).

WELDE MIKAEL SELOMON, Ras (of Hamasen; d. 1906).   Son of
the formidable Elleni (q. v.) and bitter enemy of the Tsazega
clan who had killed his mother and infant son in 1851, though
there was a brief peace between them from 1855-1859 sealed
by the marriage of his daughter (Teru) to Kefle Iyesus.   Welde
supported Kasa (Yohannes IV) whose cousin he married, and
was named governor of Hamasen and Bogos when Kasa became
emperor.   But Welde Mikael's protection of Catholics and his
contacts with Napoleon III aroused Yohannes's suspicions.   The
emperor took away his governorship and put him in prison
from 1869 to 1874, releasing him only on his promise, carried
out in November 1875, to attack the Egyptians who had occupied
Senhet.
     Two months later, Welde Mikael defected to Egypt, receiv-
ing a large batch of weapons in return.   He feigned loyalty to
Yohannes for a few months early in 1879 but, seeking to regain
his lands, continued to attack governors sent to Hamasen by
Yohannes.   He and two of his sons were captured later that
year and, after a trial for treason, were imprisoned on Amba
Selama for a 12-year term.   They were released after Yohannes'
death in March 1889.   He had 13 children from wives Absara
and Culladehab and other unknown women.

WELE BETUL, Ras (?-1918).   The eldest of the Betul Hayle Maryam family who considered themselves the hereditary lords of
Semen.   Wele and his brother Alula (d. 1882) escaped Tewodros
II's fortress at Meqdela in 1867 and joined their fellow prisoner,
Menilek, who had escaped two years earlier, in Shewa.   In
1876 Menilek exceeded his prerogatives by appointing Wele as
governor of Yejju (where Wele had relations through his grandmother, Hirut Gugsa) angering Yohannes IV, but Wele managed
to tread a line that did not bring him into conflict with the emperor while being loyal to Menilek.   In 1883, Wele's sister
Taytu married Menilek.   Wele's domain was extended to include
Lasta and Begemder, a vast increase, in 1889 when Menilek
became emperor and gave him the title of Ras.   This placed
Wele in a status equal to Ras Mengesha Yohannes of Tegray;
Wele was given the task of preventing any bitter enemies, though
his daughter, Kefey, was required to marry Mengesha in 1896
as part of his political peace with Menilek II after the 1895-96
war with Italy.   Wele was deputed to govern half of Tegray and
keep an eye on Mengesha; in 1898, his son Gugsa was also
deputized to Tegray.   After Mengesha's arrest in 1899, Wele
was appointed governor of all Tegray which he ruled from 1900
to 1903 when he returned to Yejju.   Gugsa Wele married

Menilek's daughter, Zewditu (q. v.) in 1900 and in 1901, his
daughter Mentewab, still a child, was married to the elderly
widower Ras Mekonnen (q. v.). Wele's sister, the empress,
was the architect of these marital alliances, as she tried to
place at least one of her relations in line for the throne on
Menilek's death. When Taytu was deposed in 1910, Wele tried to
come to her aid, fighting government troops from June to November when he decided to surrender. He lived under detention until he died June 1918, a few months after his sister.

WELETTE PETROS, Saint (c. 1594-1643). One of the women who
left the comfortable life of a noblewoman to arouse the people
against the Roman Catholic conversion of Emperor Susneyos
(q. v.). Though banished from the vicinity of the royal court,
she and her sister nuns who lived a rigorously ascetic life,
abetted the agitation that forced Susneyos to appoint his son in
his place. She is a saint of the church; though accounts of her
life are hagiographic, they also provide glimpses of the day-to-
day life of the period.

WELLO. Oromo migrants in the 16th century settled in these fertile highlands and created a strong, prosperous buffer state between the north (Lasta, Begemder, Tegray) and south (Shewa).
Their leaders (very active slave traders) adopted Islam in the
18th century and the traditional gada system (q. v.) was modified into dynastic inheritance.   The mountains and ravines of
Wello encouraged their separation into seven houses, or clans,
which became mutually hostile. This disunity was exploited, particularly by the kings of Shewa, who made occasionally successful attempts to annex the province by war and diplomacy.
    Wello military power is recorded in 1581, 1590 and 1622.
Peace was obtained by the marriage of Iyasu II (1730-1755) to
the daughter of a Wello leader and her relations became the
royal guards at Gondar until they were supplanted by another
Oromo group, the Yejju (q. v.) about 1780.
    Tewodros II after his coronation in 1855 inflicted terrible
casualties in Wello, made Meqdela his storehouse and state
prison, but guerrilla actions constantly harassed his armies.
The Wello, under Queen Werqitu, aided the escape of Menilek
(q. v.) from Meqdela in 1865 and her soldiers escorted him safely to Shewa where he reclaimed his father's kingdom.   Tewodros
revenged himself by the brutal murder of Werqitu's son and 24
other Wello captives whom he was holding as hostages at Meqdela.   A rival Wello queen, Mestawet was awarded fortress
Meqdela after the Anglo-Indian army razed it in April 1868, in
the name of her son, Abba Watew. Queen Werqitu took refuge
in Shewa, until Menilek's conquest regained her fief. It took
Menilek almost five years of war before the province fell to
him, July 1876. He appointed Muhammad Ali, the stepson of
Werqitu to be paramount, and gave Mestawet's son a district.
    Yohannes IV recognized Menilek's suzerainty over Wello in
1878 but insisted on a vigorous Christianizing campaign.   Both
Abba Watew (who died 2 years later) and Muhammad Ali agreed

to be baptized and Ali was made a Ras. Mikael was loyal to Emperor Yohannes though Menilek was called "King of Shewa and Wello, " and swore fealty to Menilek only when he became emperor in 1889. Wello regiments participated in all of the wars of conquest and the defensive wars against Egypt, the Mahdists, and the first war with Italy (1895-96). By the time of the second war with Italy (1935-36) the Wello had been so ill-used only ferocious methods would induce them into the Ethiopian army. From the downfall of Ras Mikael in 1916 (when his son Lej Iyasu was deposed by the coalition that brought Teferi Mekonnen (Hayle Sellase) to power) an army was quartered on Wello and in certain areas farmers had to give up three quarters of their crops to feed them. In 1930, Wello was the personal fief of Hayle Sellase and he sent Crown Prince Asfa Wessen as governor. It is doubtful that Asfa Wessen's Wello connections (his mother was the granddaughter of Ras Mikael) meant much in Wello. After the occupation, Asfa Wessen was again posted to Wello until 1947 when he became absentee governor. In 1942, the province of Wello was enlarged to include Yejju and Lasta, with Desse as the capital. Though the population (estimated 2.3 million) is largely Muslim, many Christians live in Wello, and Amharic is widely spoken. A famine in Wello 1958-59 was a precursor of an even more disastrous one in 1972-73. The mishandling of this tragedy was one of the factors leading to the deposition of Hayle Sellase.

WELWEL INCIDENT (5 December 1934). This watering hole is 60 miles inside the Ethiopian border abutting on Italian Somaliland. An Anglo-Ethiopian Commission accompanied by 600 troops working on border definition between British Somalia and Ethiopia approached the wells in late November and were refused permission to camp there by the Italian captain. The Ethiopians camped anyhow, but the two British officers withdrew. Who fired the first shot has never been established, but firing and casualties occurred. Mussolini chose to make it a casus belli, demanding unacceptable reparations. Indeed Ethiopia had passively accepted the Italian presence at Welwel for five years. Hayle Sellase registered an appeal with the League of Nations on 11 January 1935; the League decided, in May, it would not interfere; in September Italy rejected the League's recommendation for a peaceful solution as her troops were ready for war.

WERQNEH ESHETE, Dr. Martin (c. 1865-c. 1957). Found abandoned at Meqdela in April 1868 by two officers with the Anglo-Indian expedition, he was taken back to India and educated under the name of one of his benefactors as "Charles Martin." After graduating from Lahore Medical College 1882 he joined the Indian Medical Service and after more training in Edinburgh he was assigned to the Burma medical service.

Menilek II was informed by the British mission of 1897 of the existence of this Ethiopian-born doctor who had tried to return to Ethiopia to help during the Italo-Ethiopian war of

1895-96. Not long after he arrived in late 1899 (as legation doctor) he was identified from scars by his grandmother. Unable to come to agreement over salary he returned to the Burma service; returned for five more years 1908-1913 during which time he attended Menilek for six months in 1910, tried several business ventures, married and started a family. He returned to the Burma service 1913-1919 then finally settled in Ethiopia. Immune from the traditional restraints on behavior because of his cosmopolitan background, he put his hand to various projects in addition to his medical work: model farms; a flour mill; printing; hot springs therapy; road construction; the freeing of slaves and a school for them once freed. He wrote a geography in Amharic for his students, went on two missions abroad (to the U.S. to seek aid for a dam project in 1927 and to India directly after to recruit teachers) and was named governor of Tchertcher district in 1930 where he had a reservoir built, piped water, roads, bridges, and a dispensary. In 1933 he was named ambassador to London, eloquently protesting in 1935 the Italian invasion. Two of his sons were shot in the aftermath of the attempt on the life of Marshal Graziani (February 1937) in Addis Ababa. His surviving son, Yohannes, became a doctor; among his patients was Hayle Sellase.

WETCHALE, TREATY OF (2 May 1889). Signed by Menilek II at this settlement in Wello for Ethiopia and Pietro Antonelli for Italy--in this treaty Italy recognized Menilek as emperor (Yohannes IV was dead, but Menilek was not yet crowned) in exchange for his recognition of their occupation of Massawa and Hamasen. Ras Mekonnen went to Italy to witness ratification and in October 1889 signed an additional convention which rectified the border on the basis of actual occupation (Italy had moved inland since the previous May); Italy agreed to a loan of four million lira. On 12 October Italy notified Britain, France, Russia, Germany and the United States that under Article XVII of the treaty of 2 May, the foreign affairs of Ethiopia would be in their hands, an interpretation soon disputed by Ethiopia (see ARTICLE XVII).

WILDLIFE. Elephants, for their ivory, and lions for their skins, have been largely depleted. Rhinoceros are common in the southern highlands, and hippopotamus, crocodiles, Nile monitor lizards, and otter are plentiful in lakes and rivers. Spotted and black leopards, hyenas, monkeys, lynx, wolves, wild dogs, jackals, wart hogs are seen in many parts, though leopards have been hunted without restraint for their skins. Giraffe and zebra are found in some areas as are antelope and gazelle. Civet have been plentiful and their musk has been an export for many centuries. Pythons, cobras and puff adders are common. Many kinds of birds, butterflies and insects abound, some as yet unclassified. A variety of ostrich is common, as well as the marabou, crane, heron, and parrot.

Rare animals native to Ethiopia--the walia ibex and the mountain nyala--are almost extinct, as are the gelada baboon and the Semen fox, despite an attempt to preserve them by es-

tablishing the Semen National Park in 1966.   Other protected
areas are Omo Reserve in Kefa, Gambela Reserve in Ilubabor,
Lake Shamo Reserve in Gemu Gofa, Danakil Reserve in Wello,
Awash Reserve in Hararge and Shewa and the Rift Valley Lake
Reserve in Shewa.   No recent information is available on enforcement of regulations which a number of game wardens
brought in from other countries found almost impossible to
maintain against illegal hunting and sales of animal skins.   It
is speculated that close control over firearms by the peasant
associations (q. v.) since 1975 has given wild animals some
breathing and breeding space.

WOMEN, STATUS OF.   The Christian-Amhara-Tegray women have
      had equal rights in law and in inheritance of land for centuries,
      and gained suffrage with the same limitations as men in 1957
      (see ELECTIONS).   They do not change their names upon mar-
      riage, and can initiate divorce as easily as men.
         On the other hand, women are represented in folklore as
      untrustworthy, flighty, and prone to sexual temptation unless
      carefully watched.   Virginity upon marriage is required for
      girls, and if not proven they are a disgrace to their parents.
      A woman's adultery is judged more severely than a man's.   In
      case of divorce, custody goes to the father if he wishes it,
      after the child is about four.   The women of the privileged
      classes could break all rules pertaining to traditional behavior
      (subservience) though overtly respecting decorum.
         The Amhara-Tegray woman of the peasant class is restricted
      to domestic labor; the aristocratic women managed their servants,
      did occasional spinning, rarely exercised and their consequent obe-
      sity was considered a compliment to their husband's status.   Mar-
      riage at an early age was more common among the rich than the
      poor, as the arrangement of the bond was usually political and eco-
      nomic and weddings were expensive affairs.   The general run of
      women labor from dawn until dark, are divorced by their husbands
      if they do not provide a child, preferably a boy, have little chance
      at education let alone the rudiments of literacy.
         Women are excluded from public assemblies among the Beni
      Amer, Afar, Somali, Borana, Guji, Sidamo, Konso, Kefa, Dorze
      and Kunama, and a generally pejorative view of women charac-
      terizes these societies, except among the Borana.
         After World War II, despite the aura of "maternalism" the
      patronage of the women of the royal family produced great strides
      in education, medical services and women's welfare.   Women be-
      came doctors, lawyers, nurses, teachers, civil servants and for-
      eign service officers.   These were urban developments, and little
      changed in the life of women in rural areas.
         The women convey to their children the duties and manners
      that will be expected of them as adults, the respect for religion,
      thus are the prime carriers of culture and tradition.   The af-
      fection between mother and son appears to endure in a stronger
      way than with her daughters who leave home and become part of
      their husband's families.   The standard mother-in-law jokes are
      also part of Ethiopian life.   Behind their generally depressed

status in a factual sense, there exist de facto power and influence that most Ethiopian males concede. (See also CIRCUMCISION; MARRIAGE.)

WORLD BANK (International Bank for Reconstruction and Development). One of Ethiopia's prime sources for development capital, which has been used for highways, agriculture, education, telecommunications and development finance institutions. The Bank's first loan to Ethiopia, in 1950 for a highway project, was also its first to any African country. Since then, including agreements with the current military-run government of the Derg, some 35 loans or credits have been negotiated--from the IBRD and the International Development Association, a Bank affiliate--for a total of around $400 million (US). Bank officials rate Ethiopia's record of repayment as good.

In recent years, most of this financing has been to assist Ethiopia's agricultural development, such as irrigation, road construction for better distribution of farm products, improving livestock. As the urban sector comprises about 12 percent of the total population, it has received less IBRD attention; this is aimed at increasing the cities' linkage with and support of rural farm development.

- Y -

YARED, Saint (6th century). Born at Aksum during the active evangelization of the "nine saints." His hymnary, Mazqaba Degwa, is the oldest literary work written in Ge'ez and he is said to have introduced music into the Ethiopian Church. His hymns, dedicated to each of nine saints, are still sung. He composed in three modes: Ge'ez, the plain chant for ordinary days; 'Ezel, a more measured beat for funerals; and araray, a lighter, freer mood for great festivals.

YEJJU. This province was settled, like Wello (q.v.), in the 16th century by the Oromo, who retained their language, became Muslim, and adapted the gada system (q.v.) into a ruling family, the Were Shaikh. The hybrid name probably represents a mutual absorption between them and their Afar-Saho neighbors in the plains. They penetrated by conquest the central provinces while the Amhara and Tegray lords were preoccupied in civil war, gave military service as it suited them and generally held the balance of power. Their leaders became Christian (the first to be baptized was Ali "the great," d. 1788) to make their rule over the weak royal house at Gondar more palatable (see GUGSA MERSU).

Ras Ali Alula (1831-1853) found his Yejju relations often in rebellion against him, but they came to his aid in his war with Webe Hayle Maryam (q.v.) in 1842 and in 1853 they were with him in defeat, and he fled back to Yejju with them.

The Yejju (under Faris Ali and Ali Beru) refused submission to Tewodros II and to Tekle Giyorgis despite many expeditions between 1855 and 1871. Imam Ahmad, their chief in 1874-75 offered cooperation to the Egyptians in their attempted conquest. After that fiasco, Yejju was relatively quiet. The appointment in 1876 of Wele Betul (q.v.) to govern Yejju, was heralded by Menilek's chronicler as the return of a province to its rightful heir citing that Wele's great-grandfather, Gugsa Mersu came from the Yejju ruling house. Wele had to do considerable fighting before his control was secure, but he did rule it (plus Lasta and Wadela) for some 34 years and Yejju had the reputation of being completely self-sufficient in growing cotton for clothing, animals for food and leather goods, making their own pots and baskets, and doing ironwork. It was incorporated into the province of Wello in 1942.

YEKATIT 66 IDEOLOGICAL SCHOOL. Named for the Ethiopian month that runs from 9 February to 9 March, during which time in 1974 riots and strikes by students, teachers, taxi drivers and army enlisted men gave the impetus to the coming revolution. It was set up in May 1976 as a companion organization to POMOA (q.v.) and was charged with "radicalizing the intelligentsia." By March 1979 some 8,000 government officials, army people and union members had taken courses lasting from one to three months. They studied Marx, Engels, and Lenin; scientific socialism; socialist countries that had failed or succeeded; how to build a communist party; and a variety of agitation and propaganda techniques based mostly on the Soviet model.

YEKUNO AMLAQ, Emperor (1270-1285). He is considered the first Solomonic king, assisted to the throne by St. Tekle Haymanot (q.v.) after the reign of the Zagwe (q.v.); and that in gratitude he gave Tekle Haymanot one-third of the kingdom which the church claimed ever after. He wrote the sultan of Egypt in 1274/75 asking him to use his influence with the Coptic Patriarch to have a bishop sent who was honest, well-educated and not greedy for gold and silver, and promised good treatment for Muslims. The sultan refused. Yekuno Amlaq continued the building of churches in Lasta; one church there bears an inscription with his name. His administrative base was at Tegulet in Shewa.

YELMA DERESSA (1907-1974). Related to the Oromo ruling family (Moroda) of Welega; he was educated in England and for many years was the only Ethiopian with training in economics. Detained in Italy during the occupation, he returned to become Minister of Finance 1941-49. He married Elsie, one of the daughters of Dr. Werqneh Eshete (Martin) (q.v.). He was Minister of Commerce 1949-53, Ambassador to the U.S. 1953-58, Minister of Foreign Affairs 1958-60, Minister of Finance 1960-69, and Minister of Commerce, Industry and Tourism in 1969 until he was executed in 1974 by the Derg (q.v.). Using oral traditions, he authored a book (1967) on the history of the Galla (Oromo) in Amharic.

YEMEN and Ethiopia. Semitic migrations from south Arabia (today
   it is divided as North and South Yemen) about the 7th century
   B.C. brought the Sabean language (adapted into Ge'ez), knowledge
   of the use of metals, certain domestic animals, new plants, advanced systems of irrigation and agriculture, and the art of
   writing into the highlands of Ethiopia and the rise of a new civilization once they fused with the original inhabitants.
       Even before the kingdom at Aksum adopted Christianity
   (c. A.D. 331) there were Christian and Jewish settlements in
   Yemen. A Christian survivor of persecution by a Himyar (one
   of Yemen's ancient kingdoms) leader who had embraced Judaism,
   got word to the two protectors of Christianity, Justinian and
   Kaleb (q.v.), of Aksum. Kaleb being closer (it was three hours
   by dhow from the Ethiopian port of Adulis) responded and after
   two expeditions imposed a Christian viceroy over Yemen, Abreha, who ruled from about 524 to about 585. Abreha's attempt
   to conquer Mecca led to the reconquest in 590 by the Persians,
   and Christianity was stamped out permanently.
       Trade revived, especially in slaves, leading to formation
   of a dynastic kingdom of ex-slaves called "Abyssinian Mamluks"
   (or "Najahids") who ruled at Zebid from 1021-1159.
       After the fall of Zagwe dynasty in Ethiopia in 1270, Yekuno-
   amlaq had cordial relations with the Imam of Yemen whose good
   offices he employed to secure a new bishop from Egypt; and
   Fasiledes (after the expulsion of the Jesuits) cordially urged the
   Yemen ruler in 1642 to banish or kill any Portuguese that
   crossed his path and invited him to send Muslim missionaries
   to Ethiopia if he liked. One was sent in 1648 but Fasiledes had
   to send him back with compensatory gifts as the church hierarchy
   was enraged. Yemenite traders had more success spreading the
   message of Islam in the 19th century, especially among the Oromo; poverty in their homeland kept up a steady flow of immigrants who did not bring their families, but made liaisons
   with local women. In Jimma, there was a large settlement of
   Yemenites, and their descendants by Oromo women continued to
   remain a distinct element from the rest of the population.
   Between Hayle Sellase and Imam Yahya an agreement was reached
   that they should be under Ethiopian government administrative
   law; those who came from Aden or Hadramawt would be under
   British protection. (Those areas were occupied in Yemen by the
   British from 1839-1968.) Until direct diplomatic relations were
   established in Addis Ababa in 1897, most of Ethiopia's communications went through Aden. Marxist South Yemen (which consists
   of the former Aden protectorate) maintains relations with the
   present government. North Yemen claims that the "Queen of
   Sheba" came from there, but no evidence has been found to support this.

YESHAQ, Bahr-negash ("king of the sea") (c. 1540-1580). When his
   father, Bahr-negash Degana, defected to the side of Ahmad ibn
   Ibrahim (see ISLAMIC CONQUEST) in 1535, Yeshaq remained
   loyal to the defeated emperor, Lebna Dengel (q.v.). Yeshaq
   welcomed the leader of the Portuguese expedition, Christovão da

Gama at Massawa in 1541 and fought with him to defeat the Muslim armies.   When the Ottomans occupied Massawa in 1557, Yeshaq prevented them from coming into the highlands, but three years later he asked their help (muskets) in order to fight Emperor Minas (1559-1563) and in 1575 allowed them to build a fort at Debarwa (a few miles from present day Asmara) to help keep up his resistance against Minas' successor Sartsa Dengel (q.v.). Sartsa Dengel crushed him and his ally the king of Adal by 1580 and the territories of the <u>Bahr-negash</u> were much reduced. Sartsa Dengel emphasized his control of Tegray by being re-crowned at Aksum.

YODIT EMRU. A daughter of <u>Ras</u> Emru (q.v.) who became the highest ranking woman in the Foreign Affairs ministry in the 1960s and served as Ambassador to Sweden.   Both she and her father were spared by the Derg, in the executions of the old regime in November 1974.

YOHANNES IV, Emperor (1872-1889).   Born in 1831 to Mercha, <u>shum</u> of Temben (district of Tegray) and Selas Dimtsu (descended from Mikael Sehul (q.v.)), he was often called by his "horse" name (see ONOMASTICS), "Abba Bezbez Kasa." He declared himself in opposition to Tewodros II who had appointed Kasa and his brother Gugsa to govern certain districts in Tegray in early 1864 as soon as he heard that the emperor had imprisoned the head of the church in November that same year. By the time the Anglo-Indian forces had made camp at Senafe in December 1867, Kasa controlled most of Tegray.   Upon understanding that the foreign army's purpose was solely to punish Tewodros and rescue the European captives, he gave his full cooperation to the expedition.   In gratitude, Kasa was given about 800 muskets, and some light artillery expeditionary force as it left the country, 25 May 1868.

Kasa Mercha, a very religious widower of austere personal habits, had sent money for a new <u>abun</u> (bishop) from Egypt in February 1869 but when he arrived in August, Kasa refused to send him on to the erstwhile emperor, Tekle Giyorgis (q.v.) who was also his brother-in-law.   Tekle Giyorgis attacked him at Adwa 11 July 1871 and Kasa defeated him.   Kasa Mercha was crowned Yohannes IV at Aksum 21 January 1872.   In two years he managed to acquire the loyalty of four provinces but had to take an army to Shewa in 1878 to secure Menilek's submission; Yohannes was indisputably the strongest as his armies had just defeated two Egyptian invasions in 1875 and 1876.   His son Araya (d. 1888) was married to Menilek's daughter Zewditu (q.v.) in 1882.

Deeply committed to religious unity (there were several heresies current in the Ethiopian Church) Yohannes innovatively secured four bishops, instead of the customary one, from Egypt in 1881; one to stay at his side, and the others to oversee orthodoxy in the provinces.   He had already banished foreign missionaries.   In 1878 he announced a forced conversion campaign for Muslims and animists which was not a success.

Despite settling his problems with Egypt by treaty with its occupying power, Great Britain (see ADWA, TREATY OF, 1884) and meeting all the terms of his commitment, Yohannes was betrayed when Italy occupied the port of Massawa with Britain's full knowledge in February 1885. Their inevitable expansion inland was checked briefly by Ras Alula (q.v.) in 1887. Preparing to give battle to Italy in late 1888, but weakened by a threatened coalition against him by Menilek and Tekle Haymanot (q.v.) Yohannes suddenly offered mediation to Italy. At his back were the Mahdist armies, whom he wheeled to attack. Though the Mahdists retreated after the battle (9 March 1889) they retreated with the head of Yohannes, which was paraded on a spike before a cheering mob in Khartoum (see MENGESHA YOHANNES).

- Z -

ZAGWE DYNASTY (Ze-Agew, Zegwe). There is disagreement about the duration of this dynasty; figures vary from 133 years to 375, but it is accepted that it ended in 1268-1270. "Zagwe" most probably refers to the area that the Agew (q.v.) were settled in. Church history calls them usurpers because they did not belong to the tribe of Israel, i.e., the liaison of Solomon and the "Queen of Sheba." The Zagwe purveyed the rationalization that they were descended from Solomon's dalliance with a maid servant of the Ethiopian queen. In any case the Zagwe kings were devoutly Christian and maintained contacts with Egypt and Jerusalem to ensure delivery of the bishops of the church. Two versions tell of the downfall of the dynasty: one is that St. Tekle Haymanot (q.v.) arranged his abdication peacefully and the other is that Yekuno-Amlaq restored the Solomonic line by killing the last usurper in 1270.

ZEMECHA (Expedition). The military campaigns of Menilek II (and previous sovereigns) to extend the kingdom of Shewa were called zemecha. They occurred twice a year (October-November and March-April) as a rule. Mobilization began a month or two weeks before with the slow beat of drums, accompanied by dire threats if men and their women did not appear with their food, mules and weapons. Women accompanied every expedition playing the role of burden-carrier, "thigh-maid," fire-maker, cook and exhorter to bravery. The word was converted to a peaceful slogan by the Derg in 1975-76 when it sent students into the countryside to organize the rural population into peasant associations (see DEVELOPMENT THROUGH COOPERATION CAMPAIGN).

ZEMENE MESAFINT (Era of the Princes, or Judges). A phrase from the Bible (Judges 21:25) that is used to define the period from about 1769 to 1855 when the emperor was only a puppet in the hands of his regents, and each of the provinces--Begemder, Tegray, Wag-Lasta, Damot, Semen and Shewa--acted as a sovereign power. Parallel with the breakdown of central authority, doctrinal factions of the church fought each other, aggravating the general disunity. Though the anarchy was initiated by Tegray's ruler, Ras Mikael Sehul (q. v.), a Christian who murdered two emperors within a six-month period in 1769, a Yejju Oromo family of superficially converted Christians took control of the symbolic center, Gondar. From about 1800 to 1825, the Yejju chief, Ras Gugsa Mersu (q. v.) maintained supremacy, marrying his daughters wisely to regional lords to achieve an effective network. His sons, Yeman, Marye, and Dori, who succeeded each other in turn, did not have Gugsa's judgment and all were dead by 1831. It was Gugsa's widowed daughter-in-law, Menen Ali Leben (q. v.), who through regency for her 13-year-old son Ras Ali Alula, had the strongest influence until he came of age. Ali Alula kept a shaky hold over Begemder and Gojam from 1831 to 1853 with his mother's help. In 1853, his army was defeated by Kasa Haylu of Qwara whose rule as Tewodros II (q. v.) is considered the end of the Zemene Mesafint, though the turbulence during his reign was such that some historians prefer to think the Zemene Mesafint did not end until Yohannes IV took power in 1872.

ZENEB, Aleqa. The keeper of the royal archives for Tewodros II and the author of his chronicle covering only his early years and the first four years of his reign, i. e. 1825-1859. It was the first chronicle to be written in Amharic instead of Ge'ez, thus an early example of Amharic prose writing in addition to its historical importance. He was a Protestant convert and went to Cairo with Johann Flad, one of the European captives freed in 1868, and returned the following year. He went to live in Shewa in 1872 at the Protestant mission where he died in 1876. Zeneb also translated the scriptures into Oromo (1870-77 edition printed in Switzerland), not J. L. Krapf as is generally credited.

ZERA YAQOB (Emperor 1434-1468). A son of Dawit (q. v.) and Queen Egzi Kebra who succeeded to the throne only after his brothers had died. At no other time in Ethiopian history were there so many female governors and titled women; Zera Yaqob appointed his daughters and his sisters to high office, nor did he spare their lives when three of his daughters were accused of condoning un-Christian practices. Monastery-educated, he is also called "the scholar king" and wrote or caused to be written some of the basic texts of the orthodox faith. He initiated contacts with Christian Europe when he sent delegates to the Council of Florence (1431-1445) and also sent an embassy to Cairo in 1443 to protest the persecution of Christians there.

One of his wives (see ELLENI) was powerful during his life and after his death. Despite his ruthlessness, he has been called the "greatest ruler since Ezana. "

ZEWDE GEBRE SELLASE (1927-   ). The son of Dejazmach Gebre Sellase, onetime governor of Tegray and Welette Israel,

daughter of Ras Seyum Mengesha.   His mother subsequently
married Crown Prince Asfa Wessen (q. v.), from whom she
was later divorced.   Educated at Oxford he became Minister of
Public Works 1955-57; Mayor of Addis Ababa 1957-60; Ambassador to Somalia 1960-61; Minister of Justice 1961-62.
Thwarted in his efforts toward democratic reforms, he exiled
himself to St. Anthony's College, Oxford where he earned his
doctorate with his history of Yohannes IV (see the Bibliography),
his ancestor.   He returned to government in 1972-73 as Ambassador to the United Nations; became Deputy Prime Minister
and Foreign Affairs Minister and was confirmed by the Derg
(q. v.) in 1974.   He condemned the mass executions of 23-24
November 1974 in a public statement and became a political
refugee in the United States, and is presently employed by the
United Nations.

ZEWDITU MENILEK, Empress (1916-1930).   The first woman to
rule Ethiopia since the legendary Queen of Sheba announced that
after herself only men should rule.   Zewditu, daughter of
Menilek II and Weyzero Benchi (or Abichu), was a compromise
choice, once the deposition of her nephew Lej Iyasu (q. v.) was
determined.   She was to be supervised by Teferi Mekonnen
(Hayle Sellase I), her second cousin, who was named regent and
heir at the same time (25 September 1916).   On assuming the
throne she was required to divorce her husband, Gugsa Wele, a
move aimed at thwarting the power of the Betul family (see
TAYTU and WELE BETUL).   Zewditu had no surviving children
from her previous marriages to Araya Yohannes (son of Yohannes IV), Gwangul Zagwe and Webe Atenaf Seged.

A test of her authority came on 6 September 1928 when a
24-gun salute was heard in Addis Ababa.   Regent Teferi, who
had not given his permission (it was to celebrate the birth of
a child to a relation of hers) used it as a pretext to demand
the title of negus (king) and was given that crown on 6 October
1928.

On 1 April 1930, after three years of war (commanded by
the Regent) against her rebellious ex-husband, Gugsa Wele, she
died of pneumonia, complicated with diabetes, two days after
his death in battle.

BIBLIOGRAPHY

The bibliography has been sorted into these categories:

We have omitted Catalogues of the Ethiopic manuscripts in European and U. S. collections, Geology, Geography, Linguistics, Archaeology, and unpublished dissertations, with a few exceptions that we judged appropriate.   Again, with the occasional exception, neither newspaper references, nor Government reports, nor unpublished diplomatic or missionary archives have been cited.   Royal Chronicles are grouped under the headings of History (A) and (B) not listed by their translator's name.

LIST OF ABBREVIATIONS

AAS	Asian and African Studies
AAW	Aus Allen Weltteilen
ABC	African Bibliographic Center, Washington, D. C.
AbhKAW	Abhandlungen der Kaiserliche und Köngliche Geographischen Gesellschaft in Wien
AC	Agricoltura Coloniale
ACISE	Atti di Congresso Internazionale di Studi Etiopici.
(1959)	Accademia Nazionale dei Lincei, Rome: 1961
ACISE	Atti di Congresso Internazionale di Studi Etiopici.
(1972)	Accademia Nazionale dei Lincei, Rome: 1974
AE	Annales d'Ethiopie
AGE	Allgemeine Geographische Ephemeriden
AION	Annuario dell'Istituto Orientale di Napoli
AJPA	American Journal of Physical Anthropology
ALS	African Language Series
ANL	Accademi Nazionale dei Lincei
AnnDEVS	Annalen der Erd-, Völker- und Staatenkunde
AQ	Anthropological Quarterly
ASA	African Studies Association, Brandeis University, Waltham, Mass. 02154
ASC, MSU	African Studies Center, Michigan State University, East Lansing, Mich. 48824
ASR	African Studies Review
ASSB	Annales de la Société de Bruxelles
AttiCGI	Atti del Congresso Geografica Italiana
B	Bulletin, Bolletino
BGHD	Bulletin de Géographie Historique et Descriptive
BGSPhil	Bulletin of the Geographic Society of Philadelphia
BIE	Bulletin de l'Institute Egyptien
BJRL	Bulletin of the John Rylands Library
BRSGI	Bolletino Reale Società Geografica Italiana
BSAC	Bulletin de Société d'Archéologie Copte
BSG	Bulletin de Société de Géographie (Paris)
BSGCHavre	Bulletin de la Société de Géographie Commerciale du Havre
BSGLille	Bulletin de la Société Géographie de Lille
BSGLyons	Bulletin de la Société Géographie de Lyons
BSAI	Bolletino della Società Africana d'Italia
BSGest	Bulletin de la Société de Géographie de l'Est
BSGI	Bolletino della Società Geografica Italiana
BSGM	Bulletin de la Société de Géographie de Marseille
BSKG	Bulletin de la Société Khédeviale Géographie
BSNG	Bulletin de la Société Neuchâteloise de Géographie
BSNorG	Bulletin de la Société Normande Géographie

BSRBelge	Bulletin de la Société Royale Belge Géographie
BUP	Boston University Press
BZ	Byzantische Zeitschrift
CEA	Cahiers d'Etudes Africaines
CGIN	Congresso Geografica d'Italiana Napoli
CRSG	Comte Rendu Congrès Internationale Société Géographie
CSCO	Corpus Scriptorum Christianorum Orientalium
CUP	Cambridge University Press, Cambridge, England
DKAW	Denkschriften der Kaiserliche Akademisch der Wissen-schaften
DRGS	Deutsche Rundschau für Geographie und Statistik
EC	Esploratore Commerciale
E. C.	Ethiopian Calendar
EER	Ethiopian Economic Review
EGJ	Ethiopian Geographical Journal
EJE	Ethiopian Journal of Education
EMJ	Ethiopian Medical Journal
EN	Ethiopianist Notes
EO	Ethiopia Observer
FAO	Food and Agriculture Organization, United Nations
FDUP	Fairleigh Dickinson University Press
GII	Geograficheskiia Izviestiia Imperatorskago Russkago Geograficheskago Obshchestva
GJ	Geographical Journal
Gli Annali	Gli Annali dell'Africana Italiana
GM	Geographical Magazine
GPO	Government Printing Office, Washington, D. C.
GR	Geographical Review
GSAI	Giornale delle Società Asiatica Italiana
Harvard UP	Harvard University Press
HIBS	Hoover Institution Press, Bibliographical Series. Stan-ford, California
HIP	Hoover Institution Press
HMSO	His (Her) Majesty's Stationery Office
HSIU	Hayle Sellase I University
HUP	Howard University Press
IAI	International African Institute, London, England
IJAHS	International Journal of African Historical Studies
IzIR	Izvïestiïa Imperatorskago Russkago Geograficheskago Obshchestva
JA	Journal Asiatique
JAH	Journal of African History
J. A. S.	Journal of African Studies
JAS	Journal of the Asiatic Society
J. des A.	Journal des Africanistes
JEL	Journal of Ethiopian Law
JES	Journal of Ethiopian Studies
JFVG	Jahresbericht des Frankfurter Vereins für Geographie und Statistik
JG	Journal of Geography
JGEG	Jahresbericht der Geographisch-Ethnographischen Ge-sellschaft in Zürich
JHMAS	Journal of the History of Medicine and Allied Sciences

JMAS   Journal of Modern African Studies
JMH   Journal of Modern History
JRAI   Journal of the Royal Anthropological Institute
JRAS   Journal of the Royal African Society
JRGS   Journal of the Royal Geographic Society
JRSA   Journal of the Royal Society of the Arts
JRUSI   Journal of the Royal United Service Institution
JSA   Journal de Société des Africanistes
JSOR   Journal of the Society of Oriental Research
JSS   Journal of Semitic Studies
JTGS   Journal of the Tyneside Geographical Society
MAE   Ministero Affari Esteri, Roma, Italia
Mem. SGI   Memorie Società Geografica Italiana
MGGJ   Mitteilungen der Geographischen Gesellschaft (für
            Thuringen) zu Jena
MIT   Massachusetts Institute of Technology Press
MKKGG   Mitteilungen der Kaiserliche und Köngliche Geographi-
            schen Gesellschaft in Wien
MSU   Michigan State University, East Lansing, Mich.
MUP   Manchester University Press, Manchester, England
MVE, L   Mitteilungen des Vereins für Erdkunde zu Leipzig
n. d.   no date
n. p.   no publisher
NAS   Northeast African Studies (formerly Ethiopianist Notes)
NAV   Nouvelles Annales des Voyages, de la Géographie, de
            l'Histoire, et de l'Archéologie
Nor UP   Northwestern University Press
NUP   Negro Universities Press, in conjunction with Green-
            wood Press, Westport, Connecticut 06880
OCP   Orientalia Christiana Periodica
OM   Oriente Moderno
OSU   Ohio State University, Columbus, Ohio
OUP   Oxford University Press
P. 1st   Proceedings of the First United States Conference on
  USCES   Ethiopian Studies, 1973 (African Studies Center,
            Michigan State University, East Lansing, Mich.
            48824: 1975)
P. 3rd   Proceedings of the Third International Conference on
  ICES   Ethiopian Studies, March-April 1966, Addis Ababa.
            3 vols. (Hayle Sellase I University, Addis Ababa:
            1969-1970)
P. 5th   Proceedings of the Fifth International Conference on
  ICES   Ethiopian Studies. Session B, April 13-16, 1978,
            Chicago, USA. (Office of Publications Services,
            University of Illinois at Chicago Circle, Robert L.
            Hess, Editor: 1979)
P. RGS   Proceedings of the Royal Geographic Society
PUF   Presses Universitaires de France
PUP   Princeton University Press, Princeton, N. J.
QIC   Quaderni dell'Istituto Italiano di Cultura
RA   Rural Africana
RAL   Reale Accademie dei Lincei
RAOS   Rerum Aethiopicarum Scriptores Occidentales

RCI	Rivista delle Colonie Italiane
Rd'Eth.	Revue d'Ethnographie et Traditions Populaires
RDM	Revue des Deux Mondes
REC	Rassegna Economica delle Colonie
Rev. GCB	Revue Géographie Commerciale de Bordeaux
RG	Revue Géographie
RI	Rassegna Italiana
Riv. CI	Rivista Colonie Italiane
Riv. GI	Rivista Geografica Italiana
Riv. PL	Rivista Politica e Litteraria
Riv. SO	Rivista Studi Orientali
RO	Revue de l'Orient
ROC	Revue de l'Orient Chrétien
RRAL	Rendiconti dei Accademia dei Lincei
RS	Revue Semitique
RSAI	Rassegna Sociale dell'Africa Italiana
RSE	Rassegna di Studi Etiopici
RSO	Rassegna di Studi Orientale
RSSA	Royal Society of South Africa
RUSIJ	Royal United Service Institution Journal
SGM	Scottish Geographic Magazine
SKW	Sprachenkommission der Kaiserliche Akademie der Wissenschaften
SOAS Bull.	Bulletin of the School of Oriental and African Studies, University of London, England
SUP	Stanford University Press, Palo Alto, Calif.
TM	Le Tour de Monde
Trans. BGS	Transactions of the Bombay Geographical Society, India
TV	A Travers le Monde
UCAAESB	University College of Addis Ababa Ethnological Society Bulletin
UCLA	University of California at Los Angeles, Calif.
UCP	University of Chicago Press
UCPress	University of California Press, Los Angeles, Calif.
UCR	University College Review, Addis Ababa, Ethiopia
UP	University Press of North America
USAID	United States Agency for International Development
UWP	University of Wisconsin Press
ZA	Zeitschrift für Assyriologie
ZAE	Zeitschrift für Allgemeine Erdkunde
ZDMG	Zeitschrift der Deutschen Morgenländischen Gesellschaft
ZE	Zeitschrift für Ethnologie
ZGEBerlin	Zeitschrift der Gesellschaft für Erdkunde zu Berlin
ZK	Zeitschrift für Kulturaustausch (Sonderausgabe: 1973)

GENERAL WORKS

Area Handbook for Ethiopia (U.S. G.P.O.: 1971, 2nd ed.) Irving
    Kaplan, Mark Farber, Barbara Marvin, James McLaughlin,
    Harold D. Nelson, Donald Whitaker.

Atnafu Makonnen. Ethiopia Today (Tokyo: Radiopress, 1960).

Budge, E. A. Wallis. A History of Ethiopia, Nubia and Abyssinia,
    2 vols. (Oosterhout N.B., The Netherlands: Anthropological
    Publications, 1966).

Buxton, David R. The Abyssinians (New York: Praeger, 1970).

Cambridge History of Africa. 5 vols. (to date). See vol. 2
    (c. 500 B.C.-A.D. 1050) P. L. Shinnie, "The Nilotic Sudan
    and Ethiopia," and "Christian Nubia"; vol. 3 (c. 1050-c. 1600)
    Tadesse Tamrat, "Ethiopia, the Red Sea and the Horn"; vol. 4
    (c. 1600-c. 1790) M. Abir, "Ethiopia and the Horn of Africa";
    and vol. 5 (1790-1870) S. Rubenson, "Ethiopia and the Horn of
    Africa."

Cerulli, Enrico. Studi Etiopici, 4 vols. (Rome: Istituto per
    l'Oriente, 1936-1963).

Conti Rossini, Carlo. Etiopia e gente di Etiopia (Florence: 1937).

Coulbeaux, J. B. Histoire politique et religieuse d'Abyssinie, 3
    vols. (Paris: Paul Geuthner, 1929).

Davy, André. Ethiopie: d'hier et d'aujourdhui (Paris: Le Livre
    Africain, 1971).

Deribéré, Paulette. L'Ethiopie, berceau de l'humanité (Paris:
    Société Continentale d'Editions Modernes Illustrées, 1972).

_____. Histoire Sommaire de la Corne Orientale de l'Afrique
    (Paris: P. Geuthner, 1972).

Doresse, Jean. Ethiopia (trans. New York: Putnam's, 1959).

_____. Histoire de l'Ethiopie (Paris: PUF, 1970).

Encyclopaedia Africana, Dictionary of African Biography, Vol. I:
    Ethiopia-Ghana (New York: Reference Publications, 1977).

Gailey, Harry A. History of Africa from 1800 to Present (New York: Holt, Rinehart and Winston, 1972).

Haberland, Eike. Athiopiens (Stuttgart: Kohlhammer Verlag, 1963).

Hammerschmidt, Ernst. Athiopien: Christliches Reich zwischen Gestern und Morgen (Wiesbaden: Harrassowitz, 1967).

Hess, Robert L. Ethiopia: The Modernization of Autocracy (Ithaca, N. Y.: Cornell University Press, 1970).

Hotten, J. C. Abyssinia and Its People (London: 1868. Reprinted: Greenwood, Westport, Conn., 1970).

Jones, A. H., and Monroe, E. A History of Abyssinia (Oxford: 1935, and 1955. Reprinted Westport, Conn., Greenwood Press, 1976).

July, Robert W. A History of African People (New York: Scribners, 1970), 43-49, 89-100, 334-343.

Langer, Villiam L. Encyclopedia of World History (Boston: Houghton Mifflin, 1968).

Last, Geoffrey, and Pankhurst, Richard. A History of Ethiopia in Pictures (Addis Ababa: OUP, 1969).

Levine, Donald. Wax and Gold (Chicago: UCP, 1965).

_____. Greater Ethiopia (Chicago: UCP: 1974).

Lipsky, George A. Ethiopia: Its People, Its Society, Its Culture (New Haven: HRAF Press, 1962).

Lord, Edith. Queen of Sheba's Heirs (Washington, D. C.: Acropolis Books, 1974).

Luther, Ernest W. Ethiopia Today (Stanford: SUP, 1958).

Markakis, John. Ethiopia, Anatomy of a Traditional Polity (Clarendon: OUP, 1974).

Mathew, David. Ethiopia, the Study of a Polity, 1540-1935 (London: 1947, Reissued 1974 by Greenwood Press, Westport, Conn.).

Mesfin Wolde-Mariam. An Introductory Geography of Ethiopia (Addis Ababa: Berhanena Salem, 1972).

Morié, L. J. Les civilisations africaines. Histoire de l'Ethiopie (Nubie et Abyssinie) depuis les temps les plus reculés jusqu'à nos jours (Paris: 1904).

Pankhurst, Richard. See listings under each section.

Pankhurst, Sylvia.   Ethiopia: A Cultural History (Lalibela, 1955).

Perham, Margery.   The Government of Ethiopia (Evanston, Ill.:
    NUP, 1969).

Pétridès, S. Pierre.   Le Livre d'Or de la Dynastie salomonienne
    d'Ethiopie (Paris: Plon, 1964).

Rubenson, Sven.   The Survival of Ethiopian Independence (London:
    Heinemann, 1976).

Sabelli, Luca dei.   Storia di Abissinia.   4 vols (Rome: 1936-1938).

Saxena, Nawal I.   Ethiopia Through the Ages (Calcutta: B. K.
    Saxena, 1968).

Schwab, P.   Decision-Making in Ethiopia (Rutherford, N. J.:   FDUP,
    1972).

Shack, William A.   The Central Ethiopians: Amhara, Tigriña and
    Related Peoples (London: International African Institute,
    1974).

Simoons, Frederick J.   Northwest Ethiopia: Peoples and Economy
    (Madison, Wisc.:   UWP, 1960).

Talbot, David A.   Contemporary Ethiopia (New York: Philosophical
    Library, 1952).

Tekla Tsadeq Makuriya.   Ye-Ityopya Tarik, Ke-Atse Tewodros eska
    Germawi Hayla Sellase (Addis Ababa: Qeddus Giyorgis Print-
    ing Press, E. C. 1954 (1961)).

Trimingham, J. S.   Islam in Ethiopia (London: Frank Case, 1965).

Ullendorff, Edward.   The Ethiopians (London: OUP, 1960).

TRAVEL AND EXPLORATION
(The underlined date is the period of observation)

Abargués de Sostén, J. V.   Notas del viaje del Sr. D. J. V.
    Abargués de Sostén por Etiopia, Xoa, Zenul, Uolo, Galas, etc.
    (Madrid: Imp. de Fortanet, 1883).   1881

Abbadie, Antoine Thompson d'.   "Lettre écrite du pays d'Onarya à
    M. d'Avezac," BSG, 3 (1845), 52-67.   1843

_____ .   Géographie de l'Ethiopie. (Paris: G. Mesnil, 1890).
    1838-1848

Abbadie, Arnauld d'. Douze Ans dans l'haute-Ethiopie. (Paris: 1868). 1838-1848 (see also J. Tubiana below).

Acquaye, A. A. Ethiopia in Pictures (New York, Sterling: 1972).

Albertis, E. A. d' Una gita all'Harar. (Milan: 1906). 1905

Aleme Eshete. "European political adventurers in Ethiopia at the turn of the 20th century," JES, 12: 1 (1974).

Almeida, Manuel. Some Records of Ethiopia, 1593-1646. (Edited and translated by C. F. Beckingham and G. W. B. Hunting- ford (London: Hakluyt Society, 1954). 1624-1634

Alvarez, F. Narrative of the Portuguese Embassy to Abyssinia (trans. and edited by Lord Stanley of Alderley; Hakluyt So- ciety, London, 1881). 1520-1526

Alype, Pierre. L'empire de Négus. (Paris: Plon, 1925). c. 1924

Amodeo, M. ed. "I Rapporti tra Italia e Abissinia nell '89 e nell '89 in un carteggio inedito di Ottorino Rosa, con Porro, Guasconi, Sacconi e Cecchi," Gli annali, 4: 3 (1941).

Annaratone, Carlo. In Abissinia (Rome: 1914). 1903-1912

Antinori, O. Il Marchese Orazio Antinori e la spedizione geographi- ca italiana; nell 'Africa equatoriale (Perouse: 1883). 1876- 1882

_____, O. Beccari, and A. Issel. "Relazione sommaria del viaggio nel Mar Rosso," BSGI, 5 (1870).

_____, and A. Cecchi. [Letter on area near Mt. Zukuala] BSGI, 19 (1882).

Antonelli, Pietro. "Il primo viaggio di un Europeo attraverso l'Aussa," BSGI, 26 (1889). 1879-1891

_____. [Letters from Ethiopia of Nov. 6, 1879 and March 29, May 8, 1880], BSGI, 17 (1880), 56-57, 455-463.

_____. Rapporti sullo Scioa (1883-1888) (Rome, Tipografica Ministero Affari Esteri: 1890).

_____. "Scioa e Scioani," BSGI, 19 (1882) 69-92.

_____. [Letter from Ethiopia of 3 June 1883], BSGI, 20 (1883).

_____. "Il mio viaggio da Assab allo Scioa," BSGI, 20 (1883).

Asinari di San Marzano, R. see San Marzano

Athill, L. F. I. "Through South-Western Abyssinia to the Nile,"
    GJ, 56: 5 (1920).

Aubert, L. "Fragment sur Gondar et le Négus," BSG, 10 (1838)
    145-157.

_____. "Communication faite à la société de géographie sur le
    voyage commerciale en Abyssinie et sur la mer rouge de
    MM. Dufey et Aubert," BSG, 13 (1840) 280-90. 1837-38

Aubry, Alphonse d'. "Une Mission au Choa et dans les Pays
    Gallas," BSG extr. (1887). 1883-1885

Audon, H. "Voyage au Choa," TM, 2° sem. (1889). 1884-1887

Austin, H. H. "Survey of the Sobat region," GJ, 17: 5 (1901).
    1898

Avanchers, Father Léon des. (Lettres à M. Antoine d'Abbadie),
    BSG, 17 (1859), 20 (1860), 3 (1862), 12 (1866), 17 (1869).
    1859-1879

Azaïs, Father. "Exploration archéologique en Ethiopie méridionale
    (Mai-Nov. 1926). La Géographie, 48 (1927).

Baeteman, J. "Au pays de Menelik," BSGL, 60 (1913) 249-63.
    1903

Baker, R. St. B. Sahara Conquest (London: Lutterworth Press,
    1966). 1964

Baker, Samuel. "Journey to Abyssinia in 1862," JRGS, 33 (1863)
    237-241.

_____. The Nile Tributaries of Abyssinia and the Sword Hunters
    of the Hamran Arabs (London: 1867).

Baldacci, Luigi. "L'oro nell'Eritrea," BSAI, 16 (1897) 56-7.

Baldet, Henri. "Along the Salt Trail," EO, 15: 4 (1972) 227-234.
    1971

_____. "Seven Days on the Roof of Africa," EO, 16: 2 (1973)
    70-75. 1972

Baratti, Giacomo. The Late Travels of S. Giacomo Baratti, an
    Italian Gentleman, into the Remote Countries of the Abissins,
    or of Ethiopia Interior (London: 1670). c. 1655-

Bardey, Alfred. "Notes sur le Harar," BGHD, (1897) 130-80.
    1880

Barker, W. C. "Extract Report on the Probable Geographical Position of Harrar; with Some Information Relative to the Various Tribes in the Vicinity," JRGS, 12 (1842).

Barois, Jules. "Impressions de voyage en Abyssinie," BIE, 5, ser. 2 (1908). 1907

Barradas, Manoel. "Tractatus tres historico-geographici," in RASO, IV (1906). 1624-1633

Bartleet, E. J. In the Land of Sheba (Birmingham: 1934). 1928

Baum, J. E. Savage Abyssinia (London: 1928). 1926

Beccari, Camillo. Il Tigrè descritto da un missionario gesuita del seculo XVII (Rome: 1909).

Beke, C. T. "Appendix to Messrs. Isenberg and Krapf's Journal. Routes in Abyssinia and the neighboring countries, collected from Natives," JRGS, 10 (1841) 580-86.

_____. "On the Countries South of Abyssinia," JRGS, 13 (1843) 254-269.

_____. "Mémoire justicatif en réhabilitation des Pères Pierre Paes et Jérôme Lobo, missionaires en Abyssinie, en ce qui concerne leurs visites à la source de l'Abai (le Nil) et la cataracte d'Alata," BSG, 9 (1848) 145-886, 209-39.

_____. "Route from Ankobar to Dima," JRGS, 12 (1842) 245-260.

_____. "Abyssinia: being a continuation of routes in that country," JRGS 14 (1844) 1-64.

Belloni, Giuseppe. "Da Barentu al Setit, e a Godofelassi," EC, 19 (1904) 232-41.

_____. "In viaggio, dall'Eritrea alla Somalia," EC, 19 (1904).

Bent, J. T. The Sacred City of the Ethiopians, being a record of travel and research in Abyssinia in 1893 (London: 1896).

Bergsma, S. Rainbow Empire: Ethiopia Stretches out Her Hands. (Grand Rapids, Michigan: 1932).

Berlan, E. Addis Abeba la plus haute ville d'Afrique (Grenoble: 1963).

_____. "L'eucalyptus a Addis Abeba et au Choa," Revue de Géographie Alpine, 39 (1951).

_____. "La vigne en Ethiopie," Revue de Géographie Alpine, 40 (1952).

Bermudes, João. Breve relaçao da embaixada que o patriarcha
D. João Bermudes trouxe do imperador da Ethiopia volgar-
mente chamado Preste João dirigida a el-rei D. Sabastião
(Lisbon: 1875). 1520-c. 1550 (see Whiteway below)

Berry, LaVerle, and Smith, Richard. "Churches and Monasteries
of Lake Tana, Ethiopia, 1972," Africa (Rome) March-June
1979, 1-34.

Beurmann, Moriz von. "Reisen in Nubien und dem Sudan, 1860
und 1861: Suakin und Massua," Petermanns, 8 (1862) 95-98.

Bianchi, Gustavo. Alla Terra dei Galla (Milan: 1884). 1879-
1880

_____. "Fra i Soddo-Galla," BSAI, 1 (1882) 6-13.

_____. Letter from Asmara, 14 March 1883. BSGI, 20 (1883)
385-388.

_____. Letters of 10 July, 23 September 1884. BSGI, 22
(1885), 24-25, 28-30.

Bieber, F. J. "Die österreichische Expedition nach Kaffa," DRGS,
28 (1906). 1905

_____. "Reiseeindrücke und wissenschaftliche Beobachtungen aus
Gallaland und Kaffa," Globus, 89 (1906).

_____. "Von Addis Ababa über den Assabot nach Dschibuti,"
DRGS, 30 (1908) 13-22, 66-74.

_____. "Durch Südäthiopien zum Nil," Globus, 97 (1910).

_____. "Reise nach Harar und Adis Ababa," DRGS, 32 (1910).

_____. "Reise durch Äthiopien und den Sudan," MKKGG, 53
(1910).

Bisson, Raoul du. "Relation de l'Expedition faite en 1863-64 ...
aux frontières de l'Abyssinie," NAV, 184 (1864).

Blanc, Henry. "From Metemma to Damot, Along the Western
Shores of the Tana Sea," JRGS, 39 (1869) 36-50. 1864-1868

Blanchard, D. H. Ethiopia: Its Culture and Its Birds (San Antonio, Texas, Naylor: 1969).

Blandford, W. T. Observations on the Geology and Zoology of
Abyssinia made During Progress of the British Expedition to
That Country in 1867-68. (London: 1870).

Blashford-Snell, J. Where the Trail Runs Out (London: Hutchinson, 1974). 1969

Blondeel von Cuelebroeck, E. Rapport générale de de Blondeel sur son expédition en Abyssinie (Brussels: 1839-42).

Blundell, H. Weld. "A Journey Through Abyssinia to the Nile," GJ, 15 (1900) 97-120.

_____. "Exploration in the Abai Basin, Abyssinia," GJ, 27 (1906) 529-51. 1898 and 1905

Bolton, M. Ethiopian Wildlands. (London: Collins and Harvill, 1976).

Bonchamps, C. de "Une mission vers le Nil Blanc," BSG, 19 (1898) 404-31. 1897

Bongiovanni, W., and de Vita, A. "Escursioni in Eritrea tra Meder e Adi Cajèh," BSGI, 38 (1901) 554-61.

Borelli, Jules. Ethiopie méridionale. Journal de mon voyage aux pays Amhara, Oromo et Sidama, septembre 1885 a novembre 1888 (Paris: 1890).

_____. "Souvenirs d'un voyage dans les pays des Gallas du sud et de Sidama," BSKG, 3 (1889) 147-175.

_____. "Il fiume Omo e l'Etiopia meridionale," BSAI, 9 (1890), 171-73.

Bottego, Vittorio. "Nella terra dei Danakil, giornale de viaggio," BSGI, 29 (1892) 403-18, 480-94.

_____. L'Esplorazione del Giuba (Rome: 1900). 1892-1893

Boulvin, Fritz. Une Mission Belge en Ethiopie (Bruxelles: Société Belge d'études coloniales, 1906).

Bourg de Bozas, Robert du. Mission scientifique de la Mer Rouge à l'Atlantique a travers l'Afrique tropicale (octobre 1900--mai 1903).

Bourke, Dermot R. Wydham (Earl of Mayo). Sport in Abyssinia (London: 1876). 1874

Boyes, H. John. My Abyssinian Journey. (Nairobi: 1941?). First published as Part II of The Company of Adventurers (London, "East Africa," 1928). 1906

Branchi, G. Missione in Abissinia--1883 (Rome: 1889).

Brehm, Alfred. Ergebnisse meiner Reise nach Habesch im Gefolge des Herzogs Ernst II von Sachsen-Koburg-Gotha (Hamburg: 1863).

Brémond, L.-A. Lecture of 5 March 1885. BSGM, 9 (1885) 221-224. 1881 and 1884

Brenner, Richard. "Reise in den Galla-Ländern, 1867-1868," Petermanns, 14 (1868) 175-179.

Bricchetti-Robecchi, Luigi. "Dall'Harrar," BSAI, 8 (1889) 35-38.

_____. "Viaggio nel Paese dei Somali," BSGI, 27 (1890) 869-78.

_____. "La prima traversata della Penisola dei Somali," BSGI, 30 (1893).

_____. Nell'Harar. (Milan: 1896).

_____. Nel Paese degli Aromi--Diario di una esplorazione dell'Africa Orientale (Milan: 1903).

Bruce, James. Travels to Discover the Source of the Nile in the Years 1768-1773, 5 vols (2nd ed. Edinburgh: 1805), also (New York: Horizon 1964). Edited version by C. F. Beckingham (Edinburgh University Press: 1964).

Brucker, J. "L'Afrique Centrale des cartes du XVI siècle," BSGLyon, 3 (1880) 252-64. (Survey)

Brummelkamp, Jacob. Ethiopie, eiland in een continent (Meppel, Netherlands: 1956).

Brumpt, Emile. "Mission du Bourg de Bozas," BSGCHavre, 19-20 (1902-1903).

Buchholzer, J. The Land of Burnt Faces (trans. from Danish by M. Michael, London: Arthur Barker, 1955).

Buchs, Victor. "Voyages en Abyssinie, 1889-1895," BSNeuG, 9 (1896-97).

Bulatovich, A. Ot Entoto go reki Baro. Otchet o Puteschestvii v iugozapadnye oblasti Efiopskoi imperii v 1896-1897 (St. Petersburg: 1897).

_____. "Iz Abissinii cherez stranu Kaffa na ozero Rudol'fa," IzIr, 35 (1899). Abstract in BSGI, 37 (1900) 121-42.

_____ (Boulatovich). With the Troops of Menelick II (Academy of Sciences, Moscow: 1971). A translation and footnoted version of Voiskami Menelika (St. Petersburg: 1900) by E. S. Katsnelsona.

Burton, R. F. First Footsteps in East Africa, or an Exploration of Harar (London, Longmans: 1856) 2 vols. 1854-1855

_____. "Narrative of a Trip to Harar," JRGS, 25 (1885).

Busk, Douglas. The Fountain of the Sun: unfinished journeys in
    Ethiopia and the Ruwenzori (London, Max Parrish: 1957).
    1952-1956

Butter, A. E. Report on the survey of the proposed frontier between
    British East Africa and Abyssinia (London: HMSO 1904).

Buxton, David R. Travels in Ethiopia (London: 1950; reprint with
    revisions, New York, Praeger, 1967).

Caillou, Alan. Sheba Slept Here (New York: Abelard-Schuman,
    1973). 1941-

Calciati, C., and Bracciani, L. Nel paese dei Cunama: Missione
    Corni-Calciati-Bracciani in Eritrea 1922-1923 (Milan: 1927).

Candeo, Guiseppe. "Un viaggio nella penisola dei Somali," Atti
    Cong. Geog. Ital. (Genoa: 1892) v. 1.

Caprotti, L. "La Schiavitu nel Gallabat," EC, 6 (1882).

_____. "Il viaggiatore monti fra gli Aman-Niger (Galla) Abbai di
    Gudru," EC, 7 (1883).

Capucci, L., and Cicognami, L. "In Viaggio per lo Scioa," BSAI,
    4 (1885).

_____. (Travel journal and letters), BSAI, 5 (1886) 32-34, 61-
    68, 131-133, 222-226.

_____. See Zaghi, C.

Carafa d'Andria, R. "Le bellezze dell'Eritrea," BSAI, 19 (1900) 31-64.

Castanhoso (see Whiteway below).

Castro, Dr. Lincoln de. Nella Terra dei Negus. 2 vols (Milan:
    1915). 1896-1897 and 1901-c. 1913

_____. Terra, Uomini e cose (2nd ed. Milan: 1936).

_____. "De Zeila au Harar," BSKG, 5 (1898) 133-61.

_____. (Letter on excursion to Zukuala, Lake Zwai and Soddo),
    BSGI, 45 (1908).

_____. "Un covento trogloditico ad Eccà presso Addis-Abeba,"
    BSGI, 44 (1907).

_____. "La città e il clima di Addis Abeba," BSGI, 46 (1909)
    409-42, 492.

Cecchi, Antonio. "Sulla idrografi della regioni al Sud dello Scioa;
    studio," BSGI, 19 (1882) 414-422.

_____ . Relazione intorno alle ultime vicende della spedizione italiana in Africa attraverso i regni di Ghera-Gomma-Gimma-Guma (Pesaro: 1882).

_____ . Da Zeila alle frontiere del Caffa. 3 vols. (Rome: 1886-1887).

_____ . l'Abissinia settentrionale e le strade che vi conducono da Massaua (Milan: 1888).

Cecchi, Antonio, and Chiarini, Giovanni. (Letters of 6 and 20 July, 1878, and 16 and 26 June 1878.) BSGI, 16 (1879) 114-15, 410-31.

_____ . (Letters) BSGI, 18 (1881), 289-317, 691-705, 710-26; 19 (1882), 389-410.

Cecchi, Antonio, and Martini, Sebastiano. (Letters) BSGI, 14 (1877).

Celarié, Henriette. Ethiopie XXe-siècle (Paris: Hachette, 1934).

Cerulli, Enrico. Etiopia Occidentale dallo Scioa alla frontiera del Sudan: note del viaggio 1927-28. 2 vols. (Rome: 1933).

Cheesman, R. E. Lake Tana and the Blue Nile: an Abyssinian Quest. (London: Frank Cass, 1968). 1926-1934

Chojnacki, Stanislaw. "William Simpson and His Journey to Ethiopia in 1868," JES, 6: 2 (1968).

_____ . "Colonel Milward's Abyssinian Journal 1867-1868," JES, 7: 1 (1969).

Ciccodicola, F. "Escursione dall'Asmara a Mai Daro attraverso al Deca-Tesfa," BSGI, 31 (1894), 774-88.

Cipolla, Arnaldo. Nell'impero di Menelik (Milan: 1913). 1909

_____ . In Etiopia (Turin: 1933).

_____ . Pagine africane di un esploratore (Milan: 1927).

Citerni, Carlo. Ai confini meridionali dell'Etiopia (Milan: 1913).

Clapham, Christopher. "Multiethnic Ethiopia," African Affairs, 75: 298 (1976) 101-103.

Cocastelli, Carlo. (Letter, Zeila, March 22, 1886) BSGI, 23 (1886).

Colacci, Francesco. "Commercio e agricoltura in Abissinia," Cosmos, 8 (1884) 51-58. 1883

Collat, O. Abyssinie actuelle (Paris: 1906).

Colli di Felizzano, G. "Nei paesi Galla a sud dello Scioa," BSGI
42 (1905) 8-18, 100-118.

Combes, Edmond, and Tamisier, Maurice. Voyage en Abyssinie,
dans le pays des Galla, de Choa et d'Ifat ... 1835-1837.
4 vols. (Paris: 1838).

Conti-Rossini, C. "Geographica: (Part 3) Gli itinerari di Alessandro Zorzi," RSE, 3: 2 (1943).

_____. "Ricerche e studi sulla Etiopia," BSGI, 37 (1900).

_____. "Al Rágali," EC, 18 (1903) and 19 (1904). Sept. 1902

_____. "Catalogo dei nomi propri di luogo dell'Etiopia," Atti
del primo Congresso Geografico Italiano (Genoa: 1892).

Coon, C. S. Measuring Ethiopia and Flight into Arabia (London:
1936).

Cooper, C. "As in Solomon's Day," Asia, 23 (Dec. 1923) 910-913.

_____. "From King Solomon to Ras Tafari," Asia, 23 (Oct.
1923) 707-713.

_____. "Guardians of the Lion of Judah," Asia 23 (Nov. 1923)
832-837.

Corni, G. Tra Gasc e Setit; note di viaggio, Missione Corni-
Calciati-Bracciani (Ministero della Colonie: 1932). 1922-1923

Coulbeaux, Father Edouard. "Au pays de Menelik," Missions
Catholiques, 30 (1898) 344-46, 357-60, 368-72, 380-83, 393-96,
405-08, 417-20, 428-32, 437-41, 454-56, 473-77, 487-90,
501-02, 513-15, 524-26, 532-34.

Cosson, E. A. de. The Cradle of the Blue Nile, a Visit to the
Court of King John of Ethiopia (London: 1877) 2 vols.

Craig, J. I. "A meteorological expedition to Addis Abeba in 1907,"
Extr. de Cairo Scientific Journal (Alexandria, 1909).

Cranworth, B. F. Gurdon. Kenya Chronicles (London: Macmillan,
1939). (Some chapters are on Ethiopia c. 1911.)

Crosby, Oscar T. "Abyssinia--The Country and People," National
Geographic Magazine, 12 (March, 1901) 89-104.

_____. "Notes on a journey from Zeila to Khartum," GJ, 18
(July 1901) 46-61.

_____. "Personal Impressions of Menelik," Century, 63 (April 1902).

Cuffino, Luigi. "La via da Assab all'Etiopia centrale per il Golima," Cong. GI (Naples, 1904) 337-46.

_____. "La via carovaniera di Gondar e il mercato omonimo," BSAI, 24 (1905), 137-39.

Cuomo, Carlo. "Le province equatoriale dell'Abissinia," BSAI, 19 (1900), 110-13. (Itinerary of Leontiev-d'Orleans expedition.)

Darley, H. A. Slaves and Ivory in Abyssinia: a record of adventure and exploration among the Ethiopian slave raiders (London: 1926). Reprints 1969 and 1972 (Greenwood Press, Westport, Connecticut).

Darragon, Léon. "Le Sidamo, l'Amara, le Konso, etc." Comptes-rendus des séances de la Société de Géographie, 3 (1898).

Das ist Abessinien, L'Abyssinie telle qu'elle est; 140 photographische Bilddokumente (Leipzig: 1935).

Debrosse, Emm. "Un voyage au Harrar," Rev. GCBordeaux, 36 (1913).

Decaud, H. Chasses en Abyssinie (Paris: 1904).

_____. "L'Abyssinie," RG, 54 (1904) 143-152.

Decken, Baron K. von der. Reisen in Ost-Afrika in den Jahren 1859 bis 1865. 5 vols. (Vienna: 1869-1879).

Dehérain, Henri. "Addis-Ababa, résidence de l'empereur Ménélik et son rôle dans l'exploration de l'Abyssinie," Extr. du Bulletin de la Section de Géographie de l'Institut de France (Paris: 1914).

"Die Deutsche Expedition in Ost Afrika, 1861 und 1862," Petermanns, Erganzungsband, 3: 1-4 (1863-1864).

Diana, Cesare. [Letter from Seket, July 5, 1884], BSGI, 22 (1885).

Di Lauro, R. Tre anni a Gondar. (Milan: 1936). 1932-1935

Dimothéos, Father S. Deux ans de séjour en Abyssinie ou vie religieuse des Abyssiniens (Jerusalem: 1871). 1868-1869

Doody, John. The Burning Coast (London: Michael Joseph, 1955). 1941-

Dracopoli, I. N. "Across Southern Jubaland to the Lorian Swamp," GJ, 42 (1913) 128-40.

Duchesne-Fournet, Jean. Mission en Ethiopie (1901-1903) (Paris: 1908-9).

Dufey, J.-N., and Aubert-Roche, L. "Voyage dans l'Abyssinie," RO, 1 (1853) 315 and 435.

Dufton, H. Narrative of a Journey Through Abyssinia in 1862-1863. (London: 1867). (Reprint; Greenwood Press, Westport, Conn.)

Dulio, E. "Dalla baia d'Assab allo Scioa, 1885-1886," Cosmos, 9 (1886-88).

Dunckley, F. C. Eight Years in Abyssinia (London: 1935).

Dundas, F. G. "Expedition up the Juba river through Somaliland, East Africa," GJ, 1 (1893) 209-223.

Dupuis, C. "Lake Tana and the Nile," JRAC, 35 (Jan. 1936) 18-25.

Dutton, E. Z. T. Lillibullero; or, The Golden Road. (Zanzibar, private printing: 1944). 1933

Duvernoy, ?. "Rapport sur le troisième voyage en Abyssinie de Rochet d'Héricourt," Comptes-rendus des séances de l'Acad. des Sciences (Paris: 1851).

Ehrenberg, C. G. (Letters on Hemprich expedition, April 28, 1825(?) and September 26) NAV, 29 (1826) 139-42.

Eipperle (?). "Mittheilungen aus Galabat (Abessinien)," Ausland, 36 (1863), 1181-85.

Ellsberg, E. Under the Red Sea Sun. (New York: Dodd, Mead, 1946). 1941

Emily, Dr. J. "Mission Marchand," TM, 18 (1912) 289-432. 1899

_____. Mission Marchand, journal de route (Paris: 1913).

Erlanger, Carlo von. "Uber meine fast zweijahrige Reise durch Süd-Schoa, die Galla-und Somaliländer," JFVG, 66-67 (1901-1903) 111-15.

_____. "Uber die Reise in den Galla-Ländern," VGEBerlin, 28 (1901) 240-48.

_____. (Lecture abstract April 2, 1902.) MVELeipzig (1902).

_____. "Sulla spedizione e relativo soggiorno in Abissinia e nei paesi dei Galla e dei Somali," BSGI, 39 (1902), 539-44.

_____. "Bericht über meine Expedition in Nordost-Africa in den Jahren 1899-1901," ZGEB, 38 (1904).

_____, and Neumann, Oscar. (Letters of April 17, 1900, November 1, 1900, and Nov. 14, 1900.) VGEBerlin, 27 (1900) 285-88, 477-86.

Ernst II, Duke of Saxe-Coburg-Gotha. "Von Mensa nach Keren im Lande der Bogos," Globus, 2 (1862), 236-39.

Escherich, G. Im Lande des Negus (Berlin: 1912).

Esme, Jean d'. A travers l'empire de Menelik (Paris: 1928).

"Ethiopia," Encore, 1: 5 (December 1972) 41-72.

"Ethiopia: A Tourist Paradise," EO, 8: 3 (1964) 194-208.

Ewert, Kurt. Äthiopien (Bonn, Deutsche Afrika-Gesellschaft: 1959).

Fenzel, ?. "Bericht über die von Herrn Dr. Constantin Reitz auf seiner Reise von Chartum nach Gondar in Abyssinien," Extr. from DKAW (Vienna: 1855).

Ferguson, L. Into the Blue: The Lake Tana Expedition 1953 (London, Collins: 1955).

Ferné, F. e Romagnoli, u. (Unedited diary of trip to Harar in 1885.) Bologna: 1838, Istituto Fascismo).

_____. Un lembo d'Africa (Harar) (Bologna: 1886).

Ferrand, Gabriel. "Notes sur la situation politique, commerciale et religieuse du Pachalik de Harar et de ses dépendances," BSG'est, 8 (1886), 1, 17, 231-44.

Ferrandi, Ugo. (Letter from Harar, Feb. 12, 1889.) EC, 4 (1889) 110-18.

_____. (Letters, Brava, Feb. 2, 5, Mar. 12, April 19 and undated 1891.) EC, 6 (1891), 137-39, 140-50, 171-2, 185-87, 188-89; and EC, 7 (1892) 1-20, 309-10, 373.

_____. "Viaggio nelle regioni dell Giuba," EC, 7 (1892) 35-39, 86-91, 143-45, 149-81, 189-91, 255-56, 278-83.

_____. "Da Brava a Bardera " EC, 8 (1893) 108-15, 197, 230-230-242.

_____. "La spedizione Ruspoli," EC, 9 (1894) 137-43, 364-66.

_____. (Letters, Lugh, Jan. 6 and 8, March 1 and 21, 1896.) MemSGI, 4 (1896) 157-58, 168-70.

_____. (Letter, Mogadishu, May 20, 1897.) BSGI, 34 (1897), 363-66.

_____. "Il viaggio di ritorno alla costa," EC, 13 (1898) 55-59.

Ferrari, V. e Nerazzini, Dr. C. Riepilogo della missione presso Negus Giovanni d'Abissinia (marzo-luglio 1885) (Rome: Voghera, 1885).

Ferret, P. V., and Galinier, J. G. Voyage en Abyssinie, dans les provinces du Tigré, du Samen, et de l'Amhara. 3 vols, and atlas. (Paris: 1847-1848). 1840-1842

Fesquet, Jean de. "Impressions de voyage au Harar," BSGM 21 (1897) 429-30. (Resume of a speech June 3, 1897.)

Ficalho, F. M. Viagens de Pero da Covilham (Lisbon: 1898). c. 1487-c. 1526

Flad, J. Martin. "Reise von Massaua zu Metemmah," Ausland 48 (1875) 99-100. January 1874

_____. Zwölf Jahre in Abessinien oder Geschichte des Konigs Theodoros II und der Mission unter seiner Regierung (Basel: 1869).

Forbes, Duncan. The Heart of Ethiopia (London: R. Hale and Co., 1972).

Forbes, Rosita. From Red Sea to Blue Nile (New York: 1935). 1920s

Fornari, Guido. "L'Uebi Scebeli e la sua regione," BSAI, 25 (1906), 235-60. (On Lt. W. Christopher trip in 1843.)

Förster, Brix. "Die Expedition Graf Wickenburg," Globus, 84 (1903) 308. (survey)

Foster, Sir William, ed. The Red Sea and Adjacent countries at the close of the seventeenth century (London: 1949).

Fouquet, G. Mer Rouge (Paris: J. Suse, 1946).

Fouyas, P. G. "James Bruce of Kinnaird and the Greeks in Ethiopia," Abba Salama, 2 (1971).

Franchetti, R. Nella Dancalia Etiopica; Spedizione Italiana 1928-29. (Verona: Mondadori, 1930).

Franzoj, Auguste. Continente Nero (Turin: 1885). 1882-1884

Fraser, S., and Pedersen, E. Love, Siri and Ebba (London: N. Saunders, 1973).

Fritzsche, G. F. "Die Karawanenstrasse von Zeila nach Ankober und die Kartographie der Grenzgebiete der Somali, Afar und Galla," Petermanns, 36 (1890). (Survey and critique)

Frobenius, Leo. Unter den unsträflichen Aethiopen (Berlin: 1913).

Fuertes, L. A., and Osgood, W. H. Artist and Naturalist in Ethiopia (New York: 1936). 1926

Garstin, Sir William. Report upon the Basin of the Upper Nile ... (Cairo: Imprimerie nationale, 1904). 1902-03 survey by Dupuis and Hayes.

Gatta, L. "Da Massaua a Chartum per Keren e Cassala," BSGI, 22 (1885), 398-406.

Germano, T. and Marchiori, E. "Un escursione nel Danakil," Cosmos, 13 (1897). April-May 1893

Gerster, Georg. L'Ethiopie, toit de l'Afrique (Paris: Webber Diffusion, 1974).

_____. "Searching out Medieval Churches in Ethiopia's Wilds," National Geographic, 138: 6 (1970).

Ghika, Nicolas. Cinq mois au pays des Somalis (Bâle et Genève: 1897). 1895

Ghiorghis Mellesa. "Gondar yesterday and today," EO, 12: 3 (1969) 164-176.

Gigar Tesfaye. "Reconnaissance de trois églises antérieures à 1314," JES, 12: 2 (1974) 57-75.

Girard, Alexandre. Souvenirs d'un voyage en Abyssinie (1868-1869) (Cairo: Ebner, 1873).

Giulietti, G. M. (Letter, Harar, Nov. 3, 1879) BSGI, 17 (1880).

_____. "Viaggio da Zeila ad Harar," BSGI, 18 (1881) 365-82, 425-45.

Giurcaneanu, Claudiu. Etiopia. (Bucureşti: Editura Stuntifică, 1965).

Gleichen, E. With the Mission to Menelik, 1897 (London: 1898).

Giuseppi (of Let Marefia). "Viaggio d'esplorazione d'un abissino fra l'Aussa e lo Scioa." BSGI, 24 (1887) 343.

Gizachew Adamu. "The City of Castles and 44 Churches," Ethiopian Herald, Aug. 13, 1972.

Gödel-Lannoy, Rudolf. "Das Gebiet des Dschubflusses und dessen Dependenz von Zanzibar," MKKGGWien, 14 (1871) 267-72. (Survey)

Goedorp, Victor.   "Chez les Somalis," TV, 5 (1899) 369-71.

_____. "A la cour du Negus Ménélik," et "Chez le ras Makon-
nen," Lectures pour tous, Oct., Nov. 1899.

Gonzague de Lassere, Monsignor.   "Mgr. Massaja et l'empereur
Joannês," l'Explorations, 10 (1880).

Gordon, C. G.   (Letter to Romolo Gessi, Suez, 25 Dec. 1879)
BSKG, 3 (1888).

Grabham, G. W. and Black, R. P.   Report of the Mission to Lake
Tsana 1920-1921 (Cairo, Ministry of Public Works: 1925).

Grad, Charles.   "Résultats scientifiques de la mission allemande
au Soudan oriental à la recherche de Vogel (1861-1862),"
BSG, 9 (1865).

Graham, D. C.   Glimpses of Abyssinia; or extracts from letters
written while on a mission from the Government of India to
the King of Abyssinia. 1841-1843. (London, Longmans:
1867).

Greenfield, Richard.   "Ethiopian Itineraries: some routes in
northern Ethiopia," EO, 6: 4 (1963) 313-335.

Griaule, Marcel.   Abyssinian Journey (London: 1935).

_____. Les Flambeurs d'hommes (Paris: 1934). 1928-29.

Grigg, L. B.   Three Years in Gemu Gofa (As told by Susan and
Brad Coady) (New York: Vantage Press, 1974). 1968-1971

Grixoni, G.   "I capi Bottego e Grixoni sull-alto Giuba," BSAI,
12 (1893).

Grühl, Max.   The Citadel of Ethiopia (trans. from the German)
(London: 1935).

Guida dell'Africa Orientale Italiana (Consociazione Turistica Italiana,
Milan: 1938).

Gunther, John.   Inside Africa (New York, Harpers: 1963).

Gwynn, G. W.   "A journey in southern Abyssinia," GJ, 38 (1911)
113-39. 1908

_____ and Jackson, L. C.   "Surveys on the proposed Sudan-
Abyssinian frontier," GJ, 18 (1901) 562-573.

Haggenmacher, G. A.   "Reise im Somali-Lande, 1874," Petermanns,
10 (1875-1876) 1-45.

Hahn, F. "Aufnahmen in Ostafrika; Begleitworte zur Karte der Gallalander," Petermanns, 51 (1905). (Survey of routes)

Halévy, Joseph. Travels in Abyssinia (Trans. from French) in Miscellany of Hebrew Literature (London: Society of Hebrew Literature, n. d.) 177-256.

_____. "Excursion chez les Falacha, en Abyssinie," BSG, 17 (1869) 270-94. 1868

Halldin, Viveca. Etiopien: Beskrivining av ett u-land (Stockholm: 1917).

Hallé, Clifford. To Menelik in a Motor-Car (London: 1913).

Hallett, R. "The Lure of Africa: II. Ethiopia." Geographical Magazine 35 (1963) 499-506.

Halls, J. J. The Life and Correspondence of Henry Salt (London: 1834). 1805 and 1809 (see also Salt, Henry)

Hamilton, C. E. Oriental Zigzags, or Wanderings in Syria, Moab, Abyssinia, and Egypt (London: 1875).

Haneuse, L. "Notes sur l'Erythrée," BSRBG, 17 (1893). Aug. 1892

Hanson, H. M. and Della. For God and Emperor (Mountain View, Calif. , Pacific Press: 1958). 1935-7 and 1940-

Harlan, Harry V. "A Caravan Journey Through Abyssinia: from Addis Ababa through Lalibela, the strange Jerusalem of Ethiopia, in search of new grains for American Farms," National Geographic, 47: 6 (1925) 613-33.

Harmsworth, Geoffrey. Abyssinia Marches On (London: Hutchinson, 1941).

_____. Abyssinian Adventure (London: Hutchinson, 1935).

Harris, Cornwallis W. The Highlands of Aethiopia. 3 vols. (London: 1844) (Republished by Gregg International Publishers, England, 1968). Illustrations (London: 1845).

Harrison, J. H. "A journey from Zeila to Lake Rudolf," GJ, 18: 3 (Sept. 1901) 258-275.

Harrison-Smith, F. Through Abyssinia: An Envoy's Ride to the King of Zion (London: 1890).

Hartlmaier, Paul. Golden Lion, a Journey Through Ethiopia (London: S. Paul, 1956).

Hartmann, Robert. Abyssinien und die übrigen Gebiete der Ostküste Afrikas (Leipzig-Prague: 1883).

Haskard, Dudley. "Lion Shooting in Somaliland," Travel and Exploration, 2 (1909) 342-47.

Hayes, Arthur. The Source of the Blue Nile. A record of a journey through the Soudan to Lake Tsana in western Abyssinia and of the return in Egypt by the valley of the Atbara, with a note on the religion, customs, etc. of Abyssinia and entomological appendix by E. B. Poulton (London: 1905). 1903

Hayter, F. E. In Quest of Sheba's Mines (London: 1935).

_____. The Garden of Eden (London: 1940).

_____. African Adventurer (London: 1939).

Hénin, H. Ethiopie, voyage d'exploration commerciale (Brussels: 1907). Extr. du Recueil consulaire belge, 138.

Hentze, Willy. Am Hofe des Kaisers Menelik von Abyssinien (Leipzig: 1905).

_____. Volldampf unter Palmen; erinnerungen eines Ingenieurs (Leipzig: 1928).

Herzbruch, Kurt. Abessinien. Eine Reise zum Hofe Kaiser Menelik II (Munich & Leipzig: 1925).

Heudebert, Lucien. Au pays des Somalis et des Comoriens (Paris: 1901).

Heuglin, M. T. von. Reise nach Abessinien, den Gala-Ländern, Ost-Sudán und Chartum in ... 1861 und 1862 (Jena: 1868).

_____. Reisen in Nord-Ost Afrika. Tagebuch einer Reside von Chartum nach Abyssinien, mit besonderer Rücksicht auf Zoologie und Geographie in den Jahren 1852 und 1853 (Gotha: 1857).

_____. (Letter from Gondar, Feb. 1, 1853) Ausland, 26 (1853) 813-14.

_____. "Neueste Reise durch Agypten und im Rothem Meere nach den Abessinischen Kusten-Länder," Petermanns, 3 (1857) 485-86.

_____. "Die Habab-Länder am Rothen Meere," Petermanns, 4 (1858) 370-72.

_____. "Major Graf Ludwig Thürheim's Reise in Afrika," Petermanns, 5 (1859).

_____. "Reise in Nordost-Afrika und längs des Rothen Meeres im Jahre 1857," Petermanns, 6 (1860).

_____. "Reise längs der Somali-Küste im Jahre 1857," Petermanns, 6 (1860) 418-37.

_____. "Expedition nach Inner-Afrika," Petermanns, 7 (1861).

Hildebrandt, J. M. "Ausflug in die Nord-Abessinischen Grenzländer im Sommer 1872," ZGEBerlin, 8 (1873).

_____. "Erlebnisse auf einer Reise nach Massua in das Gebiet der Afer und nach Aden," ZGEBerlin, 10 (1875).

_____. "Ausflug von Aden in das Gebiet der Wer-Singelli-Somalen und Besteigung des Ahl-Gebirges," ZGEBerlin, 10 (1875) 266-95.

Hindlip, C. A. Sport and Travel; Abyssinia and British East Africa. (London: 1906).

Hodson, Arnold W. Seven Years in Southern Abyssinia (London: 1927). Reprinted Greenwood, Westport, Conn.

_____. "Southern Abyssinia," GJ, 53: 2 (Feb. 1919).

_____. "Notes on Abyssinian Lakes," GJ, 60 (July 1922).

_____. Where Lions Reign. An account of Lion Hunting and Exploration in southwest Abyssinia (London: 1929).

Hohler, Sir Thomas. Diplomatic Petrel (London: 1942). 1906-1908

Höhnel, Ludwig R. von. Discovery of Lakes Rudolf and Stefanie--a narration of Count Samuel Teleki's exploring and hunting expedition in Eastern equatorial Africa in 1887 and 1888 (Trans. from German) (London: 1893).

_____. "In Mission bei Kaiser Menelik-1905," in Mein Leben zur See, auf Forschungs reisen und bei Hofe (Berlin: 1926).

Holtz, Arnold. Im Auto zu Kaiser Menelik (Berlin: 1908).

Hoyos, Ernst. Zu den Aulihan. Reise und Jagderlebnisse in Somaliland (Vienna: 1895).

_____. "La spedizione Hoyos e Coudenhove nel paese dei Somali," EC, 9 (1894) 260-61. (Abstract from the German original in MKKGGWien, 38 (1894)).

Hunter, F. M., and Fullerton, J. D. Reports on Somali Land and the Harar Province (Simla, India: 1885).

Hoskins, G. A. Travels in Ethiopia Above the Second Cataract of the Nile, exhibiting the State of that country and its various inhabitants under the Dominion of Mohammed Ali, and Illustrating the Antiquities, Arts, and History of the Ancient Kingdom of Meroe (London: 1835).

Isenberg, Karl W. "Reise in Abyssinien von Zeylah, im Hintergrund des Meerbusens von Aden, nach Ankobar, der Hauptstadt des Königreichs Schoa, durch das Land Adal, " Ausland, 21 (1848).

_____. The Journals of the Rev. Messrs. Isenberg and Krapf, Missionaries of the Church Missionary Society, detailing their proceedings in the Kingdom of Shoa, and Journeys in Other Parts of Abyssinia, in the Years 1839, 1840, 1841, and 1842 (London: 1843).

Issel, Arturo. Viaggio nel Mar Rosso e tra i Bogos, (1870) (2nd ed. , Milan: 1876).

Jacobis, Farther Justin de. (Letters from Adwa June 18, 1843 and Nov. 1844), NAV, 107 (1845), 207-08.

_____. (Excerpts from letter published in Annales de la Propagation de la Foi) NAV, 124 (1849) 353-67.

Jacoby, C. M. On Special Mission to Abyssinia (New York: 1933).

Jaenen, C. J. "Contemporary Ethiopia, " JG, 57 (Jan. 1958), 31-38.

James, F. L. The Unknown Horn of Africa: an Exploration from Berbera to the Leopold River (London: 1888).

Jansen, P. G. Abissinia di oggi (Viaggio in Ethiopia) (Milan: 1935).

Jessen, B. H. "South-western Abyssinia, " GJ, 25: 2 (Feb. 1905) 158-71.

Johnson, Martin. "Addis Ababa from the air, " EO, 6: 1 (1962), 17-31.

Johnston, Charles. Travels in Southern Abyssinia Through the Country of Adals to the Kingdom of Shoa During the Years 1842-43 (London: 1844).

Jumilhac, Comtesse E. B. Ethiopie modern (Paris: 1933).   1930

Junker, Wilhelm. Travels in Africa During Years 1875-1886 (London: 1890).

Kallenberg, C. "Die Leiden der Italiener am Rothen Meer, " Ausland, 58 (1885) 991-93. Massawa 1884-1885

Katte, A. von. Reise in Abyssinien im Jahre 1836 (Stuttgart: 1838).

Keller, Conrad. "Neue Nachrichten über die Expedition Bottego," Globus 72 (1897) 110-11.

_____. "Die neuesten Expeditionen in Innern des afrikanischen Osthorns," Globus, 66 (1894) 252-56. (Survey)

_____. "Reisestudien in den Somaliländern," Globus, 69 (1896).

Kenny, N. T. "Ethiopian Adventure," National Geographic, 127: 4 (1965).

Kersten, Otto. Baron Carl Claus von der Deckens Reisen in Ost-Africa. 2 vols. (Leipzig: 1869-).

Kielmeier, C. "Nachrichten über Abyssinien," Ausland, 12 (1839). 1836-1838, see Katte above.

Kirk, R. "Report on the Route from Tajurra to Ankobar Travelled by the Mission to Shwa, under Charge of Captain W. C. Harris, 1841," JRGS, 12 (1843) 221-238.

Koettlitz, Reginald. "A Journey Through Somali Land and Southern Abyssinia to the Berta or Shangalla Country and the Blue Nile, and Through the Sudan to Egypt," JTGS, 4 (1901) 323-43. 1900

Kolmodin, A. "Meine Studienreise in Abessinien, 1908-1910," Le Monde Oriental, 4 (1910).

Koner, W. "Der Anteil der Deutschen an der Entdeckung und Erforschung Afrika's," ZGEBerlin, 8 (1873), 386-432. (A survey)

Krafft, Walter. "Wayname Kidana Meherat, Little Known Gojam Church," EO, 15: 2 (1972).

Krapf, J. L. Travels, Researches and missionary labours during an 18 Years' Residence in Eastern Africa (London: 1860). Reprint 1972.

_____. "Extracts from a Journal, kept at Ankóbar, from 7th June to 2nd October, 1839," JRGS, 10 (1841) 469-88.

_____. "Abstract of a Journal kept by the Rev. Messrs. Isenberg and Krapf, on their Route from Cairo, through Zeila to Shwá and I'fât, between the 21st of Jan. and 12th June, 1839," JRGS, 10 (1841) 66-70.

_____. "Seereise an der südarabischen Küste von Aden bis Sihut, an der von Cap. Guardafui bis zur Insel Sansibar; unternommen am 10 Nov. 1843, und vollendet am 7 Jan. 1844, " Ausland, 30 (1857).

_____. "Abessinische Notizen, " Ausland, 32 (1859).

_____. "Reise von Tadschurra durch das Afer-Land nach Schoa, im Jahre 1839, und Aufenthalt daselbst, " Ausland, 33 (1860).

Kretschmar, J. A. Van. Ethiopië (Amsterdam: 1954).

Kropp, Wilhelm. "Die Beschiffung des Rothen Meeres, " MKKGG-Wien, 15 (1872) 348-63.

Kulmer, Friedrich von. Im Reiche Kaiser Meneliks: Tagebuch einer Abessinischen Reise (Leipzig: 1911). (Ed. by E. Mattl-Löwenkreuz.)

Kuo, Leslie. "Ethiopia, " Focus, 5: 10 (1955).

Kürchhof, D. "Alte und neue Handelsstrassen und Handelsmittelpunkte an den afrikanischen Küsten des Roten Meeres und des Golfes von Aden, Sowie in deren Hinterländern, " GZ, 14 (1908). (Survey)

Kurze, G. "Die schwedische Gallaexpedition, " MGGJ, 1 (1882).

Lacetti, B. "Cinque mesi in Eritrea, " BSAI, 31 (1912) 116-134.

Lachin, M. L'Ethiopie et son destin (Paris: 1935).

Lagana, Gino. "Abissinia, " BSAI, 34 (1915) 250-77. 1911

Lambie, T. A. Abayte! or Ethiopia's Plea: a Record of Missionary Beginnings in Ethiopia (Abyssinia) with Special Reference to the Sudan Interior Mission (London, S. I. M.: 1935).

Lande, L. L. "Un voyageur français dans l'Ethiopie méridionale, " RDM, 15 Dec. 1878, 15 Jan. 1879. Pierre Arnoux 1874-1876

Landini, Lorenzo. Due anni col Marchese Antinori (Citta di Castello: 1884). 1876-77

Landor, A. Henry Savage. Across Wildest Africa. 2 vols (New York and London: 1907).

Last, Geoffrey. "Some Notes on the Scenery of the Ethiopian Rift Valley, " EO, 5: 3 (1961) 194-202.

Latham, Hubert. "Au Sidamo et chez les Gallas Aroussi, " La Géographie, 26: 1 (1912).

Lauribar, Paul de (pseud.). Douze Ans en Abyssinie (Paris: 1898).

Lebrun, H. Voyages en Abyssinie et en Nubie, recueillis et mis en ordre (Tours: 1840).

Leclerq, Claude. L'Empire d'Ethiopie (Paris: Berger-Levrault, 1969).

Lefebvre, C. T. Voyages en Abyssinie Exécuté Pendant Les Années 1839, 1840, 1841, 1842, 1843. 6 vols. (Paris: 1845-1851).

Lega, Manlio. "Su Dancalia e in Abissinia, " BSGI, 48 (1911), 368-88, 444-75. 1910

Leiris, M. L'Afrique fantôme (Paris: 1934). 1931-33

Lejean, Guillaume. Voyage en Abyssinie, exécuté de 1862 à 1864. (Paris: 1870).

_____. "Gallabat et adabhi, deux républiques nègres au N. O. de l'Abyssinie, " NAV, (1864).

_____. "Notes d'un voyage en Abyssinie, " TM, (1864).

_____. "Le Sennaheit, souvenirs d'un voyage dans le désert Nubien, " RDM, 1 (June 1865).

_____. "Voyage en Abyssinie (1862-1863), " TM, 2 sem. 1865 and 1 sem. 1867.

Leontieff, N. "Exploration des provinces équatoriales d'Abyssinie, " La Geographie, 2 (1900).

_____. See also Elets, Yu. in History c. 1760-c. 1930 section.

Lepsius, Richard. Letters from Egypt, Ethiopia and the Peninsula of Sinai (London: 1853, re-edition Wilmington, Delaware: Scholarly Resources, Inc., 1974).

Le Roux, Hugues. Ménélik et nous (Paris: 1902).

_____. Chasses et gens d'Abyssinie (Paris: 1903).

_____. Chez la reine de Saba (Paris: 1917).

_____. "Voyage au Ouallago, Itineraire d'Addis-Ababa au Nil Blue, " La Géographie, 4 (1901) 217-34.

_____. "Reconnaissance du lac Zouaï, de ses îles et de ses archives, " La Géographie, 11 (1905), 66-69.

_____. "Voyages d'actualité, Harar, " Le Globe Trotter, 13 (1908), 206.

Leslau, Wolf. "Impressions of Ethiopia, " Middle Eastern Affairs,
    1: 11 (Nov. 1950), 316-320.

Leymarie, H.   Un Dieppois en Abyssinie (Dieppe: 1898).

_____.   "En Abyssinie.   Mission du Comte Leontieff, " TM,   4
    (1899).

Liano, Alejandro.   Ethiopie, empire des Nègres blancs (Paris:
    1929).

Licata, G. B.   In Africa.   Scritto postumo (Florence: 1886).

_____.   Assab e i Danachili.   Viaggio e Studii (Milan: 1885).

_____.   "Obok ed Assab, " BSAI,   1 (1882) 1-23.

Littmann, Enno.   Abessinien (Hamburg: 1935).

_____.   "Preliminary Report of the Princeton University Expe-
    dition to Abyssinia, " Zeitschrift für Assyriologie, 20 (1906).

Lobo, Father J.   A Voyage to Abyssinia (A translation by Dr.
    Samuel Johnson in 1735 from the 1673 French translation by
    Le Grand from the original Portuguese Historia de Etiopia
    (Coimbre: 1669).

Longbois, Capt.   "Rapport sur une mission scientifique au Choa, "
    Archives des missions scientifiques et littéraires, 13 (1887).

Loti, Pierre.   "Obock, " Revue pol. et parl. (Feb. 1887).

Lovelace, A. E.   "Some Notes on the Climb of Ras Dashan, " EO,
    5:3 (1961).

Luchsinger, H. R.   "Von Schoa zum Stefaniesee und zu den
    Borangalla, " JGEG (1906-07).

Lulseged Lemma.   "Ethiopia: an interpretative essay, " Negro
    History Bulletin, 35: 1 (Jan. 1972) 6-8.

Macaire, Mgr.   "Mon voyage en Abyssinie, " BSKG,   4 (1897).

MacCreagh, Gordon.   The Last of Free Africa: The Account of
    an Expedition into Abyssinia (New York: 1928).

MacDermot, B. H.   Cult of the Sacred Spear: the story of the
    Nuer Tribe in Ethiopia (London: Robert Hale, 1972).

Magretti, P.   "Dall'Eritrea, " EC,   15 (1900), 65-66.

Mahoney, Kevin O'.   "The Salt Trail, " JES,   8: 2 (1970) 147-154.

Maindron, Maurice. "Une mission scientifique dans la baie de Tadjourah, " Revue Encyclopédique, (1 Oct. and 1 Nov. 1894).

Majo, Carlo F. di. "Una ricognizione a Keren, " BSAI, 8 (1889), 23-24.

Malécot, Georges. Les Voyageurs Français et les relations entre la France et l'Abyssinie de 1835 à 1870. (Paris, Société Française d'Histoire d'Outre-Mer: 1972).

Mannweiler, David. "Ethiopia: Africa's Odd Man Out, " Holiday, 54: 1 (1973).

Marini, Angelo. "La Valle del Gherghèr (Colonia Eritrea), " BSGI, 39 (1902) 987-1003.

Martinelli, R. Sud: rapporto di un viaggio in Eritrea ed Etiopia (Florence: 1930).

Martini, Ferdinando. Nell'Africa Italiana. Impressioni e ricordi (Milan: 1891).

Martini, Sebastiano. Ricordi d'escursioni in Africa dal 1878 al 1881. Diario geografico e topographico (Florence: 1886).

Masland, Frank E. "A Survey of Ethiopia, " Explorers Journal, 46: 2 (June, 1868) 120-127.

Massaja (Massaia), Father Gugliemo. (Letter to Antoine d'Abbadie from Keffa Oct. 7, 1860). BSG, 1 (1861) 328-31; (Letter from ? December 1, 1861) BSG, 3 (1862) 378-81.

_____. I miei trentacinque anni di missione nell'alta Ethiopia. 12 vols (Rome: 1885-1895; re-issued 1921).

Mattaucci, Pellegrini. Spedizione Gessi-Mattaucci. Sudan e Gallas (Milan: 1879).

Matthew, A. F. "Slavery in Abyssinia, " The Church Overseas, 6 (1933).

Maud, Phillip. "Exploration in the Southern Borderland of Abyssinia, " Proceedings RGS, 23 (1904), 552-79.

Maydon, H. C. Simen, its Heights and Abysses, a Record of Sport and Travels in Abyssinia (London: 1925).

_____. "Across Eritrea, " GJ, 63 (1924).

Mayo, Earl of see Bourke, Dermot

Meisler, Stanley. "Ethiopia, " The Atlantic, 229: 6 (June 2, 1972).

Melladew, H. (Account of journey by Melladew and Captain Gascoigne.) Petermanns, 28 (1882) 314.

Mellon, James. "The Abyssinian Ibex, or Walia," "The Mountain Nyala," "Quest for the Nile, or Mrs. Gray's Lechew," African Hunter (New York: Harcourt, Brace, Jovanovich, 1975) 186-196, 197-204, 205-212.

Mendez, A., and Paez, P. Lettere di Ethiopia del 1624, 1625 e 1626 scritte al M. R. P. Mutio Vitelleschi (Rome: 1628). (Translated into French as Histoire de ce qui s'est passé au royaume d'Ethiopie années 1624, 1625, 1626, Paris: 1629.)

Menges, Josef. "Am Rothen Meere: Massawa," AAW, 8 (1877) 182-85.

_____. (Letter from Berbera, Jan. 27, 1884.) Petermanns, 30 (1884) 151.

_____. "Jagdzug nach dem Mareb und obern Chor Baraka, Marz und April 1881," Petermanns, 30 (1884) 162-69.

_____. "Ausflug in das Somali-Land," Petermanns, 30 (1884) 401.

_____. (Letter from Berbera, Jan. 2, 1885.) Petermanns, 31 (1885) 67.

_____. "Zweite Reise in das Somaliland und Besteigung des Gan-Libach," Petermanns, 31 (1885), 449.

_____. "Die Küstenlandschaft des Somalilandes östlich von Berbera, nebst Bemerkungen über die Folgen der englishchen Herrschaft," Petermanns, 37 (1891) 41-44.

_____. "Streifzüge in dem Küstenlande der Habr Auel," Petermanns, 40 (1894) 227-234.

Mérab, Dr. P. Impressions d'Ethiopie. 3 vols. (Paris: 1921, 1922 and 1929).

Messing, Simon D. "Changing Ethiopia," Middle East Journal, 9: 4 (1955).

Michel, Charles. Vers Fachoda à la rencontre de la mission Marchand à travers l'Ethiopie (Paris: 1900).

_____. "Vers Fachoda," BSGLyon, 15 (1898-99).

_____. "Résultats Géographiques de la Mission de Bonchamps," La Géographie, 2 (1900) 25-34.

_____. "Dans les brousses de l'Ethiopie et du Soudan. Mon

raid de Djibouti à Khartoum, " Lectures pour tous, 15 March 1921.

_____. "De la Mer Rouge au Nil, à travers les plateaux éthiopiens et la vallée du Nil Blue, " L'Illustration, 11 June 1921.

Miklukho-Maklaĭ, N. N. (Account of trip taken in 1869 to Red Sea Coast.) Izviestiia Irgo, 5 (1869) 277-87.

Miles, S. B. "On the neighbourhood of Bunder Marayah, " JRGS, 42 (1872).

Mitchell, L. H. "Journal Officiel de la reconnaissance géologique et minéralogique, " BSKG, 3 (1889).

Mitzakis, Demosthenes. Voyage en Abyssinie (in Greek) (Athens: 1889).

_____. Report on the Seizure by the Abyssinians of the Geological and Mineralogical Reconnaissance Expedition. (Cairo: 1878).

Mohammed-Moktar Bey. "Notes sur le pays de Harrar, " BSKG, 4 (1877).

_____. "Une reconnaissance au pays des Gadiboursis, " BSKG, 7 (1880).

Mondon-Vidailhet, C. (Letters from Abyssinia) Le Temps (newspaper). 1 May, 12 June, 2 Nov. 1892; 29 April, 18 July, 28 July, 17 August, 20 August, 30 August 1893; 27 April 1895; 23 and 30 Jan. , 2 April, 4 April, 26 April, 11 May, 11 June, 1 July, 13 Sept. , 2 Nov. 1896; 17 April, 16 June, 2 Oct. , 28 Oct. , 17 Nov. , 1897; 22 March, 25 March, 31 May, 29 June, 18 Nov. , 1 Dec. 1898.

Monfreid, H. de. Pearls, Arms and Hashish; Pages from the Life of a Red Sea Navigator (London: 1930).

_____. Le Lépreux (Paris: 1935).

_____. Secrets of the Red Sea (London: 1934).

_____. Sea Adventures (London: 1937).

_____. Hashish (London: 1935).

_____. Abdi. L'homme à la main coupée (Paris: 1937).

_____. L'enfant sauvage (Paris: 1938).

_____. La poursuite du Kaipan (Paris: 1934).

_____ . Ménélik tel qu'il fut (Paris: 1954).

_____ . Les lionnes d'or d'Ethiopie (Paris: 1964).

_____ . Vers les terres hostiles de l'Ethiopie (Paris: 1933).

Montandon, George. Au pays Ghimirra, Récit de mon voyage à
    travers le Massif éthiopien (1909-1911) (Paris: 1913).

Monty, Christian. Ethiopie: Dernier empire des visages brûlés
    (Paris, L'école des loisirs: 1968).

Moorehead, Alan. The Blue Nile (London, Hamish Hamilton: 1962).

Muller, J. von. "Tagebuch einer Reise durch das Gebiet der Ga-
    dabursi-Somali und Noli-Galla nach Harrar," ZGEBerlin, 19
    (1884) 73-80.

_____ . "Tagebuch einer Reise durch das Gebiet des Habab und
    Beni-Amer," ZGEBerlin 18 (1883) 412-38.

Munzinger, Werner. Ost-Afrikanische Studien (Schaffhausen: 1864).
    (Translated into Italian as Studi sull'Africa Orientale, Rome:
    1890)

_____ . "Die nordöstlichen Grenzländer von Habesch," ZAE, 3
    (1857).

_____ . "Die Schohos und die Beduan bei Massua," ZAE, 6
    (1859).

_____ . "Auszüge aus Werner Munzinger's Tagebuch, angefangen
    den 13 Juli 1861 bei der Abreise von Mocullu (Om Kullu),
    vollendet den 15 Oktober in Keren," ZAE, 12 (1862) 162-74,
    356-63.

_____ . "Die Inselstadt Massua im Rothen Meer," Ausland, 37
    (1864) 1079-80.

_____ . "Narrative of a Journey through the Afar Country,"
    JRGS, 39 (1869) 188-232.

Munzinger, W., Heughlin, Th. von, and Kinzelbach, Th.   "Die
    deutsche Expedition in Ost-Afrika 1861 und 1862." Petermanns,
    13 (1864).

Murphy, D. In Ethiopia with a Mule (London, John Murray: 1968).

Mylius, Alph. von. "Reise nach Kaffa und Dauro," Extr. des
    MKKGG, 49 (1907).

Nalty, Bernard C. Guests of the Conquering Lion: The Diplo-
    matic Mission to Abyssinia, 1903 (Washington, D.C., U.S.
    Marine Corps: 1959).

Nerazzini, Dr. Cesare. "Itinerario in Etiopia (1885), " BSGI, 26 (1889) 968-86; 27 (1890), 54-81, 140-72.

Nesbitt, L. M. Desert and Forest: the Exploration of the Abyssinian Desert (London: 1934). 1927-1928

Neumann, Oskar. (Letter from Jimma, March 29, 1901.) VGEBerlin, 28 (1901), 325-26.

_____. "From the Somali Coast Through Southern Ethiopia to the Sudan, " JTGS, 5 (1903). (Translated from ZGEBerlin (1902).)

Nicholson, T. R. A Toy for the Lion (London, William Kimber: 1965). (Automobile trip of Bede Bentley in 1907)

Nicol, C. From the Roof of Africa (London: Hodder & Stoughton, 1971).

Nikolopoulos, Dimitri. Addis-Abeba ou "Fleur nouvelle." Souvenirs et contes d'Ethiopie (Marseille: 1923). (Translated from Greek)

Norden, H. Africa's Last Empire: Through Abyssinia to Lake Tana and the Country of the Falasha (London: 1930). 1928-1929

Nurse, Charles G. "A Journey Through Part of Somali--Between Zeila and Bulhar, " Proc. RGS, 13 (1891) 657-63.

Odorizzi, Dante (pseud. "Ghibellino"). "Lettere dall'Etiopia, " BSAI, 23 (1904), 92-104, 123-30, 139-45, 162-71, 201-206; 24 (1905), 204-10, 233 and 240, 284-92.

Ogilvie, Grant. On the Birds Collected During an Expedition Through Somaliland and South Abyssinia to Lake Zwai (London: 1901).

Orléans, Henri d'. Une visite à l'empereur Ménélick (Paris: 1898).

Osgood, W. H. "Nature and Man in Ethiopia, " National Geographic, 54; 2 (1928).

O'Shea, J. J. "An Old Monarchy and a Young Republic, " Amer. Catholic Quarterly, 29 (July, 1904), 533-550.

Ouanno, Jane and Jean. L'Ethiopie, pilote d'Afrique (Paris: Maisonneuve, 1952).

Paez, Pero see Mendez

Pagne, Leon. Mon voyage en Abyssinie et séjour chez les Somalis (St. -Quentin: 1900).

Pakenham, T.   The Mountains of Rasselas; an Ethiopian Adventure
(London, Weidenfeld and Nicolson: 1959). 1955

Pankhurst, Richard K. P., ed. Travellers in Ethiopia (London,
OUP: 1965).

Parazzoli, A. "Sulle odierne condizioni dell'Eritrea," EC, 16
(1901) 249-52, 265-69.

Pariset, Dante. Al tempo di Menelik (Milan: 1947). (Memoirs of
M. et Mme. Stévinin)

Parisis, Dr. N. L'Abissinia (translated from Greek) (Milan: 1888).

Park, L. "Life's Tenor in Ethiopia," National Geographic, 67
(June 1935) 783-793.

Parkyns, Mansfield. Life in Abyssinia, being notes collected during three years residence and travels in that country (London:
1853).

Parmentier, Jean. "De Khartum à Addis-Abeba," La Géographie,
25 (1912) 231-246. 1907

Paul, Elisabeth. "Notizie Preliminare Sulla Spedizione dell'Istituto Frobenius in Abissinia (1950-1951)," Rivista di Antropologia, 39 (1951-1952).

Paulitschke, Philipp. Die geographische Erforschung der Adal
Länder und Harar's in Ost Afrika. Mit Rücksicht auf die
Expedition des Dr. med. Dominik Kammel, Edlen von Hardeg-
ger (Leipzig: 1884).

_____. Harar. Forschungsreise nach den Somal und Galla-
Landern Ost-Afrika (Leipzig: 1888).

_____. "Major Heaths und Leutenant Peytons Reise von Harar
nach Berbera, Juni 1885," Petermanns, 32 (1886).

_____. "Kapitän J. S. Kings Reisen im Lande der Ejssa und
Gadaburssi-Somâl, 1886," Petermanns, 33 (1887).

_____. (Letter about Harar) Petermanns, 31 (1885), 98.

_____. (Letters about Harar), BSGI, 22 (1885) 673-79, 937-38.

_____. "Reise nach Harar und in die nördlichen Galla-Länder,
1885," Petermanns, 31 (1885).

_____. "Relazione sulle condizioni dell'Harar nel Gennaio 1885,"
BSGI 23 (1886), 397-99, and additional in BSAI, 4 (1886)
259-62.

_____. "Giudizio sul paese del Somali e sull'eccidio della nostra spedizione," EC, 1 (1886), 161.

_____. "Harar," BSAI, 7 (1888), 171-73, 212-15; 8 (1889), 10-18, 142-47.

_____. "Kulturbilder aus den Somâl- und Gallaländern von Harar," Globus 56 (1889).

_____. Reise des Fursten Demeter Ghika Comaneşti im Somâl-Lande 1895-96," Petermanns, 42 (1896).

Pearce, F. B. Rambles in Lion-Land; three month's leave passed in Somaliland (London: 1898).

Pearce, Nathaniel. The Life and Adventures of Nathaniel Pearce written by himself during a residence in Abyssinia from the Years 1810 to 1819 (London: 1831). 2 vols.

Pease, A. E. Travel and Sport in Africa. 3 vols. (London: 1902) 1896-1897 and 1900-1901.

_____. "Some Account of Somaliland: with Notes on Journeys Through the Gadabursi and Western Ogaden Countries, 1896-1897," SGM, 14 (1898).

Pennazzi, Luigi. Dal Po ai due Nili (Milan: 1882). 2 vols.

_____. Sudan e Abissinia (Bologna: 1887).

_____. "Esplorazioni Baudi e Candeo nell'Ogaden," EC, 6 (1891) 274-277.

_____. "Il viaggio dell'ing. Robecchi-Bricchetti," EC, 6 (1891) 343-345.

Perham, M., and Simmons, J. African Discovery: An Anthology of Exploration (Northwestern U. P.: 1963), 35-70 and 149-179.

Perini, Ruffillo. "Un escursione nello Scoiattè-Ansebà," BSGI, 31 (1894).

_____. Di qua dal Marèb (Marèb-mellàsc) (Florence: 1905).

Perl, Lila. Ethiopia: Land of the Lion (New York: Morrow, 1972).

Pestalozza, G. "Alula," BSAI, 20 (1901). (coastal exploration)

Philip, Hoffman. Abyssinian Memories (Pvt. printing, Santa Barbara: 1948).

Piaggia, Carlo. "Relazione di viaggio nell'Abissinia e nel Goggiam," BSGI, 12 (1875).

_____. "Il Tsana e il Goggiam, " BSGI, 12 (1875).

Piazza, G. Alle corte di Menelik: lettere dall'Etiopia (Ancona: 1912).

Pick, Emil von. Reisenbriefe eines osterreichischen Industriellen aus Abessinien, Indien und Ostasien (Prague: 1910).

Playne, Beatrice. Saint George for Ethiopia (London, Constable: 1954).

Plowden, W. C. Travels in Abyssinia and the Galla Country with an Account of a Mission to Ras Ali in 1848 (London: 1868).

Polydenot, G. Obock, une station de ravitaillement pour la marine française (Paris: 1889).

Poncet, Charles. "Relation abrégée du voyage que M. Charles Poncet fit en Ethiopie en 1698, 1699 et 1700. Lettres édifiantes et curieuses écrites des missions étrangères par quelques missionaires de la Compagnie de Jesus. IV recueil, II partie, 251-443. (Paris: 1704). English translation in Foster, W. (see above).

Poncins, Edm. de. "Abyssinie. Mission du Prince Henri d'Orleans, " RF, 22 (1897) 415-421.

Porquier, Georges. "L'Ethiopie et la question éthiopienne, " BSGLille, 45-46 (1906) 163-75. 1904-1905

Porro, G. P. "Ultime lettere di Porro, Zanini, e Licata, " EC, 1 (1886), 147-152.

_____. "Notizie della nostra spedizione, " EC, 1 (1886) 33-34, 65-71, 97-102.

_____. (Letters) BSGI, 23 (1886) 402-405.

Portal, Gerald H. An Account of the English Mission to King Yohannis of Abyssinia (Winchester: 1888). Re-issued London: 1892 as My Mission to Abyssinia. Reprinted Greenwood Press, Westport, Conn.: 1975.

Potocki, J. Sport in Somaliland (London: c. 1900).

Pottier, Louis. "Note de route d'Aden au Choa, " BSGM, 2 (1878) 142-146.

Powell, E. A. Beyond the Utmost Purple Rim: Abyssinia, Somaliland, Kenya Colony, Zanzibar, the Comoros, Madagascar (London: 1925).

Powell-Cotton, P. H. G. A Sporting Trip Through Abyssinia (London: 1902).

Prée, H. de. "Notes of a Journey on the Tana River, July to September 1899," GJ, 17 (1901) 512-516.

Prorok, B. K. Dead Men Do Tell Tales (London: 1943). 1930s

Pucci, G. Coi "negadi" in Etiopia; note di viaggio (Florence: 1934).

Radford, William. "Mr. Jenner's Expedition from Kismayu to Logh (Luch) on the Juba," GJ, 14 (1899) 637-39.

Raffray, Achille. "Voyage en Abyssinie, à Zanzibar et aux pays des Ouarika," BSG, 10 (1875) 291-313. Aug-April 1873

_____. "Voyage en Abyssinie et au pays des Gallas Raias," BSG, 3 (1882), 324-52.

_____. Abyssinie (Paris: 1876).

Ragazzi, Vincenzo. "Relazione sul suo viaggio dallo Scioa ad Harar," BSGI, 25 (1888) 66-80.

Rampone, O. A Souvenir Book on a Journey in Ethiopia (Addis Ababa: Commercial Bank of Ethiopia, 1973).

Ramsauer, A. "Land und Leute in Abessinien," Ausland, 61 (1888) 292-94.

Rasmussen, J. Welcome to Ethiopia (Addis Ababa, Ethiopian Tourist Organization: c. 1965).

Rassam, Hormuzd. "Extracts of a letter to Colonel Playfair," Proc. RGS, 10 (1865-66) 295-300.

_____. Narrative of the British Mission to Theodore, King of Abyssinia. 2 vols. (London: 1869).

Ratjens, Karl. "Ein Kirchgang mit dem Abuna Petros von Abessinien," Globus, 94 (1908), 154-58.

_____. "Beiträge sur Landeskunde von Abessinien," MGGMünchen, 6 (1911).

Rava, Maurizio. Al Lago Tsana (Il Mar profondo d'Etiopia) (Rome: 1923).

Ravenstein, E. G. "Somal and Galla Land; embodying information collected by the Rev. Thomas Wakefield," Proc. RGS, 6 (1884).

_____. "Italian explorations in the Upper Basin of the Jub," GJ, 3 (1894), 134-38. (A survey)

Rayne, H. Sun, Sand and Somalis: Leaves from the Note-Book of a District Commissioner in British Somaliland (London: 1921).

Rebeaud, H. Chez le roi des rois d'Ethiopie (Neuchatel, Paris: 1935). 1920s

Reil, Otto. "Reise von Suakin nach Massua durch die Gebiete der Hadendoa, Beni-Amer und Habab, 1868," Petermanns, 15 (1869) 368-73.

Rein, G. K. Abessinien. Fine Landes-Kunde nach Reisen und Studien in den Jahren 1907-1913 (Berlin: 1919-1920) 3 vols.

Rémond, Georges. "Excursions et Chasses en Abyssinie," TM, 17 (1911) 409-80.

_____. "Renseignements pratiques pour un voyage en Abyssinie. Centres d'exploration et itinéraires," TV, 17 (1911), 400.

_____. "En Abyssinie. L'agonie de l'empereur Menelik," Le Correspondant, 25 Juillet 1911.

_____. La route de l'Abbaï noir. Souvenirs d'Abyssinie (Paris: 1924).

Rennell-Rodd, J. Social and Diplomatic Memories, 1894-1901; Egypt and Abyssinia (London: 1923).

Révoil, Georges. "Voyage au pays des Medjourtines," BSG, 19 (1880) 254-69.

_____. "Voyage au pays des Çomalis," BSG, 20 (1880) 566-68.

_____. "Voyage au pays Çomali," BSGMarseille, 5 (1881) 329-52.

_____. "Voyage chez les Benadirs, les Çomalis et les Bayouns en 1882 et 1883," TM, 49 (1885) 1-80; and 50 (1885) 129-208; and 56 (1888), 385-416.

Rey, C. F. In the Country of the Blue Nile (New York, NUP: 1969). Originally published 1927 in London.

_____. The Real Abyssinia (New York, NUP: 1969). Originally published 1935 as an updated version of Unconquered Abyssinia as it is Today which was published in London, 1923.

Reynolds-Ball, Eustace. "Tourist Travel," (Addis Ababa) Travel and Exploration, 1 (1909), 451-52.

Riboni, P. "Alcune altre notizie sulle miniere d'oro dell'ualega," BSGI, 40 (1903), 778-81.

Ricchieri, G. "La spedizione Ferrandi al Giuba mandata della 'Società d'esplorazione commerciale in Africa di Milano,'" Compte Rendu Cong. Int. Soc. Geog. (Berne: 1891), 732-40.

Rigby, C. P. "Remarks on the North-east Coast of Africa, and the various tribes by which it is inhabited," Trans. Bombay GS, 6 (Sept. 1841-May 1844), 69-91.

Rimbaud, Arthur. "Rapport sur l'Ogadine," Comptes rendus SG (Paris: 1884).

_____. Lettres de J. A. Rimbaud, Egypt, Arabie, Ethiopie (Paris, Soc. du Mercure de France: 1899).

_____. Voyage en Abyssinie et au Harrar (Paris, La Centaine: 1928).

Riola, G. "Keren," BSAI, 7 (1888) 35-58.

_____. "Zula," BSAI, 7 (1888) 162-64.

Rittlinger, Herbert. Ethiopian Adventure; from the Red Sea to the Blue Nile (London: Odhams Press, 1959).

Rivera, ?. "Informazioni sui territori attorno a Beilul e Gubbi," BSAI, 9 (1890), 10-14.

Rivoyre, B. L. Denis de. Mer Rouge et Abyssinie (Paris: 1880).

_____. Obock, Mascate, Bouchire, Bassorah (Paris: 1883).

Roberts, L. B. "Travelling in the Highlands of Ethiopia," National Geographic, 68 (1935).

Rochet d'Héricourt, C. E. X. Voyage sur la côte orientale de la Mer Rouge, dans le pays d'Adal et le royaume de Choa (Paris: 1841).

_____. Second voyage sur les deux rives de la Mer Rouge, dans le pays des Adels et le royaume de Choa (Paris: 1846).

_____. "Considerations géographiques et commerciales sur le golfe Arabique, le pays d'Adel et le royaume de Choa (Abyssinie méridionale)," BSG, 15 (1841), 269-93.

_____. (Lecture of 23 Nov. 1849) Revue de l'Orient (December 1849).

Rodatz, Albert. "Auszug aus dem Tagebuche des Capitän Alb. Rodatz Schiff 'Alf,' betreffend einen Besuch von Massowah aus bei Dr. Schimper im Innern von Abyssinien, und Weiterreise von Massowah bis zur Umschiffung des Cap Guardafui," Ausland 19 (1846).

Rodatz, Johannes. "Wanderungen von Massawa, Hafenstadt in Abyssinien nach den Gebirgen und Aufenthalt zu Halai auf der Taranta im Jahre 1847; aus dem Tagebuche," Ausland, 22 (1849).

Rohlfs, F. G. Meine Mission Nach Abessinien auf Befehl Sr. Maj. des Deutschen Kaiser, Im Winter 1880-81 (Leipzig: 1883). (Translated into Italian in 1885)

_____. "Der Aschangi-See in Abessinien," ZGEBerlin, 3 (1868) 229-32.

_____. "Nach Axum uber Hausen und Adua," ZGEBerlin, 3 (1868).

_____. "Von Magdala nach Lalibala, Sokota, und Antalo, April/Mai 1868," Petermanns, 14 (1868).

_____. (Undated letter, probably in late 1880) Petermanns, 27 (1881) 73.

_____. "Klimatisches und Meteorologisches vom Roten Meere und aus Abessinien," Ausland, 54 (1881) 578-80.

_____. "Ergebnisse meiner Reise nach Abessinien; Bemerkungen zur Karte," Petermanns, 28 (1882).

_____. "Liegt ewiger Schnee in Abessinien?" Ausland, 57 (1884).

Romano Scotti, V. "Nell Eritrea inesplorata; itinerario attraverso il paese dei Baza," BSAI, 19 (1900).

Roncaglia, G. "Viaggio del Sig. Darragon dallo Scioa al paese dei Boran e viceversa," Extr. BSGI, 6 (1898).

Rondani, Armando. (Letters from Harar; March 1 and July 26, 1888) BSGI, 25 (1888), 579-81 and 948-49.

Rosa, Ottorino. Storie vecchie e nuove sull'Abissinia (Brescia: 1908).

_____. L'Impero del Leone di Giuda (Brescia: 1913).

_____. (Letter from Asmara, Aug. 21, 1901). EC, 16 (1901).

Rosen, Dr. Felix. Eine deutsche Gesandtschaft in Abessinien (Leipzig: 1907).

Rossetti, Carlo. "Una punta in Etiopia dalle frontiere del Sudan," BSGI, 47 (1910) 955-85.

Rossi, A. La nostre conquiste in Africa. Impressioni e note di un viaggio secondo fatto durante l'occupazione delle Agamè. (Milan: 1895).

Rothschild, Maurice de. Voyage en Ethiopie et en Afrique orientale anglaise (1904-1905). Résultats scientifiques. Animaux articulés (Paris: 1922) 2 vols.

Roumar, Paul. "Au Pays du Ras Makonnen," TM, 12 (1906), 117-18.

Roux, Hugues Le see Le Roux

Rüppell, Wilhelm P. Reise in Abyssinien. 2 vols (Frankfurt: 1838-1840).

_____. "Eineges über Abyssinien," Ann. D. Erd., Volkerund Staat, 12 (1835) 239-45.

Ruspoli, M. Eugenio. "La spedizione Ruspoli: Lettere," Extr. from BSGI, 30 (1893).

Russ, Kamill. "Aufzeichnungen in Bezug auf den Aegyptische-Abessinischen Krieg," Petermanns, 23 (1877) 157-58.

_____. "Abyssinia," GM, 5 (1878), 228-30.

Russel, Stanislas. Une mission en Abyssinie et dans la Mer Rouge, (23 Oct. 1859-7 mai 1860) (Paris: 1884).

Ruyters, André. "D'Addis-Abeba a Djibouti," La Nouvelle Revue Française, (1 Oct., 1 Dec. 1911 and 1 May 1912).

Sacconi, Gaetano (and Pietro). Letters from Harar 1 Dec. 1882, 2 Jan., 14 and 15 Feb., 17 June, 1883, l'Esploratore, 2 and 7 (1883); June 3, 6 and July 16 and 21, 1886, Esplorazione Commerciale, 2 (1887). (see also Amodeo, M.)

Saint-Ivens, G. "L'Erythree italienne," BSGM, 22 (1898), 23 (1899).

Salimbeni, Augusto. (Letters) BSGI, 22 (1885) 326; 23 (1886) 279; 24 (1887) 101-106, 180-92, 290-97.

_____. "Tre Anni di Lavoro nel Goggam," Extr. BSGI, ser. 2, 11 (Rome: 1886).

_____. "Diario d'un pioniere africano," Nuova Antologia, 384 (16 Mar., 10 and 16 April, 1936).

_____. "Il viaggio del Conte Salimbeni per raggiungere S. M. Menelich, Negus Neghest," BSAI, 9 (1890), 168-71.

_____. (Diary of Salimbeni, edited and annotated by Carlo Zaghi) Crispi e Menelich nel diario inedito del conte Augusto Salimbeni (Turin: 1956).

Salkeld, R. E. "A Journey across Jubaland," GJ, 46
     (1915).

Salt, Henry. A Voyage to Abyssinia and Travels into the Interior
     of that Country (London: 1814).

San Marzano, R. di. Dal Giuba al Margherita (Rome:
     1935).

_____. Dalla piano Somalia all'altipiano etiopico (Rome:
     1935).

Sapeto, Giuseppe. Etiopia (Rome: 1890).

_____. Viaggio e Missione Cattolica fra I Mensa I Bogos E Gli
     Habab con un Cenno Geografico e Storico dell'Abissinia (Rome:
     1857).

_____. "Ambasciata mandata nel 1869 dal governo francese a
     Negussie--Memorie," BSGI, 6 (1871), 22-71.

_____. "Notizie sopra Assab," Cosmos, 4 (1877), 226-30.

Savage-Landor see Landor

Savoia-Aosta, Luigi Amedeo di. La esplorazione dello Uabi-Uebi
     Schebeli dalle sue sorgenti nella Etiopia meridionale alla So-
     malia italiana (1928-1929) (Milan: 1932).

Schimper, Wilhelm. Berichte aus und über Abessinien (Vienna:
     1852).

_____. "Nachrichten von dem Reisenden Schimper," Ausland, 11
     (1838) 279.

_____. "Meine Gefangenschaft in Abessinien," Petermanns, 14
     (1868), 294-98.

_____. "Die geologischen und physikalischen Verhältnisse des
     Districts Arrho und der Salzhandel in Abyssinien," ZGEBerlin,
     12 (1877), 109-116.

Schoenfeld, E. D. Erythräa und der Ägyptische Sudan (Berlin:
     1904).

Schöller, ?. Mitteilungen uber meine Reise in der Colonia Eritrea
     (Berlin: 1895).

Schuver, Juan Maria. (Excerpts from letters sent from Fadasi,
     Sept. 10, October 18, 1881) Petermanns, 28 (1882).

_____. "Reisen im oberen Nilgebiet; Erlebnisse und Beobachtungen
     auf der Wasserscheide zwischen Blauem und Weissem Nil und

in den ägyptisch-abessinischen Grenzländern, 1881 und 1882, " Petermanns, Erganzungsband 16 (1883-84), 1-95.

Schwarz, Herbert. Die Entwicklung der völkerrechtlichen Beziehungen Äthiopiens zu den Mächten seit 1885 (Breslau: 1937).

Schweinfurth, Dr. G. Beitrag zur Flora Aethiopiens (Berlin: 1867).

_____. "Was die Deutschen in Abessinien treiben, " Petermanns, 12 (1866).

_____. "Il Dr. G. Schweinfurth in Eritrea, " BSAI, 10 (1891).

_____. "Einige Mitteilungen über seinen diesjährigen Besuch in der Colonia Eritrea (Nord-Abessinien, 2 Juli 1892), VGEBerlin, 19 (1892), 332-60.

_____. "Escursione nel Dembelas, " BSAI, 13 (1894), 54-58.

_____. "Viaggio dei Dott. G. Schweinfurth e M. Schoeller in Eritrea, " BSAI, 13 (1894). Translation from Verhandlungen der Gesellschaft für Erdkunde zu Berlin, 21 (1894), 279-231.

Scognamiglio, Paola. "Etiopia: Un Paese in movimento, " Africa (Rome), 28 (June 1973), 311-316.

Seno, Emilio dal. (Letter of March 27, 1893) BSAI, 12 (1893) 123-24.

Seyoum Tegegn Worq. "The Ethiopian Ports. " EO, 12: 4 (1969), 242-43.

Shatte, T. C. "Ethiopia: General Survey, " African Hunter (New York, Harcourt, Brace, Jovanovich: 1975), 173-185.

Shaw, J. H. Ethiopia (New York: Acme Photo Offset Corporation, 1936).

Shchusev, P. V. Iz puteshestviia v Abissiniiu (St. Petersburg: 1897).

_____. "Kistokam Golubogo Nila, " GII, 36 (1900), 198-217.

Simon, Gabriel. Voyage en Abyssinie et chez les Gallas-Raïas (Paris: 1885).

Skinner, Robert P. Abyssinia of Today (New York: 1906) Reprint, Greenwood Press, Westport, Connecticut: 1970.

_____. "An Expedition Between Lake Rudolf and the Nile, " BGSPhiladelphia, 2 (1900).

Smith, H. F. H. see Harrison-Smith

Snailham, R.   The Blue Nile Revealed, the Story of the Great Abbai Expedition 1968 (London, Chatto and Windus: 1970).

Soleillet, Paul.   (Letter from Gallau, Sept. 2, 1883) BSGI, 21
(1884), 244-45.

_____.   "Obock et l'Ethiopie Méridionale," BSGLyon, 5 (1884-
85).

_____.   Voyages en Ethiopie (Jan. 1880-Oct. 1884) (Rouen: 1886).

_____.   Obock, le Choa, le Kaffa; une exploration commerciale
en Ethiopie.   Récit anecdotique (Paris: 1886).

Sommer, J. W.   "Ethiopia," Focus 15 (1965) 1-6.

Sorrentino, Giorgio.   "Ricordi del Benadir," BSAI, 26 (1907); 27
(1908); 28 (1909).

Soudan de Pierrefitte, ?.   "En Abyssinie," BSNormandeG, 18
(1896), 150-83.   1886

Spencer, Diana.   "Trip to Wag and northern Wallo," JES, 5: 1
(1967) 95-108.

_____.   "St. Luke ikons in Ethiopia, in search of," JES, 10: 2
(1972), 67-96.

_____.   "Travels in Gojjam: St. Luke ikons and Brancaleon re-
discovered," JES, 12: 2 (1974) 201-220.

Stecker, Anton.   (Letters from Debra Tabor, June 21, 1881 and
Ashangi, August 9, 1881).   Petermanns, 27 (1881), 472-74.

_____.   (Letter from Mekelle, Nov. 1881).   Globus, 41 (1882),
223.

_____.   (Letter from Massawa, July 4, 1883).   VGEBerlin, 10
(1883) 434-35.

_____.   (Undated letter) Petermanns, 29 (1883), 356.

_____.   "Dr. Anton Steckers Reisen in den Galla-Ländern, 1882;
nach seinen Tagebuchnotizen zusammengestellt von G. E.
Fritzsche," Petermanns, 37 (1891).

_____.   "Die Steckers Expedition.   Berichte des Reisenden.
Aufnahme des Tana-Sees," Mittheilungen der Afrikanischen
Gesellschaft, 3 (1881-1883).

Stefanini, G.   Saggio di una carta geologica dell'Eritrea, della
Somalia, e dell'Etiopia (Florence: 1936).

Stella, Father Giovanni. Abissinia: Storia (Rome: Propaganda Fide, 1850).

Stepunin, Alekseĭ N. Efiopiîa. (Moscow: 1965).

Stern, Henry A. Wandering among the Falashas in Abyssinia with a Description of the Country and Its Various Inhabitants (London: 1862). Reprinted: London, Frank Cass: 1968).

_____. The Captive Missionary (London: 1868).

Steudner, Hermann. "Bericht des Herrn Dr. Steudner an Dr. H. Barth über seine Reise von Djedda bis Keren," ZAE, 12 (1862), 46-73.

_____. "Besuch des Klosters Zad'Amba (Sept. 10-Oct. 2, 1861)," ZAE, 12 (1862), 205-15.

_____. "Reise von Keren nach Adoa, vom 28 Oktober bis 14 Nov. 1861, sowie Besuch von Axum," ZAE, 12 (1862), 326-40.

_____. (Letter from Khartoum, Sept. 14, 1862). ZAE, 13 (1862) 423-28.

_____. "Reise von Adoa nach Gondar, 26 Dezember 1861-Januar 1862," ZAE, 15 (1863) 43-141.

_____. "Herrn Dr. Steudner's Bericht über seine abessinische Reise," ZAE, 17 (1864), 22-112.

Stévenin, M. et Mme. see Pariset above

Stigand, Chauncey Hugh. To Abyssinia, Through an Unknown Land (London: 1910). Reprinted New York, NUP, 1969.

Swayne, Frances. A Woman's Pleasure Trip in Somaliland (London: 1907).

Swayne, H. J. E. Seventeen Trips Through Somaliland. A Record of Exploration and Big Game Shooting, 1885-1893 (London: 1895).

Tagliabue, Enrico. "Da Massaua a Keren per la via del Lebca," EC, 4 (1889), 34-39.

_____. "Egiziani e Abissinesi," EC, 5 (1881).

Tamisier, Maurice see Combes and Tamisier

Tanca, G. "Sulla Somalia meridionale," Cong. GI (6°, Venezia, 1907) 2, 9-33.

Tancredi, A. M. "Una cucina barbara; come mangiano gli Abissini d'Eritrea," BSGI, 44 (1907), 960-82, 1088-1113.

_____. "La missione della Società Geografica italiana in Etiopia settentrionale, " BSGI, 45 (1908), 1199-1250.

_____. "La missione Italiana al Lago Tzana, " EC, 23 (1908).

_____. "Nel Piano del Sale, " BSGI, 48 (1911) 57-84, 150-78.

Tarchi, Arturo.   (Letter from Assab, March 11, 1888).   BSAI, 7 (1888).

Taurin de Cahagne, Father.   (Letter from Litche, Sept. 12, 1868). BSG, 19 (1870), 381-8.

_____. (Letter from Harar 28 Nov. 1880).   Explorations, 13 (1881-82) 342.

_____. "Mission Galla; corr. de Mgr. Taurin et autres missionaires avec R. P. Salvator de Bois Hubert, 1865-1892, " Bibliothèque Franciscaine Provincial, No. 185.

_____. (Letters from Father Taurin to Antoine d'Abbadie in the Bibliothèque Nationale, Paris, d'Abbadie Collection N. A. 10222.)

_____. "l'Harar negli ultimi secoli, " BSGI, Ser. 2, 8 (1883).

Tedesco Zammarano, V.   Alle sorgenti del Nila azzuro.   (Rome: 1922).

Teleki, Samuel.   "Graf Teleki's Entdeckungsreisen in Ostafrica, " Ausland, 62 (1889), 189-92.

Tellez, Baltazar.   "Histoire de la Haute-Ethiopie écrite sur les lieux par le R. P. Manoel d'Almeida, " Relations de divers voyages curieux qui n'ont pas été publiées.   Vol. 4 (Paris: 1673).   See d'Almeida for English translation.

Terracciano, Achille.   "Escursione botanica alle terre degli Habab, " BSGI, 29 (1892).

Tommaso di Savoia, Duke of Genoa.   "Il commercio di Alula, " BSAI, 19 (1900).   1877

Tonkin, Thelma.   Ethiopia with Love.   (London,   Hodder and Stoughton: 1972).

Toy, Barbara.   "A Night on the Princes' Prison Mountain, " Mademoiselle, 54 (Jan. 1962) 98-99.

_____. In Search of Sheba: Across the Sahara to Ethiopia. (London, Murray: 1961).

Toynbee, A. J.   Between Niger and Nile.   (London, OUP: 1965).

Traub, Paul. "Voyage au pays du Bogos et dans les provinces septentrionales de l'Abyssinie, " BSNeuG, 4 (1888). 1878

Traversi, Leopoldo. "Appunti sui Danakili, " BSGI, 23 (1886), 516-27.

_____. (Letter from Entotto, July 15, 1887). BSAI, 6 (1887), 274-75.

_____. "Profili da Ancober a Let-Marefia, " BSGI, 24 (1887), 197-99.

_____. "Viaggi negli Arussi, Guraghi, ecc. , " BSGI, 24 (1887), 267-77. (In letter dated Entotto, Sept. 5, 1886.)

_____. "Da Entotto al Zuquala, " BSGI, 24 (1887), 581-95.

_____. (Letter from Entotto, Aug. 10, 1887). BSGI, 25 (1888), 122-26; (Letter from Finfinni, Nov. 15, 1887), 126-27.

_____. "Escursione nel Gimma, " BSGI, 25 (1888), 901-23.

_____. "Lo Scioa ed i paesi limitrofi, " BSGI, 26 (1889), 703-35.

_____. "Notizie dallo Scioa, " (Let Marafia, Dec. 23, 1891 and Jan. 12 and 14, 1892), BSGI, 29 (1892), 224-31.

_____. "Sulla regione dei Danakili, " BSGI, 30 (1893), 105-108.

_____. "Itinerario Aussa-Doué, " BSGI, 30 (1893).

_____. "La antichità di Uorcamba nello Scioa, " BSGI, 30 (1893), 681-84. (Letters of June 5 and 19, 1893.)

_____. "Sul corso del Golima; sulle origini del Guiba, " BSGI, 30 (1893), 684-88. (Letters of July 8 and April 24, 1893.)

_____. "Informazioni geografiche dallo Scioa, " BSGI, 31 (1894), 390-93. (Letters Nov. 1, 1893 and 24 January 1894.)

_____. "Sul corso dell'Omo, " BSGI, 31 (1894), 465-66. (Letter of 29 April 1894.)

_____. Let Marefia. (Milan: 1931).

_____. L'Italia e l'Etiopia da Assab a Ualual (Bologna: 1935).

Treat, Ida. "With the Slave Traders of Abyssinia, " Travel, 57 (June, 1931), 32-36 and 72.

Trémaux, Pierre. Voyage en Ethiopie au Soudan Oriental. (Paris: 1862).

Tubiana, Joseph. "Fragments du Journal de Voyages d'Antoine d'Abbadie," Cahiers de l'Afrique et l'Asie, 5 (1959).

_____. "Deux fragments du tome second de 'Douze Ans dans la Haute Ethiopie' d'Arnauld d'Abbadie," Rocznik Orientalistycny, 25, 2 (Warsaw: 1961).

V. G. "Pâques chez Menelich," Le Globe Trotter, 1 (1902).

Valenti, Gino. "Condizioni e problemi della Colonia," Riv. GI, 20 (1913), 553-54.

Valentia, Viscount (George Annesley). Voyages and Travels to India, Ceylon, The Red Sea, Abyssinia and Egypt, in the Years 1802-1806. 3 vols. (London: 1809).

Vanderheym, J. Gaston. Une Expedition Avec Le Negous Menelik. (Paris: 1896).

Vannutelli, L., and Citerni, C. "Relazione preliminare sui resultati geografici della II. spedizione del Capt. V. Bottego nell'Africa orientale," BSGI, 34 (1897), 320-330.

_____. L'Omo, Seconda Spedizione Bottego (Milan: 1899).

Vayssière, Alexandre. "Scenes de Voyage dans L'Hedjaz et L'Abyssinie," RDM, (Oct. Nov. Dec.: 1850).

_____. Souvenirs d'un voyageur en Abyssine. 2 vols. (Brussels and Leipzig: 1857)

Vedova, F. "Nota sulla Carta della regione tra lo Scioa ed Harar," BSGI, 25 (1888), 56-65.

Veitch, Sophie see Zander, Edward

Vignéras, Sylvain. Une Mission Française En Abyssinie (Paris: 1897).

Vigoni, Pippo. "Keren e Sanhit," EC, 2 (1887).

_____. "Massaua e il Nord dell'Abissinia," EC, 3 (supplement to Jan. 1888) 1-18.

_____. Abissinia: Giornali di un viaggio (Milan: 1881). 1876

Villespy, Seraphin de. "La mission du Kaffa, autrefois et aujourd' hui," Les Missions Catholiques, vol. 36 (Paris: 1904).

Vita, A. de see Bongiovanni

Vitta, Umberto. "Nei Maria," BSAI, 10 (1891), 71-75, 81-89.

Vivian, Herbert. Abyssinia: Through the Lion-land to the Court of the Lion of Judah (London: 1901). Reprint Greenwood Press, Westport, Connecticut.

Vladykin, B. V. "Osobennosti sovremennago obraza zhizni abis-sintsev i ikh Imperatora Menelika II, " IzIr, 43 (1907).

Vollbrecht, H. Im Reiche des Negus Negesti Menelik II: eine Gesandtschaftsreise nach Abessinien. (Stuttgart, Berlin, Leipzig: 1906).

Waldmeier, Theophilus. Autobiography. Being an Account of Ten Years Life in Abyssinia and Sixteen Years in Syria (London: 1886). (Translated from German).

Waugh, Evelyn. Remote People. (London: Duckworth, 1931).

_____. Waugh in Abyssinia (London: 1936).

_____. When the Going Was Good (London: 1948).

Weir, V. "The Changing Face of Ethiopia, " African World (April 1967), 7-8.

Wellby, M. S. 'Twixt Sirdar and Menelik: An Account of a Year's Expedition from Zeila to Cairo through Unknown Abyssinia (London, New York: 1901). Reprint Greenwood Press, West-port, Connecticut, 1970.

_____. "King Menelik's Dominions and the Country Between Lake Gallop (Rudolf) and the Nile Valley, " GJ, 16 (1900), 292-304.

Whiteway, R. S., ed. and trans. The Portuguese Expedition to Abyssinia in 1541-1543, as narrated by Castanhoso, with some contemporary letters. The Short Account of Bermudez, and Certain extracts from Correa (London: 1902).

Wickenburg, Eduard. (Letters from Harar in 1897). BSAI, 16 (1897), 115-118.

_____. "Reise des Grafen Wickenburg, " MKKGGWien, 45 (1902), 22-24.

_____. "Von Dschibuti bis Lamu, " Petermanns, 49 (1903).

_____. Wanderungen in Ost-Africa (Vienna: 1899).

_____. "Abessinien, " Deutsche Rundschau, 32 (1908).

Wild, G. Von Kairo nach Massaua. Eine Erinnerung an Werner Munzinger (Olten: 1879).

Wilkins, Henry St. Clair. Reconnoitering in Abyssinia (London: 1870).

Wilkinson, J. Gardner. "Account of the Jimma country," JRGS,
    25 (1855), 206-14.

Winstanley, W. A Visit to Abyssinia. An Account of Travel in
    modern Ethiopia (London: 1881). 2 vols. Reprint Greenwood
    Press, Westport, Conn. (1973).

Wolf, ?. "Narrative of Voyages to explore the shores of Africa,
    Arabia and Madagascar. Performed in His Majesty's Ships
    Leven and Barracouta; under direction of Capt. W. F. W.
    Owen, R. N., " JRGS, 3 (1833), 197-223.

Wolynsky, Decio. (Letters from Holl Holl, August 17, 1903 and
    from Dire Dawa, Nov. 10, 1903, and from Jibuti.) EC, 18
    (1903), 282, 372-77.

_____. "Note dall'Harrar," EC, 19 (1904).

Wolverton, Lord. Five Months' Sport in Somaliland (London: 1894).

Wylde, Augustus. '83 to '87 in the Soudan. With an Account of
    Sir William Hewett's Mission to King John of Abyssinia. 2
    vols. (London: 1888).

_____. Modern Abyssinia (London: 1901). Reprint Greenwood
    Press, Westport, Conn. (1974).

Zaghi, C. "L'Italia e l'Etiopia alla viglia di Adua nei dispacci
    segreti di Luigi Capucci," Gli annali dell'Africana, 4: 2 (1941).

_____. "Il diario inedito della spedizione Capucci e Cicognani
    all'Aussa nel 1885, " BRSGI, 12 (1935).

_____. "La spedizione Capucci e Cicognani in Abissinia, "
    Riv. CI, 8 (1934).

_____. "l'Italia, Francia e Inghilterra nel mar rosso dal 1880-
    1888 in una memoria inedita di Cesare Nerazzini a Francesco
    Crispi," Gli annali dell'Africana, 3 (1940).

Zahn, W. Adami Tullu: Apotheker, Pionier und Zauberer im Lande
    des Negus (Stuttgart: Deutsche Volksbucher: 1951). 1914-
    1940's

Zander, Edward. Views in Central Abyssinia with Portraits of the
    Natives of the Galla Tribes, Taken in Pen and Ink under Cir-
    cumstances of Peculiar Difficulty, by T. E. (sic) a German
    Traveller Believed at Present to be One of the Captives There.
    With descriptions by Sophie F. F. Veitch (London: 1868).

Zantrop, S. Glimpses from My Flying Carpet: Jet-Age Tales
    (Munich: printed privately by Leyers, 1971). (Trans. from
    German.)

Zichy, Count Wilmos. "Die salzebene Asale im Danakil-Land an der africanischen Ostküste, " Ausland, 48 (1875), 820-22.

_____. "Die Danakil-Küste, " Petermanns, 26 (1880), 133-35.

Zintgraff, Alfred. Der Tod es Löwen von Juda (Berlin: 1932).

HISTORY (A)
Ancient and Medieval

Abd el-Kader, Chihab Ed-Din Ahmed (surnommé: Arab-Faqih). Histoire de la conquête de l'Abyssinie (XVI siècle). Texte arabe et traduction française et notes par René Basset. 8 vols. (Paris: 1897-1901).

Aboul Feda. Géographie d'Aboulféda (Paris: 1848) Tome 2, part 1.

Acanfora, M. Ornella. "Avanzi di civiltà antica Debre Tsièn (Asmara), " RSE, 6 (1947), 23-28.

Admassou Shiferaou. "Rapport sur la découverte d'antiquités trouvées dans les locaux du gouvernment general de Magallé, " AE, 1 (1965), 11-15.

Agostino Tedla, Abba. "A proposito di alcuni passi oscuri negli scritti teologici etiopici dei secoli XVI-XVII pubblicati da E. Cerulli, " Proc. Third International Conference of Ethiopian Studies, Addis Ababa, 1966. Vol. 2 (Addis Ababa: Institute of Ethiopian Studies, 1970).

Akalou Wolde, Michael. "The Impermanency of Royal Capitals in Ethiopia, " Yearbook of the Association of Pacific Coast Geographers, 28 (1966), 147-156.

Alimen, H. Préhistoires de l'Afrique (Paris: N. Boubée, 1955).

Anastos, M. "The Alexandrian Origin of the Christian Topography of Cosmas Indicopleutes, " Dumbarton Oaks Papers, No. 3 (1946).

Anfray, Francis. "Aspects de l'archéologie éthiopienne, " JAH, 9: 3 (1968), 343-366.

_____. "Notre connaissance du passé éthiopien d'après les travaux archéologiques récentes, " JSS, 9: 1 (1964), 247-249.

_____. "Les Rois d'Axoum d'après la numismatique, " JES, 6: 2 (1968), 7-38.

_____. "Une nouvelle inscription grecque d'Ezana, roi d'Axoum, " Journal de Savants (Oct.-Dec. 1970).

Aubin, J. "L'ambassade du Prêtre Jean à Don Manuel," Mare-Luso-Indicum 3 (1976).

Bahrey. "History of the Galla," Trans. in Beckingham-Huntingford, Some Records of Ethiopia, 1593-1646 (London, Hakluyt Society: 1954).

Bahru Demissie. "External Policy of Zagwe Kings," History Journal (Addis Ababa), 2: 2 (1968), 32-36.

Bailloud, Gerard. "La préhistoire de l'Ethiopie," Tarik, 2 (1963).

Baldet, Henry. "Some aspects of the Pre-History of Ethiopia: Melka Kontoure and the Omo Valley," EO, 15: 1 (1972), 45-50.

Baratelli, Elvira. "Le leggenda del re serpente in Etiopia," Atti del Terzo Congresso di Studi Coloniali, 6 (1937), 7-18.

Bartnicki, Andrezej and Mantel-Niécko, Joanna. "The Role and Significance of the Religious Conflicts and People's Movements in the Political Life of Ethiopia in the Seventeenth and Eighteenth Centuries," RSE, 24 (1971), 5-39.

Basset, René. Etudes sur l'Histoire d'Ethiopie (Paris: 1882).

Beardsley, G. H. The Ethiopian in Greek and Roman Civilization. (Johns Hopkins University, Baltimore: 1922).

Beccari, C. Notizie e saggi di opere e documenti inediti riguardanti la storia di Etiopia durante i secoli XVI, XVII, e XVIII. Vol. 1 of series Rerum Aethiopicarum Scriptores Occidentales Inediti a Saeculo XVI ad XIX.

Beckingham, Charles F. "Amba Geshen and Asirgarh," JSS, 2 (1957), 182-188.

_____. "A Note on the Topography of Ahmad Gran's Campaigns in 1542," JSS, 4: 4 (1959), 362-373.

_____. "The Travels of Jerónimo Lobo," JES, 4: 1 (1966), 1-4.

_____. "Pantaleao de Aveiro and the Ethiopian Community in Jerusalem," JSS, 7 (1962).

Béguinot, Francisco, ed. and trans. La Cronaca Abbreviata d'Abissinia (Rome: 1901).

Berchet, G. "Lettera sulle cognizioni che i Veneziani avevano dell'Abissinia," BSGI, 2 (1889).

Berry, LaVerle. "Factions and Coalitions During the Gonder Period, 1630-1755," P. 5th ICES, (Chicago: 1979).

Biasutti, Renato. "Egiziani ed Etiopici," Aegyptus, 6: 1 (1925).

Blundell, H. Weld, ed. and trans. The Royal Chronicle of Abyssinia, 1769-1840 (Cambridge, England: 1922).

Bosi, Roberto. "Appunti per una proto-storia d'Etiopia," Africa (Rome), 13: 6 (1958).

Braukämper, Ulrich. "Islamic Principalities in Southeast Ethiopia Between the Thirteenth and Sixteenth Centuries," EN, 1: 1 (1977) and 1: 2 (1977).

Brown, Clifton. The Conversion Experience in Axum During the Fourth and Fifth Centuries. 2nd ser. Historical Publications, 11, History Dept., Howard University, Washington, D.C., 1973.

Buder, W. "Das Reich von Aksum," Zeitschrift fur Kulturaustausch (Aethiopien--Sonderausgabe: 1973), 29-37.

Budge, E. A. W., ed. and trans. The Book of the Saints of the Ethiopian Church: A Translation of the Ethiopian Synaxarium. 4 vols. (Cambridge, England: 1928).

_____. The Life and Exploits of Alexander the Great; Being a Series of Ethiopic Texts (London: 1896).

Buxton, D. R. "The Christian Antiquities of Northern Ethiopia," Archaeologia, 42 (1948), 1-42.

Caix de Saint-Aymour, Amédée de. La France en Ethiopie. Histoire des relations de la France avec l'Abyssinie chrétienne sous les règnes de Louis XIII et de Louis XIV (1634-1706), d'après des documents inédits du Ministère des Affaires étrangères (Paris: 1886).

Caquot, Andre. "Ethiopie et Cyrenaique?" AE, 3 (1959).

_____. "Histoire amharique de Gran et des Gallas," AE, 2 (1957).

_____. "L'Homélie en l'Honneur de l'Archange Raguel (Dersana Ragu'el)," AE, 2 (1957), 91-122.

_____. "La Reine de Saba et le bois de la croix, selon une tradition Ethiopienne," AE, 1 (1955), 137-147.

_____. "La Royauté sacrale en Ethiopie," AE, 2 (1957), 205-218.

Cerulli, Enrico. Documenti arabi per la storia dell'Etiopia (Rome: 1931).

_____. "L'Etiopia medievale in alcuni brani di scrittori arabi," RSE, 3 (1943), 272-294.

_____. "L'Imperatore Na'od e gli Stefaniti a Gerusalemme in un documento inedito (Vaticano Etiopico 298)," Proc. Third Int'l Conference of Ethiopian Studies, Addis Ababa, 1966. Vol. 2 (Addis Ababa, Institute of Ethiopian Studies, 1970), 243-253.

_____. "Gli Abbati di Dabra Libanos, capi del monachismo etiopico, secondo la 'lista rimata' (sec. XIV-XVIII)," Orientalia, 12 (1943), 13 (1944).

_____. "Gli Atti de Batra Maryam," RSE, 4 (1944), 5 (1945).

_____. "Gli Atti di Zena Maryam monaca ethiopica del secolo XIV," Riv. SO, 21 (1946).

_____. "Il sultanato dello Scioa nel secolo XIII secondo un nuovo documento storico," RSE, 1 (1941).

_____. "Il Libro etiopico dei miracoli di Maria e le sue fonti nelle letterature de medio evo latino," Vol. 1, Studi Orientali Pubblicata cura della Scuola Orientale, Università di Roma, 1943.

_____. "La Nubia cristiana, i Baria ed i Cunama, nel X secolo, secondo Ibn Hawqal, geografo arabo," Istituto Universitario Orientale di Napoli Annali, 3: 1 (1949), 215-222.

_____. "Vestigia di antiche civilta in Eritrea e in Somalia," L'Africa Orientale Italiana e Il Conflitto Italo-Etiopico (Rome: 'La Rassegna Italiana,' 1936).

Chaîne, Marcel. La Chronologie des temps chrétiens de l'Egypt et de l'Ethiopie (Paris: 1925).

_____. "Jean Bermudez, patriarche d'Ethiopie (1540-1570)," Revue de l'orient Chrétien, 14 (1909).

Chatterji, S. K. India and Ethiopia from the 7th Century B.C. (Calcutta, Asiatic Society, monograph no. 15, 1968).

Chavaillon, Jean. "L'Ethiopie avant l'histoire: une trace vers les premiers hommes," Archeologia, 64 (1973), 11-19.

Chhabra, Hari Sharan. "Ancient Indo-Ethiopian Relations," EO, 4: 10 (1960), 343-346.

Chittick, Neville. "Excavations at Aksum: A Preliminary Report," Azania, 9 (1974), 159-206.

Christides, Vassilios. "The Himyarite-Ethiopian War and the Ethiopian Occupation of South Arabia in the Acts of Gregentius (c. 530 A.D.)," AE, 9: 2 (1972), 115-146.

Chronicles, Royal (c. 1270-c. 1769)
    Vie de Lalibala, roi d'Ethiopie. Trans. J. Perruchon (Paris:
        1892.)

    "Histoire d'Eskender, d'Amda Syon et de Naod," JA (1894)
        Trans. J. Perruchon.

    "Histoire des Guerres d'Amda Syon," JA (1889). Trans.
        J. Perruchon.

    The Glorious Victories of Amda Seyon, King of Ethiopia
        (Oxford: 1965). Trans. G. W. B. Huntingford.

    Les Chroniques de Zar'a Ya'eqob et de Baeda Maryam, rois
        d'Ethiopie de 1434 à 1478. Trans. J. Perruchon (Paris:
        1893).

    "The Chronicle of Ba'eda Mariam." English translation of
        Perruchon (above) in EO, 6: 1 (1962), by L. Haber.

    "The Chronicle of the Emperor Zara Yaqob (1434-1468)."
        English translation by L. Haber of Perruchon (above) in
        EO, 5: 2 (1961).

    "Le Règne de Lebna Dengel," RS, 1 (1893). Trans. J. Perruchon.

    "Storia di Lebna Dengel Re d'Etiopia," RRAL, Vol. III (Rome:
        1894). Trans. C. Conti Rossini.

    "Le Règne de Galawdewos (Claudius) ou Asnaf-Sagad," RS, 1
        (1894). Trans. J. Perruchon.

    Chronique de Galawdewos (Claudius, 1540-1559). Trans. W.
        E. Conzelman (Paris: 1895).

    "Règne de Minas ou Admas-Sagad (1559-1563)," RS, 4 (1896).
        Trans. J. Perruchon.

    "Règne de Sarsa Dengel ou Malak Sagad I," RS, 4 (1896).
        Trans. J. Perruchon.

    Historia Regis Sarsa Dengel (Malak Sagad). CSCO: SA, ser.
        altera, 3 (Paris: 1907). Trans. C. Conti Rossini.

    "Règne de Yaqob et Za-Dengel," RS, 4 (1896). Trans. J.
        Perruchon.

    "Règne de Susneyos," RS, 5 (1897). Trans. J. Perruchon.

    "Règne de Fasiladas," RS, 6 (1898). Trans. J. Perruchon.

    "Règne de Iyasu I, Roi d'Ethiopie," RS, 9 (1901). Trans. J.
        Perruchon.

Annales Iohannes I, Iyasu I et Bakaffa. CSCO: SA, ser. altera, 5. 2 vols. (Paris: 1903). Trans. I. Guidi.

"Iyasu I Re d'Etiopia e Martire," RivSO, 20 (1942), 65-128. Trans. C. Conti Rossini.

"Règne de Yohannes I. roi d'Ethiopie de 1667 à 1682," RS, 6 (1898). Trans. J. Perruchon.

Annales Regum Iyasu II et Iyo'as. CSCO: SA, ser. altera, 6 (Paris: 1910, text) (Rome: 1912, trans. by I. Guidi).

Clark, J. D. "A Kenya Fauresmith Factory and Home Site at Gondar, Northern Abyssinia," Transactions RSSA, 31 (1945), 19-27.

_____. Prehistoric Cultures of the Horn of Africa (Cambridge: CUP: 1954).

Contenson, Henri de. "Les principales étapes de l'Ethiopie antique," Cahiers d'études Africaines, 2: 1 (1961) 12-23.

_____. "Les Subdivisions de l'archaéologie éthiopienne état de la question," Revue Archaéologique (1936), 189-191.

_____. "Relations entre la Nube chrétienne et l'Ethiopie axoumite," Proc. Third Int'l Conference of Ethiopian Studies, Addis Ababa, 1966. (Addis Ababa: Institute of Ethiopian Studies, 1969), 17-18.

Conti Rossini, Carlo. "Appunti ed Osservazione sui Re Zague a Takla Haymanot," RRAL, ser. 5, 4 (1895), 341-359.

_____. "Aethiopica," RivSO, 9 (1922), 365-381, 449-468.

_____. "La Caduta della dinastia Zague e la versione amarica del Be'ela Nagast," RRAL, ser. 5, 31 (1932), 279-314.

_____. "Expeditions et possessions des Habasat en Arabie," JA, ser. 11, 18 (1921), 1-36.

_____. "I Castelli di Gondar," BRSGI, ser. 3, 4 (1939), 165-168.

_____. "Ieha, Tsehuf Emni e Dera," RSE, 6 (1947), 12-22.

_____. "Il Libro di Re Zara'a Ya'qob sulla custodia del mistero," RSE, 3: 2 (1943), 148-166.

_____. "Les listes des rois d'Aksoum," JA, ser. 10, 10: 14 (1909), 263-320.

_____. "Meroe ed Aksum ne romanzo di Eleodoro," RivSO, 8 (1919-20), 233-239.

_____. "La Regalità Sacra in Abissinia e nei Regni dell-Africa Centrale ed Occidentale," Studi e Materiali di Storia delle Religioni, 21 (1948), 12-31.

_____. "Seppellimento in vasco," RSE, 7: 1 (1948), 114-115.

_____. "Sulla dinastia Zague," Extr. de L'Oriente, 11 (1897).

_____. See Chronicles, Royal (of Libna Dingil, Sartsa Dengel and Iyasu I)

_____. "Due Squarci Inedici di Cronaca Etiopica," RRAL, ser. 5, 2 (1893).

_____. "Il Convento di Tsana in Abissinia e le sue laudi alla Vergine," RRAL, ser. 5, 19 (1910), 581-91.

_____. "Di un nuovo Codice della Cronaca Etiopica Pubblicata da R. Basset," RRAL, ser. 5, 2 (1883).

_____. "Sulla Missioni Domenicane in Etiopia nel secolo XIV," RRAL, ser. 7, 1 (1940).

_____. "Tre piccoli testi etiopici," Riv. SO, 23 (1946).

Coppet, Maurice de. "Sanctuaires et pélerinages chrétiens d'Ethiopie," L'Illustration, 4239 (1924), 531-532.

Crawford, O. G. S., ed. Ethiopian Itineraries: circa 1400-1524. (Hakluyt Society, ser. 2, 109 CUP: 1958).

Crowfoot, J. Grafton. "Christian Nubia," J. of Egyptian Archaeology, 13 (1927) 141-150.

Crummey, Donald. "Gondarine Rim Land Sales: An Introductory description and Analysis," Proc. of Fifth Int'l Conference on Ethiopian Studies, April, 1978, Chicago, USA. (Publications Services, U. of Illinois at Chicago Circle: 1979).

_____. "Women and Landed Property in Gondarine Ethiopia," No. 78-16 (1978), African Association, Brandeis University, Waltham, Massachusetts.

Da Costa, Manuel G. "Jeronimo Lobo Reveals Ethiopia to Europe in the middle of the XVIIth Century," P. 3rd ICES, Addis Ababa, 1966, Vol. 1.

Davis, Asa J. "Background to the Zaaga Lab Embassy: an Ethiopian Diplomatic Mission to Portugal (1527-1539)," Studia, 32 (1971), 211-302.

_____. "The Relevance of Negusa Negast (King of Kings) in an Arabic Text," Ibadan, 26 (1959), 68-72.

_____. "The Sixteenth Century Jihad in Ethiopia and Its Impact on Culture," J. of Historical Society of Nigeria, 2: 4 (1963), 567-592.

Deramey, I. "Une lettre d'Ignace de Loyola à Claudius, roi d'Ethiopie ou d'Abyssinie," Revue de l'Histoire des Religions, 28 (1893).

Dictionary of Ethiopian Biography. Vol. 1 From early times to the End of the Zagwé Dynasty c. 1270 A. D. (Institute of Ethiopian Studies, Addis Ababa University, 1975).

Dillmann, C. F. A. "Zur Geschichte des Axumitischen Reiches vierten bis sechsten Jahrhundert," Abh. der Kön. Akad. der Wis. (Berlin: 1880).

Doresse, Jean. "Ethiopie in the Early Christian and Byzantine Era," Abba Salama, 2 (1971), 108-118.

_____. "La Découverte d'Asbi-Dera. Nouveaux documents sur les rapports entre l'Egypte et l'Ethiopie a l'époque axoumite," Atti del convegno internazionale di studi etiopici (Rome: 1959), 411-434.

_____. L'Empire du Prêtre-Jean (Paris, Plon: 1957).

_____. La Vie quotidienne des Ethiopiens chrétiens (aux XVIIe et XVIIIe siècles). (Paris, Librairie Hachette: 1972).

Drewes, A. J. and Schneider, R. "Documents épigraphiques de l'Ethiopie," AE, 7 (1967) and 8 (1970).

Drouin, E. "Les listes royales éthiopiennes et leur autorité historique," Extr. de la Revue archéologique (1882).

_____. "Deux chroniques éthiopiennes (Jean de Nikiou et la Chronique de Basset)," Museon, 3 (1884).

Duchesne, L. "Note sur le massacre des chrétiens himyarites au temps de l'empereur Justin," Revue des Etudes Juives, 20 (1890).

Duensing, H. "Ein Brief des Abessinischen Königs Asnaf Sagad (Claudius) an Papst Paul III aus dem Jahre 1541," Gottinger Nachrichten, Phil.-hist. Klasse (1904).

Edwards, Frederick A. "Early Ethiopia and Songhay," Asiatic Quarterly Review, 32: 64 (1911).

Ehret, C. "On the antiquity of agriculture in Ethiopia," JAH, 20: 2 (1979).

Ellero, Giovanni. "Note sull'Enderta," RSE, 1 (1941), 146-172.

_____. "Il Uolcait," RSE, 7 (1948), 89-112.

Euringer, S., ed. and trans. "Die Geschichte von Narga: ein Kapitel aus der abessinischen Kulturgeschichte," Zeitschrift für Semitistik und verwandte Gebeite, 9 (1935); 10 (1935). Reprinted in Wiesbaden, 1967.

Fawzy Mikawy. "Aksumite influence on Beja cult in the middle ages," JES, 12: 1 (1974) 183-184.

Fernandes, André, and Louys Azebede, R. R. Pères. Sommaire des Lettres Ecrites de l'Ethiopie au R. Père Andre Palmiee ... du mois de Mars 1623 et de celles du Roy de l'Ethiopie, dit Preste-Ian, au R. Père Louys de Cordoba, Provincial de la Compagnie de Iesus en l'Inde Orientale (Lyon: 1625).

Ficalho, Francisco Manuel Carlos de Mello. Viagens de Pedro de Covilham (Lisbon: 1898).

Foti, C., ed. and trans. "La Cronaca Abbreviata dei Re d'Abissinia in un Manoscritto di Dabra Berhan di Gondar," RSE, 1 (1941), 87-123.

Fourier, B. "Uber die Oasen," AGE, 6 (1800), 30-44 (on Poncet and Lenoir du Roule).

Grébaut, Sylvain. "Note sur la Princesse Zir Ganela," JA, 1 (1928).

Guidi, Ignazio. "Di Due Frammenti Relativi alla Storia di Abissinia," RRAL, ser. 5, 2 (1893), 579-96.

_____. "Le canzoni Ge'ez-Amarina in onore di re abissini," RRAL, ser. 4, 4 (1889), 53-66.

_____. "Bisanzio e il regno di Aksum," Studi Bizantini, ser. 2, 5 (1924), 134-139.

_____. "L'Abissinia antica," Nuova Antologia, 63 (1896).

_____. "Due Nuovi Manoscritti della 'Cronaca Abbreviata' di Abissinia," RRAL, ser. 6, 2 (1926), 357-421.

Gumprecht, T. E. "Die Reise des Paters Krump nach Nubien in den Jahren 1700-1702 und dessen Mittheilungen über Abyssinien," Monatsberichte der Gesellschaft für Erdkunde zu Berlin, 7 (1850).

Haberland, Eike. Untersuchungen zum Aethiopischen Königtum (Wiesbaden: 1965).

_____. "The Influence of the Christian Ethiopian Empire on Southern Ethiopia," JSS, 9 (1964), 235-38.

Halévy, Joseph.   Trans.   La Guerre de Sarsa-Dengel contre les
    Falachas.   Extr. de Revue Sémitique (1907).

_____.   "Remarque sur un point contesté touchant la persécution
    des chrétiens de Nedjran par le roi juif des Himyarites,"
    Revue des Etudes Juives, 21 (1890).

_____.   "L'alliance des Sabéens et les Abyssins contre les Him-
    yarites," RS, 4 (1896).

_____.   "Traces d'influence indoparsie en Abyssinie," RS, 4
    (1896).

Hansberry, W. L.   "Ancient Kush, Old Aethiopia, and the Balad es
    Sudan," J. of Human Relations, 8 (1960), 357-387.

_____.   "Ethiopian Ambassadors to Latin Courts and Latin Emis-
    saries to Prester John," EO, 9: 2 (1965), 90-99.

Harris, Joseph, ed.   Pillars in African History; the William Leo
    Hansberry African Notebook.   Vol. 1 (Wash. D.C., HUP:
    1974).

Hartmann, M.   "Der Nagasi, Ashama und sein Sohn Arma," ZDMG,
    49 (1895).

Heeren, A. H.   Historical Researches into the Politics, Intercourse,
    and Trade of the Carthaginians, Ethiopians, and Egyptians.
    2 vols.   (Oxford: 1832) Re-issued New York: NUP: 1969.

Helena (Empress).   Epistola Helenea aviae Dauidis Preciosi Joannis,
    Aethiopum imperatoris, ad Emmanuelem Lusitanorum, & regem,
    scripta anno 1519 (Ponta Delgada: 1907).

Heliodorus.   Aethiopica.   Trans. M. Hadas (MSU Press: 1957).

Henning, R.   "Frumentius und Aedesius im Reiche Aksum," Terrae
    incognitae, 1 (1944).

Hess, Robert L.   "The Itinerary of Benjamin of Tudela: a 12th
    century Jewish description of North-east Africa," JAH, 6: 1
    (1965).

Honigmann, E.   "Un évêque d'Adoulis?"   Byzantion, 20 (1950).

_____.   "Evêques et Evechés monophysites d'Asie anterieure au VI
    siecle," CSCO, 2 (Louvain: 1951).

Horvath, R. J.   "The Wandering Capitals of Ethiopia," JAH, 10: 2
    (1969).

Huntingford, G. W. B.   "Arabic Inscriptions in Southern Ethiopia,"
    Antiquity, 29 (1955), 230-233.

_____, ed. The Land Charters of Northern Ethiopia (Addis Ababa, Institute of Ethiopian Studies and the Faculty of Law, HSIU, 1965).

_____. "The Lives of Saint Takla Haymanot, " JES, 4: 2 (1966), 35-40.

_____. "Lost Province of Ethiopia, " Proc. Third Int'l Conference of Ethiopian Studies, Addis Ababa, 1966. Vol. 1 (Addis Ababa: Institute of Ethiopian Studies, HSIU, 1969), 113-115.

_____. "The Wealth of Kings and the end of the Zague Dynasty, " SOAS Bull., 18 (1965), 1-23.

Ibn Haukal, Muhammad. Configuration de la terre. Trans. J. H. Kramers and G. Wiet (Paris: Beyrouth, Commission Internationale pour la Traduction des Chefs-d'oeuvre: 1964), 2 vols.

Jackson, H. C. Ethiopia and the Origin of Civilization. (New York: 1939).

Jaeger, Otto A. Antiquities of North Ethiopia (Stuttgart: Brockhaus, 1965). (2nd ed. with Ivy Pearce: 1974).

Jones, William. "A Conversation with Abram, an Abyssinian, concerning the city of Gwender and the Sources of the Nile, " Asiatik Researches: Transactions of the Society Instituted in Bengal, 1 (1788), 383-388.

Jorga, N. "Cenni sulle relazioni tra l'Abissinia e l'Europa Cattolica nei secoli XIV-XV, " Centenario della nascita di Michelle Amarit, 1 (Palermo: 1910).

Kammerer, Albert. "Bermudes: Pseudo-Patriarche d'Abyssinie, 1535-1570, " Tirage à part du Bulletin de la Société de Géographie de Lisbonne, 1940.

_____. Essai sur l'histoire antique d'Abyssinie; le royaume d'Aksum et ses voisins d'Arabie et de Meroe (Paris: 1926).

_____. La Mer Rouge, l'Abyssinie et l'Arabie aux XVIe et XVIIe siècles et la cartographie des portulans du monde orientale. 3 vols (Cairo: Société Royale de Géographie d'Egypte, 1947-1952).

Kibre Negest (Glory of Kings) see Budge, E. A. W.

Kobischanov, Yurii M. Aksum (Moscow: Izdatelstvo 'Nauka, ' 1966).

_____. "The Sea Voyages of Ancient Ethiopians in the Indian Ocean, " Proc. Third Int'l Conference of Ethiopian Studies. Vol. 1 (Addis Ababa, Institute of Ethiopian Studies, HSIU, 1969), 19-23.

Krump, Theodore. Hoher und Fruchtbahrer Palm Baum des
    Heiligen Evangelij ... In einem Diario oder Täglich und or-
    dentlicher Reiss-Beschreibung ... Sendlingen aus dem Orden
    des H. S. Vatters ... so Anno 1700 von der P. H. Innocen-
    tio XII aus bis zu dem Grossmächtigen Abyssiner-Kaiser
    Adiam Saghed Jasu (Augsburg: 1710). (see also Gumprecht)

Krzeczunowicz, George. "The Law of Filiation in Ethiopia," Proc.
    Third Int'l Conf. Eth. Studies. Vol. 3 (1970), 184-196.

Kur, S. "Actes de Iyasus Mo'a, abbe du couvent de St.-Etienne de
    Hayq," CSCO, SA, 49 (Louvain: 1965).

La Croze, Mathurin Veyssière. Histoire du Christianisme d'Ethio-
    pie et d'Arménie (La Haie: 1739).

Lasteyrie, F. de. "Notice sur une ancienne croix éthiopienne con-
    servée à Florence," Extr. Memoires de l'Acad. des Inscr.
    & Belles-Lettres, 28, Iére partie (Paris: 1884).

Lefevre, R. "Documenti pontifici sui rapporti con l'Etiopia nei
    secoli XV e XVI," RSE, 5 (1946).

_____. "Note su alcuni pellegrini etiopi in Roma al tempo di
    Leone X (1516)," RSE, 21 (1965).

_____. "Presenze etiopiche in Italia prima del Concilio di Fi-
    renze del 1439," RSE, 23 (1969).

_____. "Documenti e notizie su Tasfa Syon e la sua attivitá
    romana nel secolo XVI," RSE, 24 (1971).

Lenoir du Roule see Roule

Lewis, I. M. "The Somali Conquest of the Horn of Africa," JAH,
    1: 2 (1960), 213-229.

L'Huillier, Th. "Un voyageur officiel envoyé en Ethiopie sous
    Louis XIV. Correspondance et documents inédits relatifs à
    Lenoir du Roule," Extr. des Mémoires lus a la Sorbonne en
    1890, section de géographie (Paris: 1890).

Littmann, Enno. Publications of the Princeton Expedition to Abys-
    sinia. 4 vols. in 5. (Leyden: Brill: 1910-1915).

_____. "The Legend of the Queen of Sheba in the Tradition of
    Aksum," Bibliotheca Abessinica, 1 (1904) (Leyden: Brill).

_____. "La leggenda del dragone di Aksum in lingua Tigrai,"
    RSE, 6: 1 (1947).

_____. Zar'a-Jacob, Ein einsamer Denfer in Abessinien (Berlin:
    1916).

Lockman, John. Travels of the Jesuits into Various Parts of the World: Particularly China and the East-Indies. 2nd ed. 2 vols (London: 1743).

Ludolphus, Job. A New History of Ethiopia, Being a Full and Accurate Description of the Kingdom of Abessinia, Vulgarly, though Erroneously, Called the Empire of Prester John (Trans. from Latin publication in Frankfurt in 1681 by J. P. Gent) (London: 1684).

_____. Commentarius ad suam Historiam Aethiopicam (Frankfurt: 1691).

McCann, James. "The Ethiopian Chronicles as Documentary Tradition: Description and Methodology," P. 5th ICES (Chicago: 1975).

_____. "The Ethiopian Chronicles: An African Documentary Tradition," NAS 1: 2 (1979).

McCrindle, J. W., trans. and ed. The Christian Topography of Cosmas: An Egyptian Monk (London, Hakluyt Society: 1897 and New York: Franklin, 1967).

Maly, Zbynek. "The Visit of Martin Lang, Czech Franciscan, in Gondar in 1752." JES, 10: 2 (1972), 17-27.

Manzi, L. Il commercio in Etiopia, Nubia, Abissinia, Sudan, etc. dai primordi alla dominazione Musulmana (Rome: 1886).

Maqrizi, Ahmad ibn-Ali al-. Historia rerum islamiticarum in Abyssinia (Trans. from Arabic into Latin by F. T. Rinck) (Leyden: 1790).

Markham, C. R. "The Portuguese Expeditions to Abyssinia in the Fifteenth, Sixteenth and Seventeenth Centuries," JGS, 38 (1969), 4-12.

Martin, B. G. "Mahdism, Muslim Clerics, and Holy Wars in Ethiopia. 1300-1600," P. 1st USCES (ASC, MSU: 1975).

Matthaeus. 1517-1518: Cartas do bispo Matthaeus a el-rei D. Manoel. (Coimbra: Imprensa da Universidade, 1907).

Matthews, D. H., and Mordini, A. "The Monastery of Debra Damo, Ethiopia," Archaeologia, 97 (1959).

Mauro Da Leonessa, P. "Un trattato sul Calendario redatto al Tempo di re 'Amda Syon I," RSE, 3 (1943), 302-326.

_____. Chronologia e calendario etiopico (Tivoli: 1934).

Mechinau, Père. "L'histoire religieuse de l'Abyssinie aux XVIe et

XVIIe siècles." Etudes de la Compagnie de Jesus, 72 et 73 (1897).

Meinardus, Otto F. A. "Ein portugiesischer Altar in Bahar Dar Gyorgis," AE, 6 (1965), 281-284.

_____. "Ecclesiastica Aethiopica in Aegypto," JES, 3: 1 (1965), 23-25.

Merid Wolde Aregay. "Two unedited Letters of Galawdewos, Emperor of Ethiopia (1540-1559)," Studia, 13-14 (Jan.-July 1964), 363-376. (See also Unpublished theses.)

Methodios Fouyas, Most Rev. "The Introduction of Christianity into Aksum," Abba Salama, 1 (1970), 186-190.

Michaelis, J. H. Sonderbarer Lebens-Lauf Herrn Peter Heylings Aus Lubec, Und dessen Reise nach Ethiopien ... Aus des ... Rath Ludolfs Edirten Schriften und andern noch nicht gedruckten Documenten ... herausgegeben (Halle: 1724).

Mikawy see Fawzy

Minucci, Minuccio. Storia inedita dell'Etiopia. Scritta nel 1598 da Archivescovo di Zara, Minuccio Minucci (Rome, Il Mariani: 1968).

Mittwoch, Eugen. "Dschanhoi, die amharische Bezeichnung für Majestät," ZA, 25 (1911).

Moberg, A. The Book of the Himyarites. Fragments of a hitherto unknown Syriac Work (Lund: 1924).

Molignoni, Gigliola. "La storia di re Bacaffa nel racconto di James Bruce," RSE, 6 (1947).

Monneret de Villard, Ugo. "Note sulle influenze asiatiche nell' Africa Orientale," RSO, 17 (1938).

_____. Aksum, ricerche di topografia generale (Rome: 1938).

_____. See listing under Missions and Missionaries.

_____. "Aksum e i quattro re del mondo," Annali Lateranensi, 12 (1948).

Mordini, Antonio. "Su di un nuovo titolo regale Axumita," RSE, 8 (1949).

_____. "Un tissu musulman du Moyen Age provenant du Couvent de Dabra Dammo," AE, 2 (1957).

_____. "Gli aurei kushana del convento di Dabra Dammo un indizio sui rapporti commerciali fra l'India e l'Etiopia nei primi secoli dell'Era Volgare," ACISE (Rome: 1960).

_____. "I Tessili medioevali del convento di Dabra Dammo," ACISE (Rome: 1960).

Muir, W. The Life of Mahomet (London: 1861).

_____. The Life of Mohammad from Original Sources (Edinburgh: 1923).

Muthanra, I. M. Indo-Ethiopian Relations for Centuries (Addis Ababa, Artistic Press: 1971).

Nerazzini, Dr. Cesare. La conquista musulmana dell'Etiopia nel secolo XVI (Italian translation of Abd-el-Kader, Chihab Ed-din Ahmed) (Rome: 1891).

Osei, G. K. Africans in Europe. Vol. 2 of History of the African People (London: African Publication Society, 1971) 56-67.

Pankhurst, R. K. P. "The Advent of Fire-Arms in Ethiopian Ecclesiastical Manuscripts," EO, 15: 1 (1972).

_____. "An Early Fourteenth Century Persian Representation of Ethiopian Emperor Armah and His Court," EO, 14: 1 (1971).

_____. "Ethiopia in the Seventeenth and Early Eighteenth Centuries: The Report of Ambassador Mikael and the Imaginary Description of John Campbell," EO, 16: 2 (1973).

_____, ed. The Ethiopian Royal Chronicles (Addis Ababa, OUP: 1967).

_____. "Caves in Ethiopian history: cave sites in environs of Addis Ababa," EO, 16: 1 (1973).

_____. "Famine and pestilence in Ethiopia prior to the founding of Gondär," JES, 10: 2 (1972).

_____. "Fire-arms in Ethiopia prior to the 19th century," EO, 11: 2 (1967).

_____. "Gregorius and Ludolf," EO, 12: 4 (1969).

_____. "Historical and economic geography of the Mesewa area (1520-1885)," JES, 13: 1 (1975).

_____. "Horsemen of Old-time Ethiopia," EO, 13: 1 (1970).

_____. "Letter writing and use of royal and imperial seals in Ethiopia prior to 20th century," JES, 11: 1 (1973).

_____. "Linguistic and cultural data on penetration of fire-arms into Ethiopia," JES, 9: 1 (1971).

_____. "Measures, weights and values, a preliminary history," JES, 7: 1 and 2 (1964).

_____. "Primitive money in Ethiopia," JSA, 20 (1963).

_____. "Greek coins of Aksum," Abba Salama, 6 (1975).

_____. "The Golden age of Graeco-Egyptian discoveries on the Horn of Africa, the rise and fall of the elephant trade, and the introduction of iron into the region," ΕΚΚΩΗΣΙΣΤΙΚΟΣ ΦΑΡΟΣ, (1976).

_____. State and Land in Ethiopian History (Nairobi, OUP: 1966). Monographs in Ethiopian Land Tenure, No. 3, Institute of Ethiopian Studies and Faculty of Law.

_____. "Notes for a history of Ethiopian agriculture," EO, 7: 3 (1964).

_____. "Wild life and forests in Ethiopian history," EO, 7: 3 (1964).

_____. "Some historical aspects of land tenure in Ethiopia," Ministry of Land Reform and Administration, Seminar Proceedings on Agrarian Reform (Addis Ababa: 1970).

_____. "Greek land-holding in 18th and early 19th century Ethiopia," Abba Salama, 4 (1973).

_____. "The earliest history of famine and pestilence in Ethiopia and a Note on the 'Egyptian deaths' of 17th and 18th century Ethiopia," EMJ, 11: 3 (1973).

_____. "Demetros and Giyorgis: Two Greeks in early eighteenth century Ethiopia," Abba Salama, 8 (1977).

_____. "Ethiopia, an independent African state in the age of Vasco da Gama," Studies on Developing Countries, Planning and Economic Development. (Polish Scientific Publishers, Warsaw: 1964), 1.

_____. "Reflections on the importance of Graeco-Ethiopian studies," Abba Salama, 1 (1970).

_____. "Echoes of the Greek fable in Ethiopia," Abba Salama, 7 (1975).

_____. "Echoes of the Alexander story in Ethiopian royal chronicles, Abba Salama, 8 (1977).

_____ . "The inscriptions and royal chronicles of Ethiopia, " Tarikh (Ibadan), 2: 3 (1967).

_____ . "Peter Heyling, Abba Gregorius and the Foundation of Ethiopian Studies in Germany, " ZK, 1973.

_____ . "The Beginnings of Oromo studies in Europe, " Africa, 31: 2 (1976).

_____ . "Ethiopia, " Chapters 11 and 28, Vol. VII, UNESCO, General History of Africa.

_____ . "Linguistic and cultural data on the penetration of fire-arms into Ethiopia, " JES, 9: 1 (1971).

Pankhurst, R. K. P. , and Pearson, Tony. "Remedius Prutky's 18th century account of Ethiopian taenicides and other medical treatment, " EMJ, 10: 1 (1972).

Pankhurst, Sylvia and Pankhurst, Richard. "Special Issue on the Queen of Sheba, " EO, 1: 6 (1957).

Papi, Maria R. "Una santa abissina anti-cattolica: Walatta-Petros, " RSE, 3: 1 (1943).

Paribeni, Roberto. Ricercha nel luogo dell'antica Adulis. RRAL, 1908.

Peiser, F. E. Zur Geschichte Abessiniens im 17. Jahrhundert: Der Gesandtschaftsbericht des Hasan ben Ahmed El-Haimi (Berlin: 1898).

The Periplus of the Erythraean Sea: Travel and Trade in the Indian Ocean by a Merchant of the First Century. Trans. from Greek and annotated by W. H. Schoff (New York: 1912).

Perruchon, J. see Chronicles, royal

Pétridès, S. P. "The Empire of Ethiopia in the XVth and XVIth Centuries: Its Powers, Grandeur and Extent as Recorded by Arab, Italian and Portuguese Travellers and Cartographers, " EGS, 2: 2 (1964).

_____ . "Essai sur l'Evangelisation de l'Ethiopie, sa date et son protagoniste, " Abba Salama, 2 (1971).

Phillips, Wendell. Qataban and Sheba: Exploring the Ancient King-doms on the Biblical Spice Routes of Arabia (New York: 1955).

Picca, Paolo. "Antiche relazioni italo-abissine, " Nuova Antologia, 136 (1908).

Plante, Julian G. "The Ethiopian Embassy to Cairo of 1443, " JES; 13; 2 (1975), 133-140.

Playne, Beatrice. "Suggestions on the Origin of the False Doors of the Axumite Stelae," AE, 6 (1965).

Pollera, Alberto. Storie Leggende e Favole del Paese dei Negus. (Florence: 1936).

Praetorious, F. "Ein arabisches Document zür äthiopischen Geschichte," ZDMG, 39 (Leipzig, 1885).

Prideaux, W. F. "The Coins of the Axumite Dynasty," Numismatic Chronicle, 4 (1884), and 5 (1885).

Renaudot, E. Historia Patriarcharum Alexandrinorum. (Paris: 1713).

Revelli, P. "Una relazione inedita sull'Abissinia nel 1578," Extr. BSGI, 10 (1910).

Rey, Charles F. The Romance of the Portuguese in Abyssinia (London: 1929). Reissued 1969, New York, NUP.

Ricci, Lanfranco. Trans. Vita di Walatta Pietros. CSCO, SA, 316: 61 (Louvain: 1970).

Richard, J. "L'Extrême-Orient légendaire au Moyen Age. Roi David et Prêtre Jean," AE, 2 (1957).

Romanet du Caillaud, F. "Les tentatives des Franciscains au moyen âge pour pénétrer dans la Haute-Ethiopie," BSG, 7e serie, 17 (1896).

Rosenfeld, Chris Prouty. "Gossip, Proclamation and Women as revealed in the Royal Chronicles (1500-1900)," #79-81 (1979) (ASA, Brandeis U., Waltham, Mass.)

Roule, Lenoir du. "Mémoire et Lettres au Chancelier de Pontchartrain sur sa mission en Ethiopie," BGHD (1891).

Rubenson, Sven. "The Lion of the Tribe of Judah: Christian Symbol and/or Imperial Title," JES, 3: 2 (1965).

Russell, Michael. Nubia and Abyssinia Comprehending their Civil History, Antiquities, Arts, Religion, Literature, and Natural History (Edinburgh and London: 1833; New York: 1845).

Sanceau, Elaine. The Land of Prester John: A Chronicle of Portuguese Exploration (New York: 1944).

Sawirus ibn-al-Mukaffa. History of the Patriarchs of the Egyptian Church Vol. I in "Patrologia Orientalis," I, V, X; Vol. 2 published in 3 parts, Cairo: 1943, 1948, 1959.

Schefer, C. Le voyage d'outremer de Bertrandon de la Brocquière (Paris: 1892).

Schneider, Madeleine.   "Notes au sujet de l'épitaphe du premier
    sultan de Dahlak, " JES, 11: 2 (1973).

Schneider, Roger.   "Documents épigraphiques de l'Ethiopie, " AE,
    9: 2 (1972).

Sergew Hable Sellassie.   Ancient and Medieval Ethiopian History to
    1270 (Addis Ababa: 1972).

_____.   "Church and State in the Aksumite Period, " Proc. Third
    Int'l Conf. of Ethiopian Studies, Vol. 1 (Addis Ababa: Insti-
    tute of Ethiopian Studies, 1969).

_____.   "The Problem of Gudit, " JES, 10: 1 (1972).

_____.   "Die Aethiopische Kirche im 4 bis 6 Jahrhundert, " Abba
    Salama, 2 (1971).

_____.   "New Historical Elements in the 'Gedle Aftse', " JSS, 9:
    1 (1964).

Serjeant, R. B.   "South Arabia and Ethiopia--African Elements in
    the South Arabian Population, " Proc. Third Int'l Conf. of Eth.
    Studies, Vol. 1 (1969).

Shinnie, P. L. and M.   "New Light on Medieval Nubia, " JAH, 6:
    3 (1965).

Simoons, F. J.   "Some Questions on the Economic Prehistory of
    Ethiopia, " JAH, 6: 1 (1965).

Snowden, Frank M.   Blacks in Antiquity: Ethiopians in the Greco-
    Roman Experience (Cambridge, Mass., Harvard UP: 1970).

Somigli di S. Detole, Father Teodosio.   "L'Itinerarium del P.
    Remedio Prutky ... e il suo viaggio in Abissinia, 21 Feb.
    1752-22 Aprile 1753. " Studi Francescani, 22 (Florence:
    1925).

Stitz, Volker.   "The Amhara Resettlement of Northern Shoa during
    the 18th and 19th centuries, " Rural Africana, 11 (East Lansing,
    Michigan: 1970).

Strabo.   The Geography of Strabo, ed. H. L. Lewis (London: Heine-
    mann, 1917-1933; New York: Putnam, 1917-1933).

Taddesse Tamrat.   Church and State in Ethiopia: 1270-1527 (Oxford,
    Clarendon Press: 1972).

_____.   "The Abbots of Däbrä-Hayq, 1248-1535, " JES, 9: 1 (1970).

_____.   "Hagiographies and the Reconstruction of Medieval Ethio-
    pian History, " Ethiopia: Land and History, eds. H. G. Marcus
    and D. E. Crummey (Rural Africana #11:   1970).

_____. "A Short Note on the Traditions of Pagan Resistance to the Ethiopian Church (14th and 15th centuries), " JES, 10: 1 (1972).

_____. "Some Notes on the Fifteenth Century Stephanite Heresy in the Ethiopian Church, " RSE, 22 (1968).

Taye, Aleqa. Ye-Ityopya Hezb Tarik (History of the Ethiopian People). (Asmara, Swedish Mission: 1922).

Tedeschi, Salvatore. "L'Etiopia nella storia dei patriarchi alles- sandrini, " RSE, 23 (1968).

_____. "Poncet et son Voyage en Ethiopie, " JES, 4: 2 (1966).

_____. "Profilo storico di Dayr as-Sultan, " JES, 2: 2 (1964).

Tekle Tsadik Mekuriya. Ya-Ityopya Tarik. (Addis Ababa: E. C. 1954).

_____. Les Noms propres, les Noms de baptême et l'Etude généalogique des rois d'Ethiopie (XIIIe-XXe siècles) a travers leurs noms patronymiques (Belgrade: 1966).

Temple, R. C. The Itinerary of Ludovico di Varthema of Bologna from 1502 to 1508 as translated from Italian edition of 1510 (London, Hakluyt Society: 1928).

Traselli, C. "Un Italiano in Etiopia nel secolo XV: Pietro Rombu- lo di Messina, " RSE, 1 (1941).

_____. "Un sovrano musulmano citato nel Libro etiopico dei mi- racoli di Maria, " Bull. SAC, 21 (1975).

Ullendorff, E. Ethiopia and the Bible (London: OUP: 1968).

_____. "Candace (Acts 8:27) and the Queen of Sheba, " New Tes- tament Studies, 2 (1955-1956).

_____. "The Queen of Sheba, " John Rylands Library Bull., 45 (1963).

Van Donzel, E. Foreign Relations of Ethiopia: 1642-1700 (Istanbul, Nederlands Historisch-Archaeologisch Instituut: 1979).

Varenbergh, J., ed. and trans. "Studien zur abessinischen Reichs- ordnung Ser'ata Mangest, " ZA, 30 (1915-1916).

Vasiliev, A. "Justin I (518-527) and Abyssinia, " BZ, 33 (1933).

Von Endt, D. W. "Was Civet used as a perfume in Aksum?" Azania, 13 (1978).

Vycichl, Werner. "Le Titre de Roi des Rois, étude historique et comparative sur la monarchie en Ethiopie," AE, 2 (1957).

Wansleben, J. M. A Brief Account of the Rebellions and Bloodshed Occasioned by the Anti-Christian Practices of the Jesuits and Other Popish Emissaries in the Empire of Ethiopia (London: 1679).

Wendt, Kurt. "Das Mashafa Berhan und Mashafa Milad," Orientalia, 3 (1934).

Wiedemann, A. L'Ethiopie au temps de Tibère et la trésorier de la reine Candace (Louvain: 1884) Extr. du Muséon, 3 (1884).

Wiet, G. "Les relations égypto-abyssines sous les sultans mamelouks," BSAC, 4 (1938).

Witte, C. M. de. "Une ambassade éthiopienne à Rome en 1450," OCP, 21 (1956).

Yabetz, A. "Roman Campaigns in Ethiopia and the Policy of Augustus," EO, 9: 2 (1965).

Yilma Deressa. Ye-Ityopya Tarik Be-asra Sedestegnaw Kefle Zemen. (Ethiopian History of the 16th century). (Addis Ababa: Berhanena Selam press: 1949 E. C.).

Zaborski, A. "Some Remarks Concerning the Ezana Inscriptions and the Beja tribes," Folia Orientalia, 9 (1968).

HISTORY (B)
Circa 1760-Circa 1930

This section includes Zemene Mesafint, reigns of Tewodros II, Yohannes IV, Menilek II; the war with Egypt, the British expedition of 1868 and the first war with Italy (1894-1896).

Abbadie, Antoine d'. L'Abyssinie et le roi Théodore (Paris: 1868).

Abbadie, Arnauld d' see Travel and Description

"The Abyssinian Difficulty," Westminster Review, 89 (1868).

Abir, Mordechai. Ethiopia: The Era of the Princes (New York, Praeger: 1968).

_____. "Trade and Christian-Muslim Relations in Post-Medieval Ethiopia," P. 5th ICES (Chicago: 1979).

_____. "The Emergence and Consolidation of the Monarchies of

Enarea and Jimma in the First half of the 19th century, " JAH, 6: 2 (1965).

_____ . "Brokerage and Brokers in Ethiopia in the first half of the 19th century, " JES, 3: 1 (1965).

_____ . "The Origin of the Ethiopian-Egyptian Border Problem in the 19th Century, " JAH, 8: 3 (1967).

_____ . "Salt, Trade and Politics in Ethiopia in the 'Zämänä Mäsäfent', " JES, 4: 2 (1966).

Abraham Demoz. "Emperor Menelik's Phonograph Message to Queen Victoria, " SOAS Bull. , 32: 2 (1969).

_____ . "The Many Worlds of Ethiopia, " African Affairs, 68 (1969).

Acton, Roger. "The Abyssinian Expedition, " Illustrated London News, 1868.

Afewerq Gebre Yesus. Guide du voyageur en Abyssinie (Rome: 1909).

_____ . Il Dagmawi Menilek (Rome: 1910). Trans. by Luigi Fusella in RSE, 17 (1961) and 19 (1963).

"Agordat," Miscellanea, Etiopia ed Eritrea varia (Firenze: 1902).

Akalu Walda Mikael see listing under History, ancient and medieval.

Akisheva, A. P. "The Expedition of N. N. Kurmakov (1904), " Russia and Africa (USSR Acad. of Sciences, Africa Institute, Moscow: 1966).

Aleme Eshete. "Une ambassade du Ras Ali en Egypte: 1852, " JES, 9: 1 (1970).

_____ . "The Role and Position of Foreign-Educated Interpreters in Ethiopia (1800-1889), " JES, 11: 1 (1973).

_____ . "European Political Adventurers in Ethiopia at the turn of the 20th Century, " JES, 12: 1 (1974).

_____ . "Alaqa Taye Gabra Mariam (1861-1924), " RSE, 25 (1974).

_____ . "Ethiopia and the Bolshevik revolution, 1917-1935, " Africa, 32: 1 (1977).

Allen, Bernard. "Gordon and Abyssinia, " JRAS, 35: 139 (1936).

Amato, Dr. N. d'. Da Adua ad Addis Abeba, ricordi di un prigioniero (Salerno: 1898).

Amero, Constant. Le Negus Ménélik et l'Abyssinie Nouvelle (Paris: 1897).

Amulree, Lord Basil. "Prince Alamayou of Ethiopia," EO, 13: 1 (1970).

Andrzejewski, B. W. "A Genealogical Note Relevant to the dating of Sheikh Hussein of Bale," SOAS Bull., 38: 1 (1975).

Angoulvant, G. and Vigneras, S. Djibouti, Mer Rouge, Abyssinie (Paris: 1902).

Antonelli, Pietro. Menelik, imperatore d'Etiopia (Rome: 1891).

_____. Taitu, imperatrice d'Etiopia (Rome: 1891).

_____. "Nell'Africa Italiana," Extr. Nuova Antologia (July 1891).

_____. See listings under Travel and Exploration and in Atti Parlamentari below.

Arce, Laurent d'. L'Abyssinie. Etude d'actualité (1922-1924). (Avignon: 1925).

Arimondi, E. "The Italian Operations at Agordat," (translation) JRUSI, 38 (1894).

Armandy, Andre. La désagréable partie de campagne. Une incursion en Abyssinie (Paris: 1930).

Armbruster, Stephana. Life and History of John Bell and his descendants (Palma de Mallorca: Imprenta Mossen Alcoves, 1966).

Arnoux, Pierre see Lande, L. L.

Assaggakhan, Debtera see L. Fusella and C. Conti Rossini

Atti Parlamentari, XVI Legislatura, seduta del 17 dicembre, 1889. "Etiopia, XV (1890), documenti diplomatici," and "L'occupazione di Keren e dell'Asmara," XVI (1890).

Ayandele, E. A. "The Sudan and Ethiopia since 1898," Growth of African Civilization; the Making of Modern Africa. Vol. 2 (New York, Humanities Press: 1971).

Bairu Tafla. "Four Ethiopian biographies: Däjjazmač Gärmamé, Däjjazmač Gäbrä-Egzi'abehér Moroda, Däjjazmač Balčä and Käntiba Gäbru Dästa," JES, 7: 2 (1969).

_____. "Land tenure and taxation in Sälalé under Ras Dargé, 1871-1900," JES, 12: 2 (1974).

_____. "Marriage as a political device; an appraisal; of a socio-
political aspect of the Menilek period 1889-1916," JES, 10: 1
(1972).

_____. "Ras Dargé Sahlä-Sellasé c. 1827-1900," JES, 13: 2
(1975).

_____. "Three portraits: Ato Asmä Giyorgis, Ras Gobäna DaČi
and Sähafé Tezaz Gäbra Selassé," JES, 5: 2 (1967).

_____. "Two Ethiopian biographies: Wahni Azaj Wäldä Sadeq,
Abba Menzir, 1838-1909 and Fitawrari Habte Giyorgis Abba
Mechal, 1853-1926," JES, 6: 1 (1968).

_____. "Two of the last provincial kings of Ethiopia: Negus
Täklä Haymanot Abba Tanna of Gojjam, 1850-1901 and his
sons; Negus Wäldä Giyorgis Abboyyé Abba Säggäd c. 1859-
1918," JES, 11: 1 (1973).

_____. "Civil Titles and Offices in the Reign of Emperor Mene-
lik II, 1889-1913," P. 4th ICES, Rome, 1972.

_____. "Chronicle of Yohannes IV" see Chronicles, Royal

Baldacci, A. "Italian Colonial Expansion: its origin, progress and
difficulties," United Empire, 2 (1911).

Baratieri, O. Memorie d'Africa (1892-1896) (Turin: 1898).

_____. "Operazioni militare nella colonie eritrea 15 Dec. 1895-
20 Jan. 1895," Miscellanea; Etiopia ed Eritrea varia (Istituto
per l'Africa: n. d.).

_____. "L'Africa nella secolo XX," Extr. La Settimana, 6 (12
and 24 March 1901). Miscellanea; Etiopia ed Eritrea varia.

_____. "Les Anglais au Soudan et la question d'Abyssinie,"
RDM (15 Jan. 1899).

Bardi, A. Trentacinque anni vissuti in Eritrea e Abissinia (San
Remo: 1936).

Bardi, P. Pioneri e soldati d'Abissinia (Milan: 1936).

Bardone, R. L'Abissinia e i paesi limitrofi (Florence: 1888).

"Le Bataille d'Adua," (d'après relations d'Abyssinien). Gazette
Géographique 21: 215 (1896).

Bates, Darrell. The Abyssinian Difficulty. [1868] (London, OUP:
1979).

Battaglia, R. La prima guerra d'Africa (Turin: 1958).

Beke, C. T. Abyssinia: a statement of facts relating to the
    transactions between the writer and the late British Political
    Mission to the Court of Shoa (London: 1845).

_____ . The British Captives in Abyssinia (London: 1867).

_____ . The Sources of the Nile (London: 1860).

_____ . "Extract from a Journal of Lieut. W. Christopher, "
    JRGS, 14 (1844).

Bell, J. G. "Extracts from a Journal of Travels in Abyssinia, "
    Miscellanea Aegyptica 1 (1842).

_____ . "Extrait du Journal d'un voyage en Abyssinie, dans les
    années 1840, 1841 et 1842, " NAV, 112 (1846).

Bellavita, Emilio. Adua i precedenti-la battaglia, le consequenze
    (1881-1931) (Genoa: 1931).

Berkeley, G. F. H. The Campaign of Adowa and Rise of Menelik
    (London: 1902, revised ed. 1935; reissued New York, NUP, 1969).

Bertin, G. "Les Européens en Abyssinie, " TM, 14 (22 Feb. 1908).

Bieber, F. J. Kaiser Menelik und sein Reich (Berlin ?:   1914).

Bizzoni, Achille. "The Battle of Adowa of 1896:   a contemporary
    Italian view, " EO, 14: 2 (1971).

Blanc, H. J. A Narrative of Captivity in Abyssinia (London: 1868).

Blerzy, H. "La guerre d'Abyssie, l'expédition anglaise et la chute
    de Théodore II, " RDM (15 July 1868).

Bodini, Cesare. L'Abyssinia degli Abissini, ossia la vera opinione
    della Gran Maggioranza del paese sul fatto e da farsi (Turin: 1888).

Borelli, G. La battaglia di Abba Garima (Milan: 1901).

Boulvin, F. "Une mission belge en Ethiopie, " Société Belge
    d'études coloniales Brussels (1906).

Braukamper, U. "La conquête et l'administration éthiopienne du
    Kambatta au temps de Ménélik II, " 5th Congrès International
    des Etudes Ethiopiennes, Nice, France, December 1977.

Brinton, J. Y. "The American Effort in Egypt; a chapter in diplo-
    matic history in the 19th century, " SOAS Bull. , 8: 9 (1972).

Bronzuoli, Anacleto. Adua (Rome: 1935).

Brunialti, A. "Menelik, re di Scioa e le sue recenti conquiste, "
    Nuova Antologia, 8 (1887).

[Cagnassi, Eteocle]. Tredici anni di missione in Eritrea. (Published anonymously Turin: 1898).

Caix, Robert de. Fachoda. La France et l'Angleterre (Paris: 1899).

_____. "Menelik, " RDM (1 June 1911).

Caix de St. -Aymour, Vicomte de. Les intérêts français dans le Soudan éthiopien (Paris: 1884).

Camperio, M. Da Assab a Dogali. Guerre Abissine (Milan: 1887).

Canevari, Emilio. Il generale Tommaso Salsa e le sue campagne coloniale (Milan: 1935).

Carlo, Giannini. "La conquista Scioana dell'Aussa, " RSE, 3 (1943).

Castellani, Ch. Vers le Nil; Français avec la mission Marchand (Paris: 1899).

Caulk, Richard A. "The occupation of Harar: January 1887, " JES, 9: 2 (1971).

_____. "Religion and State in 19th Century Ethiopia, " JES, 10: 1 (1972).

_____. "Yohannes and the Mahdists: Mere Pawns in European Diplomacy or unsuspected Collaborators with Colonialism, " History Journal, 2: 2 (1968), Addis Ababa.

_____. "Firearms and Princely Power in Ethiopia in the 19th Century, " JAH, 12: 4 (1972).

_____. "Territorial competition and the Battle of Embabo, 1882, " JES, 13: 1 (1975).

_____. "Dependency, Gebre Heywet Baykedagn, and the Birth of Ethiopian Reformism, " P. 5th ICES, Chicago, U. S. A., 1978, (Chicago: 1979).

_____. "Ernest Work on Ethiopian Education, " EJE, 8: 1 (1975).

_____. "The Army and Society in Ethiopia, " Ethiopianist Notes (ASC, MSU), 1: 3 (1978).

Cerulli, E. "La fine dell'Emirato di Harar in Nuovi documenti, storici, " Annali Istituto Universitario Orientali di Napoli, n. s. 14: 1 (Naples: 1964).

_____. Etiopia in Palestina. 2 vols. (Rome: 1943).

_____. "Menelik, " Enciclopedia Italiana (1934).

Chaine, M. see Chronicles, Royal

Chiarini, Giovanni. "Memorie sulla storia recente dello Scioa,
    della morte di Sahle Selassie sini ad oggi (Nov. 1877),"
    BSGI Memoria, 2 (1878).

Chojnacki, C. "Forests and forestry problems as seen by some
    travellers in Ethiopia," JES, 1: 1 (1963).

_____. "Notes on the History of the Ethiopian Flag," JES 1:2 (1963).

_____. "A Second Note on the Ethiopian National Flag, with
    comments on its Historical and Sociological Sources," P. 3rd
    ICES, vol. 1 (Addis Ababa: 1969).

Chronicles, Royal.
    "La Cronaca Reale dell'Abissinia dall'anno 1800 all'anno 1840,"
    RRAL (1917). Trans. C. Conti Rossini.

    The Royal Chronicle of Abyssinia, 1769-1840 (Cambridge:
    1922). Trans. H. Weld Blundell.

    Ye-Atse Tewodros Tarik (Rome: 1959) trans. into Italian by
    Luigi Fusella as La cronaca dell'Imperatore Teodoro II di
    Etiopia in un manoscrito amarico (Annali d'Istituto Universi-
    tario di Napoli, 6 (1957-59).

    Zeneb, Debtera. Ye-Tewodros Tarik, ed. and pub. in Amharic
    by Enno Littmann as The Chronicle of King Theodore (Prince-
    ton: 1902). Trans. into Italian by M. M. Moreno as
    "La cronaca di re Teodoro attribuita al dabtara 'Zaneb,'"
    RSE, 2 (1942).

    Welde Maryam. (Amharic manuscript) Published by C. Mondon
    Vidhailet as Chronique de Theodros II, roi des rois d'Ethio-
    pie (Paris: n. d.).

    "Histoire du règne de Iohannès IV, roi d'Ethiopie (1868-1889),"
    Trans. M. Chaine. Revue Sémitique, 21 (1913).

    "Una cronaca del regno di Yohannes IV," (trans. L. Ricci)
    RSO, 22 (1947).

    Lemlem, Aleqa. (Amharic chronicle of reigns of Tekle Giyor-
    gis (1868-71) and Yohannes IV (1871-1889) in Mondon-
    Vidhailet Collection, Bibliothèque Nationale, Paris.

    Foti, C. "La cronaca abbreviata dei Re d'Abissinia in un
    manoscritto di Dabra Berhan di Gondar," RSE, 1 (1941).

    Chronicle of Yohannes IV, trans. and annotated by Bairu Tafla
    with reference to 4 other unpublished chronicles: Aleqa
    Lemlem's in Mondon-Vidhailet Collection, Bibliothèque
    Nationale, Paris. Ms. collection of Institute of Ethiopian

Studies, Addis Ababa, Ethiopia; Manuscript Library of Church of Seyon, Aksum Church of Debre Berhan, Adwa. (Wiesbaden, Franz Steiner Verlag: 1977).

Guèbré Sellassié. Chronique du règne de Ménélik II, Roi des Rois d'Ethiopie. 2 vols. Trans. Tèsfa Sellassié, annotated by Maurice de Coppet (Paris: 1930 and 1932).

Collins, R. O. The Partition of Africa; illusion or necessity (New York, John Wiley: 1969). See speeches by Ferdinando Martini, June 3, 1887 and Francesco Crispi, Dec. 19, 1895, 125-132 and 123-124.

Colombo, A. "L'Assedio di Makalle in una lettera-diario del maggiore Giuseppe Galliana," Rassegna Storica del Risorgimento (April 1935).

Combes, Paul. L'Abyssinie en 1896; le pays, les habitants, la lutte italo-abyssinie (Paris: 1896).

Constantin, Vicomte Henri de. L'archimandrite Paisi e l'Ataman Achinof (Paris: 1891).

_____. "Une Expedition Religieuse in Abyssinie," La Nouvelle Revue (Feb. 1891).

Conti Rossini, C. Italia ed Etiopia dal trattato d'Uccialli alla battaglia di Adua (Rome: 1935).

_____. L'Abissinia (Rome: 1929).

_____. "L'editto di Ras Gugsa sui feudi," La Rassegna Coloniale, 1 (1921).

_____. "La fine di Re Teodoro in un documento abissino," Nuova Antologia, (1935).

_____. "Vicende dell'Etiopia, e delle missioni cattoliche ai tempi di Ras Ali, deggiac Ubié e re Teodoro secondo un documento abissino," RRAL, ser. 5, 25 (1916).

_____. "Epistolario del Debterà Aseggachègn di Uadla," RRAL, ser. 6, 1 (Rome: 1925). (Amharic text)

_____. "Nuovi documenti per la storia d'Abissinia nel secolo XIX," RRAL. ser. 8, 2 (1947).

_____. "Testi in Lingua Harari; Cronaca di Harar," Riv. SO, 9 (1910).

_____. "La relazioné di Pietro Felter sullo sgombero di Macale," RSE, 3: 2 (1943).

_____. See also Chronicles above.

Coppet, Maurice de. Appendices to Chronique de Menelik (see Chronicles, Royal) on: Le Tabot, Languages of Ethiopia, Ethiopian antiquities, Ethiopian calendar, Origin and history of the Gallas, Christianity of Ethiopia, Fasting in Ethiopia, Ethiopian money, Where do they get custom of eating raw meat. Ownership of land in Shoa, Slavery in Ethiopia, the Ethiopian Flag and Ethiopia from 1909-1916. Vol. II.

Cora, G. "L'Ethiopia durante la prima guerra mondiale," RSE, (1942).

Coulbeaux, Father Jean Baptiste. Histoire politique et religieuse de l'Abyssinie. 3 vols (Paris: 1929).

Coursac, J. de. Le règne de Johannes, d'après les papiers de M. de Sarzec, v. consul de France a Massawa (Paris: 1926).

Crabites, Pierre. Americans in the Egyptian Army (London: 1938).

Crispi, F. La prima guerra d'Africa (Milan: 1914).

Crummey, Donald E. "Initiative and Objectives in Ethio-European Relations, 1827-1862," JAH, 15: 3 (1974).

_____. Priests and Politicians: Protestant and Catholic Missions in Orthodox Ethiopia, 1830-1868 (London, OUP: 1972).

_____. "Tewodros as Reformer and Modernizer," JAH, 10: 3 (1969).

_____. "The Violence of Tewodros," JES, 9: 2 (1971).

_____. "Shaikh Zäkaryas: an Ethiopian prophet," JES, 10: 1

_____. "Cacaho and the politics of the northern Wällo-Bägémder border," JES, 13: 1 (1975).

_____. See Negaso Gidada.

Cumming, D. C. "The History of Kassala and the Province of Taka," Sudan Notes and Records, 20: 1 (1937); 23: 1 (1940); 23: 2 (1940).

Darcy, Jean. France et Angleterre--Cent années de rivalité coloniale (Paris: 1903).

Darkwah, Kofi. "Emperor Theodore II and the Kingdom of Shoa, 1855-1865," JAH, 10: 1 (1969).

_____. Menelik of Ethiopia. African Historical Biographies, 1 (London, Heinemann: 1972).

_____. "Some Developments in Ethiopia during the Era of the Mesafint," Research Review, 6: 2 (1970).

_____. Shewa, Menilek and the Ethiopian Empire (London, Heinemann: 1975).

Dehérain, H. La colonisation italienne dans l'Erythrée (Paris: 1904).

_____. Les katamas dans les provinces méridionales de l'Abyssinie (Paris: 1914). (Extr. du B. de la Section de Géographie de l'institute de France (1914).

_____. "La carrière africaine d'Arthur Rimbaud," Extr. de la Revue de l'histoire des Colonies françaises (Paris: 1917).

Despagnet, ?. "Le conflit entre l'Italie et l'Abyssinie," Extr. de la Revue de Droit internationale publique, 4 (1897).

Le Docteur Nouvellement Venu (Imprimerie St. Lazaire, Diré Daoua: 1909).

Documents on Ethiopian Politics. Eds. B. G. Steffanson and R. K. Starrett. 3 vols. 1. Decline of Menelik II to emergence of Ras Tafari, 1910-1919. 2. Consolidation of power of Haile Selassie 1920-1929. 3. Foreign powers in Ethiopia. The role of England, France, Italy, Germany and the United States in internal Ethiopian affairs 1920-1929 (Salisbury, North Carolina; Documentary Publications: 1976-1977).

Documents relatifs au coup d'état d'Addis Abeba du 27 Septembre 1916. (Imprimerie St. Lazaire, Diré Daoua (Abyssinie).

Douin, G. Histoire du règne de Khédive Ismail. 3 vols. (Cairo: 1936-1941).

Duchesne, Albert. Le consul Blondeel von Cuelebroeck en Abyssinie (Brussels: 1953).

Dye, William McE. Moslem Egypt and Christian Abyssinia; or military service under the Khedive, in His Provinces and Beyond their Borders as Experienced by the American Staff (New York: 1880, reissued New York, NUP, 1969).

E. B. "La battaglia di Adua dal campo Abissino e da fonti russe," Rivista Mil. Italiana (1897).

Edwards, Frederick. "The New Ethiopia," Imperial Asiatic Review, 23 (1912).

Effendi (X). "Le Maadhi, l'Egypte et l'Abyssinie," Revue Britannique, 1 (1884).

Elenco dei principali capi etiopici (Ministero delle colonie, Tipografica nazionale di G. Bertero: 1913).

Elets, Yu. Imperator Menelik i voina ego s italei, po dokumentam i poxordnym dnevnikam, N. S. Leont'eva (St. Petersburg: 1898).

Erlich, Haggai. "Alula, 'the son of Qubi, ' a 'King's Man' in
Ethiopia (1875-1897), " JAH, 15: 2 (1974).

_____. "A contemporary biography of Ras Alula: a Ge'ez manu-
script from Mänäwe, Tamben, " SOAS Bull. 3: 1 and 2 (1976).

Falkenegg, Baron A. von. Abessinien--Wissenwertes über Land und
Leute der Afrikanischen Schweiz (Berlin: 1902).

Felcourt, Etienne de. "Conditions actuelle du commerce à Addis-
Abeba, " Suppl. 681, Moniteur officiel du Commerce (23 Janv.
1908).

_____. L'Abyssinie. Agriculture. Chemin de fer (Paris: 1911).

Falcone, E. Menelich II, l'Etiopia e la relazione con l'Italia
(Naples: 1941).

Farina, G. Le Lettere del Cardinale Massaia dal 1846-1886 (Turin:
1936).

Fasolo, Francesco. L'Abissinia e le Colonie Italiane sul Mar Rosso.
(Caserta: 1887).

Felter, Pietro. "La relaxione di Pietro Felter sullo sgombero di
Macalè, " RSE, 3: 3 (1943).

Ferry, René. "L'Ethiopie et l'expansion européene en Afrique
orientale, " Annales des Sciences politiques, 25 (1910).

Flad, J. M. "Neuste Nachrichten aus Abessinien, " Ausland, 31 (1858).

Florio-Sartori, F. "I capi ribelli Abissini, " BSAI, 6 (1887).

Fornari, G. "La crisi italo-etiopica del 1914, " Rassegna Italiana,
28 (1951) and 29 (1952).

Foti, C. see Chronicles, Royal

Franchetti, L. L'Italia e la sua colonia africana. (Città di Castello: 1891).

Fusella, L. "Les lettere del dabtara Assaggakañ, " RSE, 13 (1954).

_____. "Menelik e l'Etiopia in un testo amarico del Baykadan, "
Annali dell'Istituto Universitario Orientale di Napoli, 4 (1952).

_____. See Chronicles, Royal and Afewerq Gebre Yesus

_____. "L'ambasciata Francese a Nĕgusĕ, " RSE, 7 (July-Dec.
1948).

Gabre Negus. "Sensazioni africane una presagio, " Riv. PL, 6: 4 (1902).

_____. "Eritrea and its new borders," Riv. PL, 6: 3 (1902).

Gaibi, Agostino. La guerra d'Africa, 1895-1896 (Rome: 1930).

Gamba, P. "L'Azione russa in Etiopia," Gli Annali dell'Africa Italiana, 1: 1 (1938).

Gamerra, G. Ricordi di un prigionero di guerra nello Scioa (Florence: 1897).

_____. Fra gli ascari d'Italia a ricordi di Mohammed Idris (Bologna: 1899).

Gardiner, A. L. "The Law of Slavery in Abyssinia," J. Comparative Legislation and International Law, 15 (1933).

Gaselee, S. The Beginning of Printing in Abyssinia (London: 1930).

Gebre Heywat Baykedagn see Fusella, L.

Getachew Haile. "A Note on Writing History from Forgotten Documents," NAS, 2: 1 (1980).

Giaccardi, A. "La colonizzazione abissina nell'Etiopia occidentale," Gli Annali, 2 (1939).

Giannini, C. "La conquista Sciona dell'Aussa (ricordi di missione)," RSE, 3: 2 (1943).

Giglio, Carlo. "Article 17 of the Treaty of Uccialli," JAH, 6: 2 (1965).

_____, ed. L'Italia in Africa--Etiopia Mar Rosso. (Istituto poligrafico dello stato: 1958 Vol. 1, "1857-1885, testo"; 1959 Vol. 2 "Documenti, 1859-1882," 1960 Vol. 3 "Documenti, 1883-1885"; 1966 Vol. 5 "Documenti, 1885-1886."

_____. Il Trattato di pace italo-etiopico del 26 Ottobre 1896," P. 3rd ICES, Vol. 1 (Addis Ababa: 1969).

_____. L'Impresa di Massawa (1884-85) (Rome: 1955).

_____. La politica africana dell Inghilterra nel XIX secolo (Padua: 1950).

_____. L'articolo XVII del trattato di Uccialli (Como: 1967).

Gilmour, T. L. Abyssinia, the Ethiopian Railway and the Powers (London: 1906).

Girma-Selassie Asfaw, David L. Appleyard and E. Ullendorf. The Amharic Letters of Emperor Theodore of Ethiopia to Queen Victoria and Her Special Envoy (OUP for British Academy: 1979).

Giudici, Barbaro lo. "I preliminari de Pace di Faras-Mai del 1896," RSE, 2: 1 (1942).

Giustiani, F. "Considerazioni sull'Italia e la baia di Assab," (Rome: 1879) in Miscellanea. Etiopia ed Eritrea, varia (Istituto per l'Africa, Rome).

Goedorp, Victor. "L'Abyssinie et la France," Revue des Revues, 15 July, 1 August, 1901.

Goj, Luigi. Adua e prigiona fra i galla (Milan: 1901).

Goldmann, W. Das ist Abessinien (Leipzig: 1935).

Gordon, Charles G. Equatoria under Egyptian Rule. The unpublished correspondence of Col., afterwards Major-Gen., C. G. Gordon with Ismail, Khedive of Egypt and the Sudan, during the years 1874-1876. Ed. M. F. Shukry (Cairo: 1953).

_____. Colonel Gordon in Central Africa 1874-1879. Ed. G. B. Hill (London: 1881). See also Nutting, A.

Guêbrè Sellassié see Chronicles, Royal

La Guerra italo-abissina (1895-1896), documentata ed illustrata (Milan: 1896).

Guillain, C. Documents sur l'histoire, la geographie et la commerce de l'Afrique orientale (Paris: 1856-57).

Haile Gabriel Dagne. "The Gebzenna Charter, 1894," JES, 10: 1 (1972).

_____. "The Letters of Emperor Teodros to Itege Yetemegnu," EO, 7: 2 (1963).

Hamilton, David. "Schedule of International Agreements Relating to the Boundaries of Ethiopia," EO, 16: 2 (1973). (1827-1972)

Hans, A. "L'Armée de Ménélik," RDM, June 15, 1896.

Harris, Joseph E. "Soliaman Bin Haftoo: Ethiopian imposter in India?," JES, 7: 1 (1969).

Hayle Sellase see Teferi, Ras

Hecht, Elisabeth-Dorothea. "A Note to the Lists of the Emperors of Ethiopia, Ba'eda Maryam II (1795-1826)," JES, 7: 1 (1969).

Hendécourt, Louis d'. "L'expedition d'Abyssinie en 1868," RDM, 1 April 1869.

Hénin, H. "Ethiopie," Recueil Consulaire Belge, 138 (1907).

Henty, G. A. The March to Magdala (London: 1868).

Hertslet, Edward. Map of Africa by Treaty. 3 vols. (London: 1909).

Heruy Welde Sellase. Ityopyana Metemma: Ye-Atse Yohannes Tarik. (Ethiopia and Metemma, A History of Emperor Yohannes) (Addis Ababa: 1917-18).

_____. Ye-heywet Tarik [Biographies] behwala Zemen le- minew Lejoch Mastaeiya (Addis Ababa, E. C. 1915, European calendar 1922-23).

Hesseltine, W., and Wolf, H. C. The Blue and the Gray on the Nile (Chicago, UCP: 1961).

Hill, G. B. see Gordon, C. G.

Holland, T. J., and Hozier, H. M. Record of the Expedition to Abyssinia, Compiled by Order of the Secretary of State for War. 2 vols. (London: 1870).

Holt, P. M. The Mahdist State in the Sudan, 1881-1898 (Oxford: Clarendon, 1958).

Honeyman, A. M. "Letters from Magdala and Massawa," Bull. JRL, 44 (1962).

Hooker, J. R. "The Foreign Office and the Abyssinian Captives," JAH, 2: 2 (1961).

Huntingford, G. W. B. "Note on the dating of two Ethiopian manuscripts, JSS, 8: 1 (1963).

Ilg, Alfred. "Die äthiopische Heeresorganisation," Schweizerische Monatschrift für Offiziere aller Waffen, 8: 4 (1896).

_____. "Uber die Verkehrsentwicklung in Äthiopien," JGEG, 1 (1899-1900).

_____. "Zür Geschichte der äthiopischen Eisenbahnen," JGEG, 10 (1909-10). See also Keller, C. and Loepfe, W.

"The Italians at Kassala," Saturday Review, 78 (July 28, 1894).

Jackson, H. C. Osman Digna (London: 1926).

Jaenen, Cornelius. "Blondeel: the Belgian attempt to colonize Ethiopia," African Affairs, 55 (1956).

Jaja, G. "Etiopia commerciale," BSGI, 46 (1909), 13-36, 129-72.

Jennings, J. W. & Addison, C. With the Abyssinians in Somaliland (London: 1905).

Jesman, C. The Russians in Ethiopia (London, Chatto and Windus:
    1958).

_____. "The Tragedy of Magdala: an Historical Study, " EO, 10:
    2 (1966).

_____. "Theodore II of Ethiopia, " History Today, 22: 4 (1972).

Jonquière, C. de la. Les Italiens en Erythrèe (Paris: 1895).

Keefer, Edward C. "Great Britain and Ethiopia, 1897-1910: com-
    petition for Empire, " IJAHS, 6: 3 (1973).

Keller, Conrad. Alfred Ilg, sein Leben und sein Wirken (Freuen-
    feld: 1918).

Keller-Zschokke, J. V. Werner Munzinger Pascha, sein Leben und
    Wirken (Aarau: 1891).

Klobukowski, Antoine. "La question de l'Abyssinie, " La Revue de
    Paris, 18 (15 Sept. 1926).

Kodolitsch, H. Bericht über die englische Armee in Abyssinien
    1867 bis 1868 (Vienna: 1869).

Koubel, Lev. "Données sur les rapports socio-économiques chez
    les peuples de l'Ethiopie dans les oeuvres de A. K. Boulato-
    vitch (voyage des années 1896-1899), " P. 3rd ICES, v. 3
    (Addis Ababa: 1970).

Krindach, F. Russkii Kavalerist v Abissinii. Iz Dzhibuti v Kharar
    (St. Petersburg: 1898, 2nd ed.).

Labrousse, H. "La Neutralité Ethiopienne pendant la Première
    Guerre Mondiale: l'incident Holtz-Karmelich (1917), " P. 5th
    ICES (Chicago: 1979).

Lambert, Henri see L. Simonin

Lamlam, Alequa see Chronicles above

Lande, L. L. "Un voyageur français [Pierre Arnoux] dans l'Ethiopie
    méridionale, " RDM, (15 Dec. 1878 and 15 Jan. 1879).

Lazarevic, A. S. "Researches of the Seljan brothers in Ethiopia, "
    P. 3rd ICES, vol. 1 (1969).

Lejean, Guillaume. Théodore II, le Nouvel Empire d'Abyssinie et
    les intérêts français dans le sud de la mer Rouge (Paris: 1865).

Lemmi, F. Lettere e diari d'Africa (Rome: 1937).

Leontiev, N. see Elets above

Lesseps, Ferdinand de.   "L'Abyssinie, " La Nouvelle Revue, 27
    (March 1884).

Lindley, A. F.   The Abyssinian War from an Abyssinian Point of
    View (London: 1868).

Littman Enno see Chronicles, Royal

Loepfe, Willi.   Alfred Ilq und die äthiopische Eisenbahn (Zürich,
    Atlantis Verlag: 1975).

Loring, W. W. A Confederate Soldier in Egypt (New York: 1884).

Luciano, G. B.   La Colonizzatione e l'Ordinamento Militare nell'
    Eritrea (Rome: 1891).

Luzeux, General.   Etudes critiques sur la guerre entre l'Italie et
    l'Abyssinie (Paris: 1896).

McClellan, C. W.   "The Ethiopian occupation of Northern Sidamo--
    Recruitment and Motivation, " P. 5th ICES, Chicago, 1978.

_____.   "Perspectives on the Neftenya-Gabbar System.   The
    Example of Darasa, " Africa (Rome) (1980?).

Mahteme Sellase Welde Mesqel.   Zekra Neger (Things remembered),
    Addis Ababa: 1949-50.

_____.   Ye-Ityopya Bahl Tenat: Tche Belew (Addis Ababa, E. C.
    1961), Reprinted JES, 7: 2 (1969).   ("Study of Horse-names in
    Ethiopian culture. ")

Maindron, M.   "Ménélick et son empire, " Revue de Paris, (15
    June 1896).

Makonnen, Endalkachew.   Taytu Betul.   (Privately printed, Addis
    Ababa: 1957).

Mantegazza, V.   Gli Italiani in Africa (Florence: 1905).

_____.   Da Massaua a Saati (Milan: 1888).

_____.   La guerra in Africa (Florence: 1896).

_____.   Menelik--L'Italia e l'Etiopia (Milan: 1910).

Marcus, Harold G.   "The End of the Reign of Menelik II, " JAH,
    11: 4 (1970).

_____.   "Ethio-British Negotiations Concerning the Western Bor-
    der with the Sudan, 1896-1902, " JAH, 4 (1963).

_____.   "The Foreign Policy of the Emperor Menelik 1896-1898:
    a rejoinder, " JAH, 7: 1 (1966).

_____. "A History of the Negotiations Concerning the Border Between Ethiopia and British East Africa, 1897-1914, " Boston University Papers on Africa, vol. 2 (Boston, BUP: 1966).

_____. "The Last Years of the Reign of the Emperor Menelik, 1906-1913, " JSS, 9: 1 (1964).

_____. The Life and Times of Menelik II: Ethiopia 1844-1913 (Oxford, Clarendon: 1974).

_____. "Motives, Methods and Some Results of the Unification of Ethiopia during the Reign of Menelik II, " P. 3rd ICES, Addis Ababa, 1966. V. 1.

_____. "A preliminary History of the Tripartite Treaty of December 13, 1906, " JES, 2: 2 (1964).

_____. "The Rodd Mission of 1897, " JES, 3: 2 (1965).

_____. "Menilek II, " Leadership in Eastern Africa; Six Political Biographies. Ed. Norman R. Bennett (Boston, BUP: 1968).

_____. "Some Reflections on the Development of Government and Taxation in Southern Ethiopia around the turn of the Century, " ANL, 371: 191 (1974) I.

_____. "Disease, Hospitals, and Italian Colonial Aspirations in Ethiopia, 1930-1935, " NAS, 1: 1 (1979).

Markham, Clement. A History of the Abyssinian Expedition (London: 1869).

Martini, Ferdinando. Nell'Africa Italiana. Impressioni e ricordi (Milan: 1891).

_____. Cose africane. Da Saati ad Abba Garima. Discorsi e scritti (Milan: 1896).

_____. Il diario eritreo. 4 vols (Florence: 1946).

Martini, Sebastiano. Ricordi ed escursioni in Africa dal 1878-1881 (Florence: 1886).

Martino, G. de. La Somalia italiana nei trei anni del mio Governo (Rome: 1912).

Mashcov, V. "Il secondo viaggio in Abissinia del Mashcov (1891-92), " BSGI, ser. 3, 7 (1894). Trans. from Novoe Vremia.

Massaia, Father G. see Travel and Description section

Matteucci, P. In Abissinia, viaggio (Milan: 1880).

Melli, B.   La Colonia Eritrea (Parma: 1899).

_____.   La Battaglia d'Adua (Parma: 1901).

_____.   L'Eritrea dalle sue origini a tutto l'anno 1901 (Milan: 1902).

Menarini, G.   La brigata Dabormida alla battaglia di Adua (Naples: 1898).

Menilek, King then Emperor.   Letters from him published in BSGI, 13 (1876) 671; 16 (1879) 354-5; 18 (1881) 168-9; 20 (1883) 510-11; 23 (1886) 515; 28 (1891) 22; 29 (1892) 769-70; 37 (1900) 7-8 and BSAI, 9 (1890) 138 and Exploration, 1 (1876) and in Heruy, Ityopyanna Metemma 81-88 (cited above) trans. into English by Zewde Gabre Sellassie, Appendix C of Yohannes IV of Ethiopia (cited below).

Mérab, P.   see   History c. 1760-1913 and Medical history

Mercatelli, L.   "Nel Paese di Ras Alula," Corriere di Napoli, 13-14 May 1891.

Methodios Fouyas, Bishop.   "A Contract between the Ethiopian government and P. Myriallis concerning the construction of St. Georges Cathedral in Addis Ababa, Dec. 26, 1909," Abba Salama (Athens) 2 (1971).

_____.   "Letters of the Greek Patriarchs of Alexandria to Ethiopia," Abba Salama, 1 (1970).

_____.   "A letter of Emperor Yohannes of Ethiopia (1871-1889) to the Greek Patriarch Sophronios of Alexandria (1870-1899)," Abba Salama, 2 (1971).

"The Mission to Menilek," The Spectator (Feb. 27, 1897).

Mitchell, L. H.   Report of the Seizure by the Abyssinians of the Geological and Mineralogical Reconnaisance Expedition (Cairo: 1878).

Moltedo, G.   L'Assedio di Maccalé (Rome: 1901).

Mondon-Vidhailet, C.   see   Chronicles, Royal this section and Travel and Description

Moorehead, Alan   see   Travel and Exploration

Moreno, M. M.   see   Chronicles, Royal this section

Morgan, Margaret.   "Continuities and Traditions in Ethiopian History: an investigation of the reign of Tewodros," EO, 12: 4 (1969).

Myatt, Frederick. The March to Magdala: The Abyssinian War of 1868 (London, Leo Cooper: 1970).

Nabokov, Vladimir. Eugene Onegin, Vol. 3, Appendix 1 on Abram Gannibal (New York, Random House: 1964).

Napier, Lord Robert. Abyssinia and Theodore (London: 1869).

Naretti, Giacomo. (Letter from Mekelle) BSGI, 19 (1882).

Natsoulas, Theodore. "The Hellenic Presence in Ethiopia, a study of a European minority in Africa (1740-1936)," Abba Salama, 8 (1977).

Negaso Gidada with Donald Crummey. "The Introduction and Expansion of Orthodox Christianity in Qēlēm Awraja, Western Wāllā-ga from about 1896 to 1941," JES, 10: 1 (1972).

Negussay Ayele. "Rhetoric and Reality in the making of boundaries on the Horn of Africa in 1897," EO, 13: 1 (1970).

Nicoletti-Altimari, A. Fra gli Abissini; ricordi di un prigionero del Tigrê (Rome: 1897).

Noir, Louis. Au pays des Lions noirs, La mission Marchand en Abyssinie (Paris: 1899).

Nutting, A. Gordon: Martyr and Misfit (London: 1966).

"Les occupations de Mênêlik," TM, 15 (1909).

Osio, Egidio. "Spedizione inglese in Abissinia; estratto del giornale di viaggio," BSGI, 2 (1869).

Pankhurst, Richard. See also General Works, History (A) and Medical.

_____. "The Emperor Theodore and the Question of Foreign Artisans in Ethiopia," Boston University Papers on Africa, vol. 2 (Boston, BUP: 1966).

_____. "The Emperor Theodore of Ethiopia," EO, 8: 3 (1964).

_____. "The Emperor Theodore's Amulet: a Note," EO, 6: 3 (1962).

_____. "Ethiopia and the Red Sea and Gulf of Aden Ports in the 19th and 20th Centuries," EO, 8: 1 (1964).

_____. "Ethiopia in the 19th Century," EO, 7: 1 (1963).

_____. "Ethiopian Noblemen's Seals of the Late 19th and early 20th Centuries: a First Selection," EO, 15: 3 (1972).

_____. "The Ethiopian Slave Trade in the 19th and early 20th Centuries," *JSS*, 9: 1 (1964).

_____. "Fire-arms in Ethiopian History (1800-1935)," *EO*, 6: 2 (1962).

_____. "The Franco-Ethiopian Railway and Its History," *EO*, 6: 4 (1963).

_____. "The Great Ethiopian famine of 1888-1892: a new assessment," *JHMAS*, 21: 2 and 3 (1966).

_____. "The Historic Battle of Adowa," *Addis Reporter*, 2: 4 (1970).

_____. "The History of Fire-Arms in Ethiopia Prior to the 19th Century," *EO*, 11: 3 (1967).

_____. "The History of Famine and Pestilence in Ethiopia prior to the founding of Gondar," *JES*, 10: 2 (1972).

_____. "The history and principles of Ethiopian Chess," *JES*, 9: 2 (1971).

_____. "The History of Ethiopian-Armenian Relations," *Revue des Etudes Arméniennes*, 12 (1977) and 13 (1978-79).

_____. "The Illustration of Menelik's Letter of 1867 to Queen Victoria," *EO*, 14: 2 (1971).

_____. "An Enquiry into the Penetration of Fire-Arms into Southern Ethiopia in the 19th Century Prior to the Reign of Menelik," *EO*, 12: 2 (1968).

_____. "Italian Settlement Policy in Eritrea and Its Repercussions, 1889-1896," *Boston University Papers on Africa*, vol. 1 (1964).

_____. "Letter Writing and the Use of Royal and Imperial Seals in Ethiopia Prior to the 20th Century," *JES*, 11: 1 (1973).

_____. "Linguistic and Cultural Data on the Penetration of Fire-Arms into Ethiopia," *JES*, 9: 1 (1971).

_____. "Menelik and the Foundation of Addis Ababa," *JAH*, 2: 1 (1961).

_____. "Menelik and the Utilisation of Foreign Skills in Ethiopia," *JES*, 5: 1 (1967).

_____. "Nineteenth and early Twentieth Century Population Guesses," *JES*, 5: 2 (1961).

_____. "Popular Opposition in Britain to British Intervention Against Emperor Tewodros of Ethiopia (1867-1868)," EO, 16: 3 (1973).

_____. "Pushkin's African Ancestry: a Question of Roots," History Today, (Sept. 1980).

_____. "Robert Skinner's Unpublished Account of the First American Diplomatic Mission to Ethiopia," EO, 13: 1 (1970).

_____. "The Role of Foreigners in 19th Century Ethiopia, prior to the Rise of Menelik," Boston University Papers on Africa, vol. 2 (1966).

_____. "Sir Robert Napier's Comments on Clements Markham's History of the Abyssinian Expedition," EO, 12: 1 (1969).

_____. "Special Issue on the Battle of Adowa," EO, 1: 11 (1957).

_____. "Three 19th Century Ethiopian Profiles: Sahle Sellassie, Ras Wube and Yohannes IV," EO, 9: 3 (1965).

_____ and Germa-Selassie Asfaw. Tax Records and Inventories of Emperor Tewodros of Ethiopia (1855-1868). Fontes Historiae Africanae, Series Aethiopica (1980).

_____. "Two Forgotten Ethiopian Scholars of the Late 18th and Early 19th Centuries: Abu Rumi and Liq-Atsqu," EO, 12: 2 (1968).

_____. "Pushkin's Ethiopian Ancestry: Introduction," EO, 1: 8 (1957).

_____. "The Visit of Ras Makonnen to Europe in 1902 and the 'Spy' Cartoon of Him," EO, 14: 4 (1971).

_____. "The Hapshis of India," EO, 4: 10 (1960).

_____. "Banyan" or Indian Presence at Massawa, Dahlak Islands and the Horn of Africa," JES, 12: 1 (1974).

_____. "Mahbuba, the 'Beloved': The Life and Romance of an Ethiopian Slave-Girl in Early 19th Century Europe," J. African Studies, 6: 1 (1979).

_____. "William H. Ellis--Guillaume Enriques Ellesio: First Black American Ethiopianist," EO, 15: 2 (1972).

_____. "The History of Prostitution in Ethiopia," JES, 12: 2 (1974).

_____. "Misoneism and Innovation in Ethiopian History," EO, 7: 4 (1964).

_____. "The Kwer'ata Re'esu: History of an Ethiopian Icon, " Abba Salama, 10 (1979).

_____. "The foundations of education, printing, newspapers, book production, libraries and literacy in Ethiopia, " EO, 6: 3 (1962).

_____. "Education, language and history: an historical background to post-war Ethiopia, " EJE, 7: 2 (1975).

_____ (with Adi Huka). "Early nineteenth century Oromo childhood reminiscences, " EJE, 7: 2 (1975).

_____. "An early 19th century attempt at teaching Greek at Adwa (Ethiopia), Abba Salama, 9 (1978).

_____. "Reflections on the importance of Graeco-Ethiopian studies, " Abba Salama, 8 (1977).

_____. "The inscriptions and royal chronicles of Ethiopia, " Tarikh (Ibadan), 2: 3 (1967).

_____. "'Tewodros': the question of a Greco-Roman or Russian Hermit or Adventurer in 19th century Ethiopia, " Abba Salama, 5 (1974).

_____. "Yohannes Kotzika, the Greek and British intervention against Emperor Tewodros, " Abba Salama, 3 (1972).

_____. "The Reign of Menelik, and era of innovation, " Tarik (Addis Ababa) 1: 2 (1963).

_____. "The Genesis of Photography in Ethiopia and the Horn of Africa, " British Journal of Photography, 41-44 (1976).

_____. "The independence of Ethiopia and her import of arms in the 19th Century, " Présence Africaine, 6: 2 (1962).

_____. "The Ethiopian Army in Former Times, " EO, 7: 2 (1963).

Pankhurst, Rita. "The Franco-Ethiopian Railway and its History, " EO, 1: 12 (1958).

_____. "Library of Tewodros dispersed far and wide, " SOAS Bull., 36: 1 (1973).

_____. "Three Notable Ethiopian Women, " EO, 1: 3 (1957).

Pegolotti, B. "Un Italiano alla corte di Menelik, " Sebastiano Castagna. Storia Illustrata, 148 (March 1970).

Pellenc, Capitaine. "Les Italiens en Afrique (1880-1896), " Extr. Revue Militaire de l'Etranger (Paris: 1897).

Perino, E. Vita e gesta di Ras Alula (Rome: 1897).

Petetin, Lt. Col. "La bataille d'Adoua," Etude tactique (Paris: 1901).

Petridus, Pierre. Le Héros d'Adoua: Ras Makonnen, Prince d'Ethiopie (Paris, Plon: 1963).

Piano, Federico. "Appunti militari sull'Abissinia; La Spedizione egiziana contro l'Abissinia, 1876," Relazione al Ministro della guerra (Rome: 1876).

_____. Da Massua all'altopiano etiopico. Con alcune note sull'ordinamento militare dell'Abissinia (Rome: 1887).

Pierre-Alype, F. Les grands problèmes coloniaux. L'Ethiopie et les convoitises allemandes. La politique anglo-franco italienne (Paris: 1917).

_____. "La situation vraie de l'Ethiopie," L'Afrique française (May, 1922).

_____. Sous la couronne de Salomon. L'empire des Negus. De la reine de Saba à la Societé des Nations (Paris: 1925).

Pigli, Mario. l'Etiopia nella politca Europea (Padua: 1936, 3rd ed.).

_____. Etiopia, l'incognita africana (Padua: 1935).

Pinon, René. "La résurrection d'un état africain," RDM, 1 and 15 April 1901.

Pollera, Alberto. L'Abissinia di ieri; osservazioni e ricordi (Rome: 1940).

_____. La Battaglia di Adua del 1 Marzo 1896 narrata nei luoghi ove fu combattuta (Florence: 1928).

_____. "La circolazione monetaria nell'Eritrea ed il commercio etiopico," Rivista coloniale, 22: 5 (1925).

_____. Lo stato etiopico e la sua Chiesa (Rome-Milan: 1926).

_____. "Il regime della proprietà terriera in Etiopia e nella Colonia Eritrea," Monografie e Rapporti coloniali, 13 (1913).

Poncins, Edmond de. "The Menelik Myth," Nineteenth Century, 45 (1899).

Pougeois, Abbé. L'Abyssinie. Son histoire naturelle, politique et religieuse depuis les temps les plus reculés jusqu'à la chute de Théodoros. (Paris: 1968).

Prasso, A. Raccolta di scritti e documenti relativi ad Alberto
     Prasso (Rome: 1939).

Quaranta di Sanserverino, F. Ethiopia, an Empire in the Making
     (London: 1918).

Ragazzi, Dr. V. (Letters from Ethiopia) BSGI, 23 (1886) 340-42
     and 391; 24 (1887) 195-96; 25 (1888) 66-80; 26 (1889) 964 and
     967; EC, 2 (1887) 96.

Raït, Maria. "Les voyageurs et savants Russes en Afrique," Les
     Africanistes Russes parlent de l'Afrique (Présence Africaine,
     date?)

Rao, Vasant. "Siddis: African Dynasty in India," Black World,
     24: 10 (1975).

Ravier, Theodore. L'Ethiopie et l'expansion européen (Lyons:
     1910).

Record of the Expedition to Abyssinia (HMSO: 1870).

"Le retraite de Ménélik et la situation en Ethiopie," TM, 16 (1910).

Ricci, L. see Chronicles above

Riguzzi, A. Macallé, Diario. Quarantacinque giorni di assedio
     (Palermo: 1901).

Riola, G. "Da Saati a Metemma," BSAI, 8 (1889).

Robbins, Jerrold. "The Americans in Ethiopia," American Mercury,
     29 (1933).

Robinson, A. E. "The Egyptian-Abyssinian War of 1874-1876,"
     JRAS, 26 (1927).

Roeykens, R. P. A. "Les préoccupations missionaires du consul
     belge Edouard Blondeel von Cuelebroeck en Abyssinie (1840-
     1843)," B. de l'Académie Royale des Sciences Coloniales
     (1959), 1135-54.

Rosenfeld, Chris Prouty. "Empress T'aitu Bitoul, Lioness of
     Judah," P. 1st USCES, East Lansing, Michigan, 1973.
     (ASC, MSU: 1975).

_____. A Chronology of Menilek II of Ethiopia, 1944-1913 (ASC,
     MSU: 1976).

_____. "Eight Ethiopian Women of the Zemene Mesafint
     (c. 1769-1855)," NAS, 1: 2 (1979).

_____. The Medical History of Menilek II, Emperor of Ethiopia;

a case of medical diplomacy (Munger Africana Library Notes, Calif. Inst. of Technology, Pasadena, Calif.: 1978).

Rossetti, Carlo. Storia diplomatica dell'Etiopia durante il regno di Menelik II (Turin: 1910). See Ullendorf in Bibliographies for index to this work.

_____. "Quaranta lettere inedite di Oreste Baratieri ad Antonio Cecchi," Gli annali dell'Africana, 3: 4 (1940).

Rubenson, Sven. "Professor Giglio, Antonelli and Article XVII of the Treaty of Wichale," JAH, 8 (1966).

_____. Wichale XVII (HSIU Dept. of History, Historical Study #1, Addis Ababa, 1964).

_____. King of Kings Tewodros of Ethiopia (HSIU and OUP: Nairobi 1966).

_____. "The Adwa Peace Treaty of 1884," P. 3rd ICES, vol. 1 (Addis Ababa: 1969).

_____. "Aspects of the Survival of Ethiopian Independence 1840-1896," Nineteenth-Century Africa, ed. P. J. McEwan (London, OUP: 1968).

_____. The Survival of Ethiopian Independence (London, Heinemann: 1976).

Sambon, L. L'escercito abissino; usi et costumi (Rome: 1896).

_____. "Etiopia militare," BSAI, 9 (1898).

San Marzano, Roberto di. "Relazione a S. E. il Ministro della Guerra sulla operazione militare eseguita nell'inverno del 1887-88 per la reoccupazione di Saati," Extr. Rivista Militare Italiana (1888).

_____. Le Terre del nostro impero. 2 vols. (2nd edita, Rome: 1937).

Sanderson, G. N. "The Foreign Policy of the Negus Menelik, 1896-1898," JAH, 5: 1 (1964).

_____. "Menelik and the European Powers," Nineteenth-Century Africa, ed. P. J. McEwan (London, OUP: 1968).

Sanguinetti, J. Essais de pénétration européene en Ethiopie 1885-1906 (Montpellier: 1907).

Sapelli, Alessandro. Memorie d'Africa 1883-1906 (Bologna: 1935).

_____. "Ricordi di un vecchio soldato d'Africa: 1887-1896," Nuova Antologia, (Mar.-Apr. 1935 and May-June 1935).

Sapeto, G. see Travel and Exploration

_____. Osservazione sulla spedizione inglese in Abissinia (Messina: 1868).

Schneider, R., and J. Vanderlinden. "A propos d'un manuscrit de Casimir Mondon-Vidhailet addressé à Menelik II," JES, 7: 2 (1969).

Scholler, Heinrich. "Letters Exchanged Between Ethiopian and German Emperors," P. 5th ICES, Chicago, 1978 (Chicago: 1979).

Schrenzel, E. H. Abessinien, Land ohne Hunger, Land ohne Zeit (Berlin: 1928).

Seckendorff, G. B. Meine Erlebnisse mit dem englischen Expeditionscorps in Abessinien 1867-1868 (Potsdam: 1869).

Seifu Metaferia. "Sixteen Letters of Ras Makonnen and his sons to Haji Ahmad Abonn of Harar," JES, 12: 2 (1974).

Selamu Bekele and Vanderlinden, J. "Introducing the Ethiopian Law Archives: some documents on the first Ethiopian Cabinet," JEL, 4 (1967).

Sengal, E. "Condizioni ed esigenze dell'Etiopia dopo il '96 secondo uno scrittore Abissino," Atti del terzo congresso di studi coloniali (Firenze: 1937).

Shepherd, A. J. The Campaign in Abyssinia. Bombay, Times of India: 26 (1868).

Sillani, Tomaso. l'Africa Orientale Italiane e il conflitto Italo-Etiopico (Rome: 1936).

Simone, Ed. "The Amhara Military Expeditions Against the Shawa Galla (1800-1815): a Reappraisal," P. 1st USCES, MSU, 1973 (ASC, MSU: 1975).

Smith, Homer. "Hannibal and Russian Arms," EO, 1: 8 (1957).

_____. "Pushkin's Ethiopian Ancestor," EO, 1: 8 (1957).

Spedizione Militare Italiane in Abissinia," Miscellanea, Etiopia ed Eritrea varia (Rome: 1887).

Stanley, H. M. Coomassie and Magdala: The story of Two British Campaigns in Africa (London and New York: 1874).

Starkie, Enid. Arthur Rimbaud in Abyssinia (Oxford, Clarendon Press: 1937).

Stitz, Volker. "The Amhara Resettlement of Northern Shoa During the 18th and 19th Centuries, " Rural Africana, 11 (East Lansing, Michigan: 1970).

Strelcyn, S. "Contribution à l'histoire des poids et des mesures en Ethiopie, " Rocznik Orientalistyczny, 28 (1965).

Stumm, F. Meine Erlebnisse bei der englischen Expedition in Abessinien (Frankfurt: 1868).

"Taitou, the Abyssinian Empress, " Harpers Weekly, 40: 318 (1896).

Tedone, Giovanni. I recordi di un prigionero di Menelik dopo il disastro di Adua (Rome: 1915; reissued 1964).

[Teferi, Ras]. "Two versions of proclamation of July 1913 of Dej. Tafari, governor of Harar to counteract certain abuses of tax collection under which peasants chafed, " SOAS Bull., 37: 2 (1974).

Terrefe Woldesadik. "The Unification of Ethiopia (1880-1935) Wällä-ga, " JES, 6: 1 (1968).

Traversi, L. "Il conte Pietro Antonelli e la politica scioana, " Riv. PL, 5 (1901).

_____. "Gli eredi di Menelik, " Riv. PL, ser. 2, 6 (15 March 1902).

_____. See listings under Travel and Exploration.

Tristan, H. "Les relations postale de l'Ethiopie, " Revue de l'Académie de Philatée, 7: 35 and 38; 9: 43 (1970).

Triulzi, Alessandro. "Gudru Oromo and their neighbours in the two generations before the battle of Embabo, " JES, 13: 1 (1975).

_____. "The Background to Ras Gobana's Expeditions to Wälläga in 1886-1888: a review of the evidence, " P. 1st USCES (ASC, MSU: 1975).

_____. "Trade, Islam and the Mahdia in Northwestern Wallagā, Ethiopia, " JAH, 11: 3 (1970).

Tsehai Berhane Selassie. "The Question of Damot and Wälamo, " JES, 13: 1 (1975).

_____. "Life and Career of Däjazmač Balčä Aba Näfso, " JES, 9: 2 (1971).

Tubiana, J. "Quatre généalogies royales éthiopiennes, " Cahiers d'etudes Africaines, 2 (1962).

_____. "Turning Points in Ethiopian History, " RSE, 21-22 (1965-66).

_____ . "Théodore II d'Ethiopie, " RSE, 19 (1963).

Ullendorff, E.   "Some Early Amharic Letters, " SOAS Bull. , 35: 2 (1972).

_____ . "Queen Victoria's Phonograph Message to the Emperor Menilek of Ethiopia, " SOAS Bull. , 32 (1969).

_____ , and C. F. Beckingham.   "The First Anglo-Ethiopian Treaty, " JSS, 9: 1 (1964).

_____ . "The 1897 Treaty between Britain and Ethiopia, " RSE, 22 (1966).

Underhill, G. E.   "Abyssinia under Menelik and After, " Quarterly Review, 237 (1932).

Valle, C. della.   "Tappe italiano in Africa: la vittoria di Agordat (21 Dicembre 1893) da lettere inedite, " Riv. C. , 7 (1933).

Venkataram, Krishnamurthy.   "Foreign Policy of Theodore II of Ethiopia: an interpretation, " Transafrican JAH, 3: 1-2 (1973).

Villari, G.   "I'gulti della regione di Axum, " Rassegna Economica dell' Africa Italiana, 16 (1938).

Vitalien, J.   Pour l'independence de l'Ethiopie (Paris: 1919).

Wadhawan, G. N.   "Indians in Ethiopia, " EO, 4: 10 (1960).

Wagner, Ewald.   "Three Arabic documents on history of Harar, " JES, 12: 1 (1974).

Walker, C. H.   "The Emperor of Abyssinia and his Army, " African Observer, 4 (1936).

_____ . "The Road in Abyssinia, " African Observer, 2 (1932).

Weld-Blundell, H.   see   Chronicles, Royal

Wigny, P. , and M. Borboux.   "Belgique et Abyssinie, " La Vie Economique et Sociale (Nov. 15, 1935).

Wild, G.   "Werner Munzinger Pascha, " Petermanns, 22 (1876).

Wilson, E. T.   Russia and Black Africa Before World War II (New York, Holmes and Meier: 1974).

Wolde Tsadek, Azaj.   (Letter to Antonelli from Ankobar 18 Nov. 1882) BSGI, ser. 2, 8 (1883), 284.

Yaltasamma (pseud.).   Les Amis de Menilek II ... avec documents sur la conquête du Nil par les Anglais et l'incident de Fachoda (Paris: 1899).

Yaqob Beyene. "L'imperatore Giovanni IV in alcune composizioni tigrine, " AION, 34 (1974).

_____. "Ras Sebhat in alcune composizioni tigrine dell'Agama, " AION, 33 (1973).

Yohannes IV, Emperor. (Letters of: see Zewde Gabre Sellassie's Yohannes IV of Ethiopia and Bairu Tafla's Chronicle of Yohannes IV, listed under Chronicles, Royal.)

Zaghi, C. "I fratelli Naretti, " Riv. C, 9 (1935).

_____. "Rimbaud in Africa e le sue relazione col viaggiatori italiani, " Nuova Antologia (16 Agosto, 1933).

_____. I Russi in Etiopia. 2 vols (Naples, Guida Editori: 1972).

_____. Crispi e Menelich (Turin: 1956) (see Salimbeni).

_____. Le Origini della colonia Eritrea (Bologna: 1934).

_____. "Cesare Diana e la spedizione Bianchi alla luce di nuovi documenti, " Nuova Antologia, 10: 1 (1936).

_____. L'Ultima spedizione africana di Gustavo Bianchi. 2 vols. (Milan: 1930).

_____. "La missione del maggiore Salsa at campo sciona prima di Adua, " Riv. C, 10 (1936).

_____. "La conquista di Cassala, " Nuova Antologia, ser. 8, (Sept. -Oct. 1934).

_____. "Lo sbarco italiano a Zeila e l'attegiamento inglese durante la campagna del 1895-96, " Riv. C., 9: 2 (1935).

Zervos, Adrien. L'empire d'Ethiopie, le miroir de l'Ethiopie moderne 1906-1936 (Alexandria: 1936).

Zewde Gabre Sellassie. Yohannes IV of Ethiopia (Oxford, Clarendon: 1975).

Zewditu, Empress. (See Documents relatifs au coup d'état d'Addis Abeba du 27 Sept. 1916.)

Zoli, C. Etiopia d'oggi (Rome: 1936).

_____. Cronache etiopiche (Rome: 1930).

HISTORY (C)
Circa 1930-1974:   Reign of Hayle Sellase

General Works

Asfa Yilma, Princess.   Haile Selassie, Emperor of Ethiopia
(London: 1936).

Clapham, C.   Haile Selassie's Government (New York: Praeger,
1969).

Gilkes, Patrick.   The Dying Lion: Feudalism and Modernization
in Ethiopia (New York, St. Martin's Press: 1975).

_____.   "Haile Selassie: How Much Money Did He Salt Away?"
African Development, 8: 12 (1974).

Gorham, Charles.   The Lion of Judah: a life of Haile Selassie I. ; Emperor of Ethiopia (New York: Farrar, Straus and Giroux: 1966).

Greenfield, Richard.   Ethiopia, a new Political History (London,
Pall Mall Press: 1965).

Haile Selassie I.   Volumes 1-16 of the Ethiopia Observer, 1956-
1974 contain speeches, statements, appointments and travels
of the emperor.

_____.   "Ethiopian Independence," Vital Speeches of the Day, 1:
22 (1935).

_____.   "Ethiopia's Position, " Vital Speeches of the Day, 2: 1
(1935).

_____.   My Life and Ethiopia's Progress, 1892-1937.   Trans.
and edited by E. Ullendorff from the Amharic publication in
Addis Ababa, 1973-74 (London, New York; OUP: 1976).

_____.   "Towards African Unity, " JMAS, 1: 3 (1963).

Hess, Robert L. see General Works

Jaffe, Andrew.   "Haile Selassie's Remarkable Reign, " Africa Report
16: 5 (1971).

Juniac, G. de.   Le dernièr roi des rois (Paris, Plon: 1979).

Legum, Colin.   Ethiopia: The Fall of Haile Sellassie's Empire
(London, Rex Collins: 1975).

_____.   Ethiopia (New York, Africana Publishing Company:
1975).

MacLean, Robinson. John Hoy of Ethiopia (New York: 1936).

Makonnen Endalkatchu. Why Was the Lion of Judah Defeated? (Jerusalem: 1939).

Marcus, Harold. "The Infrastructure of the Italo-Ethiopian Crisis: Haile Sellassie, the Solomonic Empire, and the World Economy, 1916-1936, " P. 5th ICES, Chicago, 1978.

Moore, W. R. "Coronation Day in Addis Ababa, " National Geographic, 56: 6 (1931).

Moraitis, George. "The Autobiography of Haile Sellassie as a Psychological Document, " P. 5th ICES, Chicago, 1978.

"Mort de l'Ex-empereur Haile Sélassié (27 Août 1975), " Afrique Contemporaine, 81 (1975).

Mosley, Leonard O. Haile Selassie: The Conquering Lion (London, Weidenfeld and Nicolson: 1964).

Norberg, V. H. Swedes in Haile Sellassie's Ethiopia, 1924-1952 (Uppsala, Scandinavian Institute of African Studies: 1977).

Nouaille-Degorce, Brigitte. "L'Heritage de l'Empereur Haile Sélassié, " Revue Française d'Etudes Politiques Africaines (July, 1975).

Pankhurst, R. "Decolonization of Ethiopia, 1940-1955, " Horn of Africa, 1: 4 (1978).

_____. "Emperor Haile Sellassie's litigation in England to reassert the independence of Ethiopia during the Italian occupation in 1937-38, " EO, 14: 1 (1971).

_____. "Ethiopian national anthem in 1940: chapter in Anglo-Ethiopian relations, " EO, 14: 3 (1971).

Perret, M. "L'Ethiopie moderne, de l'avènement de Menelik II à nos jours, " Rev. Fr. d'Etudes Politiques Africaine, 158 (1979).

"Ras Tafari of Abyssinia, " Current Opinion, 77 (1924).

Said, Abdulkadir N. "The Man in the Rolls Royce, " New Directions (Howard University), 2: 4 (1975).

Sandford, Christine. The Lion of Judah Hath Prevailed: being a biography of H. I. M. Haile Selassie I (New York, Macmillan: 1955. Reprint, Greenwood Press, Westport, Connecticut.)

Sbacchi, Alberto. "Haile Selassie and the Italians, 1941-1943, " ASR, 22: 1 (1979).

Schwab, Peter, ed.   Ethiopia and Haile Selassie (New York, Facts
    on File, 1972).

_____. "Haile Selassie: Leadership in Ethiopia," Plural Socie-
    ties, 6 (1975).

Skinner, Elizabeth and James.   Haile Selassie: Lion of Judah
    (London: Thomas Nelson and Sons, 1967).

Spencer, John H.   "Haile Selassie: Triumph and Tragedy," Orbis,
    18 (1975).

_____. "Haile Selassie: Leadership and Statesmanship," EN,
    2: 2 (1978).

Sterling, Claire.   "The Aging Lion of Judah," The Reporter, 36
    (1967).

Ullendorff, E.   "Haile Sellassie at Bath," JSS, 42: 3 (1979).

Italian Invasion and
Occupation: 1935-1941

Abraham, E.   "Abyssinia and Italy--the case for Ethiopia," JRAS,
    37 (Oct. 1935).

The Abyssinian Campaigns (London, HMSO: 1942).

Agostino Orsini di Camerota, Paolo d'.   Perche andiamo in Etiopia?
    (Rome: 1935).

Angell, Norman.   "The Politics and Morals of Mustard Gas," Time
    and Tide (1936).

Annali dell'Africa Italiana, 2: 1 (1939) (War bulletins reproduced).

"L'Armee ethiopienne," Revue Militaire Française, 170: (1935).

Arnold, A. C.   "Italo-Abyssinian Campaign," RUSIJ (Feb. 1937),
    71-88.

Asante, S. K. B.   "The Catholic Missions, British West African
    Nationalists and the Italian Invasion of Ethiopia, 1935-36,"
    African Affairs, 73 (April, 1974).

_____. Pan-African Protest: West Africa and the Italo-
    Ethiopian crisis, 1934-1941   (Legon Hist., 1977).

Askew, W. C.   "The Secret Agreement between France and Italy
    on Ethiopia, January 1935," JMH, 25 (Mar. 1953).

Auer, Paul de.   "The Lesson of the Italo-Abyssinian Conflict,"
    New Commonwealth Quarterly, 1 (Mar. 1936).

"L'Azione coloniale," Che cosa è l'Africa Orientale? (Rome: 1935).

Badoglio, Pietro. The War in Abyssinia (London: 1937). Trans. from Italian edition of 1936.

Baer, G. W. The Coming of the Italian-Ethiopian War (Cambridge, HUP: 1967).

Baravelli, G. C. The Last Stronghold of Slavery: What Abyssinia Is. (Rome: 1935).

Barker, A. J. The Civilizing Mission: A History of the Italo-Ethiopian War of 1935-1936 (New York, Dial Press: 1968).

_____. The Rape of Ethiopia, 1936 (New York, Ballantine: 1971).

Barnes, James Strachey. Half a Life Left (London: 1937).

Bastin, Jean. L'Affaire d'Ethiopie et les diplomates, 1934-1937 (Brussels, l'Edition Universelle: 1938).

Benelli, Sem. Io in Africa (Milan: 1937).

Beonio-Brocchieri, V. Cieli d'Etiopia (Milan: 1936).

Berio, Alberto. "L'Affare etiopico," Rivista di Studi Politici Internazionali, 25 (Apr.-June 1958).

Bidou, Henry. "La Conquête de l'Ethiopie," RDM, 33: 8 (1936).

Blomgren, G. D. 'Ethiopia, here I come' says Mussolini (Waterloo, Iowa: 1936).

Bonneuil, Marie Edith de. Bivouacs aux étoiles (Paris: 1938).

Bottai, Giuseppe. Vent'anni e un giorna (2nd ed.) (Rome: 1949).

Bova, Pasquale. Il Criterio 'razziale' nella politica imperiale d'Italia (Naples: 1937).

Braddick, Henderson B. "New Look at American Policy During the Italo-Ethiopian Crisis: 1935-1936," JMH, 34 (Mar. 1962).

Briggs, Asa. They Saw It Happen (Oxford, Blackwell & Mott: 1960).

Burgoyne, Clarissa. "The Incorruptible Ethiopia," (Makonen Demisse), EO, 10: 3 (1966).

_____. "Lost Month in Ethiopia," EO, 11: 4 (1967).

Burns, Emile. Ethiopia and Italy (New York: 1935).

Caimpenta, Ugo. L'Impero Abissino (Milan: 1935).

Caioli, Aldo. L'Italia di fronte a Ginevra (Rome, Volpe: 1965).

"Un Camp militaire Abyssinia, " J. Société des Africanistes, 4: 1 (1934).

"La campagna 1935-1936. " Africa Orientale, vol. 1.

Carbone, Adriano. Questa è l'Etiopia (Naples: 1936).

Carter, Boake. Black Shirt, Black Skin (Harrisburg, Pa.: 1935).

Castellani, Sir Aldo. "Hygienic Measures and Hospital Organization of the Ethiopian Expeditionary Forces, " JRSA, 86 (1938), 289-302.

Caviglia, Enrico. Diario, aprile 1925-marzo 1945 (Rome: 1951).

Chaplin, W. W. Blood and Ink (an Italo-Ethiopian War Diary) (New York: 1936).

Charles-Roux, François. Huit ans au Vatican, 1932-1940 (Paris: 1947).

Christopolous, G. La Politique extérieure de l'Italie fasciste (Paris: 1936).

Ciasca, Raffaele. Storia coloniale dell'Italia contemporanea (Milan: 1940).

Cibot, L. J. L'Ethiopie et la Société des Nations (Paris: 1939).

Cimmaruta, Roberto. Ual Ual (Milan: 1936).

Cipolla, A. L'Abissinia in armi (Florence: 1935).

Coffey, T. M. Lion By the Tail (New York, Viking Press: 1974).

Cohen, Armand. La Société des Nations devant le conflit italo-éthiopien (Dec. 1934-Oct. 1935) (Geneva: 1960).

Comryn-Platt, T. The Abyssinian Storm (London: 1935).

Il Conflitto italo-etiopico: documenti (Milan, Istituto per gli studi di Politica Internazionale: 1936).

Conti Rossini, Carlo. "L'Etiopia e' incapace di progresso civile, " Nuova Antologia, 303 (16 Sept. 1935).

Cora, Giuliano. Attualità del trattato italo-etiopico del 1928 (Florence: 1928).

_____ . L'Italia e Etiopia (Florence, 1951. Università degli Studi di Firenze, Centro Studi Coloniali, Pub. #39).

_____ . "Il trattato italo-etiopico del 1928," Rivista di Studi Politici Internazionali, 15 (Apr. -June 1948).

_____ . "Un diplomatico durante l'era fascista," Storia e politica, 5 (Jan. -March 1966).

Currey, Muriel. A Woman at the Abyssinian War (London: 1936).

Davies, D. D. Nearing the Abyss: The Lesson of Ethiopia (London: 1936).

Dean, Vera M. The League and the Italian-Ethiopian Dispute (Geneva Research Center: 1935).

De Bono, Emilio. Anno XIII: The Conquest of an Empire (London: 1937).

_____ . La Preparazione e le prime operazioni (3rd ed.) (Rome: Istituto Nazionale Fascista di Cultura: 1937).

Del Boca, Angelo. The Ethiopian War: 1935-1941 (Chicago, U. of Chicago Press: 1969). Translated by P. D. Cummins from the Italian edition of 1965.

Delgado, Luis H. Italia en Africa: Seis conferencias de un ciclo de conferencias internacionales sobre el conflicto italo-etiope (Lima, Peru: 1935).

Deschamps, H. "Griaule, Mandel et l'Ethiopie," JES, 4: 1 (1966).

Diel, Louise. "Behold our New Empire"--Mussolini (London: 1939) Trans. from the German edition.

Documenti: Il Conflitto italo-etiopico, 2 vols. (Istituto per gli studi politica Internazionale, Milan: 1936).

Documents on Italian War Crimes, 2 vols. (Ethiopia, Ministry of Justice, 1940-1950). (Submitted to the U. N. War Crimes Commission.)

Dorigo, P. P. Ginevra o Roma? (Pisa: 1934).

Driberg, J. H. "Conditions of warfare in Abyssinia," New Statesman, 10 (Aug. 31, 1935).

Dubois, W. E. B. "Inter-Racial Implications: a Negro View," Foreign Affairs, 14 (Oct. 1935).

Dugan, J., and L. Lafore. Days of Emperor and Clown: the Italo-Ethiopian War, 1935-36 (New York, Doubleday: 1973).

Duprey, A. G. De l'invasion à la libération de l'Ethiopie (Paris:
    1955).

"The Ethiopian Patriots as seen at the time," EO, 3: 12 (1959); 4:
    1 (1959).

L'Ethiopie et les puissances; textes diplomatiques collationnés par
    Michel Pobers (Geneva: Geneve-Informations, Agence Inter-
    Nationale de Press, 1935).

Etiopico (pseud.). "Che cosa è il soldato abissino?" Italia Coloni-
    ale, 12 (1935).

Farago, L. Abyssinia Stop Press (London: 1936).

_____. Abyssinia on the Eve (New York: 1936).

Favagrossa, C. F. Perchè perdemmo la guerra (Milan: 1946).

Frangipiano, Agenore. L'equivoco abissino (Milan: 1936).

Garratt, G. "Abyssinia," JRAS, 36 (1937).

_____. Mussolini's Roman Empire (London: 1938).

Gentizon, Paul. La Conquête de l'Ethiopie (Paris: 1936).

_____. La Revanche d'Adoua (Paris: 1936).

Giglio, Guido. "Sguardo ai rapporti fra Badoglio e Mussolini fino
    alla crisi etiopici del 1935-36," Appendix 1 of V. Vailati,
    Badoglio Risponde (Milan: 1958).

Gingold-Duprey see Duprey

Goiffon, Paul. Les clauses coloniales dans les accords franco-
    italiens de 7 janvier 1935 (Lyons: 1936).

Graziani, Rodolfo. Il Fronte sud (Milan: 1938).

Griaule, Marcel. La peau de l'ours (Paris: 1936).

_____. Le Problème Ethiopien (Paris, Société d'Etudes et d'In-
    formations Economiques: 1935).

"La Guerre Italo-Ethiopienne," L'Illustration (Paris: 1936).

Haile Sellassie I. La vérité sur la guerre Italo-Ethiopienne.
    (Trans. from Amharic by Marcel Griaule. Paris: 1936)
    Also published as supplement to Vu (Paris: 1936) as "Une
    victoire de la civilisation."

_____. Address to the League of Nations. Full text in New

Times and Ethiopia News (London: July 1936). Excerpts in EO, 3: 10 (1959).

Halden, Leon G. "The Diplomacy of the Ethiopian Crisis," J. Negro History, 22 (1937).

Hamilton, Edward. The War in Abyssinia (London: 1936).

Hardie, Frank. The Abyssinian Crisis (Hamden, Conn., Archon Books: 1974).

Harris, Brice, Jr. The United States and the Italo-Ethiopian Crisis (Stanford University Press, Palo Alto, Calif.: 1964).

Haskell, Daniel C. Ethiopia and the Italo-Ethiopian Conflict (New York Public Library: 1936).

Haynes, G. E. "Negroes and the Ethiopian Crisis," Christian Century, 52 (1935).

Henson, H. H. Abyssinia: Reflections of an Onlooker (London: 1936).

Hiett, Helen. Public Opinion and the Italo-Ethiopian Dispute: The Activity of Private Organizations in the Crisis (Geneva, Switzerland, Geneva Research Center: 1936).

Hoare, Sir Samuel. Nine Troubled Years (London, Collins: 1954).

_____. Italy and Ethiopia, Collective Action for Security Demanded (New York, Carnegie Endowment for International Peace: 1935).

Hollis, M. Christopher. Italy in Africa (London: 1941).

Hubbard, Wynant D. Fiasco in Ethiopia (New York: 1936).

Iadarola, Antoinette. "The Anglo-Italian agreement of 1925: Mussolini's 'Carte Blanche' for War Against Ethiopia," NAS, 1: 1 (1979).

L'Italie et l'Abyssinie (Rome, Società editrice di Novissima, 14 1936).

The Italo-Ethiopian Controversy (New York, Italian Historical Society, 1935).

Italy and Abyssinia (1897-1935) (Calcutta, Indian Daily News Press: 1936).

Italy and Ethiopia, International Conciliation (New York, Carnegie Endowment for International Peace: 1935).

Junod, Marcel. Le Troisième combattant (Paris: 1936).

Kane, Thomas L. "The Nasi-Ras Abbäbä Arägay truce according
    to two Amharic sources, " SOAS Bull., 39, part 1 (1976).

Kebede Tesemma. Yatarik Mastawasha (Historical Memoirs) (Addis
    Ababa: 1962).

Klein, Fritz. Warum Krieg um Abessinien? (Leipzig: 1935).

Konovaloff, Theodore E. Con le armate del Negus (Bologna: 1936).

Koren, William. "The Italian-Ethiopian Dispute, " Geneva Special
    Studies, 6: 4 (1935).

Lahse, Erich. Abessinien: Der Brennpunkt der Weltpolitik (Leip-
    zig: 1935).

Langer, W. L. "The Suez Canal in Time of War, " Foreign Af-
    fairs, 14 (Oct. 1935).

Laurens, Franklin D. France and the Italo-Ethiopian Crisis, 1935-
    1936 (The Hague: Mouton, 1968).

Lechenberg, H. P. "With the Italians in Eritrea, " National Geo-
    graphic, 68: 3 (1935).

Lefevre, Renato. "Etiopi precursori dei rapporti con l'Italia, "
    Sestante, 6: 1 (1970).

Legionarius (pseud.). The Grounds for the Serious Charges Brought
    by Italy Against Abyssinia (Rome: 1935).

Leroux, E.-L. Le Conflit italo-éthiopien devant la Société des
    Nations (Paris, Librairie Technique et Economique: 1957).

Lessing, P. "The Fall of Mussolini's East African Empire, " His-
    tory of the Second World War, Part 14 (1973), 365-373.

_____. "Italian Collapse in Somaliland, " Ibid, part 12 (1973),
    332-336.

Lessona, Alessandro. Memorie (Florence: 1958).

Lingelback, W. E. "Italy: A Nation in Arms" "Italy Mobilizes for
    War, " "The Strain on Italian Finance, " Current History, 42
    (April-Sept. 1935).

Lixia, Dr. Alberto. P. R. Giuliani, per Cristo e per la Patria
    (Salani: 1937).

Lloyd, H. P. "The Italo-Abyssinian War, the Operations: Massa-
    wa-Addis Ababa, " R.A.F. Quarterly, 8 (1937), 357-367.

MacCallum, E. P. Rivalries in Ethiopia (New York, World Peace
    Foundation: 1935).

MacGregor-Hastie, Roy. The Day of the Lion (New York, Coward
    McCann: 1964).

Magistrati, Massimo. "La Germania e l'impresa italiana di Etiopia
    (Ricordi di Berlino), " Rivista di Studi Politici Internazionali,
    17 (Oct. -Dec. 1950).

Makin, W. J. War Over Ethiopia (London: 1935).

Mantoux, Paul, et al. The World Crisis (London: 1938).

Marcus, Harold. "Disease, hospitals, and Italian Colonial Aspira-
    tions in Ethiopia, 1930-1935, " NAS, 1: 1 (1979).

Mariotti, Delio. In armi sulle Ambe (Milan: 1937).

Martelli, George. Italy Against the World (London: 1937; New
    York: 1938).

Matthews, Herbert. Eyewitness in Abyssinia (London: 1937).

_____. Two Wars and More to Come (New York: 1937).

Melly, John M. "Ethiopia and the War from the Ethiopian Point of
    View, " International Affairs, 15 (Jan. -Feb. 1936).

Mennevée, Roger. Les Origines du conflit italo-éthiopien et a So-
    ciété des Nations (Paris: Documents Politiques, 1936).

Migliorini, Elio. L'Italia in Africa (Rome: 1955).

Miller, Webb. I Found No Peace (London: 1937).

Modica, Giovanni. Cinghia (Turin: 1937).

Monfreid, Henri de. Le Masque d'or; ou le dernier négus (Paris:
    1936).

_____. Les guerriers de l'Ogaden (Paris: 1936, 2nd ed.).

_____. Le drame Ethiopien (Paris: 1935).

Montanelli, Indro. XX Battaglione Eritreo (Milan: 1936).

Monti, A. Gli Italiani e il canale di Suez (Rome: 1937).

Morgan, T. B. Spurs on the Boot (London: 1942).

Mussolini, Benito. "Declaration of Purpose, " (speech to troops at
    Salerno, July 6, 1935); "Italo-Ethiopian Relations, " (speech to

Senate May 14, 1935); "Italy's Foreign Policy," in Vital Speeches of the Day, 1: 22 (July 29, 1935) and 1: 18 (June 3, 1935).

Mussolini, Vittorio. Voli sulle Ambe (Florence: 1937).

Nanni, Ugo. Che cosa è l'Etiopia (Milan: 1935).

Nelson, K., and A. Sullivan, eds. John Melly of Ethiopia (London: 1937).

Nemours, Gen'l. Alfred. Craignons d'être un jour l'Ethiopie de quelqu'un (Port-au-Prince: Collège Vertières: 1945).

Nevins, Allan. "Italy's Aims in Abyssinia," and "Italy's Gamble for Ethiopia," Current History, 42 (Apr.-Sept. 1935).

Newman, E. W. Polson. Ethiopian Realities (London: 1936).

_____. Italy's Conquest of Abyssinia (London: 1937).

_____. New Abyssinia (London: 1937).

Orano, Paolo. Rodolfo Graziani, generale scipione (Rome: 1936).

Ortega y Gasset, Eduardo. Etiopia: El Conflicto italo-abisinio (Madrid: 1935).

Padmore, George. "Ethiopia and World Politics," Crisis, 42: 5 (1935).

Pankhurst, Richard. "A Chapter in Ethiopia's Commercial History: developments during the Fascist Occupation of 1936-41," EO, 14: 1 (1971).

_____. "Economic Verdict on the Italian Occupation of Ethiopia, 1936-1941," EO, 14: 1 (1971).

_____. "The Ethiopian Patriots and the Collapse of Italian Rule in East Africa," EO, 12: 2 (1969).

_____. "The Ethiopian Patriots: the lone struggle," EO, 13: 1 (1970).

_____. "Fascist Racial Policies in Ethiopia: 1922-1941," EO, 12: 4 (1969).

_____. "Italian and 'Native' Labour during the Italian Fascist Occupation of Ethiopia, 1935-1941," Ghana Social Science Journal, 2: 2 (1973).

_____. "Italian Fascist Claims to the port of Jibuti, 1935-1941: an historical note," EO, 14: 1 (1971).

_____. "The Italo-Ethiopian War and the League of Nations Sanctions, 1935-1936," Genève-Afrique, 13: 2 (1974).

_____. "Italy and Ethiopia: The First Four Years of the Resistance Movement (1936-1941)," Africa Quarterly, 9: 4 (1970).

_____ see Medical section

_____. "Old Stones--the Loot of Ethiopian Antiquities during the Italian invasion of 1935-36," Dialogue, 3: 1 (1970).

_____. "A Page of Ethiopian History: Italian Settlement Plans during the Fascist Occupation of 1936-1941," EO, 13: 2 (1970).

_____. "The Perpetuation of the Maria Theresa Dollar and Currency Problems in Italian-occupied Ethiopia," JES, 8: 2 (1970).

_____. "Plans for Mass Jewish Settlement in Ethiopia (1936-1943)," EO, 15: 4 (1972).

_____. "Secret History of Italian fascist occupation of Ethiopia," Africa Quarterly, 16: 4 (1977).

_____. "The text-books of Italian colonial Africa," EO, 11: 4 (1973).

Pankhurst, Sylvia. "The Genesis of the Italo-Ethiopian War," EO, 3: 12 (1959) and 4: 1 (1960).

_____. "Special Issue on the Ethiopian Patriots," EO, 3: 10 (1959).

_____. New Times and Ethiopia News, editor (London, May 9, 1936-May 1956).

Pesenti, G. La Prima Divisione Eritrea alla battaglia dell'Ascianghi (Milan: 1937).

Pierotti, Francesco. Vita in Etiopia, 1940-1941 (Bologna: 1959).

Pigli, Mario. L'Etiopia nella politica europea (Padua: 1936).

_____. Etiopia, l'incognita africana (Padua: 1935).

Pignatelli, L. La Guerra dei sette mesi (Naples, Mezzogiorno: 1961).

Poggiali, Ciro. Diario Africana Orientale Italiana (Milan, Longanesi: 1971).

Potter, Pitman B.   The Wal Wal Arbitration (Washington, D. C. , Carnegie Endowment for International Peace, 1938).

Procházka, Roman.   Abyssinia: The Powder Barrel (London: 1936). Translated from German edition of 1935.

Rampone, Oscar.   Il Mareb era un confine (Asmara: Corriere Eritreo, 1936).

Ridley, Francis A.   Mussolini Over Africa (London: 1935).

Rochat, Giorgio.   Militari e politici nella preparazione della campagna d'Etiopia (Milan, Franco Angeli: 1971).

Roghi, Bruno.   Tessere verde in Africa Orientale (Milan: 1936).

Ross, Red.   "Black Americans and Italo-Ethiopian Relief 1935-1936, " EO, 15: 2 (1972).

Rosso, Augusto.   Italy's Conflict with Ethiopia: The Facts in the Case (New York, American League for Italy, 1935).

Rouard de Card, E.   L'Ethiopie au point de vue du droit international (Paris: 1928).

Rousseau, Charles.   Le conflict italo-éthiopien devant le droit international (Paris: 1938).

Rowan-Robinson, Major-Gen'l H.   England, Italy and Abyssinia (London: 1935).

Salome Gabre Egziabher.   "The Ethiopian Patriots: 1936-1941, " EO, 12: 2 (1969).

_____.   "The Patriotic Works of Dejazmatch Aberra Kassa and Ras Abebe Aragaye, " P. 3rd ICES, Addis Ababa, 1966, Vol. 1 (1969).

Salvatorelli, Luigi.   Vent'anni fra due guerra (Rome: 1941).

Salvemini, Gaetano.   Prelude to World War II (London: 1953).

_____.   "The Vatican and the Ethiopian War, " in Neither Liberty nor Bread, ed. F. Keene (New York: 1940).

Sanctis, Gino do.   La mia Africa (Milan: 1938).

Sandri, Sando.   Sei mesi di guerra sul Fronte Somalo (Anconia: 1936).

Savoia-Genova, Filiberto di.   La prima divisione Camicia Nere 23 marzo (Milan: 1938).

Sbacchi, Alberto. "Secret Talks for the submission of Haile Selassie and Prince Asfaw Wassen, 1936-1939," IJAHS, 7: 4 (1974).

_____. "Legacy of Bitterness: Poison Gas and Atrocities in the Italo-Ethiopian War, 1935-1936," Genève-Afrique, 13: 2 (1974).

_____. "Ethiopian opposition to Italian Rule, 1936-1940," P. 5th ICES, Chicago, 1978.

_____. "Italy and the treatment of the Ethiopian Aristocracy 1936-1940," IJAHS, 10: 2 (1977).

_____. "The Price of Empire: Towards an enumeration of Italian casualties in Ethiopia 1935-40," EN, 2: 2 (1978).

Scaetta, H. "Geography, Ethiopia's Ally," Foreign Affairs, 14 (1935).

Schaefer, Ludwig F., ed. The Ethiopian Crisis: Touchstone of Appeasement? (Boston, Heath: 1961, London, Harrap: 1961).

Scott, W. R. "Malaku E. Bayen: Ethiopian emissary to black america (1935-1936)," EO, 15: 2 (1972).

_____. "Colonel John C. Robinson: the Brown Condor of Ethiopia," Pan-African Journal, 5: 1 (1972).

Shenk, Calvin E. "The Italian attempt to reconcile the Ethiopian Orthodox Church; the use of religious celebrations and assistance to churches and monasteries," JES, 10: 1 (1972).

Sillani, Tomaso, ed. "L'Africana orientale italiana e il conflitto italo-etiopico," Rassegna Italiana, 1936.

Smith, Alan. "The Open Market: The Economy of Kenya's Northern Frontier Province and the Italo-Abyssinian War," East Africa Journal, 6: 11 (1969).

Starace, Achille. La marcia su Gondar (Milan: 1936).

Steer, George L. Caesar in Abyssinia (London: 1936 and Boston: 1937).

_____. "Dejazmatch Afewerk, Hero," EO, 1: 1 (1959).

Tanghe, Raymond. Le conflit italo-éthiopien (Montréal: 1936).

Taylor, A. J. P. The Origins of the Second World War (London, Hamish Hamilton: 1961 and New York, Atheneum: 1962).

Taylor, Frank W. "Interview with Mussolini," Vital Speeches, 1: 24 (1936).

Terlinden, Charles. Le Conflit italo-éthiopien et la Société des Nations (Liège, Belgium: 1936).

Thomas, Norman M. War: No Glory, No Profit, No Need (New York: 1935), Chap. 5 and 6.

Thompson, A. "The Water Problems of Abyssinia and Bordering Countries," International Affairs, 14 (1935).

Tomaselli, C. Con le colonne celeri dal Mareb allo Scioa (Milan: 1936).

Toscano, Mario. "Eden's Mission to Rome on the Eve of the Italo-Ethiopian Conflict," Studies in Diplomatic History (London: 1961), 126-152.

Toynbee, Arnold. "Abyssinia and Italy," in Survey of International Affairs vol. 2 (1935).

_____. "The Italian Dispute," in Twentieth-Century Africa, ed. P. M. M. McEwan (New York, OUP: 1968).

Tsehai Berhane Silassie. "Women Guerrilla Fighters," NAS, 1: 3 (1979-80).

Varanini, Varo. "Le Forze armate dell'Abyssinia," Gerarchia, 15 (1935).

_____. L'Abissinia attuale sotto tutti i suoi aspetti (Turin: 1935).

Vecchi, B. V. Il crollo dell'impero del leone di Guida (Milan: 1936).

Villari, Luigi. "The Italian case," JRAS, 34 (Oct. 1935).

_____. Italy, Abyssinia and the League (Rome: Dante Alighieri Society, 1936).

_____. Storia diplomatica del conflitto Italo-Etiopico (Bologna: 1943).

_____. Italian Foreign Policy under Mussolini (New York: 1956).

Villella, Giovanni. Italia chiama Africa (Ethiopia 1885-1941) (Rome: C. E. N., 1968).

Virgin, Gen'l Eric. The Abyssinia I Knew (London: 1936). Translated from Swedish by N. Walford.

Vitali, Giovanni. Le guerre Italiane in Africa (Milan: 1936).

Volta, Sandro. Graziani a Neghelli (Florence: 1936).

Waley, D.   British Public Opinion and the Abyssinian War, 1935-36. (London, Maurice Temple Smith: 1975).

Walker, C. H.   "The Emperor of Abyssinia and his Army," Africa Observer, 4 (1935).

Water, Monk.   "The Battle of Amba Aradam," EO, 10: 3 (1966).

Weerts, Maurice L.   "The Late Mr. Antonin Besse and the Ethiopian Resistance during the years 1935-1940," JES, 8: 2 (1970).

Weisbord, R. G.   "Black America and the Italian-Ethiopian Crisis: an episode in Pan-Negroism," The Historian, 34: 2 (1972).

_____.   "British West Indian Reaction to the Italian-Ethiopian War: an episode in Pan-Africanism," Caribbean Studies, 10: 1 (1970).

Wesley, C. H.   "The Significance of the Italo-Ethiopian Question," Crisis, 18: 5 (1935).

Wilson, Hugh R.   For Want of a Nail.   The failure of the League of Nations in Ethiopia (New York, Vantage Press: 1959).

Wingate, O. C.   "Appreciation of the Ethiopian Campaign (1941)," EO, 15: 4 (1972).

Woolbert, R. G.   "Italy in Abyssinia," Foreign Affairs, 13: 3 (1935).

Woolf, Leonard S.   The League and Abyssinia (London, 1936).

Work, Ernest.   "Italo-Ethiopian Relations," J. Negro History, 20 (1935).

_____.   Ethiopia, A Pawn in European Diplomacy (Pvt. printing, New Concord, Ohio: 1935).

Wright, Patricia.   "Italy's African Dream," History Today, 23: 4 and 5 (1973).

Xylander, Rudolf.   La conquista dell'Abissinia (Milan: 1937).

Zangandri, R.   Il lungo viaggio attraverso il fascismo (Milan, Foltrinelli: 1962).

Zoli, Corrado.   La conquista dell'impero (Bologna: 1937).

Government and Political Analysis

Berket Habte Selassie.   "Constitutional Development in Ethiopia," J. African Law, 10 (1966).

_____ . The Executive in African Governments (London, Heinemann: 1974). 93-112.

Castagno, Alphonse. "Ethiopia: Reshaping an Autocracy," Africa
Report, 18: 9 (1963).

Clapham, Christopher. "The December 1960 Ethiopian Coup d'Etat,"
JMAS 6 (1968).

_____ . "Centralization and Local Response in Southern Ethiopia,"
African Affairs, 74: 294 (1975).

_____ . "The Functions and Development of Parliament in Ethiopia," P. 3rd ICES, vol. 3 (Addis Ababa: 1970).

_____   see Hayle Sellase

_____ . "Imperial Leadership in Ethiopia," African Affairs, 68:
(1968).

Cohen, John M. "Ethiopian provincial elites and the process of
change (Celalo awraja, Arussi)," JES, 11: 2 (1973).

"Constitution of 1931," EO, 5: 4 (1962).

"Constitution of 1955," EO, 5: 4 (1962).

"Development of the Ethiopian Constitution," EO, 5: 4 (1962).

Dow, Thomas E. and Peter Schwab. "Imperial Leadership in Contemporary Ethiopia," Genève-Afrique, 12: 1 (1973).

Ellis, Gene. "The Feudal Paradigm as a Hindrance to Understanding
Ethiopia," JMAS, 14: 2 (1976).

_____ . "Feudalism in Ethiopia: a further comment on paradigms
and their use," NAS, 1: 3 (1979-80).

"Ethiopia--Feudal Symbol of African Advance," Barclays Bank Review (Feb. 1965).

"The Ethiopian Budget," EO, 10: 3 (1966).

Ewing, W. H. "Some Observations on Ethiopian Legislative Development," P. 1st USCES (ASC, MSU: 1975).

"First Ethiopian General Election: The Electoral Law," EO, 1: 7
(1957).

Haberland, Eike. Untersuchungen zum äthiopischen Königtum (Wiesbaden: Franz Steiner Verlag: 1965).

Hadis Alemayehu. Ityopya Men Aynet Astedader Yasfelegetal (What type of Administration does Ethiopia Need?) (Addis Ababa: Berhanena Selam: 1974).

Hess, R. L. "The Ethiopian No-Party State," American Political Science Review, 58 (1964).

_____ see General Works

Howard, William E. H. Public Administration in Ethiopia; a study in retrospect and prospect (Groningen: J. B. Wolters: 1955).

Huntingford, G. W. B. "The Constitutional History of Ethiopia," JAH, 3: 2 (1962).

Ianni, Francis. "Ethiopia: a special case," in The Transformation of East Africa: Studies in Political Anthropology. Ed. S. Diamond and F. Burke (New York: 1966).

"Imperialism in Ethiopia," African Red Family, 1: 2 (1973).

Jandy, E. C. "Ethiopia Today: A Review of its Changes and Problems," Annals of the American Academy of Political and Social Sciences, 306 (July, 1956).

Johnson, Willene. "Food and Politics: A Case Study of Ethiopia," Horn of Africa, 2: 1 (1979).

Korten, D. C. and F. Planned Change in a Traditional Society: Psychological Problems of Modernization in Ethiopia (New York: Praeger: 1972).

Lefever, E. W. Spear and Scepter: Army, Police and Politics in Tropical Africa (Washington, D. C. , Brookings Institution: 1970). Chapter 4.

Legesse Lemma. "The Ethiopian Student Movement 1960-1974: a challenge to the monarchy and imperialism in Ethiopia," NAS, 1: 2 (1979).

Levine, D. M. "Class Consciousness and Class Solidarity in the New Ethiopian Elites," in The New Elites of Tropical Africa. Ed. P. C. Lloyd (London, OUP: 1966), 312-327.

_____. "The Roots of Ethiopian Nationhood," Africa Report, 16: 5 (1971).

_____. "Ethiopia: Identity, Authority and Realism," in Political Culture and Political Development. Ed. L. Pye and S. Verba (Princeton, PUP: 1965).

_____. "The Military in Ethiopian Politics: Capabilities and

Constraints," in The Military Intervenes: Case Studies in Political Development. Ed. Henry Bienen (New York, Russell
Sage Foundation: 1968).

Lewis, W. H. "Ethiopia: The Quickening Pulse," Current History,
54 (Feb. 1968).

_____. "The Ethiopian Empire: Progress and Problems,"
Middle East J. 10: 3 (1956).

_____. "Ethiopia's Revised Constitution," Middle East J., 10:
2 (1956).

Logan, Rayford W. "Ethiopia's Troubled Future," Current History,
44 (1963).

Markakis, John. "An Interpretation of Political Tradition in Ethiopia," Présence Africaine, 66 (1968).

_____. "Social Formation and Political Adaptation in Ethiopia,"
JMAS, 11: 3 (1973).

_____ and Asmelash Beyene. "Representative Institutions in
Ethiopia," JMAS, 5: 2 (1967).

_____ see General Works

Melesse Ayalew. "Beyond an Ideology of Powerlessness," in The
African Reader: Independent Africa. Ed. W. Cartey and M.
Kison (New York: Random House: 1970).

"The Military and Politics in Ethiopia," Strategic Survey 1974 (London, International Institute for Strategic Studies: 1975).

Nicolas, Dildas. "Peasant Rebellions in the Socio-Political Context
of Today's Ethiopia," Pan-African J., 7 (1974).

"The Order of 1966 Defining the Powers and Duties of Ministers,"
EO, 10: 1 (1966).

Paul, James C. and Christopher Clapham. Ethiopian Constitutional
Development: a sourcebook (Addis Ababa, Faculty of Law,
HSIU: 1966).

Perham, Margery see General Works

Ricci, L. "The Organization of the State and Social Structures in
Ethiopia," in Twentieth Century Africa. Ed. P. J. McEwan
(New York, OUP: 1968).

Rosen, Charles B. "The Governor-General of Tigre Province:
Structure and Antistructure," P. 1st USCES (ASC, MSU: 1975).

Schwab, Peter. "Rebellion in Ethiopia: a Study of Gojam Province," East African J., 6: 11 (1969).

Shepherd, Jack. Politics of Starvation (New York, Carnegie Endowment for International Peace: 1975).

International and Pan-African Relations

Abir, Mordechai. "The Contentious Horn of Africa," Conflict Studies, 24 (1972).

_____. "Red Sea Politics," Conflicts in Africa. #94 (London, International Institute for Strategic Studies: 1972).

Alype, P. Sous la couronne de Salomon. L'Empire des Negus de la reine de Saba à la Société des Nations (Paris: 1925).

Befekadu Tadessa. "Africa and the World," EO, (special issue, April 1958).

Bell, J. Bowyer. The Horn of Africa (New York, Crane, Russak Co.: 1973).

Bentwich, Norman. "Ethiopia at the Peace Conference," Pan-Africa, 1: 2 (1947).

Brown, D. J. L. "Ethiopia-Somaliland Frontier Dispute," International and Comparative Law Quarterly, 5 (1956).

_____. "Recent Developments in the Ethiopia-Somaliland Frontier Dispute," Ibid, 10 (1961).

Chukumba, Stephen U. The Big Powers against Ethiopia (Wash. D.C., University Press of America: 1977).

Clapham, Christopher. "Ethiopia and Somalia," Conflicts in Africa. #93. (London, International Institute for Strategic Studies: 1972).

Clifford, E. H. M. "The British Somaliland-Ethiopia Boundary," GJ 87 (1936).

Contee, Clarence G. "Ethiopia and the Pan-African Movement before 1945," Black World, 21: 4 (1972).

_____. "Ethiopia and the Pan-African Movement, 1945-1963," Negro History Bulletin, 33: 5 (1970).

Drysdale, John. "The Intractable Frontier," Twentieth-Century Africa. Ed. P. J. McEwan (New York, OUP: 1968).

_____. Somali Frontier Dispute (New York, Praeger: 1964).

"Effects of the Suez Crisis in Ethiopia," EO, 2: 7 (1958).

"Emperor Haile Sellassie." Visits to India, EO, 1: 6 (1957); 4: 10 (1960); in Ogaden, 1: 7 (1956); Tour of India, Burma, Japan, 1: 4 (1957); on Economic Commission for Africa, 3: 7 (1959); speech to Pan-African students, 3: 3 (1959); visits to Sudan, UAR, USSR, Czechoslovakia, Belgium, France, Portugal, West Germany and Yugoslavia, 3: 12 (1960); visit from Kwame Nkrumah, 4: 1 (1960); world tour, 4: 2 (1960); United Nations address, 7: 4 Part 1 (1964); East African visits, 8: 2 (1964); visit to China 14: 4 (1971); speech to O. A. U., 4: 9 and 10: 3 (1966); visit of Queen of Holland, 12: 4 (1969); visit of Queen Elizabeth, 9: 1 (1965).

Endalkachew Makonnen. "Ethiopia at the Security Council: the speeches of H. E. Endalkachew Makonnen," EO, 13: 2 (1970).

_____. "Ethiopia's Role in Africa and the World," EO (special issue April 1958).

_____. "Ethiopia and Africa; the Economic Aspect," EO, 8: 2 (1964).

"Ethiopia--Ex-Italian Somaliland Boundary: the Treaty of 1908," EO, 1: 9 (1957).

Farer, Tom J. War Clouds on the Horn of Africa: a Crisis for Detente (N. Y. and Wash., D. C., Carnegie Endowment for International Peace: 1976).

Fechter, Rudolf. "History of German Ethiopian Diplomatic Relations," ZK, (1973).

Gayda, V. Italia, Inghilterra, Etiopia (Rome: 1936).

Gross, Ernest A.; D. P. de Villiers; Endalkatchew Makonnen; and R. A. Falk. Ethiopia and Liberia vs. South Africa: The South West Africa Case. (Los Angeles, California; African Studies Center, UCLA: 1968).

Gulavi, S. J. "The Development of Friendship between Ethiopia and her Southern Neighbour," EO, 3: 3 (1959).

Haggag, J., and R. J. H. Church. "Ethiopia, Eritrea, and Somalia," GR, 43 (1953).

Hamilton, David. "Imperialism Ancient and Modern: a study of

English attitudes to Sovereignty on the Northern Somali Coastline, " JES, 5: 2 (1957).

_____. "Schedule of International Agreements Relating to the Boundaries of Ethiopia, " EO, 16: 2 (1973).

"The Horn: Somalia Calculates Anew, " Africa Confidential (Feb. 1979). Reprinted Horn of Africa, 2: 1 (1979).

Hoskyns, Catherine, ed. The Ethiopia-Somalia-Kenya Dispute 1960-1967. (Case Studies in African Diplomacy, no. 2, Dar-es-Salaam, OUP: 1969).

Jaenen, C. J. "The Case for a Federated Somalia, " EO, 9: 3 (1963).

King, K. J. "Some Notes on Arnold J. Ford and New World Black Attitudes to Ethiopia, " JES, 10: 1 (1972).

Labrousse, H. "La Neutralité Ethiopienne pendant la première Guerre Mondiale: l'incident Holtz-Karmelich (1917), " P. 5th ICES (Chicago: 1979).

"Letter from Jeddah: an interview with Western Somali Liberation Front, " [by an 'American Professor'], Horn of Africa, 1: 2 (1978).

Mamo Zeleke. "Ethiopie: Machine de guerre contre la Somali, " Afrique Asie, 29 (1973).

_____. "Kagnew: Rester ou partir?" Afrique Asie, 47 (1974).

Manheim, F. J. "The United States and Ethiopia: a study in American Imperialism, " J. Negro History, 17 (1932).

Marcus, Harold. "Transitions; Britain, America and Ethiopia (1941-1961). " (in press--CUP)

Mesfin Wolde Mariam. "The Background of the Ethio-Somalia Boundary Dispute, " JMAS, 2: 2 (1964).

Morgan, Edward. "The 1977 Elections in Djibouti: a tragi-comic end to French Colonial rule, " Horn of Africa, 1: 3 (1978).

Oudes, Bruce. "Viewpoint: The Lion of Judah and the Lambs of Washington, " Africa Report, 16: 5 (1971).

Pankhurst, Richard. "Controversies on the Horn of Africa, " EO, 1: 1 (1956).

_____. "Ethiopia, Africa and the United Nations, " EO (special issue, April 1958).

_____. "Ethiopia and League of Nations Sanctions," EO, 10: 1 (1966).

Pankhurst, Sylvia. "Ethiopia, Africa and the League of Nations," EO, (special issue, April 1958).

_____. "Ethiopia's Part in the Geophysical Year," EO, 2: 7 (1958).

_____. "Somaliland Problems," EO, 1: 1 (1956) and 9: 3 (1958).

Pierre-Alype, F. J. see Listing under History (B) c. 1760-c. 1930

Potholm, Christian P. Liberation and Exploitation: The Struggle for Ethiopia (Washington, D. C., University Press of America: 1976).

Reisman, W. M. "The Case of Western Somaliland: an international legal perspective," Horn of Africa, 1: 3 (1978).

Rubenson, Sven. "The Genesis of the Ethio-Somali Conflict," P. 5th ICES (Chicago: 1979).

Said Yusuf Abdi. "The Mini-Republic of Djibouti: problems and prospects," Horn of Africa, 1: 2 (1978).

_____. "Self Determination for Ogaden Somalis," Horn of Africa, 1: 1 (1978).

Shinn, David. "A Survey of American-Ethiopian Relations Prior to the Italian Occupation of Ethiopia," EO, 14: 4 (1971).

Silberman, Leo. "Ethiopia: Power of Moderation," Middle East J., 14: 2 (1960).

Skordiles, K. Kagnew: the story of the Ethiopian Fighters in Korea (Tokyo, Radiopress: 1954).

Spencer, J. H. Ethiopia, the Horn of Africa and U.S. Policy (Institute for Foreign Policy Analysis Inc., Cambridge, Mass.: 1977).

_____. "A Reassessment of Ethiopian-Somali Conflict," Horn of Africa, 1: 3 (1978).

_____. "Ethiopia, the Horn of Africa and U.S. Policy," IJAHS, 11: 3 (1977).

Thompson, Virginia, and R. Adloff. Djibouti and the Horn of Africa (Stanford UP, Calif.: 1968).

Thompson, W. Scott. "The American-African Nexus in Soviet Strategy," Horn of Africa, 1: 1 (1978).

Thurston, R. L. "The United States, Somalia, and the Crisis in the Horn," Horn of Africa, 1: 2 (1978).

Vali, Ferenc A. Politics of the Indian Ocean Region: the Balances of Power (New York, The Free Press: 1976).

Work, Ernest. Ethiopia: A Pawn in European Diplomacy (New York, Macmillan: 1935).

Yakobson, Sergius. The Soviet Union and Ethiopia: a case of Traditional Behavior (Indiana, The University of Notre Dame Press: 1965).

Yodfat, Ayreh. "The Soviet Union and the Horn of Africa," NAS, 1: 3 (1979) and 2: 1 (1980).

Yonas Kebede. "Legal Aspects of Ethiopian-Somali Dispute," Horn of Africa, 1: 1 (1978).

AGRICULTURE, LAND TENURE, RURAL DEVELOPMENT
(with a selected listing under "Coffee")

Abate Temesgen see Goering

Afanasiev, Michel. Trial of Indigenous and Exotic Trees in Harar Province (Alemaya Experiment Station Bulletin, 16 (n. d.).

Aklilu Afework see Goering

Ambaye Zekarias. Land Tenure in Eritrea (Addis Ababa, Addis Printing Press: 1966).

"American Cooperation in Agricultural Education and Research," EO, 1: 10 (1957).

Assefa Dula. "Land Tenure in Chercher Province," EO, 12: 2 (1969).

"Bela Tit Fetai (Diabaco Cotton Company)," EO, 1: 5 (1957).

Berhanou Abbebe. Evolution de la propriéte foncière au Choa (Ethiopie) (Paris: 1971).

Betru Gebregziabher. Integrated Development in Rural Ethiopia: an Evaluative Study of the Chilalo Agricultural Development Unit (Indiana University, Bloomington, Indiana: 1975).

Bieber, F. J. "Die Bodenkultur in Kaffa," DRGS, 31 (1909).

"Bishoftu Agricultural Research Station," EO, 1: 10 (1957).

Brown, Leslie H. Conservation for Survival: Ethiopia's Choice
(Addis Ababa, HSIU: 1973).

Capucci, Luigi. "Condizioni dell'agricoltura nello Scioa," BSAI, 6
(1887) and 7 (1888).

Carlson, Dennis G. "Eucalyptus Trees, Tin Roofs and Intra-uterine
Devices: Indicators of Modernization in Traditional Rural Ethiopian Community," P. 1st USCES, MSU, 1973.

Christensen, H. Fertilizer and Variety Trials and Demonstrations in
Ethiopia, 1972-73 (Addis Ababa, Ministry of Agriculture: 1973).

Coffee
       "An Evaluation of Ethiopia's Production and Consumption of
           Coffee," EER, 6 (April, 1963).

       "Coffee not Derived from Ethiopia," EO, 4: 6 (1960).

       "Coffee Production and its Problems," EO, 4: 6 (1960).

       "Coffee, the Main Crop," EO, 2: 7 (1958).

       "Ethiopian Coffee," EO, 4: 6 (1960).

       "The Ethiopian Coffee Board," EO, 4: 6 (1960).

       "Ethiopia's Coffee Problems," EO, 2: 7 (1958).

       "How Ethiopian Coffee Spread Through the World," EO, 4: 6 (1960).

       Cortesi, F. "Il caffe etiopico," Gli Annali dell'Africa
           Italiana, 1 (1939).

       Pankhurst, Sylvia. "Coffee Cultivation and Processing," EO,
           1: 10 (1957).

       Schumacher, Gunther. Der Kaffeeanbau in Äthiopien (Köln:
           Kölnische Verlagsdruckerie, 1963).

       Siemienski, Z. "Impact of the Coffee Boom on Ethiopia,"
           Middle East Journal, 9: 1 (1955).

       Sylvain, Pierre G. "Ethiopian Coffee; its significance to World
           Coffee Problems," Economic Botany (1958).

       Taye Gulilat. "Coffee in the Ethiopian Economy," University
           College Review (Addis Ababa), 1: 1 (1961). Part 2 in JES,
           1: 1 (1963).

       Teketel Haile-Mariam. "The Impact of Coffee on the Economy
           of Ethiopia," Commodity Exports and African Economic De-
           velopment. Eds. Scott R. Pearson and John Cownie (Lex-
           ington, Mass., Lexington Books: 1974).

Vayssière, Paul. "L'Ethiopie, pays d'origine du caféier d'Arabie," Café-cacao-thé, 2 (1961).

Winid, J. B. "The History of Ethiopian Coffee," African Bulletin (Warsaw), 10 (1969).

Cohen, John M. "Rural Change in Ethiopia: The Chilalo Agricultural Development Unit," Economic Development and Cultural Change, 22 (1974).

_____. "Ethiopia after Haile Selassie: the government land factor," African Affairs, 72: 289 (1973).

_____. "Effects of Green Revolution Strategies on Tenants and Small-scale Landowners in the Chilalo Region of Ethiopia," J. of Developing Areas, 9: 3 (1975).

Demissie Gebre, Michael. Land Tenure in Bale (Dire Dawa, College of Agricultural and Mechanical Arts, HSIU: 1966).

Dessalegn Rahmato. "Conditions of the Ethiopian Peasantry," Challenge, 10: 2 (1970).

"Dilemma of Famine in Ethiopia," Combat, 2: 2 (1974).

Dimbleby, Jonathan. "Too Little, Too Late," Atlas World Press Review, 21: 5 (1974).

Disney, Richard. "Some Measures of Rural Income Distribution in Ethiopia," Development and Change, 7 (1976).

Dula Abdu. "Land Reform in Ethiopia: a Prelude to Socialist Development," P. 5th ICES (Chicago, 1979).

Dunning, H. C. "Land Reform in Ethiopia: A Case of Non-Development," UCLA Law Review, 18: 2 (1970).

Ellis, Gene. "Agricultural Development Strategy in Ethiopia: on reaching the peasant sector," P. 1st USCES, MSU, 1973.

_____. "Land Tenancy Reform in Ethiopia: a retrospective analysis," P. 5th ICES, Chicago, 1978.

"Ethiopian Tobacco Monopoly," EO, 1: 5 (1957).

"Famine in Ethiopia--the Starving Granary of the Middle East," African Red Family, 1: 5-6, 1974 (?).

Gebre-wold Ingida Worq. "Ethiopia's Traditional System of Land Tenure and Taxation," EO, 5: 4 (1962).

Gentry, R. L. Wheat Research: Debre Zeit and Alemaya 1955-1962 (Experiment Station Bulletin, 28 (n. d.) Research Department of College of Agriculture, Alemaya, Harar).

Gill, G.   Readings on the Ethiopian Economy (Addis Ababa, Institute
     of Development Research: 1974).

_____.   "Improving Traditional Ethiopian Farming Methods: Mis-
     conceptions, Bottlenecks, and Blind Alleys," Rural Africana,
     28 (1975).

Goering, T. J.; Aklilu Afework; and Abate Temesgen.   "The Re-
     sponse of Ethiopian Farmers to Changes in Product Prices,"
     EO, 15: 3 (1972).

Goldsmith, A. A.   see   Cohen

Green, D. A. G.   Ethiopia: An Economic Analysis of Technological
     Change Four Agricultural Production Systems (East Lansing,
     Michigan; ASC, MSU: 1974).

Haile Menkerios.   "The Present System of Land Tenure in Ethiopia:
     an introduction," Challenge, 10: 2 (1970).

Haile Selassie I.   "Ethiopia's Second Five Year Plan and envisaged
     Land Reform," (speech).   EO, 6: 4 (1963).

Hapte-ab Bairu.   "The Livestock Processing Industry," EO, 4: 4
     (1960).

"Harar Agricultural College," EO, 1: 2 (1957).

Harbeson, J. W.   "Afar Pastoralists and Ethiopian Rural Develop-
     ment," Rural Africana, 28 (1975).

Hoben, Allan.   Land Tenure Among the Amhara of Ethiopia: the
     Dynamics of Cognatic Descent (Chicago, UC Press: 1973).

_____.   "Land Tenure and Social Mobility among the Damot Am-
     hara," P. 3rd ICES, Addis Ababa, 1966.   Vol. 3 (1970).

_____.   "Social Anthropology and Development Planning--a case
     study in Ethiopian Land Reform Policy," JMAS, 10: 4 (1972).

Holm, Henrietta M.   The Agricultural Economy of Ethiopia (USGPO:
     1956).

Huffnagel, H. P., ed.   Agriculture in Ethiopia (Rome, FAO: 1961).

"Imperial College of Agricultural and Mechanical Arts," EO, 1: 10
     (1957).

Jones, David R. H.   "Some Aspects of Eritrean Fruit Production,"
     Sudan Notes and Records, 46 (1965).

Karsten, Detlev.   "Entwicklungstendenzen der Ethiopischen Wirts-
     chaft," ZK (1973).

Koehn, Peter. "Ethiopia: Famine, Food Production, and Changes in the Legal Order," ASR, 22: 1 (1979).

Lalevich, D. and I. "Agricultural Possibilities of the Awash River Valley," EO, 2: 10 (1958).

"Land Distribution and Farm Financing," EO, 4: 12 (1961).

"Land Tenure and Taxation from Ancient to Modern Times," EO, 1: 9 (1957).

Lawrence, J. D. C. and H. S. Mann. "F.A.O. Land Policy Project (Ethiopia)," EO, 9: 4 (1966).

Mahteme Selassie Wolde Maskal. "The Land System of Ethiopia," EO, 1: 9 (1957).

Mellor, J. W. see Cohen

Nadel, S. F. "Land Tenure on the Eritrean Plateau," Africa, 18: 1 (1946).

Nekby, B. CADU: An Ethiopian Experiment in Development Peasant Farming (Stockholm, Prisma: 1971).

Nicholson, G. E. Cotton in Ethiopia (Addis Ababa, Ministry of Agriculture: 1956).

Odorizzi, Dante. "Notizie sull'ordinamento della proprietà terriera in Etiopia e nella Zona Abissina della Colonie Eritrea," BSAI, 25 (1906).

Olmstead, Judith. "Agricultural Land and Social Stratification in the Gamu Highland of Southern Ethiopia," P. 1st USCES, MSU, 1973. (1975)

Orent, Amnon. "From the Hoe to the Plow: a study in Ecological Adaptation," P. 5th ICES, Chicago, 1978.

Ottaway, Marina. "Land Reform in Ethiopia, 1974-1977," ASR, 20: 3 (1977).

Pankhurst, Richard. "Ethiopian Agriculture," EO, 1: 10 (1957).

_____. "Notes for a History of Ethiopian Agriculture," EO, 7: 3 (1964).

Pankhurst, Sylvia. "Agricultural Extension Services," EO, 3: 2 (1959).

_____. "Agricultural Station at Debra Zeit," EO, 3: 2 (1959).

_____. "Ambo Agricultural School," EO, 1: 10 (1957).

_____. "Ethiopian Agriculture in Retrospect and Prospect," EO, 1: 9 (1957).

_____. "Farmer on whom the Ethiopian Economy Depends," EO, 4: 4 (1960).

Pausewang, Siegfried. "Land, Market, and Rural Society (Rural Ethiopia 1840-1976)," P. 5th ICES, Chicago, 1978.

Pike, Clarence E. "Ethiopia's Expanding Agriculture," Foreign Agriculture, 2: 4 (1956).

Pittwell, L. R. ; Haile Sellassie Gebregzie; Solomon Jiru. "Trace Elements in Some Ethiopian Food Grains," EO, 15: 1 (1972).

Reimer, Richard. "Ethiopian Agricultural Exports: a brief survey," RA, 28 (1975).

Rouk, Hugh F. , and Haile Mengesha. The Cultivated Sorghums of Ethiopia, Ethiopia Civet (Civettictis Civetta), and An Introduction to T'ef (Eragrostis Abyssinica Schard): A Nutritious Cereal Grain of Ethiopia (Experiment Station Bulletins, 6, 21 and 26; Research Dept. of College of Agriculture, Alemaya, Harar).

Rowse, E. A. "The Tibilla Estate of the Prize Trust," EO, 8: 2 (1964).

Savouré, A. L'Abyssinie agricole (Addis Ababa, Imprimerie Ethiopienne: 1912).

Schiller, A. A. "Customary Land Tenure Among the Highland Peoples of Northern Ethiopia: a Bibliographic Essay," African Law Studies, 1 (1969).

Seleshi Sisaye. "The Role of Social Sciences in Rural Development Planning: the case of Ethiopia," ASR, 21: 3 (1978).

Shiberu, W. Mariam. Development of a Castor Bean Sheller for Ethiopian Farmers (Experiment Station Bulletin, 25; Research Department of College of Agriculture, Alemaya, Harar).

"Slaughterhouse," EO, 1: 5 (1957).

Stahl, M. Contradictions in Agricultural Development: a study of Three Minimum Package Projects in Southern Ethiopia (Uppsala, Scandinavian Institute of African Studies: 1973).

_____. Ethiopia: Political Contradictions in Agricultural Development (Uppsala: 1976; Distributed by Africana Pub. Co. , New York).

Stiehler, W. "Studien zur Landwirtschafts--und Siedlungsgeographie Äthiopiens," Erdkunde, 2: 4/6 (1948).

"Sugar Production, " EO, 2: 7 (1957).

Tesfai Tecle. The Evolution of Alternative Rural Development
    Strategies in Ethiopia: Implications for Employment and in-
    come Distribution (East Lansing, Michigan; Department of
    Agricultural Economics, MSU: 1975).

_____. "An approach to Rural Development: a case study of the
    Ethiopian Package Projects, " RA, 28 (1975).

"To Awasa, a Future City, Farming and Cadastral Survey, " EO, 4:
    12 (1961).

Watson, R. "The Food and Agriculture Organization in Ethiopia, "
    EO, 2: 9 (1958).

Wells, Milton. Selection and Breeding for Improved Performance of
    Livestock (Experiment Station Bulletin, 19; Research Depart-
    ment College of Agriculture, Alemaya, Harar).

Westphal, E. Agricultural Systems in Ethiopia (Agricultural Research
    Reports, 826: Centre for Agricultural Publishing and Documen-
    tation, Wageningen, Netherlands, 1975).

"Wheat for Ethiopia, " EO, 3: 1 (1959).

Wolf, J. D. Commercial Poultry Production in Ethiopia (Experi-
    ment Station Bulletin, 12; Research Department of College of
    Agriculture, Alemaya, Harar).

Young, Maurice de. "The Internal Marketing of Agricultural Pro-
    ducts and its Influence on Agricultural Productivity and In-
    come, " EO, 11: 1 (1967).

ARTS, ARCHITECTURE, MUSIC

"Afewerk Tekle, " (editorial), EO, 6: 3 (1962), and interview, EO,
    7: 4 (1964).

Alemayehu Bizuneh see Chojnacki, S.

Ashenafi Kebede. "The Krar, " EO, 11: 3 (1967).

_____. "Musical Innovation and Acculturation in Ethiopian Cul-
    ture, " #79-51 ASA, Brandeis U., Waltham, Mass.

Ayele Tekle Haymanot. "Indagine sulle origini della città' santa di
    Lalibela, " Sestante, 4 (1968).

Barriviera, L. Bianchi. "Le chiese in roccia di Lalibela e di altri
    luoghi del Lasta, " RSE, 19 (1963).

Berhan Mehary <u>see</u> Chojnacki, S.

Bidder, Irmgard. <u>Lalibela</u> (Cologne; DuMont Schauberg: 1958).

Buxton, David. "Ethiopian architecture in the Middle Ages,"
    <u>Churches in Rock: Early Christian Art in Ethiopia</u>. Ed.
    Georg Gerster (London, Phaidon; 1970).

_____. "Ethiopian Medieval Architecture--the present state of
studies," <u>JSS</u>, 9 (1964).

_____. "Ethiopian rock-hewn churches," <u>Antiquity</u>, 20 (1946).

Cassièrs, Anne. "Ethiopian Pottery," <u>African Arts</u>, 4: 3 (1971).

Cerulli, E. "Il Gesu percosso nell'arte etiopica," <u>RSE</u>, 6: 2
    (1947).

Chojnacki, Stanislaw. "Alemayehu Bizuneh," <u>EO</u>, 14: 4 (1971).

_____. "Berhane Mehary," <u>EO</u>, 14: 2 (1971).

_____. "Gebre Kristos Desta," <u>EO</u>, 11: 3 (1967) and 14: 1
(1971).

_____. "The Iconography of Saint George in Ethiopia," <u>JES</u>, 11:
1 and 2 (1973) and 12: 1 (1974).

_____. "The Nativity in Ethiopian Art," <u>JES</u>, 12: 2 (1974).

_____. "Note on the early Iconography of St. George and related
Equestrian Saints in Ethiopia," <u>JES</u>, 8: 2 (1975).

_____. "Notes on Art in Ethiopia in the 15th and early 16th
Century," <u>JES</u>, 8: 2 (1970).

_____. "Notes on Art in Ethiopia in the 16th Century," <u>JES</u>,
9: 2 (1971).

_____. "Notes on a Lesser-known type of St. Mary in Ethiopian
Painting," <u>Abba Salama</u>, 1 (1970).

_____. "A Short Introduction to Ethiopian Painting," <u>JES</u>, 2: 2
(1964).

_____. "Skunder: His first Addis Ababa Exhibition," <u>EO</u>, 10:
3 (1966).

_____. "A Survey of Modern Ethiopian Art," <u>ZK</u> (1973).

_____. "Note on the early imagery of the Virgin Mary in Ethio-
pia," <u>Ethnologische Zeitschrift Zurich</u>, 2 (1977).

Conti Rossini, C. "Incisioni Rupestri all'Hagghar, " RSE, 3 (1943).

Cowen, Chester R. "Wooden Sculpture among the Konso and Gato of Southern Ethiopia, " P. 5th ICES, Chicago, 1978.

Findlay, Louis. The Monolithic Churches of Lalibela in Ethiopia (Cairo, Société d'Archéologie Copte: 1944).

"Gebre Kristos Desta. " See S. Chojacki, Solomon Deressa and Sidney Head, also EO, 14: 1 (1971).

Gerster, Georg. L'Art Ethiopien (Boston, Newbury Books: 1969).

_____, ed. of Churches in Rock: Early Christian Art in Ethiopia with contributions by David R. Buxton, Ernst Hammerschmidt, Jean Leclant, Jules Leroy, Roger Schneider, André Caquot, Antonio Mordini and Roger Sauter. Trans. by Richard Hosking of German edition of 1972.

Gigar Tesfaye see Travel and Description

Head, Sydney. "Art Exhibition of 40 Paintings by Gabre Kristos, " EO, 4: 11 (1966).

Heldman, Marilyn E. "Christ's Entry into Jerusalem, " P. 1st USCES, MSU, 1973.

_____. "The Kibran Gospels: Ethiopia and Byzantium, " P. 5th ICES, Chicago, 1978.

Jager, Otto A. "Ethiopian Manuscript Painting, " EO, 4: 11 (1960).

Keller, Conrad. "Uber Maler und Malerei in Abessinien, " JGEG, 4 (1903-04).

Kifle Beseat. An Introduction to Abstract Painting in Ethiopia (Addis Ababa, United Printers: 1970).

Kimberlin, Cynthia Tse. "The Bägänna of Ethiopia, " EN, 2: 2 (1978).

Krafft, Walter. "Kirchenbauten in Athiopien, " ZK (1973).

Lepage, C. "Découverte d'un art étonnant: Les églises éthiopiennes du Xe au XVIe siècles, " Archeologia, 64 (1973).

_____. "Histoire de l'ancienne peinture ethiopienne, " Comptes-rendus des Séances de l'Académie des Inscriptions et Belles-Lettres (Avril-juin 1977).

Leroy, Jules. "Les étapes de la peinture éthiopienne révélées par les manuscrits illustrés et les églises peintes, " JSS, 9: 1 (1964).

_____ . Ethiopian Painting (New York, Praeger: 1967).

_____ . "Notes d'archéologie et d'iconographie étiopiennes, " AE,
6 (1965).

_____ . See also G. Gerster, Churches in Rock.

Lindahl, Bernard. Architectural History of Ethiopia in Pictures
(Addis Ababa, The Ethio-Swedish Institute of Building Technology: 1970).

Matthew, A. F. "The Monolithic churches of Yekka, " JES, 7: 2
(1968).

Matthews, D. H. "The Restoration of the Monastery Church of
Debra Damo, " Antiquity, 23 (1949).

Menghestu Lemma. "Snatch and Run (a play) on Marriage by Ab-
duction, " EO, 7: 4, Part 2 (1964).

Mohammad Ali. (art work) EO, 14: 3 (1971).

Mondon-Vidhaillet, C. "La musique éthiopienne, " Encyclopédie de
la Musique et Dictionnaire du Conservatoire, 5 (Paris: 1922).

Monti della Corte, A. A. I Castelli di Gondar (Rome: 1938).

Mordini, Antonio. "L'architecture religieuse chrétienne dans
l'Ethiopie du moyen age; un programme de recherches, " Cahiers d'Etudes Africaines, 2: 5 (1961).

_____ . "Un riparo sotto roccia con pitture rupestri nell'Amba
Focada, " RSE, 1 (1941).

_____ . "Il soffitto del secondo vestibolo dell'Enda abuna Aragāwe
in Debra Dammô, " RSE, 6 (1947).

_____ . "La chiesa di Aramô, " RSE, 15 (1960).

_____ . "Informazioni preliminari sui risultate delle mie ricerche
in Etiopia dal 1939 al 1944, " RSE, 4 (1946).

_____ . See also chapter in G. Gerster's Churches in Rock.

Pankhurst, Richard. "Ethiopian Manuscript Illustrations: The Four
Evangelists, " EO, 9: 2 (1965).

_____ . "Some Notes for a history of Ethiopian secular art, " EO,
10: 1 (1966).

_____ . "Queen of Sheba in European Art, " EO, 1: 6 (1957).

_____ . "Traditional Ethiopian Art, " EO, 5: 4 (1961).

Bibliography 328

Pankhurst, Sylvia. "Imrahanna Kristos," EO, 4: 7 (1960).

_____. "The Monolithic Churches of Lalibela," EO, 4: 7 (1960).

_____. "The Changing Face of Addis Ababa," EO, 4: 5 (1960).

Pearce, Ivy. "An Andrews Adventure and Pearce's Pilgrimage to the Cave and rock churches of Lasta," EO, 12: 3 (1969).

_____. "The Cave, Rock-Hewn churches of Goreme, Turkey and the Cave and Rock-Hewn Churches of Tigre, Ethiopia," EO, 13: 1 (1970).

_____. "Pearce's Pilgrimage to the Rock-Hewn Churches of Tigre," EO, 11: 2 (1967).

Plant, Ruth. "Notes on 17 Newly discovered Rock-Hewn Churches of Tigre," EO, 16: 1 (1973).

_____. "Painter's Pattern Book, Makelle, Tigre Province, Ethiopia," EO, 17: 3 (1973).

_____. "Rock-hewn Churches of the Tigre Province. Additional Churches by David R. Buxton," EO, 13: 3 (1969).

_____. "Ancient and Medieval Architecture of Tigre Province in the Light of Present Evidence," P. 5th ICES, Chicago, 1978.

Playne, Beatrice. "In Search of Early Christian Paintings in Ethiopia," GM, 8 (1950).

Sárosi, Bálint. "Melodic Patterns in the Folk Music of the Ethiopian People," P. 3rd ICES, Addis Ababa, 1966, Vol. 2.

"Skunder Bogassian," see Chojnacki

Solomon Deressa. "Skunder: In Retrospect Precociously," EO, 10: 3 (1966).

Staude, W. "Les Peintures de l'église d'Abba Antoine, Gondar, Abyssinie," Gazette des Beaux-Arts (1934).

Stratton, Howard Fremont. "Coptic Art: Its Origin and Transfer into the Arabic," Art and Archaeology, 23: 6 (1927).

Talbot, David. "The Art of Gabre Kristos Desta," EO, 9: 4 (1966).

Tewelde Medhin Joseph, Abba. "Introduction générale aux églises monolithes du Tigraï," P. 3rd ICES, Addis Ababa, 1966, vol. 1.

"Traditional Ethiopian Art in Pictures," EO, 5: 4 (1962).

Tsegaye Gebre Medhin. "Azmari," EO, 9: 3, part 2 (1965).

_____. "Tewodros," EO, 9: 3, part 2 (1965).

_____. Collision of Altars; a play set in sixth century Axum
    (London, Rex Collins: 1976).

Tubiana, J. "Peintures populaires éthiopienne," Revue Municipale
    d'Antibes et de Juan-les Pins, 5 (Oct.-Dec. 1979).

UNESCO, Ethiopia: illuminated Manuscripts (Distributed by New
    York Graphic Society, 1961).

Villard, U. Monneret de. "Note sulle più antiche miniature abis-
    sine," Orientalia, 8 (1939).

Warren, H. and A. "The Film Artist in a Developing Nation:
    Ethiopia," Horn of Africa, 1: 1 (1978).

"Yohannes Tessema," Agricultural Scenes by. EO, 8: 3 (1964).

                COMMUNICATIONS, MEDIA, TRANSPORT

Abel, Alfred, and Pasteau, M. "Arrival of the first aeroplane in
    Ethiopia," JES, 10: 2 (1972).

Aleme Eshete. "A Page in the History of Posts and Telegraphs in
    Ethiopia: 1899-1903," JES, 8: 2 (1975).

Arens, Gustav. See listing under Missions, for history of printed
    books.

"A Brief History of the Imperial Highway Authority," EO, 5: 2
    (1961).

Burdick, C. C. "Highways in Ethiopia," EO, 1: 12 (1957).

Coles, R. L., and J. J. Heierle. "International Civil Aviation in
    Ethiopia," EO, 2: 9 (1958).

"The Development of Telecommunications," EO, 4: 5 (1960).

Dubois, H. P. Cheminot de Djibouti a Addis-Abeba, le chemin de
    fer franco-éthiopien (Paris, Librairie Académique Perrin:
    1959).

"Ethiopian Civil Aviation Department," EO, 2: 1 (1957).

Gabriel Tedros, Girma Dessalegn, Kidane Wolde Georgis et al.
    "International Telecommunications Union in Ethiopia," EO, 2:
    9 (1958).

Geiger, Theodore. TWA's Services to Ethiopia (Wash. D.C.,
National Planning Association: 1959).

Gilmour, T. L. See reference under History (B).

Head, Sydney. "The Beginnings of Broadcast Audience Research in
Ethiopia," JES, 6: 2 (1968).

"The Imperial Highway Authority," EO, 5: 3 (1961).

"The Initiation of Ethiopia's Postal Service," EO, 2: 1 (1957).

Kollbrunner, Ulrich. "Die Eisenbahn von Djibouti nach Harar,"
JGEG, 4 (1903-1904).

Le Hérissé, ?. Rapport fait au nom de la commission des affairs
extérieures, des protectorats et des colonies chargée d'examiner
le projet de loi relatif au chemin de fer de Djibouti à Addis
Abeba. (Chambre des Députés, No. 2362, annexe au procès-
verbal de la séance du 5 mars 1909).

Loepfe, W. See his listing under History (B).

Lovelace, A. E. "Ethiopian Airlines and Tourism," EO, 5: 3 (1961).

_____. "The History of the Ethiopian Airlines," EO, 5: 3 (1961).

Marcus, Harold. See listing under Bibliographies. There are more
than 100 references to the history of the railroad; and others
on the postal service, telegraph and telephone in the index to
this volume.

Olagnier, G., and A. Hesse. La concession du chemin de fer
franco-éthiopien. (Paris, Librairie génerale de droit et de juris-
prudence: 1921).

Pankhurst, Richard. "Internal Freight," EO, 5: 3 (1961).

_____. "Transport and Communications in Ethiopia, 1835-1935,"
J. Transport History, 5: 2-3 (1961-62).

_____. See listing under Education for reference on history of
printing, etc.

Pankhurst, Sylvia. "Ethiopian Telecommunications," EO, 2: 1
(1957).

_____. "Imperial Highway Authority," EO, 1: 12 (1957).

_____. "The Initiation of Ethiopia's Wireless Communications,"
EO, 2: 1 (1957).

_____. "Road Transport for Passengers and Freight," EO, 1:
12 (1957).

_____. "Telephone Service 1894-1935," EO, 2: 1 (1957).

_____. "Training for Road Construction and Maintenance," EO, 1: 12 (1957).

Schimberg, A. W. "Highways in Ethiopia: an introduction," EO, 5: 2 (1961).

Tristan, H. "Les relations postale de l'Ethiopie," Revue de l'Académie de Philatée, 7: 35, 38 (1968) and 9: 43 (1970).

Zanutto, S. See listing under Bibliographies for periodical printing.

ECONOMY, BUSINESS, TRADE, LABOR

Abir, M. See listings under History c. 1760-c. 1930.

Ahooja, Krishna. "The Bank of Abyssinia: a portrait," EO, 8: 4 (1965).

_____. "Banking Legislation in Ethiopia," EO, 8: 4 (1965).

_____. "The Banks of Modern Ethiopia," EO, 8: 4 (1965).

_____. See listing under Law.

Assefa Bequele and Eshetu Chole. A Profile of the Ethiopian Economy (Addis Ababa, OUP: 1969).

_____. "The State of the Ethiopian Economy: a structural survey," Dialogue, 1: 1 (1967) and 1: 2 (1968).

_____. See listing under Education.

Austen, Ralph A. "The Islamic Red Sea Slave Trade: an effort at Quantification," P. 5th ICES (Chicago: 1979). (Covers data from 970s to 1920s.)

"The Banking Proclamations of 1963," EO, 8: 4 (1965).

Baudissin, G. "An Introduction to Labour Developments in Ethiopia," JEL, 2: 1 (1965).

Brietzke P. H. see Harbeson below.

"Census of Industrial Production," EO, 2: 7 (1958).

Cherian, K. A., ed. Agriculture, Industry and Commerce in Ethiopia and Eritrea (Asmara: 1957).

"Co-operative Technical and Economic Programmes of the Imperial Ethiopian Government and Point Four," EO, 3: 1 (1959).

"The Dam: [Koka]: Its Power and Potentialities," EO, 4: 8 (1960); see also EO, 2: 7 (1958).

Debebe H. Yohannes. "The Addis Ababa Bank," EO, 8: 4 (1965).

"The Development Bank," EO, 8: 4 (1965).

Duggar, J. W. "Monetary Development in Ethiopia since 1931," EO, 10: 3 (1966).

Duri Mohammed. "Private Foreign Investment in Ethiopia (1950-1968)," JES, 7: 2 (1969).

Eshetu Chole. "Taxation and Economic Development in Ethiopia," EO, 11: 1 (1967).

_____. See also Assefa Bequele.

"Ethiopia: an Economic Survey," African Development, 8: 5 (1974).

"Ethiopia: The Spotlight Country," African Business, 1: 1 (1967).

"Ethiopian Currency and Exchange Control Proclamations," EO, 8: 4 (1965).

"Ethiopian Exports and Imports," EO, 2: 7 (1958).

"Ethiopian Handicraft Industry," EO, 2: 7 (1958).

"The Ethiopian Investment Corporation," EO, 10: 1 (1966).

"The Ethiopian Population and Economic Planning," EO, 5: 2 (1961).

"Ethiopian Trade and Production," EO, 2: 7 (1958).

"Ethiopia's Imports of Motor Vehicles," EO, 2: 7 (1958).

"Ethiopia's New Oil Refinery," EO, 11: 1 (1967).

"Expanded Coverage of Price Statistics," EO, 2: 7 (1958).

Fanuel Deggie. "Small-scale Industries in Ethiopia," EO, 11: 3 (1967).

Felcourt, Etienne de. "Conditions actuelles du commerce à Addi Abeba," Suppl. au Moniteur officiel du Commerce, 681 (Jan. 1908).

_____. L'Abyssinie. Agriculture. Chemin de fer (Paris: 1911).

Fidel, Camille. "Les voies commerciales de l'Abyssinie, " B. du
    Comité de l'Afrique française (Paris: 1914).

Garretson, Peter P. "The Näggädras, Trade, and Selected Towns
    in Nineteenth and Early Twentieth Century Ethiopia, " 12: 3
    (1979).

Ginzberg, Eli, and H. A. Smith. Manpower Strategy for Developing
    Countries: Lessons from Ethiopia (New York, Columbia UP:
    1967).

Gray, Clive S. "Comparative Performance of Monetary G. D. P. and
    Money Supply in 'Explaining' Ethiopian Imports, " EO, 15: 3
    (1972).

Gryziewicz, S. "Main Determinants of Ethiopian Economic Develop-
    ment Policy, " EO, 7: 3 (1964).

_____, Legesse Tickeher; and Mammo Bahta. "An Outline of
    the Fiscal System in Ethiopia, " EO, 8: 4 (1965).

Hagos Tsehay. "Fluctuation of Share Quotations Over-the-Counter:
    The Case of the Ethiopian Investment Corporation Share Com-
    pany, " Dialogue, 1: 1 (1967).

Halpern, J. "La planification et le développement en Ethiopie après
    la deusième guerre mondiale, " Cultures et Développement, 6:
    4 (1974).

Harbeson, J. W. , and Brietzke, P. H. , eds. "Rural Development
    in Ethiopia, " Rural Africana, 28 (1975).

Hershfield, A. F. "From Point Four, " EO, 4: 4 (1960).

Ilg, Alfred. "Über die Verkehrsentwicklung in Äthiopien, " JGEG,
    1 (1899-1900).

"The Investment Bank, " EO, 8: 4 (1965).

Karsten, Detlev. "Problems of Industrialisation in Ethiopia, " EO,
    11: 1 (1967).

Kloos, Helmut. See listing under Medical.

Kouri, Nooman. "Situation commerciale du Harar en 1904, " Suppl.
    au Moniteur officiel du Commerce, 512 (5 Avr. 1906).

Liebenthal, Robert. "Certain Development Issues in Ethiopia and
    their Relationship to Rural/Urban Balance: a perspective based
    on World Bank Experience, " EN, 1: 3 (1978).

Lilliefelt, Theodor. "United Nations Technical Assistance, " EO, 2:
    9 (1958).

"Money Supply," EO, 2: 7 (1958).

Montandon, George. L'esclavage en Abyssinie. Rapport rédigè à la demande de la Ligue suisse pour la défense des indigènes pour être présenté au Conseil federal suisse en vue du débat sur l'esclavage à la IVe assemblée de la Société des Nations (Geneva: 1923).

Morehouse, Lynn G. "Ethiopian Labour Relations: Attitudes, practice and law," JEL, 7: 1 (1970).

Naggiar, J. P. "Mouvement commercial de l'Ethiopie en 1907-1908 par Dirre-Daoua et Djibouti," Suppl. au Moniteur officiel du Commerce, 799 (1 Juillet 1909); 911 (1910).

"New Ethiopian Legislation on Employment," EO, 6: 4 (1963).

Pam, K. V. "British Government: Finance Capital and the Franco-Ethiopian Railway (1898-1910)," (Sherbrooke, Quebec, Canada: Canadian Assoc. of African Studies).

Pankhurst, Richard. "Monetary and banking innovations in 19th and 20th Centuries," JES, 1: 2 (1963).

_____. "The Advent of the Maria Theresa Dollar in Ethiopia, its Effect on Taxation and Wealth accumulation, and other Economic, Political and Cultural Implications," NAS, 1: 3 (1979-1980).

_____. "Ethiopian monetary history in the phase of post-war reconstruction (1941-45); a collation of Ethiopian, British and American documents," EO, 16: 4 (1974).

_____. "Some Notes for an economic history of Ethiopia, 1800-1935," EO, 11: 1 (1967).

_____. "Some Notes on the Historical and Economic Geography of the Mesewa area (1520-1885)," JES, 13: 1 (1975).

_____. "A Preliminary History of Measures, Weights and Values," JES, 7: 1 (1964).

_____. "Tax Documents of the early 20th Century," JES, 11: 2 (1973).

_____. "The Trade of Central Ethiopia in 19th and early 20th Centuries," JES, 2: 2 (1964).

_____. "The Trade of Northern Ethiopia in 19th and 20th centuries," JES, 2: 1 (1964).

_____. "The Trade of Southern and Western Ethiopia and Indian Ocean ports in 19th and early 20th centuries," JES, 3: 2 (1965).

_____. "Trade of the Gulf of Aden Ports of Africa in the 19th and early 20th Centuries," JES, 3: 1 (1965).

_____. "Indian Trade with Ethiopia, the Gulf of Aden and the Horn of Africa in the 19th and early 20th Centuries," Cahiers d'Etudes Africaines, 14: 3 (1974).

_____. "Tribute, taxation and Government Revenues in 19th and early 20th Century Ethiopia," JES, 5: 2 (1967); 6: 1 (1968); 6: 2 (1968).

_____. "Status, Division of Labour and Employment in 19th century and early 20th century Ethiopia," UC of AA ESB, 2 (1961).

_____. "The History of Currency and Banking in Ethiopia from the Middle Ages to 1935," EO, 8: 4 (1965).

_____. Economic History of Ethiopia, 1800-1935 (Addis Ababa: HSIU: 1968).

"Point Four: Its Concept and Development," EO, 3: 1 (1959).

Pollestri, Edoardo. Dinamica dell'economica in Etiopia (Asmara: 1968).

Quinn, Harold A. "The Mineral Industry of Ethiopia," EO, 6: 3 (1962).

"Revised Presentation of Export Statistics Due to Federation of Eritrea," EO, 2: 7 (1958).

Seleshi Sisaye see Urban Areas

_____. "The Role of Social Sciences in Rural Development Planning: The Case of Ethiopia," ASR, 21: 3 (1978).

Seyoum G. Selassie. "Manpower needs for social welfare; new approaches," EO, 14: 2 (1971).

"Special Issue on Ethiopia's Five-Year Plan," EO, 3: 4 (1959).

Tafara Degeffe. "The Commercial Bank of Ethiopia," EO, 8: 4 (1965).

_____. "Credit Institutions in Ethiopia; an historical outline," EO, 8: 4 (1965).

"The Third Five Year Plan, 1968-1973," EO, 13: 4 (1970).

Trade Reports, Great Britain HMSO. (1897) Trade and Finance of Abyssinia, Trade of Harrar; (1899-1900) Trade of Addis Ababa and Harar; (1905-06) Trade of Abyssinia; (1910) Trade of

Abyssinia; (1911-12) Trade of Abyssinia; (1911) Trade of Gambela; (1911-12) Trade of Consular District of Harrar; (1912/13) Trade of Consular District of Harrar.

Wadhawan, G. N. "The Indo-Ethiopian Textile Mill," EO, 4: 10 (1960).

"Where do Ethiopian Exports Go? Whence do Ethiopia's Imports Come?" EO, 2: 7 (1958).

"The Work of the United Nations in Ethiopia," EO, 2: 9 (1958).

Young, Maurice de. "Pricing Practices for Selected Commodities in the Addis Ababa Markato," P. 3rd ICES, vol. 3 (Addis Ababa: 1970).

EDUCATION, LIBRARIES

Abdu Mozayen. "The Use of Mass Media in Language Teaching," 505-519, Language in Ethiopia (see Bender, et al.).

"Abyssinia," Education in East Africa: a study of East, Central and South Africa by the Second African Education Commission under the Auspices of the Phelps-Stokes Fund (New York: 1925). 316-336.

Aklilu Habte, Menguesha Gebre Hewit, Monika Kehoe. "Higher Education in Ethiopia," JES, 1: 1 (1963).

Alemayehu Moges. "Language Teaching and Curricula in Traditional Education of the Ethiopian Church," EJE, 6 (1973).

Assefa Bequele. "The Educational Framework of Economic Development in Ethiopia," EO, 11: 1 (1967).

Ayalew Gabre Sellassie. "Three Years Experience in Education," EO, 8: 1 (1964).

Beek, E. S. Report on Education for the Building Trade in Ethiopia (Addis Ababa: Ethio-Swedish Institute of Building Technology: 1962).

Bender, M. L., J. D. Bowen, R. L. Cooper and C. A. Ferguson, eds. Language in Ethiopia (London, OUP: 1976).

Bowen, J. D. "Organization, Methodology, and Supervision," 434-460 in Language in Ethiopia (see Bender et al.).

_____. "Teacher Training and Problems of Staffing the Schools," 461-481 in Language in Ethiopia (see Bender et al.).

Bricklin, Barry, and Carter Zeleznik. "A Psychological Investigation of selected Ethiopian Adolescents by means of the Rorschach and other Projective Tests," Human Organization, 22: 4 (1963-64).

Brooks, Kenneth. "Literacy Programmes in Ethiopia," 520-534 in Language in Ethiopia (see Bender et al.).

Comhaire, Sylvain. "Higher Education and Professional Training of Women in Ethiopia," P. 3rd ICES, Addis Ababa, 1966, Vol. 3.

Cooper, R. L. and Michael King. "Language and University Students, " 273-280 in Language in Ethiopia (see Bender et al.).

Desta Asyeghn. "Schooling and inequality in pre-revolutionary Ethiopia, " EN, 2: 2 (1978).

"Education Report: Analysis of Developments in Recent Years," EO, 5: 1 (1960).

"The Elementary School Curriculum," EO, 2: 4 (1958).

Eriksson, O. "Education in Abyssinia," Africa, 5 (1932).

"Ethiopia: Rationalising Education," Africa, 14 (1972).

"Ethiopian State Secondary School-Leaving Certificate Examination," EO, 2: 5 (1958).

Giel, R. , and J. N. Van Luijk. "A Follow-up of 1066 Freshman at Haile Sellassie I University, " JES, 8: 1 (1970).

Girma Amare. "Government Education in Ethiopia, " EO, 6: 4 (1963).

_____. "Memorization in Ethiopian schools, " JES, 1: 1 (1963).

Haile Gabriel Dagne. "Non-Government Schools in Ethiopia, " 339-370 in Language in Ethiopia (see Bender et al.).

Haile Woldemikael. "Government Schools in Ethiopia, " 324-338, ibid.

Hanson, J. W. Secondary Level Teachers: Supply and Demand in Ethiopia (East Lansing, Michigan: Institute for International Studies in Education and ASC, MSU, 1976).

"Higher Education in Ethiopia, " EO, 2: 6 (1958).

Hoerr, O. D. "Educational Returns and Educational Reform in Ethiopia, " East African Economic Review, 6 (1974).

Imbakom Kalewold, Aleka. Traditional Ethiopian Church Education.

Trans. by Menghestu Lemma (New York, Teachers College Press: 1970).

Kehoe, Monika see Aklilu Habte

Korten, David C. "Evidence of an important Social Change in Ethiopia: Motivations and Career Objectives of Students Studying in the Haile Sellassie I University, College of Business Administration," Business Journal, 2 (1965).

_____, and Frances F. Korten. "Ethiopia's Use of National University Students in a Year of Rural Services," Comparative Education Review 10: 3 (1966).

Last, Geoffrey C. "The Aims and Purpose of Geography Teaching," EO, 2: 5 (1958).

_____. "Geographical Field Work with Secondary School Students," EGJ, 3: 2 (1965).

Lord, Edith. "Education--What For," EO, 2: 4 (1958) and 5: 2 (1961).

Ludwig, Marvin J. "Positive Physical Education," EO, 2: 7 (1958).

Madsen, Harold S. "Language Examinations in Ethiopia," 482-504 in Language in Ethiopia (see Bender et al.)

Menguesha Gebre Hewit see Aklilu Habte

Million Neqniq. "The Most Urgent Needs in the Expansion of Ethiopian Education," EO, 2: 4 (1958).

Mulugeta Wodajo. "Ethiopia: Some Pressing Problems and the Role of Education in their Resolution," J. Negro Education, 30 (1961).

_____. "Postwar Reform in Ethiopian Education," Comparative Education Review, 2 (1959).

Naomi Gebrat. "Girls' Education," EO, 1: 3 (1957).

O'Connor, Lillian. "Some Aspects of the Language Problem," EO, 2: 4 (1958).

Pankhurst, Richard. "The Foundations of Education, Printing, Newspapers, Book Production, Libraries and Literacy in Ethiopia," EO, 6: 3 (1962).

_____. "Historical Background of Education in Ethiopia," 305-323 in Language in Ethiopia (see Bender et al.).

Pankhurst, Rita. "Leadership in Ethiopian Post-war Library Development: The National Library vs. the University Library," P. 5th ICES, Chicago, 1978.

_____ (Eldon). "The National Library of Ethiopia," EO, 1: 11 (1957).

Pankhurst, Sylvia. "Education in Ethiopia: Secondary Education," EO, 2: 5 (1958).

_____. "History of Ethiopian Schools," EO, 2: 4 (1958).

_____. "Problems of Ethiopian Education," EO, 2: 4 (1958).

Paulos Milkias. "Traditional Institutions and Traditional Elites: the role of Education in the Ethiopian Body-Politic," ASR, 19: 3 (1976).

Resources and Needs for Training Facilities for Africans in British Africa, Ethiopia and Liberia (Washington, D. C.: Ruth Sloan Associates, September 30, 1955).

Schools: Individual Institutions.
    "Amba Desta," "Asfa Wossen," "Empress Menen Orphanage," "Haile Sellassie I Day School," "School for Blind Boys," "Schools of Addis Ababa," "Women's Vocational School," EO, 2: 4 (1958).

    "Empress Menen School for Girls," "Gabre Mariam Lycée," "General Wingate Secondary School," "Haile Sellassie I Secondary School," "Medhane Alem School," "Menelik II School," "Tafari Makonnen School," EO, 2: 5 (1958).

    "Imperial Ethiopian Institute of Public Administration," EO, 2: 9 (1958) and "Institute of Public Administration," EO, 5: (1961).

    "College of Engineering and Technical School," "Debra Berhan Community School," "The Vocational Building School," EO, 1: 7 (1957).

    "Empress Menen Handicraft School," "Empress Menen Girls' School," EO, 1: 3 (1957).

    "Debra Berhan Community Training School," EO, 2: 10 (1958).

    "School of Home Economics," EO, 4: 4 (1960).

    "Imperial College of Agricultural Education and Research," "Jimma Agricultural School," EO, 1: 10 (1957).

    "The Institute of Building Technology," EO, 1: 11 (1957).

    "The New Theological College," "Holy Trinity Theological College," EO, 2: 6 (1958).

    "Prince Makonnen School, Massawa," EO, 3: 9 (1959).

Schools: Individual Institutions (Cont'd.)
   "The Model School, Harar, " 2: 4 (1958).

   [German school.]   Asfa-Wossen Asserate.   "Die Deutsche
      Schule in Addis Abeba--aus äthiopischer Sicht, " and Buttner,
      Manfried.   "Die Deutsche Schule Addis Abeba in Rahman
      des deutschen Auslandsschulwesens, " ZK (1973).

"Alliance Française in Ethiopia, " EO, 4: 2 (1960).

"The Secondary School Curriculum, " EO, 2: 5 (1958).

Senedu Gabru.   "Girls' Education, " EO, 1: 3 (1957).

Seyoum G. Selassie.   "New Approaches for Meeting Manpower needs
   for Social Welfare in Ethiopia, " EO, 14: 2 (1971).

Shack, William A.   "Organization and Problems of Education in
   Ethiopia, " J. Negro Education, 28 (1959).

Sjostrom, R. and M.   YDLC: A Literacy Campaign in Ethiopia;
   an introductory Study and a Plan for Further Research (Uppsala, Scandinavian Institute of African Studies: 1973).

Solomon Inquai.   "Adult Literacy in Ethiopia--a Profile, " JES, 7: 1
   (1969).

Tadesse Tereffe.   "Progress, Problems and Prospects in Ethiopian
   Education, " EO, 8: 1 (1964).

Teshome G. Wagaw.   "Access to Haile Sellassie I University, " EO,
   14: 1 (1971).

_____ .   Education in Ethiopia: Prospect and Retrospect (Ann Ar-
   bor, Michigan; University of Michigan Press: 1979).

"University College Examinations, " EO, 2: 6 (1958).

"University College Publications, " EO, 2: 6 (1958).

Vollprecht, Dieter.   "Das Goethe-Institut in Addis Abeba, " ZK
   (1973).

Wright, S.   "National Libraries of Ethiopia, " UCR (Addis Ababa) 1
   (1961).

ERITREA
(See references under Law, Medicine, Ethnography, and
and History categories)

Alamanni, E.   La Colonia Eritrea e i suoi commerci (Turin: 1891).

"L'Andamento d'agricultura in Eritrea durante il 1933," REC, 22
(1934).

Baldrati, I.   "I Prodotti del suolo coltivati e spontanei in Eritrea,"
REC, 20 (1932).

_____.   "Lo sviluppo dell'agricoltura in Eritrea nei ciquant'anni
di occupazione italiana," RCI, 7 (1933).

Bartolotti, D.   "Lo sviluppo commerciale della colonia Eritrea,"
BSAI, 24 (1915).

Boyce, Frank.   "The Internationalizing of Internal War: Ethiopia,
the Arabs, and the Case of Eritrea," J. International and Comparative Studies, 5: 3 (1972).

Breutz, P. L.   "Know Africa: Confederation of Ethiopia and Eritrea," Bantu, 9 (Dec. 1954).

Bruchhausen, Karl von.   "Der Handel Erythraeas," DRGS, 17
(1895).

Campbell, J. F.   "Background to the Eritrean Conflict," Africa Report, 48 (Apr. 1970).

_____.   "Rumblings along the Red Sea: The Eritrean Question,"
Foreign Affairs, 48 (Apr. 1970).

Cherian, K. A., ed.   Ethiopia and Eritrea (Bombay: 1954).

Cumming, D. C.   "The Disposal of Eritrea," Middle East J. 7: 1
(1953).

El Gamal, R.   "The Eritrean Conflict: Middle East Hot Spot," The
Plain Truth (Jan. 1972).

Ellingson, Lloyd.   "The Origins and Development of the Eritrean
Liberation Movement," P. 5th ICES (Chicago: 1979).

Enahoro, Peter.   "Africa's Forgotten Wars," Africa, 7 (1972).

"Eritrea," Handbook 126.   Spanish and Italian Possessions: Independent States (Peace Handbooks, Historical Section, Foreign Office, London; vol. 20, 1920).   Reissued New York, Greenwood
Press, 1969.

The Eritrean Revolution, 16 Years of Armed Struggle. Sept. 1, 1977. (Eritrean Liberation Front Foreign Information Center, Beirut, Lebanon: 1977).

Ford, Alan. "Russian Attempt to Control Red Sea Behind Eritrean Movement," National Review, 18 (Apr. 5, 1966).

Gabrielli, A. "Il nuovo ordinamento organico per l'Eritrea e le sue norme giuridiche," Oltremare, 8 (1934).

Getahun Dilebo. "Historical Origins and Development of the Eritrean Problem, 1889-1962," Current Bibliography on African Affairs, 7: 3 (1974).

"Una grande impresa industriale in Eritrea: le saline di Uachiro," RCI, 5 (1931).

Grundy, Kenneth W. "Nationalism and Separatism in East Africa," Current History, 54 (1968).

Guiolotti, R. "Boschi e servizio forestale in Eritrea," AC, 28 (1934) and REC, 22 (1934).

Haile Wolde Emmanuel. "Concession Agriculture in Eritrea," EGJ, 2: 1 (1964).

Hayle Sellasie. (Speeches on Eritrea) EO, 6: 3 (1963); 6: 4 (1963).

"L'Industria della pesca in Eritrea nel 1932," REC, 21 (1933).

Kramer, Jack. "Africa's Hidden War," Evergreen, 15: 94 (1971).

"La legge sulla Colonia Eritrea al Senato," BSAI, 21 (1902).

Lessona, Alessandro. "L'Eritrea e la Somalia nei fini dell'espansione," RI, 35 (1933).

_____. La Missione dell'Italia in Africa (Rome: 1936).

Licata, G. B. see Travel and Exploration

Lobban, Richard. Eritrean Liberation Front: A Close-up View (Munger Africana Library Notes, 13; California Institute of Technology, 1972).

Longrigg, Stephen A. A Short History of Eritrea (Oxford, Clarendon Press: 1945). (Reissued New York, Greenwood Press: 1974).

Martini, Ferdinando. Relazione sulla Colonia Eritrea del R. Commissario Civile. 4 vols. (Rome: Tipografia della Camera dei Deputati, 1913-1914).

_____. See Listings under History, c. 1760-1930.

Massa, L.   "Le Piante da frutto coltivate in Eritrea," AC, 28 (1934).

Morgan, E.   "A Geographic evaluation of the Ethiopian-Eritrea conflict," JMA, 15: 4 (1977).

Morrison, Godfrey.   "The Southern Sudan and Eritrea; Aspects of Wider African Problems," in The Fourth World: Victims of Group Oppression.   Ed. Ben Whitaker (New York, Schocken Books: 1973).

"Il Movimento commerciale carovaniero dell'Eritrea nel 1933," and "Il Movimento commerciale marittimo dell'Eritrea," REC, 21 and 22 (1933 and 1934).

Muhammad Yunus.   "The Lone Voice of Eritrea," Yageen International, 17: 15 (1968).

Nadel, S. F.   See listing under Agriculture.

Nouaille-Degorce, Brigitte.   "L'Impasse militaire en Erythrée," Revue Française d'Etudes Politiques Africaines (Mar. 1975).

Odorizzi, D.   See listing under Agriculture and Land Tenure.

Ostini, G.   "L'Avvenire marittimo di Massaua e la nostra espansione economica dell'Est Africa Centrale," RC, 14 (1919).

Paladino, G.   "Documenti per la storia della colonia Eritrea," L'Africa Italiana, 37 (1918).

Pankhurst, Sylvia.   British Policy in Eritrea and Northern Ethiopia (Woodford Green, England: 1946).

_____.   "Eritrea on the Eve.   The Past and Future of Italy's 'First Born' Colony, Ethiopia's Ancient Sea Province," New Times and Ethiopia News (1952).

_____.   Special issues of Ethiopia Observer on Eritrea.   3: 5, 6, 7, 8 (1959).

_____, and Richard Pankhurst.   Ethiopia and Eritrea: The Last Phase of the Reunion Struggle, 1941-1952 (Woodford Green, Lalibela House: 1953).

Parazzoli, A.   "Sulle odierne condizioni dell'Eritrea," EC, 16 (1901).

Parpagliolo, A.   "La nuova legge organica dell'Eritrea e della Somalia," RCI, 8 (1934).

Peninou, J. L.   Eritrea: The Guerrillas of the Red Sea (New York: EFLNA, 1976?).

Pliny the Middle-Aged (pseud.). "Eclectic Notes on the Eritrean Liberation Movement: E Pluribus Unum?" EN, 2: 2 (1978).

Pollera, Alberto. "Le Vicende della colonizzazione agricola Eritrea," RCI, 8: 7 (1934).

_____. Le Populazioni Indigene dell'Eritrea (Bologna: 1935).

Puglisi, G. Chi è? dell'Eritrea (Asmara: 1952).

Rava, Maurizio. L'Eritrea: la nostra colonia primogenita (Rome: 1923).

"Reunion of Eritrea Proclamation," EO, 6: 4 (1963).

Robbs, Peter. "Battle for the Red Sea," Africa Report, 20: 2 (1975).

Rossi, Giacinto. La Prefettura Eritrea (Genoa: 1895).

Sapeto, G. Asseb e i sui critici (Genoa: 1879).

_____. See listings under Travel and Description and History c. 1760-c. 1930.

Schweinfurth, G. A. Il Presente e l'avvenire della Colonia Eritrea (Milan: 1894).

Semeraro, G. "L'Ordinamento e il funzionamento della giustizia militare nella colonia Eritrea," RC, 14 (1919).

Sertoli, S. R. L'Ordinamento fondiario dell'Eritreo (Padua: 1932).

Sherman, Richard. "Eritrea: a survey of Social and Economic Change," Horn of Africa, 1: 3 (1973).

Sillani, Tomaso, ed. L'Africa Orientale Italiana (Eritrea e Somalia) (Rome: 1913).

"Lo sviluppo economico dell'Eritrea nel cinquantennio dello sua esistenza," AC, 26 (1932).

Tekle Fessehatzion. "The Eritrean Struggle for Independence and National Liberation," Horn of Africa, 1: 2 (1978).

Trevaskis, G. K. N. Eritrea: A Colony in Transition: 1941-52 (London, OUP: 1960).

Troll, C. "Escursioni scientifiche nella colonia Eritrea," BRSGI, 12 (1935).

Zaghi, C. Le Origini della colonia Eritrea (Bologna: 1934).

ETHNOGRAPHY, SOCIOLOGY, FOLKLORE, REGIONAL STUDIES

Abaineh Workie. "Minority Group Perceptions of the Amharas, Tigres, and Oromos (Research Notes)," P. 5th ICES (Chicago: 1979).

Abbadie, Antoine d'. "Notes sur les Nègres de l'Ethiopie," BSG, ser. 4, 27 (1859).

_____. "Notice sur la Kafa, les Woratta, Limmou, Gonda, etc.," BSG, ser. 5, 2 (1861).

_____. "Sur les Oromo, grande nation africaine designée souvent sous le nom de Galla," ASSB, 4 (1880).

Abdulla Abdurahman, et al. "Ethiopian food," UCAAESB, 3 (1954).

Abdurahman Mohamed Korram. "Oromo Proverbs," JES, 7: 1 (1969) and 10: 2 (1972).

Abebe Ambatchew. "Betrothal among the Säwan Amhara," UCAAESB, 5 (1956).

Abeles, A. and M. "L'organisation sociale de l'espace à Ochollo (Ethiopie méridionale)," J. des A., 46: 1-2 (1976).

Abeles, Marc. "L'organisation sociale et politique des Ochollo (Ethiopie méridionale)," P. 5th ICES (Chicago: 1979).

Abir, M. "The Emergence and Consolidation of the Monarchy of Enarea and Jimma in the first half of the nineteenth Century," JAH, 6: 2 (1965).

Abraham Demoz. "Language and Society in Ethiopia," ZK (1973).

Aescoly, A. Z. "Les noms magiques dans les apocryphes chrétiens des Ethiopiens," JA, (1929).

Akalu Walda-Mikael. "Buhe," UCAAESB, 7 (1957).

Alemayehu Seifu. "Eder in Addis Ababa: a sociological study," EO, 12: 1 (1968).

Almagor, U. "Name-Oxen and Ox-Names among the Dassanetch of southwest Ethiopia," Paideuma, 18 (1972).

_____. "Tribal Sections, Territory and Myth: Dassanetch Responses to variable ecological conditions," AAS, 8: 2 (1972).

_____. See Baxter below.

_____. "Pastoral Partners: affinity and bond partnerships among the Dassenetch of southwest Ethiopia," (MUP: in press, 1980).

Andargatchew Tesfaye. "The Funeral Customs of the Kottu of Harrar," UCAAESB, 7 (1957).

Andrezejewski, B. W. "Ideas about Warfare in Borana Galla Stories and Fables," ALS, 3 (1962).

_____. "Sheikh Hussein of Bali in Galla oral traditions," ACISE, Rome, 1972; ANL (Scienza e Cultura), 191 (1974).

Anfray, Francis. "Les Sculptures rupestres de Chabbè dans le Sidamo," AE, 7 (1967).

Armstrong, W. H. and Fisseha Demoz Gebre Egzi. "Amharic Proverbs," EO, 12: 1 (1968).

Asfaw Damte. "Ekub," UCAAESB, 8 (1958).

Asmarom Legesse. "Class Systems Based on Time," JES, 1: 2 (1963).

_____. Gada: Three Approaches to the Study of African Society (New York, Free Press: 1973).

Ayele Tekle Haymanot, Abba. "Il Wata, una tipica figura folclorista dell'Etiopia e la sua professione interdetta," P. 3rd ICES, vol. 2 (Addis Ababa: 1970).

Azais, Rev. P. "Folklore Oromo," Rd'Eth., 6: 22 (1925).

_____. "Le paganisme en pays gouraghe," Rd'Eth. 6, 23 (1926).

_____. "Etude sur la religion du peuple Galla," Rd'Eth. 7: 25 (1926).

Azais, R. P., and Chambard, R. "Notes sur quelques coutumes observées au Gouraghe," Rd'Eth. 8: 29-30 (1927).

_____. Cinq annees de recherches archéologiques en Ethiopie. 2 vols. (Paris: 1931).

Bachrach, Shlomo. Ethiopian Folk-Tales (Addis Ababa: OUP, 1967).

Barnicot, N. A. "A Survey of Some Genetical Characters in Ethiopian Tribes," AJPA, 20: 2 (1962).

Bartels, L. "Birth Customs and Birth Songs of the Macha Galla," Ethnology, 8: 4 (1969).

_____. "Studies of the Galla in Wälläga: Their Own View of the Past," JES, 8: 1 (1970).

_____. "Dabo: a Form of Cooperation between Farmers among the Macha Galla of Ethiopia, Social Aspects, Songs and Rituals," Anthropos 70: 5-6 (1975), and 72: 3-4 (1977).

_____. "Galla to the east of Nekemte," UCAAESB, 6 (1957).

Basset, Rene. "Folk-lore d'Ethiopie," Rd'Eth., 2 (1911).

_____. "Contes d'Abyssinie," Rd'Eth. (July 1902).

Bauer, Dan F. "For Want of an Ox ...: Land, Capital, and Social Stratification in Tigre," P. 1st USCES (ASC, MSU: 1975).

Baxter, P. T. W. "Repetition in Certain Boran Ceremonies," African Systems of Thought, ed. Fortes, M. and Dieterlen, G. (London, OUP: 1965), 64-76.

_____. "Stock Management and the Diffusion of Property Rights among the Boran," P. 3rd ICES, Vol. 3 (Addis Ababa: 1970).

_____. "Some Preliminary Observations on a type of Arsi Song, Wellu, which is popular with Young Men," ACISE, tomo I, Sezione Storica, 1974.

_____. "'Atete' in a Highland Arssi Neighborhood," NAS, 1: 2 (1979).

Baxter, P. T. W., and Almagor, U., eds. Age, Generation and Time: Some Features of East African Age Organizations (London: Hurst, 1980).

Bekele Nadi. "Adoption Among the Oromo of Säwa," UCAAESB, 8 (1958).

Bender, M. L. "The Languages of Ethiopia: A New-Lexico Statistic Classification and Some Problems of Diffusion," Anthropological Linguistics, 13: 5 (1971). See also 14: 5 (1972).

_____. "Omotic: A New Afroasiastic Language Family," (Carbondale: Southern Illinois University Museum Series, 3 (1975).

_____. "The beginnings of Ethnohistory in Western Wellegga: The Mao Problem," Patterns in Language Culture and Society: Sub-Saharan Africa. Ed. R. K. Herbert (Working Papers in Linguistics, 19, OSU Dept. of Linguistics, Columbia, Ohio).

_____. The Non-Semitic Languages of Ethiopia. Monograph 5 (ASC, MSU: 1976).

Bender, M. L., and Mulugeta Eteffa. "Galla," Language in Ethiopia (London, OUP: 1976).

Biasutti, Renato. "La posizione antropologica degli etiopici," Atti del Terzo Congresso di Studi Coloniali, 5 (1937).

Bieber, F. Kaffa, ein Altkuschitisches Volkstum in Inner Africa: Nachrichten uber Land und Volk, Brauch und Sitte der Kaffitscho oder Gonga und das Kaiserreich Kaffa. 2 vols (Munich: 1920 and Vienna: 1923).

Blackhurst, H. "Continuity and Change in the Shoa Galla Gada System," in Age, Generation and Time: Some Features of East African Age: Some Features of East African Age Organisations. Eds. Baxter and Almagor (London: Hurst, 1980).

Bliese, Loren F. "Lexicon--a key to culture; with illustrations from Afar word lists," JES, 8: 2 (1970).

_____. "The Tragedies of Three Afar Girls," EN, 2: 3 (1978-1979).

Bogale-Walalu. Yawalamo Tarikena Barenatem Endet Endatawagada (The History of Walamo and How Slavery Was Abolished) (Addis Ababa: Artistic Press, n. d.).

Bondestam, Lars. "People and Capitalism in the Northeastern Lowland of Ethiopia," JMAS, 12: 3 (1974).

Borello, M. "Proverbi Galla," Studi Raccolti da Conti Rossini (Rome: Istituto per l'Oriente, 1945). 111-130.

_____. "Proverbi Galla II, III and IV," RSE, 5 (1946) 103-121; 7 (1948) 66-88; 24 (1970) 40-73.

Bowditch, T. E. An Essay on the Superstitions, Customs and Arts Common to the Ancient Egyptians, Abyssinians and Ashantees (Paris: 1821).

Braukämper, U. "The Correlation of Oral Traditions and Historical Records in Southern Ethiopia: A Case Study of the Hadiya Sidamo Past," JES, 11: 2 (1973).

Brogger, I. Cultivators and Hersmĕn. Notes on a Predatory History of the Sidama (Copenhagen: 1973).

_____. "Spirit Possession and the Management of Aggression Among the Sidamo," Ethnos, 40: 1-4 (1975).

Brooke, C. H. "The Galla of Northwestern Africa," GR, 47 (1957).

_____. "The Rural Village in the Ethiopian Highlands," GR, 49 (1959).

Brotto, E. "I Magianghir," RSE, 6: 1 (1947).

Brown, R. L. & Awad Abdullah. "Sociological Needs of Ethiopia,"
EO, 11: 3 (1967).

Bubbamo Arficio see Haile Bubbamo Arficio

Bureau, J. "Le statut des artisans en Ethiopie," Ethiopie d'aujourd-
'hui: la terre et les hommes (Paris, Musée de l'Homme: 1975).

Burley, Dexter. "The Despised Weavers of Addis Ababa," P. 5th
ICES (Chicago: 1979).

Carr, C. Societal/Environmental Interactions as a System: the
Dasanetch of Southwest Ethiopia (UC, Monographs in Geography, 180 (1977).

_____. Pastoralism in Crisis. The Dasanetch and their Ethiopian
Lands (Chicago: 1977).

Casotto, G. da. "Note sulle popolazioni dell'alto e medio Galana,"
Studi etiopici raccolti da C. Conti Rossini (Rome, Istituto per
l'Oriente: 1945), 150-181.

Cerbella, G. Aspetti etnografici della casa in Etiopia (Rome, Istituto Italiano per l'Africa: 1963).

Cerulli, E. "The Folk-Literature of the Galla of Southern Abyssinia," Harvard African Studies, 3 (1922), 9-228.

_____. "I Riti della Iniziazione della tribu Galla," RSO, 9
(1923).

_____. "Note su alcune populazioni Sidama dell'Abissinia meri-
dionale," RSO, 10 (1925).

_____. "Notizia preliminare dei risultati scientifici del mio vi-
aggio nell'Etiopia occidentale," OM, 8: 7 (1928).

_____. "La poesia popolare amarica," BSAI, 35 (1916) 172-79
and 237-51.

_____. "La Dea Mater ed il suo culto presso le genti dell'Etiopia
Meridionale (Galla Caffo)," Rivista di Antropologia, 43 (1956).

_____. Etiopia occidentale (Rome: 1933) 2 vols.

_____. "Two Ethiopian tales on the Christians of Cyprus," JES,
5: 1 (1965).

Cerulli, Ernesta. Peoples of South-West Ethiopia and its Borderland (London, Int'l African Institute: 1956).

Chambard, R. "Notes sur quelques croyances des Galla," Rd'Eth.,
7 (1926).

Bibliography 350

Cittadini, M. "Magia e ossessione presso i Sidamo, " QIC, 4 (1969).

_____. "Inferie e pianto funebre Cunama, " QIC, 5 (1970).

_____. "Primitivo stanziamento estra eritreo dei Cunama, " P. 3rd ICES, vol. 2 (Addis Ababa: 1970).

Close, D. F. , ed. Stories from the Arussi Hills (New York, Vantage Press: 1973).

Cohen, Marcel. Etudes d'éthiopien méridional (Paris: 1931);

_____. Nouvelles études d'Ethiopien Méridional (Paris: 1939).

_____. "Couplets amhariques du Choa, " JA, 205 (1924), 1-100.

_____. Documents éthnographiques d'Abyssinie (Paris: 1920).

_____. "Jeux abyssins, " JA, 18 (1911).

Comhaire, J. L. "La condition féminine en Ethiopie, " Mélanges d'Islamologie, Correspondance d'Orient No. 13 (Brussels: 1975).

Conforti, E. "La regione dei Guraghe, " Aq. Col. 35 (1941).

Conti Rossini, C. "Popoli dell'Etiopia occidentale, " RRAL, 22, 7-10 (1920).

_____. "Il popoli dei Magi nell'Ethiopia meridionale e il suo linguaggio, " ACSC, 6 (1927).

Cooper, R. L. , and Horvath, R. J. "Language, Migration and Urbanization in Ethiopia, " Anthropological Linguistics, 15: 5 (1973).

Crummey, Donald. "Society and Ethnicity in the Politics of Christian Ethiopia during the Zamana Mesafent, " IJAHS, 8 (1975).

Doresse, Jean. "Le mois de Genbôt, " L'Ethiopie d'aujourd'hui, 1: 1 (1962) (Paris, Musée de l'Homme).

Dupont, L. "La culture de l'ensete chez les Wollamo, " L'Ethiopie d'aujourd'hui (Paris, Musée de l'Homme, 1975).

Eadie, J. An Amharic Reader (Cambridge: 1924).

Ehret, C. Ethiopians and East Africans (Nairobi: East African Publishing House, 1974).

Ellero, Giovanni. "I Conventi dello Scirè e le loro leggende, " BSGI, 7: 4 (1939).

_____. "Una regione etiopica: lo Scire," BSGI, 7: 6 (1941).

Englebert, V. "The Danakil: nomads of Ethiopia's Wasteland,"
    National Geographic, 137: 2 (1970).

Ephraim Isaac. "The Hebraic Molding of Ethiopian Culture," Mo-
    saic, 6: 1 (1965).

Eshete Tadesse. "Preparation of Tej among the Amhara of Sawa,"
    UCAAESB, 8 (1958).

Ezra Gäbra-Mädhen. "Wedding Customs Practiced in Shoa,"
    UCAAESB, 3 (1954).

Faitlovich, Jacques. "Proverbs abyssins, traduits, expliqués et an-
    notés," (Paris: 1907).

_____. "Nouveaux proverbes abyssins traduits et expliqués,"
    Riv. SO, 2 (1908).

_____. "Versi abissini," GSAI, 23 (1910).

Fasika Bällata. "The Death Customs Among the Amharas of Shoa,"
    UCAAESB, 7 (1957).

Fecadu Gadamu. "Social and Cultural Foundation of Gurage Asso-
    ciation," P. 3rd ICES, Vol. 3 (Addis Ababa: 1970).

Fellman, Jack. "Amhara verbal behavior," Anthropological Lin-
    guistics, 18: 1 (1976). See also Hoben, Susan.

Fisseha H. Maskal. "Atete," UCAAESB, 9 (1959).

Flemming, H. C. "Recent Research in Omotic-Speaking Areas,"
    P. 1st USCES (ASC, MSU: 1975).

_____, and Lewis, H. S. "Concerning Haberland's Comments on
    Review of 'Altvoelker Sued-Aethiopiens: a rejoinder,"
    American Anthropologist 65: 5 (1963).

"Forschungsreise des Frobenius-Instituts 1970/71 nach Sued Aethio-
    pian: Verlauefiger Bericht," Paideuma, 17 (1971).

Forster, J. "Economy of the Gamu Highlands (Ethiopia)," GM, 41
    (1969).

Francaviglia, A. "Osservazioni sulla regione del Guraghe occiden-
    tale (A. O. I.)," L'Universo, 21 (1940).

Franzoj, A. "I Danachili e loro usanze," BSAI, 5 (1886), 209-17.

Fuchs, V. E. "The Lake Rudolf Rift Valley Expedition," GJ, 86
    (1935).

Fusella, L. "Proverbi amarici," RSE, 3 (1942).

Gallagher, J. P. "The Preparation of Hides with Stone Tools in South Central Ethiopia," JES, 12: 1 (1974).

_____. "Contemporary stone tools in Ethiopia: implications for archaeology," J. Field Archaeology, 4: 4 (1977).

Gamst, F. C. "Peasantries and Elites without Urbanism," Comparative Studies in Society and History, 12: 4 (1970).

_____. Peasants in Complex Society (New York, Holt, Rinehart and Winston: 1974).

_____. "Wayto Ways: Change from Hunting to Peasant Life," P. 5th ICES (Chicago: 1979).

_____. The Qemant: a Pagan-Hebraic peasantry of Ethiopia (New York, Holt, Rinehart and Winston: 1969).

Gedamu Abraha. "Wax and Gold," EO, 11: 3 (1967).

Giaccardi, A. "La popolazioni del Boran e del Sidamo," Riv. C, 2 (1937).

Giel, R., and Van Luijk, J. N. "Patterns of Marriage in a Roadside Town in South-western Ethiopia," JES, 6: 2 (1968).

Graham, D. C. "Reports on the Manners, Customs and Superstitions of the People of Shoa, and on the History of the Abyssinian Church," JAS (Bengal), 12 (1843).

Griaule, Marcel. "Mythes, Croyances et coutumes du Bégamder (Abyssinie)," JA (1928).

_____. "Coutumes abyssines relatives au lait de vache," Lait, 209-10 (1941).

_____. Jeux et divertissements abyssins (Paris: 1935).

_____. "Noms propres d'animaux domestiques d'Abyssinie," Jdes A, 12 (1942).

_____. Silhouettes et Graffitti Abyssins (Paris: 1933).

_____. Le Livre de recettes d'un dabtara abyssin (Paris, Institut d'éthnologie: 1930).

Grottanelli, V. L. "I Niloti dell'Ethiopia allo stato attuale delle nostre conoscenze," BSGI, 20 (1937), 561-588.

_____. "Tra le genti primitive dell'estremo occidente etiopico," RSAI, 5: 5 (1942).

_____. "Acconciatura e vestiaria dei Coma al confine etiopico-sudanese," Annali Lateranesi, 9 (1945).

_____. "Burial among the Koma of Western Abyssinia," Primitive Man, 20: 4 (1947).

_____. "I pre-niloti. Un'arcaica provincia culturale in Africa," Annali Lateranesi, 12 (1948).

Guidi, G. "Nel Sidamo orientale, I paesi del Mondo," BSGI, ser. 7, 14 (1939).

Guidi, I. "I popoli e le lingue di Abissinia," Extr. Nuova Antologia (1887).

_____. "Proverbi, strofe e favole abissine," GSAI, 5 (1891).

_____. Proverbi, strofe e racconte abissini. RAL (Rome: 1894).

_____. "Proverbi abissini," OM, (April, 1894).

_____. "Leggende storiche di Abissinia," RivSO, 1 (1907).

Haberland, E. "Uber einen unbekannten Gunza stamm in Wallega," RSE 12 (1954).

_____. Galla Sud-Aethiopiens (Stuttgart: 1963).

_____. "Aethiopien-Expedition des Frobenius Institutes 1950-52," Remedia Casella Curta, 4: 3 (1954).

_____. "Aethiopische Dachaufsaetze," Jahrbuch des Museums für Volkerkunde, 17 (1960) and 19 (1962).

_____. "Bemerkungen zur Kultur und Sprache der 'Galila' im Wonci-see (Mittel Athiopien," RSE, 16 (1960).

_____. "Zum Problem der Jaeger und besonderen Kasten in Nord-ost und Ost-Afrika," Paideuma, 8 (1962).

_____. "The Influence of the Christian Ethiopian Empire on Southern Ethiopia," JSS, 9 (1964).

_____. "Recenti ricerche etnologiche in Etiopia," Africa (Rome), 29 (1974).

_____. "Special castes in Ethiopia," P. 5th ICES (Chicago: 1979).

Hadt, C. "Contribution a l'histoire ethnobotanique d'une plante stimu-lante, le kat en Ethiopie," Ethnographie, 65 (1971).

Haile Bubbamo Arficio. "Notes on Traditional Hadiya Women," JES, 11: 2 (1973).

Haile Michael Mesghinna. "Salt Mining in Enderta," JES, 4: 2 (1966).

_____. "Betrothal and Marriage customs in Endärta," UCAAESB, 8 (1958).

Hailu Gabre-Hiot. "Omens in Ethiopia," UCAAESB, 8 (1958).

Hailu Mengesha and Bob Lee. Domestic Implements of Ethiopia: A Brief Survey of Hand Tools, Household and Farming Implements of Harar Province (Experiment Station Bulletin, 5 (Nov. 1960), College of Agriculture, Alemaya).

Hallpike, C. R. "The Status of Craftsmen among the Konso of South-West Ethiopia," Africa, 38: 3 (1968).

_____. "Konso Agriculture," JES, 8: 1 (1970).

_____. "The Principles of Alliance Formation between Konso Towns," Man, 5 (1970).

_____. The Konso of Ethiopia. A Study of the Values of a Cushitic People (London, OUP: 1972).

_____. "Two Types of Reciprocity," Comparative Studies in Society and History, 17 (1975).

Halperin, R., and Olmstead, J. "To Catch a Feastgiver: Redistribution among the Dorze of Ethiopia," Africa, 46: 2 (1976).

Hamer, J. "Voluntary Associations as Structures of Change among the Sidamo of Southwestern Ethiopia," AQ, 40: 2 (1967).

_____. "Prerequisites and Limitations in the Development of Voluntary Self-Help Associations: an Example from Ethiopia," AQ, 49 (1976).

_____. "Sidamo Generational Class Cycles: a Political Gerontocracy," Africa, 40: 1 (1970).

_____. "Development of Self-Help and Cooperative Associations," (Sidamo) P. 5th ICES (Chicago: 1979).

_____. "Dispute Settlement and an Ethiopian Example," AQ, 45: 4 (1972).

_____. "Folktales, Socialization and the content of Social Relationships: an Ethiopian Example," Anthropos, 67: 3-4 (1972).

_____. "Myth, Ritual and the Authority of Elders in an Ethiopian Society," Africa, 46: 4 (1976).

_____. "Crisis, Moral Consensus, and the Wando Magano Movement among the Sidama of Southwest Ethiopia," Ethnology, 16: 4 (1977).

_____, with I. Hamer. "Spirit Possession and its Socio-Psychological Implication among the Sidamo of Southwest Ethiopia," Ethnology 5: 4 (1966).

Hentze, Paul. "Lake Zway and its islands; an Ethiopian lake where a unique Christian culture has survived since medieval times," EO, 16: 2 (1973).

_____. "Patterns of cultural survival on the islands in Ethiopia's highland lakes," EO, 16: 2 (1973).

Hill, Bob G. "Cat (Catha edulis Forsk)," JES, 3: 2 (1965).

Hinnant, J. "Spirit Possession and Social Change. Current Research in Southern Ethiopia," Rural Africana, 1970. #11.

_____. The Guji of Southern Ethiopia. 2 vols (MRAF Books: 1975).

Hoben, Allan. "Social Stratification in Traditional Amhara Society," Social Stratification in Africa, eds. Arthur Tuden and L. Plotnikob (New York: Free Press: 1970).

Hoben, Susan. "Kin Terms of Reference and Kin Terms of Address in Amharic of Menz," P. 1st USCES, MSU, 1973 (ASC, MSU: 1975).

_____. "Amhara Verbal Behavior; a commentary," Anthropological Linguistics, 8: 8 (1976).

Hoffman, Hans. "Markov Chains in Ethiopia." Exploration in Mathematical Anthropology.   Ed. Paul Kay (Cambridge, M.I.T. Press: 1971).

Holcomb, Bonnie K. "Oromo Marriage in Wälläga Province, Ethiopia," JES, 11: 1 (1973).

Hosken, Fran P. Genital Mutilation of Women in Africa (Munger Africana Library Notes, 36 (Oct. 1976) (California Institute of Technology).

_____. The Hosken Report: Genital/sexual mutilation of Females (WIN News, Lexington, Mass., 1979).

Huber, A. "Weibliche Zirkumzision und Infibulation in Aethiopien," Acta Tropica, 23: 1 (1966).

Huntingford, G. W. B. The Galla of Ethiopia, the Kingdoms of Kaffa and Janjero (London, IAI: 1955).

Hylander, G. "Onesimus Nesib--Some Remarks on Cerulli's 'The Folk Literature of the Galla,' " JES, 7: 2 (1969).

Irwin, Lee. "Notes on Saysay Culture," JES, 6: 1 (1968).

Jackson, R. T. "Land Use and Settlement in Gamu Gofa, Ethiopia," Occasional Paper, 17 (Kampala, Makerere University: 1970).

_____. "Some Observations on the von Thünen Method of Analysis: with reference to Southern Ethiopia," East African Geographical Review, 8 (1970).

James, W. "Sister Exchange Marriage," Scientific American, 223: 6 (1975).

Jousseaume, F. Impressions de voyage en Apharras (Afars) 2 vols. (Paris: 1914).

_____. "Sur l'infibulation ou mutilation des organs génitaux de la femme chez les peuples de la Mer Rouge et du Golfe d'Aden," R. d'Anthropologie 4 (1889).

Kapeliuk, Olga. "Traitement special du corps et de l'âme dans la syntaxe Ethiopienne," JES, 11: 1 (1973).

Karsten, D. "The Luwa System of the Garbicco Subtribe of the Sidama (Southern Ethiopia) as a special case of an age set system," Paideuma, 14 (1968).

_____. "Die Ensete (Falsche Banane), ein Beispiel zur Ernaehrungswirtschaft in Aethiopien," Afrika Spectrum, 1 (1968).

_____. The Economics of Handicrafts in Traditional Societies: an investigation in Sidamo and Gemu Goffa Province, Southern Ethiopia (Munich: Weltforum-Verlag, 1972).

_____. "Problems of Industrialisation in Ethiopia," EO, 11: 1 (1967).

Kieran, J. "A Route to the Galla," Hadith, 3 (1971).

Kifle Wodajo. "Wedding Customs Among the Amhara," UCAAESB, 2 (1953).

Klausberger, F. "Die Leqa-Hordo: ein Beitrag zur Geschichte der Galla in Aethiopien," Wiener Ethnohistorische Blaetter, 7 (1973).

Klingenheben, A. "Zur amharischen Poesie," RSE, 15 (1960).

Knuttson, E. E. Authority and Changes: a study of the Kallu Insti-

tution Among the Macha Galla of Ethiopia #29 (Goteborg, Etno-
grafiska Museet: 1963).

_____. "Social Structure of the Mecca Galla," Ethnology, 2
(1963).

_____. "Dichotomisation and Integration in South-Ethiopia," Ethnic
Groups and Boundaries. Ed. F. Barth (Oslo: 1969).

_____. "Possession and Extra-Institutional Behavior; an essay on
Anthropological Micro-Analysis," Ethnos, 40: 1-4 (1975).

Kobishchanov, Y. M. "Les données primordiales sur les chasseurs-
cueill-eurs de l'Ethiopie," VIIe Congrès international des
Sciences anthropologiques et ethnologiques, Moscow, 1964 (pub.
1970).

Koehn, Peter and Waldron, S. R. Afocha: a Link between Community and Administration in Harar, Ethiopia. Foreign and Comparative Studies/African Series 31 (Syracuse University, Max-
well School: 1978).

Kolmodin, Joh. Traditions de Tsazzega et Hazegga (Uppsala: 1912-
1916).

_____. "Meine Studdienreise in Abessinien 1908-1910," Le Monde
Oriental, 4.

Lange, W. Gimira, Remnants of a Vanishing Culture (Frankfurt/
Main: 1975).

_____. Dialectics of Divine "Kingship" in the Kafa Highlands
(Los Angeles, ASC, U. of California: 1976). Occasional
Paper #15.

_____. Domination and Resistance: Narrative Songs of the Kafa
Highlands. Monograph #8 (ASC, MSU: 1979).

_____. "Relations of Production in Feudal Kafa and Sheka," P.
5th ICES, Chicago: 1978 (pub. 1979).

Lauro, Raffaele di. "Panorama politico-economico dei Galla e Sidama: Tradizioni indigene e realta," REC, 26 (1938).

Lebel, P. "On Gurage Architecture," JES, 7: 1 (1969).

_____. "Oral Tradition and Chronicles on Gurage Immigration,"
JES, 1: 2 (1963).

_____. "Economic and Social Indicators as Predictors of the
Ethiopian Revolution of 1975," P. 5th ICES, Chicago, 1978
(pub. 1979).

LeClant, Jean. "Deux têtes de pierres dressées du Sidamo," AE, 1 (1955).

Leiris, M. "Un rite medico-magique éthiopien," Aethiopica, 3 (1945).

_____. "Le Culte des Zars à Gondar," Aethiopica (1933).

Leslau, Wolf. "Ethiopic Documents: Gurage," Viking Fund Publications in Anthropology, 14 (1950).

_____. "Observations on Gurage Documents," Word, 6 (1950).

_____. "Observations on Gurage Notes," Africa, 21 (1951).

_____. "The Gurage and their Social Life," American Anthropologist, 59 (1957).

_____. "An Ethiopian Argot of a Gurage Secret Society," J. of American Oriental Society, 79 (1959).

_____. "An Ethiopian Argot of People Possessed by a Spirit," Africa, 19 (1949).

_____. "An Ethiopian Merchant's Argot," Language, 25 (1959).

_____. "An Ethiopian Minstrel's Argot," J. American Oriental Society, 72 (1952).

_____. "Ethiopic proverbs in Chaha," Word, 5 (Aug. 1949).

_____. "Asat, the soul of the Gurage," Africa, 39: 3 (1969).

_____. "Harari idioms," RSE, 19 (1963).

_____. with S. Chojnacki. "On Mule-back through Gurage in Ethiopia," Canadian Geographical Journal, 58: 3 (1959).

_____. Documents Tigriña (éthiopien septentrional) (Paris: 1941).

_____, and C. Leslau. African Poems and Love Songs (Mt. Vernon, N. Y., Peter Pauper Press: 1970).

_____, and H. Courlander. The Fire on the Mountain and other Ethiopian Stories (New York, Holt, Rinehart: 1956).

Lester, P. "Etude anthropologique des populations de l'Ethiopie," l'Anthropologie, 1-4 (1928).

Levine, Donald. "The Concept of Masculinity in Ethiopian Culture," Int'l J. of Social Psychiatry, 12 (1966).

_____. "Menilek and Oedipus: further observations on the Ethiopian National Epic," P. 1st USCES (ASC, MSU: 1973).

Lewis, H. S. "Historical Problems in Ethiopia. The Horn of Africa." Annals of New York Academy of Science, 96 (1962).

_____. "A Reconsideration of the Socio-Political System of the
Western Galla," JSS, 9: 1 (1964).

_____. A Galla Monarchy. Jimma Abba Jifar, 1830-1932 (Madi-
son, U. of Wisconsin Press: 1965).

_____. "Kud'Arfan--a Multi-Function Institution among the
Western Galla," P. 3rd ICES, Addis Ababa, 1966, Vol. 3
(Addis Ababa: 1970).

_____. "The Origins of Galla and Somali," JAH, 7: 1 (1966).

_____. "Wealth, influence and prestige among the Shoa Galla,"
Social Stratification in Africa. Ed. Tuden and Plotnicov
(New York: Free Press, 1970).

_____. "Neighbors, Friends and Kinsmen. Principles of Social
Organization among the Cushitic-Speaking Peoples of Ethiopia,"
Ethnology, 13: 2 (1974).

Lifchitz, Deborah. Textes Ethiopiens magico-religieux (Travaux et
Mémoires de l'Inst. d'Ethnologie: 1940).

Lonfernini, B. "Il grande piano (Sidamo lamenti)," Nigrizia, 85: 1
(1967).

_____. "Eva e stata uno sbaglio (Sidamo)" Nigrizia, 87: 1 (1969).

_____. "I Sidamo," Nigrizia, 87: 6 (1969).

_____. "Calendario Sidama," Nigrizia, 87: 6 (1969).

_____. "Amore e morte nei canti Sidamo," Nigrizia, 87: 12
(1969).

Lord, Edith. "The Impact of Education on Non-scientific Beliefs in
Ethiopia," J. of Social Psychology, 47 (May, 1958).

Lortat-Jacob, B. "Notes sur la musique des Dorze d'Ethiopie méridionale," Ethiopie d'aujourd'hui, la terre et les hommes (Paris:
Musée de l'Homme, 1975).

Lydall, Jean; Strecker, Ivo. The Hamar of Southern Ethiopia. 3
vols. (Renner: Hohenschaft-larn, 1979-1980).

MacDermot, B. H. Cult of the Sacred Spear: The Story of the Nuer
Tribe in Ethiopia (London: Hale, 1972).

MacGaffey, Wyatt. "Concepts of Races in the Historiography of
Northeast Africa," JAH, 7: 1 (1966).

McLaughlin, J. "Tentative Time Depths for Nuer, Dinka and Anuak," JES, 5: 1 (1967).

Mahteme Sellassie Wolde Maskal. "Portrait retrospectif d'un gentilhomme éthiopien," P. 3rd ICES, Vol. 3 (Addis Ababa: 1970).

_____. "Study of the Ethiopian culture of Horse-names," (Amharic text) JES, 7: 1 (1969).

_____. "Bulga: study of an Ethiopian culture," (Amharic text) JES, 6: 1 (1968).

Martial de Salviac, Père. Un peuple antique ou une colonie gauloise au pays de Ménélik; Les Galla, grande nation africaine (2nd ed., Paris: 1902).

Mercier, J. Les rouleaux magiques éthiopiens (Paris, Seuil: 1979).

Mesfin Wolde Mariam. "The Population of Ethiopia, A Review," EGJ, 4: 2 (1967).

Messing, Simon. "The Abyssinian Market Town," Markets in Africa. Ed. P. Bohannan and G. Dalton (Evanston, NUP: 1962).

_____. "Role Differentiation in the Amhara Family in Ethiopia," J. Human Relations, 8: 3-4 (1960).

_____. "Group Therapy and Social Status in the Zar Cult of Ethiopia," American Anthropologist, 60 (1958).

_____. "A Modern Ethiopian Play--Self Study in Culture Change," AQ, 33: 3 (1960).

_____. "Ethiopian Folktales Ascribed to the Late Nineteenth Century Amhara Wit, Aleka Gabre Hanna," J. American Folklore, 70 (1957).

Mikael Hailu. L'Ethiopia descritta da un etiope: usi natalizi nell' Amara (Naples: 1890).

Million Tesfaye. "Mutual Aid Associations among the Kottu-Galla of Harar," UCAAESB, 2: 1 (1961).

Mizzi, A. Genni etnografici galla, ossia organizzazione civile, usi e costumi oromonici (Malta: 1935).

_____. I Proverbi Galla (prima serie) (Malta: 1935).

Mondon-Vidhailet, C. "Proverbs Abyssins," JA, 3-4 (1904).

_____. "La rhétorique étiopienne," JA, 9-10 (1907).

_____. "Etude sur le Harari," JA (1901-1902).

_____. "Etudes sur le Guragiè (d'après notes par Erich Wein-
zinger) SKW, 5 (1913).

Moreno, M. M. "Alcuni racconti galla," Riv. SO, 16 (1935).

_____. Favole e rime galla (Rome: 1935).

_____. Cent Fables amhariques mises en écrit par le Dabtara
Kenfê (Paris: 1948).

Morton, Alice. "Mystical Advocates. Explanation and Spirit-
sanctioned Adjudication in the Shoa Galla Ayana Cult," P. 1st
USCES (ASC, MSU: 1975).

Munzinger, W. Dei costumi e del diritto dei Bogos (trans. from
German) (Rome: 1891).

Needham, R. "Gurage Social Classification: Formal Notes on an
Unusual System," Africa, 39: 2 (1969).

Nicoletti-Altimari, A. "Tradizione e leggende abissine," Riv. d'Italia,
1 (1903).

Oddy, D. J., and Baker, J. D. "Socio-economic structure of two
towns in the Semên region," JES, 11: 1 (1973).

Offeio, Father. Dall'Eritrea. Lettere sui costumi abissini (Rome:
1904).

_____. "Proverbi Abissini in lingua tigray," Anthropos, 3
(1906).

Olmstead, J. "The Dorze House: A Bamboo Basket," JES, 10: 2
(1972).

_____. "The Versatile Ensete Plant: Its Use in the Gamu High-
lands," JES, 12: 2 (1974).

_____. "Agricultural Land and Social Stratification in the Gamu
Highlands of Southern Ethiopia," P. 1st USCES (ASC, MSU:
1975).

_____. "Father's Wife, Weaver's Wife: Women and Work in
Two Southern Ethiopian Communities," ASR, 18: 3 (1975).

_____, and James A. Sugar. "Ethiopia's Artful Weavers,"
National Geographic, 143: 1 (1973).

Orent, A. "A New Hypothesis for the Cultural Similarities between
the Horn and the Interlacustrine Culture Areas of East Africa,"
P. 3rd ICES, vol. 3 (Addis Ababa: 1970).

_____. "From the 'Good King' to the 'Good Chief': the evolution of Micro-Politics in Kafa, Ethiopia," (Mimeo: African Studies Association, Brandeis U., Waltham, Mass.).

_____. "Three Kafa Songs: an Insight into Sex and Marriage," (Mimeo: Northeastern Anthropological Assn., Brown University, 1969).

_____. "Folk Songs and Sociological Interpretations: a Kafa case study," (Mimeo: Int'l Meeting on African Studies, Montreal, 1969).

_____. "Dual Organization in Southern Ethiopia: Anthropological Imagination or Ethnographic Fact," Ethnology, 9: 3 (1970).

_____. "Cultural Factors inhibiting population growth amongst the Kafa of Southwest Ethiopia," Social Organization, Population and Ecology: Cross Cultural and Evolutionary Perspectives, ed. N. Moni (The Hague: Mouton, 1975).

Pankhurst, R. "Status, Division of Labour and Employment in Nineteenth and Early Twentieth Century Ethiopia," UCAAESB, 2: 1 (1967).

_____. "Gabata and Related Board Games in Ethiopia and the Horn of Africa," EO, 14: 3 (1971).

_____. "Early Nineteenth Century Oromo Childhood Reminiscenses," EJE, 7: 2 (1975).

_____. "Ethiopian Slave Reminiscences of the 19th Century," Transafrican Journal of History, 5: 1 (1976).

_____. "The History of Prostitution in Ethiopia," JES, 12: 2 (1974).

_____. "Misoneism and Innovation in Ethiopian History," EO, 7: 4 (1964).

_____. "The Old-time Handicrafts of Ethiopia," EO, 8: 3 (1964).

_____. "The role of fire-arms in Ethiopian culture (16th to 20th centuries)," J. des A., 47: 2 (1977).

_____. "Some Factors Depressing the Standard of Living of Peasants in Traditional Ethiopia," JES, 4: 2 (1966).

_____ and Andreas Eshete. "Self-help in Ethiopia," EO, 9: 3 (1958).

Parker, Enid. "Afar stories, riddles and proverbs," JES, 9: 2 (1971).

Pecci, D. "Note sul sistema delle Gada e delle classi di eta presso le popolazioni Borana," RSE, 1 (1941).

Perrini, R. I Bani Amir (Rome: 1895).

Plazikowsky-Brauner, H. "Historisches über die Hadiya," ZE, 82 (1957).

_____. "Über die Wallamo," ZE, 85: 1 (1960).

_____. "Die Schinascha in West-Aethiopien," ZE, 35: 1 (1970).

Plowman, C. "Notes on the Gadamoch Ceremonies among the Boran," J. of the African Society, 18 (1919).

Pollera, Alberto. La donna in Etiopia (Rome: 1922).

_____. I Baria e i Cunama (Rome: 1914).

Read, R. N. D. "The Gidicho Islanders of Ethiopia," GM, 34 (1962).

Reminick, R. A. "The Evil Eye Belief Among the Amhara of Ethiopia," Ethnology, 13: 3 (1974).

_____. "The Structure and Functions of Religious Belief Among the Amhara of Ethiopia," P. 1st USCES (ASC, MSU: 1975).

Ricci, M. "Usanze matrimoniali, etica sessuale e credenze degli Arbore, degli Amar e dei Gheleba," Studi Etiopici Raccolti da C. Conti Rossini (Rome, Istituto per l'Oriente: 1945).

_____. "Notizie etnografiche sugli Arbore," RSE, 9 (1950).

Rodinson, Maxime. "Les Interdictions alimentaires étiopienne," P. 3rd ICES, Addis Ababa, 1966, vol. 3 (Addis Ababa: 1970).

_____. Magie, Médecine et possession à Gondar (Paris: 1967).

_____. "Sur la question des 'influences juives' en Ethiopie," JSS, 9: 1 (1964).

Rosen, C. B. "Tigrean Political Identity: an explication of Core Symbols," P. 5th ICES (Chicago: 1979).

Roubet, Colette. "Prospection et découvertes de documents préhistoriques en Dankalie (Ethiopie septentrionale)," AE, 8 (1970).

Ruggieri, R. "Strane genti d'Etiopia: i Como adoratori e protettori dei cani," L'Italia d'oltremare (1939).

Sacchetti, A. "Sull'antropologia degli Arbore," RSE, 3: 3 (1943).

Sahle Selassie. Shinega's Village (Berkeley, U. of Calif. Press: 1964).

Salome Gebre Egziabher.   "The Changing Position of Women in
    Ethiopia, " ZK, 1973.

Sárosi, Bálint.   "Melodic Patterns in the Folk Music of the Ethio-
    pian People, " P. 3rd ICES, vol. 2 (Addis Ababa: 1970).

Savard, Georges C.   "Cross Cousin Marriage among the Patrilineal
    Afar, " P. 3rd ICES, Addis Ababa, 1966.

_____. "War Chants in Praise of Ancient Afar Heroes, " JES, 3:
    1 (1965).

_____. "The Peoples of Ethiopia, " EO, 5: 3 (1961).

Schmidt, W.   "Die Religion der Galla, " Annali Lateranensi, 1
    (1937).

Schulz, A.   "Sidamo-Voelker in Abessinien, " Paideuma, 2-3 (1942).

Seifu Metaferia Ferewe.   "Terminology for "servant" (slave) in Am-
    haric tradition, " (Amharic text) JES, 10: 2 (1972).

Shack, Dorothy M.   "Nutritional Processes and Personality Develop-
    ment among the Gurage of Ethiopia, " Ethnology, 8: 3 (1969).

Shack, William A.   The Gurage: A People of the Ensete Culture
    (London, OUP: 1966).

_____. "Hunger, Anxiety, and Ritual Deprivation and Spirit Pos-
    session among the Gurage of Ethiopia, " Man, 6: 1 (1971).

_____. "The Masqal-pole: Religious Conflict and Social Change
    in Gurageland, " Africa, 38: 4 (1968).

_____. "Notes on Occupational Castes among the Gurage of
    South-West Ethiopia, " Man, 54 (1964).

_____. "On Guragé Judicial Structure and African Political The-
    ory, " JES, 5: 2 (1967).

_____. "Religious Ideas and Social Action in Gurage Bond-
    Friendship," Africa, 33: 3 (1963).

_____. "Some Aspects of Ecology and Social Structure in the En-
    sete Complex in South-West Ethiopia, " JRAI, 93: 1 (1963).

_____. "Guilt and Innocence: Problem and Method in the Gurage
    Judicial System, " Ideas and Procedures, 1969.

_____. "Occupational Prestige, Status and Social Change in
    Modern Ethiopia, " Africa, 46: 2 (1976).

_____ and Habte-Mariam Marcos, trans. and eds.   Gods and

Heroes: Oral Traditions of the Gurage of Ethiopia (Oxford, Clarendon Press: 1974).

Simoons, F. J. "The Forked Digging Stick of the Gurage," ZE, 84 (1959).

_____. "The Agricultural Implements and Cutting Tools of Begemder and Semyen, Ethiopia," Southwestern J. Anthropology, 14: 4 (1958).

Singer, N. "The Dissolution of Religious Marriage in Ethiopia," JEL, 4: 1 (1967).

Smeds, H. "The Ensete Planning Cultures of Eastern Sidamo, Ethiopia," Acta Geographica, Helsinki, 13: 4 (1955).

Sophie Desta. "Cottage Crafts," EO, 1: 3 (1957).

"Special Issue on Harar," EO, 2: 2 (1958).

Sperber, Dan. "La notion d'ainesse et ses paradoxes chez les Dorze d'Ethiopie méridionale," Cahiers internationaux de Sociologie, 56 (1974).

_____. "Paradoxes of Seniority among the Dorze," P. 1st USCES, MSU, 1973 (ASC, MSU: 1975).

_____. "The Management of Misfortune among the Dorze," P. 5th ICES, Chicago, 1978 (Chicago: 1979).

Stanley, S. "The Political System of Sidama," P. 3rd ICES, Addis Ababa 1966, Vol. 3 (Addis Ababa: 1970).

Stauder, J. The Majangir. Ecology and Society of a Southwest Ethiopian People (Cambridge, CUP: 1971).

_____. "Anarchy and Ecology, Political Society among the Majangir," Southwestern J. Anthropology, 28 (1972).

Stinson, L. "Folk-tales of the Hadiya," JES, 3: 2 (1965).

Stitz, Volker. "The Western Argobba of Yifat, Central Ethiopia," P. 1st USCES, MSU (ASC, MSU: 1975).

Strecker, Ivo see Lydall, Jean

Strelcyn, Stefan. Prières magiques éthiopiennes pour délier les charms (Warsaw: 1955).

Tadesse, Mary. "The Rights of Women," EO, 1: 3 (1957).

Tedeschi, S. "Note storiche sulle isole Dahlac," P. 3rd ICES, 1966 (Addis Ababa: 1969) Vol. 1.

Tegegne Yetesha-work. "Talla," UCAAESB, 7 (1957).

Tekestebrahan Gabremedin, Abba. "Il Matrimonio consuetudinario in Etiopia, suoi aspetti giuridici--suo valore," P. 3rd ICES (Addis Ababa: 1970) Vol. 2.

Temesgen Gobena. "Gege, Dabo and other Communal Labours mainly among the Oromo of Western Sawa and Wallaga," UCAAESB, 7 (1957).

Teqebba Biru, Zena Adal and Roger Cowley. "The Kunfäl People and their Language," JES, 9: 2 (1971).

Terrefe Ras-Work. "Birth Customs of the Amharas of Säwa," UCAAESB, 7 (1957).

Teshager Wube. "The Wandering Student," UCAAESB, 9 (1959).

Todd, D. M. "Caste in Africa?" Africa, 47: 4 (1977).

_____. "Herbalists, Diviners and Shamans in Dinam," Paideuma (1977).

_____. "Problems of Comparative Ecstasy," NAS, 1: 3 (1979-80).

Tornay, S. "Langage et perception. La denomination des couleurs chez les Nyangatom du sud-ouest éthiopien," L'Homme, 13: 4 (1973).

_____. "Le culture materielle des Nyangatom," L'Ethiopie d'aujourd'hui, la terre et les hommes (Paris, Musée de l'Homme, 1975).

Torrey, E. F. "The Zar Cult in Ethiopia," P. 3rd ICES, 1966, Vol. 3 (Addis Ababa: 1970).

Torry, W. I. "Life in the Camel's Shadow," Natural History, 83: 5 (1974).

_____. "Residence Rules among the Gabra Nomads: some Ecological Considerations," Ethnology, 15: 3 (1976).

Tsehaye Teferra and David Beyl. "Personal pronouns in Tigrinya: a socio-linguistic study," Ethiopianist Notes, 2: 3 (1978-79).

Tubiana, J. "Un document amhara sur les Galla Karayu," Neue afrikanistische Studien. Ed. J. Lukas (1966).

_____. Un Culte des genies agraires en Ethiopie (Inst. Français d'Anthro.: 1953).

Turton, D. A. "The Relationship between Oratory and the Exercise of Influence among the Mursi," Political Language and Oratory in Traditional Society. Ed. M. Bloch (London, Academic Press: 1976).

_____. "Agreeing to Disagree: On the Measurement of Duration in a Southwestern Ethiopian Community," Current Anthropology, 19: 3 (1978).

Turton, E. R. "Bantu, Galla and Somali Migrations in the Horn of Africa: a reassessment of the Juba/Tana area," JAH, 16: 4 (1975).

Ullendorff, E. "Gurage Notes," Africa, 20: 4 (1950).

Vadasy, T. "Ethiopian folk-dance," JES, 8: 2 (1970); Tegrē and Guragē (folk-dance) JES, 9: 2 (1971); Wallo and Galla (folk-dance) JES, 11: 1 (1973).

Walker, C. H. The Abyssinian At Home (London: 1933).

_____. "Abyssinian Superstitions and Customs," African Observer, 4 (1936).

Wilkinson, J. Gardner. "Account of the Jimma Country," (by a native of that place who was a slave in Cairo), JRGS, 25 (1855).

Yilma Workneh. "An essay on Community Life," UCAAESB, 2: 1 (1961).

Young, Allan. "Magic as a 'Quasi-profession': the organization of Magic and Magical Healing among Amhara," Ethnology, 14: 3 (1975).

Yusuf Ahmed. "An Inquiry into some aspects of the economy of Harar and the records of the household economy of the Emirs of Harar (1825-1875)," UCAAESB, 10 (1960).

_____. "Afocha," JES, 3: 2 (1965).

Zanni, P. L. "La tribu dei Gumus: note etnografiche," Nigrizia (1939-40).

Felasha

Abbadie, Antoine. "Les Falacha ou Juifs de l'Ethiopie," BSG, ser. 3, 4 (1845), 43-57, 65-74.

_____. "Réponse des Falasha dits juifs d'Abyssinie aux questions faite par M. Luzzatto, orientalist de Padoue," Archives Israélites, 12 (1851).

Adelman, K. L. "The Black Jews of Ethiopia," Christian Century
    (Jan. 15, 1975).

Aeŝcoly, A. Z. "Notices sur les Falacha ou Juifs d'Abyssinie,
    d'après 'Le Journale de Voyage' d'Antoine d'Abbadie," CEA,
    2: 1 (1961).

_____. "Recueil de textes Falachas," Travaux et mémoires de
    l'Institute d'ethnologie, 55 (1951).

Borchardt, Paul. "Die Falaschajuden in Abessinien im Mittelater,"
    Anthropos, 16-17 (1923-24).

Conti Rossini, C. "Appunti di storia e letteratura Falascia," Riv.
    SO, 8 (1919-1920).

Faitlovitch, Jacques. Notes d'un voyage chez les Falachas. Rap-
    port présenté à M. Le Baron Edmond de Rothschild (Paris,
    Leroux: 1905). A summary is in Globus, 90 (1906) 163.

_____. Quer durch Abessinien. Meine zweite Reise zu den Fa-
    lachas (Berlin: 1910).

"Falashas." Encyclopedia Judaica. Vol. 6 (New York, Macmillan
    and Co.: 1970).

"The Falashas," Jewish Quarterly Review, 17 (1905).

Flad, J. M. 60 Jahre in der Mission unter den Falaschen in Abes-
    sinien: Selbstbiographie (Giessen und Basel: 1922).

_____. A Short Description of the Falashas and Kamants in Abys-
    sinia, together with an outline of the elements and a vocabulary
    of the Falasha Language (Chrischona Mission Press, Basel,
    Switzerland: 1866).

_____. Mikael Aragawi (Basel: 1952).

Godbey, Allen H. The Lost Tribes, a Myth--suggestions towards
    Rewriting Hebrew History. Chap. 9 "Yemen Jews and Falashas,"
    (Durham: Duke University, 1930).

Goldstein, Israel. "Falashas: Ethiopia's Jews," National Jewish
    Monthly (Dec. 1969).

Halèvy, J. (see under Travel and Description). "Travels in Abys-
    sinia," in A. L. Lowy, ed. Miscellany of Hebrew Literature,
    ser. 2, 2 (1877), 227.

_____. "La guerre de Sarsa-Dengel contre les Falashas, extrait
    des annales de Sarsa-Dengel," RS, 14 (1906).

_____. "Nouvelles prières des Falachas," RS, 19 (1922).

Hess, R. L. "An Outline of Falasha History," P. 3rd ICES, 1966 vol. 1 (Addis Ababa: 1969).

_____. "Toward a History of the Falasha," Eastern African History, vol. 2, 107-132. Eds. D. F. McCall, N. R. Bennett and J. Butler (New York, Praeger: 1969).

Krempel, Veronika. "Eine Berufskaste in Nordwest Aethiopien--die Kayla Falascha," Sociologus, Zeitschrift für Empirische Ethnosoziologie und Ethnopsychologie, 24 (1974).

Leslau, Wolf. "The Black Jews of Ethiopia," Commentary, 7 (1949).

_____. Coutumes et croyances des Falachas; Juifs d'Abyssinie (Paris, Institut d'Ethnologie: 1957).

_____, ed. Falasha Anthology: The Black Jews of Ethiopia (New York, Schocken Books: 1951).

_____. "A Falasha Religious Dispute," P. Academy for Jewish Research, 16 (1947).

Luzzato, P. "Mémoire sur les Juifs d'Abyssinie ou Falashas," Archives Israélites, 12-15 (1851-1854).

Marcus, Louis. "Notice sur l'époque de l'établissement des Juifs en Abyssinie," Extr. Nouveau Journal asiatique (Paris: 1829).

Mendelssohn, Sidney. The Jews of Africa: especially in the 16th and 17th Centuries (London: 1920).

Messing, Simon D. "Journey to the Falashas," Commentary, 22 (July, 1956).

Norden, Hermann. "The Black Jews of Abyssinia," Travel, 59 (Jan. 1930).

_____. See also listing under Travel and Description.

Quirin, J. "The Beta Israel (Felasha) and the Process of Occupational Caste Formation, 1270-1868," P. 5th ICES (Chicago: 1979).

Rathjens, Carl. Die Juden in Abessinien (Leipzig: 1921).

Shelemay, Kay Kaufman. "Rethinking Falasha Liturgical History," P. 5th ICES (Chicago: 1979).

Stein, L. Die Juden in Abessinien (Falaschas). Ihr Ursprung, ihre geschichtliche, Entwicklung und ihre gegenwartigen Zustande. (Eine Quellenstudie (Amsterdam: 1881).

Stern, Henry A. See listing under Travel and Description.

Ullendorff, E.   "The 'Death of Moses' in the Literature of the
    Felashas, " SOAS Bull, 24 (1961).

Wurmbrand, Max.   "Remarks on the Text of the Falasha 'Death of
    Moses', " SOAS Bull, 25 (1962).

LAW

Abbadie, Antoine d'.   "La procédure en Ethiopie, " Extr. Nouvelle
    Revue histoire de droit français et étranger, " (Paris: 1888).

Ahooja, Krishna.   "Law and Development in Ethiopia, " EO, 10: 2
    (1966).

Beckstrom, J. H.   "Transplantation of Legal Systems: an early
    report on the reception of western Laws in Ethiopia, " Ameri-
    can J. Comparative Law, 21 (1973).

Bieber, F. J.   "Das Recht der Kaffitscho, " Globus, 92 (1907).

Brown, Robert L.   "Comparative Statistics on Crime: Ethiopia and
    the United States, " ASR, 16: 3 (1973).

_____.   "Juvenile Delinquency in Ethiopia, " EO, 14: 2 (1971).

Capomazza, Ilario.   Il diritto consuetudinario dell'Acchelè-Guzai
    (Asmara: 1909).

Castro, Lincoln de.   "Criminali, guidici e tribunali etiopici, " BSGI,
    48 (1911).

Consolidated Laws of Ethiopia: an unofficial compilation of National
    Laws in effect as of September 10, 1969.   2 vols (Faculty of
    Law, HSIU: 1972).

Corpus iuris Abessinorum.   Ed. Johannes Bachman (New York:
    1890).

Costanzo-Beccaria, Giuseppe A.   "Traditions, Legislation and Cus-
    tomary Law in Ethiopia, " P. 3rd ICES, vol. 3 (Addis Ababa:
    1970).

David, René.   "A Civil Code for Ethiopia: Considerations on the
    Codification of the Civil Law in African Countries, " Tulane
    Law Review, 37: 2 (1963).

_____.   Le Droit de la famille dans le code civil éthiopien (Mi-
    lan: Istituto Giuridico, Università degli Studi di Camerino:
    1967).

Fetha Nagast, (The Law of the Kings). Trans. by Abba Paulos
    Tzudua. Ed. Peter L. Strauss (Addis Ababa, Faculty of Law,
    HSIU: 1968).

Fusella, Luigi. "Il nuovo codice penale etiopico," JSS, 9: 1 (1964).

_____. "Lo statuto del Barequa," RSE, 6 (1947).

Gabre Sadik Dagafou. Die völkerrechtliche Lage Athiopiens seit
    1941 (Bonn, Reinischen Friedrich Wilhelm Universitat: 1961).

Graven, Jean. Le Code pénal de l'Empire d'Ethiopie du 23 Juillet
    1957 (Paris, Centre Français de Droit Comparé: 1959).

Graven, Phillippe. An Introduction to Ethiopian Penal Law (Addis
    Ababa; Faculty of Law, HSIU: 1965).

Guadagni, Marco. Ethiopian Labour Law Handbook (Asmara; Il
    Poligrafico P. L. C.: 1972).

_____. "Note sulle fonti del diritto etiopico (con particolare ri-
    ferimento all'istituto del divorzio)," Africa, 28 (Sept. 1973).

Ilg, Alfred. "Uber das Gerichtswesen in Athiopien," JGEG, 12
    (1911-1912).

Krzeczunowicz, George. "The Ethiopian Civil Code: its usefulness,
    Relation to Custom and Applicability," J. African Law, 7: 3
    (1963).

_____. "The Law of Filiation in Ethiopia," P. 3rd ICES, vol. 3
    (Addis Ababa: 1970) (see also JEL, 3 (1966)).

_____. "A new Legislative Approach to Customary Law: The
    'repeals' Provisions of the Ethiopian Civil Code of 1960,"
    JES, 1: 1 (1963).

_____. "Ethiopian legal education: retrospect and prospect,"
    JES, 1: 1 (1963).

Lowenstein, Steven. Materials for the Study of the Penal Law of
    Ethiopia (Addis Ababa, Faculty of Law, HSIU: 1963).

_____. "Ethiopia" 35-57 in African Penal Systems (New York,
    Praeger: 1969).

Marein, Nathan. The Ethiopian Empire; Federation and Laws
    (Rotterdam; Royal Netherlands Printing and Lithography Co.:
    1954).

_____. Handbook of the Laws of Ethiopia (Addis Ababa: 1949).

_____. The Judicial System and the Laws of Ethiopia (Rotterdam, Royal Netherlands Printing and Lithographing Co.: 1951).

_____. "Laws Affecting Women," EO, 1: 3 (1957).

Moreno, M. M. "La terminologia dei nuovi codici etiopici," RSE, 20 (1964).

O'Donavan, Katherine. "Void and Voidable Marriages in Ethiopian Law," JEL, 8: 2 (1972).

Pankhurst, Sylvia. "The New Ethiopian Penal Code," EO, 2: 8 (1958).

Paul, James C. "Problems of Public Law and Political Development," P. 1st USCES (ASC, MSU: 1975).

_____. See also listing under Government.

Plater, Zyg B. see Government

"The Prison Farm at Robi," EO, 4: 12 (1960).

Pollera, A. L'Ordinamento della giustizia e la procedure indigena in Etiopia e in Eritrea (Rome: 1913).

Redden, Kenneth R. The Law Making Process in Ethiopia (Addis Ababa, Faculty of Law, HSIU: 1966).

_____. The Legal System of Ethiopia. Vol. 1, Legal Systems of Africa (Charlottesville, Va., Michie Co., 1969).

Russell, Franklin F. "The New Ethiopian Penal Code," American J. of Comparative Law, 10 (1961).

Sedler, Robert A. The Conflict of Laws in Ethiopia (Addis Ababa, Faculty of Law, HSIU: 1965).

_____. Ethiopian Civil Procedure (Addis Ababa, Faculty of Law, HSIU and OUP: 1968).

Selamu Bekele and J. Vanderlinden. "Introducing the Ethiopian Law Archives: some documents on the First Ethiopian Cabinet," JEL, 4: 2 (1967).

Singer, Norman J. "A Traditional Legal Institution in a Modern Legal Setting: The Atbia Dagnia of Ethiopia," UCLA Law Review, 18: 2 (1970).

_____. "Ethiopia: Human Rights, 1948-1978," P. 5th ICES (Chicago: 1979).

_____. "The Use of Courts as a Key to Legal Development: an

analysis of Legal Attitudes of the Cambata of Ethiopia," P. 1st USCES (ASC, MSU, 1975).

Sperry, David. "Law and the Religious Community," P. 1st USCES (ASC, MSU: 1975).

Strauss, Peter L. "On Interpreting the Ethiopian Penal Code," JEL, 5: 2 (1968).

"Study of respect for the law in Amharic literature," (in Amharic) JES, 8: 1 (1970).

Seyoum Gebregziabher. Collection of Labour Laws of Ethiopia (Addis Ababa, Federation of Employers: 1967).

Vanderlinden, J. An Introduction to the Sources of Ethiopian Law. (Addis Ababa, Faculty of Law, HSIU: 1966).

_____. See also listing with Selamu Bekele.

Yohannes Berhane. Delict and Torts: An Introduction to the Sources of the Law of Civil Wrong in Contemporary Ethiopia (Asmara, Il Poligrafico: 1969).

LITERATURE
(Titles of religious or secular works are not included)

Beylot, R. "Notes de littérature éthiopienne," Semitica, 27 (1977).

Cerulli, E. "Nuove idee nell'Etiopia e nuova letterature amarica," OM, 6 (1926).

_____. "Nuove pubblicazioni in lingua amarica," OM, 12: 6 (1932).

_____. La letteratura etiopica (Florence: 1958) (3rd edition, 1968).

Chaine, Marius. "La poésie chez les Ethiopiens: poésie amharique," Revue de l'Orient Chrétien, ser. 3, 2: 3 and 4 (1923).

Cohen, Marcel. "La naissance d'une litterature imprimée en amharique," JA, 206 (Avr.-juin, 1925).

_____. "La langue littéraire amharique," Comptes rendus du groupe linguistique d'Etudes chamito-semitiques, 2 (1937).

Comba, Pierre. "Le roman dans la littérature éthiopienne de langue amharique," JSS, 9: 1 (1964).

_____. "Une année de publications en langue Amharique," AE, 2 (1957).

_____. "Bref aperçu sur les debuts de la litterature de la langue amharique et sur ses tendences actuelle," EO, 2: 3 (1958).

Conti Rossini, Carlo. "Notes per la storia letteraria abissinia," RRAL (Scienze Morali...) ser. 5, 8 (1900).

Cowley, Roger W. "The Beginnings of the andem Commentary Tradition," JES, 10: 2 (1972).

_____. "Old Testament Introduction in the Andemta Commentary Tradition," JES, 12: 1 (1974).

_____ and Aleme Teferu. "The study of Geez manuscripts in Tégre province," JES, 9: 1 (1971).

_____. "Preliminary notes on the balaandem commentaries," JES, 9: 1 (1971).

Doresse, Jean. "Littérature éthiopienne et litterature occidentale au moyen-age," B. Société d'Archéologie Copte, 16 (1962).

Gerard, Albert G. "Amharic Creative Literature: The early phase," JES, 6: 2 (1968).

_____. Four African Literatures: Xhosa - Sotho - Zulu - Amharic (Berkeley, California, UC Press: 1971).

Getachew Haile. "Remarks on the Contents of Ge'ez Literature of Ethiopia," History Journal (Addis Ababa), 2: 3 (1968).

Grébaut, S. "Note sur la poésie ethiopienne," ROC (1909).

Guidi, Ignazio. Breve storia della Letterature Etiopica (Rome, Istituto per l'Oriente: 1932).

_____. "Le odierne letterature dell'Imperio Etiopico," Atti del Reale Istituto Veneto di Scienze, Lettere ed Arti, 92 (1932-33).

_____. "Contributi alla storia letteraria di Abissinia," RRAL, ser. 6, 31: 3-4 (1922).

Harden, J. M. An Introduction to Ethiopic Christian Literature (London Society for Promoting Christian Knowledge: 1926).

Hecht, Elisabeth-Dorothea. "The Kebra Nagast: Oedipus and Menilek; a comparison of two myths," P. 5th ICES (Chicago: 1979).

Kane, Thomas L. Ethiopian Literature in Amharic (Wiesbaden, Harrassowitz: 1975).

_____ . "Arabic Translations into Amharic, " SOAS Bull. 37, part 3 (1974).

Kebra Negest (Glory of the Kings) Trans. into English by E. A. W. Budge as The Queen of Sheba and Her Only Son Menyelek (London: 1922).

Lantschoot, A. "Abba Salama, Métropolite d'Ethiopia (1348-1388), et son role de traducteur, " ACISE (Rome: 1959).

Littman, Enno. "Specimens of Popular Literature of Modern Abyssinia, " J. American Oriental Society, 23 (1902).

_____ . "The Legend of the Queen of Sheba in the Tradition of Axum, " Biblioteca Abessinica, 1 (Leyden: 1904).

Menghistu Lemma. "From Traditional to Modern Literature in Ethiopia, " ZK (1973).

Mittwoch, "Literarisches Morgenrot in Abessinien, " Deutsche Literatur, 45 (1973).

Moreno, M. M. "Letteratura etiopica, " Civiltà dell'Oriente, ed. G. Tucci (Rome: 1957).

Pankhurst, R. "The Foundation of Education, Printing, Newspapers, Book Production, Libraries and Literacy in Ethiopia, " EO, 6: 3 (1962).

Pankhurst, Sylvia. "Biblical Commentaries and the Schools, " EO, 2: 3 (1958).

Ricci, Lanfranco. Letterature dell'Etiopia (Milan: 1969).

_____ . "Romanzo e novella: due esperimenti della letterature amarica attuale, " JSS, 9: 1 (1964).

Sengal, Elena. "Note sulla letteratura moderna amarica, " Annali dell'Istituto Universitario Orientale di Napoli, 2 (1943).

Spencer, Meredith. "Structural Analysis and the Queen of Sheba, " P. 5th ICES (Chicago: 1979).

Teferra Shiawl. "Aethiopiens zeitgenossische Literatur, " Afrika-Heute (Dec. 15, 1965).

_____ . "Ethiopia's Literature Today: a brief Survey, " Afrika (Cologne) 7: 1 (1966).

Tsegaye Gabre Medhin. "Literature and the African Public, " EO, 11: 1 (1967).

MEDICINE, HEALTH, AND SOCIAL SERVICES

Barkhuus, A. "Diseases and Medical Problems of Ethiopia," Ciba Symposia (1947).

Barry, B. Oscar. "Rehabilitation in Ethiopia," EO, 5: 1 (1957).

Blanc, Henry Jules. Notes médicales recueillies durant une mission diplomatique en Abyssinie (Paris, Gazette hebdomadaire des médicine: 1974).

Brielli, D. ; V. Calo; and A. Bevilacqua. Note di Patologia etiopica (Monografie e Rapporti Coloniali, Rome: 1913).

Cacciapuoti, Raffaele. "Medicina e farmacologia indigena in Etiopia," RSE, 1: 3 (1941).

Castro, Lincoln de. "Contributo allo psicopatologia d'Etiopia," Estratto dell'Archivo di Psichiatria, 30: 2 (Turin: 1911).

_____. "L'arte di Esculapio tra gli Abissini," BSGI, 45 (1908), 880-90.

_____. "Medicina vecchia e nuova in Abyssinia," BSGI, 45 (1908) 1070-92.

Chang Wen-Pin. "Development of Basic Health Services in Ethiopia," EO, 12: 4 (1969).

_____. "Population Studies in Ethiopia: Knowledge, Attitudes and Practice Surveys in Population and Health," JES, 12: 1 (1974).

Ehrenstrale, Hans. "Better Milk Utilization in Ethiopia: toward a National Nutrition Policy," EO, 4: 4 (1960).

"Ethiopian Women's Welfare Work," EO, 1: 1 (1956).

"Ethiopia's First National Seminar on Social Welfare," EO, 9: 4 (1966). "Family and Child Services in Ethiopia" Helene Castel; "Youth Welfare in Ethiopia" by M. J. Ludwig; "Philosophy and Trends in Development of Rural Life and Institutions" by E. Burke; "Urban Community Development" by Shimelis Adugna; "The Problem of Juvenile Delinquency in Ethiopia" by Mebratu Yohannes; "Treatment and Rehabilitation of Orthopaedically Handicapped" by Oscar Barry; "Social Aspects of Rehabilitation of the physically handicapped" by Nados Tessema.

Gabre Kristos Legesse. "Milk Control," EO, 4: 4 (1960).

Garraud, R. , and Ruth Imru. "Community Development Training at Majete," EO, 2: 9 (1958).

Getachew Wolde Hanna.   "School Nutrition and Gardening," EO, 4:
4 (1960).

Han Lee-Min.   "A Historical Sketch of the Public Health College
and Training Center, Gondar," EO, 10: 3 (1966).

"Home School for Lepers," EO, 2: 4 (1958).

Kloos, H.   "The Geography of Pharmacies, Druggist Shops and Rural Medicine Vendors and the Origin of Customers of such
Facilities in Addis Ababa," JES, 12: 2 (1974).

_____.   "Preliminary studies of medicinal plants and plant
products in markets of central Ethiopia," Ethnomedizin, 4:
1-2 (1976-77).

_____.   "Medicine Vendors and their Products in Markets in
the Ethiopian Highlands and Rift Valley," EN, 2: 2 (1978).

Mason, J. B. , et al.   "Nutritional Lessons from the Ethiopian
Drought," Nature, 248 (April, 1974).

Mérab, Paul.   Médicins et Médicine en Ethiopia (Paris: 1912).

Messing, Simon.   "Disease and Development in Ethiopia," #78-60
(1978), African Studies Association, Brandeis University,
Waltham, Mass.

Misrar Teferra.   "The Uses of Milk and Milk Products in the
Home," EO, 4: 4 (1960).

"Mother and Child Welfare," EO, 4: 4 (1960).

O'Brien, Henry R.   "Mapping a Program of Public Health for
Ethiopia and Eritrea," Public Health Reports, 68: 10 (1953).

Pankhurst, Richard.   "The Beginnings of Modern Medicine in
Ethiopia," EO, 9: 2 (1965).

_____.   "Some Factors influencing the Health of Traditional
Ethiopia," JES, 4: 1 (1966).

_____.   "The History and traditional treatment of smallpox in
Ethiopia," Medical History, 9: 4 (1965).

_____.   "The History of Cholera in Ethiopia," Medical History,
12: 4 (1968).

_____.   "The History of Typhus in Ethiopia," Medical History,
12: 3 (1968).

_____.   "Some Notes for the History of Influenza in Ethiopia,"
Medical History, 21: 2 (1977).

_____ . "The History and Traditional Treatment of Rabies in Ethiopia, " Medical History, 14: 4 (1970).

_____ . "The Hedar Bäšeta of 1918, " JES, 13: 2 (1975).   (flu epidemic)

_____ . "The Traditional Taenicides of Ethiopia, " J. History of Medicine and Allied Sciences, 24: 3 (1969).

_____ . "Traditional Ethiopian treatments for syphilis (17th to 20th century), " J. History of Medicine and Allied Sciences, 30: 3 (1975).

_____ (with Tony Pearson).   "Remedius Prutky's 18th century account of Ethiopian taenicides and other medical treatment, " EMJ, 10: 1 (1972).

_____ .   "Dr. A. Brayer and Europe's discovery of Kosso, " EMJ, 13: 4 (1975).

_____ . "An historical note on Ethiopian terminology for syphilis, " Afrika und Ubersee, 59: 1 (1974).

_____ . "An historical examination of traditional Ethiopian Medicine and Surgery, " EMJ, 3: 4 (1965).

_____ . "An outline of traditional Ethiopian medicine, " in Science and Humanity Yearbook (Moscow: 1964).

_____ . "The Medical History of Ethiopia during the Italian Fascist Invasion and Occupation (1935-1941), " EO, 16: 2 (1973).

Pankhurst, Sylvia.   "The Ethiopian Women's Welfare Association, " EO, 4: 2 (1960).

_____ . "The Gandhi Memorial Hospital: an Indian Gift, " EO, 4: 10 (1960).

_____ . "The Social Service Society, " EO, 4: 2 (1960).

Rochet d'Héricourt, C. E. X.   "Notes sur la racine employée dans le nord de l'Abyssinie (à Devratabor) contre l'hydrophobie, communiquée à l'Académie des Sciences, " NAV, 124 (1849).

Roundy, R. W.   "The Cultural Geography of Communicable Disease Transmission in Ethiopia, " P. 1st USCES, MSU, 1973.

"St. Paul's Hospital for the Poor, " EO, 3: 1 (1959).

Sandford, R. H. D.   "Milk and Cattle, " EO, 4: 4 (1960).

Seyoum G. Selassie see Education section

Singer, C. "Notes on Cases met in South-Western Abyssinia, " J.
    Tropical Medicine, 12 (1909).

Solomon Ayalew. "Macro evaluation of Health Expenditure in Ethio-
    pia, " EO, 16: 3 (1973).

Stiller, Josef. "Das Leprösen--Hospital Bisidimo, " ZK (1973).

Strelcyn, Stefan. "Les Ecrits Médicaux Ethiopien, " JES, 3: 1
    (1965).

_____. "Ethiopian Medical Treatises as source for the study of
    early Amharic, P. First International Congress of Africanists
    (Accra: 1962).

_____. Médecine et plantes d'Ethiopie (Warsaw: 1968).

_____. "Un traité éthiopien d'hygiène et de diététique, " African
    Bulletin (Warsaw: 1964).

_____. "Les Médecines du Bégamder et du Tchelgas (Ethiopie)
    d'Abbaba Garred, " African Bulletin (Warsaw: 1966).

_____. Mission scientifique, en Ethiopie (Conference faite le 28
    mars 1956) (Rome, A. Signorelli: 1959).

Tayetch Wolde Georgis. "Home Economics in Ethiopia, " EO, 4: 4
    (1960).

"Toward Better Health, " EO, 3: 1 (1959).

"UNICEF and the Children in the Future of Ethiopia, " EO, 2: 9
    (1958).

"Voluntary Social Work in Ethiopia, " EO, 4: 2 (1960).

Weithaler, Kurt L. "Die deutsche Medizin in Athiopien, " and
    "Moderne Medizin und Gesundheitsdienst in Athiopien, " ZK
    (1973).

"The World Health Organisation in Ethiopia, " EO, 4: 4 (1960).

Wurtz, R. "Hygiène publique et privée en Abyssinie, " La Semaine
    Médicale (7 Dec. 1896).

Yemed Alemu. "A Brief Report on a Nutrition Survey, " EO, 4: 4
    (1960).

Yeshimebet Tafari. "The Pre-School Children Feeding Program, "
    EO, 4: 4 (1960).

Young, Alan. "The Practical Logic of Amhara Traditional Medicine," Rural Africana (Winter, 1974-75).

MISSIONS AND MISSIONARIES

Agostini, D. d'. Storia della vita del venerabile Giustino de Jacobis, apostolo dell'Abissinia (Naples: 1910).

Alays, Père. Capucins missionaires en Afrique Orientale. Pays
Galla, en Ethiopie, Cote Française des Somalis (Toulouse:
Les Voix Franciscaines: 1931).

Aleme Eshete. Activités Politiques de la Mission Catholique (Lazariste) en Ethiopie (sous la règne de l'Empereur Johannes,
1869-1889). (Paris, Etudes Documentaires: 1970).

_____. La Mission Catholique lazariste en Ethiopie (Aix-en-
Provence, Faculté des Lettres et Sciences Humanines, Institut
d'Histoire des Pays d'Outre-mer: 1972).

Anderson, W. B. Ambassadors by the Nile: The Church in North
East Africa (London, Lutterworth Press: 1963).

Annales de la congrégation de la Mission (Lazarist). All vols. from
1840.

Arata, S. Abuna Yakob, Apostolo dell'Abissinia (Mons. Giustino de
Jacobis C. M.) 1800-1860 (Rome, 2nd ed. 1934).

Aren, Gustav. Evangelical Pioneers in Ethiopia; origins of the Evangelical Church Mekane Yesus (Uppsala, Studia Missionalia Up-
saliensia 32: 1978).

Azais, Bernardin. "Lettres," L'Echo de St. François, 5 (1898);
10 (1902).

_____. "Lettres." Missions Catholiques, 31 (1899).

_____. "Lettres." Petit Messager de St. François, 6 (1901).

"The Baha'i in Ethiopia," EO, 5: 2 (1961).

Bernoville, G. Monseigneur Jarosseau et la Mission des Gallas.
Mission d'Ethiopie (Paris: 1950).

Betta, Luigi. "Fondazione della Missione Lazzarista in Abissinia
(1838)," Annali della Missione, 62: 45 (1955).

_____. "Il B. Giustino de Jacobis, Prefetto Apostolico dell'
Etiopia," Annali della Missione, 67 (1960); 68 (1961).

Bockelman, W. and E. Ethiopia: Where Lutheran Is Spelled
    "Mekane Yesus." (Minneapolis, Augsburg Pub.: 1972).

Canton, W. History of the British and Foreign Bible Society.
    4 vols (London: 1904 and 1910).

Carouge, A. de. Une Mission en Ethiopie d'après les mémoires
    du Cardinal Massaia et d'autres documents (Paris: 1902).

"The Catholic Church in Ethiopia," African Ecclesiastical Review,
    13 (1971).

Chalais, Martial. "Les anciens missionaires Capucins de
    l'Ethiopie et science," Etudes Franciscaine, 5 (1902).

_____. "Mission des Gallas," Mission Catholiques Françaises,
    2 (1900).

Church Missionary Record, detailing the Proceedings of the Church
    Missionary Society, 1-15 (1830-44).

Cleland, C. S. "Seen in Abyssinia," The Missionary Review of
    the World, 47: 12 (1924).

Constantius II Augustus. "Letter of Constantius to the Ethiopians
    against Frumentius." In Nicene and Post-Nicene Fathers of
    the Christian Church. Vol. 4, 2nd. ser. (Grand Rapids,
    Michigan: 1953).

Conti Rossini, C. "Lo Hatata Zar 'a Ya' qob e il Padre Giusto da
    Urbino," RRAL, ser. 5, 29 (1920).

_____. "Il libro delle leggende e tradizioni abissine dell'ecciaghe
    Filpos," RRAL, ser. 5, 26 (1917).

_____. See Conti Rossini under History, ancient and Medieval.

Cotterell, F. P. Born at Midnight (Chicago, Moody Press: 1973).

_____. "An Indigenous Church in Southern Ethiopia," B. Society
    for African Church History, 3: 1-2 (1960).

Coulbeaux, J.-B. "Abouna Salama," Revue Anglo-romaine, 1
    (1895).

_____. Un Martyr abyssin, Ghebra-Michael de la Congrégation
    de la Mission (Lazariste) (Paris: 1902). Revised as Vers la
    lumière, Le Bienheureux Abba Ghèbrè-Michael, prêtre de la
    mission martyrisé en Ethiopie (Paris: 1926).

Crummey, Donald. "Foreign Missions in Ethiopia, 1829-1868," B.
    Society for African Church History, 2: 1 (1965).

Bibliography   382

_____. Priests and Politicians; Protestant and Catholic Missions
in Orthodox Ethiopia 1830-1868 (Oxford, Clarendon Press:
1972).

Davis, Raymond J. Fire on the Mountains: The Story of a Miracle
--The Church in Ethiopia (Grand Rapids, Michigan: 1966).

"Développement et évangelisation--une analyse éthiopienne, " L'Afrique
Urbaine, 45 (1974).

Farina, G. Le Lettere del Cardinale Massaia dal 1846 al 1886
(Turin: 1936).

Le Figlie di S. Anna in Etiopia in 1866-1966 (Rome: 1966).

Flad, J. M. Notes from the Journal of F. (sic) M. Flad, one of
Bishop Gobat's Pilgrim Missionaries in Abyssinia (London:
1860) ed. Rev. W. D. Veitch.

_____. See also under Travel and Description, and Felashas.

Giacchero, G. and Bisogni, G. Vita di Giuseppe Sapeto. L'ignota
storia degli esordi coloniali italiani rivelata da documenti
inediti (Florence: 1942).

Gimalac, Paul. "Le vicariat apostolique d'Abyssinie (1839-1931), "
Revue d'histoire des missions, 9 (1932).

Gobat, Samuel. Journal of a Three Years' Residence in Abyssinia,
in furtherance of the objects of the Church Missionary Society.
(London: 1834). Reprinted 1969 NUP, Greenwood.

Gondal, I. L. Il Christianismo nel paese di Menelik (Rome: 1908).

Groves, C. P. The Planting of Christianity in Africa (London,
Lutterworth Press, 1964) 4 vols. See Vol. 2, 85-91; 290-293.

Hailu, G. Y. "Un Manoscritto Amarico sulle Verità della Fede, "
ACISE (ANL: 1960).

Hayla-Dengel, Abba. "Lettre d'un prêtre indigène de la Mission
Galla, " L'Echo de St. François et de St. Antoine de Padoue,
15: 183 (1926).

Herbert, Lady Mary E. Abyssinia and its Apostle (de Jacobis) (London: 1867).

Isenberg, K. and Krapf, J. L. See under Travel and Description.

Iwanson, Jonds. Notizie storiche e varie sulla Missione Evangelica
Svedese dell'Eritrea, 1866-1916 (Asmara: Missione Evangelica
Svedese, 1918).

Jarosseau, André. "L'Apostolat Catholique au Kaffa de Kaffa de
    1861 à 1912," Revue Histoire Missions, 9 (1932).

_____. "L'Ethiopie au Vatican; l'Apostolat du Cardinal Massaia
    et de ses successeurs," Analecta Ordinis Minorum Cappoccino-
    rum, 41 (1925).

_____. "Précis historique et chronologique des principaux événe-
    ments depuis la fondation de la mission des Gallas (1846)
    jusqu'à nos jours," Analecta Ordinis Minorum Cappoccinorum,
    43 (1927) and 44 (1928).

Krapf, J. L.   Travels, Researches and Missionary Labours (London:
    1860). (Reprinted London, Frank Cass: 1968).

Lambie, Thomas A.   "Pioneer Missions in Abyssinia," Bibliotheca
    Sacra, 85 (1928).

Larigaldie, G.   Le vénérable Justin de Jacobis (Paris: c. 1910).

Lass-Westphal, Ingeborg.   "Protestant Missions during and after the
    Italian-Ethiopian War, 1935-1937," JES, 10: 1 (1972).

Lauro, Raffaele di.   "Etiopia Vecchio Regime: Il Massacro dello
    Missione Canadese nel 1936," Gli Annali, 1 (1938).

Lefèvre, Renato.   "L'Abissinia nella politica orientale di Gregorio
    XIII," Gli Annali, 1 (1938).

Light for Dark Ethiopia.   Christ for the World Material for 1962 in
    three studies (Board of Foreign Missions, Chicago, Ill., 1962).

Lombard, Pascal.   "Nouvelles de nos missions d'Abyssinie,"
    L'Echo de St. François, 26: 297 (1936).

Mario da Abiy-Addi' (Ayyala Takla Haymanot).   La dottrina della
    Chiesa etiopica dissidente sull'Unione Ipostatica.   #147 in series
    Orientalia Christiana Analecta (Rome, Pont. Institutum Orien-
    talium Studiorum: 1956).

Martial de Salviac, Père.   "Mission des Galla," Les Missions Catho-
    liques Françaises, 2 (1901).

Massaia, Father Gugliemo.   See listing under Travel and Descrip-
    tion.

_____. "Un ami et bienfaiteur de l'Ethiopie: Justin de Jacobis.
    Lettre inedité de Mgr. Massaia," Revue d'histoire des Mis-
    sions, 12 (1935).

_____   see   Farina, G.

Meinardus, Otto F. A.   "Peter Heyling in the light of Catholic His-
    toriography," Ostkirchliche Studien, 18: 1 (1969).

_____. "Peter Heyling, History and Legend," Ostkirchliche Studien (1965).

Metodio da Nembro, Padre. La Missione dei Minori Cappuccini in Eritrea (1894-1952) (Rome: 1953).

_____. Vita missionaria in Eritrea (Rome: 1953).

Mezzabotta, Ernesto. Il Cappuccino Eritreo. Episodii drammatici della querra d'Africa (Rome: 1896).

"Missionaries and the Law," EO, 4: 2 (1960).

"Missionary Work in Ethiopia," EO, 4: 3 (1960).

Mojoli, Giuseppe. La Chiesa in Etiopia: Note e ricordi di un nunzio (Rome: 1973).

Monneret de Villard, Ugo. "L'origine dei più antichi tipi di chiese abissine," Atti del 3rd Congresso di Studi Coloniali a Firenze, 1937.

_____. Storia della Nubia cristiana (Rome: 1938).

_____. "Su una possibile origine delle danze liturgiche nella chiesa abissina," OM, 22 (1942).

_____. "Perchè la chiesa abissina dipendeva dal patriarchato d'Alessandria," OM, 23 (1943).

_____. See other listings under History, ancient and medieval.

Mordini, A. "Il convento di Gunde Gundiè," RSE, 12 (1953).

Murad Kamil. "Letters to Ethiopia from the Coptic Patriarchs, Yo'annas XVIII (1770-1796) and Marqos VIII (1796-1809)," B. SAC, 8 (1942). (Arabic texts)

Offeio, Francesco da. I Cappuccini nella Colonia Eritrea: Ricordi (Rome: 1910).

Othmer, Fr. Cajus O. F. M. "P. Liberatus Weiss, O. F. M. Seine Missionstaetigkeit und Sein Martyrium (3 Marz 1716)," Archivum Franciscanum Historicum, 20 (Florence: 1927).

Oudenrijn, Marc-Antoine van den. "L'évêque dominicain fr. Barthélemy fundateur supposé d' un couvent dans le Tigrê au 14e siècle," RSE, 5 (1946). (pseudo-ethiopica)

Pacelli, M. Viaggi in Etiopia del P. Michelangelo da Tricarico, Minore Usservante, ne'quali si descrivono le cose più rimarche-voli, ed osservabili incontrate in quella regione sulle orme del Ludolf, De La Croix, ed altri celebri scrittori di quei luoghi (Naples: 1797). (Mission of Father Tobias)

Pane, S. Il Beato Giustino de Jacobis della Congregazione della
     Missione. Vescovo Titolare di Nilopoli. Primo Vicario Apos-
     tolico di Abissinia (Storia critica sull'ambiente e sui documen-
     ti) (Naples: 1949).

Pankhurst, Richard. "The Saint Simonians and Ethiopia," P. 3rd
     ICES, vol. 1 (Addis Ababa: 1969). (See also Combes and
     Tamisier under Travel and Description.)

Pankhurst, Rita. "Mikael Aragawi: Ethiopia's First Protestant Mis-
     sionary," EO, 10: 3 (1966).

Paton, W. and Sinclair, M. "Survey of Missions in Ethiopia,"
     Int'l Review of Missions, 32: 125 (1943).

Rasmussen, Lester. "The Seventh-Day Adventist Mission," EO, 4:
     3 (1960).

Rayner, DeCourcy H. "Persecution in Ethiopia," Christianity Today,
     7: 3 (1972).

Richard, J. "Les Premiers missionnaires latins en Ethiopie (XIIe-
     XIVe siècles)," ACISE (Rome: 1959).

Roehrich, L. Samuel Gobat, ancien missionnaire en Abyssinie
     et évêque anglican de Jerusalem (Paris and Basel:
     1880).

Roeykens, R. P. A. See under History, c. 1670-1930.

Saeveräs, O. On Church-Mission Relations in Ethiopia, 1944-69,
     with Special Reference to Evangelical Church Mekane Yesus and
     the Lutheran Missions (Drammen: 1974).

Sapeto, G. See listing under Travel and Description.

Sergew Hable Selassie. Beziehungen Äthiopiens zur griechisch-
     römischen Welt (Bonn: 1963).

I Settanti anni della Missione Cattolica dei Padri Cappucini in
     Eritrea (1894-1964) (Asmara, Schola Tipografica Francescana,
     1964).

Sidler, W. Mission in der Krise. Aus der Sicht eines Missionars
     in Aethiopien (Giessen and Basel: 1968).

Stern, H. A. See listing under Travel and Description.

Stjarne, Per. "The Swedish Evangelical Mission in Ethiopia," EO,
     4: 3 (1960).

Stock, E. The History of the Church Missionary Society. 4 vols.
     (London, 1899 and 1916).

"The Sudan Interior Mission, " EO, 4: 3 (1960).

Takla Hāymānot, Abba. Episodi della vita apostolica di Abuna Jacob
    ossia il venerabile Padre Giustino de Jacobis raccontati da un
    testimonio Abba Teclà Haimanot prete cattolico abissino.
    Trans. from French by Father Celestino da Desio (Asmara:
    1915).

_____. See also his work listed under the translators, Conti
    Rossini, "Vicende, " and Fusella "L'ambasciata" in History
    c. 1760-c. 1930.

_____. Lettere di Abba Tecla Haymanot di Adua. 4 vols. pub-
    lished and edited by Mauro da Leonessa (Rome: 1939).

Tellez, B. See listing under Travel and Description.

Trimingham, J. S. The Christian Church and Missions in Ethiopia
    (including Eritrea and the Somalilands) (London, World Do-
    minion Press: 1950).

Valori, F. Guglielmo Massaia (Turin: 1957).

Willmott, Helen M. The Doors Were Opened: the Remarkable Ad-
    vance of the Gospel in Ethiopia (London, Sudan Interior Mis-
    sion: n. d.).

Yaqob Beyene. "Un manoscritto cattolico tigrino del XIX secolo, "
    AION, 35 (1976).

_____. "Un opuscolo cattolico di polemica teologica in tigrino
    del XIX secolo, " AION, 36: 1 (1976). Supplement 6.

RELIGION
(Ethiopian Orthodox Church and the
Ethiopian Community in Jerusalem)

Aescoly, A. Z. "La colonie éthiopienne à Jerusalem, " Aethiopica
    3 (1935).

"The Ancient, Serene Ethiopian Church, " Time (Jan. 6, 1967).

Andersen, Knut. Ethiopiens Orthodokse Kirke (Dansk Ethiopei Mis-
    sion, Copenhagen: 1971).

Arnhard, Carl von. "Die Wasserweike nach dem Ritus der Äthio-
    pischen Kirche, " Zeitschrift der Deutschen Morgenlandischen
    Gesellschaft, 41 (1887).

Aymro Wondmagegnehu, and Joachim Motovu, eds. The Ethiopian

Orthodox Church (Addis Ababa, The Ethiopian Orthodox Mission: 1970).

Beylot, Robert. "Un Episode de l'histoire ecclésiastique de l'Ethiopie, le mouvement Stéphanite. Essai sur sa chronologie et sa doctrine," AE, 8 (1970).

_____. "Le millénarisme, article de foi dans l'Eglise éthiopienne, au XVe siècle," RSE, 25 (1974).

Bezold, Carl. Äthiopische Religion. Extr. Archiv. fur Religionswissenschaft (Leipzig and Berlin: 1912).

Blyth, E. M. E. "The Church of Ethiopia," Hibbert J., 34 (Oct. 1935).

Brightman, F. E., ed. Liturgies: Eastern and Western. Vol. 1 (Oxford, Clarendon Press: 1965).

Brown, C. F. "The Ethiopian Orthodox Church," Negro History Bulletin, 35: 1 (1972).

_____. The Conversion Experience in Axum during the fourth and fifth centuries, (Dept. of History, Howard University: 1973).

Browne, P. W. "Ethiopia in its Ecclesiastical Aspects," Ecclesiastical Review, 94: 2 (1936).

Caquot, André. "Un Texte Ethiopien sur les enseignés du camp d'Israel," AE, 2 (1957).

Cerulli, Enrico. Scritti teologici etiopici dei secoli XVI-XVII. 2 vols (Biblioteca Apostolica Vaticana: 1958-1960).

_____. Etiopia in Palestina. 2 vols (Rome: 1943 and 1947).

Chaine, Marius. "Le Rituel du baptême," Bessarione, 17: 123 (1913).

The Church of Ethiopia: an introduction to the Contemporary Church. (Addis Ababa, Ethiopian Orthodox Church: 1973).

Cleret, Maxime. Ethiopie: Fidèle à la Croix (Paris, Editions de Paris: 1967).

Cohen, Marcel. "Ceremonies et croyances abyssines," Revue de l'Histoire des Religions, 66: 33 (1912).

Conti Rossini, Carlo. "Pergamene di Debra Dammo," Riv. SO, 19 (1940).

_____. "Il convento di Tsana in Abissinia e le sue Laudi alla Vergine," RRAL, ser. 5, 19 (1910).

Coppet, Maurice de. "Le Tabot," Appendix to Chronique du Règne de Ménélik II, by Guèbrè Sellassiè, Vol. 2 (Paris: 1932).

Cowley, Roger W. "The Ethiopian Church and the Council of Chalcedon," Sobernost, 6: 1 (1970).

Croze, M. V. de la. Histoire du Christianisme d'Ethiopie et d'Arménie (La Haie: 1739).

Crummey, D. See under Missions, Foreign.

Davis, Asa J. "The Church-State Ideal in Ethiopia: A Synopsis," Ibadan, 21 (1965).

_____. "The Orthodoxy of the Ethiopian Church," Tarikh, 2: 1 (1967).

Deramy, J. "Introduction et restauration du christianisme en Abyssinie (330-480)," Extr. de la Revue de l'Histoire des Religions, 31 (1895).

Doresse, Jean. "Les Fêtes d'Axoum," Connaissance du Monde (1956).

_____. "La Saison et ses fêtes: de Noel au Timkat," L'Ethiopie d'aujourd'hui, 8 (1963).

Dowling, T. E. The Abyssinian Church (London: 1907).

Duensing, H. "Die Abessinier in Jerusalem," Zeitschrift des Deutschen Palatinat-Vereins (1916).

Eadie, D. G. "Chalcedon Revisited," J. Ecumenical Studies, 10: 1 (1973).

Endalkachew Makonnen. "Religion of our Forefathers," Abba Salama, 1 (1970).

Ephraim Isaac. The Ethiopian Church. (Boston, H. N. Sawyer Co.: 1968).

_____. "An Obscure Component in Ethiopian Church History: an examination of various theories pertaining to the problem of the Origin and Nature of Ethiopian Christianity," Muséon, 85: 1-2 (1972).

_____. "Social Structure of the Ethiopian Church," EO, 14: 4 (1971).

"Ethiopian Church: Obstacle to Progress," Christianity Today, 14: 14 (Apr. 10, 1970).

"Ethiopian Patriarch visits World Council of Churches," Ecumenical Press Service, 40: 17 (June, 1973).

Funk, F. X. "Die Liturgie der äthiopischen Kirchenordnung,"
    Theol. Quartalschrift, 80: 4 (1898).

Gabre Yesus Haylu, Abba. "Considerations théologiques sur le
    Melke'a Sellase de Abba Sebhat Le'ab," P. 3rd ICES, vol. 2
    (Addis Ababa: 1970).

Gillard, J. T. "Are There any Colored Saints?" The Catholic
    World, 144: 859 (1936).

Girma Beshah and Merid Wolde Aregay. The Question of the Union
    of Churches in Luso-Ethiopian Relations 1500-1632 (Lisbon,
    Junta de Investigacoes de Ultramar Centro: 1964).

Glenday, D. K. "Mary in the Liturgy; an Ethiopian Anaphora,"
    Worship, 47 (1973).

Gondal, I. L. "Le Christianisme au pays de Ménélik," Science et
    Religion, 161 (1908).

Gragg, Gene B. "A Magic Prayer of Henoch from the Manuscript
    of the Goodspeed Collection of the University of Chicago,"
    P. 1st USCES, (ASC, MSU: 1975).

Grébaut, S. "Sargis d'Aberga (controverse judeo-chrétienne),"
    Patrologia Orientalis (Paris: ?).

Gregorious, Bishop. "The Sacraments of Baptism and Chrism in
    the Rite of the Coptic Orthodox Church," Abba Salama, 2
    (1971).

Griaule, M. "Règles de l'Eglise: documents éthiopiens," JA (July-
    Sept. 1932).

Guidi, Ignazio. "La chiesa Abissin e la chiesa russa," Nuova An-
    tologia, ser. 3, 26 (16 April 1890).

_____. "L'Eglise d'Abyssinie," Dictionnaire d'Histoire et de
    Géographie Ecclésiastique, 1 (Paris: 1912).

_____. "La chiesa abissina," OM, 2 (1922).

Haberland, Eike. "Christian Ethiopia," in The Middle Age of African
    History (New York, OUP: 1967), ed. Roland Oliver.

Hammerschmidt, Ernst. "Jewish Elements in the Cult of the Ethio-
    pian Church," JES, 3: 2 (1965).

_____. "The Liturgical Vestments of the Ethiopian Church: a
    tentative survey," P. 3rd ICES, vol. 2 (Addis Ababa: 1970).

_____. Stellung und Bedeutung des Sabbats in Äthiopien (Stutt-
    gard: 1963).

_____. "Zur Christologie der Äthiopischen Kirche," Ostkirchliche Studien, 13 (1964).

Harden, J. M. The Anaphoras of the Ethiopic Liturgy (London Society for Promoting Christian Knowledge: n. d.).

_____. The Ethiopic Didascalia (New York: 1920).

Heidt, A. M. "L'Eglise éthiopienne orthodoxe d'aujourd'hui. Interview avec l'abuna Théopolos, patriarche d'Ethiopie et l'abuna Samuel," Irénikon, 46 (1973).

Hempel, Christa, and E. Hammerschmidt. "Position and Significance of Sabbath in Ethiopia," Mundus, 1: 4 (1965).

Heyer, Friedrich. Die Kirche Athiopiens (Berlin, W. de Gruyter: 1971).

_____. "The Teaching of Tergum in the Ethiopian Orthodox Church," P. 3rd ICES, vol. 2 (Addis Ababa: 1970).

Hyatt, H. M. The Church of Abyssinia (London: 1928).

Kallimachos, D. "The Patriarchate of Alexandria in Abyssinia," Abridged and translated into English by Metropolitan Methodios Fouyas. Abba Salama, 2 (1971).

Karpozilos, Apostolos D. "Anglican and Orthodox Relations to 1930," Abba Salama, 1 (1970).

Littmann, Enno. "Aus dem abessinischen Klöstern in Jerusalem," Zeitschrift für Assyriologie, 16 (1902).

The Liturgy of the Ethiopian Church (in English and Arabic) trans. Marcos Daoud; ed. Marzie Hazen (Egyptian Book Press: 1959).

Löfgren, Oscar. "The Necessity of a Critical Edition of the Ethiopian Bible," P. 3rd ICES, vol. 2 (Addis Ababa: 1970).

Mara, Yolande. The Church of Ethiopia: the National church in the making (Asmara, Ethiopia, Il Poligrafico: 1972).

Marcos Daoud. Church Sacraments (Addis Ababa: 1952).

_____. The Liturgy of the Ethiopian Church (Addis Ababa: 1954).

Marsie Hazen, Blatta. "The Ethiopian Church," Ecumenical Review, 1: 2 (1949).

Matthew, A. F. "The Abyssinian Church," The Christian East, 14: 3 (1933).

_____. The Church of Ethiopia During the Italian Occupation (Addis Ababa: 1943).

_____ . The Church of Ethiopia, 1941-1944 (Addis Ababa: 1944).

_____ . The Teaching of the Abyssinian Church, as set up by the Doctors of the Same (London, The Faith Press: 1936).

Meinardus, Otto. "Ecclesiastica Aethiopica in Aegypto, " JES, 3: 1 (1965).

_____ . "Notizen über das Eustathische Klöster Debra Bizen, " AE, 6 (1965).

_____ . The Copts in Jerusalem (Cairo: 1960).

Mercer, Samuel. Translations of Anaphoras in J. SOR, 1: 1 (1917); 3: 1 (1919); and 7: 1 (1923).

_____ . The Ethiopic Liturgy: Its Sources, Development, and Present Form (New York: AMS Press, 1970).

Methodios, Metropolitan. "The First Meeting of the Orthodox-Anglican Theological Sub-Commissions of Joint Doctrinal Discussions in Chambésy, Sept. 12-14, 1972, " Ekkleseastikos Paros, 55: 1 (1973).

_____ . "Patriarch Basilios of Ethiopia in Memoriam, " Abba Salama, 2 (1971).

_____ . Christianity and Judaism in Ethiopia, Nubia and Meroe (1979 by author, Athens, Greece).

Mitchell, Ella P. "The Hebrew Christian Tradition in Ethiopia, " Freeing the Spirit (National Office of Black Catholics) 4: 1 (1975).

Molnar, E. C. The Ethiopian Orthodox Church: a contribution to the Ecumenical Study of less known Eastern Churches (Pasadena, Calif.; Bloy House Theological School: 1969).

Moore, Dale H. "Christianity in Ethiopia, " Church History, 5: 3 (1936).

National Festivals in Ethiopia: Kulubi (Ministry of Information, Addis Ababa: 1967).

Negaso Gidada see History c. 1760-1930

Nelson, J. Robert. "No Myopia in Ethiopia, " Christian Century, 88: 6 (1971).

"New Patriarch Enthroned, " Amer. Review of Eastern Orthodoxy, 17: 6 (1971).

Nicolas, Archbishop of Aksum. Church's Revival: Emancipation from 1600 Years' Guardianship; Free Church in Free State Achieved by His Majesty Haile Selassie I (Cairo: 1955).

O'Hanlon, Douglas. Features of the Abyssinian Church (London Society for Promoting Christian Knowledge: 1946).

O'Leary, D. E. The Ethiopian Church (London Society for Promoting Christian Knowledge: 1936).

Pawlikowski, J. T. "The Judaic Spirit of the Ethiopian Orthodox Church: a case study in Religious Acculturation," J. Religion in Africa, 4: 3 (1972).

Philippos, Abuna. Know Jerusalem. (Addis Ababa, Berhanena Selam Printing Press: 1972).

Poladian, Bishop T. "The Doctrinal Position of the Monophysite Churches," EO, 7: 3 (1964).

Pollera, Alberto. Lo Stato etiopico e la sua chiesa (Rome: 1926).

Post, Ken. "The Bible as Ideology: Ethiopianism in Jamaica, 1930-1938," African Perspectives. Ed. Christopher Allen and R. W. Johnson (CUP: 1970).

Ranger, T. O. "African Religion in the History of Ethiopia," African Religious Research, 3: 1 (1973).

Rees, A. H. "Ethiopia and Her Church," East and West Review, 2 (1936).

Rochet d'Héricourt, C. E. X. "Les moeurs religieuses dans le royaume de Choa," BSG, 4 (1845).

Samuel, V. C. "The Fourth unofficial consultation of theologians belonging to the Eastern and the Oriental Church," Abba Salama, 3 (1972).

_____. "Proceedings of the Council of Chalcedon and its Historical Problems, a paper written from a critical point of view," Abba Salama, 1 (1970).

Schodde, G. H. "The Rules of Pachomius Translated from the Ethiopic," Presbyterian Review, 6 (1885).

Schultz, H. J. "Reform and Reaction in Ethiopia's Orthodox Church," Christian Century, 85 (1968).

Sergew Hable Selassie. The Church of Ethiopia. A Panorama of History and Spiritual Life (Addis Ababa, Ethiopian Orthodox Church: 1970).

Sperry, D. See listing under Law.

Stan, Liviu. "L'église d'Ethiopie, Nouveau Patriarcat," Abba
    Salama, 2 (1971).

Strelcyn, Stefan. "La Chrétienté dans la region de la Mer Rouge,"
    J. Religion in Africa, 5: 3 (1973).

Sumner, Claude. "Ethiopic liturgy: an analysis," JES, 1: 1 (1963).

Tadesse Tamrat. See listing under General Works.

Tedeschi, Salvatore. "Profilo storico di Dayr as-Sultan," JES, 2:
    2 (1954).

"Theophany in Ethiopia," Amer. Review of Eastern Orthodoxy, 17:
    2 (1971).

Thurston, H. "Abyssinian Devotion to Our Lady," Dublin Review,
    198: 396 (1936).

Tito Lipisa, Abba. The Cult of Saints in the Ethiopian Church
    (Rome: Typis Pontificiae Universitatis Gregorianae: 1963).

_____. "The Three Modes and the Signs in the Ethiopian Liturgy,"
    P. 3rd ICES, vol. 2 (Addis Ababa: 1970).

Tubiana, Joseph. "Le Frère de Saint Lâlibalâ," Objets et Mondes,
    3 (1963).

Ullendorff, Edward. Ethiopia and the Bible (New York, OUP: 1965).

_____. "Hebraic-Jewish Elements in Abyssinian (Monophysite)
    Christianity," JSS, 1: 3 (1956).

Velat, Bernard. "Chantres, poètes, professeurs: Les Dabtara
    éthiopiens," Les Cahiers Coptes, 5 (1954).

_____. Etudes sur le Me'eraf commun de l'office divin éthiopien.
    Introduction, commentaire liturgique et musical. Patrologie
    Orientalis (Paris), 33 (1966).

_____. "Un grand dignitaire de l'Eglise Ethiopienne: l'Abouna,"
    Les Cahiers Coptes, 4 (1953).

_____. "Fuoco sacro ed acque prodigiose a Gerusalemme e nel
    Gélo Makādā," RSE, 7: 2 (1948).

Villard, Monneret de. "La Majestas Domini in Abissini," RSE, 3:
    1 (1943).

Ware, Timothy. The Orthodox Church (Penguin: 1963).

Wendt, Kurt. "Der Kampf um den Kanon Heiliger Schriften in der
    äthiopischen Kirche der Reformen des XV. Jahrhunderts,"
    JSS, 9: 1 (1964).

Weyer, Robert van de. "The Monastic Community of Ethiopia, " EO, 16: 1 (1973).

Yaqob Beyene. "Controversie cristologische in Etiopia, " AION, 37: 2 (1977). Supplement 11.

Islam

Abraham Demoz. "Moslems and Islam in Ethiopic Literature, " JES 10: 1 (1972).

Braukamper, U. See listing under History (A).

Cassanelli, Lee V. "Migrations, Islam and Politics in the Somali Benadir, " P. 1st USCES, (ASC, MSU; 1975).

Cederquist, Karl. "Islam and Christianity in Abyssinia, " Moslem World, 2 (1912).

Cerulli, Enrico. "Islam u Ethiopi, " Prezeglad Orientalistyczny 1/65 (1968).

Crummey, D. E. "Shaikh Zäkaryas: an Ethiopian Prophet, " JES, 10: 1 (1972).

Dye, W. M. See listing under History (B).

Hasselblatt, Gunnar. "Der Islam in Äthiopien, " ZK (1973).

_____. "Islam i Etiopien: overs B. Hallgren, " Svensk Mission-stidskrift 59: 4 (1971).

Iwarson, Jonas. "Islam in Eritrea and Abyssinia, " Moslem World, 18 (1928).

_____. "Moslem Mass Movement Toward Christianity in Abyssinia, " Moslem World, 14 (1924).

Lambie, T. A. "Islam in Southern Ethiopia, " Moslem World, 25: 1 (1925).

Littmann, Enno. "Bemerkungen über den Islam in Nordabessinien, " Der Islam, 1: 1 (1910).

Maqrizi. See listing under History (A).

Martin, B. G. "Mahdism, Muslim Clerics, and Holy Wars in Ethiopia, 1300-1600, " P. 1st USCES (ASC, MSU: 1975).

Massaia, G. Della Propaganda Mussulmana nell'Africa e nelle Indie (Turin: 1859).

Müller, Walter W. "Abessinier und Ihre Namen und Titel in Voris-
lamischen Südarabischen Texten," P. 5th ICES (Chicago: 1979).

"Muslims in Ethiopia Raise the Standard of Revolution," Yaqeen International, 18: 24 (1970).

Mengin, F. Histoire sommaire de l'Egypte sous le gouvernement de
Mohammed Aly (Paris: 1839).

Oman, G. "La necropoli islamica di Dahlak Kebir nel Mar Rossi,"
Africa, 29 (1974).

Schneider, Madeleine. "Stèles funéraires musulmanes de la province
du Choa," AE, 8 (1970).

_____. "Notes au sujet de l'épitaphe du premier sultan de
Dahlak," JES, 11: 2 (1973).

Shihab ad-Din. Futuh al-Habasha. Ed. and trans. by R. Basset as
Histoire de la conquête de l'Abyssinie (Paris, l'Ecole des
Lettres d'Alger: 1897-1909).

"Taulud," EO, 3: 9 (1959).

Trimingham, J. S. "North-eastern Ethiopic Zone," The Influence of
Islam Upon Africa (New York, Praeger: 1968) p. 26-30.

_____. See his listing under General Works.

URBAN AREAS AND URBANIZATION

Akalu Wolde Michael. "Some Thoughts on the Process of Urbanization in Pre-Twentieth Century Ethiopia," EGJ, 4: 2 (1967).

_____. "Urban Development in Ethiopia (1889-1925), early
phase," JES, 11: 1 (1973).

Amos, Francis J. C. "A Development Plan for Addis Ababa," EO,
6: 1 (1962).

Belletetch Iyakem and Torvald Akesson. Survey of Housing Conditions in Tekla Haimanot and Lidetta District of Addis Ababa,
1962. (Addis Ababa, Ethio-Swedish Institute of Building Technology: 1962).

Comhaire, Jean. "Urbanization in Ethiopia," Dialogue, 1: 1 (1967).

_____. "Wage Pooling as a form of Voluntary Association in
Ethiopia and other African Towns," P. 3rd ICES, vol. 3 (Addis
Ababa: 1970).

Cooper, R. L., and R. J. Horvath. See study under Ethnography.

Ghiorghis Mellessa. "Gondar Yesterday and Today," EO, 12: 3 (1969).

Guida, Guido. "Addis Abeba e la sua popolazione," BRSGI, 7: 5 (1940).

Horvath, R. J. "Addis Ababa's Eucalyptus Forest," JES, 6: 1 (1968).

_____. "The Process of Urban Agglomeration in Ethiopia," JES, 8: 2 (1970).

_____. "Towns in Ethiopia," Erkunde, 22 (1968).

_____. "Von Thunen's Isolated State and that Area around Addis Ababa, Ethiopia," Annals of the Association of American Geographers, 59 (1969).

Koehn, Eftychia and Peter. "Edir as a Vehicle for Urban Development in Addis Ababa," P. 1st USCES (ASC, MSU: 1975).

Mesfin Wolde Mariam. "Problems of Urbanization," P. 3rd ICES, Vol. 3 (Addis Ababa: 1970).

_____. "The Rural-Urban Split in Ethiopia," Dialogue, 2: 1 (1968).

_____. "Some Aspects of Urbanization in Pre-Twentieth Century Ethiopia," EGJ, 3: 2 (1965).

Oddy, D. J. and J. D. Baker. See listing under Ethnography, etc.

Pankhurst, Richard K. "The City 50 Years Ago," EO, 9: 3 (1958).

_____. "The Foundation and Early Growth of Addis Ababa to 1935," EO, 6: 1 (1962).

_____. "Three Urban Precursors of Gondar: Emfraz, Gorgora and Danqaz," P. 5th ICES (Chicago: 1979).

_____. "Notes for the History of Gondar," EO, 12: 3 (1969).

_____. "Notes on the Demographic History of Ethiopian Towns and Villages," EO, 9: 1 (1965).

_____. "The History of Däbrä Tabor (Ethiopia)," SOAS Bull. 40: 2 (1977).

Pankhurst, Sylvia. "Addis Ababa Today," EO, 9: 3 (1958).

_____. "The Changing Face of Addis Ababa," EO, 4: 5 (1960).

Seleshi Sisaye. "Urban Migration and the Labor Movement in
    Ethiopia, " P. 5th ICES (Chicago: 1979).

Shack, William A.   "Notes on Voluntary Associations and Urbaniza-
    tion in Africa, with Special Reference to Addis Ababa, Ethio-
    pia, " African Urban Notes, ser. B, 1 (1974-1975).

"Sir Patrick Abercrombie's Town Plan, " EO, 9: 3 (1958).

"Town Planning in Ethiopia, " EGJ, 4: 2 (1966).

Wang, C. K.   "The Population of Ethiopia's Metropolis, " EO, 9: 3
    (1958).

Young, Maurice de.   "An African Emporium: The Addis Märkato, "
    JES, 5: 2 (1967).

Zewde Gabre-Sellassie.   "Problems and Plans of Addis Ababa, " EO,
    3: 2 (1959).

REVOLUTION AND AFTER

Addis Hiwet.   Ethiopia: from Autocracy to Revolution.   #1 (London,
    Review of African Political Economy: 1975).

Aryeh Y. Yodfat.   "The Soviet Union and the Horn of Africa, " NAS, 2:
    2 (1980).

Baissa, Marilyn H.   "Civil-Military Elite Interaction in the Ethiopian
    Revolution: the role of Students, " P. 5th ICES (Chicago:
    1979).

Bereket Habte Selassie.   "Evolution of the principle of self-determi-
    nation, " Horn of Africa, 1: 4 (1978).

Brietzke, Paul.   "Law, Revolution and the Ethiopian Peasant, " Rural
    Africana, 28 (1975).

_____.   See also Scholler below.

Cohen, John M.   "Traditional Politics and the Military Coup in
    Ethiopia, " African Affairs, 74: 295 (1965).

_____; A. A. Goldsmith; John W. Mellor.   Revolution and Land
    Reform in Ethiopia: Peasant Associations, Local Government
    and Rural Development (Ithaca, N. Y., Center for International
    Studies, Rural Development Committee, Cornell University:
    1976).

_____; _____; _____. "Rural Development Issues Following Ethiopian Land Reform," Africa Today, 22: 2 (1976).

_____, and Peter Koehn. "Rural and Urban Land Reform in Ethiopia," African Law Studies, 14 (1977).

_____, and _____. Ethiopian Provincial and Municipal Government: Imperial Patterns and Postrevolutionary Changes. (ASC, MSU: 1980).

_____, and Seleshi Sisaye. "Research Priorities for the study of Socioeconomic Change in Ethiopia's Rural and Urban Sectors," EN, 1: 3 (1978).

_____, and _____. Research on Socioeconomic Development in Ethiopia: Past Problems and Future Issues in Rural-Urban Studies (Ithaca, New York; Department of Rural Sociology, Cornell University: 1977).

_____, and Dov Weintraub. Land and Peasants in Imperial Ethiopia: the Social Background to a Revolution (Assen, The Netherlands: Van Gorcum and Co.: 1975).

Dereje Deressa. "Ethiopia Fallen," The New Republic, 183: 13 (Sept. 27, 1980).

Dula Abdu. See listing under Agriculture, Land Tenure.

Ellis, Gene. "After the Revolutions: the Development Paths of Ethiopia and Peru Compared," EN, 2: 3 (1978-79).

_____. "Land Tenancy Reform in Ethiopia: A Retrospective Analysis," P. 5th ICES (Chicago: 1979).

Erlich, Haggai. "The Establishment of the Derg: The Turning of a Protest Movement into a Revolution," P. 5th ICES (Chicago: 1979).

_____. "Ethiopia and Islam in Postrevolution Perspective," EN, 1: 1 (1977).

"Ethiopia: Crisis Diary," Africa, 33 (1974).

Getatchew Mekasha. "Remarks on the Ethiopian Revolution: a personal view," P. 5th ICES (Chicago: 1979).

_____. An Inside View of the Ethiopian Revolution. Munger Africana Library Notes, 39 (July 1977).

Gilkes, Patrick. "Ethiopia--the Beginning of Change?" Contemporary Review, 225 (July, 1974).

_____. "The Coming Struggle for Ethiopia," Africa Report, 20: 3 (1974).

_____. "Ethiopia: A Real Revolution?" World Today, 31 (Jan. 1975).

_____. See other listings under Hayle Sellase.

Goddard, Ian. "An Interview with Ethiopia's Foreign Minister," Horn of Africa, 1: 2 (1978).

Goldsmith, A. A. See Cohen above.

Grey, Robert D. "Post Imperial Ethiopian Foreign Policy: Ethiopian Dependence," P. 5th ICES (Chicago: 1979).

Hamilton, D. "Ethiopia embattled revolutionaries," Conflict Studies, 82 (Apr. 1977).

Harbeson, John W. "Toward a Political Theory of the Ethiopian Revolution," P. 5th ICES (Chicago: 1979).

_____. "Perspectives on the Ethiopian Revolution," EN, 1: 1 (1977).

_____. "Socialism, Traditional, and Revolutionary Politics in Contemporary Ethiopia," Canadian J. African Studies, 11: 2 (1977).

_____. "Ethiopia and the Horn of Africa," NAS, 1: 1 (1979).

_____. "Revolution and Rural Development in Ethiopia," RA, 28 (1975).

_____. "Afar Pastoralists and Ethiopian Rural Development," RA, 28 (1975).

Hoben, Allan. "Perspectives on Land Reform in Ethiopia: the Political Role of the Peasantry," Rural Africana, 28 (1975).

_____. Social Soundness Analysis of Agrarian Reform in Ethiopia (Washington, D.C., USAID, Feb. 1976).

Jones, W. "Problems of the Ethiopian Revolution," The African Communist, 69 (1977).

Kapeliuk, Olga. "Marxist-Leninist Terminology in Amharic and in Tigrinya," NAS, 1: 2 (1979).

Katz, D. R. "Children's Revolution: A Bloodbath in Ethiopia," Horn of Africa, 1: 3 (1978).

Koehn, Peter. "Ethiopian Politics: Military Intervention and Prospects for Further Change," Africa Today, 22 (Apr.-June, 1975).

_____. "Ethiopia; Famine, Food Production, and Changes in the Legal Order," ASR, 22: 1 (1979).

_____. See also Cohen above.

Lapiso D. Dilebo. "Land Tenure, Underlying Cause of the Ethiopian Revolution," P. 5th ICES (Chicago: 1979).

LeBel, Phillip. "Economic and Social Indicators as Predictors of the Ethiopian Revolution of 1975," P. 5th ICES (Chicago: 1979).

Legesse Lemma. See listing under Government and Political Analysis.

Legum, Colin. See listing under Hayle Sellase.

"A Letter to Cubans in Harar," [from] Oromo Liberation Front. Horn of Africa, 2: 1 (1979).

Malécot, Georges R. "L'Ethiopie à la croisée des chemins," Afrique Contemporaine, 80 (1975).

Mamo Zeleke. "Dernières convulsions," Afrique Asie, 62 (1974).

_____. "Ethiopie: Au bord de la guerre civile," Afrique Asie, 56 (1974).

_____. "La Ronde de prétendants," Afrique Asie, 47 (1974).

Markakis, John and Nega Ayele. Class and Revolution in Ethiopia. (Nottingham, England; Spokesman: The Review of African Political Economy: 1978). (See also Brietzke review in NAS, 1: 3 (1979-80).)

Mellor, John. See Cohen above.

"The Military and Politics in Ethiopia," Strategic Survey 1974 (London, International Institute for Strategic Studies: 1975).

Morgan, E. See listing under Eritrea.

Nega Ayele. See Markakis above.

Ottaway, Marina. "Land Reform and Peasant Associations: A Preliminary Analysis," Rural Africana, 28 (1975).

_____. "Democracy and New Democracy: The Ideological Debate in the Ethiopian Revolution," ASR, 21: 1 (1978).

_____. "Land Reform in Ethiopia, 1974-1977," ASR, 20: 3 (1977).

_____, and David Ottaway. Ethiopia: Empire in Revolution (New York, Africana Publishing Co.: 1978).

Pausewang, Siegfried. Peasants and Local Society in Ethiopia: Land Tenure, Social Structure, and Land Reform (Bergen, Norway; Michelsens Institute, Working Paper 105: 1978).

_____. See also listing under Agriculture.

Pliny the Middle-Aged (pseud.) "The PMAC: Origins and Structure," EN, 2: 3 (1978-79).

Rapoport, Louis. "There's Hope for Ethiopia," Horn of Africa, 2: 1 (1979).

Revolution in Eritrea: The Ethiopian Military Dictatorship and Imperialism (Eritreans for Liberation in North America: 1975).

"Revolution in Ethiopia," Monthly Review, 29: 3 (1977).

Scholler, H. and P. Brietzke. Ethiopia: Revolution, Law and Politics (Munich, Weltforum Verlag: 1976).

Seleshi Sisaye. "The Political and Economic Perspectives of Union Members in Addis Ababa, Ethiopia, during the 1974 General Strike," EN, 1: 2 (1977).

_____. See also Cohen above, and listing under Economy.

Singer, Norman. "Legal Development in Post-Revolutionary Ethiopia," Horn of Africa, 1: 2 (1978).

_____. "Ethiopia: Human Rights, 1948-1978," P. 5th ICES (Chicago: 1979).

Stahl, Michael. New Seeds in Old Soil: A Study of the Land Reform Process in Western Wollega, Ethiopia, 1975-76 (Uppsala: Scandinavian Institute of African Studies, #40: 1977).

Thomas, Tony. "Ethiopia: The Empire Trembles," International Socialist Review, 35: 5 (1974).

Thompson, Blair. Ethiopia: The Country That Cut Off Its Head (London, Robson Books: 1975).

Tubiana, J. "Ethiopie: fin de l'empire ou fin de la société impériale," Herodote, 10 (1978).

"Violation of Rights of Man in Ethiopia," Amnesty International (Nov. 1978).

Vivó, Raúl Valdés. Ethiopia's Revolution (New York, International Publishers: 1977).

Weintraub, Dov. See Cohen above.

Yohannes Abate. "Military Administration and Intra-Military Conflict," #79-1 (ASA, Brandeis University, Waltham, Mass.: 1979).

BIBLIOGRAPHIES, INDEXES, STUDY AIDS

Aesčoly, A. Z. The Falashas: a Bibliography (Jerusalem: 1937).

Alula Hidaru and Desselegn Rahmato. A Short Guide to the Study of Ethiopia (Westport, Connecticut; Greenwood Press).

Baylor, Jim. Ethiopia: A List of Works in English (Berkeley, California: 1967).

Bell, Pamela M. Land Tenure in Ethiopia: Bibliography (HSIU Library: 1968).

Bender, Marvin L., Head, Sydney and Cowley, Roger, eds. "The Ethiopian Writing System," Language in Ethiopia, 120-129 (London, OUP: 1976).

"A Bibliography of Publications on Agriculture of Ethiopia," EGJ, 2: 1 (1964).

Black, George F. Ethiopica & Amharica: A List of Works in the New York Public Library (New York Public Library: 1928).

Bombaci, Alessio. "Notizie sull'Abissinia in fonti turche," RSE, 3: 1 (1943).

Brown, Clifton F. Ethiopian Perspectives. A Bibliographical Guide to the History of Ethiopia (Westport, Connecticut and London, England, Greenwood Press: 1978).

Chojnacki, S., and Mergia Diro. Ethiopian Publications in 1961 Ethiopian and 1969 Gregorian Calendar (Addis Ababa, Institute of Ethiopian Studies: July, 1970).

_____, and Pankhurst, R., eds. Register of Current Research on Ethiopia and the Horn of Africa (Addis Ababa, Institute of Ethiopian Studies: 1969).

Comba, Pierre. Inventaire des livres dans la collection éthiopienne à la bibliothèque de l'Université College d'Addis Ababa (HSIU Library: 1961).

Conti Rossini, C. Bibliografia Etiopica (1927-giugno 1936) (Milan: 1936).

_____. "Pubblicazioni etiopistiche dal 1936 al 1945," RSE, 4: 4 (1946).

_____. "Catalogo dei nomi propri di luogo dell'Etiopia," Atti del primo Congresso Geografico Italiano (Genoa: 1892).

_____. "Recerche e studi sull'Etiopia," BSGI, 2 (1900).

_____. "Di alcuni recenti pubblicazioni sull'Etiopia," Oriente, 2 (1897).

_____. Tabelle comparativo del calendario Etiopico col calendario Romano (Rome: 1948).

Contribution to an Italian Bibliography on Ethiopia 1935-1950 (Istituto Agronomico per l'Africa Italiana, Florence: 1952).

Dainelli, G., Marinelli, O., and Mori, A. "Bibliografia geografica della Colonia Eritrea," Riv. GI, 14 (1907).

Darch, Colin. A Soviet View of Africa; an annotated Bibliography on Ethiopia, Somalia and Djibouti (G. K. Hall, 70 Lincoln Street, Boston, Mass.: 1980).

Delany, Annette. Ethiopian Survey: A Select Bibliography (Special Bibliographic Series, ABC, Wash., D.C.: 1964).

Duignam, Peter. Guide to Research Works on Sub-Saharan Africa (Palo Alto, California; HIP: 1971).

Ethioconcord. [for calendar conversion] (Sophia-Antipolis, Valbonne, Laboratoire Peiresc: 1977).

Ethiopia, 1950-1962: A Select Bibliography (Africa House, Washington, D.C.: 1963).

Fumagalli, Guiseppe. Bibliografia ethiopica. Catalogo descrittivo e ragionata degli scritti pubblicati della invenzione della stampa fino a tutto il 1891 interno alla Ethiopia e regione limitrofe (Milan: 1893).

Fusella, Luigi. "Recenti pubblicazioni amariche in Abissinia," RSE, 5 (1946).

Garretson, Peter P. "Some Amharic sources for modern Ethiopian history, 1889-1935 (with notes by Richard Pankhurst)," SOAS Bull., 41: part 2 (1978).

Gasbarri, Carlo. "Fondi archivistici e bibliografici relativi all' Africa esistenti a Roma: l'Archivio Storico del soppresso Ministero dell'Africa Italiana," Africa (Rome), 28 (Sept. 1973).

Geshekter, Charles. "Some Archival sources concerning Modern Somali History: an Introduction," P. 5th ICES (Chicago: 1979).

Grébaut, Sylvain. Catalogue des manuscrits Ethiopiens de la collection Griaule (Paris, Institut d'Ethnologie: 1938).

_____. "Les manuscrits étiopiens de M. E. Delorme," ROC, 2 (1912) and 2 (1914).

Guérinot, A. "Les principales publications relatives à l'Ethiopie en 1908 et en 1909," JA, 14 (1909), 15 (1910).

Guida delle fonti per la storia dell'Africa a sud del Sahara esistenti in Italia (Zug: 1973).

Guide to the sources of the history of Africa. Vol. 3. Source de l'histoire de l'Afrique au sud du Sahara dans les archives et bibliothèques françaises. International Council on Archives (Zug: 1971).

Halstead, J. P., and Porcari, S. Modern European Imperialism: a bibliography of books and articles 1815-1972. Vol. 2. (Boston, Mass., G. K. Hall: 1974).

Hammerschmidt, E. "Die Äthiopistischen studien in Deutschland (von ihren Anfängen bis zur Gegenwart)," AE, 6 (1965).

Hansberry, W. L. "A Survey of Native Documentary Sources Available for the Study of Ancient Ethiopian History," Howard University Studies in History, 11 (n. d.).

Hartwig, G. W., and W. M. L'Barr. Student Africanist's Handbook (New York, John Wiley: 1975).

Haskell, D. C. Ethiopia and the Italo-Ethiopian Conflict, 1928-1935. [a bibliography] (New York: 1936).

Heruy Welde Sellassie. Catalogue des livre redigés en langue gueeze et amharique (Addis Ababa: 1928).

Hess, R. L., and Coger, D. M. A Bibliography of Primary Sources for Nineteenth-Century Tropical Africa as Recorded by Explorers, Missionaries, Traders, Travellers, Administrators, Military Men, Adventurers and Others. Hoover Bibliographical Series, 47 (HIP: 1972).

Höjer, Christianne. Ethiopian Publications 1942-1962 (Addis Ababa, HSIU: 1974).

Izarn, R. R. "Les documents Arnauld d'Abbadie (in Vatican Library)," P. 3rd ICES, vol. 1 (Addis Ababa: 1969).

Jones, Ruth. Africa Bibliography Series: Northeast Africa, Ethiopia (London: 1959).

Kassahun Checole. "Eritrea: a preliminary bibliography," Africana Journal, 6: 4 (1975).

Kinefe-Rigb Zelleke. "Bibliography of the Ethiopic Hagiographical
Traditions," JES, 8: 2 (1975).

Koehn, Peter. "Selected Bibliography: The Municipality of Addis
Ababa, Ethiopia," African Urban Notes, ser. B (1975).

Langer, William. An Encyclopedia of World History.   4th ed.
(Boston, Houghton Mifflin: 1968).

Lasor, W. S.   A Basic Semitic Bibliography (annotated) (Wheaton,
Illinois: Van Kampen Press, 1950).

Leslau, Wolf.   An Annotated Bibliography of the Semitic Languages
of Ethiopia (The Hague, Mouton: 1965).

_____. "Ethiopian Studies in the United States Since World War
II," P. 1st USCES (ASC, MSU: 1975).

Lewis, H. S.   "Historical Problems in Ethiopia and the Horn of
Africa," Annals of the New York Academy of Sciences, 96
(1962).

Lockot, H. W.   "German Literature on Ethiopia in the Libraries of
Addis Ababa," EO, 11: 1 (1967).

McCann, James, and McClellan, C.   "A Note on Ethiopianist source
material in Chicago's Field Museum of Natural History," EN,
2: 2 (1978).

Macomber, W. F.   A Catalogue of Ethiopian Manuscripts Microfilmed
for the Ethiopian Manuscript Microfilm Library, Addis Ababa
and The Monastic Manuscript Microfilm Library, Collegeville,
Minn. vol. 1 (Collegeville, Minn., St. John's Abbey and University: 1975).

Marcus, Harold G.   The Modern History of Ethiopia and the Horn of
Africa: A Select and Annotated Bibliography (Palo Alto, Calif.,
HIP: 1972).

Matthews, Daniel G.   A Current Bibliography on Ethiopian Affairs: A
select bibliography from 1950-1964 (Wash. D.C., ABC: 1965).

Matthews, Noel, and Wainwright, M. D.   A Guide to Manuscripts and
Documents in the British Isles Relating to Africa (London, OUP:
1971).

Moscati, S.   "Bibliographie sémitique," Orientalia 16 (1947); 17
(1948); 19 (1950); 22 (1953).

Pankhurst, Richard K. P.   "Short Bibliography on Lalibela," EO, 4:
7 (1960).

_____, and Pankhurst, Rita. "Bibliography of Ethiopian Travel Books," Africana Journal, 9: 3 (1978).

Paulitschke, P. Die Afrika-Literatur in der Zeit von 1500 bis 1750 N. Chr. (Vienna: 1882).

Peltier-Charrier, M-C., and Abeles, Marc. "Bibliographical Notes on Ethnological Research in Southern Ethiopia," P. 5th ICES (Chicago: 1979).

Petracek, Karel. "Ceský prinos k pozáni Ethiopu a jejich zeme," [Czech contribution to the knowledge of the Ethiopians and their country] Ceskoslovenska Etnografie, 6: 1 (1958).

Pétridès, S. Pierre. "Etiologie et finalité des généalogies éthiopiennes," P. 3rd ICES, vol. 1 (Addis Ababa: 1969).

Pollera, A. Piccola bibliografia dell'Africa Orientale con speciale Riguardo all'Eritrea e paesi confianti (Asmara: 1933).

Porter, Dorothy B. A Catalogue of the African Collection in the Moorland Foundation, Howard University Library, Washington, D.C. (HUP: 1958).

Roberts, A. D. "Documentation on Ethiopia and Eritrea," J. Documentation, 1: 4 (1946).

Roberts, Ursula, and Solomon Amde. Medicine in Ethiopia: Bibliography (HSIU Library: 1970).

Rosenfeld, Chris Prouty. "Index to the First Ten Years of Ethiopia Observer," EO, 10: 4 (1966).

_____. "Combined Index to Ethiopia Observer (1967-1974) and Journal of Ethiopian Studies (1963-1975) by subject and author," (NAS, 2: 1 [1980]).

Rubenson, Sven. "Ethiopian Historical Studies in Addis Ababa," Ethiopia: Land and History. Rural Africana, #11 (ASC, MSU: 1970).

Schwab, Peter. "Bibliography on Ethiopia," Genève-Afrique, 12: 2 (1973).

Sergew Hable Sellassie. Bibliography of Ancient and Medieval Ethiopian History (HSIU, History Department: 1969).

Simon, Jean. "Bibliographie éthiopienne," Orientalia, 21 (1952).

Sommer, John. A Study Guide for Ethiopia and the Horn of Africa (Boston University: 1969).

Tubiana, Joseph. "Ouvrages manuscrits concernant l'Ethiopie à la Bibliothèque Nationale de Paris," RSE, 15 (1960).

_____. "Calendrier éthiopien et grégorien ou l'informatique au service des sciences sociales," Revue Français Etudes Politiques Africaines, 160 (1979).

Turaiev, Boris. "Teste etiopici in manoscritti di Leningrado," RSE, 7: 1 (1948).

Ullendorff, E., and Kelly, Anne. "Index of C. Conti Rossini's "Storia d'Etiopia," RSE, 18 (1962), 97-141.

Wright, Stephen. "Book and Manuscript Collections in Ethiopia," JES, 2: 1 (1974), 11-24.

_____. "Transliteration of Amharic," JES, 2: 1 (1964).

Wright, William. Catalogue of the Ethiopic Manuscripts in the British Museum Acquired Since the Year 1847 (London: 1877).

Yarley, D. H. A Bibliography of Italian Colonisation in Africa with a section on Abyssinia (Folkestone, England, Dawsons of Pall Mall: 1970).

Zanutto, Silvio. Bibliografia Etiopica (Rome: 1936).

_____. "La stampa periodica etiopica," RivCI, 9 (1935).

Zotenberg, Hermann. Catalogue des Manuscrits Ethiopiens (Ghêez et Amharique de la Bibliothèque Nationale (Paris: 1877).

INDEX TO THE DICTIONARY

An underscored page number indicates that an index entry is also a main entry in the Dictionary on that page.